# CORPORATE GOVERNANCE

# Corporate Governance

## Robert A.G. Monks and Nell Minow

The most comprehensive examination and commentary on corporate governance that I have yet seen . . . If I had to choose one book among the dozens available to explain and illuminate the complexities of corporate governance, this definitive treatise would be it.
*Hugh Parker*

*Corporate Governance* is a lucid and comprehensive introduction to a subject that is of critical importance to anyone interested in business. Everyone, from student, to scholar, to corporate employee, officer, director, or shareholder, will find it valuable.
*Donald Jacobs, Dean, Kellogg School of Business, Northwestern University*

This is what we've needed – a solid text on corporate governance written by two of the real stars in the field.
*D. Jeanne Patterson, former Associate Professor of Public and Environmental Affairs, Indiana University*

. . . a fresh, thoughtful, and timely look at the problem of corporate governance . . . a little gem.
*Joseph A. Grundfest, Professor of Law, Stanford Law School*

Exactly what's needed for MBA students and management professionals.
*Gordon Clark, Dean, Faculty of Arts, Monash University*

The MBA student seeking real world examples will be well satisfied with this material . . . a major strength of the book is the practitioner perspective that the authors bring to the area.
*Stuart L. Gillan, The University of Texas at Austin*

. . . authoritative and informative, with some fascinating case vignettes . . . A monumental work.
*Bob Tricker, Editor,* Corporate Governance

. . . carefully blends economic and legal aspects of corporate governance. Highly recommended for use in seminars on board practices, MBA programs, and corporate governance forums. *Cornelis A. de Kluyver, former Dean, School of Business Administration, George Mason University*

Highly useful . . . illuminates the current issues facing managers, boards of directors, and shareholders, as well as explaining their respective roles in the corporation.
*Ira M. Millstein, Weil, Gotshal & Manges; Lester Crown Visiting Faculty Fellow, Yale School of Management*

Provides a strong theoretical framework for the subject. It gives meaning to the important public policy issues by numerous examples, case studies, and policy statements.
*Professor J. Fred Weston, UCLA*

(Praise for the first edition)

# CORPORATE GOVERNANCE

## Third Edition

## Robert A.G. Monks
## Nell Minow

**Blackwell**
Publishing

© 2004 by Robert A.G. Monks and Nell Minow

350 Main Street, Malden, MA 02148-5020, USA
108 Cowley Road, Oxford OX4 1JF, UK
550 Swanston Street, Carlton, Victoria 3053, Australia

First published 1995 by Blackwell Publishing Ltd
Second edition published 2001, reprinted 2002 (twice), 2003 (twice)
Third edition published 2004

*Library of Congress Cataloging-in-Publication Data*

Monks, Robert A. G., 1933–
    Corporate governance / Robert A.G. Monks and Nell Minow. – 3rd ed.
        p. cm.
    Includes bibliographical references and index.
        ISBN 1–4051–1698–6 (pbk. : alk. paper)
        1. Corporate governance – United States.    I. Minow, Nell.    II. Title.

HD2745.M66 2003
658.4–dc21                                                                2003007769

A catalogue record for this title is available from the British Library.

Set in 10/11.5pt Bembo
by Graphicraft Limited, Hong Kong
Printed and bound in the United Kingdom
by T J International, Padstow, Cornwall

For further information on
Blackwell Publishing, visit our website:
http://www.blackwellpublishing.com

To the future: Max, Mariah, and Megan
R.A.G.M.

To David, Benjamin, and Rachel
N.M.

# Contents

# Cases in Point

# ACKNOWLEDGMENTS

First and foremost, we want to thank Kit Bingham, former editor of the indispensable magazine *Corporate Governance*, without whom this book would still be just a dream. His tireless, thorough, creative, and even cheerful diligence provided most of the case studies and supporting material, and he made even the more tedious aspects of research and writing a genuine pleasure. Professor Emerita D. Jeanne Patterson did a masterful job of reading through hundreds of academic papers and assembling the material for the Enron supplement. Holly Gregory of Weil, Gotshal, and Manges LLP created the incomparable materials on corporate governance in emerging and established economies, and we are immeasurably grateful to her for allowing us to share them with our readers.

We are also very grateful to the heroic scholars whose work instructed and inspired us, especially Jonathan Charkham, Sir Adrian Cadbury, David Walker, Robert Clark, Alfred Conard, Peter Drucker, Melvin Eisenberg, Shann Turnbull, Betty Krikorian, Margaret Blair, Jeffrey Sonnenfeld, Adolf Berle and Gardiner Means, and James Willard Hurst.

We have also learned a great deal from our colleagues, clients, and friends, including the widely disparate group of institutional investors all joined together by their commitment to the beneficial owners they serve as fiduciaries and the corporate managers they monitor as shareholders. It also includes the corporate managers, lawyers, regulators, commentators, and individual shareholders who care enough about making things work better to make a difference. These are also our heroes. They include Kayla Gillan, Linda Crompton, Carol Bowie, Peter Clapman, Stephen Davis, Olena Berg, Tom Horton, Dale Hanson, Rich Koppes, Ned Regan, Tom Pandick, Harrison J. Goldin, Carol O'Cleireacain, Patricia Lipton, Nancy Williams, Ned Johnson, Dean LeBaron, Dick Schleffer, Janice Hester-Amey, Phil Lochner, the late Al Sommer, Cathy Dixon, Martin Lipton, Ira Millstein and Holly Gregory, Luther Jones, Roland Machold, Michael Jacobs, the late John and Lewis Gilbert, Peg O'Hara, Mort Kleven, Alan Lebowitz, Karla Scherer, Kurt Schacht, Beth Young, Abbot Leban, Bill Steiner, Bob Massie, Tom Flanagan, Bill McEwen, David Greene, Alan Towers, Ann Yerger, Anne Simpson, Alyssa Machold, Roger Raber, Peter Gleason, Deborah Davidson, and Alan Kahn.

We are also especially grateful to our dear friends Sarah A.B. Teslik, Executive Director of the Council of Institutional Investors, and Ralph Whitworth, of Relational Investors, who provided the leadership, support, and intellectual foundation for most of the developments in this area over the past few years. We have also learned a great deal from scholars, including Joe Grundfest, Charles Elson, Bernie Black, Mark Roe, and Jack Coffee. John

M. Nash and the late Jean Head Sisco, former Director and Chair of the National Association of Corporate Directors, deserve special thanks for their labors in the field of governance.

We are grateful to those who permitted us to use their material in this book, which added inestimably to its value. Thanks to Holly Gregory, Chancellor William Allen, Ira Millstein, Shann Turnbull (apologies for failing to provide an appropriate credit in the first edition), Martin Lipton, Jay Lorsch, Cyrus F. Freidheim, Hugh Parker, Oxford Analytica, Jeanne Patterson, Paul Hodgson, Aaron Brown, Joe Grundfest, Jamie Heard, Sophie L'Helias, Howard Sherman, Bruce Babcock, and Geoff Mazullo. Dave Wakelin was most generous with his time in bringing us up to date on the Maine State Retirement System. Cathy Dixon guided us through the thorny securities law issues with patience, good humor, and unbounded expertise. Beth Young contributed the superb WorldCom case study and Paul Lee of Hermes allowed us to use his equally superb case studies of Premier Oil and Trinity Mirror. We are deeply grateful.

Becky Lawler, Jessica Thomas, Michelle Gayton, Beth Young, Jackie Cook, and Paul Hodgson of the Corporate Library were generous, knowledgeable, and completely indispensable in giving us the latest data and analyses. Carol Bowie of IRRC gave us important statistics about shareholder votes on compensation proposals. Ric Marshall, our trusted colleague, developed the website that has made it possible for us to include and update the book's supporting materials. Manpower CEO Mitchell Fromstein was most generous not only with useful material but also his own time. Newton Minow and the late Stanley Frankel constantly sent us clippings and gave us thoughtful advice.

There is a special section of heaven for those who are willing to trudge through early drafts and provide comments. Thanks very much to Margaret Blair, Alfred Conard, Wayne Marr, Jane Zanglein, and Stu Gillan.

We want to thank our colleagues, including everyone at the three companies we have worked at together: Institutional Shareholder Services, Lens, and the Corporate Library. Barbara Sleasman is the finest professional with whom we have ever worked. Cheri Gaudet was wonderfully diligent on updating and organizing the manuscript. We would also like to thank the people at Blackwell's, including Linda Auld, Rhonda Pearce, and Rosemary Nixon. Alexandra Lajoux was a brilliant (and tactful) editor.

*Note from Bob Monks*: I sometimes feel like Samuel Taylor Coleridge's famed wedding guest "who stoppeth one of three" and proceeds to regale each with his memorable tale. In view of my utter preoccupation with this book and its subject matter, I am profoundly grateful for the civility and forbearance of friends and family and the love and understanding of my wife – Milly – and partners – Barbara and Nell.

*Note from Nell Minow*: Thanks and love to my extended family, including all of the Minows and Apatoffs; my friends Kathy and Andrew Stephen, Kristie Miller, Patty Marx, Jeff Sonnenfeld, Jesse Norman, Tom Dunkel, Judy Viorst, Sarah Teslik, Adam Frankel, Judy Pomeranz, Cynthea Riesenberg, the Klein and Marlette families, Nadine Prosperi, Deborah Baughman, Jon Friedman, Desson Howe, Deborah Davidson, John Adams, Shannon Hackett, David Drew, Beth Young, Ann Yerger, Terry Savage, Bill Pedersen, Gary Waxman, Sarah Kavenaugh, Jane Leavy, Isabel Contreras, Steve Wallman, Sam Natapoff, Toby Kent, Michael Kinsley, Parvané Hashemi, Ken Suslick, Ellen and Sandy Twaddell, Steve Friess, Duncan Clark, Ellen Burka, Jim Richter, Michael Deal, and Stuart Brotman. Very special thanks to two very special girls, Lauren Webster and Alison Anthes. Thanks, as ever, to Bob Monks, the perfect partner.

Most of all, I want to thank my family – my children, Benjamin and Rachel, and my husband, David, still the best person I know.

# INTRODUCTION

The importance of corporate governance became dramatically clear in 2002 as a series of corporate meltdowns, frauds, and other catastrophes led to the destruction of billions of dollars of shareholder wealth, the loss of thousands of jobs, the criminal investigation of dozens of executives, and record-breaking bankruptcy filings. Seven of the 12 largest bankruptcies in American history were filed in 2002 alone. The names Enron, Tyco, Adelphia, WorldCom, and Global Crossing have eclipsed past great scandals like National Student Marketing, Equity Funding, and ZZZZ Best. Part of what made them so arresting was how much money was involved. The six-figure fraud at National Student Marketing seems almost endearingly modest by today's standards. Part was the colorful characters, from those who were already well known, like Martha Stewart and Jack Welch, to those who became well known when their businesses collapsed, like Ken Lay at Enron and the Rigas family at Adelphia. Part was the breathtaking hubris – as John Plender says in his 2003 book, *Going Off the Rails*, "Bubbles and hubris go hand in hand." And then there were the unforgettable details, from the $6,000 shower curtain the shareholders unknowingly bought for Tyco CEO Dennis Kozlowski to the swap of admission to a tony pre-school in exchange for a favorable analyst recommendation on ATT at Citigroup.

Another reason for the impact of these stories was that they occurred in the context of a falling market, a drop off from the longest, strongest bull market in US history. In the 1990s we saw billions of dollars of fraudulently overstated books at Cendant, Livent, Rite Aid, and Waste Management, but those were trivial distractions in a bull market fueled by dot.com companies. Those days were so heady and optimistic that you didn't need to lie. Why create fake earnings when an honest disclosure that you had no idea when you were going to make a profit wouldn't stop the avalanche of investors ready to give Palm a bigger market cap than Apple on the day of its IPO?

But the most important reason these scandals became the most widely reported domestic story of the year was the sense that every one of the mechanisms set up to provide checks and balances failed at the same time.

All of a sudden, everyone was interested in corporate governance. The term was even mentioned for the first time in the president's annual State of the Union address. Massive new legislation, the Sarbanes-Oxley Act, was quickly passed by Congress and the SEC had its busiest rulemaking season in 70 years as it developed the regulations to implement it. The New York Stock Exchange and NASDAQ proposed new listing standards that would require companies to improve their corporate governance or no longer be able to trade their securities. The rating agencies, S&P and Moody's, who had failed to issue early warnings on the bankrupt companies, announced that they would factor in governance in their future analyses. Corporate governance is now and forever will be properly understood as a element of risk – risk for investors, whose interests may not be protected by ineffectual or corrupt managers and directors, and risk for employees, communities, lenders, suppliers, and customers as well.

Just as people will always be imaginative and aggressive in creating new ways to make money legally, there will be some who will devote that same talent to doing it illegally, and there will always be people who are naive or avaricious enough to fall for it. Scam artists used to use faxes to entice suckers into Ponzi schemes and Nigerian fortunes. Now, they use e-mail. Or, sometimes, they use audited financial reports.

Were the scandals of 2002 any worse in scope or magnitude than they have ever been before? Most of the focus has been on less than a dozen of the thousands of publicly traded companies, and the overwhelming majority of executives, directors, and auditors are on the level.

If the rising tide of a bull market lifts all the boats, then when the tide goes out some of those boats are going to founder on the rocks. That's just the market doing its inexorable job of sorting. Some companies (and their managers and shareholders) got a free ride during the 1990s due to overall market buoyancy. If the directors and executives were smart, they recognized what was going on and used the access to capital to fund their next steps. If they were not as smart, they thought they deserved their success. If they were really dumb, they thought it would go on for ever.

One factor that can make the difference between smart and dumb choices is corporate governance. In essence, corporate governance is the structure that is intended to make sure that the right questions get asked and that checks and balances are in place to make sure that the answers reflect what is best for the creation of long-term, sustainable value. When that structure gets subverted, it becomes too easy to succumb to the temptation to engage in self-dealing.

# Case in point: Should the Chicago Cubs play night games?

Can CEOs decide not to pursue opportunities that will increase revenues? In 1968, some shareholders of the Wrigley Corporation sued the company and its directors for failing to install lights in Chicago's Wrigley Field. The shareholders claimed that the company's operating losses for four years were the result of its negligence and mismanagement. If the field had lights, the Cubs could play at night, when revenues from attendance, concessions, and radio and television broadcasts were the greatest. The shareholders argued that the sole reason for failing to install the lights was the personal opinion of William Wrigley, the president of the company, that baseball was a daytime sport, and that night games would lead to a deterioration of the neighborhood. "Thus," the complaint concluded, "Wrigley and the directors who acquiesced in this policy were acting against the financial welfare of the Cubs in an arbitrary and capricious manner, causing waste of corporate assets. They were not exercising reasonable care or prudence in the management of the corporation's affairs."[1]

The court ruled against the shareholders. As long as the decision was made "without an element of fraud, illegality, or conflict of interest, and if there was no showing of damage *to the corporation*, then such questions of policy and management are within the limits of director discretion as a matter of business judgment," the court ruled (emphasis added).

*Do you agree with this result? Should the management of a public corporation (a company receiving capital from the public) be able to forgo additional returns to shareholders on the basis of a CEO's personal opinions about the company's product? How relevant are concerns about whether baseball should be played at night and the impact on the neighborhood? More important, who is in the best position to decide how relevant those concerns are? Does it affect your answer to know that every other major league playing field had night games? Does it affect your answer that Mr. Wrigley, at the time of this case, held 80 percent of the company's stock? If it does change your answer, how? And why?*

# Case in point: Should AT&T owners pay for propaganda?

Is a corporation entitled to free speech? A Massachusetts statute prohibited corporations from making expenditures to influence the vote on "any questions submitted to the voters, other than one materially affecting any of the property, business, or assets of the corporation." The law made it clear that this prohibition extended to all tax issues, even those that did "materially affect" the company. The statute was declared unconstitutional because it infringed the First Amendment rights of the company to freedom of speech.[2] Two justices of the Supreme Court who heard a case raising some similar issues had opposite reactions.

Justice William Brennan did not want corporate management to use the shareholders' money to promote their ideas: "The State surely has a compelling interest in preventing a corporation it has chartered from exploiting those who do not wish to contribute to the Chamber's political message. 'A's right to receive information does not require the state to permit B to steal from C the funds that alone will enable B to make the communication.'"[3]

Justice Anton Scalia thought it was worthwhile to bring ideas to the marketplace, and he did not worry that the extra support for those ideas from the corporate bank account would sway anyone otherwise unwilling to buy them: "The advocacy of [AT&T or General Motors] will be effective only to the extent that it brings to the people's attention ideas which – despite the invariably self-interested and probably uncongenial source – strike them as true."[4]

*Do you agree with this result? What do you think was the rationale for such a statute in the first place? Should the management of a public corporation be able to use the shareholders' money to express its views (or further its political agenda) when those views may not be shared by the people who are paying the bill? A corporation is an entity created by law that has some of the same rights as individuals – does that include all of the freedom of speech rights granted to individuals by the Constitution?*

The Supreme Court has expanded the protections for the oxymoronic "commercial free speech" since this ruling. In a 2002 case called Thompson v. Western States Medical Center, the court invalidated a statute that prohibited the advertising of "compounded" drugs, medications created for specific patients by combining two approved drugs. Because the combined form of the drugs had not received FDA approval, the law permitting their manufacture prohibited their being advertised. But the court found that the government cannot legitimately deny the public truthful commercial information to prevent the public from making bad decisions with the information. *Why not? How does this fit with the traditional justification for freedom of speech?*

Authors Russel Mokhiber and Robert Weissman argue, "If the Court is going to justify commercial speech protections based on the public's right to know, as opposed to the speaker's right to speak, it makes sense for the government to make determinations about whether the commercial information actually will educate the public to advance public policy goals. It is hardly a revelation that advertising contains promotional elements that may drown out its educational benefits."[5]

But the California Supreme Court found that Nike's inaccurate reports about pay and working conditions in its overseas factories were not protected as commercial speech, even though they addressed what might be considered political matters rather than just advertising its products. The intention of the statement was to encourage people to buy sneakers, so the court ruled that they were entitled only to the narrower protection given to advertising and other forms of commercial speech. The United States Supreme Court has deferred its ruling pending further fact finding.

---

# Case in point: Who pays the penalty when babies drink sugar water?

How do you punish a corporation? The president and vice-president of Beech-Nut admitted that they knowingly permitted adulterated apple juice to be sold for babies. The babies who drank the juice, of course, had no way of knowing that the juice was not right, and no way of communicating it if they did. The company pled guilty to 215 counts of violating federal food and drug laws, and paid a $2 million fine. According to the *New York Times*, its market share dropped 15 percent. The president and vice-president were not fired. On the contrary – the company paid all of their legal fees and their salaries until their appeals ran out. No one from the company ever went to jail or paid a fine out of his own pocket. On the witness stand, one of the executives explained his decision to continue to market the adulterated juice: "What was I supposed to do? Close down the factory?"

*Is this the right result? What would be the result if the men involved had sold adulterated apple juice from a street corner or a local store, without the protection of the corporate structure? Is it fair for the shareholders to pay the fine in addition to suffering the reduction in share value? What was the executive supposed to do? Once he found out that the juice was adulterated, should he have closed down the factory? What reporting structure or incentive structure or set of guidelines for employees would be most likely to achieve the best result? Who will or should go to jail because of the frauds at Enron, Global Crossing, WorldCom, Adelphia, and the others?*

There is one theme to all three of these cases, and indeed to all problems of corporate governance, and that is the issue of agency costs. The price we all pay for the benefits of the corporate structure is our loss of control. Investors lose control over the use of their capital. Managers lose control over their sources of funding. Other participants in the corporate structure – employees, creditors, and so forth – also lose some measure of control. The board has the oversight responsibility. It monitors the extent to which the various corporate participants retain control, the costs and benefits of their attempts to do so, and the resulting balance of powers among them.

---

# Case in point: A CEO's perspective

These excerpts are from a speech by a leading CEO at a 1999 conference on ethics and corporate boards:

[A] strong, independent, and knowledgeable board can make a significant difference in the performance of any company. . . . [O]ur corporate governance guidelines emphasize "the qualities of strength of character, an inquiring and independent mind, practical wisdom and mature judgment . . .". It is no accident that we put "strength of character" first. Like any successful company, we must have directors who start with what is right, who do not have hidden agendas, and who strive to make judgments about what is best for the company, and not about what is best for themselves or some other constituency . . .

[W]e look first and foremost for principle-centered leaders. That includes principle-centered directors. The second thing we look for are independent and inquiring minds. We are always thinking about the company's business and what we are trying to do. . . . We want board members whose active participation improves the quality of our decisions.

Finally, we look for individuals who have mature judgment – individuals who are thoughtful and rigorous in what they say and decide. They should be people whom other directors and management will respect and listen to very carefully, and who can mentor CEOs and other senior managers. . . . The responsibility of our board – a responsibility which I expect them to fulfill – is to ensure legal and ethical conduct by the company and by everyone in the company. That requirement does not exist by happenstance. It is the most important thing we expect from board members . . .

What a CEO really expects from a board is good advice and counsel, both of which will make the company stronger and more successful; support for those investments and decisions that serve the interests of the company and its stakeholders; and warnings in those cases in which investments and decisions are not beneficial to the company and its stakeholders.

---

That speech, "What a CEO Expects from a Board," was delivered by then Enron CEO Kenneth Lay. The company's code of ethics is similarly impressive. The company got high marks from just about everyone for best corporate governance practices.

The board looked good on paper: the former dean of the Stanford business school was chairman of the audit committee. Another director was formerly a member of the British House of Lords and House of Commons, as well as Energy Minister. In addition, the board included one of the most prominent business leaders in Hong Kong, the co-founder and former president of Gulf and Western, two sitting CEOs of large U.S. corporations, and the former head of the Commodities Futures Trading Corporation, who was an Asian woman with an economics Ph.D., and married to a prominent Republican congressman. There was also a former professor of economics and a former head of General Electric's Power Division worldwide, a senior executive of an investment fund with a Ph.D. in mathematics, the former president of Houston Natural Gas, the former head of M. D. Anderson, the former head of a major energy and petroleum company, and a former Deputy Secretary of the Treasury and Ph.D. economist.

That shows that it is easy to achieve the letter of good corporate governance without achieving the spirit or the reality. While it is tempting to engage in checklists of structural indicators, there is no evidence that intuitively appealing provisions like independent outside directors rather than people whose commercial or social ties might create conflicts of interest, or annual election of directors rather than staggered terms have any correlation to the creation of shareholder value or the prevention of self-dealing. Therefore, it is important to keep in mind throughout this book that corporate governance is about making sure that the right questions get asked and the right checks and balances are in place, and not about some superficial or theoretical construct.

William Donaldson, Chairman of the Securities and Exchange Commission, made this point in a 2003 speech at the Washington Economic Policy Conference:

> a "check the box" approach to good corporate governance will not inspire a true sense of ethical obligation. It could merely lead to an array of inhibiting, "politically correct" dictates. If this was the case, ultimately corporations would not strive to meet higher standards, they would only strain under new costs associated with fulfilling a mandated process that could produce little of the desired effect. They would lose the freedom to make innovative decisions that an ethically sound entrepreneurial culture requires.
>
> As the board properly exercises its power, representing all stakeholders, I would suggest that the board members define the culture of ethics that they expect all aspects of the company to embrace. The philosophy that they articulate must pertain not only the board's selection of a chief executive officer, but also the spirit and very DNA of the corporate body itself – from top to bottom and from bottom to top. Only after the board meets this fundamental obligation to define the culture and ethics of the corporation – and for that matter of the board itself – can it go on and make its own decisions about the implementation of this culture.

In this book we will focus on the three most significant players in the corporate process: shareholders, managers, and directors. Together, these forces shape a corporation's focus, its direction, its productivity and competitiveness, and ultimately, its viability and legitimacy. First, however, we will begin with an inquiry into the nature of the corporation itself.

# Ideas about corporations

Concentration of economic power in all-embracing corporations represents a kind of private government which is a power unto itself – a regimentation of other people's money and other people's lives. *Franklin Roosevelt*

The myth that holds that the great corporation is a puppet of the market, the powerless servant of the consumer, is, in fact, one *of* the services by which its power is perpetuated. *John Kenneth Galbraith*

Merchants have no country. The mere spot they stand on does not constitute so strong an attachment as that from which they draw their gains. *Thomas Jefferson*

By making ordinary business decisions [corporate] managers now have more power than most sovereign governments to determine where people will live; what work they will do, if any; what they will eat, drink, and wear: what sorts of knowledge, schools, and universities they will encourage; and what kinds of society their children will inherit. *Richard J. Barnet and Ronald Mueller*

Corporations, especially the large and complex ones with which we have to live, now appear to possess some of the qualities of nation states including, perhaps, an alarming capacity to insulate their members from the moral consequences of their actions. *Paul Eddy, Elaine Potter, and Bruce Page*

## NOTES

1.  *Shlensky v. Wrigley*, 95 Ill. App. 2d 173, 237 (1968).
2.  *First National Bank of Boston v. Bellotti*, 435 US 765 (1978).
3.  *Austin, Michigan Secretary of State, et al. v. Michigan State Chamber of Commerce*, Brennan's concurring opinion, p. 7.
4.  Ibid., Scalia's dissent, p. 5.
5.  "The Final Call," Sept. 24, 2002. <http://www.finalcall.com/perspectives/free_speech09-24-2002.htm>.

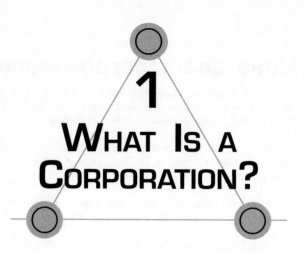

# 1
# WHAT IS A CORPORATION?

Definitions of the term *corporation* reflect the perspectives (and the biases) of the people writing the definitions. Anyone who tries to come up with a definition is like the blind men who tried to describe an elephant – one feeling the tail and calling it a snake, one feeling the leg and calling it a tree, one feeling the side and calling it a wall. Similarly, some lawyers and economists describe the corporation as simply "a nexus (bundle) of contracts," arguing that the corporation is nothing more than the sum of all of the agreements leading to its creation.[1] Here are some other attempts to describe or define the corporation:

## DEFINITIONS

"The business corporation is an instrument through which capital is assembled for the activities of producing and distributing goods and services and making investments. Accordingly, a basic premise of corporation law is that a business corporation should have as its objective the conduct of such activities with a view to enhancing the corporation's profit and the gains of the corporation's owners, that is, the shareholders." *Melvin Aron Eisenberg*[2]

"A corporation is an artificial being, invisible, intangible, and existing only in the contemplation of the law. Being the mere creature of the law, it possesses only those properties which the charter of its creation confers on it, either expressly or as incidental to its very existence. These are such as are supposed best calculated to effect the object for which it was created. Among the most important are immortality, and, if the expression be allowed, individuality; properties by which a perpetual succession of many persons are considered the same, and may act as a single individual." *Chief Justice John Marshall*

"A body of persons granted a charter legally recognizing them as a separate entity having its own rights, privileges, and liabilities distinct from those of its members." *American Heritage Dictionary*

"An artificial person or legal entity created by, or under the authority of, the laws of a state . . . The corporation is distinct from the individuals who comprise it." *Black's Law Dictionary, 6th edition, 1990*

"When they [the individuals composing a corporation] are consolidated and united into a corporation, they and their successors are then considered as one person in law . . . for all the individual members that have existed from the foundation to the present time, or that shall ever hereafter exist, are but one person in law – a person that never dies: in like manner as the river Thames is still the same river, though the parts which compose it are changing every instant." *Blackstone*

"An ingenious device for obtaining individual profit without individual responsibility." *Ambrose Bierce, The Devil's Dictionary*

*What do these definitions tell you about the corporation? Are any of them incompatible, or do they differ only in their emphasis? Can you think of a better definition?*

All of these definitions have some validity, and all, including the one from *The Devil's Dictionary*, reflect the corporation's key feature – its ability to draw its resources from a variety of groups and establish and maintain its own persona separate from all of them. As Henry Ford once said, "A great business is really too big to be human."

In our view, a corporation is a mechanism established to allow different parties to contribute capital, expertise, and labor, for the maximum benefit of all of them. The investor gets the chance to participate in the profits of the enterprise without taking responsibility for the operations. The management gets the chance to run the company without taking the responsibility of personally providing the funds. In order to make both of these possible, the shareholders have limited liability and limited involvement in the company's affairs. That involvement includes, at least in theory, the right to elect directors and the fiduciary obligation of directors and management to protect their interests.

This independent entity must still relate to a wide variety of "constituents," including its directors, managers, employees, shareholders, customers, creditors and suppliers, as well as the members of the community and the government. Each of these relationships itself has a variety of constituents. The corporation's relationship to its employees varies, for example, depending on the circumstances: whether or not they are members of a union, whether or not they are pension plan participants. And each of these relationships affects the direction and focus of the corporation. The study of corporate governance is the study of the connection of those relationships to the corporation and to one another.

## EVOLUTION OF THE CORPORATE STRUCTURE

While, in law, a corporation is, at least for some purposes, considered to be a fictional "person," at its core each corporation is in fact a structure. The corporate structure was developed to meet particular needs that were not being met by earlier forms available to business. It evolved through a Darwinian process in which each development made it stronger, more resilient, and more impervious to control by outsiders.

As we examine that evolutionary pattern, it will become clear that every change the corporate form has undergone has been directed toward the corporation's own perpetuation and growth. The advantages and disadvantages of this fact of business life are discussed throughout this book.

In their earliest Anglo-Saxon form, municipal and educational corporations were granted perpetual existence and control over their own functions as a way of insuring

**Figure 1.1**   The Company Corporation advertisement
Reproduced with permission from *The Company Corporation*

independence from the otherwise all-encompassing power of the king. By the seventeenth century, corporations were created by the state for specific purposes, like the settlement of India and the American colonies. Their effectiveness is credited as one of the principal explanations for Europe's half-millennium domination of the globe. Limiting investors' liability to the amount they actually invested was a critical factor in attracting the necessary capital for this unprecedented achievement.[3]

Even as recently as 1932, US Supreme Court Justice Louis Brandeis argued that "The privilege of engaging in such commerce in corporate form is one which the state may confer or may withhold as it sees fit."[4] He emphasized the importance of making sure that states conferred the privilege of the corporate structure only in those cases where it was consistent with public policy and welfare, as, for example, "as a means of raising revenue; or, in order to procure for the community a public utility, a bank, or a desired industry not otherwise attainable; or . . . an instrumentality of business which will facilitate the establishment and conduct of new and large enterprises deemed of public benefit."[5] He noted that:

> The prevalence of the corporation in America has led men of this generation to act, at times, as if the privilege of doing business in corporate form were inherent in the citizen, and has led them to accept the evils attendant upon the free and unrestricted use of the corporate mechanism as if these evils were the inescapable price of civilized life, and hence, to be borne with resignation. Throughout the greater part of our history, a different view prevailed. Although the value of this instrumentality in commerce and industry was fully recognized, incorporation for business was commonly denied long after it had been freely granted for religious, educational, and charitable purposes. It was denied because of fear. Fear of encroachment upon the liberties and opportunities of the individual. Fear of the subjugation of labor to capital. Fear of monopoly. Fear that the absorption of capital by corporations, and their perpetual life, might bring evils similar to those which attended mortmain.[6] There was a sense of some insidious menace inherent in large aggregations of capital, particularly when held by corporations. So at first the corporate privilege was granted sparingly; and only when the grant seemed necessary in order to procure for the community some specific benefit otherwise unattainable. The later enactment of general corporation laws does not signify that the apprehension of corporate domination had been overcome.[7]

Brandeis points out that the decision to remove the strict requirements imposed on corporations was not based on the legislators' "conviction that maintenance of these restrictions was undesirable in itself, but to the conviction that it was futile to insist on them; because local restriction would be circumvented by foreign incorporation."[8] In other words, the characteristics of the corporate form were so important to people in business that legislators recognized that they could not beat them, and therefore might as well join them, or at least permit and then tax them.

What made the corporate form so appealing, so essential? According to Dean Robert Clark of Harvard Law School, the four characteristics essential to the vitality and appeal of the corporate form are:

1. limited liability for investors;
2. free transferability of investor interests;
3. legal personality (entity–attributable powers, life span, and purpose); and
4. centralized management.[9]

He adds that three developments, starting in the late nineteenth century, made these attributes particularly important. The first was the need for firms far larger than had previously been the norm. Technological advances led to new economies of scale. For the first time it made sense to have firms of more than a dozen people, and suddenly there were companies employing hundreds, then thousands. The second was the accompanying need for capital from a range of sources broader than in the past, when the only game in town was a small group of wealthy individuals who had previously invested by private negotiation. The third condition was that private ownership of investment property had to be "accepted as a social norm." The concept hardly seems revolutionary now, but it was radical, even a century ago, when it was widely assumed that most property would belong to the state, the church, or a select number of wealthy people. While this tradition was challenged from time to time, as, for example, during the Colonial and Revolutionary period of US history, the idea of widespread private property is essentially a modern one.

Let's look at Clark's four characteristics.

*1. Limited liability.* The notion of limited liability goes back to at least 2000 BC, when merchants provided the financing for seagoing vessels. But the English courts first spelled it out during the fifteenth century. It means that the corporation is separate from its owners and employees; what is owed to the corporation is not owed to the individuals in the group that make up the corporation; and what the group owes is not owed by the individuals that make it up. Hence, if a corporation goes bankrupt and is sued by its creditors for recovery of debts, the individual members of the corporation are not individually liable.

If a dozen people pool their funds to create a partnership, they risk losing not just their stakes, but everything they have. Partners who operate a restaurant are personally liable for debts to unpaid creditors and employees, for any injuries to a patron who sues after falling down the restaurant stairs, and for the misconduct of fellow partners, even of which they had no knowledge or control. Investors in a corporation that operates a restaurant have no such risk. If Beech-Nut (see case in point in the introduction) had been a partnership, all of the partners could have been liable to pay the fine as well as for any damages the court might award to the consumers who purchased the adulterated juice.

This kind of shared liability may work well when the partnership is small enough to enable everyone to keep an eye on everyone else and share in all decisions, and when the personal investment of each partner is big enough to give each one the same incentive for low risk and high returns.[10] But this oversight and incentive would be impossible in a setting of not just dozens, but millions of "partners" investing in a company. No one would buy stock in a large corporation if the risk of loss were unlimited. One of the primary advantages of investing in stock is the certainty that whatever happens, the risk of loss is limited to the amount of the investment.

There is a catch here, however. With limited liability comes limited authority. A partner has a co-equal right to run the company with all of the other partners (unless the parties have agreed to another arrangement by contract). It is the partner's high level of control that makes the high level of liability acceptable. And it is the shareholder's low level of risk that makes the low level of control acceptable.

One other note on limited liability. During the 1980s, another form of limited liability became popular, as a result of revisions in the bankruptcy law, giving shareholders a second chance to profit from failing enterprises. Airline companies were able to avoid union contracts and asbestos companies were able to avoid tort liability. Most prominently of all, Texaco was able to negotiate down the damages assessed against it arising out of the Pennzoil acquisition. It became expedient even for companies with substantial assets to declare bankruptcy because of the protections – and the extra time – it gave them. Ultimately, many of these companies emerged from bankruptcy with their liabilities better organized, and the shareholders – whose downside liability was always limited – were given a second chance to profit.

*2. Transferability.* Just as important as limited liability in achieving an acceptable level of risk is the ability to transfer one's holding freely. A partnership interest is complicated and difficult to value, and there is no stock exchange where partnership interests can be traded. By contrast, stock is almost as liquid as cash. A shareholder who is concerned that the stock may be losing value can sell almost immediately.

Transferability is also a function of limited authority. It is as though the shareholder says, "I will put my money at risk, with little authority to control the enterprise, as long as I can control my own risk by selling out any time I want to."

*3. Legal personality.* A partnership dies with its partners. Or it dies when one partner decides to quit (unless there are explicit contractual provisions to the contrary). Continuing after the death or resignation of the partners can be complicated and expensive. A corporation lives on for as long as it has capital. This is a fairly recent development. Business corporations in the United States during the nineteenth century usually had a life limited to a term of years. As Justice Brandeis wrote in *Liggett v. Lee*, only in the most recent times have people assumed that perpetual existence was a necessary – to say nothing of a desirable – attribute of corporations.

Legal personality has other benefits as well. One is demonstrated by the Beech-Nut example in the introduction, where actions that would result in a penalty for an individual, perhaps even a jail sentence, have no such result when the individual commits them as part of a corporation. Another is in the First Amendment example in the introduction, where corporate management is allowed to use investors' money to promote a political agenda with which they may not agree. Another is ownership. It is because corporations are defined as legal persons that they may own property, including real estate, copyrights, and other assets.

This aspect, too, depends on limited authority by investors. To the extent the investors do have authority, they jeopardize the company when they are unavailable to exercise it. Legal personality allows the corporation to act, to own, and to continue past the life span of any individual or group.

*4. Centralized management.* Partnerships are managed by consensus or majority vote (unless partners explicitly agree otherwise). The point is that every partner has, if he wants it, a co-equal say in the affairs of the company. In a corporation, the power to determine the company's overall direction is given to the directors and the power to control its day-to-day operations is given to the managers.

This is another aspect of the limited authority given to investors. In order to allow the company to operate with maximum efficiency, the shareholders give up the right to make decisions on all but the most general issues facing the company.

Initially, a corporation was not permitted to engage in any activity unless it was specifically approved by the state in granting its charter. The original rule was based on the state's presumption *against* corporate activity; every undertaking had to be explicitly justified and approved. But as the corporate form became increasingly popular, the presumption shifted. By the late nineteenth century, business corporations were permitted to organize for any lawful purpose, without requiring the prior approval of the government.

Just as dramatic – and just as important – as this shift in the relationship between the corporation and the government was the shift in the relationship between the corporation and its shareholders. As corporations grew in size and age, their ownership became increasingly fractionated and markets developed to assure almost total immediate liquidity. This increased their strength and scope, but it reduced their accountability. In the early days, when the directors sat around a real board, they represented the shareholders because they *were* the shareholders. As corporations grew in size and complexity, the law tried to develop a standard of performance for directors that would encourage the same sense of duty and care that they would naturally use when they were representing themselves.

## THE PURPOSE OF A CORPORATION

Corporations are such a pervasive element in everyday life that it is difficult to step back far enough to see them clearly. Corporations do not just determine what goods and services are available in the marketplace, but, more than any other institution, corporations determine the quality of the air we breathe and the water we drink, and even where we live. It helps to spend some time talking about the purposes that corporations serve.

### Human satisfaction

Business corporations provide an outlet for the satisfaction of essential human drives – quests for fulfilment, success, and security, for creative expression and for the competitive spirit. The corporate structure allows value to be placed on differing contributions that combine together so that the whole is greater than the sum of its parts. Through corporations, skills and experience can be competitively marketed and rewarded according to their contribution to value. Corporations have provided a means for the ambitious to achieve, the enterprising to prosper, and the ingenious to be enriched beyond their fondest expectations – the role played by the church or the military or the crown at other times and in other cultures. Ideally, money invested buys perpetual ownership in a cornucopia of self-renewing abundance. Only the amount invested is at risk, and, if an investor buys ownership in several companies, that risk can be spread, and a portfolio corporation can be divested at any time to reduce significantly the possibility of loss.

Above all else, creating a structure for the agglomeration of talent and capital has permitted an increasing number of individuals the opportunity to create wealth for themselves and their descendants.

### Social structure

Human beings have created social structures since their cave days, in order to foster co-operation and specialization. Corporations offer lasting and resilient social structures. For centuries, these structures were devoted to goals that were not (necessarily) financial. For example, during the Dark Ages and the Middle Ages, Western man was organized under the single church. Toward the end of the medieval era, signs of this "church triumphant" system abounded. Under its banner, whole populations committed themselves for decades to the Crusades. The gross national product of the continent was devoted to the construction of magnificent houses of worship. Then, in a remarkable turn of events aided by religious protest, Henry VIII abruptly asserted the primacy of civil authority. For several centuries, up to the end of World War I, civil order based on hereditary rulers dominated the West.

At about this time, power in the form of ability to create wealth through goods and services desired by a population willing to pay passed to an entirely new type of entity, the huge worldwide corporations (see the Standard Oil case study in chapter 2).

### Efficiency and efficacy

Corporations enable people to get things done. The words "businesslike," "professional," and "enterprise" are synonymous with beneficial efficiency and efficacy. The translation of an idea into a product; human ingenuity into bricks, mortar, and equipment; and savings into "growth stocks," has materially enhanced the lives of many people in democratic capitalist societies.

The challenge has been to adapt the corporate form to the needs of society. To this end, the state has maintained the original corporate model, chartering special-purpose corporations to achieve a particular objective. For example, in order to assure better control by America of its fuel needs, the US Congress created the United States Synthetic Fuels Corporation in 1980 and attempted to use private sector personnel and techniques to solve a public problem. Similarly, organizations such as the Federal National Mortgage Association show the government's recognition that if it is going to compete with Wall Street, it must be through a private, for-profit organization. That organizations own corporate governance problems in 2003 – the abrupt departure of the top three executives amid accusations of accounting problems – shows that this public–private combination is no better at preventing abuse than one that is strictly government or strictly private.

This works both ways, of course. It is an understatement to say that the government does not hesitate to regulate corporations for a variety of reasons, some tangential to the corporation's activities. Society can induce or restrain particular corporate activities through tax and regulatory "fine-tuning." For example, much New Deal legislation attempted to achieve social goals while pursuing economic ones. The Davis–Bacon Act of 1931 is one of three labor statutes passed in the 1930s to protect workers employed on government contracts. Davis–Bacon provides minimum wage requirements and fringe benefits for government-employed construction workers. More recent examples include laws and regulations designed to promote safety in the workplace and prohibiting discrimination on the basis of age, race, gender, and disability, rules requiring employers to grant "family leave" to those who required it, and rules enlisting private companies to help gather information on suspected terrorists.

## Ubiquity and flexibility

Corporations give individuals a greater and more lasting sphere of action. Corporations have no boundaries in time or space. A corporation continues despite the death or retirement of its highest officers. A corporation that is chartered in Delaware can do business anywhere in the world. Corporations can be moved. They can be transformed by a revision to their legal or financial structure. A corporation's officers and directors can change its place of incorporation, close existing places of business and open new ones virtually without restraint, and reallocate investment capital. American companies change their state of incorporation to receive the benefits of favorable laws, or reincorporate offshore for tax reasons. The free trade agreements in Europe and Northern America are creating a "borderless world" in which a company's legal domicile relates to nothing but its own convenience.

An individual may decide to refrain from certain risky actions for several reasons. He may fear blame, shame, liability, even prison. But corporations, though they may be fined, cannot be jailed. This makes the corporate form a way of transferring enterprise liabilities to society as a whole. With their ability to provide jobs, corporations are aggressively courted by competing locations and states and countries, who "race to the bottom," imposing fewer and fewer constraints on profit potential. The state anti-takeover laws enacted hastily to protect local companies from the prospect of a contest for control (even, as in Massachusetts, signed by the governor in the headquarters of the company in question) are just one example.

## Identity

Indeed, corporations have a life, and even citizenship, of their own, with attendant rights and powers. They appear to have personalities. We speak of "Ma Bell" and "Big Blue."

Corporations are "persons" within the meaning of the United States Federal Constitution and Bill of Rights. They are entitled to protection against the taking of their property without due process of law. They are entitled (at least to some extent) to freedom of speech. They can contribute money to political causes and campaigns, though some restrictions apply, due to post-Watergate reforms.

As the source of jobs, and therefore of the livelihood for people who vote, they have significant political capital. Corporations, therefore, are powerful participants in the deliberations of our lawmakers.

Corporations also decide what products and services will be available. This applies not just to laundry soap and toothpaste, but also to medications and safety equipment. They decide investment priorities. They establish workplace conditions. They set prices.

## THE CORPORATION AS A "PERSON"

Author and reporter William Greider describes the development of corporate "personalities":

> The great project of corporate lawyers, extending over generations, has been to establish full citizenship for their business organizations. They argue that their companies are entitled to the same political rights, save voting, that the Constitution guarantees to people. In 1886 the Supreme Court declared, without hearing arguments, that corporations would henceforth be considered "persons" for purposes of the 14th Amendment – the "due process" amendment that was established to protect the newly emancipated black slaves after the Civil War. Fifty years later, justice Hugo Black reviewed the Supreme Court's many decisions applying the 14th Amendment and observed that less than one half of one percent invoked it in protection of the Negro race, and more than 50 percent asked that its benefits be extended to corporations . . .
>
> In the modem era of regulation [corporate lawyers] are invoking the Bill of Rights to protect their organizations from federal laws . . . Corporations, in other words, claim to be "citizens" of the Republic, not simply for propaganda or good public relations, but in the actual legal sense of claiming constitutional rights and protections . . . Whatever legal theories may eventually develop around this question, the political implications are profound. If corporations are citizens, then other citizens – the living, breathing kind – necessarily become less important to the processes of self-government.[11]

## THE CORPORATION AS A COMPLEX ADAPTIVE SYSTEM

In the authors' first book, we said that the corporate structure was designed to be so vital and robust that it was like an "externalizing machine." There is no malice involved – it is just the flip side of its purpose of wealth generation. Therefore, it will do whatever it can to hang on to its earnings and push its costs off of its balance sheet. This can be done, for example, through legislation that increases barriers to entry for its competitors or limits its liabilities. The self-perpetuating life force built into the corporate structure fights the systems intended to impose accountability, and through that, legitimacy.

"Externality" is the vocabulary of economics. Another way to think about this is to use the vocabulary of science and call it a "complex adaptive system."

These systems, whether in physics, biology or economics, can be analyzed as patterns and modes of behavior that can inform activity in other fields. One cannot literally find in corporate behavior a repetition of the interaction of subatomic particles; one can, however, notice living patterns that seem to replicate in corporate experience – tendencies towards immortality, for unlimited size, unlimited power, unlimited license.

Only when one understands that corporations have adaptive characteristics does it become clear that modification of their behavior must come from within the organizations. It has not been convenient for society to recognize the general ineffectiveness of external restraints on corporate activity. Neither government nor marketplace has the capacity to require corporate functioning to conform to society's interests. Large corporations retain the services of the most talented professionals, the most persuasive lobbyists: former Senator George Mitchell, "hero" of the Irish peace talks, is the principal lobbyist for the tobacco industry. They control the most influential newspapers, TV (all three American networks are owned by diversified conglomerates – GE, Disney, and Westinghouse) and magazine outlets, and the best lawyers. With such competitive strength, it is difficult for the widely dispersed elements that comprise society to effectively assert a contrary view. They even control their own shareholders; the corporations themselves are the largest investors through their pension funds, often the greatest asset and liability even a major corporation has on its balance sheet. For example, in 2001, General Motor's pension assets of $74 billion were worth 271 percent of the company's market capitalization. And in 2003 the *Washington Post* reported that the $19 billion under-funding of GM's pension fund was driving the company to slash car prices to raise money quickly. This astonishing development – a pension deficit as the driver of corporate strategy – had a predictable result. GM's competitors also discounted prices, resulting in reduced margins and earnings for the entire sector. The only way in which to attempt societal harmony with corporations is to understand that they are complex adaptive systems and change must come from within.

## THE CORPORATION AS A "MORAL PERSON"

Thomas Donaldson provides an analytical structure to consider how a corporation can be structured to make "moral" decisions:

> In order to qualify as a moral agent, a corporation would need to embody a process of moral decision making. On the basis of our previous discussion, this process seems to require at a minimum:
>
> 1. The capacity to use moral reasons in decision-making.
> 2. The capacity of the decision-making process to control not only overt corporate acts, but also the structure of policies and rules.
>
> [The first] is necessary to raise the corporation above the level of a mere machine. To be a moral agent, something must have reasons for what it does, not simply causes for what it does, and for something to be a moral agent, some of those reasons must be moral ones. Obviously, corporations are unable to think as humans, but they can employ reasons of a sort, and this is shown by the fact that they can be morally accountable. That is, with the proper internal structure, corporations, like humans, can be liable to give an account of their behavior where the account stipulates which moral reasons prompted their behavior.[12]

Can business "do well by doing good?" This is a perennial question. On one end of the scale, companies such as Body Shop and Ben and Jerry's have made social responsibility (or, at least, their view of social responsibility) part of their marketing strategy. Consumers can feel less guilty about buying arguably decadent products like make-up and ice cream if they know that by doing so they are supporting good causes. But can companies thrive when the cost of social responsibility raises prices too high, instead of making the products more marketable making them less so? Clearly, there is some point past which the company's goods and services will become too expensive.[13]

At one end of the scale are the most basic aspects of social responsibility, like compliance with the law. At the other end of the scale are activities so unrelated to the goods and services sold that pursuing them is considered by the marketplace to be irrelevant, even detrimental, to the company's productivity.

Look again at the very first example in this book – the lawsuit challenging the decision not to put lights in Wrigley Field. This decision, which deprived the fans of night games and the investors of a substantial source of revenue, was made on the basis of management's notion of social responsibility. Later we will consider the example of Stride Rite, which profited from its (well-deserved) reputation for commitment to the community, while it was making the (economically necessary) decision to move jobs out of the community.

The key question here, one of the core issues of corporate governance, is "Who decides?" A CEO can decide that the company's social responsibility is best met by making a substantial charitable donation to his or her alma mater, which then shows its gratitude by giving the CEO an honorary degree and a box at the school's football games. There is also a very happy and congenial member of the board of directors when the university's president is invited to the board. But is this "social responsibility?"

*Who is in the best position to make sure that any expenses not directly associated with identifiable and quantifiable returns are at least related closely enough to have a cost-effective impact on long-term value maximization? Who is in the best position to make sure that the company's definition of social responsibility is an accurate reflection of the definition of the owners? Of the community?*

# Case in point: Union Carbide and Bhopal – what happens when the company is bought out?

This is how a successor/purchaser corporation characterized a devastating chemical spill, acknowledging the tragic consequences, absolving itself of responsibility, but portraying itself as a generous and concerned entity.

From the Dow Chemical website <http://www.bhopal.com/position.htm>:

What happened in Bhopal 18 years ago was a tragedy of unprecedented gravity and human cost, which no one in industry will ever forget.

During the early hours of December 3, 1984, methyl isocyanate gas (known as MIC) leaked from a storage tank sited at a pesticide manufacturing facility in Bhopal. As it escaped, the gas drifted across the neighboring communities with devastating consequences. According to the Indian government, some 3,800 people died and thousands more were injured as a direct result of exposure to the lethal fumes.

When the disaster occurred, the Bhopal plant was operated by Union Carbide India Limited (UCIL), a 51 percent affiliate of Union Carbide Corporation. At that time, Dow had absolutely no connection with either the facility or any of the companies linked to the incident.

But 16 years after the tragedy, on February 6, 2001, Dow acquired Union Carbide's shares. Before doing so, as you might expect, the company conducted an exhaustive assessment to ensure there was absolutely no outstanding liability in relation to Bhopal. There was none; the company Dow acquired retained absolutely no responsibility for either the tragedy or for the Bhopal site.

That conclusion was based on a number of key facts:

- On February 14, 1989, a settlement agreement was reached between Union Carbide, Union Carbide India Limited and the Indian government through which Union Carbide paid $470 million in compensation, covering all claims relating to the incident.
- On October 3, 1991, the Supreme Court of India announced the findings of its review of the settlement agreement. They upheld the settlement – concluding that the amount was just, equitable and reasonable.
- Within those same findings, the Supreme Court also directed that the Government of India make up any shortfall which might in the future arise in the settlement fund and ordered it to purchase a group medical insurance policy to cover 100,000 citizens of Bhopal in case of future illnesses. These measures were specifically put in place to address any potential future issues arising from the tragedy.
- Two years later, on October 4, 1993, the US Supreme Court reaffirmed earlier US Court rulings that the only State with jurisdiction in the case against Union Carbide on matters relating to the Bhopal tragedy was India. They based this decision on the fact that UCIL was a separate and independent legal entity, managed and operated exclusively by Indian citizens in India.
- In November 1994 – more than six years before Dow acquired Union Carbide – Union Carbide sold its interest in Union Carbide India Limited to MacLeod Russel (India) Ltd. of Calcutta (later renamed Eveready Industries India Ltd. – or EIIL). As a consequence of that sale, Union Carbide retained no interest in or liability for the Bhopal site. EIIL took exclusive possession of the land under lease from the government of Madhya Pradesh. The money from this transaction was used to fund a hospital in Bhopal which now provides specialist care to victims of the tragedy.
- In 1998, the government of Madhya Pradesh revoked the EIIL lease for the Bhopal site, reclaiming the property "as is" and stating it would take responsibility for managing any cleanup or remediation work required on the site.

All of this means that when Dow completed its stock acquisition in February 2001, Union Carbide retained no responsibility whatsoever in relation to the tragedy.

But of course there is also an entirely separate humanitarian question – that is: can Dow, in its role as a corporate citizen, help to address any of the present day needs which are apparent in Bhopal?

That is why, for some time, Dow has been exploring various initiatives which might address some of those needs – just as we do in other parts of the world where we have business interests. This work continues and we remain hopeful that we can find an appropriate initiative in the not too distant future.

The issues surrounding Bhopal are extremely emotive. It is a tragedy that should never have happened. Like the rest of industry, Dow has an obligation to learn from what took place that terrible night and to take whatever measures are necessary to prevent anything like it from ever happening again.

# Case in point: Imperial Chemical Industries plc

In 1993, Sir Denys Hendersen explained to his shareholders why he was proposing to downsize Imperial Chemical Industries (ICI), a dominant company in one of the most important worldwide industries – the chemical and pharmaceutical business. ICI had sales in the tens of billions of dollars, earnings in the billions and employees in the hundreds of thousands. Yet in 1993 it proposed a "demerger" of a major unit, Zeneca.

A detailed proposal was sent to shareholders to explain the move. The company cited "important, broader trends," including "intensified competition in industrial chemicals, most notably from the Middle East and Asia Pacific, increased costs of maintaining and developing new technology, especially in the bioscience areas, together with the adverse effects of the worldwide economic recession which began in 1990" as reasons for the demerger. In response to these trends, ICI pledged "to reshape its operations . . . focusing on those businesses and territories where it enjoyed strong market positions, reducing costs in order to remain competitive and disposing of non-strategic operations. These measures continue to be vigorously implemented, although the profit improvement benefits to date have been more than offset by the impact of the economic recession."

Henderson continued in the traditional language of business and finance, explaining, "In recent years, ICI's bioscience activities have expanded rapidly and have become increasingly distinct from its traditional chemical operations, and both face very different opportunities and challenges in the years ahead. The bioscience activities employ different technologies, are more R&D intensive and serve a largely separate customer base. The Chemicals businesses are, in contrast, for the most part capital intensive, volume driven and based on large scale process technology."

What was more important, however, was what Henderson left out. He did not mention Hanson Industries, whose purchase of a significant stock position in ICI was widely credited with being the prime cause of the demerger. ICI had performed poorly for some years, and its stock price had become heavily discounted as a result. Hanson was a known raider, and when the company announced its substantial holding in ICI, commentators asked when, not if, Hanson would attempt to take over the chemical giant.

The ICI demerger pre-empted the possible bid. Hanson, had he taken over ICI, would almost certainly have completed a similar break-up. The fact that ICI restructured on its own volition made the company a far less tempting target, since the company was able to realize the kinds of values that a raider would look to achieve. Thus, the threat of takeover forced ICI to split itself into two smaller, leaner, more competitive companies.

Not that Hanson Industries applauded the demerger. As Lord White, Hanson's chairman said: "If ICI had not spent so much time during the last year fighting a bid that was never made and spent it on seeing how it could improve shareholder value it might have come up with a better solution a lot earlier."[14] (See also the Sears case study.)

Lords Hanson and White were the bearers of the new wisdom. Even the largest and richest of corporations needs to assess its position constantly and to make whatever changes are necessary to be competitive. The basis of a corporation's existence is wealth maximization – this is its reason for being. There is no such thing as a "good" corporation that is not competitively profitable. Corporations live in a world where the market determines what people will buy and what they will pay. A corporation that does not produce goods that people want at a price they are willing to pay has no reason to exist.

## THE CORPORATION IN SOCIETY

Before we evaluate the effectiveness of the major players in corporate governance, we should look at corporations from the perspective of what our society wants and needs from them. We want jobs that pay a decent wage and goods and services that meet our needs. We want challenges to our creativity and ingenuity, and when we meet those challenges, we want to feel proud of the results, and we want to be rewarded. We want corporations to work with us to keep the workplace and the environment safe. We want a continual sense of progress and growth from our corporations. We want our interest in the company – whether as employee, shareholder, customer, supplier, creditor, or neighbor – to be designed for the long term.

Two connected sets of laws govern the relationships of these constituent groups to the corporation. One is comprised of the laws imposed by the legislature and the other is private law established in agreements between the corporation and its employees, customers, suppliers, investors, and community. Ideally, the public laws would exist only as a kind of floor or backstop to establish minimum standards, permitting maximum flexibility for the corporation and its constituents to devise optimal arrangements between them. In other words, the government should step in only when the system of corporate governance cannot be assured of producing a result that is beneficial to society as a whole. To go back to our original criteria for determining who is in the best position to make a particular decision, the government should set the standards when it has better information and fewer conflicts of interest than any (or all) of the other parties who play a role in setting the course for the corporation.

In practice, however, corporations have influenced government at least as much as government has influenced business. The corporate "citizen," with the right to political speech (and political contributions) has had a powerful impact on the laws that affect it. In theory, corporations support the free market, with as little interference from government as possible. In reality, whenever corporations can persuade the government to protect them from the free market, by legislating barriers to competition or limiting their liability, they do so.

> People of the same trade seldom meet together but the conversation ends in a conspiracy against the public, or in some diversion to raise prices. *Adam Smith*

To the extent that corporate governance standards are established by public law, one could argue that these provisions' greatest value is in providing the illusion of accountability. For example, an article written by two thoughtful observers of corporate governance, one a law professor, one a judge, points to mandatory corporate governance provisions to support their argument that these rules provide a solid foundation for real (and informed) freedom of choice for investors. The rules that inspire this confidence are:

> States almost uniformly forbid perpetual directorships; they set quorum rules, which typically require a third of the board and sometimes half of the investors to participate on critical decisions; they require "major" transactions to be presented to the board (occasionally shareholders too) rather than stand approved by managers or a committee; they forbid the sale of votes divorced from the investment interest and the accumulation of votes in a corporate treasury; they require managers to live up to a duty of loyalty to investors. Federal law requires firms to reveal certain things when they issue securities, and public firms to make annual disclosures.[15]

The authors go on to acknowledge that, "Determined investors and managers can get 'round' many of these rules, but accommodation is a sidelight."[16] Throughout this book, there are examples of getting "round" these rules. It does not mean much to "forbid perpetual directorships" if management continues to re-nominate the same people. The General Motors case study reveals that the GM board, in the middle of the company's troubles in 1992, had one member who had been on the board for 20 years, and two who had served for 15. Requiring the approval of a third of the board or half the shareholders does not mean much if the board is entirely selected by and beholden to management, and the shareholders do not have the ability to overcome the obstacle of collective choice to make informed decisions. (See chapters 2 and 3 for further discussion of these issues, as well as the "duty of loyalty", the one-share, one-vote issue, and the relevance of required disclosures.)

Many of the laws that govern corporations are designed to make it possible for them to externalize their costs. These laws vary tremendously from state to state and country to country. The tendency for states to try to outdo each other in accommodating business has been called a "race to the bottom" competition because of the way that the states compete for corporate chartering business through increasingly diluted provisions for oversight.[17] In the US, most corporations that operate nationwide or even worldwide are incorporated in Delaware, famous for its extensive and management-friendly laws and judicial decisions governing corporations. Globalization may expand the "race to the bottom," resulting in most of the world's major corporations incorporating in the world equivalent of Delaware, perhaps the Cayman Islands. Or, if providers of capital are able to communicate their concerns by directing their funds to enterprises governed by more investor-friendly laws, competition for capital could turn the race to the bottom into a race to the top.

## The marketplace

Corporations also operate under the laws of the marketplace. While these laws can be influenced to some extent by the legislature, the marketplace is the ultimate arbiter of corporate performance. No matter where a company is located and what it produces, these laws affect, even determine, every decision made by its directors and officers. We would call this the law of economics, if we could use that term without then limiting ourselves to the narrow vocabulary and assumptions of that academic specialty, so we will just call them the laws of capitalism.

This set of laws reacts to and influences the first set. When a company changes its state of incorporation for tax reasons, for example, that is a function of economics. So too is a company's consideration of the differing social laws of states and nations, such as varying regulations governing occupational safety and environmental standards. Like a consumer selecting a car, the corporation's choice of domicile is based on an evaluation of the costs and benefits of all of the options. The same kind of evaluation applies to decisions about whether to invest in research and development or whether to update a local factory (or retrain local workers) versus reducing costs by moving the operation abroad.

## FUTURE DIRECTIONS

As corporations expand their operations and markets into virtually all parts of the world, we must begin to develop a more consistent and coherent approach. In order to do that, we must, whenever possible, integrate the most important legislated standards with the realities of the economic laws, so that all incentives promote the five overall goals outlined above, or at least so that they do not conflict with them. The law should be process-oriented, not substantive. Its focus should be the relationships between the corporation and its constituents, to reduce conflicts of interests (agency costs) and make sure that the right people are making the decisions (or at least are able to monitor the results of the decisions) that affect them most.

One of the problems that is presented by this task is finding some way to balance the need for long-term planning with the need for present-day assurances that whatever is planned for the long term is indeed likely to happen. Corporations must have as their primary and overriding goal the generation of long-term value. A commitment to the satisfaction of employees, suppliers, customers, and the community is essential for achieving this goal. But calibrating that commitment to achieve maximum value in the long term is a daunting task. No one can predict the future. In the last decade alone we have seen both new and long-established corporations achieve market dominance and extraordinary growth and vitality, only to fall into disaster, sometimes beyond recovery. How do we know that today's commitment to a long-term research and development project is going to produce a Dell instead of an Atari? More important, how can our laws best be designed to increase the likelihood that it will be the former instead of the latter?

The World Bank has an extensive governance program for developing economies that the established economies would do well to follow. Instead of prescriptive structures, the World Bank encourages countries to develop their own systems that meet three key goals: transparency, independent oversight, and accountability. The Global Corporate Governance Forum (<http://www.gcgf.org/>), co-sponsored by the World Bank and the OECD, is a new international initiative which will bring together the leading bodies engaged with governance reform worldwide: multilateral banks active in developing countries and transition economies, international organizations, country groupings engaged with governance reform, alongside professional standard-setting bodies and the private sector.

The Forum has been established to provide assistance to developing transition economies on corporate governance. It has three functions: to broaden the dialogue on corporate governance; to exchange experience and good practice; and to coordinate activities and identify and fill gaps in the provision of technical assistance.

Through other international efforts, from the International Accounting Standards Board to the International Corporate Governance Network, global corporations and investors are working to develop systems that meet the needs of individual cultures and economies while making the best possible use of international capital sources.

## CORPORATE POWER AND CORPORATE PERFORMANCE

We grant legitimacy and authority to the exercise of public (government) power through accountability. We are willing to defer to the authority of elected officials because we put them there, and if we do not like what they do we can replace them. In the US, the checks and balances of the three branches of government add to the credibility and legitimacy of the government. Any of the three branches that goes too far can be curbed by one of the others.

In theory, the legitimacy and authority of corporate power is also based on accountability. Corporate governance also has its checks and balances (including the government). In order to maintain legitimacy and credibility, corporate management needs to be effectively accountable to some independent, competent, and motivated representative. That is what the board of directors is designed to be.

Corporations exercise vast power in a democratic society. In a thoughtful and enduring essay, "The Corporation; How Much Power? What Scope?",[18] Carl Kaysen outlines the various alternative modes for containing corporate power, asking whether and how corporate power can be "limited or controlled."

> Broadly, there are three alternative possibilities. The first is limitation of business power through promoting more competitive markets; the second is broader control of business power by agencies external to business; the third, institutionalization within the firm of responsibility for the exercise of power. Traditionally, we have purported to place major reliance on the first of these alternatives, in the shape of antitrust policy, without in practice pushing very hard any effort to restrict market power to the maximum feasible extent. I have argued elsewhere that it is in fact possible to move much further than we have in this direction, without either significant loss in the overall effectiveness of business performance or the erection of an elaborate apparatus of control. While this, in my judgment, remains the most desirable path of policy, I do not in fact consider it the one which we will tend to follow. To embark on a determined policy of the reduction of business size and growth in order to limit market power requires a commitment of faith in the desirability of the outcome and the feasibility of the process which I think is not widespread. What I consider more likely is some mixture of the second and third types of control.[19]

Kaysen is pessimistic about the prospects for corporate self-regulation. "The development of mechanisms which will change the internal organization of the corporation, and define more closely and represent more presently the interest to which corporate management should respond and the goals toward which they should strive is yet to begin, if it is to come at all."[20]

But, as the scandals of 2002 have shown us again, the theory is often far from the practice. While the details of each of those failures differed, each was above all a failure of accountability, that cornerstone of the markets that permits one group to provide the capital and another to put it to use.

How do we make sure that corporate power is exercised in the best interests of society? How do we measure corporate performance? How should society measure corporate performance? Those two questions are closely related, but their answers are worlds apart. For example, imagine a company that has record-breaking earnings and excellent shareholder returns. This is in part made possible by a rigorous cost-cutting campaign that includes illegal dumping of toxic waste materials, thereby saving the money that had been used to meet environmental standards for disposal. The company's balance sheet and other financials will look very good. But the cost to society, in damage to the health and property of those affected by the illegal dumping, will not be factored in. Neither will the cost of investigating and prosecuting the company, which will be borne by the taxpayers. The cost of defending the company, and any fines imposed, will of course be borne by the shareholders.

# Cases in point: Some instances of corporate crime – Enron, Global Crossing, Tyco, Adelphia, and WorldCom

In 2002 and 2003, allegations about negligence and abuse, from accounting fraud to embezzlement, led to a new focus on corporate crime. We do not know at this writing whether any of those executives will go to jail.

According to *Corporate Crime Reporter*, the top corporate crimes of the 1990s were very different from those we saw in the early twenty-first century:

## The top ten corporate criminals of the 1990s

1. F. Hoffmann-La Roche Ltd.
*Type of crime*: Antitrust (price-fixing for vitamins)
*Criminal fine*: $500 million

2. Daiwa Bank Ltd.
*Type of crime*: Financial (falsification of records to cover up trading losses)
*Criminal fine*: $340 million

3. BASF Aktiengesellschaft
*Type of crime*: Antitrust (price-fixing for vitamins)
*Criminal fine*: $225 million

4. SGL Carbon Aktiengesellschaft (SGL AG)
*Type of crime*: Antitrust (price-fixing)
*Criminal fine*: $135 million

5. Exxon Corporation and Exxon Shipping
*Type of crime*: Environmental (Valdez oil spill in Alaska)
*Criminal fine*: $125 million

6. UCAR International Inc.
*Type of crime*: Antitrust (price-fixing)
*Criminal fine*: $110 million

7. Archer Daniels Midland
*Type of crime*: Antitrust (price-fixing)
*Criminal fine*: $100 million

8. (tie) Banker's Trust
*Type of crime*: Financial (appropriation of client funds)
*Criminal fine*: $60 million

9. (tie) Sears Bankruptcy Recovery Management Services
*Type of crime*: Fraud (widespread misrepresentation to bankrupt debtors)
*Criminal fine*: $60 million

10. Haarman & Reimer Corp.
*Type of crime*: Antitrust (price-fixing)
*Criminal fine*: $50 million

*When the companies paid these fines, who bore the cost? How many of the responsible parties served time in jail?*

## Some additional examples

**Alleco**. The company's CEO, Morton M. Lapides, was convicted of a price-fixing scheme that resulted in record-breaking fines. The judge found the facts of the case so disturbing that he took the unprecedented step of issuing a prison sentence to the corporation. The judge said, "I cannot imagine any company being more tied up with illegal activity." Four of its top managers were directed to spend up to two years in community service. The conviction notwithstanding, Lapides was permitted to take the company private at substantial personal profit.

**General Electric**. In 1992, GE settled with the government over charges that the company had been falsely billing the federal government for military sales to Israel during the 1980s. Company employees had conspired with an Israeli air force general to divert the money to their own pockets. GE's jet engine division was suspended from bidding for future Pentagon contracts, and the company agreed to pay fines of $69 million. GE's shares dipped $0.87 on the news.[21]

**Drexel Burnham Lambert**. In December 1988, the securities house pleaded guilty to six felony charges alleging widespread securities fraud and inside dealing. Drexel agreed to pay a fine of $650 million. The following March, the US Attorney's office in New York issued a 98-page indictment charging Michael Milken with similar crimes. Milken had single-handedly made Drexel successful via his aggressive hawking of junk-bonds, a security that financed most of the takeovers of the 1980s. So central was Milken to Drexel's success that the firm paid Milken compensation of as much as $550 million in one year alone. Roiled by the charges of fraud, and damaged by the increasing collapse of junk-bond-financed firms, Drexel filed for bankruptcy protection in February 1990. Just two months later, Milken agreed to plead guilty. In November 1990, he was sentenced to a prison term of ten years. The sentence was later reduced, and Milken was eventually released in the summer of 1993. He subsequently taught a finance course at the University of California at Los Angeles.

**A.H. Robins**. The company marketed an intra-uterine contraceptive device called the Dalkon Shield, despite the fact that the company had over 400 unfavorable reports from physicians. The device was eventually recalled after the deaths of 17 women. By mid-1985, over 14,000 product liability suits had been filed against the company, forcing it into bankruptcy. In 1987, a court ordered the company to set aside $2.4 billion in a trust fund to compensate women injured by the shield. Later, the company also agreed to pay out nearly $7 million to stockholders.[22]

**Gitano Group**. In December 1993, three Gitano executives pleaded guilty to charges that they had sought to circumvent customs duties on imported clothes. Following the charges, Gitano's largest customer – Wal-Mart Stores – announced that it would cease to do business with Gitano, adhering to strict company standards regarding vendor partners. In January 1994, Gitano's board of directors concluded that it was unlikely that the company could continue to operate without Wal-Mart's support, and the board voted to put the company up for sale.

**Waste Management**. In December 1996, Federal Judge Odell Horton in the Western District of Tennessee issued an opinion ordering a WMI subsidiary to pay a $91.5 million fraud judgment. The judge's ruling held that the officers in Chemical Waste Management had engaged in a scheme to "cheat the plaintiffs out of money" by keeping two sets of books to hide the amount of royalty payments due to the plaintiffs. The judge added, "What is troubling about this case is that fraud, misrepresentation and dishonesty apparently became part of the operating culture of the Defendant corporation."

**PG&E**. In 1997, PG&E agreed to pay $333 million dollars to settle claims from 648 residents of Hinkley, California, who had suffered a range of illnesses and injuries from chromium in their groundwater that came from a PG&E plant.

# Case in point: A UK attempt to redefine corporate manslaughter

In March 1987, a car and passenger ferry called the *Herald of Free Enterprise*, departed from the Belgian port of Zeebrugge for Dover. The ferry was owned by P&O European Ferries, a subsidiary of a large and venerable UK shipping line, P&O.

The *Herald of Free Enterprise* cleared the Zeebrugge harbor with its bow doors still open – it transpired that this was common practice by crews seeking to clear the hold of exhaust fumes. On this occasion, waves flooded the bow doors and the *Herald of Free Enterprise* capsized with the loss of 187 lives. Who was to blame?

Clearly, on an immediate level, the disaster was caused by those who failed to close the bow doors, and those who instructed the vessel to sail while the doors were still open. But the judicial inquiry identified deeper causes – a corporate culture at P&O European Ferries that ignored basic safety. The inquiry concluded that: "All concerned in management, from the members of the board of directors down to the junior superintendents, were guilty of fault in that all must be regarded as sharing responsibility for the failure of management. From top to bottom the body corporate was infected with the disease of sloppiness."

But how do you punish the body corporate? As we have discussed, you cannot put it in jail, and any fines will ultimately be paid by those who were not responsible (the shareholders).

In the UK, corporations may be prosecuted for manslaughter. But, in reality, successful prosecutions are all but impossible to achieve. In English legal history, there have been four prosecutions of corporations for manslaughter, and only one conviction.

The problems of securing a conviction were vividly highlighted by the *Herald of Free Enterprise* tragedy. Following the coroner's inquest into the disaster, the jury returned verdicts of unlawful killing in all 187 cases. P&O European Ferries was charged with manslaughter, as were seven high-ranking company officers. But the judge threw the case out, directing the jury to acquit the company and the five most senior defendants.

The judge gave this direction because English law requires that, to find a company guilty of manslaughter, the illegal acts must be committed by those "identified as the embodiment of the company itself." In a famous passage Lord Justice Denning said that, to convict a company, one must identify as guilty the person who represents "the directing mind" of the corporation.

A company cannot be considered guilty of manslaughter simply because its employees have recklessly caused death. Rather, as one British judge has written, "it is required that manslaughter should be established not against those who acted for or in the name of the company but against those who were to be identified as the embodiment of the company itself."

In the P&O Ferries example, the judge directed that in order to convict the company of manslaughter "one of the individual defendants who could be 'identified' with the company would have himself to be guilty of manslaughter." There was insufficient evidence against the individuals to meet this standard, hence the direction to acquit.

And yet disasters such as that of the *Herald of Free Enterprise* give rise to widespread public concern that the law does not do enough to hold companies to account. For this reason, the UK's Law Commission (a government-funded body that studies law reform) proposed a new law of corporate killing to replace the current, inadequate provisions for corporate manslaughter. The Commission argued that "a number of recent cases have evoked demands for the use of the law of manslaughter following public disasters, and there appears to be a widespread feeling among the public that in such cases it would be wrong if the criminal law placed all the blame on junior employees who may be held individually responsible, and also did not fix responsibility in appropriate cases on their employers, who are operating, and profiting from, the service they provide to the public, and may be at least as culpable."

Under the "directing mind" standard discussed above, it is all but impossible to convict the large modern corporation of manslaughter. As the Commission wrote, "the more diffuse the company structure and the more devolved the powers that are given to semi-autonomous managers, the easier it will be to avoid liability." The study notes "the increasing tendency of many organisations to decentralise safety services in particular." Indeed, "it is in the interests of shrewd and unscrupulous management to do so."

The inquiry into the *Herald of Free Enterprise* disaster, according to the Commission, found that "no single individual had responsibility for safety matters." The Commission comments that "if responsibility for the development of safety monitoring is not vested in a particular group or individual, it becomes almost impossible to identify the 'directing mind' for whose shortcomings the company can be liable."

The only successful prosecution for manslaughter in English legal history highlights the difficulties. In 1994, a jury convicted the owner-operator of an adventure company, in whose care some children had died while canoeing. The Commission comments: "Since the company was a one-man concern whose 'directing mind' was plainly its managing director, the company's liability was established automatically by his conviction."

The Law Commission thus concluded that the chances of ever convicting a large, complex corporation for manslaughter were minimal – even if, as in the P&O Ferries example, the manslaughter was the result not just of individual errors but of a corporate culture or management failure.

Thus, the Commission proposed a new offence of corporate killing, broadly corresponding to the individual offence of killing by gross carelessness. "For the purposes of the corporate offence," they wrote, "a death should be regarded as having been caused by the conduct of a corporation if it is caused by a failure in the way in which the corporation's activities are managed or organized." They suggested that "It should be possible for a management failure on the part of a corporation to be a cause of a person's death even if the immediate cause is the act or omission of an individual." (In the US, corporate homicide charges are equally rare. One successful prosecution involved a worker who was killed through on-the-job exposure to hazardous chemicals. The boss had actually removed the warning labels.)

Let us look again at the *Herald of Free Enterprise* example. "If circumstances such as these were to occur again," explained the Law Commission "we think it would probably be open to a jury to conclude that, even if the immediate cause of the deaths was the conduct of the assistant bosun, the Chief Officer, or both, another of the causes was the failure of the company to devise a safe system for the operation of its ferries; and that that failure fell far below what could reasonably have been expected. In these circumstances the company could be convicted of our proposed new offence."

On conviction, the court would have the power to order the cause of the offence to be remedied.

*All the stakeholders in these companies lost as a result of these actions. Corporations are supposed to be governed by a system of checks and balances to make sure that these disasters do not happen. Who failed? Who paid the price? If it is not the same people, why not?*

*If the system of checks and balances failed, why? Who was in the best position to deter this kind of mistake, and why didn't they do so? What changes would make these mistakes less likely? What changes would catch and address them sooner?*

The American Law Institute, *Principles of Corporate Governance: Analysis and Recommendations* (Proposed Final Draft, March 31, 1992)

Sec. 2.01 The Objective and Conduct of the Corporation

(a) Subject to the provisions of Subsection (b) and section 6.02 [Action to Directors That Has the Foreseeable Effect of Blocking Unsolicited Tender Offers], a [business] corporation should have as its objective the conduct of business activities with a view to enhancing corporate profit and shareholder gain.

(b) Even if corporate profit and shareholder gain are not thereby enhanced, the corporation, in the conduct of its business:

(1) Is obliged, to the same extent as a natural person, to act within the boundaries set by law:

(2) May take into account ethical considerations that are reasonably regarded as appropriate to the responsible conduct of business;

(3) May devote a reasonable amount of resources to public welfare, humanitarian, educational and philanthropic purposes.

Accountability requires not just a mechanism, but also a standard. That standard is usually described as "maximizing long-term returns for the owners." (Milton Friedman adds "within the limits of the law," but we believe that compliance with the law is assumed as a part of value maximization.) The relationship of any particular corporate action to shareholder returns does not have to be immediate or direct. Corporations can give away money, voluntarily increase their workers' compensation over required, or even competitive, levels, spoil their customers and act as benefactors in the communities where they function, all to the extent that these activities can be credibly related to increasing the long-term value of the enterprise. To the extent that they drive up costs to make the company's products and services less competitive, they cannot be credibly related to profit maximization.

The extent to which corporations can pursue objectives that are by definition not related to value generation must be severely limited, as a matter of both legislated and economic rules. Compare the current corporate system to the prevailing Western system of political legitimacy and accountability. We allow the legislature to make economic tradeoffs. We give this level of authority to the government, which derives its legitimacy from its accountability through the political process. And when it does not earn that legitimacy, the citizens disregard the laws and create a new government. We have laws allowing a certain level of permissible emissions from factories, despite documented health risks and attendant costs, after determining that those costs are exceeded by the benefits of the factory's products and jobs (and contributions to the tax base). The US has refrained from imposing especially onerous environmental laws like the German law requiring that all materials involved in the production process be recycled.

As in the political domain, in the corporate domain accountability should be based on a comprehensible standard that is widely understood. It can be argued that employees, customers, suppliers, and the residents of host communities should share with owners the entitlement to hold corporations accountable. Yet, to date, no one has developed a language of accountability that would be equally acceptable to all of these constituencies; indeed, no one has succeeded in conceiving of acceptable quantifiable standards. As Milton Friedman said, "Few trends could so thoroughly undermine the foundations of our free society as the acceptance by corporate officials of a social responsibility other than to make as much money for their stockholders as possible."[23] Friedman is too often cited in a simplistic way. He does not ask us to accept the narrowest definition of immediate profit as defined by accountants as the ultimate rudder for corporate direction. But we should recognize that the size and power of the corporate system tends to dominate the language of accountability.[24]

> I submit that you cannot abandon emphasis on the view that business corporations exist for the sole purpose of making profits for their shareholders until such time as you are prepared to offer a clear and reasonably enforceable scheme of responsibilities to someone else.[25]

In the US, the decade of the 1990s was a time in which 10 percent of the value of listed companies – roughly $1 trillion in value at the top of the market – was transferred from the shareholders to the CEOs. While shareholders did very well during that period, CEOs did much better.

## CORPORATE CRIME:
## "WITHIN THE LIMITS OF THE LAW"

Did you ever expect a corporation to have a conscience, when it has no soul to be damned and no body to be kicked? *Edward, First Baron Thurlow, Lord Chancellor of England*

By classifying particular conduct as "criminal," government gives its most unequivocal signal that particular activities are intolerable. That seems simple enough when applied to armed robbery or assault, but criminal law and corporate activity seem to exist in different media, like oil and water. Understanding the difficulty that society encounters in trying to communicate absolute standards of conduct to corporations is an essential beginning to the study of governance.

Why do corporations engage in criminal behavior? It has to be because they find that the benefits outweigh the costs. Or, to put it another way, the managers who take the risk of criminal behavior decide that the benefits accrue to the corporation, while the costs are borne elsewhere. And these costs are enormous. A single price-fixing case was found to cost the affected consumers more than all of the robberies of that year. Shareholders in particular pay the costs on all sides: as members of the community, they pay the costs of the crime itself, as taxpayers, they pay the costs of the prosecution; as shareholders, they pay the costs of the defense and any penalties.

The people who decide to violate the law, however, pay very little. There is a great disparity between the way individual criminal offenders and corporate criminal offenders are treated. One reason for this is society's perception of the crimes. We are more likely to imprison violent offenders than white-collar criminals, despite the fact that the white-collar crime, in absolute terms, is more expensive. The business judgment rule (see the discussion of legal duties in chapter 3) and the limitation on director liability restrict the shareholders' ability to get the courts to order reimbursement for the payment of these expenses or the loss in share value. Corporate managers rarely go to jail; indeed, they seldom even lose their jobs. The company pays the fines, which are seldom high enough to offset any gains, and the company pays the legal fees.

Corporations have limited economic liability, as described above, and at one time this extended to criminal activity. In modern times, at least in theory, corporations do have criminal liability. Originally, the standard for determining that a corporation (and its officers) was liable for criminal activity was *respondent superior*, vicarious liability by the corporation for the acts of its employees, as long as those acts were (1) within the scope of the employment and (2) with the intent of benefiting the corporation. This required knowledge (willfulness) on the part of the employee. He had to know what he was doing and know that it was illegal.

Recently, however, there has been a trend to criminalize a broader category of behavior, often for political reasons. This began in the health and safety area, and has expanded to include other areas of social policy concern like discrimination, and areas of political sensitivity like government contracts. Regulations established a new standard in holding corporations liable for "flagrant indifference," "neglect," or "failure to perceive a substantial risk." Ignorance of the law is no excuse. Courts have held that corporate officers are presumed to know certain things, just because of their position. And the knowledge of *any* employee can be attributed to the company as a whole, even if the employee did not inform anyone else.

The primary justifications for penalties are deterrence, incapacitation from further crimes, and rehabilitation. All of these depend on some degree of moral culpability. It is easy enough to apply them to an individual who commits a crime. A thief is sent to jail to deter him (and others) from future crime, to keep him away from society so that he cannot commit further crimes, and to give society a chance to teach him to do better. Some systems also try to incorporate compensation of some kind for the victims as well, though this has been less a priority of the criminal justice system than of the civil justice system; and in the criminal system such compensation is more likely to take the form of community service than direct compensation to the individuals who were harmed. And, as Douglas Ginsburg's example shows below, "community service" is interpreted very broadly.

No one seems to know what to do about it. It almost seems as though a certain level of corporate crime is just assumed as a real-life "cost of doing business."

The failure of our efforts to rein in criminal corporate conduct stems from trying to treat artificial entities as if they were natural persons. Legal scholar John C. Coffee Jr. of Columbia University has stated the problem succinctly: "At first glance, the problem of corporate punishment seems perversely insoluble: moderate fines do not deter, while severe penalties flow through the corporate shell and fall on the relatively blameless."[26]

## *Probation of corporations*

In March 1986, the US government prepared a "sentencing memorandum" recommending "probation" and a fine for the Bank of New England, following the bank's conviction on 31 counts. The crime involved repeated failure to file Currency Transaction Reports (CTRs), a requirement imposed in an effort to track financial transactions that may be related to illegal activities. In this case, although the bank admitted to its failure to file thousands of these forms, the prosecution centered on a bookie named McDonough, whose failure to file CTRs for his dealings with the bank made it impossible for the government to prosecute McDonough for tax and gambling offenses.

The memo pointed out that "the (bank's) misbehavior was truly institutionalized, having been engaged in by numerous employees and officers on repeated occasions over a four-year period . . . The failure to file the required CTRs involved not one, but at least ten bank employees . . . The failures to file were aggravated by the fact that some of the employees knew McDonough was a bookie and that he was trying to circumvent the CTR law . . . The bank's culpability as an institution was compounded . . . when [the] Branch Manager . . . was informed of repeated failures to file and deliberately chose not to file the forms even though she admitted to fully knowing that they were required by law . . .". Furthermore, said the memo, the bank's internal fraud officer and other senior officials were also made aware of the problems.

*How can a corporation be sentenced to probation?* The "probation" requested by the government in this case required regular reporting by the bank on its program (including the names of personnel assigned) to comply with CTR requirements.

After emphasizing the law's clear message that failure to file CTRs is a serious crime and that fines should be "severe" enough to have "some real economic impact," the memo recommended a fine that amounted to less than 0.0002 percent of the bank's asset base and 2 percent of its net income. The comparable fine for an individual would approximate to one week's salary, less taxes and expenses.

In 1986 testimony before the US Sentencing Commission, Douglas H. Ginsburg, then Assistant Attorney General for Antitrust (now chief judge on the DC Circuit Court of Appeals) bemoaned the inadequate penalties for individuals convicted of price-fixing. "There can be no doubt that price fixing is a serious crime. It cannot be inadvertently committed, it causes substantial social harm, and it creates no redeeming social benefits." He noted that the average time served for the small percentage of defendants who actually went to prison was only about 30 days. Fines for individuals averaged less than $16,000. The average fine for a corporation was about $133,000.

> The failure of our sentencing system to achieve deterrence is evident from our continuing discovery of significant numbers of price-fixing conspiracies each year. The explanation for this is also obvious. Price fixing offers the opportunity to extract huge sums from consumers, and there is a good chance that price fixers will escape detection despite our best efforts. To deter so potentially lucrative an enterprise requires much higher levels of fines and imprisonment than are currently imposed.
>
> Before addressing fines and imprisonment, however, I would like to explain why four kinds of alternative sentences or sanctions – community service, probation, debarment, and restitution – are not adequate substitutes for imprisonment and heavy fines. Such alternative sentences or sanctions often impose little hardship on offenders, and their very availability leads all too often to their substitution for more meaningful sentences, thus undermining deterrence.
>
> First, many of the community service sentences imposed in recent years were not punishment at all. One defendant's community service involved coordinating an annual rodeo for charity. A defendant in another antitrust proceeding was required to organize a golf tournament fundraiser for the Red Cross. The experience proved so pleasant that he quickly agreed to organize the golf tournament again the next year! In yet another case, the defendant was sentenced to give thirty hours of speeches explaining the economic effects of his criminal activities – punishment that in practice is more likely to frustrate than to advance the purposes of the antitrust laws. Such penalties can do nothing but trivialize the offense in the eyes of the business community and the public.[27]

Judge Ginsburg went on to explain that probation had little deterrent impact and "implies unwarranted judicial regulation of the defendant's business activities." Debarment (making the company ineligible to sell to the government) was also ineffective. "Ironically, by eliminating competitors, it can impose on society the same harm as does the crime it is designed to punish. Indeed, there could be situations in which all potential suppliers might be debarred, making the product, at least for a while, totally unavailable."

Many ingenious solutions have been suggested, including the "equity fine."[28] But all face the same obstacle: cooked books. As John Braithwaite explains in his study of the pharmaceutical industry,

> companies have two kinds of records: those designed to allocate guilt (for internal purposes), and those for obscuring guilt (for presentation to the outside world). When companies want clearly defined accountability they can generally get it. Diffused accountability is not always inherent in organizational complexity; it is in considerable measure the result of a desire to protect individuals within the organization by presenting a confused picture to the outside world. One might say that courts should be able to pierce this conspiracy of confusion. Without sympathetic witnesses from inside the corporation who are willing to help, this is difficult.[29]

Despite various efforts to place corporations "on probation," to require payments to causes that benefit society, and even to jail executives, it is plain that nothing being done at this time is effective and that the problem is becoming more acute. In 1980, *Fortune* magazine surveyed 1,043 large companies and concluded that a "surprising" and "startling" number (about 11 percent) of them had been involved in "blatant illegalities." Two years later, *US News and World Report* conducted a similar survey of America's largest 500 companies, and found that, in the preceding decade, 115 had been convicted of at least one major crime.[30] In 1990, the *New York Times* found that 25 out of the 100 largest Pentagon contractors had been found guilty of procurement fraud in the preceding seven years.[31]

After a six-week trial and ten days of deliberations, jurors convicted accounting giant Arthur Andersen for obstructing justice when it destroyed Enron Corp. documents while on notice of a federal investigation. Andersen had claimed that the documents were destroyed as part of its housekeeping duties and not as a ruse to keep Enron documents away from the regulators. (See the case study for more information.) While the jury was unable to agree on more than one employee as "corrupt persuader," the firm as a whole was held responsible. The judgment was a fine and probation, but the effect was to destroy the entire firm, which quickly folded.

On December 20, 2002, The SEC, the New York State Attorney General, the National Association of Securities Dealers, North American Securities Administrators Association, the New York Stock Exchange, and state regulators announced a $1.4 billion global settlement with the nation's top investment firms. The settlement provided for:

- The insulation of research analysts from investment banking pressure. Firms will be required to sever the links between research and investment banking, including analyst compensation for equity research, and the practice of analysts accompanying investment banking personnel on pitches and road shows. This will help ensure that stock recommendations are not tainted by efforts to obtain investment banking fees.
- A complete ban on the "spinning" of Initial Public Offerings (IPOs). Brokerage firms will not allocate lucrative IPO shares to corporate executives and directors who are in the position to greatly influence investment banking decisions.
- An obligation to furnish independent research. For a five-year period, each of the brokerage firms will be required to contract with no less than three independent research firms that will provide research to the brokerage firm's customers. An independent consultant ("monitor") for each firm, with final authority to procure independent research from independent providers, will be chosen by regulators. This will ensure that individual investors get access to objective investment advice.
- Disclosure of analyst recommendations. Each firm will make publicly available its ratings and price target forecasts. This will allow for evaluation and comparison of performance of analysts.
- Settled enforcement actions involving significant monetary sanctions.

"This agreement will permanently change the way Wall Street operates," said New York Attorney General Eliot Spitzer. "Our objective throughout the investigation and negotiations has been to protect the small investor and restore integrity to the marketplace. We are confident that the rules embodied in this agreement will do so."

Note, however, that the settlement permitted the payment to be characterized as compensation rather than a penalty, so it was tax-deductible, making it about a third less in effect than the reported amount. In *Slate Magazine*, Daniel Gross quoted New York University law professor Daniel Shaviro: "The regulators wanted the payment to be big, and the firms wanted it to be tax deductible." Gross concluded, "They both got what they wanted." And one thing they wanted was no individual consequences. No one went to jail. No one was made ineligible for future employment on Wall Street.

*Is there such a thing as capital punishment for corporations? In light of the white-collar crime problem, the questions arise: Who is in the best position to define corporate crimes, and who should determine their punishment? Who within the corporation is best situated to prevent corporate crime, and does that person/group have the authority to make it?*

There will always be a need for legal sanctions, but the job of meting out punishment should not belong to the government alone. Indeed, without self-regulation by private industry, government's power to deter crime will decline further. As Braithwaite observes, "[S]ome executives abstain from bribery because they are afraid of being punished. Most abstain from bribery because they view it as immoral. One reason that they view it as immoral is that executives who bribe are sometimes punished and held to public scorn. Do away with criminal punishment and you do away with much of the sense of morality that makes self-regulation possible. Self-regulation and punitive regulation are, therefore, complementary rather than alternatives."[32]

Self-regulation is the responsibility of all participants in the corporate governance system. Unfortunately, under the current system, the risk of engaging in criminal behavior is evaluated by corporate managers who have very little to lose, even if the company is prosecuted. The criminal justice system has not been able to provide the appropriate level of deterrence, incapacitation, and rehabilitation for white-collar offenders or compensation for their victims.

Corporate crime is not victimless. Those adversely affected include the shareholders, often thousands of them. Long-term shareholders certainly have an interest in making societal and corporate interests compatible, but they are not likely to have the resources to be able to make that interest felt throughout the company, either before or after the fact (see discussion of the collective choice problem, in the "prisoner's dilemma" section of chapter 2). They can, however, take steps to make sure that the other parties in the corporation have the right incentives and authority. "[T]he firm is better positioned than the state to detect misconduct by its employees. It has an existing monitoring system already focused on them, and it need not conform its use of sanctions to due process standards. Indeed, if the penalties are severe enough, the corporation has both the incentive and, typically, the legal right to dismiss any employee it even suspects of illegal conduct."[33]

*How can shareholders make this system work?* They have no interest – much less competency – in developing or prescribing internal corporate procedures. Yet they do have some responsibility for this area. Shareholders expect managers to run their business in a way that will encourage a supportive governmental and societal climate to capitalist enterprise, and that means that the shareholders' concern is to hold management accountable for their conduct of the business "within the rules." Shareholders share some of the responsibility for failing to establish mechanisms for preventing and responding to corporate crime in the past. In the future, shareholders need to make it unmistakably clear that continued corporate crime will not be tolerated. But it is the job of the directors and management to make sure that information flows assure that notice of potentially criminal activity is received at the appropriate level, that the company develops incentive systems to assure that compliance with the law has the clear and undivided attention of appropriate personnel, and that review structures are established to monitor, review, document and validate compliance with the law. As Judge Ginsburg said,

Shareholders should no more be insulated from the gains and losses of price fixing than from the gains or losses from any other risky management decision. Indeed, it is essential that shareholders have the incentives to institute appropriate safeguards to prevent criminal behavior.[34]

Shareholders, along with directors and officers, must see to it that companies have information systems to expose, not cover up, wrongdoing. One way to do this is by setting forth the conditions of eligibility for service on the board of directors. Unquestionably, the board of directors has the authority, indeed the responsibility, to promulgate basic corporate policies.

> More active stockholder participation might force greater corporate compliance with the law in some areas, although, as we have pointed out, their primary concern is often corporate stock growth and dividends . . . Far reaching corporate reform, however, depends on altering the process and structure of corporate decision-making. Traditional legal strategies generally do not affect the internal institutional structure . . . At present few clear functions are usually specified for corporate boards of directors; they frequently have served as rubber stamps for management. If a functional relationship and responsibility to actual corporate operations were established, directors would be responsible not only for the corporate financial position and stockholder dividends but also for the public interest, which would include the prevention of illegal and unethical activities undertaken in order to increase profits.[35]

The Sarbanes–Oxley legislation underscored the authority of the directors to establish policies requiring management to implement obedience to the law as a corporate priority. And shareholders have the authority and the means to make directors do just that. By amending the bylaws to make compliance with the law a condition of eligibility for service on the board, they ensure that the buck will stop somewhere. Directors are highly motivated to continue to be eligible to serve as directors of public companies.

One way in which a board can exert its authority is described by long-time consumer advocate Ralph Nader: "[T]he board should designate executives responsible for compliance with these laws and require periodic signed reports describing the effectiveness of compliance procedures."[36] Other reformers recommend that mechanisms to administer spot checks on compliance with the principal statutes should be created. Similar mechanisms can insure that corporate "whistle blowers" and non-employee sources may communicate to the board "in private and without fear of retaliation knowledge of violations of law."

Professor Christopher Stone's *Where the Law Ends*[37] is perhaps the best-known work on corporate criminal liability. He concludes that the suspension of directors is the most effective way of dealing with the problems of corporate criminality. He says,

> In general, though, I think it would be best if for all but the most serious violations we moved in the opposite direction, relaxing directors' liability by providing that any director adjudged to have committed gross negligence, or to have committed nonfeasance shall be prohibited for a period of three years from serving as officer, director or consultant of any corporation doing interstate business. Why is this better than what we have now? For one thing, the magnitude of the potential liability today has become so Draconian that when we try to make the law tougher on directors the more likely effects are that corporate lawyers will develop ways to get around it, judges and juries will be disinclined to find liability, and many of the better qualified directors will refuse to get involved and serve. The advantages of the "suspension" provision, by contrast, are that it is not

so easy to get around; it is not so severe that, like potential multi–million–dollar personal liability, it would strike courts as unthinkable to impose; but at the same time it would still have some effective bite in it – the suspendees would be removed from the most prestigious and cushy positions ordinarily available to men of their rank, and would, I suspect, be the object of some shame among their peers.

*The Sarbanes–Oxley legislation gives the SEC authority to debar individuals from serving on corporate boards. In 2003, the SEC used this authority to negotiate the resignation of former Xerox CEO from his other boards, even though he did not admit guilt in the $22 million settlement of accounting fraud charges at Xerox.*

*Do you agree with Judge Ginsburg that imprisonment and heavy fines can deter crimes such as price-fixing? Why or why not? Do you share his objections to sentences such as community service, probation, debarment, and restitution? Why or why not? Look again at the Beech-Nut example in the introduction. Who paid the penalty there? Who should? What could each of the major players in corporate governance do to prevent such crimes in the future?*

An alternative model appears to exist in Japan. In 1981, after a series of leakages from a nuclear power station owned and operated by the Japan Atomic Power Company, the chairman and president of the company resigned in the hope that trust in nuclear power stations would be restored under new leadership.[38]

*Can society hope to govern corporations merely by expecting executives of wrongdoing corporations to resign?*

## CORPORATIONS AND GOVERNMENT: CO-OPTING THE MARKET

Many observers have argued that corporate power has created a framework within which only the illusion of free choice exists. One example is that of the Chrysler Corporation.

## Case in point: Chrysler

In 1977, Chrysler was the tenth largest US company, and fourteenth largest in the world. Within two years, however, the company was in serious trouble. In 1979, Chrysler's new boss, Lee Iacocca, told the federal government that without huge federally guaranteed loans, the company would almost certainly fold.

Loan guarantees were a familiar element of US economic policy. In 1970, the Penn Central Railroad requested a $200 million loan under the Defense Production Act of 1950, a measure that allowed public corporations to borrow from the Treasury if the national defense was at stake. Congress refused Penn Central's request, and only after the railroad filed for bankruptcy was it granted $125 million in loan guarantees. One year later, Congress narrowly approved (by one vote in the Senate) Lockheed Aircraft's request for $250 million in guaranteed loans. In that instance, New York Senator James Buckley sonorously warned, "if the inefficient or mismanaged firm is insulated from the free-market pressures that other businesses must face, the result will be that scarce economic and human resources will be squandered on enterprises whose activities do not meet the standards imposed by the market place." Ultimately, however, the prospect of unemployment for Lockheed's 17,000 workers and the 43,000 employees of supplier companies was enough to see that Lockheed received the loans.

Senator Buckley's arguments were revived in 1979 when a similar debate broke out over Chrysler. On the one hand was America's commitment to free markets; on the other, the lives of tens of thousands of Chrysler's employees. Michael Moritz and Barrett Seaman describe the issue as it faced Congress: "The Corporation's 4,500 dealers and 19,000 suppliers were another matter. Unlike the company's, their presence was tangible and their plight immediate. There was a Chrysler dealer or supplier in every congressional district in the country. These were the merchants of the nation, men who had inherited businesses from their fathers and had, in some cases, passed them on to their sons. Family commitments stretched back to the days of Walter Chrysler, and the businesses were located in the small communities of Middle America, like Great Bend in Kansas. These weren't garish swashbucklers from Detroit, bouncing billions and tweaking communities with the flash of a calculator." The authors describe how "the company drew up computerized lists out-lining contributions in every district and showing congressmen how much local, state and federal tax was contributed by Chrysler showrooms. Working through the Dealer Councils (the officials elected by the dealers themselves), an average of two hundred dealers a day came to Washington to lobby their representatives. Coached for an hour in the early morning about what they should and should not say, the dealers spent their days roaming corridors, rapping on doors and buttonholing congressmen as well as their administrative and legislative aids. The sight of these independent small businessmen was mighty effective." As one Chrysler dealer observed: "The very survival of a lot of good people in this country and a lot of small businesses depends upon the whims of the political system."

Moritz and Seaman sum up as follows: "The underlying precept of a free economy is that unsuccessful corporations do not survive. In recent years in the United States this proposition has been subjected to violent rejection. Not only are companies such as Lockheed, which were arguably essential to national defense, 'bailed out' through political action, but such a quintessential consumer giant as Chrysler proved the modern axiom that no large company will be allowed to fail in the United States today. Rarely has the power of a large, if broke, corporation been so effectively and overtly employed as in Chrysler persuading the US government to provide special financial aid to insure its survival."[39]

This case shows that only the small companies are really at risk of any meaningful market test. In a more recent example, the Federal Reserve organized a 1998 rescue of Long-Term Capital Management, a very large and prominent hedge fund on the brink of failure. The Fed intervened because it was concerned about possible dire consequences for world financial markets if it allowed the hedge fund to fail. The founder, John Meriwether, left Salomon Brothers following a scandal over the purchase of US Treasury bonds. The fund's principal shareholders included two eminent experts in the science of risk, Myron Scholes and Robert Merton, who had been awarded the Nobel Prize for economics in 1997 for their work on derivatives, and a dazzling array of professors of finance and Ph.D.s in mathematics and physics. After taking 2 percent for "administrative expenses" and 25 percent of the profits, the fund was able to offer its shareholders returns of 42.8 percent in 1995, 40.8 percent in 1996, and "only" 17.1 percent in 1997 (the year of the Asian crisis). But in September, after mistakenly gambling on a convergence in interest rates, it found itself on the verge of bankruptcy. The Federal Reserve denied that it was a bail-out, because it did not use public funds and because LTCM investors were not made whole. But a government entity did orchestrate the soft landing for LTCM, which makes it another example of a company that is "too large to fail." (Note, however, that an effort to orchestrate the same kind of deal for Enron in late 2001 failed, partly because it did not threaten the destruction of a major bank and partly because President George W. Bush's close Texas ties to Enron would have made it a political issue.)

A corporation that is large enough cannot be allowed to go broke in a "free" capitalist society. The power of larger corporations to involve themselves in the most critical decision-making by citizens has been reaffirmed by the US Supreme Court. In *The Bank of Boston v. Bellotti*, the court upheld corporations' right to enter the arena of political advertising. The Court said that the bank could spend whatever shareholder funds it thought appropriate to influence voting on a referendum matter that was not related to its business.

Efforts to reduce the influence of corporate management on the political process have failed. For example, the Federal Election Campaign Act of 1971 (FECA) prohibits corporations from making any political campaign contributions, with very limited exceptions, like non-partisan elections. But, corporate management may establish separate segregated funds (commonly referred to as political action committees or PACs) to solicit campaign contributions and make contributions to candidates, subject to a complex set of limitations and reporting requirements.

There have been a number of widely reported violations of these rules. Beulieu of America, a carpet manufacturer, pleaded guilty to five misdemeanor counts, four involving violations of campaign finance rules. Executives of the firm directed 36 employees or spouses to contribute $1,000 each to Lamar Alexander's presidential campaign, and then reimbursed the employees with corporate funds. Juan Ortiz, chief financial officer of Future Tech International (FTI), pleaded guilty to a scheme in which he secretly reimbursed himself and eight other FTI employees with corporate funds for their individual $1,000 contributions at a 1995 Clinton–Gore fundraising event at a Miami hotel. The CEO of FTI, who had been allowed to meet with top government officials, including the president, fled the country while he was under investigation for his involvement. But, as *Slate* founder Michael Kinsley says, the crime in campaign finance is not what is illegal; it is what is legal. According to a 2002 Federal Election Commission report, the Republican and Democratic parties reported raising a total of $1.1 billion in hard and soft dollars from January 1, 2001 through November 25, 2002. Post-election reports to the Federal Election Commission (FEC) include the final soft money receipts for national parties (mostly from corporations). Soft money contributions to both parties were spiked before November 5, 2002, the cut-off date imposed by the Bipartisan Campaign Reform Act (BCRA). Receipt totals were nearly equal to the party fundraising totals in the 2000 election cycle, which included a competitive presidential campaign, and 72 percent higher than in 1997–8, the most recent non-presidential cycle. When compared with 1998, however, Democratic party hard money receipts were up 43 percent and Republican hard money receipts were 47 percent higher than their 1998 totals. The economic power of corporations is dominating the political process. And that power distorts the ability of the marketplace to discipline corporations.

Lord John Browne of British Petroleum has pledged to terminate all political contributions from that company. The elimination of "soft money" donations in the McCain legislation in the US will have some impact, though, if past experience is any indicator, it will not be long before corporations figure out some other way to continue to give money to politicians.

# Case in point: Corporate political donations in the UK

One of the issues that dominated the 1997 general election in the UK was "sleaze." Numerous Members of Parliament of the incumbent Conservative administration had, or were alleged to have, a range of consultancies and relationships with business that compromised their political work. The opposition Labour party also argued that the Conservatives received numerous foreign and undisclosed donations from not altogether "clean" sources.

Labour made a manifesto pledge that, if elected, they would appoint a commission to study the funding of political parties in the UK. Once elected, they were good as their word, and the Committee on Standards in Public Life, chaired by a senior lawyer, Lord Neill, began work. One of its tasks was to investigate donations made by public companies.

The state of the law, at that time, was that UK companies were free to donate to political parties as long as any donation over £200 (about $300) was disclosed. Companies were under no obligation to seek shareholder permission in the form of a vote at the annual meeting or explain why the gift was in the company's interests. (Shareholders could challenge the gift in court, but their chances of winning were slim and the costs would undoubtedly be greater than the benefits.)

These conditions gave UK companies considerable freedom to donate, and they made the most of it. Research by the independent London-based consultancy Pensions and Investment Research Consultants showed that companies gave about $15 million between 1991 and 1997 to political parties or groups. The average donation in 1997 was about $50,000. The largest donors were P&O and Hanson, which both donated about $150,000 in 1997. To an overwhelming extent, this history of corporate giving benefited just one party, the Conservatives. Between 1991 and 1997, the Conservatives received over 97 percent of all donations made to any of the three leading political parties.

Although, as the Neill committee began deliberations, there was a general decline in corporate political donations (perhaps mirroring the decline of the Conservative party itself), there was a considerable lobby for change. At the vanguard of this call for reform were Labour-controlled local authorities and trade-union pension funds, who were in the unhappy position of seeing funds belonging to the company they owned being donated to their political adversaries. These left-wing funds could, of course, have sold their shares. But as we have argued elsewhere in this book, that is no choice at all.

These shareholders argued that, in principle, it was wrong for companies to make donations on such an emotive and personal issue as politics without shareholder permission. The anti-donation lobby argued further that there were considerable conflicts of interest inherent in the system. For example, one of the leading donors was the insurance group Guardian Royal. One of the non-executive directors was Lord Hambro, former treasurer of the Conservative party and thus chief fundraiser for the party. Lord Hambro also served on the boards of Taylor Woodrow and P&O, which together donated more than $1 million to the Conservative party in 1997.

And what did shareholders get in return for their generosity? One political commentator found that half the political honors (peerages, knighthoods and so on) were awarded to the 6 percent of companies that made donations to political parties. In other words, were business leaders able to spend shareholders' money on securing for themselves a place in Britain's political elite?

Nor was the disclosure requirement as comprehensive as might appear. The law required companies to disclose cash gifts to political parties, but gifts to political organizations escaped the net, as did gifts in kind such as personnel, equipment or facilities. For example, groups such as Aims of Industry or the Northern Industrialists Protection Association were known to be closely allied with the Conservative party. Some companies disclosed gifts to these bodies, others did not.

In June 1993 the UK newspaper the *Independent* obtained a copy of a scheme drawn up by the Conservative Central Office to boost political donations. Companies were invited to put money into a current account with the party's bankers. The bank, instead of paying the company interest, would reduce the charges on the party's $24 million overdraft. One of the advantages cited by the Conservative Central Office? The proposed interest-free loans would not need to be disclosed to shareholders.

The Neill committee sought the testimony of some leading business figures. Stanley Kalms, chairman of electrical goods retailer Dixons, said "I have been persuaded by the argument that shareholders who represent a mixed range of views might feel that their views are not represented by a political donation."

Sir Neil Shaw, chairman of sugar manufacturer Tate & Lyle, argued that, in the absence of a national system for funding political parties, companies should make donations in order to promote the wider interests of democratic society. Tate & Lyle was one of the few companies who gave money to more than one party, although its gifts were overwhelmingly made in favor of the Conservatives.

The Neill committee published its findings in the Fall of 1998. It recommended "that Parliament enact a raft of measures to make political funding more transparent and democratic." Among the measures was the recommendation that companies wishing to make a donation first seek a general prior authority from shareholders. The committee suggested that:

- the authority be sought at least once every four years;
- disclosure should include non-cash donations; and
- an upper limit for donations should be specified.

The Labour government has promised to enact the recommendations.

*Corporations are enormously wealthy organizations and "money is the mother's milk of politics." What dangers arise from these two facts? How can companies be held accountable for their involvement in the political process? Should public companies be prevented from playing a role in the political process?*

Not only have corporations succeeded in dominating the executive and legislative branches of government in the United States, but they have made substantial inroads into the judicial branch as well. In the "race to the bottom" for corporate chartering and related legal fees, states compete to be the most attractive to corporate management. During the takeover era of the 1980s, the courts seemed to do the same, as you will see in chapter 3. Accommodating the interests of corporate management (called "the Delaware factor") is the underlying rationale for many of the decisions of Delaware's Chancery and Supreme Courts.

# Case in point: "Delaware puts out"[40]

Although Delaware is one of the smallest states in the union, more companies are incorporated there than any other state. Joseph Nocera explains why: "The degree to which Delaware depends upon its incorporation fees and taxes is really quite extraordinary: It's a $200 million a year business, comprising nearly 20 percent of the state budget."

During the 1980s, when a vigorous market for corporate control developed, management appealed to the Delaware courts for protection. What became apparent was that large corporations would do whatever it took to ensure that the Delaware courts would continue to issue opinions favorable to management. In 1990, a number of pro-shareholder decisions began emerging from the Delaware Chancery Court, forcing companies "in play" to entertain hostile bids. These decisions aroused a tough response from Martin Lipton, a corporate lawyer who made his name defending companies from takeover in the 1980s. In Nocera's words: "Marty Lipton went nuts. He lashed out at the [Delaware Chancery] court, sending scathing notes to his very long list of major corporate clients, most of whom were incorporated in Delaware. In one conspicuously leaked memo, he wrote ominously, 'Perhaps it is time to migrate out of Delaware.' Lipton acted the way bullies always act when they know they have someone by the balls: he squeezed."

As every other entity concerned with corporate governance and accountability responded to the post-Enron era with proposals for reform, the courts and legislature of Delaware, the only place with authority over the obligation of directors, was alone in making no response.

## MEASURING PERFORMANCE

We cannot tell what the future impact of corporate strategy will be on shareholder value. Will spoiling the customers produce devoted loyalty or will it drive up prices too high? Will a long-term research and development project pay off? Will cost-cutting measures expose the company to future liability claims? Will the acquisition of a new business provide synergy or cause loss of focus? *How can anyone – shareholders, directors, or managers – evaluate a company's performance if they cannot predict its future?*

In order to establish a context for the evaluation of a company's performance, it makes sense to define the ultimate purpose of a corporation as long-term value creation. This creates a framework for defining the rights and responsibilities of shareholders and directors and therefore for determining how they should be organized, how they should be motivated, and how they should be evaluated. For example, it does not mean much to set long-term value creation as the goal if we allow the people who have primary responsibility for meeting the goal to be the ones who define it; that would be like allowing students to grade their own exams.

The expressions "long-term" and "value" are subject to many interpretations. Anyone who is being evaluated has an incentive to define "long-term" as "after I am gone." Anyone who is being evaluated has an incentive to define "value" as "results from whichever financial formula makes us look most appealing this year." While far from perfect, there is an entire spectrum of concepts of economic performance. These traditionally include balance sheets and earnings statements prepared according to Generally Accepted Accounting Principles

(GAAP), the availability of cash to meet corporate needs, and the ability to raise new cash from outside sources. Management expert Peter Drucker highlights the problems of evaluating corporate performance:

> One of the basic problems is that management has no way to judge by what criteria outside shareholders value and appraise performance. The stock market is surely the least reliable judge or, at best, only one judge and one that is subject to so many other influences that it is practically impossible to disentangle what, of the stock market appraisal, reflects the company's performance and what reflects caprice, affects the whims of securities analysts, short-term fashions and the general level of the economy and of the market rather than the performance of a company itself.[41]

Drucker, along with former New York State Comptroller Ned Regan and others, has advocated periodic "business audits" by expert outside parties to provide perspective in evaluating a company's performance. *But is there such a thing as "independence" in professionals, as long as they are hired by the people they are supposed to evaluate?* Even if they are people of exceptional integrity and insight, by the time they do the study and produce the report, it may be too late.

"Performance measurement" must be a flexible and changing concept. What is suitable for one time or company is wrong for others. Therefore, the single most important structural requirement is that the standard be set by someone other than management. Yet it must be by some group vitally interested in what we have already said was the only legitimate goal – long-term value creation. For that reason, it cannot be the government or the community – they have other priorities they would be happy to have corporations address.

The best entity for establishing goals and evaluating the performance of any corporation is – in theory – its board of directors. It is in the "creative tension" between the informed, involved, motivated and empowered monitors – the board of directors in the first instance and the owners ultimately – that the corporation's performance can best be monitored on an ongoing basis.

# Case in point: The years of accounting dangerously

Arthur Levitt used his 2002 book, *Take on the Street*, as an opportunity to tell his side of some of the frustrations he faced as the longest-serving chairman of the SEC during the Clinton administration. And no one was singled out for more vituperative recrimination than the accounting industry.

On September 28, 1998, then chairman of the Securities and Exchange Commission (SEC) Levitt expressed his concerns about earnings management in a speech delivered at New York University. He focused on five questionable practices: "big bath" restructuring charges, creative acquisition accounting, "cookie jar reserves," "immaterial" misapplications of accounting principles, and the premature recognition of revenue. He called for a number of studies and reforms, including more effective audit committees, concluding that

> qualified, committed, independent and tough-minded audit committees represent the most reliable guardians of the public interest. Sadly, stories abound of audit committees whose members lack expertise in the basic principles of financial reporting as well as the mandate to ask probing questions. In fact, I've heard of one

audit committee that convenes only twice a year before the regular board meeting for 15 minutes and whose duties are limited to a perfunctory presentation.

Levitt's concern followed stunning revelations of accounting irregularities at companies like Cendant, Livent, Waste Management, and Sunbeam. Cendant Corp. executives fraudulently inflated income before charges by $500 million over three years, in large part by booking fictitious revenues. They ended up paying a $2.8 billion settlement to the shareholders. Livent Inc. allegedly kept two sets of books to mask extravagant expenses. Waste Management announced that it was reducing its estimated value by three-fifths (see the case study in chapter 6). Sunbeam "stuffed" sales, calling inventory sold when it was all but being parked with retailers. America OnLine (AOL) posted a 900 percent rise in operating profits, to $57 million. At 23 cents per share, earnings would handily beat Wall Street's estimate of 19 cents. But the excitement did not last long. The SEC was suspicious. It turned out that the numbers reflected some aggressive accounting. AOL tried to instantly write off much of the value of two companies it had just purchased. By taking a charge for "in-process R&D" under way at the companies, AOL figured it could write off fully $20 million of the $29 million it was paying for NetChannel, an internet television company, and a "substantial portion" of the $287 million it would pay for Mirabilis, a developer of real-time chat software.

Levitt convened a commission to make recommendations for improving audit committees. But accounting problems continue to make headlines. Staff at MicroStrategy worked until midnight on September 30, 1999, to be able to nail down a deal in time to report it in its third quarter numbers. The company on the other side of the deal booked it in the fourth quarter, but MicroStrategy booked it in the third, allowing it to claim a fifteenth consecutive quarter of increased revenues. Without the deal, revenues would have decreased by 20 percent. MicroStrategy's stock went up 72 percent. Its officers sold shares worth more than $82 million. Then, six months later, MicroStrategy restated its financial results. Its annual profit was actually a loss. The stock dropped 62 percent in one day, erasing $11 billion of shareholder value.

Levitt's book includes descriptions of several different battles with the accountants, including the fight over expensing stock options (discussed later in this chapter). According to Levitt, the accounting profession's defeat of the FASB proposal to expense options provided momentum for them to try to "pull off a hostile takeover of the standard-setting process." The then Financial Executives Institute (now called Financial Executives International), made up of the chief financial officers and controllers of major companies, decided that the independent foundation that governed FASB, which sets accounting standards, was too independent, and not supportive enough of business. It proposed limiting the foundation's ability to control the agenda and initiate new projects. Levitt says, "I smelled a rat. Rather than speed up and improve the standard-setting process, I believed this cabal was looking to place it in the corporate equivalent of leg irons." He believed that a large part of the incentive to try this takeover was the hope that FEI could persuade FASB to allow companies to use derivatives to smooth out their earnings. Levitt succeeded in preventing the watering down of the standards for reporting derivatives, but he had to give up some of what he was trying to accomplish on the oversight of FASB. Later, after a series of accounting scandals, Levitt convened a Blue Ribbon Commission to come up with recommendations. His description of his failed attempt to prevent firms from providing both audit and the more lucrative consulting services to the same clients is truly tragic, in light of the even more devastating accounting scandals that would be revealed after he left office. (See the Arthur Andersen case study.)

# Case in Point: Mr. Biggs testifies

The following are excerpts from the testimony of then TIAA-CREF CEO John Biggs before the US Senate Committee on Banking, Housing and Urban Affairs (February 27, 2002).

The three changes we have needed for some time and that bear directly on the circumstances of Enron are these: (1) a means of dealing with the widespread overuse and abuse of fixed price stock options; (2) the need for some basic common sense regarding auditor independence; and (3) the need for a strong regulatory model to oversee the accounting profession.

## Overuse and Abuse of Stock Options

Several accounting professionals have attempted to lay the problems of Enron's accounting on the FASB. I believe they are seriously mistaken. In fact, during the late 80's and early 90's the FASB was aware of the very issues that Enron eventually faced. Among other things, the FASB addressed the absurd policy of accounting for stock options by which they appear to be "free" even though they form a central feature of executive compensation plans and obviously have very substantial costs.

Enron used such options extensively, covering all their management employees and granting large awards to their senior executives. Sixty percent of Enron employees had options. The cost of these options was never reported in Enron's earnings statements although the exercise gains were so great that in several years Enron paid no taxes.

The IRS allows as a deduction for compensation expense the difference between the option price and the stock's price when it is exercised (for most employee stock options). But in reports to shareholders that difference, or any other amount, has never been shown as an expense. Through its long, tedious, but open process the FASB explored all theoretical aspects of stock options. It put out tentative proposals, conducted exhaustive hearings so that all participants could comment, and heard arguments pro and con. The process took several years.

Many critics now say the FASB is too slow, but at other times critics have said it was too fast, especially when the issue was an unpopular one such as stock compensation or derivatives. The final proposal would have required a charge to expense for stock options given to employees as compensation. After extensive lobbying of Congress by companies and auditing firms, and following legislative threats to the existence of private sector standard setting, the FASB and the SEC capitulated. Arthur Levitt has publicly stated that he believes this was the greatest mistake made by the SEC during his chairmanship.

In capitulating, the FASB published a rule in 1995, known as Financial Accounting Standard 123, that offers the choice of expense recognition or disclosure in footnotes. If disclosure is chosen, the income statement will show expense for options only under certain circumstances required by the Accounting Principles Board (the predecessor to the FASB) in its Opinion No. 25 (1972). The FASB said the following in FAS 123, a statement with which I completely agree: "The Board chose a disclosure-based solution for stock-based employee compensation to bring closure to the divisive debate on this issue – not because it believes that solution is the best way to improve financial accounting and reporting." (Paragraph 62) In other words, disclosure in footnotes is inappropriate reporting to shareholders of the costs of operations.

As you might expect, most corporations prefer to use the obsolete accounting model of 1972 which treats the fixed price stock option as "free" and treats performance options as potentially very expensive. Significantly, most companies use virtually no other form of stock award than the fixed at-the-money option. Note that the Black–Scholes option-pricing model was created a year later, in 1973, and forms the basis for understanding financial transactions involving uncertainty. I can assure you that high-tech executives in Silicon Valley use the Black–Scholes model to value their own options. Most companies also use Black–Scholes to communicate total compensation to employees. Those same executives know that having to show the results of that calculation to shareholders would reduce or even eliminate the earnings of their companies.

I serve as a Director of the Boeing Company, which is the only major US company to adopt FAS 123 expense, in order to report to its shareholders the true cost of its stock compensation plan. Boeing's executive compensation plan is based heavily on tough performance tests which are prohibitively expensive under the 1972 accounting model used by all other companies. For the record, Boeing adopted its plan and FAS 123 in 1996, before I became a director.

I might mention a further example of the strong-arm tactics of US corporations. Last year the Financial Executives International issued a press release threatening to withdraw funding for the newly formed International Accounting Standards Board if the Board dared to study the issue of accounting for stock-based compensation. The use of options and stock as employee compensation is a growing phenomenon overseas, with little or no accounting guidance in place. I am happy to say that both Paul Volcker, Chairman of the Foundation supporting the IASB, and Sir David Tweedie, Chairman of the IASB, are standing their ground, and the project is proceeding.

The use of questionable accounting methods for stock options has several negative results:

1. Explosive growth in the use of stock options since 1995 – huge, indeed, incredible awards to CEOs and in some companies awards to every employee. For several years, this practice has been a major concern addressed by TIAA-CREF's corporate governance program.
2. The serious distortion of earnings statements so that some companies report large earnings at the same time that no taxes are paid. This is because of peculiar accounting that results in fixed price stock options as zero "cost" in public income statements while allowing the employee gain to be shown as a "cost" for the tax return.
3. Unprecedented focus on the stock price by all the employees of the company, to the point where serious ethical dilemmas are posed for employees. When excessive stress is placed on company accountants and their auditors, malfeasance may result. Business ethics experts wonder if potential "whistle blowers" are intimidated by their colleagues' or their own concern for their stock options.
4. The dramatic decline in dividends is a direct result of so much recent attention to stock options. A dollar per share paid to a shareholder as a dividend reduces the stock price by a dollar. Can anyone wonder why corporate managers find many reasons to justify a reduction or elimination of the dividend?
5. In many companies, stock options have replaced pension plans entirely. When we protested the action of IBM in abandoning its defined benefit plan, the

company responded by pointing out that its competitors in the technology world had no pensions whatsoever.

6. There has been an almost exclusive use of the fixed price stock option in employee compensation plans. More desirable stock compensation plans could be devised that would better align management and shareholder interests. Such plans are effectively prohibited by the 1972 rules because they require that management show an expense for them. For example, a plan that requires performance better than the general market performance is not considered a "fixed price option" and results in truly onerous accounting treatment under 1972 rules. FASB Statement 123 provides sensible expense accounting for performance plans.

I have long been a strong advocate for the principle that the private sector (i.e. FASB or GASB [the Governmental Accounting Standards Board] or IASB) should set accounting standards. Congress, through the political process, should not enter into such technical issues, but it should demand a fair and open process. I stand by that view. Some expression of support by your Committee, or by the full Senate or House of Representatives – the form of which you understand better than I – might make it possible for the IASB to study the issue, and for the FASB to reopen the question.

I believe that history would see this action as an extraordinary benefit coming out of the many lessons to be learned from Enron.

### Auditor Independence

My company has two important provisions in its Audit Committee Charter. Our auditors may not do any work for TIAA-CREF other than what is directly related to the audit function (this exclusionary rule also applies to our tax work); and rotation of the auditor is considered after a five- to ten-year period. The first rule was heatedly contested by our auditors at the time we imposed it; our current auditors knew the rule when they began working for us in 1997 and now accept it. We have had two auditor rotations since I have been Chairman, and each has been not only successful but also highly energizing for our financial management work.
. . .

There seems to me a widespread lack of sensitivity to conflicts for auditors that must be addressed. And there need to be more examples of lucrative opportunities turned down than there are.

I applaud the recent changes made by the accounting profession on limiting the types of non-auditor work. Several of the firms saw the public need to do this in 2000 when the SEC proposed limitations. The others have grudgingly assented, arguing, to my astonishment, that the Andersen–Enron relationships had no independence problem.

A far more powerful antidote to this blindness to conflicts of interest would be to require auditor rotation every five to seven years. Such a requirement will be fiercely opposed by the accountants and the companies, who will see only additional costs of having to make such changes. But I can vouch from my experience that the costs can be managed and that there are many positive benefits. Even if the cost-benefit ratio were unfavorable, which I doubt, isn't such a simple solution worthwhile, given the importance to our capital markets of confidence in financial reports? . . .

## A Strong Regulatory Model

The Public Oversight Board (POB) on which I have served for the past several months, attempted to oversee a bewildering array of monitoring groups. One was the Quality Control Inquiry Committee (QCIC) that reviews auditor performance in contested audits (i.e., where a lawsuit had been filed). A second was the Peer Review Board that participates in inter-firm peer reviews.

There were others as well. The POB oversaw the Professional Ethics Executive Committee (PEEC) that reviews members' actions in all types of ethical issues. It oversaw the Auditing Standard Board (ASB) and the SEC Practice Section (SECPS). Finally, the POB had the opportunity to raise questions with the FASB if accounting standards seemed in need of repair.

Being a non-accountant and an independent director, I found the POB very hard work, especially for a sitting CEO. The other four members were retired, and I succeeded Paul O'Neill who, as you know, moved from retirement to a very active position. What was often most frustrating was our lack of authority if we found something that we thought should be changed. While the major firms and the AICPA were outwardly co-operative when the SEC demanded action, they were unwilling to change in response to any significant POB initiative. At one point, the AICPA threatened to withhold funding from the POB, but was finally forced by the SEC into an unwilling marriage, documented by a new charter that gave us assurance of being able to pay our staff. No one will really miss us after March 31.

In short, we need something better for a regulatory body . . . The investigative authority of a new accounting regulatory body needs to be clear-cut and not simply a derivative of the SEC. Accounting firms must know that they cannot refuse to open their books or prevent their staff from co-operating with this new agency. Of course, it must have the ability to keep the information gathered out of the hands of the litigating lawyers. And it must have the authority to discipline firms and individuals without the delays of an AICPA investigating process.

The new agency must have licensing authority, beyond that of the states, for individuals who will practice at the SEC bar. It should have authority, I believe, to approve or disapprove business affiliations of licensed practitioners – for example, is it appropriate for American Express or H&R Block to become major players in providing audit services? Should accounting firms with an SEC audit practice be allowed to go into all the major financial businesses that the Big Five have now entered?

The new agency should also have a reliable funding source that does not come from the accounting profession on a voluntary basis. Nor should it come from the business community through the "tin-cup" process now used by the Financial Accounting Foundation and the Foundation for the International Accounting Standards Board.

Concerning this point, I have served on fund-raising committees for both the FASB and the IASB. I can assure you that voluntary giving to support the regulation of the auditing profession will not work. Raising money for a much more benign purpose – for instance, establishing accounting principles in the private sector – has been a very tough sell. Those of us asking for the money feel compromised. The unspoken question is this: "If I give, will I have more influence on FASB decisions?" The investment community has largely refused to support either the FASB or the IASB, with a very few exceptions to that rule. The usual contributors are those with a strong sense of community interest – the major banks, investment banking concerns, and several large global businesses.

We should devise instead a fee on stock market transactions, or registrations, or some other financial activity that will be devoted to paying for auditing oversight, the work of the Financial Accounting Foundation, and perhaps even the American share of the IASB's needs.

Given the welcome demise of the POB, the ball is squarely in the court of Congress and the SEC to define a strong regulatory body. It should have real teeth, adequate funding (without membership fees from the very institutions the new body will regulate), and a fair chance of bringing a new ethic and culture to a profession that needs to change.

It is my hope that we will succeed in these three areas: First, that we can make companies provide transparent accounting for stock options; second, that we can assure greater independence of auditing through auditor rotation; and third, that a strong regulatory body can be created. If these goals are reached, I believe we may look back on Enron as being a short-term financial tragedy for its employees and the holders of its securities, but a major long-run benefit for the US capital markets.

## BALANCING INTERESTS

At some point, any long-term strategy will seem at odds with the goal of profit maximization. The same is true of any commitment to corporate constituents beyond that required by law. It is impossible to determine whether a new benefit program for employees will be justified by the increased loyalty and enthusiasm it inspires. There are so many opportunities for mistakes and even self-dealing that this area requires oversight and accountability. The way it is handled is a strong indicator of the merits of any corporate governance system.

The key is finding the right system of checks and balances. A board that will blithely approve paying for a $120 million art museum with the shareholders' money is obviously operating without such a system. So is the CEO who will spend $68 million on developing an (ultimately disastrous) "smokeless" tobacco cigarette before informing his directors. (See the discussion of both of these cases in chapter 3.)

A paper company may consider which is an appropriate method of – for example – storing bark or floating logs down a river. If management makes that determination, it is likely to be designed to impose as much of the cost as possible on someone else. The only way to make sure that corporate management cannot merely externalize its costs is to have government, accountable through the political process, make the ultimate determination when the issue involves a tradeoff of corporate profits against social goals. Government regulation is justified two ways. First, it is the government's responsibility, because the government is – at least in theory – uniquely able to balance all appropriate interests as it is equally beholden (and not beholden) to all of them. Second, if enough of the community objects to the action taken by the government, they can elect new representatives who will do better.

Directors who fail to consider the interests of customers, employees, suppliers, and the community fail in their duty to shareholders; a company that neglects those interests will surely decline. The danger lies in allowing corporate managers to make policy tradeoffs among these interests. That should be left to those who have a more direct kind of accountability – through the political process. It is the job of elected public officials, not hired corporate officers, to balance the scales of justice.

F.A. Hayek posed the alternatives this way:

> So long as the management has the one overriding duty of administering the resources under its control as trustees for the shareholders and for their benefit, its hands are largely tied; and it will have no arbitrary power to benefit from this or that particular interest. But once the management of a big enterprise is regarded as not only entitled but even obliged to consider in its decisions whatever is regarded as the public or social interest, or to support good causes and generally to act for the public benefit, it gains indeed an uncontrollable power – a power which could not long be left in the hands of private managers but would inevitably be made the subject of increasing public control.[42]

There have been long periods in recent American economic history during which large corporation managers have viewed themselves as fiduciaries for society as a whole. Ralph Cordiner, the long-time CEO of General Electric Company, exemplified this standard. He said that top management was a "trustee," responsible for managing the enterprise "in the best balanced interest of shareholders, customers, employees, suppliers, and plant community cities." This is echoed in the corporate governance credo that emblazons every copy of *Director's Monthly*: "Effective corporate governance ensures that long-term strategic objectives and plans are established, and that the proper management and management structure are in place to achieve those objectives, while at the same time making sure that the structure functions to maintain the corporation's integrity, reputation, and accountability to its relevant constituencies."[43]

In recent times, more than half of the states in the US have passed "stakeholder" laws, which permit (or even require) directors to consider the impact of their actions on constituencies other than shareholders, including the employees, customers, suppliers, and the community.[44] This is in contrast to the traditional model of the publicly held corporation in law and economics, which says that corporate directors serve one constituency – their shareholders. Many people think this is a mistake. James J. Hanks Jr., of the law firm Ballard, Spahr, Andrews & Ingersoll, has called it "an idea whose time should never have come."

Typically, these statutes "apply generally to decisions by the Board, including decisions with regard to tender offers, mergers, consolidations and other forms of business combinations."[45] Most state laws of this kind do not mandate constituency-based decision-making, and just permit these provisions to be adopted by corporations, with shareholder approval. And most make it clear that the board's authority to consider other interests is completely discretionary, and that no stakeholder constituency will be entitled to be considered.

> *Do these provisions have any meaning? Do they allow or require directors operating under them to evaluate options any differently? Should they? Evaluate a proposed plant closing or acquisition as though you were a board member operating under such a provision, and as though you were not.*

Companies cannot afford to ignore the needs of their constituencies. Indeed, in the past, "stakeholder" proposals have been occasionally submitted by shareholders, asking the board to undertake a more comprehensive analysis of proposed actions. But we agree with Hanks that "stakeholder" language, in legislation or in corporate charters, can camouflage neglect, whether intentional or unintentional, of the rights of shareholders.

It has always been permissible, even required, for directors and managers to consider the interests of all stakeholders, as long as they do so in the context of the interests of shareholder value. Courts have upheld a corporation's right to donate corporate funds to charities, for example, if it was in the corporation's long-term interests. As the American Bar Association Committee on Corporate Laws pointed out: "[T]he Delaware courts have stated the prevailing corporate common law in this country: directors have fiduciary responsibilities to shareholders which, while allowing directors to give consideration to the interests of others, compel them to find some reasonable relationship to the long-term interests of shareholders."[46] The Committee also noted that the Delaware Supreme Court's decision in the *Unocal* case (see discussion in chapter 3), which enabled directors to analyze the effects of a potential takeover on a variety of factors, including constituencies, does not suggest "that the court intended to authorize redress of an adverse 'impact' on a non-shareholder constituency at the expense of shareholders."[47] While it is useful (and cost-effective) for boards to consider the best way to meet the admittedly competing needs of the company's diverse constituencies, it is imperative for them to give shareholders first priority. Only with that as their goal can they serve the other constituencies over the long term.

The Business Roundtable seems to agree. In its 1990 report, *Corporate Governance and American Competitiveness*, it contrasts political and "economic" organizations. "Legislative bodies . . . represent and give expression to a multiplicity of constituent interests. Our political system is designed to create compromises between competing interests, to seek the broad middle ground . . . This system of governance would be fatal for an economic enterprise." In later reports it backed off, suggesting that a stakeholder approach (not coincidentally, a very effective anti-takeover protection) was the better way.

# Case in point: Protection, Pennsylvania-style

In 1990, Pennsylvania risked the consequences F.A. Hayek warned about when it adopted the notorious Act 36 of 1990, which went far beyond other stakeholder laws in moving beyond the rather benign concept of "consideration" of the interests of others to a standard with more legal bite: usurpation. Directors may consider "to the extent they deem appropriate" the impact of their decisions on *any* affected interest. They are not required "to regard any corporate interest or the interests of any particular group . . . as a dominant or controlling interest or factor" as long as the action is in the best interests of the corporation.

The previous version of the law, adopted in 1983, included a stakeholder provision similar to those adopted by many other states, but the new version went further than any other state had, so far, by expanding the list of interests that may be considered and, more important, by establishing that no interest must be controlling (including the interests of shareholders), as long as the directors act in the best interests of the corporation. Other changes to the fiduciary standard include an explicit rejection of the Delaware "heightened scrutiny" test applied to directors' actions in change-of-control situations. Note: this statute was adopted very quickly, with the strong support of a major Pennsylvania company that was then the target of a hostile takeover attempt. The attempt was ultimately unsuccessful, thanks in part to the passage of this law, which included other anti-takeover provisions as well.

In the context of a potential or proposed change-of-control transaction, a determination made by disinterested directors (those not current or former employees) will be presumed to satisfy the standard-of-care requirement unless clear and convincing evidence proves that the determination was not made in good faith after reasonable investigation. This means, as a practical matter, that directors cannot be held liable for what they do, absent some element of self-dealing or fraud. This provision required no shareholder approval; it was immediately applicable to all companies incorporated in Pennsylvania, unless they opted out within 90 days. The anti-shareholder bias of the bill was made clear during the campaign to pass the bill. In December 1989, a "fact sheet" sent to state legislators from the Pennsylvania Chamber of Commerce, which co-sponsored the bill with local unions under the banner of the AFL-CIO, contained the statement that the bill would "reaffirm and make more explicit the time-honored (and current) principle that directors owe their duties to the corporation, rather than to any specific group such as shareholders."

The new law does not say that directors are free to place greater importance on factors other than long-term profit maximization. But to give it any other interpretation would violate the foremost principle of statutory construction and assume that the legislature intended its language to have no effect.

It did have an effect, though perhaps not what the legislature intended. The *Wall Street Journal* called it "an awful piece of legislation," and it soon became apparent that many Pennsylvania companies agreed. By October 15, 1990, 99 companies – nearly 33 percent of the state's publicly traded companies – had opted out of at least some of the provisions of the bill. Over 61 percent of the Fortune 500 incorporated in Pennsylvania opted out, as did over 56 percent of those in the S&P 500. So massive was the stampede out of Pennsylvania Act 36 that a *Philadelphia Inquirer* editorial noted: "These business decisions make it all the more clear that the law was crafted not in the best interest of the state's businesses, but to protect Armstrong World Industries Inc. and a few other companies facing takeover attempts." A company spokesman for Franklin Electronics Publishers stated that its board "believes that the Pennsylvania legislation runs counter to basic American principles of corporate democracy and personal property rights."

The market also agreed. Jonathan M. Karpoff and Paul M. Malatesta at the University of Washington School of Business found that from October 12, 1989 (the date of the first national newswire report of the bill), through January 2, 1990 (when the bill was introduced in the Pennsylvania House), the shares of firms incorporated in Pennsylvania under-performed the S&P 500 by an average of 5.8 percent. Another study, by Wilshire Associates, linked enactment of the Pennsylvania anti-takeover law with a 4 percent decline in stock prices of companies incorporated there.[48]

*Are the "best interests of the corporation" the same as the "best interests of the shareholders"? When do they differ? Who defines the competing interests? Who decides how to balance them? For what purpose? Consider these questions in the context of the debate about just what a corporation is. How do the answers differ if you think of a corporation as an "imaginary person"? A "bundle of contracts"?*

Some scholars have developed what they call an "ethical contract." The ethical contract is built on the model of more traditional, operational contracts between the executives and the other stakeholders in the venture. It assumes that any executive's legitimacy can only be sustained by the interaction of these "relationships" with other stakeholders. External legitimacy of the executive and the employees must be sustained and controlled by the personal ethic of the individuals involved as well as by broader corporate and societal ethics. The personal ethic operates through conscience. The corporate and societal ethics work through the internal and external systems of scrutiny, each of which is reinforced by mechanisms for enforcement. Together, these underpin the "corporate contract" between the employee and the firm.[49]

*If you were drawing up an "ethical contract" between the corporation and the community, what substantive and procedural provisions would you want to include? What would be your enforcement mechanism? What provisions would you have for amendment?*

It seems to make the most sense to envision a hypothetical long-term shareholder, like the beneficial owner of most institutional investor securities, as the ultimate party at interest. That allows all other interests to be factored in without losing sight of the goal of long-term wealth maximization. But without a clear and direct and enforceable fiduciary obligation to shareholders, the contract that justifies the corporate structure is irreparably shattered.

In our view, the arguments advancing a "constituency" or "trustee" role for corporate functioning are miscast. It is difficult enough to determine the success of a company's strategy based on only one goal – shareholder value. It is impossible when we add in other goals. There is no one standard or formula for determining the impact that today's actions will have on tomorrow's value. The only way to evaluate the success of a company's performance is to consult those who have the most direct and wide-reaching interest in the results of that performance – the shareholders. The problem is one of effective accountability (agency costs). Only owners have the motive to inform themselves and to enforce standards that arguably are a proxy for the public interest. As Edward Mason comments:

> If equity rather than profits is the corporate objective, one of the traditional distinctions between the private and public sectors disappears. If equity is the primary desideratum, it may well be asked why duly constituted public authority is not as good an instrument for dispensing equity as self-perpetuating corporate managements? Then there are those, including the editors of *Fortune*, who seek the best of both worlds by equating long-run profit maximization with equitable treatment of all parties at issue. But to date no one has succeeded in working out the logic of this modern rehabilitation of the medieval "just price."[50]

With all of the talk of corporations being run for the benefit of shareholders, it is surprising that so little attention has been paid to the past difference and utter incompatibility of interests of different shareholding groups, ranging from index funds to highly quantitative computer models. The largest single component is the pension plan participant, and even there we have a range between those in defined benefit versus those in defined contribution plans and those who are just beginning employment, those who are nearing retirement, and those who are retired. Still, as discussed in chapter 2, it is the hypothetical pension plan participant whose long-term time horizon and wish to retire into a world with a sound economy and environment can serve as a worthwhile standard.

## GOOD AND BAD CORPORATIONS?

*Are we confident of our ability to identify a "good corporation"? How do we reconcile economic and social goals?*

# Cases in point: The "good," the "bad," and the real

Let us begin with some examples of companies that have made economic decisions with (arguably) adverse social consequences. The first case in point is an actual case. The rest are hypothetical, but adapted from real cases.

- For several decades following World War II, the great inventor Edwin Land, chairman of Polaroid Corp., pioneered project after project to promote the public good – creating work groups to determine job characteristics. Banning discrimination in employment, locating new plants in distress areas, developing new technology. In the late 1960s, it was revealed that one of Polaroid's most versatile products was producing photo identification cards. In most cases, this was a useful technology. But a controversy arose when it was revealed that Polaroid's photo ID machines were the key to enforcement of the apartheid laws in South Africa. *Did Polaroid all of a sudden become a bad company?*
- A chemical company complied with all applicable laws in the disposal of its waste chemicals, burying most of them in state-of-the-art drums in a landfill. Twenty years later, there was a statistically high rate of cancer and birth defects in the housing development located near the landfill. *Is the chemical company a bad company?*
- A small manufacturing company in a very competitive market is advised by its lawyer that it is not meeting federal environmental standards, The cost of bringing the company into compliance would more than wipe out the company's profits for the year and could drive up the cost of the company's products. None of its competitors is undertaking the expenses of meeting the standard. The odds of prosecution are low. The company decides not to comply. *Is this company a bad company?* Let's say that it decides, instead, to give its hazardous materials to a disposal firm that does not comply with environmental standards but is inexpensive. *Is this a better or worse solution than continuing to violate the standards itself?*
- A newspaper company with a liberal outlook frequently publishes strongly pro-environment editorials. It is printed on paper produced outside the US, which is cheaper than US paper, partly because the producers do not have to comply with US environmental laws. *Is the newspaper a bad company? Is the paper company it buys from a bad company?*

These were companies who made arguably anti-social decisions for economic reasons. Let us look at some examples of companies who make uneconomic decisions for social reasons.

- In a landmark 1919 case, *Dodge v. Ford Motor Co.*, a Michigan court ordered Henry Ford to pay dividends to his shareholders.[51] The case arose when Ford ceased paying out a special annual dividend of over $10 million, and the Dodge brothers sued. At the time, Henry Ford owned nearly 60 percent of the company, and the Dodge brothers owned 10 percent.

  Ford Motors was rich in surplus capital, and the company would have had no difficulty in paying the dividend. Henry Ford claimed, however, that he needed the money for expansion (he planned a second plant) and he did not wish the cost of such growth to be borne by the consumer in the form of higher car prices. Indeed, because times were tough, Ford wanted to lower the price of cars. Ford argued that the stockholders had made enough money, and that it was more important to help the working man through the Depression. (Some suggested that Ford's reasons were not so altruistic: he knew that the Dodge brothers planned to join the auto-making business, and he did not want to finance their expansion by paying dividends.)

  The Michigan Supreme Court reminded Ford of his duty to the stockholders. Its message was that Ford's generosity was all very proper, but not when he was being generous with other people's money. The Court wrote: "There should be no confusion . . . of the duties which Mr. Ford conceives that he and the stockholders owe to the general public and the duties which in law he and his co-directors owe to protesting, minority stockholders. A business corporation is organized and carried on primarily for the profit of the stockholders." *Was the Court right? Compare with the Wrigley decision, about installing lights so the Chicago Cubs could play night games (see the introduction to this book).*

- A chain of restaurants called Chick-fil-A® is closed on Sundays, because of the religious beliefs of the management. Clearly, the company (and the shareholders) are forgoing considerable revenue. But the company's mission is not stated in economic terms. It does not even mention profit. It is "To glorify God by being a faithful steward of all that is entrusted to us, To have a positive influence on all who come in contact with Chick-fil-A." *Is this a good company? If it sold shares to the public, would the courts permit management to decide to keep it closed on Sundays because it was the sabbath?*

- There was a fire in the Malden Mills textile factory in Lawrence, Massachusetts that destroyed three of its nine buildings just before Christmas in 1995. As described in the thoughtful *Edges of the Field*, by Harvard law professor Joseph W. Singer, the next day the company's founder and owner, Aaron Mordecai Feurstein, spoke to the company's more than 3,000 workers in a high school gymnasium. They feared the worst. Feurstein was 70 years old. Most local manufacturing jobs had been moved offshore. Would he rebuild? Feurstein told the workers that he would. In addition, he promised to rehire every worker who wanted a job. And he promised they would all get their $275 Christmas bonuses. He did better than that. He paid all of their salaries for several months, until he could not afford it any more. By 1998, almost all of the workers had been rehired. When asked why he did not just lay off the workers, he said, "Because it wouldn't be right." When he attracted a great deal of press attention for his response, he said, "My celebrity is a poor reflection of the values of today." *Would a publicly owned company, watched carefully by analysts and accountable to shareholders, have been able to respond this way?* Singer comments, "One might think that a publicly held company might have public obligations. The reality is that such companies are managed by professionals who are obligated under existing law to maximize return to shareholders, whether or not this is in the public interest. Existing law not only does not encourage most employers to act as Feurstein did, but may actually *prohibit* them from responding as he did." Singer suggests that, if it had been a public company, shareholders might have sued Feurstein for corporate waste. *Compare this case to Ladish Company, which in 2003 announced that due to an accounting correction it was docking the workers 10 percent of their pay to make up for profit-sharing bonuses they received due to the inflated numbers.*

- A publicly held oil company spends over $100 million to build an art museum for the CEO's collection (see the Occidental Petroleum case study). *In whose interests is this expenditure?*

Sometimes the conflict between economic and social goals is even more complicated.

- An oil company with lucrative operations in South Africa is scrupulous about imposing the highest standards of equal rights for its employees. It has therefore made jobs and wages available to black South Africans that are not available to them elsewhere. The company is pressured by some of its shareholders and by outside groups to withdraw from South Africa entirely, even though a sale of the division would be uneconomic for the company and would leave the black employees unlikely to do as well with the successor owners.
- A major consumer goods company includes among its many and widely varied charitable contributions a six-figure donation to Planned Parenthood. Employees, shareholders, and consumers who object to abortion protest this contribution, so the company cancels it. It is then confronted with employees, shareholders, and consumers who object to the cancellation, and demand that the company continue to support Planned Parenthood. At annual meetings ranging over a period of several years, more time is given to this issue than any other. *Who should decide?*

Another example of how difficult it is to use social tests of company performance is Stride Rite Corporation, a company that prided itself on its well-deserved reputation for corporate citizenship. The *Wall Street Journal* noted, "In the past three years alone, Stride Rite has received 14 public service awards, including ones from the National Women's Political Caucus, Northeastern University, the Northeast Human Resources Association and Harvard University, which praised it for improving the quality of life in its community and the nation."[52] And yet Stride Rite had to move its shoe-making jobs outside of the slum areas of Boston, indeed outside of the United States, to foreign countries where employment costs are significantly lower.

*Is it socially responsible to move jobs out of depressed areas? Is it socially responsible to stay in these areas if it means going bankrupt?*

The former chairman, Arnold Hiatt, wanted Stride Rite to be (and be seen as) a leader in socially responsible capitalism. He passionately espoused a Jeffersonian vision linking corporate and social responsibility. When Stride Rite joined 54 other companies to form Businesses for Social Responsibility, he said, "If you're pro-business, you also have to be concerned about things like jobs in the inner city and the 38 million Americans living below the poverty line . . . To the extent that you can stay in the city, I think you have to . . . [but] if it's at the expense of your business, I think you can't forget that your primary responsibility is to your stockholders."[53]

For the sake of this argument, let's define "social judgments" as explicit tradeoffs of profit maximization in favor of social goals.

*To what extent do we want corporate leaders to exercise social judgments? What is their authority to make determinations affecting the public good? Who elected them to what? To whom are they accountable?*

Doug Bandow, a former Reagan aide, offers a view from the supply side:

> Corporations are specialized institutions created for a specific purpose. They are only one form of enterprise in a very diverse society with lots of different organizations. Churches exist to help people fulfill their responsibilities toward God in community with one another. Governments are instituted most basically to prevent people from violating the rights of others. Philanthropic institutions are created to do good works. Community associations are to promote one or another shared goal. And businesses are established to make a profit by meeting people's needs and wants.
>
> Shouldn't business nevertheless "serve" society? Yes, but the way it best does so is by satisfying people's desires in an efficient manner . . . Does this mean that firms have no responsibilities other than making money? Of course not, just as individuals have obligations other than making money. But while firms have a duty to respect the rights of others, they are under no obligation to promote the interests of others. The distinction is important.[54]

Bandow goes on to say that promoting other goals (giving to charity, exceeding regulatory or industry standards for pollution control or employee benefits) is permissible if it promotes the firm's financial well-being (all of the above may create loyalty in employees and customers), or if the shareholders know (and presumably therefore approve) of the program. He uses as an example the jeans company Levi Strauss, which informed shareholders when it went public that it intended to continue its generous charitable giving program.

For another approach to charitable giving, consider Warren Buffett's Berkshire Hathaway. From 1981–2003, Berkshire allowed each shareholder to designate a charity. While admitting that his approach may not be suitable for companies with institutional investors having "short-term investment horizons," Buffett believes it is a more principled approach to corporate giving.

> Just as I wouldn't want you to implement your personal judgments by writing checks on my bank account for charities of your choice, I feel it inappropriate to write checks on your corporate "bank account" for charities of my choice . . . I am pleased that Berkshire donations can become owner-directed. It is ironic, but understandable, that a large and growing number of major corporations have charitable policies pursuant to which they will match gifts made by employees (and – brace yourself for this one – many even match

gifts made by directors) but none, to my knowledge, has a plan matching charitable gifts by owners.[55]

In 2003, a tiny anti-abortion group objected to the shareholder-designated donations to Planned Parenthood, and Berkshire shut down the program. Over 22 years, it had contributed almost $200 million to over 1200 charities, mostly schools and religious institutions. Congressman Paul Gillmor of Ohio sponsored a legislative proposal that would require companies to disclose their corporate charitable contributions, based on concerns that conflicts of interest led to contributions that might not otherwise be justified as beneficial to shareholders. Douglas L. Foshee, chairman and CEO of Nuevo Energy, agreed in a statement to the Federalist Society that: "Three things should be disclosed to the shareholders: the company's giving philosophy, the amount of charitable contributions above some threshold and a description of any potential conflicts resulting from those charitable contributions." He explained his view that charitable contributions are "a part of our corporate purpose." He said that, "I believe our contributions in these communities help ensure that they remain attractive places for our employees to work, live and raise their families. I [also] view our corporate contributions as another in a long list of employee benefits. Our employees take pride in knowing that our corporate giving dollars go to causes that are important both to them and to our company."

The corporate conflicts of interest revealed in the scandals of 2002 led to additional legislative proposals for disclosure of charitable contributions to entities affiliated with corporate directors or their spouses, but strong opposition from the non-profit community prevented it from becoming part of the package of reforms that were ultimately enacted.

## EQUILIBRIUM: THE CADBURY PARADIGM

Corporations must balance many competing considerations – long- and short-term notions of gain, cash and accounting concepts of value, democracy and authority, and, as we said in the title of our first book, "power and accountability."

The intricate equilibrium of corporations has been particularly well described by Sir Adrian Cadbury, following a tradition that extends for two generations before his birth – Sir Adrian's grandfather refused to provide Cadbury chocolate to British troops in South Africa in protest against the Boer war.

From his base in the United Kingdom, Sir Adrian has provided world-class leadership and guidance with respect to corporate governance. He has been the notably successful CEO, and then chairman, of Cadbury Schweppes, a non-executive director of IBM Europe and the Bank of England, and chairman of the Cadbury Commission, which in 1992 published governance guidelines for the UK.

In his classic study, *The Company Chairman*, Cadbury identified multiple levels of responsibility in the corporation:

In practice, it is possible to distinguish three levels of company responsibility. The primary level comprises the company's responsibilities to meet its material obligations to shareholders, employees, customers, suppliers and creditors, to pay its taxes and to meet its statutory duties. The sanctions against failure to match up to these relatively easily defined and measured responsibilities are provided by competition and the law.

The next level of responsibility is concerned with the direct results of the actions of companies in carrying out their primary task and includes making the most of the community's human resources and avoiding damage to the environment . . . Beyond these two levels, there is a much less well-defined area of responsibility, which takes in the interaction between business and society in a wider sense. How far has business a responsibility to maintain the framework of the society in which it operates and how far should business reflect society's priorities rather than its own commercial ones?[56]

*How do we determine the answer to Cadbury's question? Who should be responsible for answering it?*

# Case in point: Johnson & Johnson[57]

*How much is the confidence of the marketplace worth? How should a company "invest" in gaining and maintaining that confidence? How does a company respond when confidence has been shaken?*

Johnson & Johnson faced two crises with its Tylenol product, the first in 1982 and the second just four years later. The episodes show how a company can respond to an almost instant evaporation of consumer confidence by demonstrating to the public that it is more interested in safety than profits.

In 1982, seven people died after taking tampered Tylenol. One variety of the product was sold in capsule form, and the capsules could easily be opened. It was clear that the poison had been inserted in the capsules after they left Johnson & Johnson. Sales of the product plummeted. Johnson & Johnson recalled all of their Tylenol capsules and introduced new "tamper-resistant" packaging, so that consumers could know if a bottle had been opened prior to purchase. The company was able to regain market share despite the initial drop in sales.

By 1986 Tylenol had regained a 35 percent share of the $1.5 billion nonprescription pain-reliever market, as big a share as the product had achieved before the 1982 crisis. Tylenol was Johnson & Johnson's most profitable single brand, accounting for some $525 million in revenues in 1985. The capsule form accounted for roughly a third of that. When, in February 1986, it became known that a New York woman died of taking cyanide-laced Tylenol, those revived revenues were threatened. The incident became more serious when a second bottle of adulterated capsules was discovered in the same Westchester village.

The questions facing Johnson & Johnson were these. Should the company launch another all-out offensive to calm consumer fears, or could the company get by with less drastic damage limitation? Did a pair of contaminated bottles in a New York suburb warrant a nationwide campaign to withdraw the capsules? According to the *New York Times*, chairman James E. Burke's aim was to strike a balance "between what is good for consumers and what is good for Johnson & Johnson."

Johnson & Johnson did indeed withdraw all Tylenol capsules from the nation's shelves, and replaced them with new "caplets." These were coated tablets that were safer from contamination. The full withdrawal – which could have cost the company's shareholders $150 million, or one-quarter of Johnson & Johnson's 1985 earnings – was deemed necessary in the light of bans in 14 states on the sale of Tylenol, and a drop in sales similar to that following the 1982 crisis.

In an interview with the *New York Times*, James Burke said that the company's decision-making was argumentative and aggressive. Discussions were characterized by "yelling and screaming" he said. Some executives pressed for the withdrawal and discontinuation of the capsule product. Others argued that an isolated incident in a small town did not merit a national campaign.

The decision to withdraw the capsules was encouraged by a $4 fall in Johnson & Johnson's stock price in the days following the death of the Westchester woman.

The company launched a massive publicity campaign to defend the Tylenol product, led by James Burke himself. The company held three news conferences, and Burke made over a dozen television appearances, including one on the "Donahue" television program.

*Did Johnson & Johnson act in the interests of the company's customers or share-holders? To what extent are those interests mutually exclusive? To what extent are they inextricably linked?*

# MEASURING VALUE ENHANCEMENT

As we have noted throughout this book, the measure of corporate performance must be the creation of value. This is difficult, at best. If it is impossible to determine in the present what the impact of current decisions will be on future value, it is not much easier to determine after the fact what the impact of past decisions has been.

There are many measures of corporation value. While a full discussion of the range of measures could easily fill several books, it is useful to include at this stage a brief description of the pros and cons of some of the most popular measures. To stay within the context of a discussion of corporate governance, we examine these measures by asking two questions: (1) What does each of them contribute to (or how does each interfere with) the ability of the three primary parties to corporate governance to do their part in guiding the corporation? (2) Who is in the best position to decide when to apply which measures?

## GAAP

We begin, of course, with the Generally Accepted Accounting Principles (GAAP). Readers should note that the operative term here is "generally accepted," not "certifiably accurate."

GAAP is a language by which the assets and liabilities of corporations are recorded in balance sheets and their functioning is stated in income statements. Accounting purports to present performance in numbers; by the consistent use of a fixed set of quantitative techniques, accountants can accurately depict the course of a business over long periods of time.

Accounting rules are important because the Securities and Exchange Commission (SEC), the New York Stock Exchange (NYSE), and other regulatory bodies require that companies have "certified financial statements." The purpose of these rules is to assure a consistent (if minimal) level of disclosure. What they measure is measured consistently over time and between companies, and that has some utility. But it is crucial to remember that there is enough flexibility and room for interpretation in the GAAP to permit accounting firms to compete with each other by offering more creative approaches, and there are many clients out there who will hire the firm whose creativity is most in its own favor. Accountancy is a business, indeed, a competitive business, and one of its characteristics is the willingness to find solutions to a client's problems. One accounting firm's charges against earnings are another's "charge offs" to surplus, for example. For this reason, the numbers may not be as "apples and apples" as an outsider evaluating them would wish for.

It is best to view accounting as an invented foreign language like Esperanto – useful enough for communicating across cultures, but really not particularly helpful in day-to-day business dealings. For example, accounting has always had a hard time dealing with inflation. The "nominal" or stated value of an asset departs widely from its market value. And many items that are vitally connected to the profitability of the enterprise are not carried as assets on a balance sheet: the value of a concession to drill for oil, the value of brand names, the "goodwill" associated with a new venture launched by a household name. Accounting standards are based on a time when real property, like machinery, was the most important asset. They do not reflect the value of "human capital."

But the real problem with accounting standards is that, through their general acceptance, appearance becomes reality. New forms of measurement are rarely conceptualized or applied. And existing standards are too often seen as far more objective and meaningful than they are. For example, "earnings" are one of the critical components of value in the market-place, yet the accounting scandals of 2002–3 made it clear how subjective the standards are. Earnings are subject to manipulation. Much of it is legal and some is even appropriate, but some goes far beyond what should be acceptable. The whole concept of "managed earnings" has an oxymoronic sound. Commissioner Norman Johnson of the Securities and Exchange Commission spoke about the pressures to manage earnings in a 1999 speech:

> Fundamentally, companies may attempt to manage earnings for numerous reasons. Perhaps the single most important cause, however, is the pressure imposed on management to meet analysts' earnings projections. The severity with which the market punishes companies failing to meet analysts' expectations is extraordinary. This factor, combined with the recent increased emphasis on stock options as a key component of executive compensation has also placed greater pressure on management to achieve earnings expectations. The pressure to meet analysts' estimates and compensation benchmarks have both operated to increase the temptation for management to "fudge" the numbers. Auditors surely want to retain their clients, and are thus under pressure not to stand in the way of companies who have succumbed to these temptations . . .
>
> No one who follows the financial pages could escape awareness of the recent allegations of apparent large-scale financial fraud, often involving hundreds of millions of dollars of manufactured or "managed earnings," at many prominent public companies. While the problem is not new, it is happening with alarming frequency. Barely a week goes by without an announcement that another large company is restating its past results. There are a number of dubious practices that companies employ to manage their earnings, including such gems as: "big bath" restructuring charges, creative acquisition account-ing, "cookie jar reserves," "immaterial" misapplications of accounting principles, and the premature recognition of revenue. The names for some of these techniques may be amus-ing, but in reality they are not amusing at all.

Take "big bath" accounting as one example. This is the practice when a company decides at the end of the year that it must make a one-time-only "restructuring charge." This charge is not assessed against current earnings; it is levied against the accumulated earnings of the venture. This technique is so popular that the SEC's chief accountant reported that, in the first quarter of 1998, corporate write-offs, as a percentage of the reported earnings per share of S&P's Fortune 500 stock index, surged to 11 percent of reported earnings, their highest level in the previous ten years. Warren Buffett noted in the annual report of

Berkshire Hathaway that the 1997 earnings of the Fortune 500 companies totaled $324 billion dollars. He compared this to reports by R.G. Associates of Baltimore that the total charges for items such as asset writedowns, restructurings, and IPR&D charges amounted to a stunning $86.3 billion dollars in 1998.

There is an Alice in Wonderland character to this. The numbers make more sense if you keep in mind that accounting earnings are not economic earnings. Imagine a company that has reported over the past five years earnings of $10 a share each year; then in year 6, the company decides on a restructuring charge of $75 a share. During all of the six-year period, the company is deemed to be operating profitably from an accounting point of view. Each year has its $10 earnings; the retroactive "restructuring charge" cannot affect the five years of perceptions that have passed. Furthermore, because it is a restructuring charge, it does not alter the reported "earnings from ongoing operations" in year 6, which are, let's say, $10 a share. Thus, the company has lost money over a six-year period, and yet each annual component shows a profit at the time of reporting. This trick is especially popular for new CEOs, as it enables them to start with, if not a clean slate, a cleaner one. Research by New York University accounting professor Baruch Lev suggests that the disparity between a company's tax and financial accounting is a compelling indicator of problems.

Accounting standards are like a maze through which to work one's way. A concept as simple as "costs" can be interpreted a dozen different ways. If the CEO is a veteran who wants to show steady progress, costs may be reported one way. If she is going to re-engineer the company and be compensated according to new reported earnings, costs may be calculated another way. And if she is top gun of a defense firm that is paid only "cost plus" a percentage, costs will be calculated another way.

Consider the situation of Westinghouse Corporation, which by 1993 had taken six restructuring charges over the previous seven years. It got to the point that the "operating earnings" figures were meaningless; most analysts disregarded the company's figures and developed their own calculation of Westinghouse operations.

In many instances, the accounting conventions have a material impact on the company's decisions. For example, in the late 1980s, Westinghouse decided to expand its real-estate financing business very substantially. In order to motivate the executives, they devised a compensation package that provided an incentive for an improved return on the equity invested (ROE). The executives were so motivated that they dramatically improved the ROE by the fastest method available – they borrowed. This leverage brought increased earnings (and, hence, compensation) to the bottom line. Everyone was happy, until Westinghouse became overwhelmed by its new debts. When the real-estate commitments proved to have been carelessly assumed, the entire company (not just the real-estate division) almost went bankrupt – all from an accounting formula to create incentives for salespersons.

# Case in point: Sears Automotive

In the summer of 1992, the California Department of Consumer Affairs conducted a number of undercover investigations at the auto repair stores of Sears, Roebuck & Co. They found systematic charging and regular performance of unnecessary repairs. A similar operation in New Jersey reached similar conclusions. California consumer regulators demanded the closure of all 72 auto stores in the state. Had the closedown been enforced, Sears would have lost $200 million in annual revenue, and 3,000 employees would have lost their jobs. Sears settled the New Jersey accusations with a payment of $200,000 to a fund set up to study auto malpractice nationwide. At least a dozen class-action suits relating to the fraud were filed. Finally, the auto stores, one of Sears' most profitable operations, showed a 15 percent decline in business in the months following the scandal.

In responding to the crisis, Sears blamed the compensation practice of its auto department. In early 1990 Sears stopped paying its auto workers by the hour, and instead instructed them to perform a certain number of repairs each shift. Mechanics and repairmen would be paid a commission on the work during the shift. In other words, the employees had an incentive to perform more expensive repairs than was necessary. Complaints about the stores jumped 29 percent in the year that the new commission program was introduced, and a further 27 percent the next year, leading to the investigation by consumer regulators.

Sears' chairman and CEO Ed Brennan admitted at a press conference that the incentive scheme "created an environment where mistakes did occur."

# Case in point: Green Tree Financial

Green Tree CEO Lawrence Coss had an unusual compensation formula. Instead of tying his pay to stock price performance or a particular financial goal at the company, which specialized in high-risk mortgages, Coss received a percentage of the company's profits. Perhaps it is not surprising, therefore, that the company used very aggressive accounting techniques in its reporting of profits, hooking the returns on loans as though there would be no defaults. Ironically, the problem was not defaults but prepayments. After several years of astoundingly good results, Coss had to announce in 1997 that earnings would actually be reduced by $190 million, and that the company would retroactively cut its 1996 pre-tax earnings by $200 million. Since Coss's 1996 bonus was based on pre-tax profits, the restatement forced him to give back an estimated $40 million of his then record-setting $102 million payday.

Note: Green Tree's problems were only beginning. After more than $700 million in accounting corrections, the company was acquired by Conseco, an insurance firm. Conseco, with stock trading at under a dime a share, down from a high near $60, filed for bankruptcy in December of 2002.

The accounting practices in different countries have produced some grotesque consequences. Until recently, in the United States, the "goodwill" arising out of an acquisition – meaning the extent to which the purchase price exceeds the value of the tangible assets – could not be charged off against the ongoing earnings of the enterprise.[58] In the UK goodwill arising out of acquisitions has been amortizable. Thus, the Blue Arrow scandal involved the acquisition by a small UK company of a much larger American one on terms with which other potential American acquirers could not compete. Blue Arrow was able to take on a level of debt that could be buried in its balance sheet over a period of years; an American firm, by contrast, would have had to take a hit to its profits. As John Jay wrote in the *Sunday Telegraph*: "Thanks to the disparity between United States and British accounting rules over the treatment of goodwill, an American white knight was out of the question and Fromstein [Manpower's CEO] was reduced either to contemplating some kind of poison pill acquisition or suing for peace."[59] Arbitrary accounting rules thus generate uneconomic corporate decisions.

Increasing concerns about "pro forma" reports led to a December 2001 release from the SEC cautioning companies about misleading "pro forma" reports and, a month later, the first SEC enforcement action on pro formas, involving Trump Hotels and Casino Resorts Inc.

The SEC found that the CEO, CFO, and treasurer of Trump Hotels violated the anti-fraud provisions of the Securities Exchange Act by issuing an earnings release that was materially misleading. In its third quarter 1999 earnings release, Trump Hotels explained that the reported earnings excluded a one-time charge of $81.4 million. Exclusion of the charge was not in accordance with GAAP; therefore, the reported earnings were pro forma, though not identified as such. By comparing the pro forma earnings to analysts' expectations and to its own prior period results, which were GAAP figures, Trump Hotels suggested that, but for the exclusion, the reported earnings also were in accordance with GAAP.

Most importantly, the SEC found that, by specifically describing this exclusion, the company implied that no other significant unusual items were excluded from or included in the pro forma figures. However, the figures also included an undisclosed one-time gain of $17.2 million that, if excluded, would have effectively turned the quarter's positive operating results into a loss. Company executives compounded the problem by suggesting that the company's operating improvements led to the positive results. Yet, had the one-time gain been excluded, the figures would have shown a negative financial trend in operating results and that the company's earnings failed to meet analysts' expectations. The SEC found the undisclosed one-time gain to be material, particularly because it represented the difference between a positive and negative trend in earnings and revenues . . . and the difference between meeting and failing to meet analysts' expectations.

On January 16, 2003, the SEC adopted tougher rules on pro forma releases, requiring companies to explain exactly how the pro formas differ from what would be required under GAAP.

The long-time controversy over the best way to value stock options is a good illustration of many of the issues relating to corporate governance, including executive pay and measuring both performance and value, and the relationship of business, shareholders, government, the press, and the community in resolving these questions.

# Case in point: FASB's treatment of stock options

A stock option grant is the right to buy a company's stock at a fixed price for a fixed period. That usually means that an executive is granted the right to buy the company's stock at today's trading price for a period of ten years. If the stock goes up over that period, the executive can "cash out" the increase in the stock's trading price.

Stock option grants usually account for the multi-million-dollar executive pay packages. For example, in 1999, Disney CEO Michael Eisner took home $575.6 million, mostly in stock option gains.

Stock options first became popular in the 1960s, as a way to tie an employee's compensation – and motivation – to the shareholders' interest. At that time, an award of 30,000 options was considered generous. Options became much more popular in the 1980s and 1990s, when huge gains in the market as a whole made it possible for corporate executives to increase their pay exponentially while claiming that they were linking pay to performance. Grants in the hundreds of thousands, and even the millions, became the norm. Stock options offered a unique accounting advantage. They were not charged to earnings, and yet were tax-deductible. In other words, companies could issue stock options without recording them as an expense on the income statement, while at the same time deducting their cost from taxes paid to the federal government.

So, when a company pays a CEO in cash, that payment is treated as an expense: it is deducted from company earnings on the earnings statement, and the company claims that expense as a tax deduction. But when a CEO exercises an option – let's say on 10,000 shares, at $15 a share – and sells the shares at $35 a share, the company generally does not show any expense on its earnings. Yet the company may deduct $200,000 (the difference between $15 and $35 times the 10,000 shares) as a business expense.

When this anomaly attracted the attention of the press, shareholders, and Congress, the logical entity to resolve it was the Financial Accounting Standards Board (FASB), which is responsible for setting accounting standards for US corporations. FASB is not an independent organization, but the Securities and Exchange Commission takes its recommendations into account when issuing accounting regulations.

Through FASB, corporate managers and accountants are self-regulating. That is, FASB (made up of a board of trustees taken from managerial ranks and the accounting profession) issues accounting rules and the private sector agrees to abide by them. Historically, Congress has never legislated accounting practices because as a policy matter it was committed to having accounting principles determined without being influenced by politics.

But the issue of accounting for option grants has so far at least twice given rise to a controversy that threatened to destroy this commitment to independence. When FASB tried to address the anomaly and require companies' financial statements to reflect the fact that options have value, two US senators issued conflicting bills that would have put Congress in the position of legislating accounting rules for the first time. The political pressure from the high-tech companies was enormous.

It is undeniably difficult to put a value on options, because the value depends on what is going to happen in the future and all of our evidence is about what has happened in the past. An option grant becomes valuable only if (and to the extent that) the stock goes up. If the stock drops in value over the term of the grant, the option grant is worthless. Thus, if a company issues its CEO an option grant of 100,000 shares, the grant may, in ten years, be worth millions of dollars or it may be worth nothing. The value is determined by the performance of the stock over this term.

This was the conundrum facing FASB: how do you account for something of undetermined value? Obviously it is impossible to predict precisely the growth or depreciation of stocks over a ten-year period. Just because we do not know what the value is, however, does not mean that it has no value. The right to buy stock at a fixed price in the future clearly has value, and we can make a principled guess at the present value of the option by factoring in various known elements – the stock's historic performance, its volatility, and company earnings estimates – into an option-pricing model. Such a model gives an estimated, though far from guaranteed, idea of what an option is worth. Two widely accepted formulas are the Black–Scholes model developed by financial economists Fisher Black and Myron Scholes in the early 1970s, and the binomial pricing model.

The question before FASB was whether it should require companies to use an option-pricing model as the basis for charging the cost of the option to earnings. In other words, if a company issues an option grant to its CEO of 100,000 shares, should it produce an estimated value of that option and enter that sum as a liability on the balance sheet?

The issue of accounting for options is not a new one. FASB first proposed that the cost of options be deducted from earnings in 1984. The response from corporate America was so fierce, however, that FASB tabled it indefinitely. Eight years later they found that the debate had turned 180 degrees – FASB was criticized for its inaction.

Once again, the business community opposed possible changes to the accounting rules. Business leaders argued that a balance sheet should record known costs and expenses; it should not cover estimated sums that might or might not be a cost to the company in years to come. Companies that used options widely to compensate thousands of employees complained that they would no longer be able to be so generous with their grants. Startup companies said that options were a vital means of compensating key employees when there was insufficient cashflow to pay regular salaries and bonuses, and warned that accounting for options would render them bankrupt. Ultimately, Joseph Lieberman (D–Connecticut) sponsored a bill opposing FASB's rule change, which was passed by a vote of 88 to 9 in May 1994.

FASB faced controversy over stock option accounting again in 1999, when it proposed that companies take an expense for re-pricing options. Perhaps still stinging from its previous fight, FASB made a decision to frame this as an interpretation, rather than an amendment. Once an option is re-priced (i.e., the original exercise price is lowered), that option must be accounted for as a "variable plan," whereby subsequent increases in stock price must be recorded as an earnings charge until the option is exercised. FASB wanted companies to recognize that they were increasing the value to the employees by re-pricing the options. Over many objections from the corporate community, particularly the high-tech community, FASB issued the new ruling in March of 2000.

In his book *Take on the Street*, former SEC chairman Arthur Levitt says that he made a serious mistake in encouraging FASB to give up on requiring that stock options be expensed. According to the book, in his first months in office fully one-third of his time was taken up with people who wanted to object to the proposed rule. Senator Joseph Lieberman's 88-to-9 vote on a non-binding resolution on the issue showed that he had the support to impose a legislative override, and Levitt felt he had no choice. Levitt "worried that if [FASB] continued to push for the stock-option rule, disgruntled companies would press Congress to end the FASB's role as standard-setter . . . In retrospect, I was wrong. I know the FASB would have stuck to its guns if I had pushed them not to surrender. Out of a misguided belief that I was acting in the FASB's best interests, I failed to support this courageous and beleaguered organization in its time of need and may have opened the door to more meddling by powerful corporations and Congress."

The International Accounting Standards Board has proposed that all stock option grants be expensed. FASB is expected to try again, following indications from Congress that it would not try to obstruct the rule again. In the meantime Coca-Cola, followed by more than 300 other companies, announced that it would begin to expense stock option grants without waiting for the change in GAAP.

## Market value

*Fortune* magazine has developed and perfected the concept of annually ranking the nation's (and, in later years, the world's) companies by their size. It calculates size by volume of sales, by net earnings, and – most significantly – by the market value of their equity capitalization. What is the largest company in the world? According to *Fortune*, it is the one that is worth the most. Being considered a "Fortune 100" or "Fortune 500" company has long been considered a badge of honor. But this is changing.

Market value has statistical interest, but to whom is it really meaningful? The public's valuation of a company in the marketplace has unique value, because it is the only judgment that cannot be manipulated, at least not for long. Various notions of value based on concepts like earnings per share, book value, rate of return on reinvested capital, and the like are based on accounting principles that are so highly flexible that they have limited significance. But the fact that the market valuation is independent does not make it accurate in absolute terms. Fair market value does not tell you everything about what a company is worth, only what it is perceived to be worth.

We are all familiar with the Dutch tulip bulb mania and "Popular Delusions and the Madness of Crowds." The public can value companies on bases that in retrospect appear idiotic. Examples include conglomerates in the 1960s, the "nifty fifty" in the early 1970s, and high-tech companies with enormous losses in the 1990s. The greater the price a company can command for its shares on the market, the greater is its power to raise future capital through equity sales. But even strong current market value provides little insurance against its own future decline. Good planning on all fronts must provide that insurance.

Conglomerates face special obstacles to traditional notions of head-to-head free market competitiveness, as shown by the following case in point.

---

# Case in point: The battle of the theme parks

Six Flags theme park began an aggressive advertising campaign emphasizing what it saw as its primary advantage over Disney World: its geographic convenience. The message of the ads was that people could go to Six Flags and have a wonderful time, and still be home in time to feed the dog. Both theme parks were held by massive conglomerates, Six Flags by Time Warner and Disney World, of course, by Disney. Instead of taking out its own ads responding to Six Flags, saying, for example, that its park had more attractions, Disney went to parent company Time Warner, pulling its advertising from Time Warner publications and threatening to pull out of a joint venture for video distribution.

*What impact does this kind of response have on competitiveness and the efficiency of the market?*

---

Ultimately, what is important is the company's continuing ability to obtain the capital necessary for the profitable production of goods and services that can be sold at a profit, and there is no magic monitor of this ability. More important than the worth of a company, which measures (imperfectly) today's value, is the health of a company, which can predict tomorrow's.

## *Earnings per share*

"Isn't it more important to go from #5 to #4 en route to #1 than to increase EPS by 5 percent or 10 percent this year?"

Cyrus F. Freidheim Jr., vice-chairman of Booz-Allen & Hamilton, made a provocative presentation at a conference on corporate governance sponsored by Northwestern University's Kellogg Graduate School of Management.[60] Acknowledging that there are "a number of CEOs who won the compensation battle (by hitting specified performance formulas) but whose companies lost the competitive war," he went on to attack the popular measuring stick, earnings per share (EPS), echoing the critiques of 1980s valuation gurus like Northwestern's Alfred Rappaport (now with LEK/Alcar) and Joel Stern of the New York consulting firm Stern Stewart. Freidheim said EPS has the advantage of simplicity and clarity, but is of questionable value in determining the health of an enterprise because it is too susceptible to manipulation. EPS can be driven up by liquidating the franchise, by restructuring and weakening the balance sheet, by playing "the accounting game with acquisitions, convertible securities, switching conventions. And none of those things would improve the value of the enterprise a wit." Freidheim is similarly skeptical of "the 'Rs' – ROI, ROE, ROCE, ROA, ROS, ROT. They all have a place in managing the business . . . but each can pay off without performance if followed as *the* measure."

Using stock price as the measure puts too much emphasis on the short term, Freidheim says:

> Let's stipulate that the return on shareholders' investment is maximized if the enterprise leads its industry in growth, profitability, and competitiveness over the long-term.
>
> Let's now reduce that to a framework for evaluating the performance of the CEO and the enterprise. Performance equals:

- building the franchise, and
- achieving long-term financial results and strength . . .

> The three financial categories that should be measured are:

- earnings;
- growth in the financial base;
- financial strength.

> In measuring earnings, what should we use if not earnings per share? We should pick ones that demonstrate the effectiveness of the CEO in directing all of the companies' capital without the muddying effects of accounting changes . . . and which produce what we want: cash.
>
> The best of these could well be cash flow on investment . . . The second financial measure is simply growth in equity before dividends . . . The final financial measure focuses on financial strength . . . the balance sheet.

The late Coca-Cola CEO Roberto Goizuetta had a pillow, embroidered, "THE ONE WITH THE HIGHEST CASH FLOW WINS."

## EVA®: economic value added

A 1993 cover story in *Fortune* magazine called EVA (economic value added) "today's hottest financial idea and getting hotter." The cover headline said EVA is "the real key to creating wealth . . . and AT&T chief Robert Allen and many others use it to make shareholders rich." Stern Stewart, which *Fortune* calls EVA's "pre-eminent popularizer," says, "quite simply, EVA is an estimate of true 'economic' profit after subtracting the cost of capital." EVA is commonly defined as (ATOP–WACC) × TC (where ATOP is after-tax operating profit, WACC is the weighted average cost of capital, and TC is total capital). It cannot be reduced to a simple formula, however. As Ernst & Young EVA expert David Handlon (based in Washington, DC) advised us in an interview, "the applied meaning of EVA varies tremendously from company to company, so each company should tailor it carefully to fit its own circumstances." For example, according to its brochure,

> Stern Stewart has identified more than 160 potential adjustments in GAAP earnings and balance sheets in areas such as inventory costing, depreciation, bad debt reserves, restructuring charges, and amortization of goodwill. However, in balancing simplicity with precision, we advise most clients to make only five to fifteen adjustments. In customizing EVA to each client's specific situation, we help identify those adjustments that can meaningfully improve accuracy and, in turn, performance. The basic tests are that the change is material, that the data are readily available, that the change is simple to communicate to non-financial managers, and, most important, that making the change can affect decisions in a positive, cost-effective way.

Despite EVA's complexity, however, it has become very popular, used by companies like Coca-Cola, Premark, Sprint, and Monsanto. *Fortune* noted that stock prices track EVA more closely than earnings per share or operating margins or return on equity. "That's because EVA shows what investors really care about – the net cash return on their capital – rather than some other type of performance viewed through the often distorting lens of accounting rules." By analyzing at the division level, managers can see if they are making more than their cost of capital. And since implementing EVA also includes a compensation plan, managers not only know it, they feel it.

Not everyone is as enthusiastic, however. John Balkcom and Roger Brossy of Sibson & Co. warn of the

> hidden traps in EVA-based incentives – value increments depend on the cost of capital, which can change materially if interest rates rise or fall or if the company changes its capital structure. Our experience suggests that the combination of EVA, organizational refinement, and customized incentives unlocks value. But no one of these three elements works by itself. Many monolithic companies have introduced EVA without the complementary organizational changes enacted by the likes of AT&T and Quaker, and the result has been a new, more cumbersome "value bureaucracy" that impedes decision-making, misallocates capital, and destroys value.[61]

A 1998 Working Paper compares operating income, residual income, and EVA to determine which is more relevant to value. It concludes that all three provide information of value, but that the other two measures were slightly better correlated to explaining results.[62]

Another way of thinking about this critique is in corporate governance terms. No matter how valid the method for evaluating the company's performance and direction, it cannot work itself. It must be applied within an organizational structure permitting decisions to be made by those with the best information and the fewest conflicts.

Financial Executives International published a report by Edward J. Lusk, Ruth A. Pagell and Michael Halperin that reviewed 19 articles on the merits of EVA and the results of the authors' own survey of CFOs. They concluded that EVA was not as valid a measure as earnings in enhancing the organization's relative financial performance. Considering how highly it was rated by CFOs, the authors concluded that it might just be "the Hawthorne effect," the renewed excitement and energy that results from any new program and the renewed dedication that results from any new focus of attention.

## Human capital: "It's not what you own but what you know"

Lawyer and former Darden School of Business professor Richard Crawford, in his book *In the Era of Human Capital*, documents the movement from an industrial society to a "knowledge society." As the economy shifts from "production of standard, tangible things with a split between production and consumption," to an "integrated global economy whose central economic activity is the provision of knowledge services with more fusion of producer and consumer," the primary resource shifts from physical capital to human capital. How does this affect the way we quantify value? The GAAP still assume that physical capital is the company's most important asset, even though overall investment in human capital has been higher for almost 30 years. Standard accounting rules assign no value to human resources, although they account for about 70 percent of the resources being used by US businesses, according to Crawford. He suggests "putting human capital on the balance sheet," including "off-balance-sheet intangible assets and human capital assets." Support for efforts to account for intangible capital is growing, especially markets, intellectual property, and strategic organizational issues.

A task force of academic and corporate experts that was convened by the SEC in 2001 recommended that non-financial performance data be released to investors. Similarly, the FASB has called for further review of methods to account for intangible assets. So far, both groups have recommended that disclosure remain voluntary.

In 2001, the Brookings Institution released a report called *Unseen Wealth: Report of the Brookings Task Force on Intangibles*, co-chaired by Margaret M. Blair and Steven M.H. Wallman.

Leif Edvinsson, the world's first corporate director of Intellectual Capital at Skandia of Stockholm, Sweden, developed a system for visualizing and developing intellectual, intangible and organizational business assets. In an interview in Juergen Daum's book, *Intangible Assets and Value Creation* (John Wiley & Sons Ltd., December 2002), he described those assets this way:

> One is people. The other is what is surrounding people in an organization; that is what I call structural capital – all those intangibles left behind, when people go home, and in that I include internal processes and structures, databases, customer relationships and things like that. With structural capital you enable organizations to make their human capital more productive. It's not that people work harder. It's that people work smarter with structural capital. This is what represents really the value of an organization. Not financial capital, not human capital, but structural capital.

In another interview in the same book, New York University professor Baruch Lev criticized GAAP for relying too much on transactions to determine values. He says that a better measure is the "value chain."

> By value chain, I mean the fundamental economic process of innovation that starts with the discovery of new products, services or processes, proceeds through the development and the implementation phase of these discoveries and establishment of technological feasibility, and culminates in the commercialisation of the new products or services. And this innovation process is where economic value is created in today's knowledge based businesses from nearly all industries. So what I recommend as one important complementing element of a new accounting system is a so called Value Chain Blueprint, a measure based information system for use in both internal decision making and disclosure to investors, that reports in a structured and standardized way about the innovation process.

Cleary, the greatest challenge for financial reporting in the twenty-first century will be finding some way to account for the value of intangibles, from patents to Ph.D.s, and from client relationships to risk assessment strategies. As the ratings agencies, including S&P and Moody's, begin to factor corporate governance into their assessment of companies, even elements like the abilities and independence of the board will become items on a balance sheet.

## Knowledge capital

The current accounting system was developed at a time when a company's most vital assets were equipment and property. But in today's companies, "knowledge capital" includes assets like patents, brands, and research and development. Professor Baruch Lev of New York University is one of the leading scholars working on the thorny problem of trying to find a way to reflect the value of a company's "knowledge capital." With patents, for example, he suggests looking at how many times a patent is cited in other applications as a measure of its value. With regard to estimating overall knowledge capital costs, he takes annual normalized earnings and subtracts a number arrived at by multiplying recorded assets by their respective after-tax expected returns. The residual is earnings generated by knowledge assets.

## The value of cash

Ultimately, a company is valued because of analysts' conviction that it can generate certain levels of positive cashflow from present and future operations. Any calculation of company value necessarily is based on "guesses" as to what will happen in the future. Some of the guesswork is taken out of the projections by taking into account the strength of its past performance, the quality of its products, the positioning of its niche within its industry, the competitiveness of its technology, its ability to sustain margins, and, most critically, the vision and competence of its management. For example, when an underperforming company replaces its CEO, the market's reaction can be highly positive. See figures 1.2–1.5, which show the market's response when Goodyear and Allied Signal replaced poorly performing CEOs with well-regarded outsiders. Similarly, Lord Weinstock's announcement in July 1994 that he was extending GEC's retirement age so that he could stay on for two more years sent the company's value down significantly.

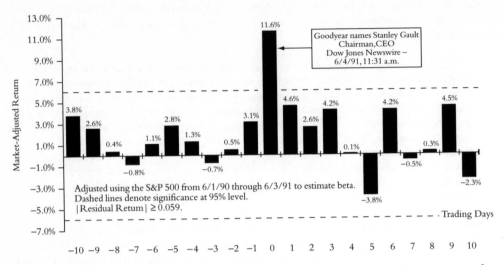

Charts from *Barbarians Inside the Gates* by Joseph Grundfest, reproduced with permission of *Stanford Law Review*.

*Sources:* Compuserve and the Center for Research in Securities Prices (CRSP), University of Chicago, daily return tapes.

**Figure 1.2**    Goodyear Tire market-adjusted returns, May 21–June 18, 1991

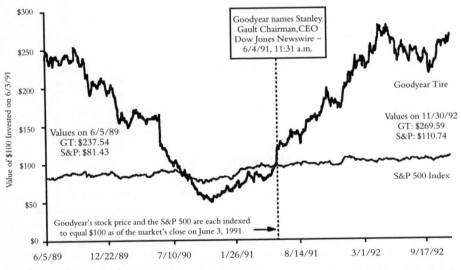

Charts from *Barbarians Inside the Gates* by Joseph Grundfest, reproduced with permission of *Stanford Law Review*.

*Sources:* Compuserve and the Center for Research in Securities Prices (CRSP), University of Chicago, daily return tapes.

**Figure 1.3**    Value of $100 invested in Goodyear Tire and the S&P 500
index on June 3, 1991 (June 5, 1988–November 30, 1992)

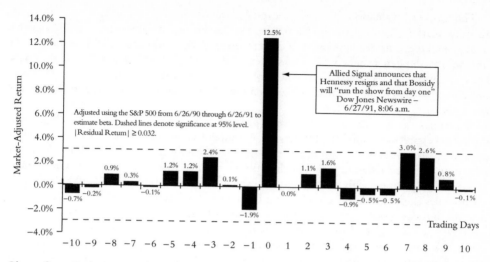

Charts from *Barbarians Inside the Gates* by Joseph Grundfest, reproduced with permission of *Stanford Law Review*.

*Sources:* Compuserve and the Center for Research in Securities Prices (CRSP), University of Chicago, daily return tapes.

**Figure 1.4**    Allied Signal market-adjusted returns June 13–July 12, 1991

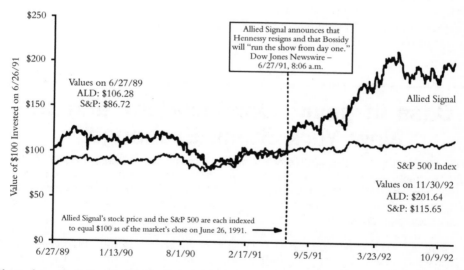

Charts from *Barbarians Inside the Gates* by Joseph Grundfest, reproduced with permission of *Stanford Law Review*.

*Sources:* Compuserve and the Center for Research in Securities Prices (CRSP), University of Chicago, daily return tapes.

**Figure 1.5**    Value of $100 invested in Allied Signal and the S&P 500 index on June 26, 1991 (June 27, 1989–November 30, 1992)

The market's valuation of human capital extends beyond the CEO slot. Eastman Kodak's market value went up $2 billion on the hiring of Christopher Steffen – the highest-ranking outsider appointed at Kodak since 1912 – and then lost $1.6 billion on the day that Steffen resigned 12 weeks later. This kind of reaction shows that the market's valuation of a company depends not just on the value of the company's assets, but also very much on the market's perception of the management's ability to manage those assets.

A company's capacity to survive and prosper is based on its ability to obtain the capital necessary to conduct its business at a competitive price. No matter how famous a company, no matter how admired its products, ultimately its worth lies in its ability to raise capital at a cost significantly less than the increase in earnings resulting from the new investment. Someone with a lower cost of capital can always buy goods, build plants, and finance sales cheaper than the competition. Business is done on the increment; a new entrant into the business creates a new reality by its cost of capital. This becomes the competitive bogey that the rest of the industry has to meet regardless of actual costs.

As Michael Jacobs argued persuasively in *Short-Term America*,[63] the international competitiveness of a country – the United States in his account – rests on its ability to provide capital to domestic companies at a rate that is internationally competitive. The perceived threat that Japanese industry would simply take over the rest of the world in the 1980s was largely based on their having virtually a zero cost of capital. Companies can survive from the earnings generated from operations in excess of depreciation and dividends. But, as even the Japanese have learned, markets change.[64] Debt that was attractive one year suddenly is non-competitive the next. Even the most financially secure company must continually have access to capital markets in order to assure that it is using the most cost-effective capital at all times.

The definition of a financially successful company might be this: one with the ability to generate returns from new investment in its business that are substantially greater than the cost of obtaining the funds, on a continuing basis.

# Case in point: Daimler-Benz and the New York Stock Exchange[65]

On March 30, 1993, Daimler-Benz announced that it would list its shares on the NYSE, making it the first German company listed on a US exchange. The move was highly significant because it showed that Daimler-Benz was prepared vastly to improve its financial disclosure in return for access to the United States' large and liquid capital markets.

The move was the result of lengthy discussions between Daimler-Benz management, NYSE chairman and CEO William Donaldson, and then SEC chairman Richard Breeden regarding disclosure requirements for the listing. And while the final agreement involved compromise on all sides, it appears that the SEC for the most part held sway over the other two parties.

In order to list its shares on the NYSE, Daimler-Benz was required to provide greater financial disclosure than is required under German law. Breeden stressed that the SEC has not changed US policy regarding disclosure requirements for foreign companies seeking listings on US stock exchanges. In fact, he referred to the agreement as a "complete rejection of the approach suggested by the [New York] stock exchange." For years, the NYSE has advocated that the SEC relax some disclosure requirements in order to attract foreign companies, but the SEC has remained steadfast.

Key aspects of the agreement included:

- Daimler-Benz AG, the parent company, proposed to adjust its earnings upward by DM4 billion ($2.42 billion) in 1992, by claiming hidden reserves of this amount as "extraordinary earnings." This move highlights one of the most controversial aspects of German company law and accounting practices, whereby companies may accumulate large hidden reserves, thereby artificially deflating the company's value. The result of this practice is that most German companies, including Daimler-Benz, are undervalued on the stock exchange. The decision to allocate these reserves indicates that the disclosure regime demanded by the SEC will provide greater transparency regarding the company's financial situation.
- Daimler-Benz will have the choice of one set of financial data for German investors and another set for US investors in accordance with SEC requirements, or a single set complying with requirements of both jurisdictions. (While German disclosure requirements are quite high in comparison with other continental European jurisdictions, they are not as stringent as SEC requirements.)
- Daimler-Benz will be required to present cashflow statements in accordance with US accounting principles.
- Daimler-Benz will not be required to offer financial information on previous years in accordance with US accounting principles.

According to the SEC, more than 200 foreign companies had listed on the US exchanges over the previous three and half years; however, no German company had ever done so. Several years ago, six of Germany's largest listed companies (Daimler-Benz AG, BASF AG, Bayer AG, Hoechst AG, Siemens AG and Volkswagen AG) approached the SEC as a united front, attempting to forge a compromise whereby German companies would not be subject to the complete SEC disclosure regime. This approach failed, and Daimler-Benz decided to "go it alone." In a March 1993 press release, Gerhard Liener, Daimler-Benz's chief financial officer, said: "We were on the way to becoming a global company and I realized that I might have been caught in an anachronistic way of thinking. Just as English has become the language of international business, Anglo-Saxon accounting has become the accounting language worldwide. I thought it was foolish to go on trying to play Don Quixote tilting at windmills."

The company's financial difficulties at the time might have contributed to a decision to create good news abroad. Net income for the group had fallen from DM1.9 billion ($1.15 billion) in 1991 to DM1.5 billion ($909 million) in 1992. Had the parent company not allocated DM4 billion ($2.42 billion) from hidden reserves in 1992, net income would have been DM703 million ($426 million) compared with DM1.19 billion ($721 million) in 1991. Unfortunately, the outlook for the following year was bleak: in April 1993, the group announced its forecast that income would fall to DM1 billion ($606 million) in 1993.

Factors affecting the German economy as a whole may also have influenced Daimler-Benz's decision. In the March press release cited above, Liener said: "[T]he agreement we have reached with the SEC gives us access to the world's largest and most dynamic stock market." In the 1980s, German companies were not strapped for capital resources since they had enough capital of their own to finance expansion. Furthermore, German companies have enjoyed solid banking relationships which are strengthened by the fact that many German banks hold substantial, long-term stakes in a wide range of publicly listed companies.

It is absolutely clear that it was the discipline of American accounting standards that made the subsequent merger with Chrysler possible. Thus, the Daimler listing carries implications for corporate governance worldwide. As competition for global capital increases, corporations will be forced to make concessions to the providers of capital,[66] Daimler, by its NYSE listing, showed that it was willing to make significant governance concessions in the quest for new and cheaper investment sources. However, this was at least in part temporary. Though it promised at the time of the merger to continue to issue US-style proxy statements, in the year following the merger it did not. It had literally the best of both worlds – the increased access to capital and markets as a result of the US presence and the decreased transparency as a result of the European domicile.

Transparency (disclosure) and good governance can produce a lower cost of capital, as equity markets increasingly recognize the value of reduced agency costs. But it may be a while before that becomes clear.

In 2000 shareholders protested as it became clear that the "merger of equals" was really a takeover. American shareholders found that they had relinquished most of their rights to protest by allowing the merged company to be organized under German law.

## *Corporate "externalities"*

Each business imposes costs that are not usually reflected in its profit and loss statements. Some of this is tradition, some of it reflects the difficulty of valuing intangible elements and some of it reflects the success of companies in having governments, regulators, and professional auditors make accommodating rules. These are "externalities," costs incurred by business but paid for elsewhere.

On his website at <http://www.ragm.com> one of the co-authors of this book has created the Brightline simulation, a simplified, accurate model of a market economy in which businesses compete against each other for a fixed pool of consumers. Brightline currently models five companies that can be customized by the user. Additionally, the shareowners (owners) of one of the five companies are given the potential to become actively involved in running the company, should the company's performance fall below their expectations. The company assigned to have potentially active shareholders will be called the "Focus" company. Variables that can be used to show different outcomes include: interest rate used for discounting, investment time horizon, customer brand loyalty, shareholder reactivity, government vigilance, supplier selection mode, shareholder anger mode, and company management aggressiveness.

## Case in point:
## Socially responsible investing

A 2002 book, *The SRI Advantage: Why Socially Responsible Investing has Outperformed Financially*, by Peter Camejo, documents the way that socially responsible funds (screening out companies that violate environmental and other laws, use child labor or sweatshops, discriminate in hiring, produce products detrimental to society, or engage in objectionable practices) have higher returns and lower risk than fund that do not screen for these factors. He predicts that "the current conflict between economic forces destroying the natural world to achieve short-term profit gains and the inevitable counter-movement to preserve natural equity and thus our economic well-being for the long term can lead to a multi-decade period of superior performance for SRI funds." He says that socially responsible investing "reveals a link between existing mass social trends and the financial performance of corporations" (emphasis omitted). He argues with Milton Friedman's claim that it is "subversive" for corporate managers to have any goal but making as much money for their stockholders as they possibly can. It may be that their views are not as diametrically opposed as Camejo thinks, however. Indeed, Camejo's use of the vocabulary of investment and economics shows that it is really not an argument about the purpose of capitalism but just an argument about how best to achieve that purpose. The very subtitle of his book makes that clear – after all, it isn't called "Why Socially Responsible Investing is a Good Thing even if You Don't Make Any Money At It."

The quotation from Adrian Cadbury earlier in this chapter speaks of a second level of company responsibility – considering the implications of a corporation's operations for the rest of society. Certainly, some corporate operations may have an adverse impact on society. In some cases, corporations pay for this cost; in others, society as a whole absorbs the cost. This is referred to as a "corporate externality." Examples include the EPA standard setting an acceptable level for the odor of emissions from paper mills, and the wrongful death statutes limiting the amount of recovery for human lives in coal-mining accidents.

In theory at least, the government is in the best position to decide which aspects of corporate cost should be charged to the enterprise. The two examples in the last paragraph illustrate this point. In the United States, environmental and occupational safety standards are set by the legislature and regulatory agencies.

Some companies have made significant, if sporadic, efforts over the last decades to reflect the "real" (in contrast to GAAP) cost of their operation. During the administration of US President Jimmy Carter, Commerce Secretary Juanita Kreps actually proposed a formal methodology for "social accounting." Her report declared that "changing public expectations of business" demanded that corporations reveal such information as "the impacts of day-to-day business activities on the physical environment, on employees, consumers, local communities and other affected interests."[67]

One attempt to design "social responsibility accounting" proposes the following characteristics of a social report:

1.  Each report should include a statement of its objectives which allows (*inter alia*) the assessment of the

- grounds for data selection;
- reasons for form of presentation chosen.

2. The objective of a social report should be to discharge accountability in the spirit of improved democracy.
3. The information should be directly related to the objectives held for the particular groups to whom it is addressed.
4. The information should be *unmanipulated* and readable by a non-expert. It must be audited.[68]

South Africa's Triple Trust Organization set forth its social accounting procedure this way:

- TTO board decision to begin social accounting process.
- Identify facilitators with social accounting expertise.
- Distill social objectives from TTO mission and values.
- Identify key organizational stakeholders.
- Consult stakeholders about social performance indicators.
- Design questionnaires or interviews to measure performance.
- Set a meaningful and manageable sampling frame for each stakeholder group.
- Gather stakeholder feedback through external facilitators and staff.
- Analyze data and write social accounts (report).
- Have external auditor verify the accounts.
- Board and management respond to issues raised in the accounts.
- Publish the accounts.

> *What are the advantages and disadvantages of these approaches? Note that in the first example, the report is to a broad "democracy" rather than to shareholders, directors, employees, the government or any other specific group. What obstacles do you see to putting this approach into practice? What liability issues does it raise? You should know that the authors themselves acknowledge that there may be some internal inconsistency between these requirements, and indeed some conflicts of interest between the intended readers of such a report. But, the authors conclude that "These are matters outside the model itself. We seek information to discharge accountability; what society does with that information has to be society's concern."[69]*

A recent study concluded that companies that make a public commitment to social responsibility outperform those that do not.[70] One example of such a public commitment is Johnson & Johnson, which has its statement on its website. It details community services that include $176 million in cash and product contributions, emphasizing programs that assist mothers and children but including programs in the area of health, safety, education, employment, the environment, culture and the arts.

Wisely, Johnson & Johnson does not try to quantify the costs, the benefits, or the net of these endeavors. Attempts to do so have looked like financial economist Ralph Estes's "comprehensive social accounting model," which follows.

# Case in point: Prototype plc[71]

The following Success Model is an excerpt of a recent attempt to provide a report that reflects social accounting at Prototype plc.

# success model – *targets & achievements...*

Key performance measures describe our success model. Here we indicate these measures for the year 2000 as they relate to our **direct stakeholders**.

| Customers | Target | Achievement | |
|---|---|---|---|
| Percentage of customers retained | 95% | 81% | |
| Share of available market | 3% | 8% | |
| Quality ratings | 90% | 81% | |
| Support services ratings | 95% | 79% | |
| Innovation ratio | 16% | 10% | |

| Shareholders | | | |
|---|---|---|---|
| Dividend payment growth | 7% | 8% | |
| Share price increase | 30% | 31% | |
| Shareholders return for the sector – 1 year | 12% | 14% | |
| – 5 years | 20% | 15% | |
| Employee shareholding | 20% | 19% | |

| Suppliers | | | |
|---|---|---|---|
| Purchases from partners | 55% | 60% | |
| Budget for co-operative development | £2.5m | £2.504m | |
| *Number of SEQUA awards | 2 | 3 | |

* (Supplier Excellence and Quality Awards)

| Employees | | | |
|---|---|---|---|
| Value of the Company's knowledge bank | 25% | 28% | |
| Morale rating | 90% | 79% | |
| Competitive pay indicators | 100% | 91% | |

# success model – *targets & achievements...*

The Company's **indirect stakeholders** also invoke measures of performance which indicate the quality of relationships with these stakeholders. For the year 2000 these are:

| Local Communities | Target | Achievement | |
|---|---|---|---|
| Budget for the coming year | £1.5m | £1.5m | |
| • Salaries | £240k | £240k | |
| • Equipment | £1.1m | £1.1m | |
| • Cash | £160k | £160k | |
| Disabled persons in Prototype training programmes | 120 | 116 | |
| Prototype employees assigned to community projects | 38 | 28 | |

| Environmental Interests | | | |
|---|---|---|---|
| Employee travel modalities | | | |
| • Car | 20% | 28% | |
| • Public Transport | 60% | 62% | |
| • Foot | 10% | 6% | |
| • Cycle | 10% | 4% | |

| Education Community | | | |
|---|---|---|---|
| Number of research projects | 10 | 11 | |
| Number of graduates recruited | 60 | 67 | |
| Number of patents applied for | 1 | 2 | |
| Budget for coming year | £1m | £908k | |

# providers of capital

| £000's | Results<br>31 December | | Actions Taken | Future Plans |
|---|---|---|---|---|
| | **1999** | **2000** | | |
| Turnover | 115,900 | 127,090 | Sales force increased Margin based commissions instituted | Continental distributions increased. More focussed benchmarking studies |
| Operating surplus (after taxation) | 14,000 | 16,950 | Value engineering programmes inaugurated | Training aimed at 20% productivity improvement |
| Revenue Investment | 2,894 | 3,770 | | |
| R&D | 1,700 | 1,860 | More academic links | Customer inspired product innovation programme |
| Training | 1,194 | 1,910 | Distance learning programmes inaugurated | Focus on technical skills and improvement in telelearning courseware |
| Net surplus accruing to the business | 11,106 | 13,180 | | Goals to improve to 20% of turnover |
| Dividends per share | 14p | 15p | Paid above market average in sector | Relate more closely with inflation indicators |
| Market capitalization | £160m | £182m | | Reach £200 million by 2002 |

The Company has created a line of credit with three European banks to provide funds for physical asset procurement, research projects and new education investment. Terms are related to market rates and vary according to the nature of the expenditure. At the year end this line of credit amounts to £15m.

## Equity Capital Ownership Profile

Among our institutional shareholders are those from outside the UK who held 21% of the capital at the year end.

Of the total shareholders, 31% have held their shares for 5 years or more. They comprise:

| | |
|---|---|
| **Employees:** | **15%** |
| **Financial institutions:** | **12%** |
| **Private individuals:** | **4%** |

**Total shareholding analysis**

# providers of capital

## Assets

|  | 1999 £'000 | 2000 £'000 |
|---|---|---|
| **Physical Assets, at cost, less amounts owed (5,000)**<br>Management analysis, valuation and independent assessment shows that the values of Prototype physical assets are greater than the amounts owed on them. | 19,000 | 21,000 |
| **Brands – at value**<br>Brand values are based upon independent multi-year research into market values of owned brands as perceived by customers, suppliers and competitors. | 1,700 | 2,000 |
| **Knowledge bank**<br>Collective improvement for future earning potential. | 2,540 | 3,900 |
| **Technology**<br>Key systems and methodologies valued at estimated cost of entry (less provision for technology change risk). | 1,000 | 1,400 |
| **Patents**<br>Valued on the basis of revenue generating expectations. | 510 | 600 |
| **Total Intangible Assets** | 5,750 | 7,900 |
| **Cash** | 1,800 | 2,190 |
|  | 7,550 | 10,090 |
| **Less liabilities** | 3,130 | 3,620 |
|  | 4,520 | 6,470 |
| **Total Assets** | 23,520 | 27,470 |

Future cash streams for Prototype depend crucially upon the exploitation of intangible assets. These assets include brands, technology and patents. In addition, the knowledge bank of the Company – which results from valuing the direction and nature of employee activity and training – represents a significant indicator of such future cash streams.

## Turnover per Employee

****** UK industry average

Based upon the number of full time equivalents

1996  1997  1998  1999  2000

## Performance Trends

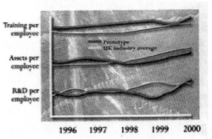

Training per employee

Assets per employee

R&D per employee

Prototype
UK industry average

1996  1997  1998  1999  2000

# employees

## Open Forum

The Company has created a "conversations" programme in which employees at all levels meet, discuss and comment upon many issues which concern the Company's future. All employees are now linked by electronic mail and internal video conferencing.

## Number of Employees

1996  1997  1998  1999  2000

• • • • • • •

Number of part time employees.

1,550 full time equivalents at the end of year 2000.

Note: Employee benefits apply equally in proportion, to both full and part time employees.

## Knowledge Bank

|  | 1999 | 2000 |
|---|---|---|
|  | £000's | |
| Total employee cost | 42,610 | 49,800 |
| Expensed | 40,070 | 45,900 |
| Deferred value★ | 2,540 | 3,900 |
| Increase in value of knowledge bank | 280 | 1,360 |

★Cost of activities and training judged to generate future cash streams

## Male / Female Ratio

1996          2000

## Employees Holding 1st Degrees

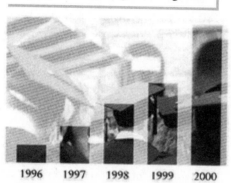

1996   1997   1998   1999   2000

Increased recruitment and focus upon outstanding graduates has enabled the Company to attract an increasing number of holders of 1st degrees – currently at 103 graduates.

In addition, the Company has inaugurated a programme for work based degrees which has proved successful.

# employees

## Morale Indicator

75% satisfied 1998
78% satisfied 1999
79% satisfied 2000

## Employee Educational Profile

Information Technology 72%

Engineering 28%

Physics 18%

Arts 35%

1st Degrees held

## Employees Completing Training Plans

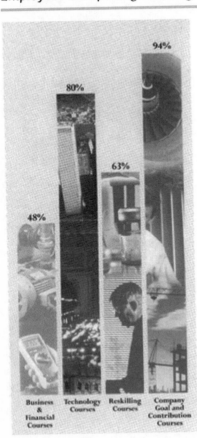

94%
80%
63%
48%

Business & Financial Courses · Technology Courses · Reskilling Courses · Company Goal and Contribution Courses

## Employee Turnover

8% 1996
8.5% 1997
8.3% 1998
9.1% 1999
10.3% 2000

## Innovation Ratio

Management measures the ratio of its expenditures on research, development, training and product branding to the value added by employees. The goal is to reach by the year 2004, value added equal to 20 times such expenditure.

| £000's | 1999 | 2000 |
|---|---|---|
| Total expenditure | 5,000 | 7,600 |
| Value added | 73,290 | 77,290 |
| Innovation ratio | 14.6 | 10.2 |

# customers

## Retained Customers

Prototype is steadily increasing the percentage of customers who are regular buyers of our products. This reflects better customer relations and improving product quality.

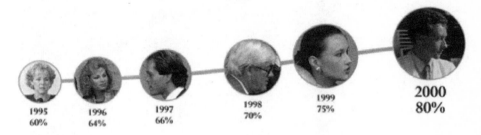

1995
60%

1996
64%

1997
66%

1998
70%

1999
75%

**2000
80%**

# Environmental Issues

## Energy Conservation

During the year 2000, Prototype completed an Energy Conservation Study. Plans are now being made to increase energy savings of 40% by the year 2005. Over this period, we will invest £350,000 and expect to achieve annual savings of £600,000.

## Employment Related Illness

Employees are monitored regularly by Prototype's medical experts and identifable work related illnesses are treated accordingly. We are finding fewer cases of RSI and other ergonomic related illnesses although air quality remains a problem. Considerable resources are addressing noise problems and a three year plan of active noise cancellation has begun.

## Communication

During the year 2000, 312 employees attended more than one seminar on environmental issues of interest to both Prototype and the communities in which we operate.

## Replaceable Materials

The increased use of electronics in the Company has led to a 27% reduction in the use of paper over the past three years. We are targeting a further reduction of 10% in the year 2001 through the adoption of electronic commerce applications.

# Environmental Issues

## Pollution

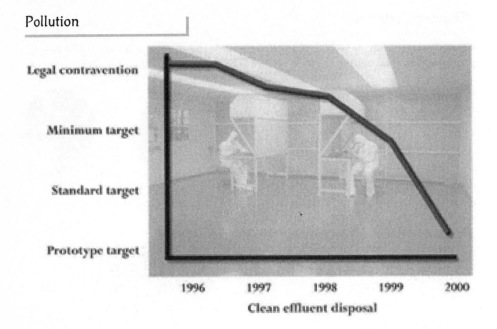

Legal contravention

Minimum target

Standard target

Prototype target

1996      1997      1998      1999      2000

**Clean effluent disposal**

## Noise Reduction in Prototype Premises

**Germany**
Noise levels have reduced by 22% over 5 years

**United Kingdom**
Noise levels have reduced by 18% over 5 years

**France**
Noise levels have reduced by 16% over 5 years

**Belgium**
Noise levels have reduced by 24% over 5 years

We aim to reach levels acceptable to our employee monitoring group by the year 2002.

All our manufacturing premises are fitted with emission controls and air quality is monitored regularly. Air purity is probably impossible, but scientific analysis is showing a continuous reduction in airborne bacteria and other noxious impurities.

# Education community

## Prototype's Licence to Operate

The Company believes it must constantly renew its licence to operate, essentially through its success and behaviour.

## Corporate Behaviour

The Company has to the best of its knowledge, conformed with all the corporate governance recommendations in Europe. It has also complied with current relevant European Directives and has advanced plans in respect of Directives in preparation.

In addition, the Company monitors on a regular basis the ethical codes which it has adopted and the internal controls which pertain to the sound running of the business.

The Company permits no discrimination on grounds of colour, race, religion, gender or age.

## Company Values

The Company's values are very important components of its way of doing business. It monitors behaviour and promptly addresses any allegations which impinge negatively upon these values, with a right of appeal directly to the Chairman of the Board.

## Contribution to Society

As a wealth generator and employer, Prototype is conscious of its opportunities to contribute to the improvement of conditions in the communities which accommodate its operations. Specific responsibilities are assumed in these communities for strong and positive relationships with people in these constituencies.

## Balanced Achievement

The Company seeks a balanced set of key performance measures which reflect economic, social and educational achievements. It holds a clear commitment to this definition of success.

# Education community

## Financial Auditor's Summary Report

We have satisfied ourselves that the business of Prototype plc has sufficient working capital to sustain its planned operations for the coming year.

We have examined the internal audit procedures and activity for the year and have concluded that the internal audit checks carried out, together with the results of those checks, provide a sufficient verification of trading activities and the assets and liabilities at the 31st December 2000.

In assessing the stated financial results, we have concluded that the management of the Company has employed a range of key performance measures with which to control the business and to fairly reflect relevant measures for all the Company's stakeholders.

**GMPK plc**

## Environmental Auditor's Summary Report

Prototype plc has complied with all the current legislation relating to environmental issues during the year under review. In addition where good practice has been the subject of public and/or professional communication, the Company has programmes in hand to meet the recommended criteria of such practice.

We have pointed out to the management of the Company the need to reach standards for noise levels and effluent quality which the 1998 European Directive has announced and which will take effect in 2002.

We have concluded that Prototype plc is in compliance with its responsibilities and that the Company's awareness programme of the issues is extensively communicated.

**WP Associates**

## Social Auditor's Summary Report

Our observations during the year 2000 lead us to conclude the Prototype's management has in its behaviour and in its procedures, endeavoured to meet its proclaimed social values.

Cases of alleged breach are referred to the Social Audit Committee and there are currently 5 unresolved cases being investigated. Prototype has established clear procedures regarding issues of ethics and discrimination which are properly communicated.

**LC & Associates**

## NON-ECONOMIC CONSIDERATIONS IN CORPORATE MANAGEMENT

*When should corporate management pursue objectives that are not directly correlated with profit maximization?* This is the third level of corporate responsibility mentioned above by Adrian Cadbury: "How far has business a responsibility to maintain the framework of the society in which it operates and how far should business reflect society's priorities rather than its own commercial ones?" Johnson & Johnson's "credo," posted on its website in dozens of languages, explicitly ranks its constituents as follows: consumers, employees, communities, and then shareholders, and concludes, "When we operate according to these principles, the stockholders should realize a fair return."

David Engel has provided a magisterial analysis of the answer to this question.[72] In the "Balancing Interests" section above, we discussed the limits to the scope of corporate managers' discretion. Nobody elected them to make social decisions. The legitimacy of corporate power requires that it be limited to business and not extend to the tradeoffs necessary to balance competing social goals. Engel concludes that there are four general areas where extra value maximization objectives are justifiable.

*1. Obey the law.* This may appear to be a relativistic command, but Engel argues that it is absolute. In many instances, a corporation can make a cost-benefit calculation and conclude that it is cheaper to break the law than to obey it. This involves weighing the costs of compliance against the probability of getting caught, plus the costs of attorneys' fees, lost time, and damages that would be awarded. Engel argues that corporations, in using such analysis, will ultimately run the risk of subverting the "legitimacy" of the societal base that is, in turn, a necessary precondition for profitable corporate operations.

The "law" underlying the legitimacy of capitalism is the existence of competition. To the extent that markets are not free, prices fixed, or territories divided, the justification for the profit structure of business disappears. The ultimate crime in recent times was the so-called "electrical price-fixing" scandal of the late 1950s. It was unusual in its scope, and even more unusual because several executives of General Electric and Westinghouse went to jail.

## Case in point: Price-fixing

In the years 1959–60, government investigators unraveled the largest price-fixing and market-rigging conspiracy in the 50-year history of antitrust law. The conspiracy aimed to divide up the $17 billion market for power-generating equipment and electrical goods. Among the indicted companies were the two giants of the industry, Westinghouse Electric Corp. and General Electric Corp.

In 1959, the Tennessee Valley Authority (TVA), which operated the largest electricity-generating capacity in the United States, asked for bids on a hydroelectric turbine generator for its Culbert steam plant. General Electric and Westinghouse offered (secret and sealed) bids of over $17.5 million. To the fury of those two companies, TVA awarded the contract to a British firm that bid a little over $12 million. General Electric and Westinghouse sought to have the award overturned as prejudicial to "national security" since they would be unable to repair foreign equipment in times of national emergency.

TVA explained why it had gone abroad for the contract: For some time, TVA has been disturbed by the rising prices of turbo generators. There are only three American firms that manufacture large turbo generators. Since 1951, the prices charged by these manufacturers for such equipment have increased by more than 50 percent while the average wholesale price of all commodities has increased only 5 percent.[73] Between 1950 and 1956, General Electric and Westinghouse had increased prices on power transformers six times, one firm copying the other's price increase within days. Between 1946 and 1957, prices on large turbines had been raised ten times.

The story instantly aroused the interest of Tennessee Senator Estes Kefauver, chairman of the Senate Subcommittee on Antitrust and Monopoly. He quickly announced an investigation into the pattern of identical bidding. An investigation into TVA's records found 24 instances of matched bids in just over three years. Some of these bids were the same down to the nearest hundredth of a cent. These were all secret, sealed bids.

The examination of TVA's records also found:

- *Circuit-breakers*: Identical bids of $21,000 were submitted by GE, Westinghouse, Allis-Chalmers and Federal Pacific.
- *Suspension circuit-breakers*: Eight identical bids of $11,900.
- *Condenser tubing*: Eight identical bids quoting prices down to the last thousandth of a cent.[74]

TVA was not the only organization to complain. Many local, state and other federal agencies backed up TVA's complaint, saying they had also received a series of similar bids.

In July 1959 the Justice Department announced that a federal grand jury in Pennsylvania was investigating the bidding for possible antitrust violations. In February 1960, the jury handed down the first seven of what would amount to 20 indictments. By the end of the summer of 1960, 29 electrical manufacturers and 45 of their executives had been indicted. The government alleged that the effect of the conspiracy had been to raise the price of electrical equipment throughout the country to high, fixed and artificial levels, as price competition was restrained, suppressed and eliminated.

As antitrust law had developed until this point, corporations generally offered one of two responses to an antitrust indictment. First, they could plead guilty and pay the fine. As one author describes, "Between 1890 and 1959, whenever a fine was imposed, it was paid, almost happily and cheerfully, as a cost of doing illicit business. Prison sentences were seldom imposed and usually suspended. Somehow the violation of the antitrust law never was considered more than a gentleman's misdemeanor – and a gentleman was never sent to jail for violating the antitrust law. Being indicted under the Sherman Act was regarded as nothing more than a bad corporate cold, which could be shaken off by the payment of a nominal number of dollars."[75]

Second, corporations could plead *nolo contendere*, literally, "I do not contest." Because this plea did not admit guilt, any party seeking damages would have to prove wrongdoing. In other words, a *nolo* plea put the burden of proof on the damaged parties. As a result, *nolo* pleas were common in antitrust cases.

Initially, Westinghouse and General Electric did not feel they had too much to worry about – just a "bad corporate cold." They had violated antitrust laws before, and would no doubt be accused of doing so in future. As the evidence grew in 1959, however, the giant electric companies began to get worried.

In March 1960, the companies were arraigned on the first seven charges, considered by the government to be the most serious. Westinghouse and General Electric pleaded not guilty; every other company pleaded *nolo*. The government believed the charges were too severe for a *nolo* settlement, and took the unusual step of asking the judge not to accept such pleas. Assistant Attorney General Robert Bicks, head of the antitrust division, told the judge: "The Attorney General states his considered judgment that these indictment charges are as serious instances of bid-rigging and price-fixing as have been charged in the more than half-century life of the Sherman Act."[76] In other words, the government wasn't charging the electric companies with mere technical violations of the act, as was usually the case. They had evidence of serious and sustained criminal activity.

The judge granted the government's request to throw out the *nolo* pleas, leaving the corporations wondering if they could possibly win at trial. As the number of indictments increased through 1960, the corporations found themselves looking at a series of trials that could last five years. Allis-Chalmers decided not to fight the battle and pleaded guilty to all charges. This undermined the defenses of the remaining companies. After the nineteenth indictment was handed down, Westinghouse and General Electric approached the government with a possible settlement. The companies would plead guilty on the most serious charges in exchange for a *nolo* plea in the remaining cases. After long negotiations, the government agreed, but insisted on guilty pleas in the seven most serious charges.

General Electric chairman Ralph Cordiner learned that GE was going to be deeply involved in the scandal in September 1959. The next January, he addressed GE's annual management conference on the subject of "Business Ethics in a Competitive Enterprise System." He said: "The system will remain free and competitive only so long as the citizens and particularly those of us with responsibilities in business life, are capable of the self-discipline required. If we are not capable of self-discipline, the power of the government will be increasingly invoked as a substitute, until the system is no longer free or competitive."[77]

In 1961, General Electric's stockholders met for their first annual meeting since the indictments. The next day, the *New York Times* editorial page carried the following comment. "Unhappily, little recognition of this responsibility [to inspire public confidence] manifested itself at the annual meeting of GE stockholders . . . For a company with nearly half a million share owners, the meeting had too much of a rubber-stamp quality to provide an inspiring demonstration of democracy at work in the corporate field. It merely supplied fresh ammunition for those who doubt the moral underpinnings of our industrial society."[78]

The Westinghouse annual meeting was not so uneventful. A shareholder made a motion from the floor for the company's three top executives to resign. A second proposal called for a committee of directors to determine if management should have known what was going on. The resolutions were defeated by overwhelming margins.

By the end of 1964, General Electric had settled about 90 percent of its lawsuits, paying out about $200 million. Westinghouse settled about the same for $110 million. The total settlements for the industry were about $500 million.

Note: Compare this to the antitrust lawsuit brought against Microsoft by the Justice Department in 1997, alleging that it violated a 1994 consent decree governing bundling of its products. The Justice Department and 17 state attorneys general asked the court to break the company into two parts: one company to develop and market the Windows operating system and the other to develop Microsoft's other software and internet holdings, including the Microsoft Office suite of programs. The court agreed, Microsoft appealed, millions of dollars were spent on legal fees, the administration changed, and the effort to split the company was abandoned.

*2. Disclose information about social impact beyond the minimum requirements of law that relate to the impact of corporation on society.* Full disclosure at the outset may result in fewer sales in the short term, but it will contribute to a society in which the legitimacy of corporate power is more generally conceded than when there are surprises. There are many recent examples of companies that learned the hard way that it is cheaper to disclose negative information than to suppress it: Dow Corning's research on the health hazards of its breast implants, A.H. Robins' research on its intra-uterine contraceptive device, tobacco companies' research on the harmful effects of tobacco, and Beech-Nut's evidence that it was manufacturing adulterated apple juice.

*3. Dramatically reduce corporate involvement in politics.* In the past decade, we have witnessed the consequences of incest between the state and its corporations with the virtual collapse of the Italian state and economy and the humiliating defeat of the LDP party in Japanese elections. In the United States, the problem is demonstrated by the level of political action committee campaign contributions, the increase in the expense and use of lobbyists, and the perception that government lacks the will and capacity to deal effectively with large companies. Corporations need to have some say in the government process affecting them, but not so much that they undercut the popular support for government in the process. And it should not be so much that they undercut the judgment of government, either. When George W. Bush appointee (and former Congressman) Donald Rumsfeld became the Secretary of Defense, he tried to push through some reforms of the procurement and weapons systems but was stopped by established government contractors and the Congressmen and Senators to whom they gave millions of dollars. Rumsfeld tried to allocate more of his budget to the development of lighter, more maneuverable conventional forces and a rapid expansion of missile defense and military space programs. But that meant scaling back existing big-ticket programs like Lockheed Martin's F-22 fighter plane and United Defense's Crusader artillery system to make way for next-generation systems. For the major contractors, this would mean giving up lucrative production contracts now for the promise of new projects down the road, a tradeoff the industry did not want to make.

Rumsfeld's reform agenda ran into a brick wall on Capitol Hill and in the military services, each of which had its own weapons procurement priorities. Then, following the terrorist attacks of September 11, 2001, the Defense Department was given an enormous budget increase. The biggest beneficiaries, however, are existing systems, many of which were designed during the Cold War and have little or nothing to do with the fight against terrorism. Similarly, the pharmaceutical corporations have 625 registered lobbyists, more than one for each member of Congress, and a combined lobbying and campaign contribution budget in 1999 and 2000 of $197 million, larger than any other industry. Following the terrorist attacks and anthrax scare of 2001, they used those resources to push through additional protections for their industry, including exemption from antitrust regulations, reduction of the timetable for getting new drugs to market for treating the ills of biological warfare, and immunity from lawsuits for any vaccines they develop to combat bioterrorism. Senator John McCain (R–Arizona) condemned this effort as "war-profiteering."

Engel's point is echoed by Andrew B. Schmookler:

> The protection of that equality, therefore, should be our first priority, even if that requires some sacrifice of other important rights. Two general principles would advance our democracy.

First, access to political speech must not be apportioned according to wealth, at least in the publicly licensed broadcast media. If a corporation like Exxon buys time to broadcast a message with political import, there should be equal time provided (perhaps at Exxon's expense) for an opposing point of view. Defining political speech might not be easy, but it should not be impossible. Our legal system continually solves definitional problems of this nature. The right of free speech is sacred, but there is no reason it should be defined in a way that subverts one of its primary purposes: the protection of democracy. Exxon has the right to be heard. But let us hear also the voices of other people, though they lack Exxon's billions, on the same policy-related questions.

Second, our political campaigns need to be completely insulated from private wealth. This is not easily achieved, but this, too, should be possible. Perhaps it could be achieved with some combination of free air time, public financing in proportion to registered voters signing petitions, and automatic public financing. In any event, it is incompatible with the principle of democracy for a candidate to have an advantage over an opponent because the supporters of the one are rich and those of the other are poor.

Let us not despair of the possibility of democracy. We have yet fully to try it.[79]

*4. Adhere to the "Kew Gardens" principle.* In the late 1960s, a young woman named Kitty Genovese returned to her apartment in the Kew Gardens section of New York City and was stabbed in broad daylight in the courtyard in full view of her neighbors, none of whom did anything to save her as she slowly bled to death. She became a symbol of the tragic consequences of failing to act. Engel argues that corporations should act when failing to do so would certainly create serious damage for society.

These four "Engel principles" form the critical basis for developing a theory of performance measurement for corporations because they reveal the need to limit corporate power to a known, definable, and limited sphere. With these principles in place, it is time to turn to the people who are responsible for monitoring corporate performance: the shareholders and the board of directors.

## NOTES

1. See, for example, Ronald Coase, "The Nature of the Firm," *Economica*, 4, 1937, p. 386, and Frank H. Easterbrook and Daniel R. Fischel, "The Corporate Contract," *Columbia Law Review*, 7, Nov. 1989, p. 1416. "The corporate structure is a set of contracts through which managers and certain other participants exercise a great deal of discretion that is 'reviewed' by interactions with other self-interested actors" (p. 1418).
2. Melvin Aron Eisenberg, Koret Law Professor at the University of California School of Law in Berkeley (*The Business Lawyer*, 48, 4, Aug. 1993, p. 1275). Professor Eisenberg gave an interesting description of the corporation in another article: "A corporation is a profit-seeking enterprise of persons and assets organized by rules. Most of these rules are determined by the unilateral action of corporate organs or officials. Some of these rules are determined by market forces. Some are determined by contract or other forms of agreement. Some are determined by law." "The Structure of Corporation Law," *Columbia Law Review*, 89, 7, Nov. 1989, p. 1461.
3. A 1993 *Wall Street Journal* article noted that a variation on the corporate structure, the limited liability company (LLC), was "arguably the hottest thing in business start-ups today." A hybrid, which offers owners "the liability protections of a traditional corporation and the tax advantages of a partnership," was, at the time of the article, permitted in 35 states, up from only 8 in 1991. A 1988 IRS ruling that permitted LLCs to be treated as

partnerships, so that each owner's profits are taxed only on his or her personal returns, and not double taxed, as with corporations, gives LLCs the advantages of partnership, and the limited liability provides the advantages of incorporation. This has not been lost on entrepreneurs or on "scam artists." Regulators have claimed that fraudulent communications technologies firms have used the LLC to avoid state and federal securities laws. *Wall Street Journal*, Nov. 8, 1993, p. B1.

4.  Opinion in *Louis K. Liggett Co. v. Lee*, 53 S. Ct. 487 (1932).
5.  Ibid.
6.  Mortmain is a legal term indicating concern that rules or restrictions established by a "dead hand" (a previous generation) would impede trade or capital allocation. Brandeis speculates in a footnote that this concern was the reason for limiting corporations to fixed terms of 20, 30, or 50 years in the early statutes.
7.  *Liggett Co. v. Lee*, p. 490. Citations omitted.
8.  Ibid., p. 493.
9.  Robert C. Clark, *Corporate Law* (Little, Brown & Co., Boston, 1986), p. 2.
10. Note, though, the widespread practice today of partners in professional firms (doctors, lawyers, etc.) each individually incorporating as a mechanism for minimizing both liability and taxes.
11. William Greider, *Who Will Tell the People? The Betrayal of American Democracy* (Simon & Schuster, New York, 1992), pp. 348, 349.
12. Thomas Donaldson, *Corporations and Morality* (Prentice-Hall, Englewood Cliffs, NJ, 1982), p. 30.
13. See, for example, Anne Murphy, "Too Good to be True?", *Inc.*, June 1994, p. 34.
14. Paul Abrahams and Roland Rudd, "ICI to float drugs unit in break-up of group interests," *Financial Times*, July 31, 1992, p. 1.
15. Easterbrook and Fischel, "The Corporate Contract," pp. 1417–18.
16. Ibid.
17. Some sources argue that there cannot be a "race to the bottom" because if Delaware, for example, permitted laws that benefited management to the detriment of shareholders, then companies incorporated in Delaware would be at a competitive disadvantage in the capital market, and ultimately in the product market. See Ralph K. Winter, "State Law, Shareholder Protection, and the Theory of the Corporation," *Journal of Legal Studies*, 6 (1977), p. 251. This argument would have more weight if shareholders were able to change the state of incorporation, instead of just refraining from investing in companies incorporated in a particular state, or selling out once the state has adopted unacceptable new legislation.
18. Carl Kaysen, "The Corporation; How Much Power? What Scope?," in Edward S. Mason (ed.), *The Corporation in Modern Society* (Harvard University Press, Cambridge, 1959), p. 103.
19. Ibid., pp. 103, 104.
20. Ibid., pp. 104–5.
21. Martin Dickson, "GE shares dip on fraud allegation," *Financial Times*, June 3, 1992, p. 17.
22. See John Braithwaite, *Corporate Crime in the Pharmaceutical Industry* (Routledge & Kegan Paul, London, 1984), p. 258; and Marshall B. Clinnard, *Corporate Corruption: The Abuse of Power* (Praeger, New York, 1990), p. 103.
23. Milton Friedman, *Capitalism and Freedom* (University of Chicago Press, Chicago, 1962), p. 133.
24. A.B. Schmookler, *The Illusion of Choice: How the Market Economy Shapes Our Destiny* (State University of New York Press, Albany, 1993), pp. 24, 25.
25. A.A. Berle Jr., "For Whom are Corporate Managers Trustees?", *Harvard Law Review*, 45 (1932), pp. 1365, 1367.

26. John C. Coffee Jr., "No Soul to Damn: No Body to Kick: An Unscandalized Inquiry into the Problem of Corporate Punishment," *Michigan Law Review*, 79 (1981), pp. 386, 387.
27. Statement of Douglas H. Ginsburg, Assistant Attorney General, Antitrust Division, before the United States Sentencing Commission, Hearings Concerning Alternatives to Incarceration, July 15, 1986.
28. "When very severe fines need to be imposed on the corporation, they should be imposed not in cash, but in the equity securities of the corporation. The convicted corporation should be required to authorize and issue such number of shares to the state's crime victim compensation fund as would have an expected market value equal to the cash fine necessary to deter illegal activity. The fund should then be able to liquidate the securities in whatever manner maximizes its return." Coffee, "No Soul to Damn," p. 413, citations omitted.
29. Braithwaite, *Corporate Crime in the Pharmaceutical Industry*, p. 324.
30. Russell Mokhiber, *Corporate Crime and Violence: Big Business and the Abuse of the Public Trust* (Sierra Club Books, 1988), p. 19.
31. Richard W. Stevenson, "Many are Caught but Few Suffer for US Military Contract Fraud," *New York Times*, Nov. 12, 1990.
32. Braithwaite, *Corporate Crime in the Pharmaceutical Industry*, p. 319.
33. Coffee, "No Soul to Damn," p. 408.
34. Douglas H. Ginsburg, testimony presented to the US Sentencing Commission, July 15, 1986.
35. Marshall B. Clinnard, *Corporate Corruption: The Abuse of Power* (Praeger, New York, 1990), p. 307.
36. Ralph Nader, Mark Green, and Joel Seligman, in *Taming the Giant Corporation* (W.W. Norton, New York, 1976), p. 120.
37. Christopher D. Stone, *Where the Law Ends: The Social Control of Corporate Behavior* (Harper & Row, New York, 1975), p. 148.
38. "Nuclear Executives in Japan Resign over Recent Mishaps," *New York Times*, May 14, 1981.
39. Michael Moritz and Barrett Seaman, *Going for Broke: The Chrysler Story* (Doubleday, New York, 1981).
40. Joseph Nocera, "Delaware Puts Out," *Esquire*, Feb. 1990, p. 47.
41. Private letter from Peter F. Drucker to Robert Monks, June 17, 1993.
42. F.A. Hayek, *Law, Legislation, Liberty*, vol. 3: *The Political Order of a Free People* (University of Chicago Press, Chicago, 1979), p. 82.
43. Published by the National Association of Corporate Directors, Washington, DC.
44. James J. Hanks, in "From the Hustings: The Role of States with Takeover Control Laws," *Mergers and Acquisitions*, 29, 2, Sept.–Oct. 1994. This was part of the protectionist surge that followed the 1987 US Supreme Court decision in *CTS Corp. v. Dynamics Corp. of America*, which permitted certain kinds of state anti-takeover statutes.
45. Ga. Code Ann. Sec. 14-2-202.5.
46. The American Bar Association on Corporate Laws, "Other Constituency Statutes: Potential for Confusion," *The Business Lawyer*, 45, 4, Aug. 1990, p. 2261.
47. Ibid., p. 2259.
48. The Wilshire study focused on 63 Pennsylvania companies with a stock market capitalization greater than $5 million. The period of study was from Jan. 1, 1989 through Aug. 15, 1990. These two studies and others like them drew fire from proponents of state anti-takeover legislation, who said the studies were biased. But in an unpublished paper dated June 17, 1994, entitled "State Takeover Legislation and Share Values: The Wealth Effects of Pennsylvania's Act 36," Karpoff and Malatesta demonstrate (again) that the "wealth effect" associated with the October 13 new announcement was "negative, large, and statistically significant."

49.  Tom Cannon, *Corporate Responsibility* (Pitman Publishing, Marshfield, MA, 1992), p. 79.
50.  Edward S. Mason, *The Corporation in Modern Society* (Harvard University Press, Cambridge, MA, 1959), pp. 11–12.
51.  James Willard Hurst, *The Legitimacy of the Business Corporation in the Law of the United States: 1780–1980* (University of Virginia Press, Charlottesville, 1970), pp. 82–3. "[I]n *Dodge Brothers v. Ford Motor Company*: Management's prime obligation was to pursue profit in the interests of shareholders and not to adopt pricing policies designed to promote the interests of wage earners or to effect wider sharing of the gains of improved technology."
52.  Joseph Pereira, "Split Personality: Social Responsibility and Need for Low Cost Clash at Stride Rite," *Wall Street Journal*, May 28, 1993, p. A1.
53.  Ibid.
54.  Doug Bandow, "Social Responsibility: A Conservative View," *Utne Reader*, Sept.–Oct., 1993, pp. 62–3. Reprinted from *Business and Society Review*, Spring 1992.
55.  1989 Berkshire Hathaway annual report, pp. 52–3.
56.  Sir Adrian Cadbury, *The Company Chairman* (Fitzwilliam Publishing, Cambridge, 1990), p. 149.
57.  Steven Prokesch, "How Johnson and Johnson Managed the Tylenol Crisis", *New York Times*, Feb. 27, 1986.
58.  Prior to passage of the 1993 Omnibus Budget Reconciliation Act (OBRA), only some types of intangibles could be written off, and of these, some had to be written off over a period of no less than 28 years. This conservative approach began to change in 1993. First, the US Supreme Court declared in *Newark Morning Ledger v. US* that if the value of an acquired asset can be measured and will appreciate over time, it can be depreciated. Then the US Congress passed OBRA, which set a maximum of 15 years for amortization of intangibles, some formerly considered non-amortizable goodwill, with even shorter periods allowed for some categories.
59.  John Jay, *Sunday Telegraph*, Feb. 4, 1990. See also Bob Hagarty, "Differing Accounting Rules Snarl Europe," *Wall Street Journal*, Sept. 4, 1992; and "Foreign Firms Rush to Acquire US Companies," *Wall Street Journal*, July 1, 1994. The last article notes that the International Accounting Standards Committee issued a new rule that will force European companies to deduct the value of goodwill from their profits, as in the US.
60.  Jan. 13, 1992. All quotes in this section are from that paper.
61.  Letter to the editor, *Fortune*, Oct. 18, 1993, p. 34.
62.  "Usefulness of Operating Income, Residual Income, and EVA®: A Value-Relevance Perspective," Shimin Chen and James L. Dodd: <http://www/drake.edu/cbpa/acctg/Dodd/mbaa/article.html>.
63.  Michael Jacobs, *Short-Term America* (Harvard Business School Press, Cambridge, MA, 1991).
64.  For an in-depth study of the growing Japanese need for equity-based capital, see Howard D. Sherman and Bruce A. Babcock, "Redressing Structural Imbalances in Japanese Corporate Governance: An International Perspective," *The Corporate Governance Advisor*, 1, 8, Dec. 1993, p. 28.
65.  This case in point has been reproduced from Geoffrey P. Mazullo, "Germany's Daimler-Benz First to List Shares on New York Stock Exchange," *ISSue Alert*, 8, 4, Apr. 1993. Used with permission.
66.  *Board Directors and Corporate Governance: Trends in the G7 Countries Over the Next Ten Years* (Oxford Analytica, UK, Sept. 1992).
67.  *Corporate Social Reporting in the United States and Western Europe*, Report of the Task Force on Corporate Social Performance, US Department of Commerce, July 1979, p. 3.
68.  Rob Gray, Dave Owne, and Keith Maunders, *Corporate Social Accounting: Accounting and Accountability* (Prentice-Hall International, Englewood Cliffs, NJ, 1987), p. 89.

69. Ibid. For the findings of a global group that explored these and other fundamental questions in governance, see the Caux Round Table report on Principles for Business, the Caux Round Table Secretariat, The Hague, The Netherlands, 1994.

70. Stephen Garone, "The Link between Corporate Citizenship and Financial Performance," the Conference Board, Feb. 8, 1999.

71. Alan Benjamin, "Prototype Plc – Core Company Report", Dec. 31, 2000.

72. David Engel, "An Approach to Corporate Social Responsibility," *Stanford Law Review*, 32, 1, Nov. 1979.

73. John Herling, *The Great Price Conspiracy: The Story of the Antitrust Violations in the Electrical Industry* (Robert B. Luce Inc., Washington, 1962), p. 3.

74. Ibid., p. 5.

75. Ibid., p. 9.

76. Clarence C. Walton and Frederick W. Cleveland, Jr., *Corporations on Trial: The Electric Cases* (Wadsworth Publishing Company Inc., Belmont, CA, 1964), p. 34.

77. Herling, *The Great Price Conspiracy*, p. 97.

78. Ibid., p. 109.

79. See Schmookler, *The Illusion of Choice*, pp. 93–4.

# 2
# SHAREHOLDERS:
# OWNERSHIP

Shareholders are often referred to as the "owners" of the corporation, but the corporation's "legal personality" raises questions about whether it can be "owned" in any meaningful and effective way. There will always be agency costs in any corporate structure in which someone other than management owns equity. Public companies have managers with agendas different from their owners'; the governance challenge is to make sure that the resolution of conflicts is an open and fair process between entities that are informed, motivated, and empowered. That challenge is primarily addressed by laws, primarily the imposition of the highest standard of procedural and substantive performance ever developed under our legal system, the fiduciary standard. Interestingly, this standard is imposed on both shareholders (institutional shareholders only) and directors, and, even more interestingly, there have been efforts to erode this standard over the past 20 years.

In order to put the role of the shareholders into context, we will spend a short time on the overall issue of "ownership" before discussing its application to stock in public corporations. Of course, this discussion does not pretend to be comprehensive, much less exhaustive, but it should provide a context for the role of the owners of public companies.

As you read through this brief background – remembering our overall question of "Who is in the best position to make this decision, and does this person/group have the authority to make it?" – keep these questions in mind:

- *What problems with traditional notions of ownership was the corporate form intended to solve?*
- *How was it intended to solve them?*
- *What have been the consequences (intended and unintended) of this corporate model?*

## DEFINITIONS

Generally, we think of "ownership" of "property" as including three elements:

- O has the right to use P as he wishes. If it is food, he can eat it or sell it. If it is land, he can build on it or grow crops on it.
- O has the right to regulate anyone else's use of P. If it is food, he can share it or not, as he pleases. If it is land, he can decide who may step over its boundaries.

- O has the right to transfer rights to P on whatever terms he wishes. If it is a product, he can limit the use of what he sells or loans. For example, he might stipulate that it may not be resold, or restrict not just the purchaser but also all future purchasers from using the land for some purpose he does not wish. If it is land, O can keep the land while he gives or sells the right to take a short cut across it or the right to extract natural gas or oil from it. This means that O's property may be subject to restrictions when he receives it, or later as a result of rights he grants or sells while he owns it. If there are apple trees on his property, and he sells to a local farmer all the produce from the trees, he may no longer pick off an apple whenever he is hungry. He may not be able to cut a tree down if it blocks his view or he needs the wood.

There is less general agreement on a fourth component of ownership:

- O is responsible for making sure that his use of P does not damage others. As one Supreme Court justice put it: "My freedom to move my fist must be limited by the proximity of your chin."[1] If P is a dog, O is responsible for taking reasonable precautions for making sure P does not bite anyone. There are often specific statutory requirements limiting the use of property. Zoning laws may provide that O may not operate a business on his property, if it is in a residential district. Other restrictions may mean that he cannot build a structure that will block his neighbor's access to sunlight, play his radio so loudly that it disturbs his neighbors' peace, or create a dangerous "attractive nuisance" that will entice children onto his property. Environmental laws restrict O's ability to dump chemicals in a river that crosses his property. Balancing the right of O to use P with the rights of the rest of O's community has challenged the imagination of lawyers and lawmakers from the earliest notions of property.

Ownership is therefore a combination of rights and responsibilities with respect to a specific property. In some cases those rights and responsibilities are more clearly defined than in others. Much of the complexity that arises from ownership comes from the responsibility side of ownership. There is little ambiguity in "owning" a dollar bill or a loaf of bread, for example. Neither imputes much in the way of responsibility to the owner (though O is not permitted to use the dollar to buy drugs or hire a hit man, and is expected to give some of it to the Internal Revenue Service).

*What does it mean to own part of something?* Stockholders, for example, are deemed to "own" the company in which they invest. But a share of stock does not translate into a specified segment of the company's assets, at least not unless the company dissolves and there is something left over after the creditors get what they are owed.[2] And shareholders have limited liability, limiting their responsibility to prevent or redress the corporation's wrongs. *What does it mean to own a share of stock? What are the rights of share ownership and what are the responsibilities?* That is what this chapter will try to answer.

Human beings relate in a special way to things that they own. Ownership is not only a measure of wealth; it is an element of personal satisfaction. Adam Smith believed that protection of an individual in his quiet enjoyment of property is one of the few legitimate activities of civil government.

Wherever there is great property, there is great inequality. For one very rich man, there must be at least five hundred poor, and the affluence of the few supposes the indigence of the many. The affluence of the rich excites the indignation of the poor, who are often both driven by want and prompted by envy to invade his possessions. It is only under the shelter of the civil magistrate that the owner of that valuable property, which he acquired by the labor of many years, or perhaps of many successive generations, can sleep a single night in security.[3]

## EARLY CONCEPTS OF OWNERSHIP

Ownership has been at issue since the dawn of human history. Disputes over property appear throughout the Bible, including bitter struggles over Joseph's coat and Jacob's inheritance. The early teachings of the Christian church were intensely hostile to individual ownership of property. The Gospels repeatedly warn that riches are a threat to salvation. "It is easier for a camel to go through the eye of a needle than for a rich man to enter the kingdom of God."[4] But these invectives against ownership failed to take hold in the West, where a tradition going back to Aristotle viewed ownership of property and its involvement in the public good as the basis of a durable society.

The later eighteenth-century notion of property involved a direct relationship between the owner and the thing owned; Locke thought of property as legitimate only to the extent that it provided enough for personal sustenance. The right of individual ownership of property was deemed important because it assured that citizens could be protected in their independence from the monarchy and centralized authority.

The central tenet of the Western concept of ownership is that, to the extent that individuals own property, they will have the incentive to manage that property in a manner that is compatible with the interests of society as a whole. Adam Smith wrote that, even if a businessman "intends only his own gain, he is . . . led by an invisible hand to promote an end which is not his intention." Indeed, Smith believed, "by pursuing his own interest, he frequently promotes that of society more effectively than when he really intends to promote it."[5] This argument is still the foundation of government policies the world over, including privatization drives in such diverse countries as the United Kingdom and Chile. Former British Prime Minister Margaret Thatcher privatized state-owned UK industries for the same reason that Chilean Labor Minister Jose Pinera privatized Chile's social security system:[6] namely, that the best way for a nation to achieve prosperity is to create a society of individual property owners pursuing their own interests.

Some cultures and some political systems are not based on ownership of property by individuals. Ownership has often been criticized throughout history as the expression of inequality in a world where fair treatment should be the highest priority. Karl Marx's *Communist Manifesto* memorably declares, "The theory of Communism may be summed up in one sentence: Abolish all private property."

There is a natural tension between freedom and equality. On one hand, human beings must be free to express their individuality, and in so doing their differences – their inequality. On the other hand is the view that only equality is an acceptable basis for a civilized state. The conflict between these two views produces uncertainty about the value of individual contributions. Should people own according to their ability to pay or according to their need? The extreme at one end is shown by the failure of communism in eastern Europe. The extreme at the other end is epitomized by Marie Antoinette, who said that if the poor had no bread they should eat cake.

## EARLY CONCEPTS OF THE CORPORATION

The corporation could not exist without a notion of private property. If everything is owned by the king, it does not matter whether the ownership is direct or indirect, or whether it is possible for many people to share in the ownership of one entity. But the corporation is a unique subset of the category of ownership, created for unique reasons, and having a unique character. It was created as a way of resolving some of the challenges presented by private ownership; it then created a new set of challenges of its own.

The first corporations were more like municipalities than businesses. They were towns, universities, and monastic orders founded in the Middle Ages. These were collective organizations – sometimes in corporate form – as a protection against the centralized power of autocrats and as a way to create a source of wealth and power that was free from royal domination. The key elements that made them corporations were that they existed independently of any particular membership, and all assets and holdings belonged to the corporation itself, distinguishing it from partnerships.

John J. Clancy, in his thoughtful book about the language we use to talk about business, noted that the development of double-entry bookkeeping in the late Middle Ages "first developed to check errors in accounts, became a technique to separate a man's business from his private life. The firm could then be seen as a separate entity, with an existence beyond the life of the owner/operator."[7] Sir William Blackstone, the great legal scholar, made his earliest reference to corporations in a judgment that King Charles I could not unilaterally abrogate the charter of the City of London.

The first joint-stock companies emerged in Britain and Holland during the early seventeenth century, in response to the rapidly emerging markets of the East Indies and West Indies. In 1602 the Dutch East India Company was granted a royal charter, with permanent capital and shares of unlimited duration. The British East India Company had received its charter from Queen Elizabeth I two years earlier. A little over a century later in response to a speculative crash in the East Indies – known as the South Sea Bubble – the British Parliament passed a law (the Bubbles Act of 1720) which forbade unchartered companies to issue stock. This meant that all commercial enterprises that wished to raise capital from stock issues had to acquire a certificate of incorporation.

Corporate organization thus meant that property could be held subject to rules that transcended royal prerogatives and power. This kind of collective establishment of an entity that could limit interference by the monarch was the basis for the modern corporation. Corporate power – although limited in time, scope, and purpose – was designed to counter the otherwise unlimited centralized authority of government.

This posed a serious threat to government. Through the ownership of corporations, individuals acquired wealth, which gave them an independent source of power. The emergence of a "private sector" threatened not only the hereditary power of princes but also the wealth of the established church. The preponderance of gross national product would no longer automatically be available for the ruler's pet projects, whether the building of great cathedrals or the launching of crusades.

> Distrust of the state as organized caused the accumulation of political powers in the hands of minor states, corporations, which excited no apprehensions because they were democratically organized . . . If the entire state had been formed and organized like the corporation, would not philosophers and political theorists have had to confess that it was an ideal state . . . ?[8]

Although the independence of the corporate structure was a threat in the short term to a powerful centralized government, ultimately the corporate form became the government's ally. (If it had not, it probably would not have been allowed to continue.) The level of independence the corporate form provided made the government's authority more acceptable. Indeed, it made it more necessary. If the state permits private property, the government must be able to protect citizens in the useful enjoyment of that property. It must provide the "civil magistrates" that Adam Smith said owners must have in order to be able to slumber peacefully.

## A DUAL HERITAGE: INDIVIDUAL AND CORPORATE "RIGHTS"

The struggle to hold property free from the demands of the state inspired European migration to the new world of the Americas, and helped to inspire the Revolutionary War for independence there. The United States Constitution and its Bill of Rights specifically protected property rights. "Property" replaced the Declaration of Independence's "pursuit of happiness" as an "inalienable" (impossible to lose or take away) right that was protected and enforced by the state. The Constitution promised "life, liberty, and property" to every (white male) citizen of the new nation.

Over time, at least a part of this guarantee was extended to corporations as well, despite the fact that, while "property" is prominently mentioned in the Constitution, the word "corporation" does not appear. Over the last century, the US Supreme Court has repeatedly ruled that certain Constitutional protections – such as "freedom of speech" and the right to the protections of "due process" in the taking of its property – extend to corporations (creatures of law) as they do to natural persons. As noted in the opening section of this book, corporations have at least some of the same inalienable rights as people.

Owners of corporations are thus heirs to a twofold tradition: on the one hand, they personally have rights as individuals and as owners of shares in a corporate entity. On the other hand, they receive the benefits of the rights extended to that entity. In this section of the book we will explore this dual heritage. Alfred Conard points out that the development of this dual tradition has been far from straightforward. "[F]or a hundred years after the Constitution was written, Congress showed little interest in exercising its commerce power. Meanwhile, throughout the nineteenth century, the states built up their idiosyncratic patterns of legislation, their separate bureaucracies for dealing with corporation documents, and their addictions to tax revenues exacted for corporation privileges."[9] In 1819, the US Supreme Court decided the case of *McCullough v. Maryland*, where Chief Justice John Marshall posed the question, "Has Congress power to incorporate a bank?" While the court was more concerned with the issue of federalism and states' rights than of corporate law, the decision has some relevance here. Marshall said,

> The power of creating a corporation, though appertaining to sovereignty, is not, like the power of making war, or levying taxes, or of regulating commerce, a great substantive and independent power, which cannot be implied as incidental to other powers, or used as a means of executing them. It is never the end for which other powers are exercised, but a means by which other objects are accomplished. No contributions are made to charity for the sake of an incorporation, but a corporation is created to administer the charity; no seminary of learning is instituted in order to be incorporated, but the corporate character is conferred to subserve the purposes of education. No city was

ever built with the sole object of being incorporated, but is incorporated as affording the best means of being well governed. The power of creating a corporation is never used for its own sake, but for the purpose of effecting something else. No sufficient reason is, therefore, perceived, why it may not pass as incidental to those powers which are expressly given, if it be a direct mode of executing them.[10]

Ownership in general – and share ownership in particular – is necessary for the organization of talent, money, and other energies critical to technological and industrial progress. Allowing fractionated "ownership" through public offerings of stock enabled the access to capital that funded modern industry. The corporate structure was as important in transforming commerce as the assembly line. Both were based on the same principle, specialization. You didn't need to know how to make a chair to work in a chair factory; all you needed to know was how to put the chair leg into the chair seat. And you didn't need to know how to make a chair to invest in a chair company. All you needed to do was buy some stock.

This notion of stock ownership has been indispensable in the extraordinary rise of western Europe and the United States over the last half-millennium. With the opportunity through ownership to achieve wealth and independence, Western man was able to successfully motivate, discipline, and organize himself in competition with other cultures. Before we continue further with the Western model for corporations in modern times, we will take a brief look at the way that the corporate ideal is being reinvented as eastern Europe tries to build it from scratch.

## THE REINVENTION OF THE CORPORATION: EASTERN EUROPE IN THE 1990s

Some argue that the "progress" that made bigger, more complicated organizations possible produced bigger, more complicated problems. This debate is being carried on today in eastern Europe and the component states of the former USSR. Their approach to property over the past three-quarters of a century was based on the communist ideal, which denied individuals most rights of ownership, leaving nearly all property in the hands of the state. The social, political, and economic failures of this system have presented the new leaders with a historic challenge – to examine the best and worst effects of the Western model of ownership and corporation laws and to devise a new system, improving it.

## Of vouchers and values

"I visited Finance Minister Vaclav Havel of the then Czechoslovakia in February 1992 to discuss his program of privatization of the nation's economy. It was an exciting time. People spoke constantly about the details of vouchers and bids, various levels of value setting and, most important, a complete change in their way of life. They aimed to convert their economy from a system of public ownership of the factories and stores in their traditionally wealthy country to one in which individuals for the first time in over half a century would become stockholders. In the West, the corporate structure evolved over time. The Czechs were starting a capitalist system from scratch. This was a moment truly worthy of the term 'revolution.'

The obstacles were enormous. All the incumbent bureaucratic managers were opposed, there was no way to set the value of the enterprises; nobody knew whether a particular business was profitable or not. How could an individual afford to investigate and make the kind of informed decision that markets depend on?

They couldn't. Instead, each Czech citizen was issued for a nominal amount a voucher book containing certificates entitling the bearer to an aggregate number of 'points.' This entitled him to 'bid' for ownership in one or more of the corporations to be privatized. Over a series of bids, values would be determined by the market place – supply and demand, the more 'bid' the higher the value, and vice-versa.

The details were overwhelming. Ultimately, in true free-market fashion, a class of 'fund managers' developed who would offer to buy the vouchers from individuals for many times their cost; the managers ultimately acquired a substantial portion of all the outstanding vouchers, giving them enormous leverage in the privatization process. All of this became clearer as events unfolded; little was known in advance. By the time of my visit, it was plain that there simply wasn't enough time or wisdom in the world to assure that the privatization process would be both 'fairly' and 'economically' administered.

I asked Minister Havel, 'But how can you assure that the process will be fair?' He replied, 'I have had to get beyond fairness. I can only hope that nothing too unfair occurs. What I have to accomplish is to get ownership into the hands of the Czech people within these precious days that my political support remains steadfast. *Once the people have become owners, nothing can stop the democratic revolution.*'" *Robert A.G. Monks*

## THE EVOLUTION OF THE AMERICAN CORPORATION

We need to go back more than 200 years before Havel's revolution to understand the way that the corporate structure evolved. America was born with a profound mistrust of power and an even more profound commitment to making sure that power drew its legitimacy from a system of checks and balances. One initial controversy that arose in the early 1830s concerned the charter of the Bank of the United States. The Bank, as originally chartered, was a private corporation, though it had the power to issue notes of exchange. The Bank was not taxed, and Congress was not allowed to charter any similar institution. In return for these favors, the government was allowed to appoint five of the Bank's 25 directors. The Bank's powers shocked democrats. Roger B. Taney, Congressman and later Chief Justice of the Supreme Court, said: "It is this power concentrated in the hands of a few individuals – exercised in secret and unseen although constantly felt – irresponsible and above the control of the people or the government . . . that is sufficient to awaken any man in the country if the danger is brought distinctly to his view."[11] This was a typical view of private, unchecked power.

In the early days of the United States, corporate charters were granted by special acts of the state legislatures. Applicants for corporate charters had to negotiate with legislators to arrive at specific charter provisions, notes Harvey H. Segal, including "the purpose of the enterprise, the location of its activities, the amount of capital to be raised by stock sales, and the power of its directory."[12] The theory was that the state should separately and specifically approve each new corporation, to guard against improper activity. But, as Segal noted, instead of oversight, this process "invited bribery and corruption." So, in 1811, New York enacted a general incorporation statute (though restricting it to manufacturing enterprises), and other states followed suit. But the state was still deeply involved.

Applications had to be approved by the state secretary, or by some other high official, who enforced firm rules such as the requirement that a minimum of capital had to be paid in before an enterprise could be launched and that delinquent shareholders would be held personally liable – up to the unpaid balances on their stock subscriptions – for any corporate debts. High taxes were levied, and there were also severe constraints on the kinds of securities – common stocks, preferred stocks, and bonds – that a corporation could issue.[13]

After the Civil War, companies began to form "trusts." It was clear that if competitors in the same line of business worked together instead of separately they could control prices. This was not illegal or even disapproved of at the time. Indeed, the directors of these new entities were called "trustees," a term that still lives on in the non-profit, banking, and securities sectors. Segal points out that, "In wielding such broad discretionary power, the trustees established important precedents for the control of corporations by professional managers rather than dominant shareholders."[14] The first antitrust laws ended the trusts, but the professional managers were there to stay.

---

# Case in point: Standard Oil and the arrival of big business

In the 1870s and 1880s, several companies achieved spectacular size, not by internal growth, but by merger. Perhaps the most famous example is the Standard Oil Company. Initially, Standard Oil was less a company than a cartel – a group of smaller, separate companies under the guidance of the largest refiner of them all, John D. Rockefeller's Standard Oil Company of Ohio.

Rockefeller initially created a trade association of refiners, and became its first president. Ultimately, this association became a massive, vertically integrated, centralized corporation. By 1880, the Standard Oil "group" or "alliance" numbered 40 separate companies. In 1882, the shareholders of these 40 companies exchanged their stock for certificates in the Standard Oil Trust. The trust authorized an office of nine trustees to "exercise general supervision over the affairs of the several Standard Oil companies." Moreover, the trust chartered local subsidiaries to take over Standard's operations in each state. This allowed Standard to avoid taxes owed by "out of state" corporations. The effect of the coordination was to allow Standard Oil to tighten its already vice-like grip on the mushrooming oil industry. By the early 1890s, Standard Oil was extracting 25 percent of the nation's crude.

Though Standard Oil was broken up by a Supreme Court order in 1891, other conglomerates avoided the antitrust axe. The United States Steel Corporation, for example, created by Andrew Carnegie in 1901, created close to 60 percent of the industry's output.[15]

---

The next stage in the evolution of the corporate structure was widespread (and therefore diffuse) ownership. Look at the description of the first public offering of Ford Motor Company stock in David Halberstam's book, *The Reckoning*:

It made ordinary citizens believe that buying stock – owning part of a giant company – was a real possibility in their lives. By purchasing stock, they became participants in American capitalism, *owners* as well as workers, junior partners of Henry Ford II . . . The news generated excitement rarely seen on Wall Street. Everyone wanted in on the issue . . . Early in the negotiations the principals had agreed that $50 per share would be satisfactory. But the fever kept building. The actual price turned out to be $64.50. Some 10 million shares were sold, and it took 722 underwriters to handle them. At a time when $100 million was considered a handsome result from a public offering, this one brought $640 million – the sheer scale of it was staggering. The fever continued, greatly inflating the stock, but though it briefly surged up near $70 it soon hit a plateau near $50. The Ford family had been joined by some 300,000 new co-owners of their company. It was, said Keith Funston of the New York Stock Exchange, "a landmark in the history of public ownership." It was a landmark in tax avoidance, too; estimates were that Eleanor Clay Ford and her four children saved some $300 million in taxes while keeping control of the company.

It also marked the beginning of a historic shift in American capitalism, a major increase in the influence of Wall Street in companies like Ford. The Street was a partner of the family now, and the family had to respond to its norms. In the old days, the Street did not demand too much of the companies whose stock it sold. But the stock market was changing now. Before the war only a small number of Americans held stocks, and they were to a large degree of the same class as the owners of the old-line companies. The market was a kind of gentlemen's club, virtually off limits to the rest of the society. People owned stocks because their families had *always* owned stocks. They invested not so much to gain but to protect . . . Those who were in the market were generally rich and were in for the long haul.[16]

This was the high-water mark of the old system. Ford became one of the last of the blue chips, just as blue-chip stocks were becoming irrelevant. Instead of a few clubby long-term investors, the postwar era created a world where the New York Stock Exchange vowed to make every American a stockholder and where stockholders could make a lot of money fast by betting on the best of a large group of entrepreneurs. Both sides were hungry and impatient: those raising capital and those who provided it. "No one talked about safe buys; there was too much action for that. Companies like Xerox and Polaroid replaced US Steel and Ford as smart buys, and they in turn were replaced by fried chicken companies and nursing home syndicates."[17]

Mutual funds allowed investors to limit the downside and take advantage of the upside. Gerry Tsai's $250,000 fund at Fidelity reached $200 million three years later. Wall Street was no longer the exclusive enclave of young men from a tiny group of "good families"; it was open to anyone (well, any white males). "Also significant for anyone involved in business – whether the investors, the managers of the companies, or the bright young men coming out of business schools – was the effect of the talent flow. One could make far more money by playing the market on Wall Street – where cleverness was rewarded imme-diately – than by joining a company and getting in line to do something as mundane as producing something. The effect of this drain on ability away from the companies themselves was incalculable."[18] One result was that companies started thinking that their product was not the product – it was the stock. Halberstam notes that, at Ford, "Not only were the top people there mainly from finance, but the bias of the (stock) market invisibly but critically bore on the company's decisions. There was a great deal of talk about the effect of production decisions on the stock."[19]

Meanwhile, a different sort of "trust" was forming in one of the states, as, for corpor-ate charters, tiny Delaware, the second-smallest state, won the "race to the bottom," and became "home" to most of America's corporations, at least on paper. In a hundred years America had gone from a country where each corporate charter had to be approved by the state legislature to a country where store fronts along the streets of Delaware's capital city are covered with signs that say "Incorporate While You Wait." Woodrow Wilson, as governor of New Jersey, persuaded the state legislature to pass the nation's first antitrust laws. Once he left to become president they were repealed.

Legal authority over corporations has always been left to the states. The federal government has very little authority over corporate governance. The theory was that the states would be "laboratories," learning from each other's successes and failures and trying to outdo each other. In reality, all of that did occur; the problem was that instead of trying to outdo each other to do what was best for the economy or the shareholders or even the community, they outdid each other in trying to attract corporations and their tax revenues.

*Should the state play a role in approving any aspect of a corporation's purpose or financial structure, or should it be left to the market? If the former, what questions should it ask and what answers should it demand? If the latter, what disclosure should it require to enable informed decision-making by the investor community?*

## THE ESSENTIAL ELEMENTS OF THE CORPORATE STRUCTURE

For debt investors and employees, everything (literally) is open to contract; for equity investors, almost everything is open to choice. Why does corporate law allow managers to set the terms under which they will govern corporate assets? Why do courts grant more discretion to self-interested managers than to disinterested regulators? Why do investors entrust such stupendous sums to managers whose acts are essentially unconstrained by legal rules? The answers lie in, and help explain, the economic structure of corporate law. The corporation is a complex set of explicit and implicit contracts, and corporate law enables the participants to select the optimal arrangement for the many different sets of risks and opportunities that are available in a large economy. No one set of terms will be best for all; hence the "enabling" structure of corporate law.[20]

What the authors are saying here is that the law gives corporate managers a great deal of flexibility in determining their capital and governance structure, relying on the market for capital to create competition that will allow shareholders to "choose" the one they think is best. In our view, this power of "choice" is hardly worthy of the term, because it all but disappears the moment it is exercised. Shareholders can "choose" which companies to invest in, and companies court them on that basis. Once shareholders have invested, however, their power to influence the company is all but vestigial, as discussed throughout this chapter. The authors of the above quotation seem to admit that, when they argue that managers and investors both "assume their roles with knowledge of the consequences."[21]

*Is it fair to assume that shareholders have that knowledge? That they can act on it in a meaningful way? What is the evidence to support your answer?*

Individual ownership evolved over time into a variety of models of collective enterprise. In Darwinian terms, the corporate model has prevailed as the legal structure of choice in modern commerce because it was the "fittest." As Dean Clark's description in chapter 1 noted, corporations combine many attractive features, among them the ability to acquire management and financial resources efficiently, the capacity to transfer holdings easily, and the ability to assert control over an under-performing venture.

Among the special attractions of the corporate form or organization are:

- A high degree of advance certitude about the ground rules of the organization. There simply isn't a lot of law on most of the other forms of doing business. In the case of entities like business trusts, the applicable law is common law, harder to determine, understand, and predict than statute.
- The financial markets have been developed to easily accommodate the mechanics of share issuance and transfer. Partnerships are more cumbersome.
- Those who put up the money can decide on the management and changes in extreme cases. In a partnership, those who put up the money cannot change the general partner.

But, as we explained earlier, perhaps the most attractive component of the corporate model is limited liability – the owner's liability is limited to the amount of his investment (or subscription).

This "limited liability" means that ventures can take very large risks and incur substantial liabilities without threatening the personal resources of their owners. Without this protection, the wealthy would be reluctant to risk their resources in risky ventures. This ability for "investors" (in contrast to active participants) to diversify their risks of investing in any single venture by investing in many is undoubtedly one of the principal reasons that capital has been available for research, innovation and technical progress during the last two centuries.

Just because the owners have limited liability doesn't mean that the risk inherent in their investments disappears or that someone else automatically pays the liabilities. The impact of business failures hits many individuals, the community, and the government. This capacity of corporations to "externalize" the costs of their actions is a continuing problem, as explained in chapter 1. And, the different investment horizons and priorities for different investors, combined with structural and economic barriers to collective action, discussed throughout this book, make it very difficult to contain the externalization.

# Case in point: Partnership vs. corporation

Let's consider an example of two failed business enterprises, one a solely owned proprietorship (an individual) and one a corporation, both owners and operators of a modern paper mill that becomes bankrupt. Suppose that the working of the mill involved the discharge of both liquid and gaseous emissions that violated environmental standards and caused great damage and financial loss to members of the community. The investigators who are responsible for enforcement of the environmental laws institute legal proceedings. So do members of the community who have been damaged.

The individual owner of the mill has no alternative – he must pay the damages up to the point of personal bankruptcy. The corporation's liability is limited to the extent of its assets. If, for example, it is leasing the plant and literally "owns" no assets, then it does not have to pay damages. The benefit of this system is that the shareholders of the corporation are protected against liability. That is, they lose what they invested, but are not liable beyond that investment. On the other hand, the individual who owns the failing paper company loses almost all of his personal assets. In both cases, the community, the employees and the customers, suppliers, and other corporate stakeholders are all damaged, but in just one do they have a chance of some recourse. The corporate form of ownership does not change the cost: it just changes the extent of the owner's responsibility.

As explained in chapter 1, the corporate form limits liability, but it does not limit risk, which extends to many "corporate externalities." None the less, the virtue of limited liability, combined with the benefits of investment diversification and the progress of technological innovations, has made it possible for corporations to grow to huge dimensions. Modern corporations are virtually unlimited in the scope of their enterprise, the size of their capital, the national reach of their operations, and even the span of their existence. It is not surprising, then, that they have acquired the capacity to influence the circumstances of the societies within which they operate. They have more money than individuals for financing elections (a serious problem in Japan, the US, and most European countries); they have more resources to expend in influencing legislation and the administration of laws; they can hire the best lawyers, lobbyists, and media consultants. All of these costs are simply passed on to the customer − and the shareholder.

Because of this ability to influence the making, interpretation, and enforcement of laws, corporations in our time are able to "externalize" many of the consequences of their operations. In our paper company example, we assume that both the company owned by an individual and the one organized as a corporation face the same marketplace and the same obligations. But the corporation has another important advantage − it is able to participate more effectively than the individual in the process that sets the legal standards regulating permissible emission levels. It is better able to organize itself and the community to fight suits by those alleging that they have been damaged by its discharge of effluents. So ownership of a large modern corporation has come to be a one-way street − the shareholders and the managers appropriate the profits and, to the extent possible, force the costs on to society as a whole.

# Case in point: The voluntary restraint agreement in the auto industry

Between 1980 and 1982, the "Big Three" automakers, General Motors, Ford, and Chrysler, lost $8 billion pre-tax, and their domestic market share sank to 71 percent.[22] Of course, in 1955 the Big Three accounted for 95 percent of the nation's sales.[23] The total market value of GM, Ford, and Chrysler stock was under $14 billion, with GM responsible for over 80 percent of that amount.[24]

Ronald Reagan, elected in 1980, made a voluntary restraint agreement (VRA) with Japan an early priority for his administration. VRAs are devices to limit foreign competitors in favor of domestic industry because, based on the argument that they do not play by the same rules, competition is unfair. The essence of the agreements is that they should be voluntary and temporary, though in reality they are neither. The beauty of it, from the importing government's point of view, is that it shelters domestic industry without appearing protectionist and it does not directly contravene GATT or domestic legislation. Because the arrangements are "informal," the traditional and expected legal protections against monopolistic behavior are simply put into suspense. This agreement limited car and truck imports from 1981 onward. While campaigning in Detroit in 1980, Reagan said, "I think the government has a responsibility that it's shirked so far. And it's a place government can be legitimately involved, and that is to convince Japan that in one way or another, and for their own best interest, the deluge of their cars into the US must be slowed while our industry gets back on its feet."[25] Within three to four years, there came about such an explosive reversal in fortunes for the Big Three auto manufacturers that all were reporting record historical profit levels and amassing huge cash reserves, For instance: in 1984 total net income from automotive operations was over $10 billion, cashflow from operating activities exceeded $20 billion, and cash on hand at the end of 1984 was over $16 billion. Market value soared to $37 billion and market share was edging back to 74 percent.[26] In the short term all of the most affected constituencies benefited. The union workers were locked into their jobs with higher than competitive-level salaries for a few more years; the companies made profits and cash; shareholder values soared. Even the Japanese companies were happy: "[T]he quotas were a boon to the Japanese manufacturers, who did extremely well and greatly strengthened their position in the US market. Thanks to the artificial hold-down of supply, they boosted their prices and profits . . . Buoyed by the profits from price premiums that often exceeded $2,000 per unit, the Japanese companies' US dealer networks got bigger and stronger."[27] There have been a number of studies of the impact of the VRA. One study estimated that the restraints produced an increase in cashflow estimated at some $6 billion, before leakages into other factor suppliers' rents. Accordingly, between 33 and 45 percent of the automobile industry cashflow for 1984–5 may be attributed to the restraints.[28] The premium for consumers has been estimated at between $500 and $2,000 per car and total consumer losses at up to $5.3 billion.[29] One study estimates that "by 1984 the restrictions led to an $8.9 billion increase in US producers' profits, virtually all of the industry's record profits of that year."[30] The VRA produced pricing increases typical of successful cartels. Consumers still purchased imported cars, but paid up to $2,000 more for them. Not surprisingly, having achieved protection from competition, the domestic manufacturers substantially increased the prices of their own cars. Thus profits for the automobile industry in the mid-1980s were really a government-mandated transfer from the American customer to the Big Three, and to the Japanese manufacturers, the unintended beneficiary of the whole exercise.

*See the General Motors case study. Did the VRA help Detroit to compete? Should the consumer bear the cost of an industry's failure to compete?*

## THE SEPARATION OF OWNERSHIP AND CONTROL PART 1: BERLE AND MEANS

The rights of ownership outlined at the beginning of this chapter are fairly simple when applied to a house, a car, or a herd of cattle. But the "owner" of a fractional share of a corporation has an intangible interest in an intangible entity. While the entity itself may have many tangible assets, the relation of those assets to the "owners" is questionable.

Only one of the ownership rights listed at the beginning of this chapter is unequivocally exercised by the stockholder – the right to transfer the interest. That is fairly simple; indeed, that has been the overwhelming priority in the development of the security markets. A share of stock is, above all, highly transferable, and the system puts a premium (in the most literal terms) on making sure that anyone who wants to sell (or buy) a share of stock can do so, immediately. Note, however, that during the takeover era even this paramount right was limited by corporate management and state government. Companies adopted "poison pills" (see the discussion in chapter 3) and other anti-takeover devices that limited the ability of the shareholders to sell to a willing buyer at a mutually agreed price. And in other cases, like the Time Warner deal, corporate management was able to prevent the shareholders from making the choice about which company was a better candidate for a business combination.

In this context, what does it mean to talk about the other two ownership rights mentioned at the beginning of this chapter? The first was the right to use the property. One does not really "use" a share of stock, beyond cashing the dividend checks or possibly using the stock to secure a loan or giving some or all of it as a gift. The shareholder does not "use" his intangible fraction of the company – even if his proportionate share of the company's assets was worth, for example, the equivalent of one desk and telephone, he cannot take it, sell it, or even use it, much less tell anyone at the company how to use it.

The shareholder–owner does not participate in the activities by which his "property" is managed. He has no relationship with the other owners; their community of interest is limited to the price of the stock. As Davis notes,

> Corporate association has reference rather to the corporate property or industry than to the persons associated. The physical element is exaggerated, the human element is depressed. The purchaser of stock considers that he is acquiring an interest in an enterprise, not so much that he is assuming common relations with the numerous other stockholders; for the most part, he does not know them and does not take the pains to learn who they are; if he "knows the property" and by what directors it is administered he is satisfied.[31] All of this "is a process which seems to be culminating in our time with a 'Cheshire Cat' disappearance of ownership in any meaningful sense of the term."[32]

The shareholder has the exclusive control of the stock itself. But as a condition of the shareholder's limited liability, the shareholder gives up the right to control use of the corporation's property by others. That right is delegated to the management of the corporation. Indeed, it is one of the benefits of the corporate organization to the investor; he can entrust his money to people who have expertise and time that he does not. But it is also one of the drawbacks. Thus it is this separation between ownership and control that has been the focus of the struggles over corporate governance.

What the owner of a corporation "owns" is a certificate representing entitlement to a proportional share of the corporation. The only thing he has is the stock certificate; the corporation itself (or maybe its subsidiary) is the owner of its own property. But the certificate entitles him to particular rights and obligations, some set by federal law, some set by the state in which the corporation is incorporated. The rights of a shareholder are classically defined as (1) the right to sell the stock, (2) the right to vote the proxy, (3) the right to bring suit for damages if the corporation's directors or managers fail to meet their obligations, (4) the right to certain information from the company, and (5) certain residual rights following the company's liquidation (or its filing for reorganization under bankruptcy laws), once creditors and other claimants are paid off.[33]

> But in the modern corporation, these two attributes of ownership [control and economic rights] no longer attach to the same individual or group. The stockholder has

surrendered control over his wealth. He has become a supplier of capital, a risk taker pure and simple, while ultimate responsibility and authority of ownership is attached to stock ownership; the other attribute is attached to corporate control. Must we not, therefore, recognize that we are no longer dealing with property in the old sense? Does the traditional logic of property still apply? Because an owner who also exercises control over his wealth is protected in the full receipt of the advantages derived from it, must it *necessarily* follow that an owner who has surrendered control of his wealth should likewise be protected to the full?[34]

Corporations today are larger and more far-reaching than anyone could have dreamed, even a century ago. In those days, industrialists such as John D. Rockefeller, Cornelius Vanderbilt, Andrew Mellon, and Andrew Carnegie ruled empires that rivaled whole countries in their size and scope – and power. The companies had public shareholders, but the men who built them held huge stakes to back their stewardship. Today, with rare exceptions like Bill Gates of Microsoft and the late Sam Walton of Wal-Mart, large companies are led by men whose stakes in the company are dwarfed by the holdings of institutional investors. The shareholders who "own" the company are so diverse and so widely dispersed that it is difficult to characterize their relationship to the venture in the terms of a traditional owner.

Most people begin the study of ownership in the context of public corporations with Columbia University professors Adolph A. Berle and Gardiner C. Means, who first recognized the separation of ownership and control in the large modern corporation.

This dissolution of the atom of property destroys the very foundation on which the economic order of the past three centuries has rested. Private enterprise, which has molded economic life since the close of the middle ages, has been rooted in the institution of private property. Under the feudal system, its predecessor, economic organization grew out of mutual obligations and privileges derived by various individuals from their relation to property which no one of them owned. Private enterprise, on the other hand, has assumed an owner of the instruments of production with complete property rights over those instruments. Whereas the organization of feudal economic life rested upon an elaborate system of binding customs, the organization under the system of private enterprise has rested upon the self-interest of the property owner – a self-interest held in check only by competition and the conditions of supply and demand. Such self-interest has long been regarded as the best guarantee of economic efficiency. It has been assumed that, if the individual is protected in the right both to use his own property as he sees fit and to receive the full fruits of its use, his desire for personal gain, for profits, can be relied upon as effective incentive to his efficient use of any industrial property he may possess.[35]

We must remember that it is not as though anyone ever made a decision that companies would work better if they separated ownership and control. There was no conscious choice in favor of treating shares of stock as though they were betting slips for races that were over at the end of each day. The wedge driven between ownership and control of American corporations was the unintended consequence of what was then thought of as progress – the technological and procedural changes made in order to meet the needs of a rapidly expanding economy. In order to make that economy work, and in order to keep it expanding, the market placed a premium on liquidity and privacy. It was not until decades later that it became clear that those priorities would create a system as shortsighted as a cat chasing its own tail.

# Case in point: The conflicted owner

A pension fund spread its assets among six to ten different money managers at any given time, in an effort to protect itself through diversification. Each had its own formula and assumptions. On any given day, half were buying United Widget stock, and the other half were selling it to them. At the end of most days, the pension fund had the same number of shares of United Widget, but was out the transaction costs. Once a year, the three to five money managers who held the stock on behalf of the pension fund on the record date received proxies. In the year when United Widget was the target of a hostile takeover attempt by International Products, some of them voted with management and some voted with the acquirer.

*Is it consistent with fiduciary obligation for the pension manager to permit this activity? Is it relevant that the fund's assets also included stock in International Products that was likely to decline after the acquisition? How does a fiduciary examine the proposed transaction when it is a stockholder in both United Widget and International Products?*

# Case in point: When is the employee stock plan obligated to step in or sell?

In theory, an ESOP or other employee stock ownership plan will make employees feel like owners, and that will be good for them, for the company, and for the non-employee shareholders. But what happens when things go wrong? As discussed in the Stone & Webster and Carter Hawley Hale case studies, when the employer company gets into difficulties, this can put the trustee (who is the employer or someone selected by the employer) into a very difficult situation. We can agree that theoretically at some point a significant block holder who is a fiduciary for the employees must either sell the stock (though at that point the stock is by definition depressed, so the transaction costs are significant) or step in to make changes in management or the board. But the hard part is knowing when that should happen and the hardest part is finding a trustee who is willing and able to do so. In early 2003, as United Airlines struggled in bankruptcy, a group of employees filed suit against the employee stock plan, which held 55 percent of the company's stock. They alleged their investment managers cost them billions by holding on to United stock as it plummeted.

The suit is reminiscent of the famous line from the Pogo comic strip: "We have met the enemy and he is us." The complaint alleges the plan's all-employee committee "was not objective in its decision" to keep the plan exclusively invested in United stock as it went into decline.

# Case in point: Who owns Hershey?

Hershey Candy was begun by a benevolent man named Milton Hershey, whose progressive views kept all of the employees on the payroll throughout the Depression. Hershey and his company practiced "welfare capitalism." The company was a pioneer in fields like occupational safety and employee benefits. The town of Hershey, Pennsylvania, with its chocolate kiss-shaped street lamps, is a reflection of his values. Hershey was deeply committed to helping orphans, and he established a school for them in Hershey. He gave the foundation that runs the school $60 million in 1918. With that as a foundation, the school expanded and became very successful, making tuition-free education and support services available to orphan boys, and then later on to poor children of both genders.

In 2002, the school's endowment was $5.9 billion, about 58.6 percent in Hershey's stock. The trustees, recognizing that their fiduciary duty was not to the Hershey Candy company but to the school and its students, decided that they needed more diversification. While this was an entirely prudent, perhaps even overdue conclusion, the announcement caused an uproar. If the foundation wanted to diversify, control would be outside of sympathetic private hands for the first time. The company could end up being sold to the highest bidder, perhaps even a non-US company like Nestlé. The impact on the town of Hershey, where most of the residents work for the company or affiliated entities, would be devastating.

The State of Pennsylvania went to court to stop the sale and got a preliminary favorable ruling. The foundation chose not to appeal. According to *Slate Magazine*'s Daniel Gross, "because Pennsylvania officials, acting on the behest of local politicians, substituted their own judgment for that of shareholders and executives, the deal is off. As a result, Hershey's stock fell today and closed at about 65. The poor kids who attend the Hershey School just lost $24 per share, or about $1 billion."

*Compare the involvement of similar foundations established by founders of major corporations, like the Hewlett and Packard Foundation's opposition to the HP–Compaq merger and the foundation that controlled Reader's Digest. How do the conflicts these relationships raise compare to the block holdings of employee stock plan and pension fund investments in employer stock?*

Every "improvement" in the system for owning stock was designed to make it easier to trade. No one seemed to notice or care that each of these "improvements" also made it harder to exercise classic ownership rights. These rights had once been thought of as equal to the right to buy and sell freely in the "invisible hand" that kept the marketplace operating efficiently.

Shareholders' ability to perform what James Willard Hurst has called "their legendary function" of monitoring has been substantially eroded. There are two primary reasons for this. First, as noted by Berle and Means, sheer numbers rob shareholders of power. Management has every incentive to increase the number of holders.[36] It increases available capital and helps transferability by keeping the prices of individual shares comparatively low.[37]

Second, increasing the number of shares has another significant advantage for corporate management: it reduces the incentive and ability of each shareholder to gather information and monitor effectively. Even the $250 million investment in General Motors by the largest equity investor in the United States, the California Public Employees' Retirement System, is not of much significance in a company with a market value of more than $30 billion. When the number of shareholders is in the hundreds of thousands – even the millions – and each of those holds stock in a number of companies, no single shareholder can monitor effectively. How much monitoring is worth the effort when your investment (and liability) is limited and when even if you did understand the issues, there was nothing you could do about them?

Professor Melvin Aron Eisenberg writes of the "limits of shareholder consent,"[38] noting that "under current law and practice, shareholder consent to rules proposed by top managers in publicly held corporations may be either nominal, tainted by a conflict of interest, coerced, or impoverished."[39] In Eisenberg's view, shareholder consent is "nominal" when (as permitted under proxy rules) the shareholder does not vote at all and management votes on his behalf, or shares held by the broker or broker's depository are voted with no direction from the beneficial owner. Shareholder consent is "tainted" by a conflict of interest when an institutional investor is pressured to vote in favor of a management proposal it would otherwise oppose, due to commercial ties to the company management (see the cases in point on Boothbay Harbor, R.P. Scherer, Citicorp, and Deutsche Asset Management).

Shareholder consent is "coerced" when, for example, management ties an action that is attractive to shareholders, like a special dividend, to passage of a provision that may be contrary to their interests. For instance, in 1989, shareholders of Ramada Inc. were asked to approve a package of anti-takeover measures, bundled with a generous cash payment.[40] And shareholder consent is "impoverished" when its choices are limited by self-interested managers. "[F]or example, shareholders may vote for a rule proposed by management even though they would prefer a different rule, because the proposed rule is better than the rule it replaces and management's control over the agenda effectively limits the shareholders' choice to the existing rule or the proposed rule."[41] This is a reflection of management's vastly superior access to the proxy, both procedurally (in terms of resources) and substantively (in terms of appropriate subject matter). Eisenberg has described shareholders as "disenfranchised."

The disenfranchisement of the modern shareholder has been developing for over a century, but it took the events of the last two decades to bring it to public attention. In the 1980s, the takeover era itself was a symptom of the problems created by the failure to link ownership and control. As we describe below in more detail, the abuses of shareholders by both managers and raiders made it clear that there was not enough accountability to shareholders, and that this lack of accountability was detrimental to the competitiveness and vitality of American companies. But, as noted above, the fact that the disconnect was inadvertent was irrelevant to one important fact – it was convenient, even ideal, for those whom it most benefited. When efforts to reconnect ownership and control began in the mid-1980s, shareholders found that the very problem of their inability to act made it all but impossible to regain their ability to hold corporate management accountable, especially when corporate management had no interest in changing a system that was working very well from their perspective.

As a result, Harvard professor Michael Jensen predicted, in *The End of the Public Corporation*, that the "ownerless" modern venture without the discipline of accountability would inevitably be unable to compete. He saw the leveraged buyouts that had reconnected management and ownership at the end of the 1980s as the model for the future.

## FRACTIONATED OWNERSHIP

In addition to the separation of ownership and control, there are several other respects in which share ownership in the modern corporation differs from traditional notions of ownership.

- *Numerical.* There are so many owners of the largest American corporations that it makes little sense to consider any one of them an "owner" in the sense of an individual with an economic interest in being informed about and involved in corporate affairs.
- *Legal.* The splitting of ownership between a legal title holder (the trustee) and beneficial owners (trust beneficiaries of all kinds, including pensioners and mutual fund participants) has created a welter of separate interests. The relationships between fiduciary and beneficiary are usually stipulated by a specific governing law. Trustees can be individuals or special-purpose corporations; beneficiaries can be individuals or classes of individuals, whose identities may not be known for many years.
- *Functional.* "It has often been said that the owner of a horse is responsible. If the horse lives he must feed it. If the horse dies he must bury it. No such responsibility attaches to a share of stock."[42]

    A corporate shareholder owns a share certificate, but this piece of paper does not accord him the rights and responsibilities traditionally associated with ownership. Berle and Means observe that, "Most important of all, the position of ownership has changed from that of an active to that of a passive agent. In place of actual physical properties over which the owner could exercise direction and for which he was responsible, the owner now holds a piece of paper representing a set of rights and expectation with respect to an enterprise. But over the enterprise and over the physical property – the instruments of production – in which he has an interest, the owner has little control. At the same time he bears no responsibility with respect to the enterprise or its physical property."[43]
- *Personal.* "The spiritual values that formerly went with ownership have been separated from it. Physical property capable of being shaped by its *owner* could bring to him direct satisfaction apart from the income it yielded in more concrete form. It represented an extension of his own personality."[44]

# Case in point: Junior invests in Boothbay Harbor

The traditional relationship between entitlement to receive the benefits from a venture and responsibility for its impact on society was charmingly put in the early twentieth century, as a father advises his son in *Main Street and Wall Street*, written in 1926:

Now, Junior, before you go to college I want to give you my investment in the Boothbay Harbor Electric Light Co. This concern serves our old neighbors and friends, and I want you to feel a continuing interest in, and a responsibility for, our share in this local enterprise. If properly managed it should be a benefit to this community; and it will yield you an income to be applied to your education through the next few years. But you must never forget that you are partly responsible for this undertaking. Our family had a hand in starting it. That responsibility is an inseparable part of your ownership. I read something the other day, in an opinion by Justice Brandeis of the US Supreme Court, which bears this out: "There is no such thing to my mind . . . as an innocent stockholder. He may be innocent in fact, but socially he cannot be held innocent. He accepts the benefits of the system. It is his business and his obligation to see that those who represent him carry out a policy which is consistent with the public welfare." He is right in that. This accountability for wealth underlies and justifies the whole institution of private property upon which the government of our great country is founded.[45]

Contrast Junior and his father with today's shareholder, who will be represented by Junior's son Trip, now an employee of Widget Co., a mid-sized manufacturing company with a "defined-benefit" pension plan. That means that, no matter what he puts in before he retires, once he does, he is guaranteed a set retirement check every month. Let's say that Trip has been with the company for 20 years, with about another 15 to go before retirement, keeping in mind that his office mates, one who just started work and one who is five years from retirement, might have very different sets of priorities. Trip and his colleagues are a far cry from Junior, who had a "sense of responsibility" for the companies he invests in; indeed, Trip could not tell you what stocks he holds, bought by several investment managers who are hired by the named fiduciary designated by the corporate chairman. Trip "owns" a minuscule fraction of perhaps thousands of publicly traded companies. He has not only no say about which securities are purchased on his behalf; he doesn't even find out until after the fact, sometimes not even then. Between Junior and Boothbay there was a reliable system of communication. Between Trip and Boothbay there is an investment manager, a custodian, a trustee, a named fiduciary, and the CEO of Trip's employer, Widget Co.

Meanwhile, Trip and the other employees whose pension money is invested really have no legally enforceable interest with respect to a particular holding of the plan. Their only right is to be paid the promised benefits. Whether that comes from stocks, bonds, or gold bullion is irrelevant to them. Trip's only right is to require that the trustee act loyally and competently in his interest. That could be complicated. The trustee, usually a bank, may have business relationships that create uncomfortable conflicts, putting it in a situation quite different from Junior's. For example, the trustee will be voting stock in the same companies it makes loans to or handles payrolls for. There have been a number of reports of cases where a trustee attempting to vote against corporate management was stopped by his own management.[46] Why fight it? After all, the shareholder has no economic interest whatsoever in the quality of his voting decision, beyond avoiding liability. No enforcement action has ever been brought and no damages have ever been awarded for breach of duty in voting proxies. Trustees earn no incentive compensation, no matter how much energy and skill they devote to ownership responsibilities.[47] And, crucially, the corporation knows how the trustee votes, while Trip has no idea. The trustee has nothing to lose, and everything to gain, from routine votes with management. Even if the trustee wanted to view its ownership responsibility more energetically, it would be all but impossible as a practical matter due to further inhibitions to shareholder activism arising out of the problems of "collective action" and "free riding," the pervasive problem of conflict of interest by institutional trustees, the legal obstacles imposed by the federal "proxy rules" and state law and state court acquiescence to management entrenchment – all described later in substantial detail.

Meanwhile, at the top of the chain, the CEO's interest in the investment in Boothbay is also quite different from Trip's or Junior's. His interest is, first and foremost, being able to pay Trip his "defined benefit" when he retires, with a minimum of contribution by Widget Co. and, probably, a minimum involvement of his own time – after all, pension benefits don't have much to do with the products or sales of the company. So the CEO will push the investment managers to provide results (while he decries the "short-term perspective" of investors with other CEOs). If he is involved, he is faced with what has been called "ERISA's Fundamental Contradiction."[48] On one hand, as a corporate manager, he would tend to favor provisions that, on the other hand, as a shareholder or director, he might find unduly protective of management.

> In the 1920s, Trip's father Junior, and his grandfather, who spoke of Boothbay Harbor with such proprietary interest, felt a real connection to the company they invested in. In the 1990s, the trustee, the custodian, the investment managers, and the CEO stand between Boothbay and Trip.
>
> *Do any of these people "feel a continuing interest in, and a responsibility for, our share in this local enterprise"? Are any of them equipped, able, or even interested in the right or responsibility of providing overall direction for the company?*
> *Given the changed nature of stock ownership today, are shareholders "failed owners"? If so, are they entitled to the benefit of having their property protected by the government? [See the quotation from Adam Smith about the "invisible hand" at the beginning of this chapter.]*

We need to keep in mind that fractionalization of ownership characteristics, although not requested by owners, has possibly served to enrich them by decreasing their accountability for corporate externalities. This may be accounted for in the value placed on the company by the marketplace – there may be a "bad governance" discount.[49] If so, this creates the basis for an obligation for fiduciary shareholders to pull together the fractions of ownership and restore value for their beneficiaries.

Perhaps instead of speaking of "failed owners," we should speak of "vestigial owners," or even "non-owners." It is important to consider the implications of corporations without owners. Bayless Manning, former dean of Yale Law School, describes the consequences:

> Assume a large modern corporation similar to its typical commercial counterpart in all respects but two. First, the model abandons the *a priori* legal conclusion that the shareholders "own the corporation" and substitutes the more restricted conception that the only thing they "own" is their shares of stock. Second, the shareholder in this model corporation has no voting rights. His position would be quite similar to that of a voting trust certificate-holder with all economic rights in the deposited stock but no power to elect or replace the trustees by vote . . . [A]s a broad generalization for use in thinking about the problems of power distribution within the publicly held corporation, the suggested model offers a much better guide than the unarticulated model we have been following – the homespun Jeffersonian image of the small business owned and operated by sturdy freeholders. Accepted as a valid working tool, the model points to the likely course of tomorrow's law governing control of the big corporation. The four areas of legal change suggested by it and outlined earlier combine to form a unified general pattern: franker acceptance that centralized managerial control is necessary, a fact and here to stay; less wishful pretense that the shareholders' vote is or can be an effective restraint; emphasis upon disclosure, free exit and transfer as the shareholder's principal protection; and development of new and extrinsic mechanics to supervise management dealings in corporate funds for non-business purposes and for itself.[50]

Almost 50 years later, Manning's description seems to be an accurate description of today's corporations. Without accountability to shareholder–owners, there is no settled notion of "new and extrinsic" mechanics to assure the accountability of management either to shareholders or to society as a whole. There is a fair measure of agreement that ownership is necessary, but there has been little consensus on how to make it meaningful or indeed how to pinpoint it. *Where are the owners?*

# THE SEPARATION OF OWNERSHIP AND CONTROL PART 2: THE TAKEOVER ERA

As explained above, one of the essential rights of ownership is the right to transfer ownership to someone else. Indeed, in making transferability a priority, owners of common stock were willing, for most of this century, to relinquish some of the other rights of ownership. In order for the stock to be freely transferable, shareholders had to have limited liability and shares had to trade at a fairly low rate. Both conditions loosened the connection between ownership and control. In order to have limited liability, shareholders had to give up control over any but the most basic corporate decisions. In order to keep trading prices low enough to ensure liquidity, shareholders had to allow their companies to issue millions of shares of stock, making it almost impossible for any one investor to hold a meaningful stake. The result was the "Wall Street Rule." Recognizing that transferability was the only real right the shareholder had, this approach provided that investors should "vote with management or sell the shares." The theory was that shareholders could send a powerful message to a company's management by selling out, ideally in enough of a block to depress the share value. Ultimately, the theory continues, the stock price would fall enough to make the company an attractive takeover target. This risk would then keep management acting in the interest of shareholders.[51] As Edward Jay Epstein points out,

[T]his economic theory requires more than a shareholder being free to sell his holdings to another investor. Merely selling shares is analogous to political refugees leaving a dictatorship by "voting with their feet." While it may solve their personal problem, it does not end, or necessarily even weaken, the dictatorship – though it might weaken the economy. Similarly, just the exchange of one powerless shareholder for another in a corporation, while it may lessen the market price of shares, will not dislodge management – or even threaten it. On the contrary, if dissident shareholders leave, it may even bring about further entrenchment of management – especially if management can pass new bylaws in the interim.

This theory works if, and only if, shareholders can sell their shares eventually to an investor who has the power to take over the company – and fire the ruling board of directors.[52]

A society of sheep must in time beget a government of wolves. *Bertrand de Jouvenel*

In the 1980s, the seismic impact of takeovers, junk bonds, and the growth of institutional investors jolted every aspect of the corporate structure down to its tectonic plates. Perhaps the most unexpected shift was the way the musty, academic question of "corporate governance" became the focus of intense debate. Once exclusively the province of scholars and theorists, the arcane vocabulary of governance was re-forged as each of the corporation's component groups blew cobwebs off the antique terminology and employed it to redefine its role and that of the corporation.

But one reason the debate had become so tangential to the reality of politics and business was that most of the theories about corporate governance bore little relation to the reality. Indeed, the theories assumed the status, and the role, of myth. And myth has both advantages and disadvantages as the basis for debate. The theory was that corporations were managed by officers, under a system of checks and balances provided by the board of directors and the shareholders. All three groups, acting in their self-interest, would maximize profit within the confines of the legal system, and all three groups would benefit, as would society as a whole, including the groups now termed "stakeholders" – employees, customers, suppliers, and the community. The reality was that there was no system of checks. Corporate governance had got completely out of balance.

That lack of balance was revealed by the collision of two developments of the 1980s, both the collateral and unanticipated results of another set of priorities. The first was the rise of the institutional investor. Even those who worked hardest for the passage of the Employee Retirement Income Security Act (ERISA) of 1974 never anticipated that in less than 20 years the funds subject to its standards would hold a third of the stock of American companies. Institutional holdings mushroomed in the 1970s and 1980s, creating a category of investor that was big, smart, and obligated as a fiduciary to exercise shareholder ownership rights if it was "prudent" and "for the exclusive purpose" of protecting the interests of pension plan participants to do so.

Meanwhile, the takeover era was giving shareholders plenty to react to. Both raiders and management took advantage of shareholder disenfranchisement and there were extraordinary abuses, which we will discuss below. All of a sudden proxy cards asked for more than approval of the auditors and the management slate of directors. The value of ownership rights became clear just as for the first time there emerged a group of owners sophisticated enough to understand them, obligated enough as fiduciaries to exercise them, and big enough that, when they did exercise them, they made a real difference. But it took them a while to do so, and during that time corporate boards and managers were able to diminish further the value of share ownership. We will come back to this issue when we discuss the role of the board as fiduciary in the next chapter, but will discuss its impact on ownership here.

As mentioned above, most of the technology and systems developed for the stock market were designed with liquidity and transferability as the primary goal. Transferability has been so important, in fact, that the market has willingly, if inadvertently, relinquished many of the other rights of ownership in order to preserve it. In the early days, stock certificates were like checks or like other kinds of property; you transferred stock by giving someone the actual certificate. As recently as the early 1950s, at least five documents were necessary for each transfer of stock, all pinned together with great ceremony by a man who worked behind a cage in the front of the office. This system worked, briefly. In the summer of 1950, for example, the market never traded over 750,000 shares in a day.

The system, however, was inadequate for the volume that would come. It was cumbersome, and too invasive of shareholder privacy. In the late 1980s, as policy-makers debated "circuit breakers" to slow down or even stop trading (as a way of preventing a stock market crash like the 500-point drop in October of 1987), the New York Stock Exchange was trading upwards of 290 million shares a day.

Universal transferability also critically changed the nature of the shareholders' relationship to the corporate structure. As an investor, the stockholder had to look to corporate performance for protection and enhancement of his investment; he had to consider the efficacy of capital investments, and he was directly influenced by how the corporation conducted itself and how society perceived that conduct. In the absence of readily available "exit," or sale, the traditional shareholder used "voice," or ownership rights.[53] "[T]he corporation with transferable shares converted the underlying long-term risk of a very large amount of capital into a short-term risk of small amounts of capital. Because marketable corporate shares were readily saleable at prices quoted daily (or more often), their owners were not tied to the enterprise for the life of its capital equipment, but could pocket their gains or cut their losses whenever they judged it advisable. *Marketable shares converted the proprietor's long-term risk to the investor's short-term risk . . ."*[54] The increased number of shares and ease of transferability acted as a vicious circle because the inability to use "voice" to influence corporate activity made "exit" the only option.

It is virtually impossible to argue that effective monitoring is cost-effective for investors whose profit is principally derived from buying and selling in the short term. The prospect of buying low and selling high is so beguiling that a lucrative industry of "active money management" has flourished, notwithstanding the reality that institutional investors are the market and, therefore, cannot hope to beat its performance. As Charles D. Ellis, one-time President of the Institute of Chartered Financial Analysts, noted: "Investment management, as traditionally practiced, is based on a single basic belief: Professional investment managers *can* beat the market. That premise appears to be false, particularly for the very large institutions that manage most of the assets of most trusts, pension funds, and endowments, because their institutions have effectively become the market."[55] William Fouse, chairman of Mellon Capital Management, says that pension fund management is "like monkeys trading bananas in trees." As he observed in an interview with *Forbes* writer Dyan Machan, "The money managers end up with a lot of the bananas."[56] The efforts by pension fund fiduciaries to find active money managers who can beat the market over time have been unsuccessful. Most pension funds give their money to whichever manager did well the previous year, and given the statistical "regression to the mean," the odds are that that manager will not do as well in the future.

An alternative strategy is "indexing," in which a fund buys every stock in a given index, such as the S&P 500. The holdings are held, not traded, so the fund neither beats the market nor under-performs it – but replicates it. A *Forbes* headline summed up the simplicity of such a strategy: "Don't Just Do Something, Sit There."[57]

For example, the S&P 500 Index beat 89.9 percent of all US stock funds in 1997. And that number goes over 99 percent when you measure the performance over several years.

Investment decisions are often based on recommendations by consultants. But consultants rarely recommend indexing. "[I]t would put them out of business if everyone did it. Pension funds pay consultants for objective advice on which funds to hire, but the same consultants charge managers fees for measuring the managers' performance . . . There are plenty of stories about managers who are recommended by the consultants on the grounds that the managers pay the consultants the biggest fees."[58] A rare contrarian exception is the General Mills pension fund, which has dared to "break entirely out of the cycle . . . Instead of firing the stock picker who happens to be performing below the mean in a given year, General Mills gives him more money, taking from the highest-ranked performer." As a result, General Mills has produced one of the best long-term records, with 17 percent annualized equity return over the 15 years ending in 1992.[59] It is therefore not surprising that a study of 135 funds with $700 billion in assets, concluded that "There was no positive correlation between performance and money spent on staff, managers, and other high-priced advice to get it."[60] Of course every investor, whether individual or institutional, hopes that it can be the exception and can beat the averages. This is reminiscent of the joke about the poker player's comment, "If we all play well, we can all make money." This hope, rather than any statistical evidence, accounts in part for the change in the way shareholders see themselves today: no longer as an owner but as a speculator.

Of course another of the incentives for a minimal sense of ownership by money managers is short-term self-interest. Active trading produces immediate transaction costs. Monitoring involves the commitment of resources for gains that are not immediately quantifiable, with the possible exception of shareholders who are large enough and aggressive enough to underwrite contests for control. In the longer term, this has involved a high price for the business system as whole.

## WAKING THE SLEEPING GIANT

Transferability has had consequences for corporations as well. It means that the interests of shareholders and managers are based on incompatible premises. The investor will want to sell at the first sign that the stock may have reached its trading peak, whereas the manager wants stable, long-term investors. The American corporate system was initially based on the permanence of investor capital. But while the capital may have remained in place, the owners kept changing. Unintentionally, the growth of the institutional investors may have served to reintroduce stability in stock ownership. But that could not happen until the institutional investors were shocked into activism by the abuses of the takeover era.

An essential part of the theoretical underpinning for the market was the notion that shareholders should sell to each other, and as often as possible keep the markets "efficient." During the takeover era, it became clear that, though the system was designed to promote transferability above all, there was one kind of transfer that the system would not tolerate: the transfer of power from one group to another. Despite a strong theoretical commitment to "the market for corporate control," as soon as the means to create a genuine market were developed, corporations, lawyers, and legislators – even judges – worked quickly to obliterate it.

One unjustifiable practice was called a "two-tier tender offer." A two-tier offer was used to accomplish what was then the largest non-oil takeover in history, R.J. Reynolds's $4.5 billion acquisition of Nabisco in 1985. In such a deal, a buyer would offer, for example, $10 per share over the market price to everyone who tendered – until 51 percent had been received. The last 49 percent to line up would be left, like Oliver Twist, asking for more. What they would get would be thinner than Oliver's gruel – such as notes for the tender not payable for 15 years. For reasons that will become clear later in this chapter, institutional investors were invariably at the front of the line in such offers – as fiduciaries, they couldn't refuse an offer of $10 now rather than $10 in 15 years.

# Case in point: One share, one vote

One of the most important (and valuable) aspects of stock ownership is the right to vote in proportion to one's ownership. The holder of 100 shares has ten times as much to say about the issues put to a vote of the shareholders as the holder of ten shares. In the mid-1980s, during the takeover era, when it seemed that every company had a permanent "for sale" sign, this system was seen as dangerous to managements trying to protect themselves (and, in some cases, their shareholders). So they decided to change the rules to make it easier for them to take away voting rights through an "exchange offer" that was something like the offer in Aladdin to trade new lamps for old. In that story, the magic in the old lamp was a genie; in this story the magic in the old stock certificate was the vote. This story is important because it raises two questions relating to ownership: *How valuable is a vote that can be bought back (for less than its true value) by the management whose accountability the vote is supposed to ensure? How meaningful is the accountability of management when management can change the rules of accountability themselves?*

In 1986, the New York Stock Exchange (NYSE) asked the Securities and Exchange Commission (SEC) for permission to drop its long-time requirement that companies listed on the NYSE have stock that gave each shareholder one vote per share.[61] One share, one vote is a shorthand reference to a form of capitalization in which the amount of investment and the amount of voting power are exactly proportional. In a dual or multiple class system, by contrast, they are not. Holders of less than 1 percent of the invested capital can, none the less, attain, through their specially classified shares, over 50 percent of the voting authority.

Under the unique system governing the securities markets, the NYSE, like the other exchanges, is a "self-regulatory organization."[62] This means that it has the authority to issues its own rules, subject to the approval of the SEC. Once they get that approval, the rules have the force of law. The SEC had always approved the exchanges' submissions as a matter of routine, mostly because the rules were routine, but this one was different.

In testimony before Congress, NYSE chairman John J. Phelan said, just months before proposing to rescind the one-share, one-vote rule, "We have consistently stated – and we repeat now – that the NYSE continues to favor the standard which we alone applied over the past 60 years: the standard of 'one share, one vote'." Phelan also admitted, in earlier testimony presented shortly before the NYSE first asked for permission to rescind the rule, that the one-share, one-vote rule was "good for its listed companies, good for their shareholders, and good for this country . . . In an ideal world, most people would probably want it to be retained." *Then why were they trying to get rid of it?* The other exchanges allowed companies to issue stock with less than one vote per share, though each had its own rules prescribing how it could be done. But most companies had only one class of stock. Traditionally, dual-class voting structures were only for companies that were traditionally family-run, like Wang and the *Washington Post*. These companies wanted access to capital without relinquishing control, and they went public with dual classes of voting stock. Investors bought in, knowing what they were getting, and paying a price that reflected their reduced voting power.

But growing concerns about institutional shareholder involvement and the prospect of real accountability led corporate management to seek ways to disenfranchise shareholders, and dual-class stock given to shareholders through a coercive exchange offer seemed like the perfect answer. The NYSE was concerned that its rule imposed a competitive disadvantage, and that its listed companies would flee to the other exchanges, which had more liberal rules. The pressure to rescind the rule came from companies who wanted to prevent takeovers by essentially taking their companies private without having to pay the full price. Chairman Phelan described the problem in his testimony: "In response to hostile takeovers, a small but growing number of listed companies have asked their shareholders to approve changes in voting rights that would, directly or indirectly, give management greater control. In some instances, this has involved creating a second class of common stock having multiple votes per share . . ."[63] The SEC was unsuccessful in trying to get all of the exchanges to agree to a consistent standard. So, despite its own misgivings, the NYSE asked the SEC to approve its abandonment of the one-share, one-vote rule. All that was needed was for the SEC to do what it has always done, approve without question the NYSE proposal.

Instead, in 1987, the SEC decided to use for the first time the authority granted to it by Congress in 1975 to impose a standard on the exchanges. This was successfully challenged in court by the Business Roundtable in the DC Circuit Court of Appeals. While the court never questioned the SEC's finding that exchange offers were coercive, it found that the rule-making exceeded the SEC's authority. The NYSE, though, voluntarily adopted the rule, and it has been in place ever since. The Business Roundtable had won the battle, but lost the war.[64] (At this writing, there is again a pending proposal to rescind the rule, however, so the war may not yet be over.)

The issue was not really whether companies could issue stock with disparate voting rights. Limited voting stock was never prohibited – preferred stock, for example, is often issued without voting rights. The issue was how that limited voting stock could be offered. What made the NYSE proposal controversial was that it allowed "exchange offers," where the company asked a shareholder to exchange stock with full voting rights for stock with lesser voting rights, usually with a "sweetener," such as a higher premium. Extensive testimony presented to the SEC in 1986–7 showed that these offers are coercive, meaning that the benefits to the individual will make it impossible to refuse the offer, even though the group as a whole will suffer. (See discussion of the prisoner's dilemma and of two-tier offers below.)

In other words, the offer could be framed in such a way that shareholders would accept, even though it was contrary to their interests. So the debate over the one-share, one-vote proposal was really about what procedural protections must be in place to ensure that limited voting stock is offered to shareholders in a way that enables them to make a fair and economically sound choice.

The shareholders argued that corporate efficiency and legitimacy depends on the managers who are, in effect, the agents of shareholder principals. To the extent that the "agency costs" of managers increase, productivity and innovation will decline. In an important analysis published in the *Journal of Law and Economics*, for example, Frank Easterbrook and Daniel Fischel argued that the separation of residual claims from voting power will always create "agency costs" that contribute to substantial inefficiencies in corporate oversight. They found that the one-share, one-vote rule ensures that no unnecessary agency costs will be created.[65] They also presented testimony that said that, as the shareholder loses even the theoretical ability to control corporations by holding their managers to account, those corporations will cease to pay attention to the need to maximize profits. Companies will become bloated and inefficient, causing dislocation in supply and demand, and performance will drop. Furthermore, if managers cannot be held responsible for meeting clear, public standards of performance such as profits, sales, or growth, then their focus of attention will shift from outside to inside the corporation. Managers will place a higher value on maintaining good relations with employees, suppliers, or local communities than on increasing market share through improved products or services. Inevitably, the primary goal of the corporation will become self-perpetuation, and the result will be a stifling level of bureaucracy.

The SEC was persuaded that the process by which shareholders are presented with a proposal for recapitalization into dual classes of voting stock is inherently coercive. Apparent efforts to provide equal value for each choice backfire, in fact, increasing the coercive character of the recapitalization. Easterbrook and Fischel envision the possibility of a market in votes: "The collective choice problem would exert a strong influence over the market price of votes. Because no voter expects to influence the outcome of the election, he would sell the vote (which to him is unimportant) for less than the expected dilution of his equity interest. He would reason that if he did not sell, others would: he would then lose on the equity side but get nothing for the vote . . . Thus, the legal rules tying votes to shares increase the efficiency of corporate organization." By enacting provisions that skew the voting power of different classes of stock and thereby protecting directors and officers from removal, management tends to make itself self-perpetuating at the expense of shareholders.

Giving any shareholders the opportunity to dilute or relinquish their votes puts them on the horns of a dilemma. Harvard Business School professor Richard Ruback has demonstrated that "[t]he terms of the dual class re-capitalization can be structured to compel individual outside shareholders to exchange even though the outside shareholders, acting *collectively*, would choose not to exchange . . ." (emphasis in original). Therefore, he reasons that "the rational choices by individual outside shareholders lead to an outcome that harms the outside shareholders." In other words, when the issue of limited voting rights is presented to shareholders, a rational, fiscally optimal choice made by an individual may, when made by enough individuals to carry the resolution, result in significant reduction in value of the holdings of all of them.

This was not the first time the one-share, one-vote issue caused controversy. This topic has played a colorful and dramatic role in American financial history. On October 28, 1925, William Z. Ripley, a Harvard University professor of political economy, warned: "the new stock, thus sold, is entirely bereft of any voting powers, except in case of actual or impending bankruptcy. General stockholders, to be sure, have always been inert, delegating most of their powers of election. But at worst they might always be stimulated to assist themselves, and, in any event, they all fared alike as respects profits or losses." In his book, *Main Street and Wall Street*, Ripley described particularly outrageous examples of abusive practices. In one, Industrial Rayon issued 600,000 shares of common stock. Only 2,000 carried voting rights. The attention Ripley drew to this kind of disparity touched off a firestorm in the public consciousness and one share, one vote became standard capitalization for the most prominent American industrial companies.[66] Disastrous experience in the 1920s with public utility companies and investment companies who consolidated control in a few voting shares, held by managers, led to the enactment of legislation to impose the one-share, one-vote rule on those companies.[67] The Public Utility Holding Company Act was a response to a 78-volume report prepared by the Federal Trade Commission (FTC). In the report, the FTC noted:

> Instead of the corporation on one side and the public, on whom it will depend for trade and revenue, on the other, as was the case originally, we have a third party of minority ownership but with management and control which may be likened to absentee landlordism. Obviously, whenever this managerial group becomes swayed with lust for power and greed for excessive profits, the many other stockholders are treated as having few, if any, rights. In many instances, such managerial groups have failed to act as trustees for their corporations and other stockholders, as in equity they are supposed to do.

The Investment Company Act of 1940 is also especially relevant here. The legislative history shows that it was enacted in response to three factors: the large proportion of investors involved (one in ten investors was a participant in an investment company, according to the SEC staff report to Congress), the serious discrepancy between equity interest and voting rights, and the consequent conflicts of interest between the senior and junior shareholders. The SEC, using its 1940

Act rulemaking and enforcement authority, found that multiple classes of stock with divergent voting rights were a major factor in the corruption and abuse prevalent in the investment industry in the 1940s. Section 18 of the act, applying one share, one vote to investment companies, was adopted in response. As Arthur Levitt, then chairman of the American Stock Exchange, and currently the chairman of the Securities and Exchange Commission, noted in 1987:

> One of the historical sources of the New York Stock Exchange rule against non-voting stock lay in the use of such shares in the public utility industry in the 1920s: non-voting stock was a key device that underlay the pyramiding of personal control in that industry and that ultimately led to collapse, to a tragic loss of public confidence in our capital markets. and to direct Federal regulation in the form of the Public Utility Holding Company Act.[68]
>
> These laws were based on the policy that management must be made accountable to shareholders who can vote them out. The one share, one vote standard was based on compelling evidence of the evils of pyramiding and otherwise separating management from the need to account to ownership. It was considered useful and efficient until the takeover era raised the specter that shareholders might be able to insist on meaningful accountability. Then the NYSE was quick to jettison it; or at least to try to.

## A FRAMEWORK FOR PARTICIPATION

The regulatory framework governing the issuance and trading of public securities and the functioning of exchanges was almost entirely set up by two landmark statutes of the New Deal era. Congress passed the 1933 Securities Act and the 1934 Securities and Exchange Act after exhaustive debate and in response to overwhelming evidence of mismanagement, deception and outright fraud during the stock market boom of the late 1920s. In the Public Utility Holding Company Act of 1935 and the Investment Company Act of 1940, multiple classes of common stock with differing voting characteristics were flatly prohibited for the affected companies. Rather than attempt with industrial companies to remedy specific mistakes or abuses, lawmakers attempted a far more difficult task; they tried to set up a process of corporate accountability – an impartial set of rules preserving the widest possible latitude for shareholders to protect their financial interests. In searching for a reliable and familiar model, they turned to America's own traditions of political accountability.

Shareholders were seen as voters, boards of directors as elected representatives, proxy solicitations as election campaigns, corporate charters and bylaws as constitutions and amendments. Just as political democracy acted to guarantee the legitimacy of governmental or public power, the theory went, so corporate democracy would control – and therefore legitimate – the otherwise uncontrollable growth of power in the hands of private individuals. Underpinning that corporate democracy, as universal franchise underpinned its political counterpart, was the principle of one share, one vote.

## OWNERSHIP AND RESPONSIBILITY

*What is the accountability of the shareholders themselves? Shareholders reap the rewards from corporate performance. What about the risks? While one of the fundamental attributes of common stock is limited liability, shouldn't they bear some responsibility for a corporation's impact on society? In other words, how limited should the liability be?*

## No innocent shareholder

Supreme Court Justice Louis D. Brandeis, who had a distinguished legal career defending both individual and public rights in large corporations, wrote passionately about the moral aspects of ownership of shares. His comments, quoted in part in the Boothbay Harbor case above, are a poignant reminder of how far modern stock ownership has strayed from its origins. They are as true today as when written almost a century ago.

To my mind there is no such thing as an innocent purchaser of stocks. It is entirely contrary, not only to our laws but to what ought to be our whole attitude toward investments, that the person who has a chance of profit by going into an enterprise, or the chance of getting a larger return than he could get on a perfectly safe mortgage or bond – that he should have the chance of gain without any responsibility. The idea of such persons being innocent in the sense of not letting them take the consequences of their acts is, to my mind, highly immoral and is bound to work out, if pursued, in very evil results to the community. When a person buys stock in any of those organizations of doubtful validity and of doubtful practices, he is not innocent; he is guilty constructively by law and should be deemed so by the community and held up to a responsibility; precisely to the same responsibility that the English owners of Irish estates have been held up, although it was their bailiffs who were guilty of nearly every oppression that attended the absentee landlordism of Ireland.

He may be innocent in fact, but socially he cannot be held innocent. He accepts the benefits of a system. It is his business and his obligation to see that those who represent him carry out a policy which is consistent with the public welfare. If he fails in that, so far as a stockholder fails in producing a result, that stockholder must be held absolutely responsible, except so far as it shall affirmatively appear that the stockholder endeavored to produce different results and was overridden by a majority. Stockholders cannot be innocent merely by reason of the fact that they have not personally had anything to do with the decision of questions arising in the conduct of the business. That they have personally selected gentlemen or given their proxies to select gentlemen of high standing in the community, is not sufficient to relieve them from responsibility.

From the standpoint of the community, the welfare of the community, and the welfare of the workers in the company, what is called a democratization in the ownership through the distribution of stock is positively harmful. Such a wide distribution of the stock dissipates altogether the responsibility of stockholders, particularly of those with five shares, ten shares, or fifty shares. They recognize that they have no influence in a corporation of hundreds of millions of dollars' capital. Consequently they consider it immaterial whatever they do, or omit to do. The net result is that the men who are in control of it become almost impossible to dislodge, unless there should be such a scandal in the corporation as to make it clearly necessary for the people on the outside to combine for self-protection. Probably even that necessity would not be sufficient to ensure a new management. That comes rarely except when those in control withdraw because they have been found guilty of reprehensible practices resulting in financial failure.

The wide distribution of stock, instead of being a blessing, constitutes, to my mind, one of the gravest dangers to the community. It is absentee landlordism of the worst kind. It is more dangerous, far more dangerous than the landlordism from which Ireland suffered. There, at all events, control was centered in a few individuals. By the distribution of nominal control among ten thousand or a hundred thousand stock-holders, there is developed a sense of absolute irresponsibility on the part of the person who holds the stock. The few men that are in position continue absolute control without any responsibility except that to their stockholders of continuing and possibly increasing the dividends.

That responsibility, while proper enough in a way, may lead to action directly contrary to the public interest.

Everyone should know that the denial of minority representation on boards of directors has resulted in the domination of most corporations by one or two men; and in practically banishing all criticism of the dominant power. And even where the board is not so dominated, there is too often that "harmonious co-operation" among directors which secures for each, in his own line, a due share of the corporation's favors.

Minority stockholders rarely have the knowledge of the facts which is essential to an effective appeal, whether it be made to the directors, to the whole body of stock-holders, or to the courts. Besides, the financial burden and the risks incident to any attempt of individual stockholders to interfere with an existing management is ordinar-ily prohibitive. Proceedings to avoid contracts with directors are, therefore, seldom brought, except after a radical change in the membership of the board. And radical changes in a board's membership are rare.

Protection to minority stockholders demands that corporations be prohibited abso-lutely from making contracts in which a director has a private interest, and that all such contracts be declared not voidable merely, but absolutely void.[69]

*And what of the institutional shareholders?* The extra overlay of fiduciary obligation requires them to act if it appears reasonably cost-effective to do so. While an individual is free to ignore both justice Brandeis' concern and his own wallet by ignoring his rights and responsibilities as corporation owner, institutions, as trustees, enjoy no such liberty. They are legally obligated to manage *all* trust assets, including those relating to ownership, prudently. And institutional investors, individually and collectively, are so large that it will be increasingly clear that oversight is not only cost-effective but a more reliable investment than many of the alternatives, including active trading.[70]

Yet it is indisputable that shareholders have largely been unable to exercise the res-ponsibilities of ownership of American corporations. In some respects, this "ownership failure" is due to the difference between tangible and intangible property.

> The capitalist process, by substituting a mere parcel of shares for the walls and the machines in a factory, takes the life out of the idea of property. It loosens the grip that once was so strong – the grip in the sense of the legal right and actual ability to do as one pleases with one's own; the grip also in the sense that the holder of the title loses the will to fight, economically, physically, politically, for "his" factory and his control over it, to die if necessary on its steps. And this evaporation of what we may term the material substance of property – its visible and touchable reality – affects not only the attitude of the holders but also that of the workmen and the public in general. Dematerialized, defunctionalized and absentee ownership does not impress and call forth moral allegi-ance as the vital form of property did. Eventually, there will be *nobody* left who really cares to stand for it – nobody within and nobody without the precincts of the big concerns.[71]

As discussed above, the liquidity of share ownership has diluted the notions of ownership and responsibility and created obstacles to their exercise.

The owner of non-liquid property is, in a sense, married to it. It contributes certain factors to his life, and enters into the fixed perspective of his landscape . . . At the same time, the quality of responsibility is always present. It is never possible, save with the irresponsible, the spendthrift, or the disabled, to decline decisions . . . So long, then, as a property requires contribution by its owner in order to yield service it will tend to be immobile. For property to be easily passed from hand to hand, the individual relation of the owner to it must necessarily play little part . . . Thus if property is to become a liquid it must not only be separated from responsibility but it must become impersonal, like Iago's purse: "'Twas mine, 'tis his, and has been slave to thousands."[72]

## TO SELL OR NOT TO SELL: THE PRISONER'S DILEMMA

The incentives driving shareholder actions can be compared to the famous logical problem called "the prisoner's dilemma." Two co-conspirators are captured and placed in separate cells by the police. They are each told that if neither confesses, they will both go to jail for five years. If one confesses, he will go free but the other will be sentenced to ten years. If both confess, both go to jail for eight years. Each must sit, unable to communicate with the other, and decide what to do. The dilemma is that an action that may benefit the individual making the choice (whether silence or confession) may have adverse consequences for the group (prison), whereas an action that benefits the group (silence) may have adverse consequences for the individual (prison, if the other confesses). This is also referred to as the problem of "collective choice" and the "free rider" problem. Any shareholder who wants to exercise ownership rights to influence a company must undertake all of the expenses, for only a pro rata share of the gains, if there are any. This problem has also produced one of this field's better oxymorons, by giving rise to the term for shareholders who deem it uneconomic to become involved in governance: "rational ignorance." This leads to votes against the investor's own interest in dual-class exchange offers, and sales against the investor's own interest in two-tier offers.

## WHO THE INSTITUTIONAL INVESTORS ARE

The largest groups of institutional shareholders had the following US equity holdings in 2001:[73]

|                                         | $ billion  |
| --------------------------------------- | ---------- |
| Private pension funds[74]               | 1,591.3    |
| State/local pension funds               | 1,100.3    |
| Mutual funds                            | 2,442.0    |
| Insurance companies                     | 990.4      |
| Bank trusts                             | 206.2      |
| Households/foundations/endowments       | 5,471.8[75] |

The increase in institutional funds has been extraordinarily rapid. In 1970, institutional assets stood at $672 billion. Over the next decade, that figure grew to $1.9 trillion. From 1980 to 1990, the value of institutional assets tripled, to $6.3 trillion. According to Carolyn

Kay Brancato of the Conference Board, US institutional investor assets increased more than 144 percent from 1990 to 1998, reaching $15 trillion. With as much as 26.5 percent of these assets in equities,[76] institutions represent a powerful stockholding force. Indeed, by 2002, institutions owned more than 60 percent of equity of most large multinational companies.[77] Institutions held 50.58 percent of Microsoft, 49.99 percent of General Electric, 51.49 percent of Intel, and 54.77 percent of Cisco Systems, and more than 90 percent of some publicly traded companies.[78] Clearly, concerns of institutional investors should be of the utmost importance to corporate management.

These institutions have one very significant thing in common. All are subject to the highest standard of care and prudence the US legal system has developed, the fiduciary standard. In Justice Benjamin Cardozo's classic terms, they must be "above the morals of the marketplace." Beyond this guiding standard, however, the groups of institutions have little in common with each other. As one observer noted, "institutional investors are by no means a monolithic group."[79]

*As you read through the descriptions of the structures, incentives, and obstacles facing each category of institutional investor, ask how that affects their ability to monitor the directors and managers of the companies in which they invest. Look for consistent themes and for individual variations, and try to determine the impact of both. Think carefully about the governance issues within the institutional investors themselves. As you do with corporate governance, ask who has the best information and the fewest conflicts of interest to make such decisions as defined benefit vs. defined contribution, passive vs. active fund management, and other fund-allocation issues, whether to sell stock in a company whose performance has been disappointing or undertake some kind of shareholder initiative, etc.*

One consistent theme is the problem of collective choice, as described in the "prisoner's dilemma" above. Another is the problem of agency costs. All institutional investors, by definition, are acting on behalf of others, whether pension plan participants, insurance policy holders, trust beneficiaries, or the less well-defined beneficiaries of charities and endowments. As you read the descriptions below, look carefully at this issue in particular. One way to begin is to ask which party has which information. For example, in almost every case, the beneficial owner of stock managed by an institutional investor has no idea how the proxies for that stock are voted. On the other hand, despite the growing popularity of "confidential voting," the corporation issuing the stock does know how the proxies are voted, and by whom. The Boothbay Harbor and Deutsche Asset Management examples illustrate this point.

## Bank trusts

Banks make up one large category of institutional investor, as trustees for everyone from pension plans to private estates. Trust administration is dominated by the complexities of federal income, gift, and estate taxes. Like other institutions, trusts have different classes of beneficiaries who have different kinds of interests.

In most instances, trusts are irrevocable, and, unless there is fraud, which is almost impossible to discover or prove, the bank can expect to continue to serve and collect fees as trustee, regardless of its investment performance. The security of the trust business may well be the reason for the traditional poor investment performance by banks. After all, in quite literal terms, they – unlike the beneficiaries – have nothing to lose. The trust contains "other people's money." *What does that mean for the way that the bank trustee votes proxies?*

Banks generally get the most profitable, and certainly the most interesting, portion of their business from prominent local corporations. The smaller the community in which the bank is located, the more completely its tone is apt to be dominated by the locally based businesses. Banks, especially trust departments, do not encourage innovation, especially positions that are contrary to corporate management's recommendations on proxies.

---

# Cases in point:
# R.P. Scherer and Citicorp

**R.P. Scherer**. A rare lawsuit exposed the conflicts of interest that can occur in these situations. In the late 1980s, Karla Scherer watched the company her father founded, R.P. Scherer Corporation, seem to lose its way under the direction of its CEO, her then husband. As a major shareholder and board member, Ms. Scherer soon realized that the inefficiently run company was more valuable to shareholders if it was sold. However, the board repeatedly refused to consider this option, forcing her to take the matter to shareholders directly in the form of a proxy fight for board seats. She filed a lawsuit, challenging the way her trust shares were being voted. Scherer recalls the most devastating blow to the ultimately successful campaign to force a sale was when she had to deal with her own trustees. "Manufacturers National Bank, the trustee of trusts created by my father for my brother and me, indicated it would vote all 470,400 shares for management, in direct opposition to our wishes. Remember the bank's chairman sat on our board and collected director's fees as well as more than half a million dollars in interest on loans to Scherer. During the trial, the then head of the bank's trust department admitted under oath that he did not know what the 'prudent man' rule was. He also stated that he had arrived at his decision to vote the stock for management in less than 10 minutes, without conferring with us and after affording management an opportunity to plead its case over lunch in a private dining room at the Detroit Club." The court initially ordered the appointment of an independent voting trustee, but the ruling was reversed.

**Citicorp**. The officer of Citicorp responsible for voting proxies determined that a proxy proposal made by Boeing management in 1987 was contrary to the interests of the shareholders, so she voted against it. She was summoned to the office of the chief executive officer to be reminded that Boeing was an important customer of the bank and expected their support. *How can a fiduciary vote proxies with prudence and diligence when there are always going to be conflicts of interest with the institution's commercial relationships?*

---

## *Mutual funds*

Mutual funds are trusts, according to the terms of the Investment Company Act of 1940, which governs them. Otherwise, they bear little resemblance to the other institutional investors because of one important difference: they are designed for total liquidity. The "one-night stands" of institutional investment, they are designed for investors who come in and out on a daily basis, or at least those who want the flexibility to do so.

The investors are entitled to take their money out at any time, at whatever the price is that day. The investment manager has no control over what he will have to pay out or when he will be forced to liquidate a holding. So he views his investments as collateral; they are simply there to make good on the promise to shareholders to redeem their shares at any time. This is not the kind of relationship to encourage a long-term attitude toward any particular company the fund happens to invest in, and if there is a tender offer at any premium over the trading price, mutual fund investment managers have to grab it.

In the face of the real need to attract new money and to retain the investors he has in a world of perpetual and precise competition, the mutual fund manager cannot concern himself with the long term, because his investors may all show up today, and he must be prepared to stand and deliver.

In 2003, the SEC issued rules that will require mutual funds and money managers to disclose their proxy voting policies and any votes inconsistent with those policies. The industry objected, claiming that it would be very expensive. But record comments in favor of the proposal led to its approval by all but one of the SEC commissioners. As the rule is implemented, we can expect to see fewer of the problems that led to the last-minute vote switch by Deutsche Asset Management on the HP–Compaq merger (see case in point later in this chapter).

# Case in point:
# T. Rowe Price and Texaco

Investment firm T. Rowe Price held substantial Texaco stock in various accounts during Carl Icahn's proxy contest for that company in 1988. Its investment managers voted the stock in one account for Icahn and the stock in another account for incumbent Texaco management. Their justification was that one fund was explicitly short-term in orientation, while the other was long term, and that this was no different from having one fund buy the stock while the other was selling it.

*Is this adequate justification? Does an investment management firm have an obligation to recognize the net impact of its proxy votes?*

## *Insurance companies*

Insurance is the only major industry that has successfully avoided any significant federal regulation, although "special accounts" and subsidiary manager investments are subject to ERISA and other federal rules. Life and casualty insurance companies prefer to deal with state legislatures, with whom they have historically had a close relationship.

State law has until most recent times severely circumscribed the extent to which insurers are allowed to invest their own funds in equities. Even today, only 14 percent of insurance fund assets are invested in common stocks. The current limit on stock is 20 percent of a life insurer's assets, or one-half of its surplus. But insurers still may not take influential blocks: life insurers may not put more than 2 percent of the insurance company's assets into the stock of any single insurer, and property and casualty insurers may not control a non-insurance company.[80]

Insurance companies, perhaps more than any other class of institutional investor, have a symbiosis with the companies in which they invest. First, they are usually holders of debt securities of any company in which they have an equity investment; debt instruments are very compatible with their needs because they have a reliable, set payout. Second, they typically have – or would like to have – a commercial relationship with the company by providing insurance or a product to meet the company's pension obligations. Third, like most other institutional shareholders, they are under no obligation to report to their customers on their proxy voting (but the companies whose proxies they vote – and with whom they do business – do know). Finally, like all other shareholders, the collective choice problem makes any form of activism uneconomic. Therefore, it is not surprising that the insurance industry consistently votes with management, regardless of the impact on share value. For example, one Midwestern insurance company wrote that its policy "is to support management positions on normal corporate policy and matters falling within the conduct of a company's ordinary business operations."[81]

### Universities and foundations

Universities and foundations are institutional shareholders because they are funded through endowments. People contribute to a fund, and the interest that fund generates is used for whatever charitable or educational purpose the endowment permits. In 1991, the J. Paul Getty Trust had $3.98 billion. The Ford Foundation had $5.83 billion, and the MacArthur Foundation had $3.13 billion. This money is put into widely diversified investments, including common stock. Although these organizations have "not for profit" status under US tax laws, they seek returns as rigorously as any other investor. But they have not been rigorous in the exercise of their stock ownership rights (or responsibilities).

Foundations and universities are no less subject to commercial pressures than banks and insurance companies. After all, their money comes from alumni, who are often business executives, and from businesses themselves. One study reported that in 1985 corporate contributions to American universities and colleges "surpassed donations from alumni for the first time."[82] Indeed, non-profits are "selling" a much less tangible product, so they must be especially diplomatic. Foundation and university trustees are usually drawn from the business community. The trustees of the Ford Foundation, of Harvard, of the New York Public Library, or of any public museum or symphony are drawn from the same list as the directors of the largest corporations. Many corporate boards include members of the academic community, whose programs and schools receive large contributions from the grateful companies.

# Case in point: Interlocking directors

The dean of a university served as head of the compensation committee of the company headed by the chairman of his university's board. The CEO and his company were both large contributors and the company funded a good deal of the university's research.

*If you were the dean, and you had to vote on the CEO's pay plan, what steps, if any, could you take to make sure that you were objective? (Of course, the same question applies to the CEO, voting on the dean's pay plan, but in that case, it is not corporate governance but university governance.)*

# Case in point: The Corporate Library's interlock tool

In 2002, The Corporate Library developed a tool for the graphic display of inter-locking relationships between directors – not just corporate relationships, but also charitable organizations, trade associations, and even the notorious all-male Augusta Golf Club. Here are two examples of highly connected directors:

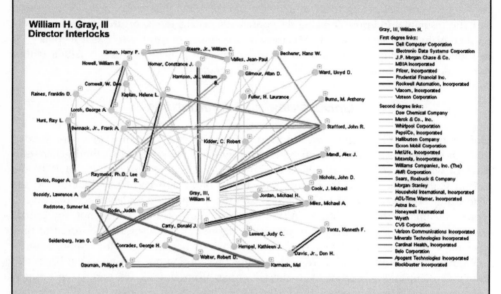

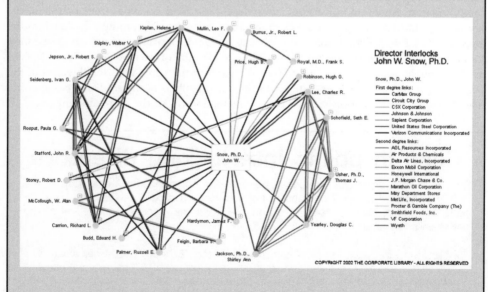

# Case in point: The Rose Foundation takes on Maxxam

The Rose Foundation for Communities and the Environment is a rare foundation that puts its endowment money where its programs are. Concerned about Maxxam's environmental and labor policies, Rose and its allies ran dissident candidates for the board in 1999 and 2000. Although they knew from the beginning that they had no chance of success, because Maxxam CEO Hurwitz had majority control of the voting shares, they believed that their campaign, which included a full-page ad calling the board a "rubber stamp," would put pressure on the Maxxam board to address their concerns.

### Pension plans

"We own the economy now," said Carol O'Cleireacain, then New York City finance commissioner and trustee of four city employee pension funds with nearly $50 billion of assets.[83] David Ball, then director of the Pension and Welfare Benefits Administration that oversees billions of dollars in pension assets, said that institutions could accurately borrow a phrase from the comic strip, Pogo: "We have met the marketplace and they is us."[84] The California Public Employees' Retirement System grows by about $1 billion every two months – "in a year more than four times the median market value of a *Fortune* 500 industrial company; in a year, enough to buy all the common stock of General Motors, with enough left to buy five tankfuls of gasoline for each vehicle it makes."[85] Because of their size and importance, we will devote the next section to pension funds.

## THE BIGGEST POOL OF MONEY IN THE WORLD

The largest institutional investors, the group that includes the largest collection of investment capital in the world, are the pension funds. One of the most important elements to understanding the current state of corporate governance, as well as its future direction and potential, is an understanding of this group. Although they are very diverse in many ways, they share several important characteristics. As we examine their impact not just on corporate governance, but also on competitiveness and productivity, we need to understand the impact of the most important characteristic they have in common: they are all trustees. A money manager who does not perform may lose clients. A trustee who does not perform may pay a fine, be permanently prohibited from managing pension money, or even go to jail. This is certainly a good way to protect the pension funds, but it is almost as certainly not a good way to move markets. The problem is that no one ever realized that the pension system would quickly take over the market, for rather Gresham-like reasons.[86]

After World War II, the US government provided generous tax incentives to encourage individuals and employers to make provision for retirement income. The program was subsidized in three ways:

- the employer's payments to the plan were deductible for federal income tax purposes;
- all transactions by the plan – buying, selling, collecting income – were exempt from tax; and
- the recipient is allowed to stagger the receipt of payments to fall into the most advantageous year from a tax point of view.

This huge federal subsidy transferred national savings from savings banks to pension systems as individuals responded to the tax incentives. They preferred to save 100-cent dollars in retirement plans rather than 50-cent dollars in the savings bank. Thus, over 30 percent of all the equity investments in the country are held in public and private pension plans. This means that the largest accumulation of investment capital in the world was the responsibility of trustees, who have a perspective (and set of incentives) very different from the strictly economic "invisible hand" of the capital markets.

The "invisible hand" is now the hand of these trustees of public (state, municipal, federal) and private (corporate and union) pension plans. Peter Drucker called this "the unseen revolution" in 1976, noting that "If 'socialism' is defined as 'ownership of the means of production by the workers' – and this is both the orthodox and the only rigorous definition – then the United States is the first truly 'Socialist' country."[87]

> Shortly before the year 2000, there will be more workers in companies that are more than 15 percent employee held than in the entire US trade union movement. *The property rights of workers will dwarf labor laws as an option for influence in corporations.* For the first time since the 1930s, America will see a new wave of employee activism – one more likely to be low key and business oriented than the early trade union movement. But this time unions will be joined by company-wide employee associations – *ad hoc* and coordinated – asking for a say because they are either the dominant shareholder or the second major shareholder in the firm.[88]

But is this "invisible hand" capable of managing the economy's rudder? While in theory the trustees are vitally committed to earning the highest possible rate of return, in reality there is little incentive for most of them to perform better than the actuarially defined return necessary to meet an actuarially defined payout (for a defined-benefit plan) or a market rate of return (for a defined-contribution plan).

A defined-benefit pension plan specifies the level of benefits it will pay, or the method of determining those benefits, but not the amount of company contributions. Contributions are determined actuarially on the basis of the benefits expected to become payable. A defined-contribution plan specifies the amount of contributions, but not the level of benefits. The size of the pension is determined by how much (or how little) is in the account at the time the plan participant retires.

The assets in a public plan are assumed by the actuaries to earn a particular rate of return. It was typically 9 percent in 1999, but many plans exceeded that level for the several years of the century-end bull market. This created a condition where most of the largest plans in 2000 were substantially over-funded. Clearly, if the plan can earn a consistently higher rate of return than the one assumed, the amount of money required to be paid in by the state from taxes can be reduced. In the case of private pension systems, this translates into higher earnings for the corporation and, presumably, bonuses for the pension manager. With public plans and civil service salaries, however, there are no bonuses (though in some cases there may be political benefits). In general, though, the individual responsible for the investment of public plan funds has no incentive to achieve beyond the mandated averages. As Edward V. Regan, former Comptroller of the State of New York, said: "Nobody ever got elected to anything by beating the S&P 500. On the other hand, for one bad investment, they'll throw you out." It is not surprising that Regan responded by investing in an "index." This meant that the state pension fund performed exactly as well as the S&P 500; in essence it *was* the S&P 500.[89] Indeed, given the inability of actively managed funds to beat the indexes, this may be the very definition of prudence. But that means that we must consider the implications of these huge passive investments. How can the market be efficient if such a large chunk of it cannot respond to good or bad performance by trading?

The defined-benefit plan is declining in popularity among private American companies. Few new ones are being started, and many existing plans are being terminated. Defined benefit plans with cost-of-living adjustments (COLAs) are an effort to insulate a particular class of citizens from the economic vagaries of the world by guaranteeing them a set level of buying power, no matter what the rate of inflation. This is a very expensive commitment, and companies and states are increasingly reluctant to assume it. The total number of defined-benefit plans increased from 103,000 in 1975 to 175,000 in 1983, and then declined precipitously to 83,600 in 1993. In contrast to the fall in defined-benefit plans, the total number of private defined-contribution plans rose steadily from 208,000 in 1975 to 618,500 in 1993. A 1997 Working Group report recommended a series of steps to make defined-benefit plans more appealing to employers.

The alternative is defined-contribution plans. Because the amount that the employer and the employee pay in is fixed, the employee has a certain control over the investment of the funds. The funds are entirely his (subject to restricted use for statutorily permitted purposes like the purchase of a residence or for education costs), and so is the risk of gain and loss. The employer ceases to play a buffering role either with respect to the performance of plan investments or with respect to inflation in the outside world.

It may appear that employees have lost financial ground in the trend toward defined-contribution plans, because of the loss of security. It is only in defined-benefit plans that the employer acts as guarantor of a set level of purchasing power after retirement. But defined-contribution plans have advantages for the plan participant as well, including the ability to change jobs and to take the benefits along. The ultimate problem lies in investment policy. As we have pointed out above, the trustee of the entire defined-benefit pool has the luxury of making the optimum long-term investment in stocks. On the other hand, the individual acting as his own "trustee" for a defined-contribution plan, worried on a day-to-day basis about preserving his retirement fund, is apt to invest in bonds. He will be satisfied with losing only a little bit as long as he avoids running the risk of losing a lot. Thus, the assets committed to an individual under a defined-contribution scheme are apt to be invested less profitably, and the aggregate will have a massive long-term impact on what funds are actually available in retirement.

As public funds gradually evolve from defined benefit to defined contribution, plan participants will have increasing involvement. Although the trustee will manage plan assets and retain ownership responsibilities with respect to plan stocks, plan participants will exercise more choice selecting investment categories (stocks or bonds), as in the FERSA example below.

# Case in point: Maine State Retirement System[90]

The Maine State Retirement System (MSRS), has a typical defined-benefit plan. Like most public pension plans in the United States, it offers participants "defined benefits" on retirement. The employee is paid an amount based on the cost of living as well as other factors. The formula takes into account expected raises, inflation, and differing retirement ages. The formula is the number of years of service times 1/50 times the average of the final three years' pay.

This produces an ideal result for a "typical" career state employee; after 35 years of service, an individual can retire at age 62 with a pension calculated as 70 percent of "final pay." Public plans generally provide for a level of "inflation protection" for payments. In Maine, there is a cap of up to 4 percent per year. The state is required to pay into the plan every year an amount calculated by actuaries to be sufficient, if invested according to the assumed returns, to produce an adequate amount of capital to pay the system's commitments as they mature.

Maine's promise to make "defined-benefit" payments to participants is enforceable whether or not there are assets in the pension plan. If the plan does not have enough, it will have to come out of tax revenues. The purpose of the plan (and the basis of the actuaries' calculations of the amount of annual payments) is to match pension payments with the benefits from the service of the participant. Like social security, it is something of a Ponzi scheme. Today's workers pay in money that is immediately sent out to today's retirees.

To make the system work, then, today's taxpayers must pay in as well. The portion of their taxes allotted to the pension system must be enough, when invested, to provide today's public employees with a suitable pension when they actually do retire. The amounts in the pension plan serve two purposes. They serve intergenerational fairness by assuring that those who receive the benefits (i.e. current citizens) pay the full costs. They also act as a buffer (if not a complete guarantee) against the changing politics and priorities of the state budgetary process. While a state can [and does] break some promises, the legislature makes it a little more difficult by segregating pension assets in an independent trust (difficult, but not impossible – see the discussion of ETIs below in this chapter).

The dynamics of a defined-benefit system are skewed heavily in favor of an individual who works until the end of the anticipated term of service. In the state of Maine system a hypothetical defined-benefit participant only begins to get a portion of the state's contribution during the last third of his term. After that, his interest soars.

*What this is doing is to "lock in" state employees for their full working lives. Neither the state nor the employee can afford flexibility. Is this what the system intends?*

The liability assumptions have been subject to great change over the past half-dozen years:

- In 1987 there was an increase of about $0.5 billion to reflect a change in assumptions as to the retirement age.
- In 1992, assumptions were changed $0.45 billion to reflect the level of pay increases at career end (and to reflect vacation and sick pay).

The Maine State Constitution requires a vote of the electorate before debt can be incurred. But the political process cannot control pension liabilities. In Maine, the level of actuarially unfunded liabilities in the MSRS approaches $2.2 billion, almost four times the amount authorized by popular vote. The aggregate level of state debt today is about $0.6 billion. (To put it bluntly, the MSRS actuaries have created more state debt over the last six years than the voters of the State of Maine have authorized in 200 years.)

State employee compensation is bargained, but pension obligations are legislated. This means that lobbying is the mode of employee involvement. In 1992, in an effort to reduce state expenditures, the legislature modified benefits for all employees with fewer than seven years' creditable service. They excluded from the definition of "earnable compensation" payment received for unused sick leave or vacation; raised the minimum age for retirement with full benefits by two years to 62; and increased the penalty for retirement before the minimum age. The state employees went to court, arguing that as soon as they accepted employment they had in effect accepted a contract providing that the state would provide them with the benefits at that time, and that they could not be reduced. Other states, like California, have ruled in favor of the employees in these challenges. The lower court in Maine did so, too, but it was reversed by the state Supreme Court, which ruled that only benefits actually due could not be changed; those merely anticipated could be. The state employees also attempted to challenge the 1992 amendments in the federal courts, but were similarly unsuccessful.

Two important developments came out of the 1992 amendments and the challenges to those amendments. In 1995, the Maine Constitution was amended: (a) to require the unfounded liability to be retired (paid down) in 31 years; (b) to prohibit the creation of any future unfounded liabilities (i.e. future benefit increases must either be prospective only or must be paid for upon enactment); and (c) to mandate that any experience losses (i.e. costs in excess of projections or investment shortfalls) must be paid off over a period no greater than ten years. These constitutional changes make it very costly and difficult to improve pension benefits within the system (and they may have the unintended consequence of "locking in" the 1992 benefit reductions).

The second significant development occurred in 1999 when the Maine legislature, the administration, and the employee unions agreed to resolve the pension contract issue by passing a statute making certain portions of the MSRS "solemn contractual commitments of the State protected under the contract clauses of the Constitution of Maine . . . and the United States Constitution" (5MRSA §17801). This enactment covers the current benefit levels and benefit structure, and ensures that benefit reductions of the type passed in 1992 could not be done in the future.

The "conventional wisdom" is that defined-benefit plans are "cheaper" than defined-contribution ones in the sense that less benefit is actually received under the former system. The reason is that so few defined-benefit plan participants actually serve the optimal period of time; the others are losers. Younger, shorter-service employees are absolute losers under the current Maine system since their own contributions, plus earnings, exceed the value of the pension promise being made to them. Most of these employees will receive no (zero) benefit from state contributions at all. Thus someone who leaves before completing five years of employment is not vested; 35 years of employment is essential for optimization.

The defined-benefit system creates winners and losers. Every employee hopes that he or she will win. Importantly for the political process, the losers are usually not available to testify, litigate, or lobby. Thus, the impression prevails that all is well, when less than 30 percent of those entering the system ultimately receive their full rewards. A defined-contribution system is transparent; you can see what is yours and what you see is what you get (and complain about).

Many employers are considering cash balance plans as a replacement for traditional defined-benefit plans. The Internal Revenue Service has recently published detailed regulations outlining the permissible scope for plans that will be eligible for favorable tax treatment. Great flexibility is encouraged, but the dominant pattern of cash balance plans involves rather larger build-ups of cash balances for employees during their early years of service than under the traditional defined-benefit arrangement. A cash-benefit plan will be more expensive for an employer wishing to provide his employees with a traditional benefit expressed as a percentage of higher pay, because the plan, as a whole, will have been diminished by those early-leaving employees. Companies have explained the change from defined-benefit arrangements to their employees as a reflection of the employment realities of the times – namely that very few employees will end their working careers with the same employer as they began, so, therefore the build-up of transferable larger cash balances is very much in their interest. Cash balance plans are easy to explain to employees, but no one should fail to note that they really are not "pensions" in the sense of guaranteeing a financial result; they are savings plans with substantial risk transferred from the company (and the US Pension Benefit Guarantee Corporation) to the employee.

A public pension system enjoys special status within governmental institutions:

- it has substantial money;
- the state can decline to make requisite payments for a sustained period of time and there is no immediate adverse impact; and
- the impact is sufficiently complex, long-range, and diffused that no one seems to be hurt by deficiencies.

Governments are increasingly being driven to extremes in efforts to balance their budgets. Roughly speaking there are three alternatives:

1. raise taxes, which can be political suicide;
2. cut back programs, which can also be politically disastrous;
3. postpone, reduce, eliminate, but – above all else – decline to pay timely the actuarially determined amounts into the pension system.

Clearly, the pension system is the easiest target. Only the raging "bull" market has obscured the extent of political profligacy over the last decade. In recent years, the percentage of equity holdings has gradually increased, so that now about 70 percent of Maine's investments are in stocks. A rising market covers all manner of sins, or has so far. Note that the Maine legislature recently increased the employee contribution from 6.5 percent to 7.65 percent. According to a newsletter published by the National Association of Public Pension Attorneys, "No sound actuarial reason was given for this increase. It is reported that the State Legislature did it simply to reduce the employer contribution so as to solve state budget problems unrelated to the retirement fund."[91] But in a bear market, the underlying problems are exposed and increased. The MSRS was briefly 100 percent funded, but the state is back on the hook for a significant proportion of its liabilities again.

The efficacy of the defined-benefit system, where no one really has a sense of owning something specific, depends ultimately on the level of discipline in the political system. Indeed, there have been challenges to the cost-of-living increases granted to defined-benefit plan participants, on the grounds that these increases should be considered "gifts." In one such suit, the challengers argued that the money belongs to the government, and not the retirees, because the government administers the plans and the government determines when or if cost-of-living increases are payable.

If one has no confidence in the capacity of government to be held to its commitments, a defined-benefit system is less desirable than a defined-contribution system where an individual has a continual sense of ownership with respect to the specific assets in their retirement account, bolstered by regular reports of its status. It seems likely that tens of thousands of participants in a defined-contribution system would be better motivated, informed, and able than defined-benefit plan participants to compel government to make the promised payments into the plan and to prevent it from wasting the assets already in the plan.

A fascinating study of the public and private pension fund cultures was described in the 1992 book *Fortune and Folly* by anthropologist William M. O'Barr and law professor John M. Conley.[92] They approached the pension fund world just as they might an unusual tribal culture. "[T]o fit better into the native environment, we exchanged our academic tweeds for field clothes – in this case, blue suits from Brooks Brothers rather than khakis from an army surplus store – and set out to live with the natives and observe their ways of life."[93] Perhaps the most interesting part of the book is its description of the cultural differences between the private and public pension funds. For example: "Private fund officials often talk about their accountability to the sponsoring corporation's bottom line, or at least to the sponsor's corporate notion of successful management. Their public counterparts talk instead about the press and the ballot box as the instruments of day-to-day accountability."[94] The result, according to the authors, is that public funds' primary goal is to avoid poor performance, while private funds try to achieve superior performance – a fine but very important distinction that is both the cause and the result of the differing incentives (pay and otherwise) of the two systems.

This distinction stems in part from what the authors call, in true anthropological terms, "creation myths." These "oral histories" about the origins of the pension system reveal, in their differing emphasis on particular aspects, what each system's assumptions and goals are. "The creation myths we heard at private funds tended to be centered around important individuals and to convey the teller's sense of the corporation's culture and personality."[95] In these stories, "cultural influences predominate over economic ones."[96] Private fund "creation myths" tend to emphasize a visionary leader who created the pension fund to provide for loyal employees and their dependants. Interestingly, these myths focus on the origins of the pension fund at the particular company and not on the establishment of the overall structure of private pension funds under ERISA, which was enacted in 1974.

O'Barr and Conley found that public fund "creation myths," too, focus on "history and politics, but the history was scandalous and the politics was external. (Ironically, much of the impetus for ERISA came from widespread corruption in the *public* pension system, which ERISA left untouched.) Once again, financial analysis was not a primary determinant of structures and strategies."[97] In contrast to the private fund managers, who see themselves as living up to the "creator's" vision of economic security for fellow workers, the public fund managers see themselves as protecting their fellow workers from those who would try to benefit themselves, politically or financially, to the detriment of the workers. While both are fiduciaries, operating under the strictest standard for integrity and loyalty imposed by the legal system, the "creation myths" reveal an important difference in the way each sees their obligations and goals.

But the authors found that there was one point on which public and private pension funds were alike – their efforts to avoid accountability for the consequences of their investment decisions. This is understandable in a field where even the most capable professionals have so little ability to control or even predict what the market will do. The 20-year effort of the federal government to gain control over the teamsters' union and the "looting" of the New York City plans created a generation of risk-averse fiduciaries.

Perhaps *Fortune and Folly*'s most important conclusion is:

> In every interview we conducted, fund executives talked at length about assuming, assigning, or avoiding responsibility. As we listened to them, it often seemed as if the funds had been designed for the purpose of shifting responsibility away from identifiable individuals. They described four specific mechanisms for displacing responsibility and avoiding blame; burying decisions in the bureaucracy, blaming someone else, blaming the market, or claiming their hands were tied by the law.[98]

## Pension plans as investors

Before we consider the question of pension funds as owners (as participants in the corporate governance system), we must take a brief look at the bigger question of pension funds as buyers and sellers. The fiduciary standard for prudent investment works fine in the situation for which it was designed, protecting the assets of a trust beneficiary, like a minor inheriting property. It does not work when it is applied to a pot of money that constitutes the largest single collection of investment capital. There are simply not enough "prudent" investments around to sustain all of that money. So what you get is what we have now, too much investment in large-capital blue-chip stocks and not enough in everything else.

This is what happens when a horde of "prudent experts" goes to the marketplace to look for diversified and seasoned investments. It is inevitable when they are faced with a choice between rational (in economic terms) or prudent (in legal terms) investments. The problem is that we need a system that invests to encourage risk, and we have a system that invests to discourage it.

The data show that pension money has not, by and large, provided new capital or new employment. During the decade of the 1980s, the S&P 500 corporations typically *reduced* their capital by buying back stock. And this (over)investment in the largest companies failed to create new jobs. Artificial inflation of investment in large-capitalization companies thus had no meaningful benefits either to those companies or to the pension beneficiary investors themselves. And of course it has provided no special benefits to participants in the pension plan, the employees and retirees. With all of the pension managers grouped together in the S&P 500, it is not surprising that none of them, over time, beats the market and that so many of them have taken the savings available by eliminating the transaction costs in active trading and investing in "index funds" that replicate the market.

*Can that essentially permanent holding give the market the feedback that it needs?*

## Pension plans as owners

The paradoxical result of passive investing is active owning, says James Dowling, chairman of Burson-Marsteller, the public relations firm that established a corporate governance practice to advise CEOs and boards on how to operate in the changed environment: "The public funds have so much money that they find it's harder to find new companies to invest in than to try to turn around poorly performing ones." Says Jennifer Morales, executive director of the Houston Firemen's Relief Retirement Fund: "We don't want to sell. If a company can be improved, why should we be the ones to leave?"[99]

Public and private pension funds are the largest single component of equity ownership – 28 percent of the total equity in the country and growing. And, with an average of 30 years from the time money comes in to the time it has to be paid out, they are the ultimate long-term holder. For that reason, we need to understand their impact on the capital markets and on corporate performance. They bring significant advantages and disadvantages over the old system of highly fractionated individual investment.

### *Advantages*

- Their size and expertise minimizes the collective choice problem discussed above. They are sophisticated enough to understand when activism is necessary and large enough to make it effective (and cost-effective) to do so. The holdings of pension funds are large enough to alleviate the free-rider problem that makes shareholder information and action economically non-rational (and therefore imprudent for fiduciaries).
- They are widely held – almost 100 million Americans have interests in employee benefit plans – so their pension trustees are good proxies for the public interest. It is virtually inconceivable that something would be in the interest of pensioners that is not in the interest of society at large.
- Pension plans are less restricted by commercial conflicts of interest than are other institutional investors, like banks, insurance companies, mutual funds, and other classes of institutional investors. (Note, however, that there are still significant commercial conflicts of interest, as shown by the Citicorp example above.)
- For political and investment reasons, pension plans are becoming increasingly "indexed" in their equity holdings. This makes them both universal and permanent shareholders. Their holdings are so diversified that they have the incentive to represent the ownership sector (and the economy) generally rather than any specific industries or companies. This endows them with a breadth of concern that naturally aligns with the public interest. For example, pension funds can be concerned with vocational education, pollution, and retraining, whereas an owner with a perspective limited to a particular company or industry would consider these to be unacceptable expenses because of competitiveness problems. Robert Reich, the Secretary of Labor, urged institutional investors against the short-term view that cutting payrolls boosted the immediate bottom line. Instead, he told institutions to adopt a long-term perspective, arguing that retraining programs and heightened employee security can enhance productivity. Reich said: "You should be aware of the full consequences of the signals you send and the positions you take, not just in the current round of play, but in the next, and the next. Stewardship of the future, after all, is the essence of your profession."[100]
- The private pension system is administered under ERISA, an existing federal law that pre-empts state involvement. The administration of this law in its definition of the scope of fiduciary responsibilities by the Pension and Welfare Benefits Administration (PWBA) of the US Department of Labor has succeeded in creating a standard that has been widely followed by the states in the operation of public pension systems. The essential legal structure needed to govern these investors is already in place.

### *Disadvantages*

The disadvantages are in general a function of what we do not know, and they can best be stated as questions.

- Who watches the watchers? Who should watch them? Who can?
- What are the qualifications of the trustees? What should they be?
- Are the trustees genuinely accountable to their own beneficiaries or are we simply substituting one unaccountable bureaucracy for another? How do we identify and then minimize the inevitable conflicts of interest of what Professor John Langbein calls "the non-neutral fiduciary"?

One way to address these questions is to make the qualifications of the trustees (like the qualifications for members of boards of directors) explicit and public. But there is another disadvantage that is more subtle and complex:

- What is the impact on the capital markets of having such a high percentage of the available capital invested by fiduciaries?

More than $2 trillion is now under the control of laws that effectively relegate pension assets to permanent yet docile holdings in large, established companies. The result is "excess diversification and insufficient innovation."[101] This means over-investment in large companies and under-investment in emerging opportunities. By nature and by law the objectives of fiduciaries are low-risk. This can hamper market efficiency, because for the first time a significant portion of the investment is managed for some goal other than maximum returns. Both public and private pension funds have thus been criticized for being under-inclusive in their investment strategy, for failing to recognize the opportunities that may be higher risk but may also be higher return. They have been encouraged to behave more like venture capitalists.

But they have also been criticized for being over-inclusive, for making investments for reasons other than returns. Social investing (or economically targeted investing) falls into this category, as well as some of the attempts to fund corporate pension funds with the corporation's own stock. Both are described in more detail in the following section. It is useful to apply the same overlay of questions in connection with the management of pension funds that we do with corporations: *Who has the best information and the fewest conflicts of interest? Who is in the best position to make the decisions, and does that person have authority to do so?*

## PUBLIC PENSION FUNDS

A small group of public pension funds has been the most visible of the institutional investors with regard to governance issues. It includes pension funds for state and municipal employees, ranging from teachers and civic workers, to firefighters and police, and oversees nearly a trillion dollars. It is important to note that of the very large group of public plans, only a handful have been actively involved in governance initiatives. One of these activists noted,

There might be lots of noise and action, and there might be talk about all the new, awakened shareholders and institutional investors, but there's really not much more than a dozen public pension funds involved. And they call the tune. In fact if you took the CalPERS and the New York City pension fund and TIAA–CREF out of the equation along with our fund [New York State] and Wisconsin, Pennsylvania and to some extent Florida, you might have very little activism at all.[102]

In terms of their own governance, the public plans are all organized differently. Some are directed by bureaucrats, some by politically appointed officials, and some by elected officials. The $133 billion California Public Employees' Retirement System (CalPERS), for example, is overseen by trustees appointed through a variety of mechanisms, who are intimately involved, whereas the New York State employees' fund is overseen by a single trustee, one of only four statewide elected officials.

The people who oversee the public pension funds come from a wider variety of backgrounds than the money managers, who are responsible for other kinds of institutional investments. The CalPERS board, for example, includes union officials and political appointees who oversee the staff (both inside and outside the civil service) and both professional money managers and staff with other kinds of expertise. They cannot compete salary-wise with other institutional investors for the top investment professionals, though, ironically, they may end up employing those same professionals by retaining their companies to manage their assets. This is because, with rare exceptions like the 1993 decision by CalPERS to give its CEO a performance-based bonus, the public plan pay schemes are designed for political, not economic reasons. As one public pension CEO said, "If I do a good job, I get $100,000. If I do a great job, I get $100,000." Several senior officials lost their jobs in the Washington state pension fund, when their very lucrative investments with LBO fund KKR came to be perceived as a political liability.

Actuaries can tell any defined-benefit plan exactly what its liquidity needs will be and how much cash it will need over the next ten years to meet retirees' entitlements. The balance of the fund really is "permanent." All of the long-term analyses of rates of return to be derived from different classes of investment prove that returns from common stocks beat the returns from bonds or money market funds – or any other investment medium for that matter. This means that it is all but impossible to justify any investment for the public plans (except for a small percentage of Treasury Bills to meet their liquidity needs), other than common equity.

So the conservative approach described by Regan prevails. The "prudent man" degenerated into a "lowest common denominator" approach. There is no incentive to do better than others, and every incentive to be safely in the middle of the pack.

In this context, let's examine the role of the public funds in corporate governance. We have already established that they are not strictly motivated by economic returns. And it is all but tautological to say that they are motivated by political concerns. To the extent that the public plans do become involved with corporate governance, they raise the very real specter of "back-door" socialism.

*What is the role of the state when it becomes a major shareholder, even the major shareholder of American business? To what extent do we really want elected officials overseeing the managers of American business?*

The incentives, expertise, and goals of business and government are so different, at such fundamental levels, that this is a complicated – and crucial – question. The trustees of public plans act on behalf of a very diverse group, including current employees (at all stages of their employment) and retirees. The trustees themselves are a diverse group, including employees, retirees, and others, including political appointees, elected officials, and a wide range of experts – investors, bankers, actuaries, insurance professionals. Usually they are paid just a nominal *per diem* fee for their work. While this attracts people with a high level of public-spiritedness, there is a certain impracticality in trying to manage the operations of a truly mammoth investment and retirement system under the direction of people whose expertise is often in other areas, and who are not paid enough to be able to devote a substantial amount of time to this task. There is also a substantial political impediment to hiring people outside the government – especially at the prices that the market demands for people who manage money. This is a significant disadvantage.

The public fund board of trustees must reach a perilous equilibrium between plan participant representatives and political appointees. There are frequent disagreements on questions of funding and investment. The plan participants' top priority is safety of the fund, and the politicians are interested in politics – on the budget side and on the investment side.

The result is a tendency toward compromise. CalPERS' success is firmly based on a realistic assessment of the limits of its practical ability to force issues. "We have a strong predisposition to accommodation," CalPERS' former CEO Dale Hanson explained in a lecture to the Harvard Business School.[103] The political realities (both internally, in Hanson's relationship with his own board and his fiduciary obligation to plan participants, and externally, as a government agency reporting to the governor) placed a premium on compromise. The economic realities ("rational ignorance") may place an even larger premium on compromise. Perhaps the public pension funds' most significant contribution has been to make the world an uncomfortable place for a director of an under-performing company. "Hanson is adamant that he does not seek to oust CEOs . . . Also CalPERS insists it does not seek to name its own people to boards, although it does push hard for independent directors."[104]

Hanson's successor, Jim Burton, maintained a much lower profile and negotiated more quietly, though CalPERS board chairman William Crist and General Counsel Kayla Gillan were publicly active in general corporate governance matters and at times with individual companies as well.

Many public funds, as well as many union funds and some corporate funds, belong to the Council of Institutional Investors (CII). The Washington-based group acts as a resource for its members, holding conferences, providing information, and acting as a clearing-house, occasionally issuing policy papers. Several corporate funds joined the Council as well, perhaps in a sort of "If you can't beat them, join them" move. It will be interesting to see which group has more of an impact on the other.

The public pension plans differ in their perspectives, their policies, and their politics. But they are all fiduciaries, obligated by law to protect the interests of their plan beneficiaries, the public employees. And they all have a high degree of independence because they are not dependent on commercial relationships with those in whom they invest. This makes it easier for them to become involved in governance issues. The Maine State Retirement System has successfully brought suit against Travelers' Insurance company to recover a portion of an investment negligently managed.

But public institutions have relationships too, and, like their private counterparts, those relationships can affect investment strategies, proxy votes, and other governance activity. They are subject to political considerations, as the cases below demonstrate.

# Cases in point:
# Public fund activism

- When the Wisconsin state pension fund wanted to object to General Motors' $742.8 million forced greenmail payment to Ross Perot, it was stopped by the governor, who was trying to get General Motors to build some plants in his state.

- When Shearson Lehman Hutton (as it was then called) assisted in the takeover of a Pennsylvania company called Koppers, many local residents (and politicians) were concerned about possible job losses. Shearson was not only acting as investment banker for the acquiring firm, but also as a participant. Shearson had loaned $500 million of its own funds to the acquirer and had agreed to purchase 46 percent of Koppers for itself if the takeover was successful. The state held some Koppers stock in its pension fund. It was not enough to stop the takeover, but it was enough to slow the effort down. The state treasurer suspended all state business, including bond business, with Shearson and its subsidiaries. Three Shearson subsidiaries were eliminated from consideration for management of state pension fund assets. The takeover was ultimately completed in a manner that satisfied the state's concerns about jobs, and the suspension was removed.

- The New York State United Teachers Fund sold its investment in the Tribune Company when employees of Tribune's *New York Daily News* went on strike in 1991. The fund stated that "our policy is not to invest in any project, corporation, or stock that is anti-union."

- Several police pension funds used the pension fund's proxies in Time Warner, parent company of Ice-T's record label, to protest the Ice-T "Cop Killer" record.

- Dr. David Bronner, manager of the Alabama state pension fund, invested $120 million to build the "Robert Trent Jones Golf Trail," seven huge golf complexes across the state. He has built so many office towers and parking garages in downtown Montgomery that he is the most active developer in that city. "Officially just the bureaucrat who manages money for teachers and state employees, Dr. Bronner has come to view himself as the personal guardian of Alabama's future."[105] He emphasizes the economic benefits to the state of his investments, arguing that the golf courses will increase tourism.

- In 2002, New York State Comptroller H. Carl McCall, North Carolina Treasurer Richard Moore, New York State Attorney General Eliot Spitzer and California State Treasurer Philip Angelides announced the launching of a major initiative to protect state taxpayer funds and public pension funds from the risks of conflicts of interest. Investment banking firms that do business with New York, North Carolina and California will be asked to adopt the conflict of interest principles set forth in the agreement that Attorney General Spitzer reached with Merrill Lynch on May 21, 2002. In addition the North Carolina Public Employees Retirement Systems and the New York State Common Retirement Fund will impose the following requirements on investment banking and money management firms that do business with the pension funds:

  - money management firms must make disclosures regarding: (a) portfolio manager and analyst compensation; (b) the firms' use of broker dealers that have adopted the Merrill Lynch principles; and (c) potential conflicts of interest arising from client and corporate parent relationships;

- money management firms must adopt safeguards to ensure that potential conflicts of interest do not influence investment decisions made on behalf of the pension funds; and
- money management firms must scrutinize more closely the auditing and corporate governance practices of companies in which pension fund moneys are invested.

- The New Jersey state pension fund, required by state law to disinvest all holdings in companies doing business with South Africa, ended up selling out of two New Jersey pharmaceutical companies whose only dealing with South Africa was the sale of medicine used exclusively by black South Africans. The *Wall Street Journal* estimated that the disinvestment policy has cost the plan between $330 and $515 million in two years.[106]

> How is this different from taking as much as $515 million out of the state budget and spending it? How do you evaluate the success of this program on moral grounds? On political grounds? On fiscal grounds? Is there any reason not to treat this as an expenditure, subject to the same procedural protections and deliberations as other expenditures of public funds?

Note that New York City's pension fund was able to adopt a more flexible policy on South Africa. It began by writing letters to express its concerns, then sponsored and supported a number of shareholder resolutions, calling for companies to adopt the Sullivan Principles making a commitment to providing equal opportunity in their South African facilities. They sold out of a limited number of companies that they determined had business dealings, such as those who do business with the police and military there. Regan, of the New York State pension fund, took a different approach. Facing annual legislative proposals along the inflexible lines enacted in New Jersey, Regan used the fund's shares to commence a massive program of shareholder resolutions calling for disinvestment from South Africa, instead of divesting. Regan's view was that mandated sale of stocks (for any reason) would impose unreasonable financial costs on the portfolio and force higher contributions from the taxpayers. By use of the shareholder franchise, he negotiated results with the companies, arguing that he met the objectives of divestment legislation without incurring the significant financial losses.

- In 1991, California governor Pete Wilson initiated what some observers called a "hostile takeover" of the state's pension funds to reduce the budget deficit and gain more control over the trustees. In 2003, a California court ruling put more than two dozen of the top officers of CalPERS on temporary status. At this writing, the legislature was considering a range of options.
- New York State Comptroller Regan voted the state pension fund's proxies in favor of management in the Texaco proxy contest. In a series of newspaper articles he was accused of basing this vote on the campaign contributions of the dissident candidate Carl Icahn. Icahn was a contributor to Regan's political opponent. Regan was subjected to a grand jury investigation.
- The inspector general of the state of Massachusetts issued a report finding that state pension fund officials had hired outside financial advisers based on friendships and political relationships rather than by competitive bidding, then created phoney, backdated documents to conceal the fact that they had not adequately researched the firms' performance in advance.

Recently, there has been an increasing number of investigations of state and city pension funds and the way they make their investment decisions.[107] Federal investigators examined the pension fund of the Commonwealth of Virginia, following the governor's (unsuccessful) attempt to use some of the pension fund's real estate for a new football stadium for the Washington Redskins. The state legislature also hired an investment firm to examine the state fund's operations, including its investment policies and procedures. In Minnesota, former state pension fund employees pled guilty to charges of embezzlement.

---

# Case in point: Myners shifts the burden of proof on activism

A commission in the UK led by Paul Myners addressed "distortions" in institutional investment. The central proposal of the review, closely modeled on the approach taken on corporate governance by the Cadbury (and subsequent) codes, is a short set of clear principles of investment decision-making. These would apply to pension funds and, in due course, other institutional investors. As with the Cadbury code, they would not be mandatory. But where a pension fund chose not to comply with them, it would have to explain to its members why not.

One of the most important of those provisions was:

* *Incorporation of the US ERISA principle on shareholder activism into UK law, making intervention in companies, where it is in shareholders' interests, a duty for fund managers* (emphasis added).

In a statement to the press on the release of the report, Paul Myners said:

"The principles may seem little more than common sense. In a way they are – yet they certainly do not describe the status quo. Following them would require substantial change in decision-making behavior and structures." The review asked the investment industry to adopt the principles voluntarily, but warned that if necessary the Government would require disclosure of the extent to which firms complied with these goals.

---

# Case in point: The Institutional Shareholders Committee

The Institutional Shareholders Committee of the UK, made up of the Association of British Insurers, the Association of Investment Trust Companies, the National Association of Pension Funds, and the Investment Management Association, adopted a statement of responsibilities and principles setting out their policy on how they will discharge their responsibilities. This includes:

* clarifying the priorities attached to particular issues and when they will take action
* monitoring the performance of, and establishing, where necessary, a regular dialogue with portfolio companies;

- intervening where necessary;
- evaluating the impact of their activism; and
- reporting back to clients/beneficial owners.

In the discussion of the obligation to intervene when necessary, the report says:

> Institutional shareholders' primary duty is to those on whose behalf they invest, for example, the beneficiaries of a pension scheme or the policyholders in an insurance company, and they must act in their best financial interests. Similarly, agents must act in the best interests of their clients. Effective monitoring will enable institutional shareholders and/or agents to exercise their votes and, where necessary, intervene objectively and in an informed way. Where it would make intervention more effective, they should seek to engage with other shareholders.
>   Many issues could give rise to concerns about shareholder value. Institutional shareholders and/or agents should set out the circumstances when they will actively intervene and how they propose to measure the effectiveness of doing so. Intervention should be considered by institutional shareholders and/or agents regardless of whether an active or passive investment policy is followed. In addition, being underweight is not, of itself, a reason for not intervening. Instances when institutional shareholders and/or agents may want to intervene include when they have concerns about:

- the company's strategy;
- the company's operational performance;
- the company's acquisition/disposal strategy;
- independent directors failing to hold executive management properly to account;
- internal controls failing;
- inadequate succession planning;
- an unjustifiable failure to comply with the Combined Code;
- inappropriate remuneration levels/incentive packages/severance packages; and
- the company's approach to corporate social responsibility.

If boards do not respond constructively when institutional shareholders and/or agents intervene, then institutional shareholders and/or agents will consider on a case-by-case basis whether to escalate their action, for example, by:

- holding additional meetings with management specifically to discuss concerns;
- expressing concern through the company's advisers;
- meeting with the chairman, senior independent director, or with all independent directors;
- intervening jointly with other institutions on particular issues;
- making a public statement in advance of the AGM or an EGM;
- submitting resolutions at shareholders' meetings; and
- requisitioning an EGM, possibly to change the board.

Institutional shareholders and/or agents should vote all shares held directly or on behalf of clients wherever it is practicable to do so. They will not automatically support the board; if they have been unable to reach a satisfactory outcome through active dialogue then they will register an abstention or vote against the resolution. In both instances it is good practice to inform the company in advance of their intention and the reasons why.

## *Economically targeted investments*

A number of states are experimenting with "social investing" (often called "economically targeted investments" or ETI), the investment of state pension funds in local companies, programs, or securities which may not meet traditional standards for risk and return. A commission convened by New York Governor Mario Cuomo released a report in 1989 called *Our Money's Worth*, recommending that the state pension fund consider the impact of its investments on the state economy as one aspect of its investment strategy. It also recommended the creation of a state agency to act as a clearing-house to find these investments, and this agency was in fact created the following year.

Former professor D. Jeanne Patterson of Indiana University published a thoughtful analysis of the ETI programs of the public pension funds in the Great Lakes states (Michigan, Illinois, Ohio, Wisconsin, Indiana) in 1992. She found that the "targeted investments" averaged about four percentage points below the S&P 500 stock index over a five-year period, and about two percentage points below the Wilshire 5,000 index during the same period. Citing Harvard professor E. Merrick Dodd's well-known argument that "It is not for the trustee to be public-spirited with his beneficiary's property," she concludes that "there will be continuing pressure for federal controls because of the excesses of a few systems."[108] She adds that "we must remember that the use of (public employee retirement system funds) to *subsidize* economic development efforts is inappropriate," citing Regan's view that "the greatest good a [state pension fund] can do for its state is to maximize return on investments and reduce the contributions necessary from taxpayers."[109] Look at the discussion of private pension funds' version of ETIs in this chapter. Compare this to claims made in a lawsuit by a group of ministers and lay employees charging that their pension funds' environmental and political investment restrictions resulted in inferior financial performance. Predictably, their complaint provoked references to the necessity of choosing between God and Mammon, but it also showed the difficulty in pinpointing which is which.

*List the risks and benefits of ETI programs. How do you ensure that these investments are not "concessionary"? Compare the efforts to expand (or "weaken," depending on who is describing it) the fiduciary standard of pension trustees and members of boards of directors, both at least ostensibly to factor in the concerns of a broader community. This is a key issue. How would you structure an ETI program to avoid both the risks of "over-investment" in enormous, mature companies and the risks of reduced economic returns from investment on the basis of non-economic goals like public housing or protecting jobs?*

# Case in point: Can a fiduciary invest in Volkswagen?

Volkswagen (VW) has a widely known and respected brand name. Its design and product qualities are at the top of the automobile industry. Innovest, the Toronto-based, strategic value-advising firm, concludes that VW will outperform the industry. In its June 2001 rating, "Volkswagen received a rating of AA, ranking 3 out of 14 Automobile companies in this sector." This suggests that Volkswagen would be an attractive investment – but it is not the whole story.

The largest shareholder in VW is the government of Lower Saxony with a little less than 20 percent (18.6 percent), which has been adequate to maintain control. Government officials have typically been on the supervisory board – Federal Chancellor Schroeder used to be chairman when he was the chief state officer – and it is clear that the company is run in large measure for the benefit of the state. Five out of its seven manufacturing plants are located there, notwithstanding a productivity of 46 cars per worker per year in contrast to 101 cars for the Japanese plants in northern England. VW stock is at approximately the same level – $45/shares – as it was in 1997, even though it rose 40 percent in 2000 representing the effect of a $2 billion stock buy-back. Using conventional investment ratios, VW is valued by the market at about half the level of its competitors – 7–8 times projected 2002 earnings as against an average of 13–14 and Daimler Chrysler at 16. VW's market capitalization $17.6 billion is 20 percent less than that of BMW, although it has twice the revenue.

VW appears twice cursed from an investment point of view. Its earnings are reduced by needlessly high operating costs dictated by non-commercial considerations, and the multiple that the market applies to even these reduced earnings is drastically lower than the industry average, representing lack of confidence that there is commitment to earnings growth. Lower Saxony as the controlling shareholder receives additional benefits of (1) subsidy of non-competitive wages and (2) subsidized tax revenues, the subsidy being extracted from the other shareholders. Like many large companies, VW has been able to finance its operations from internal sources and is, as a practical matter, not subject to the cost of capital discipline of the marketplace. It would be interesting to know the extent to which the compensation of the principal officers of VW depends on the stock price.

How can a global investor justify acquiring VW common stock? In the short term, it is always possible to "buy low and sell high," but that is not a responsible investment policy for fiduciaries. A long-term investment decision would have to be based on the conclusion that the level of political and social harmony achieved through subsidies to Lower Saxony compares favorably to the costs of competitors in achieving comparable conditions in other locations. Otherwise, the holder of VW is faced with the prospect of never being able to generate free cash, either for distribution or reinvestment, at the level of others in the industry. The global investor must evaluate the extent to which attention to non-profit-oriented values decreases the risk of continuing earnings and profits. When these values are unique to a major shareholder – like Lower Saxony in the case of Volkswagen – it would be difficult to conclude spillover benefits adequate to compensate the global investor.

# Case in point:
# Socially responsible investing

Peter Camejo's 2002 book, *The SRI Advantage: Why Socially Responsible Investing has Outperformed Financially*, asks why pension trustees fail to consider socially responsible investing, despite the fact that it has higher returns and less risk than a portfolio that does not screen for issues like compliance with environmental and labor laws. He says that the pressure for money managers hired by pension trustees to rely on short-term benchmarks leads to a kind of lowest common denominator investment strategy.

## Federal Employee Retirement System

In 1986, the US government established what will in time be the largest institutional investor in the world, the Federal Employee Retirement System (FERS). Up to that point, the federal employees had operated outside of the social security system. Like social security, the federal retirement system had no "fund" – money paid in by today's workers was immediately sent out to retirees. FERS was created in large part to help bail out social security by adding the federal employees to the pot, and by making their part of the pot a growing one. The Federal Employee Retirement System Act of 1986 (FERSA) made it possible for the first time for federal employees to create "defined-contribution plans" that they could invest in a variety of securities of their choice, including equities.

Congress wanted to allow federal employees the benefits of being allowed to invest their retirement funds in equity securities (which, as noted elsewhere in this book, according to all of the long-term analyses, have the best rate of return of all classes of available investment). The creation of FERS was not a simple matter of politics or policy, however. It raised a number of troubling issues, many of which were discussed in congressional hearings. As we have noted, widespread private ownership is viewed as an essential ingredient of democratic government and free enterprise. But the federal government already exerts enormous power over the private sector. *What would the impact be if we made Uncle Sam the country's largest shareholder as well?* Congress was reluctant to give an agency of government – the trustees of the pension fund – power over the private economy. When President John F. Kennedy became angry with the steel companies, he mobilized the government's purchasing power to force them to retract a price increase. *What could he have done if the US was also the steel industry's largest shareholder?* (For a suggested scenario, see the Koppers case in point above.)

**Table 2.1** State pension system targeted investment programs

| State | Housing debt financing | | | | Economic development debt financing | | equity financing | | |
|---|---|---|---|---|---|---|---|---|---|
| | multi-family | single family | rehab. | construction | small business | inductrial/commercial | real estate | venture indust. | env. |
| Alabama | | • | | | | | • | • | |
| Alaska | | • | | | | | | | • |
| Arkansas | | | | | • | • | | | |
| California | | • | | | • | | • | • | |
| Colorado | | | | | • | • | • | | |
| Connecticut | | • | | • | | | | • | |
| Hawaii | | • | | | | • | | | |
| Illinois (Chicago) | • | | | | | | | | |
| Massachusetts | • | • | | | • | | | • | |
| Michigan | | | | | • | | • | | • |

*Prepared by*: Center for Policy Alternatives, 1875 Connecticut Ave., NW, Suite 710 Washington, DC 20009

No one wanted to create a system in which federal officials could, through purchase or sale of the securities of a particular industry – or even, in an extreme case, a particular company – compel corporate America to comply with or even support the policies of a particular government. No one wanted federal employees with regulatory and enforcement authority over industries and companies to be able to buy and sell and vote proxies in these companies through their pension funds. Would an employee of the Environmental Protection Agency go short on a company he knew was soon to be the target of an enforcement effort? Would an employee of the Food and Drug Administration buy stock in the company whose experimental medication he was testing? Would an employee of the Occupational Safety and Health Administration over- or under-regulate a particular industry depending on what was in his portfolio? The possibilities for abuse were almost endless.

FERSA solved that problem by limiting the options for investment. The law required that equity investments be in an "index" that reflected the economy as a whole. The trustees selected the S&P 500 and appointed Wells Fargo to administer the equity fund. Wells Fargo then became part of Barclays Global, so that now the pension fund of the employees of the US government is being managed by a non-US investment firm.

That solved the issue of buying and selling, but it left the issue of voting and other corporate governance opportunities. At the legislative hearings on FERSA, the issue was raised explicitly. Republican Senator Ted Stevens from Alaska and former Social Security Commissioner Stan Ross engaged in an illuminating dialogue. It shows that everyone wished to avoid "back-door socialism." As a result, FERSA provides simply that: "The Board, other government agencies, the Executive Director, an employee, a member, a former employee, and a former member may not exercise voting rights associated with the ownership of securities by the Thrift Savings Fund."[110] The trustees were made responsible for the management of FERSA's assets and yet were prohibited from being involved in the "ownership" portion of the security. They delegated voting power to Wells Fargo.

The story of the federal retirement system's ownership of equity securities illustrates the fractionalization of ownership. The layers of ownership exemplify the evolution from the individual shareholder to the institutional shareholder.

- Trustees appointed by the President with the consent of the Senate are the legal owner of the interest in Barclay's S&P 500 index fund.
- The trustees of the index fund are the legal owners of the portfolio equity securities.
- The federal employee – the beneficial owner – has no right to make a decision about whether to buy or sell stock in a particular company. Indeed, he hasn't even chosen a particular equity index (the FERSA trustees did that); he has only elected to invest a portion of his retirement plan in the equity mode.
- Neither the federal plan trustees nor the federal employee are legally permitted to exercise their ownership rights respecting shares of common stock.
- Ownership responsibilities are dumped onto Barclays. An index fund is committed to market returns. It cannot compete with other index funds on returns. Although there is some competition between various indexes, the major basis for competition is on fees. Index funds save money because they do not have to hire analysts to follow companies and make investment decisions. Whatever resources Barclays commits to getting information in order to be able to monitor its portfolio companies effectively make it less competitive both with other index funds and other modes of equity investment. In addition, it faces the "collective choice" and "free rider" problems mentioned in the discussion of the prisoner's dilemma.

It is hard to consider an individual federal employee as the owner of portfolio companies. His interest is fractionalized among 500 companies and he is forbidden by law to make any decision with respect to the shares of a particular company. Those who are entrusted with "ownership" responsibility have a pervasive economic disincentive to discharge them in a substantively meaningful way.

> Who is the real "owner" of these companies (or even of these equity securities)? Who is best equipped to take on the responsibilities and make the most of the opportunities that accompany company share ownership?

Furthermore, the federal government has not confronted its own massive under-funding problems. "If the government were forced to adhere to the same accounting standards [as private funds], retirement programs for civilian and military employees would be under-funded by more than $1 trillion. What's more, if Uncle Sam were required to reserve for pensions as they are accrued by workers – the way corporations are – the federal budget deficit would be roughly one-third higher . . . Thanks to aging baby boomers within the civil service, the funds needed to cover annual benefit payments by 2010 are expected to nearly triple, to $160 billion."[111]

## TIAA–CREF

The Teachers Insurance and Annuity Association–College Retirement Equities Fund (TIAA–CREF) is in a category of its own, a pension fund that is neither quite public nor quite private. The $125 billion fund manages pension money for 1.5 million teachers and other employees of tax-exempt organizations. It has $273 billion in total, including over $100 billion in equities. In 2001, TIAA–CREF was among the top 100 in *Fortune* magazine's listing of the 500 largest US corporations. Its size and its unique position have given it unusual freedom from commercial or political restrictions on involvement with corporate governance. It is therefore not surprising that it has often been the first, if not the most visible, with shareholder initiatives. Its 1986 proposal to put International Paper's poison pill to a shareholder vote was the first such proposal by an institutional investor to be voted on. And it pioneered the "preferred placement" initiatives, asking companies not to offer preferred equities to "white squires" without shareholder approval.

In 1993, the fund announced a broader program, and released a detailed list of its corporate governance policies, saying "TIAA–CREF acknowledges a responsibility to be an advocate for improved corporate governance and performance discipline."[112] The policies provided the basis on which TIAA–CREF said it intended to pursue all of its portfolio companies. "The significance is not the three or four laggards you catch – it's that you get the herd to run," said chairman John Biggs. "We need to scare all the animals."[113] The policy statement also gave considerable space to a discussion of executive compensation issues – specifically, determining what constitutes "excessive" compensation, evaluating the soundness of policies and criteria for setting compensation, and deciding what constitutes adequate disclosure. There is some irony in the fact that CREF's own 1993 proxy statement, issued to its plan participant/shareholders, included a shareholder resolution concerning the executive compensation at CREF itself, complaining about the CEO's salary of over $1 million a year.

The primary focus of TIAA–CREF's policy statement was on the board of directors. They encouraged boards with a majority of outside, independent directors, and said that key board committees should be made up exclusively of independents. Moreover, TIAA–CREF did not believe that directors who have other business dealings with the corporation (as a legal representative for instance) should be considered independent.[114] Biggs said that the fund would be willing to withhold votes for directors "where companies don't have an effective, independent board challenging the CEO.[115] TIAA–CREF's website explains their current views on corporate governance:

> We acknowledge that even an ideal system of corporate governance does not guarantee superior performance. Conversely, superior performance can be achieved despite a governance system that is less than perfect. Nevertheless, TIAA–CREF believes that certain principles are the hallmark of an equitable and efficient corporate governance structure. Good corporate governance must be expected to maintain an appropriate balance between the rights of shareholders – the owners of the corporation – and the need of the board and management to direct and manage the corporation's affairs free from nonstrategic short-term influences. TIAA–CREF acknowledges a responsibility to be an advocate for improved corporate governance and performance discipline.

They also discuss their interaction with portfolio companies:

> TIAA–CREF believes that its policies on corporate governance should be shaped and allowed to evolve in collaboration with the companies in which it invests. Accordingly, we will continue to take the following steps, which have proven valuable in the past:
>
> • Provide copies of these guidelines and their updates to companies in which we invest. We will suggest that the companies distribute the guidelines to all executive officers and directors.
> • Periodically seek suggestions from companies and knowledgeable observers for ways to improve the guidelines.
> • Arrange for occasional informal forums for company managers, directors, and TIAA–CREF managers to review the guidelines.
> • Send copies of the guidelines to other large institutional investors, make them available upon request, send them to appropriate information clearinghouses, and publish them for TIAA–CREF participants and participating institutions to review and offer suggestions for change.
> • Enter into private discussions with companies regarding perceived shortcomings in governance structure or policies.

In 2002, TIAA–CREF was on the other end of shareholder activism as its own annual meeting was picketed by social justice advocacy groups, asking it to make some disclosure and corporate governance changes: revealing its proxy votes, reporting on how it takes into account social issues in its investing, and splitting the positions of Chair and CEO. The groups also asked TIAA–CREF to: (1) take action on Unocal and Singapore Technologies, two companies in its stock portfolio that are invested in Burma, a country with one of the world's worst human rights records; (2) sell its stock in Philip Morris, the world's largest tobacco corporation; (3) remove Nike from the fund's portfolio due the company's notorious sweatshop abuses; and (4) divest holdings in British Petroleum because of this company's involvement in egregious human rights violations associated with gas extraction in Chinese-occupied Tibet.

# PRIVATE PENSION FUNDS

The largest category of institutional investors is pension funds managed for the benefit of employees of private companies. ERISA, the law that governs private pension funds, was intended to encourage private companies to create pension plans, and to protect the money in those plans once they were created. The statute was designed to resolve questions of conflicts of interest and liability that had left the private pension system uncertain, even chaotic. The two public interest problems it was designed to solve were under-funded pensions and unvested pensions. "These are the institutions then that create the distinctive ERISA problems: funding, with managerial direction of the funds, and under-funding, with government guarantees of performance."[116]

ERISA funds are most often handled by outside money managers who range from one extreme to the other in their focus on proxy voting. A recent trend, endorsed by the Business Roundtable, is for plan sponsors to leave other aspects of the fund management outside, but to take the proxy voting in house. Given the natural pro-management outlook of people who are, after all, part of management, this can be expected to result in more consistently pro-management votes. But in all cases, whether the money is managed in house or outside, "The brute fact that managers control their own firms' pensions is central. Few managers want their pension more active in the corporate governance of other companies than they would want their own stockholders to be active in the firm . . . Although arising from other intentions, [ERISA's] doctrines fit well with managerial goals of shareholder passivity."[117] Despite their size, ERISA funds face the same problem of "collective choice" and "free riders" that all shareholders do: *Can it be prudent for them to expend resources, knowing that, without the ability to communicate with other shareholders, any positive results are unlikely?* Even if the results are positive, any returns to the active shareholder will only be proportionate to its holdings, all of the other shareholders getting a free ride.

For private pension funds, perhaps, this problem is presented most sharply. To the extent that a company's pension department adopts an activist posture with respect to portfolio companies, it risks retribution: retaliation in the marketplace and an invitation to other pension professionals to take an equally aggressive view of their own functioning. All the more reason, then, to do nothing, to try to maximize value by trading, despite the fact that all evidence indicates that the majority of those who do so fail to outperform the market.

ERISA fiduciaries must meet all of the obligations of prudence and diligence that any trustee must meet under the common law. The ERISA statute starts with that standard and then imposes obligations beyond those of traditional trust law. One reason for the additional obligation is that ERISA permits a "non-neutral fiduciary,"[118] which would not be allowed under the common law of trusts. Under traditional trust law, the first requirement for a trustee is that he or she must be "neutral," and must have no conflicts of interest that would interfere with the ability to administer the trust assets in the sole interest of the trust beneficiary. But it is a fact of ERISA that in pension plans, unlike traditional trusts, there is an inevitable and inherent conflict of interest. Employers and employees are both settlors (the party that provides the pension) and beneficiaries (the party that receives the pension). And the plan sponsor is the party at risk of having to make up the difference if the plan is poorly run, even if there is no negligence, a level of risk that a "neutral" trustee does not have to face.

ERISA requires that a "named fiduciary"[119] with responsibility for the plan be designated by the company, called a "plan sponsor."[120] Typically, a major corporation designates a committee of the board of directors as the "named fiduciary." ERISA recognizes that these people are too busy and important to watch over the pension fund money, so it permits them to delegate authority (and responsibility and potential liability) to an invest-ment manager. So long as the selection of the investment manager is prudent, and the plan sponsor monitors its performance, the plan sponsor company will not be liable for the investment manager's mistakes. The standard is utterly process-oriented. As long as there is a reasonable process, and it is followed, the Department of Labor (DOL) will not second-guess the results. This applies to all investment decisions, whether buy-sell deci-sions or decisions on the exercise of proxy voting and other governance rights.

The passage of ERISA in 1974 put the fear of God into trustees of private systems. There was almost as much of an impact on the public systems, which usually *de facto* hold themselves to the ERISA standard, at least in terms of process. With liability avoidance as the primary goal, the trustees developed the practice of hiring consultants of all kinds and shapes to advise the trustees. By and large these consultants have succeeded in placing a floor beneath which the trustees feel they cannot go. The stress is on "process." The "pro-cess" is simple: "Walk slowly and cover your tracks." (This is reflected in the conclusions of O'Barr and Conley cited above.) And this is the basic message of consultants' elegant presentations, often in exotic locales, to which pension fiduciaries are invited, all designed to shield the trustees from liability no matter what actually happens with their investments.[121] ERISA funds have not been noticeably active in exercising ownership rights. The issues of pension fund management (and the small subset of issues that come up for a vote on proxies) are remote from whatever goods or services the plan sponsor company produces, so it is easier to file the pension fund away under "human resources."[122] And, as we have seen in the case of the public pension funds, meaningful exercise of the ownership rights of private pension assets is thankless. No investment manager, in house or outside, ever got paid extra for voting proxies well, because that would mean a number of votes against management recommendations. For that reason, the ERISA funds have been among the least visible of institutional shareholders.

There is some evidence of change, however. In 1991, departing from their usual pro-management line, the ERISA funds sharply distinguished themselves from at least some traditional management positions in the letter to the SEC from the Committee on Investment of Employee Benefit Assets (CIEBA).[123] CIEBA's members are corporate benefit plan sponsors, representing $600 billion in collective assets managed on behalf of 8 mil-lion plan participants. The letter gave guarded backing to proxy rule changes that were often opposed by top company managements. For instance, CIEBA said that any changes to the proxy process should include giving shareholders a vote when companies want to adopt a "poison pill" or other anti-takeover defenses. But CIEBA has not been visible, much less outspoken, in any matter of corporate governance or shareholder activism since then.

# Cases in point:
# Campbell's Soup, General Motors

**Campbell's Soup**. In July of 1993, Campbell Soup Company's $1 billion pension fund became the first major ERISA plan to make a commitment to "investing" in shareholder activism. Until that point, institutional shareholder activism had been largely the province of public pension funds. Proud of its own corporate governance structure and record, Campbell's pension fund announced that it would direct the firms managing their pension fund's equity investments to vote their proxies against companies that elect more than three inside directors or re-price stock options after falling stock prices leave them with little value. Campbell's also said it would direct its money managers to vote their proxies to emphasize linking executive pay to performance.

**General Motors**. In late 1993, General Motors announced that it hoped to reduce its massive ($17 billion) pension under-funding by contributing $5.7 billion of newly issued shares of GM Class E stock (which are linked to the earnings of the EDS subsidiary) to its pension plan. The pension fund would then hold 38 percent of the EDS shares. This would require special legislation granting the company relief from tax penalties, and special rulings by the Internal Revenue Service and the Labor Department. GM at that time had the most under-funded private plan in the country, meaning the largest gap between its assets and its expected payout. In 2003, the pension fund was $19 billion under-funded, creating so much pressure on the company that it resulted in deep discounts on its cars and trucks.

At around the same time, PPG Industries announced that it would contribute 1.5 million of its shares to its pension fund, and Tenneco Inc. announced that, having already contributed 225,000 of its own shares, it would contribute the 3.2 million shares it owned in Cummins Engine Inc., a joint venture partner. A Tenneco spokeswoman said, "It was a way to achieve two things, to bring pension funding closer to where it needs to be, and to do so without using cash."[124] IBM planned to put up to 15 million shares into its pension fund. Chrysler contributed 30 million shares to its pension plans in 1991, when the stock was trading at around $10 a share, about one-fifth of what it was three years later. A Chrysler executive supports this approach: "The beauty of contributing stock to your pension fund is that the act of contributing increases the equity base of the company, and if, in fact, the stock appreciates in value, the benefit goes to the pension fund."[125] An executive at another company noted that his company saved time and investment banking fees by contributing stock to the pension fund instead of presenting it to the public equity market.

> *Who is benefiting here? Is it consistent with the fiduciary obligation of a pension fiduciary to contribute an asset to the plan when he appears unsure, if not indifferent, as to whether it will appreciate in value?*

The strongest bull market in American history led to a huge additional boost to corporate earnings as the corporate pension plans, invested heavily in equities, performed extremely well, contributing the surplus to the companies' earnings. But as the market softened, pension assumptions had to be recalibrated, and the bottom line at many companies took a hit. In John Plender's 2003 book, *Going Off the Rails*, he coins the term "pension fund glasnost," because

> the bear market had an impact not unlike that of glasnost in the Soviet Union. It exposed an economic reality that people had previously been no more than faintly aware of . . . This creates enormous corporate vulnerability to the gyrations of equity prices, especially in the more mature sectors of the economy where defined benefit schemes predominate . . . British Airways, for example, could reasonably be characterized as a hedge fund with a sideline in air transport. Its viability is even more dependent on the mood swings of the equity market than on the fortunes of the airline business.

Because accounting rules count the predicted rather than actual increase in pension assets and allow the surplus to be blended in with operating earnings, the assumptions can have a critical impact on a company's balance sheet. And no one wants to give that up, which accounts for some of the rosy predictions for pension returns that seem to bear no connection to the market's performance. According to Deepa Babington's article in a February 3, 2003 issue of *Forbes* called "Wild Optimism Rides High in Pension Accounting," "Of the first 45 S&P 100 companies to report fourth-quarter earnings [in early 2003], the 22 that spelled out their new assumptions have cut them to an average of about 8.7 percent from 9.6 percent, according to an analysis by Reuters. But the cuts in the crucial expected rate of return on pension assets may not be enough to keep pace with stock market declines . . . By contrast, investor advocate Warren Buffett, who frequently attacks high pension fund assumptions, uses a 6.5 percent rate for his company, Berkshire Hathaway Inc."

California State Controller Kathleen O'Connell has called upon the state pension funds to limit or withdraw investments from companies that take advantage of what she calls an "accounting gimmick." Analyst David Zion recommends carrying the pension fund at its actual fair market value, to minimize distortion and remove incentives for financial engineering. And S&P developed a "core earnings" calculation that removes the distortion of the pension assumptions from the balance sheet.

Westinghouse contributed 22 million shares trading at $16.50 in 1991, about $3 a share more than the stock price in 1994, when the company contributed a further 16 million shares. On the other hand, Xerox guidelines prohibit such donations. "We feel there is enough exposure on the part of the employees to the fortunes of Xerox, and there ought not to be additional exposure through the pension fund" said Myra Drucker, then assistant treasurer.[126]

> *Examine the finances and the policy of contributing the issuers' own stock to the pension fund, both from the perspective of the company and the employees. Is Drucker right?*

This is a good example of the problems of the "non-neutral fiduciary," because what is best from the perspective of the corporation's financial structure (forced sale of company stock to the friendliest and longest-term possible hands), may not be best from the perspective of the plan beneficiaries, whose pension money is tied up in stock that may not be the best possible investment.

# Case in point: "Universal Widget"

Universal Widget's pension plan holds the largest block of the company's stock. Universal's performance has been very poor over the past ten years, following a series of disastrous acquisitions and declining market share. The plan trustee is a major bank that also handles Universal's commercial accounts. It routinely votes the proxies in the pension fund for management.

> *Under what circumstances do "prudence" and "diligence" require action on the part of the trustee, either shareholder proposals, withholding votes for the board, or more aggressive initiatives? In other words, how bad does it have to get? (See also the Carter Hawley Hale and Stone & Webster case studies in chapter 6.)*

Many observers are concerned that the pension system may require a bailout that will make the savings and loan crisis look small. In 1993, the Pension Benefit Guaranty Corporation, a federal government agency that insures private pension systems, announced that the unfunded liabilities of just the worst 50 pension plans alone had grown by 31 percent in the last year, to $38 billion, of which $31.7 billion is guaranteed by the PBGC (and the taxpayers).

*Given that trustees hold a majority of the ownership of the major US companies, this collective ownership is large enough to mitigate significantly the "free rider" problem. Should the courts and the government monitoring agencies enforce the fiduciary obligation of trustees to their beneficiaries by requiring some kind of active monitoring? Collective action?*

If fiduciaries are genuinely "required" to vote independently, it will be all but impossible for commercial conflicts to interfere. Mark Roe says, "ERISA's key fiduciary restraint is *not* to force passivity but to *reinforce* whatever the prevailing practice is. ERISA mandates imitation." He recommends consideration of four possible changes to ERISA doctrine to enable more effective shareholder monitoring: a safe harbor specifying that an ERISA fiduciary could meet its diversification goals with "say, 20 or 50 stocks in different industries," "netting" for big block investments (absent wrongdoing), limiting the liability of pension funds to the business judgment rule for boardroom actions, and scrutinizing pension managers more carefully when they have conflicts of interest stemming from their position as corporate managers.

ERISA funds are also subject to the pressure for "economically targeted investments." In the early 1990s, the US government considered the establishment of a clearing-house like the one created in New York State to encourage ETI investment by ERISA funds, but the proposal was never adopted. And a report by the ERISA advisory council released in January of 1993 recommended that pension fund fiduciaries be permitted to consider "collateral benefits" (like increased employment) from their investments, though it did not say anything about collateral costs (like the costs of seeking out or monitoring these investments). On September 2, 1993, Olena Berg, Assistant Secretary of Labor for Pension and Welfare Benefits, delivered a speech to the AFL–CIO Asset Managers Conference. While emphasizing that she was in no way recommending or even countenancing "concessionary" investments (accepting a lower return in order to support some social goal), she asked pension trustees to recognize that "investments that promote a more productive, healthier economy over the long run serve the best interests of plan participants. These two objectives, of maximizing pension fund performance and investing pension fund assets in a manner which strengthens the American economy, need not be, and, indeed, are not inconsistent."[127] She urged the audience to consider "underutilized indicators" of long-term corporate performance, like "the ability to develop and retain a highly trained, high performance workplace." And she promised that the Department of Labor would study the relationship between indicators like that and long-term performance, to assist pension trustees in evaluating these data.

## THE SLEEPING GIANT AWAKENS: SHAREHOLDER PROXY PROPOSALS ON GOVERNANCE ISSUES

As noted above, some institutional shareholders became more active in exercising the rights of share ownership in the late 1980s. Initially a reaction to the abuses of the takeover era, this activism gained a life of its own as it focused on performance – and on boards of directors as the place to go when performance was unsatisfactory.

The reach and power of this trend can be seen in the number of shareholder proposals and the number of votes in favor of them. For many years these proposals were the exclusive province of legendary corporate "gadflies" like the Gilbert brothers, Evelyn Y. Davis, and Wilma Soss. Soss inspired the delightful play (later a movie) *The Solid Gold Cadillac*, still remarkably relevant to current corporate governance issues.

This small group, cheered on by a few, ridiculed by more, and dreaded by corporate management, really created the field of shareholder activism. In 1932, the late Lewis Gilbert attended the annual meeting of New York City's Consolidated Gas Co. Gilbert was unhappy with the chairman's refusal to recognize shareholder questions from the floor. He and his brother John Gilbert began buying stock (their investment policy was "never sell") and attending meetings. Their actions led to the SEC's adopting rule 14a-8 in 1942, giving shareholders the right to have their proposals included in the company's proxy statements. The early gadflies began submitting shareholder resolutions on corporate governance topics like executive compensation, cumulative voting, and the location of the annual meeting.

Public interest advocates noted this approach with approval in the 1960s, and the range of topics for shareholder proposals expanded beyond the governance realm into social activism. Public pension funds, union pension funds and church groups sponsored shareholder resolutions on "social policy" issues like investment in South Africa or the sale of infant formula. The vote of less than 3 percent for Ralph Nader's 1970 "Campaign GM" shareholder proposals was hailed as a victory of unprecedented levels for a shareholder initiative. These groups have continued to submit social policy proposals, which have received votes of 20 percent and higher. Some of these proposals have become something of a hybrid, combining elements of social policy and corporate governance. These include proposals regarding tobacco, defense manufacturing, and environmental issues, South Africa, and Northern Ireland. Members of the Interfaith Center on Corporate Responsibility, an organization that promotes corporate social accountability, sponsored many of these resolutions.

All indications are that this area will expand. The Parents' Television Council, which had urged its members to write to the sponsors of offensive television programs, began to suggest that members who own stock in those companies submit shareholder proposals, and included sample language in its newsletter. A 2000 report from Amnesty International, titled *Human Rights – Is it Any of Your Business?*, warns that advocacy groups will challenge the reputation of multinational corporations that fail to make a public commitment to fair and safe labor practices. It advises corporate board members that they cannot afford to be ignorant or neglectful on labor and environmental matters. "Companies have a direct self-interest in using their legitimate influence to protect and promote the human rights of their employees and of the community in which they are investing and/or operating," the report says.

In 1993, US District Court judge Kimba Wood overturned the SEC's determination that Wal-Mart did not have to include a shareholder resolution asking the company to issue a report on its affirmative action and equal employment opportunity programs. The resolution was sponsored by the Amalgamated Clothing and Textile Workers Union and several church groups.[128] The SEC found that the proposal concerned "ordinary business," which, as the exclusive province of corporate managers, was not appropriate for shareholder initiatives. This was a reversal of the SEC's policy before 1991, when it viewed employment issues as raising important policy questions. Judge Wood agreed with the earlier view. Similarly, in 1993, the New York City Employees Retirement System (NYC-ERS) sued the SEC after the agency allowed Cracker Barrel Old Country Store Inc. to exclude NYCERS' resolution asking the company to rescind its policy prohibiting gay employees. The SEC agreed with Cracker Barrel that the issue came under the heading of "ordinary business" and was thus not suitable for shareholder comment. NYCERS argued that the issue had broader economic implications: "Limiting the available talent pool from which a company can choose employees and managers puts that company at a disadvantage in the labor marketplace" said NYCERS chairwoman, Carol O'Cleireacain.[129]

In 1998, the Commission reversed its position, and decided to permit proposals on issues of employment discrimination. Cracker Barrel, meanwhile, had rescinded its anti-gay policy.

*Compare this to the Wrigley Field example in the introduction, and describe an optimal "ordinary business" standard.*

The United Shareholders Association (USA), founded in 1986 by T. Boone Pickens, had thousands of members in all 50 states and became a powerful force for activism by individual investors, providing information about companies, issues, and the mechanics of filing. USA members filed a large proportion of the shareholder resolutions each year, and USA was instrumental in persuading the SEC to amend the proxy rules and was a prominent commentator on executive pay issues. It closed down in 1993, following the SEC's successful overhaul of the shareholder communication rules, but some of its most active members continued to fight.

By the late 1980s, many major companies, particularly poorly performing companies, routinely had at least one shareholder resolution, sometimes as many as five or six, submitted by individuals, union pension funds, church groups, and public pension funds. Even though virtually all shareholder resolutions are precatory only, companies have increasingly responded to them, often negotiating with proponents so that the proposals are not voted on at the annual meeting. USA found, in its last year, that 29 of 50 resolutions were withdrawn after successful negotiation. CalPERS found that 11 of the 12 companies it targeted were prepared to make concessions.

As institutional investors began to use governance resolutions to fight disenfranchising anti-takeover devices corporate management installed to protect themselves from changes in control, the levels of support grew. A little more than 20 years after Campaign GM, shareholder resolutions routinely get votes ranging from 20 to 40 percent, and increasingly even majority support. In 1987, the first corporate governance resolutions from institutional investors (mostly relating to poison pills) were submitted at 34 companies, with votes in favor ranging from about 20 to 30 percent. A year later, two of these resolutions got majority votes, one concerning a poison pill, one prohibiting payment of greenmail. Both were at companies where proxy contests for control provided a good deal of visibility (and engendered a good deal of shareholder support). The more significant development that year, though, was the "Avon letter," issued by the DOL on February 23. As described in greater detail below, it was the first formal ruling by the agency with jurisdiction over the ERISA funds that the right to vote proxies was a "plan asset." Money managers across the country began to establish procedures and policies for voting proxies.

But the following year, in 1989, there was the first proxy contest that was not over director candidates, but over corporate governance. And in 1998, TIAA–CREF became the first institutional investor to run a dissident slate of candidates for the board – and the first to succeed.

# Cases in point: Honeywell and Furr's

A large individual shareholder of Honeywell joined with two public pension funds and Institutional Shareholder Services Inc.,[130] to prevent management from adopting two of management's proposed changes. The company wanted to stagger the election of directors and to eliminate the right of the shareholders to act by written consent, instead of waiting for the annual meeting. The *ad hoc* coalition circulated its own proxy card and was successful at preventing management from getting the necessary level of support. Over the three-month period of the initiative, Honeywell common stock rose 22 percent, with each state of the contest sparking a favorable market reaction. While takeover rumors played a role, the market clearly recognized the value of active shareholder involvement in an underperforming company. The individual investor who paid the costs of the solicitation got a substantial return on his investment in activism – as did the other Honeywell shareholders. Figures 2.1 and 2.2 demonstrate the impact of this effort on trading volume.

In 1998, one of the largest institutional investors in the world, TIAA–CREF, became the first to run its own slate of candidates against those nominated by management. And it was successful. The TIAA–CREF candidates received 85 percent of the vote. The company was Furr's/Bishop's, a chain of restaurants. The circumstances were unusual, and TIAA–CREF made it clear that it was not about to expand its investment strategy into Carl Icahn's territory. TIAA became the holder of 17.7 percent of the common stock of Furr's/Bishop's following the company's default on debt that was issued to TIAA and other institutional investors, resulting in a major reorganization of the company in 1996. It was indisputably clear that the costs of a proxy contest would be substantially less than the costs of inaction, permitting the company's performance to deteriorate even further. Most of the stock was held by eight shareholders – with TIAA–CREF, they held more than 84 percent of the stock. And the board was so deeply dysfunctional (one report noted that the directors spent hours debating the flavor of one item on the dessert menu) that one member defected and joined the TIAA–CREF slate.

In 1990, shareholder resolutions on governance, mostly from public pension funds, continued to receive growing support. Two resolutions got majority votes, the first majority votes without a formal proxy solicitation. But the most important corporate governance issue of the year was the battle over Pennsylvania's controversial new anti-takeover law. Like most states, Pennsylvania adopted new laws to protect companies incorporated there from takeovers. But it went further, with a second set of amendments, when local company Armstrong World became a takeover target. The 1990 amendment was objected to so strongly by shareholders that nearly one-third of the state's companies (including over 60 percent of the Fortune 500 companies located in the state) opted out of at least one of its provisions (see "Protection, Pennsylvania-style" discussion in chapter 1).

In 1991, there was an unprecedented level of cooperation and negotiation between shareholders and management. Many of the shareholder resolutions submitted by institutional investors were withdrawn, following discussions with management and agreed-upon changes. Representatives of the shareholder and corporate community negotiated a "Compact Between Owners and Directors" that was published in *Harvard Business Review*.

Significant as the compact was, however, the 1991 proxy season demonstrated that management and investors were still far apart. One of the top governance stories of the year

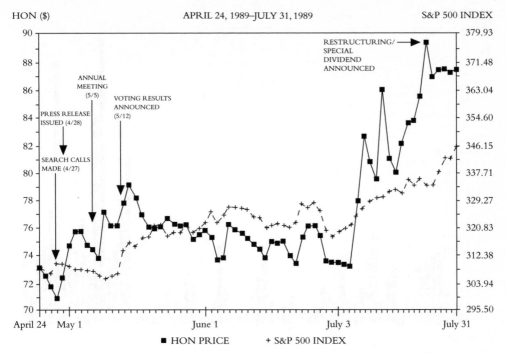

HON ($)          APRIL 24, 1989–JULY 31, 1989          S&P 500 INDEX

■ HON PRICE      + S&P 500 INDEX

*Note:* On October 31, 1989, Honeywell's closing stock price was $82^7/_8$. The closing value of the S&P 500 index was 340.36.

**Figure 2.1**    Honeywell vs. S&P 500 daily trading volume

was Robert Monks' proxy contest for one board seat at Sears, Roebuck (see the Sears case study).

And in the same year, for the first time, a corporate governance issue exploded, leaving the business pages to land on the front pages, the editorial pages, even the comic pages. The issue was, of course, executive compensation (see discussions in chapter 4). Even the business press used terms like "obscene" and "out of control" in describing the level of pay received by some top executives. Politicians and the mass media made it a central issue, and it has continued to be controversial, with pay packages that made those of a decade earlier seem paltry. Shareholders came full circle in the early 1990s, with shareholder proposals reminiscent of the proposals by the Gilbert brothers, half a century earlier. In 1991, ITT CEO Rand Araskog's pay increased by 103 percent to more than $11 million, in a year when ITT's shareholders watched the value of their stock decline 18 percent. Pressure from shareholder groups led the company to overhaul its compensation scheme for the top 500 employees, with very positive effects on the company's stock price. Also in 1991, the SEC reversed its long-term policy and allowed shareholder resolutions about pay. It gave the go-ahead to ten resolutions, all submitted by individual shareholders.

These resolutions were presented at annual meetings in the spring of 1992. While none got a majority vote, they all received substantial support, and one got 44 percent. Overall, though, the volume of shareholder proposals was down in 1992, largely because both shareholders and management were more interested in trying to find common ground through less confrontational methods. Many individual and institutional investors withdrew their proposals after successful negotiations.

SHARES (000s)        APRIL 27, 1989–JULY 31, 1989

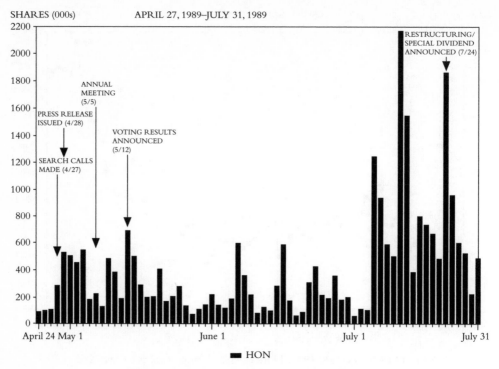

**Figure 2.2**  Honeywell daily trading volume

CalPERS, long at the vanguard of institutional shareholder activism, announced it would be, in the words of George Bush, "kinder and gentler," and it did not submit any shareholder resolutions that year. Instead it targeted a dozen under-performing companies, many with compensation schemes that had several of their widely distributed list of "danger signals" developed for them by compensation guru Graef Crystal. Although some companies stonewalled CalPERS (until their failure to respond was reported in the press), many of the companies were willing to meet and negotiate.

Boards of directors did respond to the increased levels of shareholder activism, and not just in making concessions to avoid shareholder resolutions. In just over 12 months – between October 1992 and December 1993 – the CEOs of no fewer than six major companies were pressured to resign in light of the long-term under-performance of the companies they managed. The six companies were:

- General Motors
- American Express
- Westinghouse
- IBM
- Eastman Kodak
- Borden Inc.

These resignations represented nothing less than a sea change in American governance. Boards of directors were finally holding management accountable for poor performance. Over the past decade, CEOs have been dismissed from Mattel, Scott Paper, Quaker, Sunbeam (the same CEO who was brought in to replace the one who was fired at Scott Paper),

Waste Management (two), Compaq, AT&T, Apple, Coca-Cola, and many others. As we discuss further in chapter 3, the "Pharaonic" CEO has given way to the fired CEO.

*Read the Eastman Kodak and General Motors case studies. Is pushing out the CEO a solution or just a first step in revitalizing a company? Is it just a dramatic gesture that doesn't address underlying problems with the company's operation? What are the problems associated with letting a company continue to under-perform to such a point that is it is necessary to replace the CEO? What less drastic steps can be taken earlier to ensure that the CEO need not be forced to resign? See also the discussion of "dinosaur" companies in chapter 3 for a look at those companies that remain successful for decades.*

## FOCUS ON THE BOARD

It was clear in 1992 and 1993 that large institutional shareholders, legislators, and even the corporate community have begun to look to boards to provide a more independent review of corporate performance, direction, and strategy. CalPERS CEO Dale Hanson told a group of corporate managers, "We are no longer into CEO bashing. We are now into director-bashing." After the early 1990s, shareholder focus turned from anti-takeover abuses and CEO pay-performance disparities to the perpetrators of those failures of oversight, the boards of directors.

From the shareholder perspective, the "just vote no" strategy became an increasingly important mechanism for sending a vote of no confidence. The 1 percent "withhold" vote at ITT in 1991 was overtaken in 1992 by 2 percent withhold votes at Dial and GM, 3 percent withhold votes at American Express, 4 percent at Westinghouse, Unisys, and Occidental Petroleum, 6 percent at Sears and Travelers, and a stunning 9 percent at Champion International.

Further concerns about the board have been reflected in shareholder resolutions calling for separate individuals to serve as chairman and CEO, compensation and nominating committees to be entirely made up of independent outside directors, and an overall majority of independent outside directors on the board as a whole.

Then New York State Comptroller Edward V. Regan circulated a proposal to permit large shareholders access to the company's proxy statement for brief evaluations of the performance of the board. In 1992, Robert Monks submitted a shareholder proposal at Exxon that would permit the creation of a Shareholder Advisory Committee, a group of shareholders, elected by shareholders, to meet (at company expense).[131] As with Regan's proposal, this group would be permitted to include its comments on the company in the corporate proxy statement. The California Public Employees' Retirement System negotiated the creation of such a committee with Ryder, and discussed similar committees with other companies.

Following the corporate scandals of 2002, the focus on the board became even more intense. Director and officer liability insurers, rating agencies, and even traditional investment analysts increasingly looked at the board as an element of investment risk.

## SEC'S PROXY REFORM

But the most significant development since the original adoption of the rules governing shareholder proposals was probably the October 1992 adoption of the SEC's proxy reform rule amendments. The initial proposal, in 1991, elicited an avalanche of comments. Nearly every representative of management objected; nearly every representative of shareholders supported them. The new rules make it easier for shareholders who are not seeking control of a company to communicate with each other. Previous rules required any shareholder who wants to communicate with more than ten other shareholders to have his comments approved by the SEC before they could be circulated. The new rules eliminated the SEC's role as editor/censor of this material, and required only that a copy be filed. Other aspects of the proposal made it easier for shareholders to get their material to each other.

The new rules made possible more effective shareholder oversight. But managers, directors, and shareholders must keep in mind that, just as shareholders' liability is limited, so is their agenda. The rules governing the appropriate topics for shareholder resolutions did not change, and a brief effort to do so failed. Shareholders do not have the expertise, the resources, or the right to get involved in matters of day-to-day management, and should not become involved in second-guessing "ordinary business." This is consistent with the protection of the "business judgment rule" for directors.

But as Benjamin Graham and David L. Dodd argued over a half century ago, shareholders do have the right and responsibility to focus their attention on matters where "the interest of the officers and the stockholders may be in conflict," including executive compensation.[132] Developments since the time of Graham and Dodd have shown that shareholders must also be vigilant about preserving the full integrity – and value – of their stock ownership rights. For example, their right to vote may be diluted by a classified board or by dual-class capitalization, and their right to transfer stock to a willing buyer at a mutually agreeable price may be abrogated by the adoption of a "poison pill." (For a discussion of "poison pills" and other devices adopted during the takeover era that encroached on the rights of shareholders, see chapter 3.) These kinds of issues present conflicts of interest not contemplated at the time of Graham and Dodd's first edition, as shareholders are interested in accountability, and officers and directors are interested in protecting themselves.

*Even if poison pills are good, isn't there a conflict of interests between shareholders and management in the design and timing of a pill? Who is in the best position to determine the optimal design and timing? Should pills be submitted to a shareholder vote?*

Of course, the shareholders' most important function as monitors concerns their election of the directors. As noted above, the "just vote no" strategy is an increasingly important way for shareholders to send a message of concern about the performance of a company or its board of directors. Company proxy statements reveal information about whether individual directors attend 75 percent of the meetings, how much stock they own, which committees they serve on, and whether they have other financial connections to the company. Shareholders can withhold votes for directors who do not attend meetings, who hold no stock, who serve on committees that approve bad compensation schemes, or who have conflicts of interest. While even a majority of "withhold" votes cannot keep an unopposed director candidate off the board, it can send an effective message to the board, to management, and maybe even to members of the financial community who may be considering running a dissident slate. And it can capture the attention of the press. A 1997 13 percent "withhold" vote at Disney, supported by CalPERS, helped win the board the "worst board" designation from *Business Week* that year. In 2003 the SEC proposed rules that would give shareholders "access to the proxy" for nominating director candidates. SEC Chairman William Donaldson is very committed to the proposal but corporate America is very committed to stopping it.

Investors have continued to focus on the key issues of executive compensation and board compensation and composition. In the late 1990s, accounting scandals at Waste Management, Cendant, Livent, and Sunbeam led to increased focus on the independence and competence of the audit committee. The scandals of 2002–3 led to important reforms as well.

Another important change was the passage in 1995 of legislation[133] changing the rules for shareholder lawsuits. It was intended to provide a "safe harbor" for forward-looking statements, to encourage corporate representatives to speak openly about a company's prospects without worrying about being sued if every comment they made was considered an enforceable commitment, and to give large institutional shareholders a better opportunity to represent the class of investors than the "professional plaintiffs" used by the "Delaware regular" law firms. These are firms who file dozens of lawsuits on behalf of professional plaintiffs, so they can settle quickly and move to the next case. The impact of that legislation is still being evaluated. Preliminary studies show that it has had little effect on the number of lawsuits filed, but that it has affected the jurisdiction (more filed now in state court than federal court) and the charges (more fraud-based). In a few cases, institutional investors have been able to take control of the lawsuits away from the "Delaware regulars" with good results.

---

## Case in point: SWIB and CellStar

The State of Wisconsin Investment Board (SWIB) made one of the earliest attempts to be appointed as the lead plaintiff under the new law, in a case filed against CellStar. This was a matter of the gravest concern to the usual plaintiff's counsel, who had been accustomed to controlling the cases and taking large fees. So, they objected to SWIB's filing. They were forced to concede that SWIB met the statutory standard as "presumptively most adequate plaintiff" due to the size of their investment (over 20 percent of the stock), the promptness of their filing, and their initial showing of "typicality and adequacy" as required by the law. But the law firm challenged them anyway, on grounds that they were not as "typical" and "adequate" as they appeared, in other words that they were not good representatives of the class of shareholders in CellStar. Why? Because they were too big and sophisticated and would thus not be able to represent the interests of small and ignorant investors. The judge found this claim to be unfounded.

---

Institutional investors are transforming the world of corporate governance. The issues they must consider in voting proxies are more complicated and diverse, with economic and fiduciary consequences to consider and evaluate. The priorities of the institutional investor community are evolving quickly, past the secondary (and reactive) issues of poison pills and staggered boards and toward the central (and active) concerns of board composition, independence, and effectiveness. The "New Compact Between Owners and Directors," drafted by a committee of shareholder and management representatives, shows the commitment by both parties to better board oversight.

It is not only the shareholder community that has changed in the last two decades. The corporate community has also changed, in response to the increased ownership focus of shareholders, even in cases where shareholders have not taken any overt action. John Wilcox of Georgeson Shareholder Communications Inc., one of the leading proxy solicitation firms, reports that many of his clients decided not to make certain changes that would require shareholder approval, after Georgeson advised them that they would have trouble getting a majority vote.

Many companies are restructuring their boards of directors in response to governance concerns raised by the shareholder, financial, and legal communities. Spencer Stuart's annual *Board Index* (analyzing board trends and practices at 100 major companies) shows some dramatic shifts. Between 1997 and 2002, as a result of direct shareholder activism and indirect pressures, there has been a net loss of 91 inside directorships and a net gain of two outside directorships. The median ratio of outsiders to insiders is now 3:1, and more than a quarter of the boards in the study had a ratio of 5:1 or greater. Only seven of the boards in the survey had a majority of inside directors. A survey of 653 CEOs conducted by the National Association of Corporate Directors revealed virtually unanimous support for "small, pro-active, informed and truly independent boards."[134] In many cases, companies have responded to shareholder resolutions asking for a majority of independent directors on the board, by agreeing without putting the proposal to a vote, or by capitulating.

Both institutional and individual investors are taking advantage of the new technology to become more effective in overseeing corporate managers and directors. This next case in point may turn out to be the most significant development since Lewis Gilbert persuaded the SEC to require companies to publish shareholder proposals in their proxy statements.

# Cases in point: Revolt of the Yahoos – United Companies Financial and Luby's[135]

**United Companies Financial**. UC was founded in 1946 and engaged in various businesses relating to lending money to "subprime" borrowers (people whose credit profile is unacceptable to major lenders). In 1992 it began securitizing subprime residential mortgages. That business grew very rapidly. But CEO and chairman Terrell Brown was unwilling to control operating costs and unable to come up with a long-term plan that did not depend on unlimited access to cheap capital. The stock price fell from $36 to $12 over the second half of 1997. The company put itself up for sale, and the price rebounded to $26. But there were no takers, and reversals at the company brought the price down to $4 and then to under a dollar. Two professors who were significant shareholders, Aaron Brown and Martin Stoller, attempted to get in touch with management. Stoller posted some of his concerns on the Yahoo message board assigned to the company. When he saw that other shareholders shared his concern, especially after the company filed for bankruptcy, he asked them to reveal how much stock they had. It turned out that 40 percent of the stock was represented by the participants in the Yahoo message board.

The Yahoo message board turned out to be an ideal mechanism for doing what had previously been impossible – finding and communicating with other shareholders. With the support of the other shareholders, they were able to play a role in the bankruptcy proceeding. Brown described what he learned as follows:

I believe the internet played a crucial role at three points in this story:
1. I do not think we could have gotten an Equity Committee without the large number of shares and people represented on the internet. The message board got us the SEC and newspaper interest that, in my opinion, forced the US Bankruptcy Trustee to appoint a committee. Without an Equity Committee composed of aggressive shareholders, I believe UC would have been liquidated in May 1999 with no value for shareholders.
2. The internet message board helped me find a buyer for UC in several ways. First, it got me the meeting with UC. Second, it provided detailed financial and management information that were essential to designing a plan. Finally,

I found that all the potential buyers were following the message board with a combination of amusement and awe, I got in the door of several places where I had no prior relationship, as a sort-of celebrity.
3. The message board, and the attention it generated from the SEC and newspapers, may have caused some parties to be somewhat more solicitous of shareholder interests. It had no discernible effect on UC management, however.

On the other hand, the internet postings may have caused some problems. Some of the postings were arguably illegal as stolen information, inside information, libel or invasion of privacy. There was not a lot of false information, most of that was obvious and some of it I suspect came from employees. Certainly many employees did post, most of them without revealing their status.

Although the outcome was not entirely successful as a financial matter, Brown and Stoller took what they learned and created a fund designed to use the internet to force change at under-performing companies.

**Luby's**. In 2001, Les Greenburg organized the shareholders of Luby's, a chain of Texas restaurants, primarily through an online message board. He ran a slate of four dissident directors and attracted so much support from shareholders who were unhappy about the stock's declining value that the unpopular CEO departed. The dissidents ended up with only 25 percent of the vote because many shareholders felt that the board was responding to their concerns. But the proxy contest would have been prohibitively expensive if not for the presence of a critical mass of shareholders on the message board and Greenburg's ability to do his own legal work. And, despite the directors' protestations to the contrary, it is unlikely that they would have replaced the CEO without the pressure of the contested election. The stock has continued to decline in value, so the message board may decide to try again.

As the SEC promulgated the most extensive regulatory changes in 60 years following the corporate scandals of 2002, the only major initiative not prompted by the Sarbanes–Oxley legislation was a requirement that money managers and mutual funds disclose their proxy voting policies and any votes inconsistent with those policies. This was a reflection of SEC concerns that institutional investors had too often been either negligent or corrupt in proxy voting, and that the disconnect that allowed the issuer company to know how the shareholders voted while the beneficial holders did not created perverse incentives. The tipping point may have been the decision by Deutsche Asset Management to switch votes in the hotly contested merger of Hewlett-Packard and Compaq (see case in point below).

# Case in point: DAM changes its vote

In the Fall of 2001, the boards of Hewlett-Packard and Compaq voted unanimously to merge the two companies. But then one of HP's directors, Walter Hewlett, the son of one of HP's founders, decided to oppose the deal. He was joined by David Packard, son of the other co-founder.

It was front-page news for weeks as Hewlett and the board of which he was still a member spent as much as $100 million (Hewlett spent $40 million) on lawyers, proxy solicitors, and publicity to battle each other for the support of the shareholders. HP sent out a letter to shareholders calling Hewlett "a musician and an academic . . . [whose] motivations and investment decisions are likely to be very different from your own." In the previous year's proxy statement, they had characterized him very differently: "Mr. Hewlett has been an independent software developer involved with computer applications in the humanities for more than five years."

In *Backfire: Carly Fiorina's High Stakes Battle for the Soul of Hewlett-Packard* (John Wiley & Sons, 2003), author Peter Burrows describes what happened next:

> The foundations established by the two founders of HP voted against the merger. That made getting the support of other significant shareholders essential if the deal was going to go through. Money manager Deutsche Asset Management, a subsidiary of Deutsche Bank, had 20 million votes, 1.3 percent of the stock. They originally voted against the merger. This came as a shock to HP, which had been so confident of their support that they had not even called to lobby them. They were paying Deutsche a million dollar fee to support them in getting shareholder support – with another million dollars as a bonus if the merger was approved. Furthermore, Deutsche Vice-Chairman Benjamin H. Griswold had promised that Deutsche would follow the recommendation of proxy advisor ISS, who came out in favor of the deal.

But then Deutsche decided to vote against the merger. When HP CEO Carly Fiorina got the news, she left a voicemail for HP's CFO that was later leaked and played repeatedly on the national news. She said, "Call the guy at Deutsche Bank again first thing in the morning. You need a definite answer from the vice-chairman, and if it's the wrong one, we have to swing into action. See what we can get, but we may have to do something extraordinary to bring them over the line here."

After a call from the investment banking side of Deutsche Bank and a talk with Fiorina just hours before the votes were to be counted in which she said their support was "of great importance to our ongoing relationship," the American side of Deutsche switched their vote, and when the German side balked, Deutsche's chief investment officer pushed hard, saying that "I'm not trying to put you under any undue pressure, but make sure that you have a very strong documented rationale for why you voted this way as it relates to this merger," concluding that the deal was "extremely sensitive" to Deutsche's CEO, Josef Ackerman. The German side switched, too. Later, Fiorina called to thank Griswold for his support, and said, "I'm looking forward to doing business with you in the future."

A Deutsche Bank investment banker – the banker who oversaw the Deutsche Bank–Hewlett-Packard relationship – then organized a call between Fiorina and the asset managers and participated in it. Walter Hewlett received the same privileges to discuss his side in a separate call.

Not surprisingly, the Hewlett-Packard executives did not openly threaten Deutsche Bank with a loss of business, and only discussed the merits of the transaction during the call. Nor did the Deutsche Bank asset managers make any express reference to the overall business relationship when, after the call, they decided to switch their vote to approve the merger.

The subtext, however, was very clear: the Hewlett-Packard–Deutsche Bank relationship would go dramatically south if the asset managers voted against the merger. If there were any doubt, the presence of the relationship banker on the call would have made the implicit threat clear to them.

The vote was so close that the final tally was not known for several more weeks. Ultimately, the merger won by 3 percent of the vote.

Hewlett challenged the vote in the Delaware courts and won a preliminary ruling. But ultimately, the Chancery Court found that Hewlett had not been able to demonstrate that the vote by Deutsche Asset Management was made for any reasons that were not legitimate.

In evaluating the evidence, Chancellor Chandler made every inference in favor of management's justification for the merger. He accepted Fiorina's explanation that to do "something extraordinary" was merely to make every effort to explain Hewlett-Packard's pro-merger position to the Deutsche Bank asset managers.

He also accepted the Deutsche Bank investment bankers' story that the call had not occurred to implicitly threaten the asset managers so that they would switch their vote. Rather, they said, the call was arranged because they were embarrassed at having misled Fiorina into thinking that the managers would vote for the merger.

In the end, having essentially required Hewlett to prove the threat with a "smoking gun," and seeing no smoking gun, Chancellor Chandler dismissed the vote-buying claim. A thoughtful commentary by James Fanto, "The Recent Decision on the Hewlett-Packard/Compaq Mega-Merger: How the Court Ignored the Psychological Reality of Over-Optimistic CEOs" (Findlaw.com) concludes that the court completely missed the implicit threat of retribution, and calls it "naïve" to insist on "a smoking gun" to prove coercion in a voting situation.

> Chancellor Chandler missed the psychological realities of the situation. Hewlett-Packard executives did not have to communicate openly, whether inside or outside the call, any threats to Deutsche Bank about the loss of future business. It would have been clear to everyone involved what would have happened had Deutsche Bank failed to change its vote. (It had similarly been clear to Hewlett-Packard, following Walter Hewlett's declared opposition to the merger, that it had to compensate Deutsche Bank for its support and votes by hiring it as an advisor.)
>
> It is not at all surprising that there was no express threat. One would expect that the conversation, both during the call and among the asset managers following it, would deal only with the merits of the transaction.
>
> Indeed, the managers might not even have realized they had capitulated to an implicit threat. Rather, under the influence of the groupthink mentality, the asset managers would naturally rationalize, to themselves and others, that they had made the vote switch only because of their own independent assessment of the merger. Certainly they would not have liked to think they had cravenly switched their honest opinion in order to prevent Deutsche Bank from losing business.

## SYNTHESIS: HERMES

Hermes is a UK independent fund manager investing approximately £36 billion on behalf of over 100 clients, including pension funds, insurance companies, government entities, and financial institutions. Originally an in-house pension fund of British Telecom, its continuing affiliation with that group "gives its investment management perspective a unique insight and close alignment with the needs of other long-term investors and pension funds," according to its report *Corporate Governance and Shareholder Engagement Overview*. Hermes manages money through an index/specialist approach. One of its many unique attributes, though, is its commitment to "Focus Funds" intended to "tackle the 'anxieties' brought on from owning stocks in the index." Because of its long-term holdings in index stocks, it is "therefore necessarily exposed to under-performing assets." In addition to exercising the ownership rights of these indexed securities to ensure that the clients' interests are upheld, Hermes is the first major investment institution in the world to establish "shareholder engagement funds." They invest in "under-performing companies which are fundamentally sound but poorly managed, where Hermes believes that its intervention and involvement as long-term shareholders can release the latent value that exists within the company." (See the Premier and Trinity Mirror case studies in chapter 6.)

Hermes prefers the term "engagement" to activism. And engagement occurs at the end of a series of steps that begin with communication through telephone, letters, meetings, and visits of any concerns and efforts at private, cooperative negotiation to "help resolve issues that are hindering the company's performance." This can include executive compensation, along with a broad range of other issues. Hermes will consult with and involve company advisors and other shareholders as well. Focus companies are selected on the basis of two criteria – the underlying investment value and the probability of or susceptibility to change. Because engagement is resource-intensive, no more than 15 companies are held at any one time in the Focus Fund portfolio. The idea is that engagement will produce superior returns in that portfolio and in the securities held in the portfolio company through the indexed investments as well.

## INVESTING IN ACTIVISM

Brown's and Stoller's eRaider fund demonstrates that the changes in technology and the SEC rules and in the size and kind of shareholder have changed the cost-benefit calculus of shareholder activism. The Gordon Group's *Active Investing in the US Equity Market: Past Performance and Future Prospects* (December 2, 1992) provides the most persuasive analysis to date of the value to be realized from effective shareholder activism. The report, which combines its own ground-breaking research with an exhaustive study of the massive traditional literature on the subject and considers several new approaches, concludes that, "a partnership catalyzing such activity [proxy initiatives, board candidacy] can expect to provide a return substantially above the baseline expected return on a passive equity investment." The report goes on to quantify this potential return as up to 30 percent in excess of the S&P 500.

Several sources cited earlier lend strong support to the proposition that activism is good for corporate health and shareholder value. Columbia Law School professor Bernard Black has written a thoroughly reasoned and documented argument for the efficacy of ownership involvement.[136] Former US Treasury Department Corporate Finance Director Michael Jacobs forcefully argued in *Short-Term America* that poor governance results in a higher cost of capital that in turn inhibits competitiveness.[137] This capital theme is echoed in Harvard Business School professor Michael Porter's portion of the Council on Competitiveness report released in June 1992.[138] A similar conclusion, based on global analysis, was reached by the two international governance studies mentioned in chapter 1, Oxford Analytica's *Board Directors and Corporate Governance* and the Pacific Institute's "Redressing Imbalances in Japanese Corporate Governance." The Oxford Analytica report found that, in order to compete for capital, corporations will have to give investors more of a role in governance. A McKinsey report in 2000 found that UK and US investors would be willing to pay as much as an 18 percent premium for what they perceived as good corporate governance. Investors in developing economies would be willing to pay as much as 28 percent, reflecting the discount they attribute to less rigorous governance requirements imposed by legislation. The willingness of Daimler-Benz to make governance changes to accommodate the requirements of the New York Stock Exchange, and Rupert Murdoch's rejection from the Australian Exchange, are real-life examples.

In early 1992, Wilshire Associates' Steve Nesbitt analyzed several years of CalPERS' shareholder initiatives and concluded that the effort was highly profitable to the system; a program costing $500,000 resulted in $137 million extraordinary (above the S&P 500) returns. Significantly, the initiatives did not have to be "successful" (gain majority support) in order to produce those returns.[139] And the market saw other examples of the "returns" on activism. The stock of Sears, Roebuck went up almost 10 percent on the day that the management acceded to shareholder pressure to stick to its core business and divest the financial services divisions. Honeywell stock went up 22 percent during the shareholder opposition to two management-sponsored proposals to decrease accountability to shareholders (see figure 2.1). Michael Jacobs' second book, published in 1993, argues that shareholders, even individual shareholders, can outperform the market by "breaking the Wall Street rule" and exercising ownership rights instead of buying and selling.[140] To the extent that it becomes part of the "conventional wisdom" that a corporation with informed and effectively involved owners is worth more in the marketplace than one without them, a burden is placed on pension fund trustees – who are, after all, the majority owners of American corporations – to develop the ability to act as owners. *How can they do this?* Informed and effective participation by shareholders in today's equity markets requires new structures and procedures. Few exist already, and those are still in the very earliest stages of development.

This gap between governance forms and the reality they confront is not new. In 1960, Harvard law professor Abram Chayes wrote that "Ownership fragmented into shares was ownership diluted. It no longer corresponded to effective control over company operations." He found that there were no "institutional arrangements" that could "make it possible for many scattered individuals to concert their suffrages on issues sufficiently defined to warrant meaningful conclusions about an expression of their will."[141]

## NEW MODELS AND NEW PARADIGMS

In the absence of effective mechanisms for channeling shareholder power, some individuals and institutions have sought a way to hold management accountable – often by joining it.

# Cases in point: From DuPont to relationship investing

**DuPont at General Motors.** In an article in *Harvard Business Review*, William Taylor held out Pierre S. du Pont (the first in the distinguished industrial lineage) as a large shareholder and chairman of a troubled General Motors corporation. Du Pont was both the substantial owner and the chief executive of the DuPont Company, which in turn owned a substantial stake in General Motors. Acting as an owner, much along the lines Brandeis contemplated for "Junior's" father at Boothbay Harbor, du Pont was able to provide the focus and energy to ensure that General Motors emerged as the dominant force in the world automotive industry for a half century. But du Pont's very effectiveness raised questions. In 1957, in the context of the trust-busting concerns of that era, the United States Supreme Court ordered the DuPont Company to divest itself of its holdings of General Motors on the grounds that the relationship violated the nation's laws against restraint on competition (see case study in chapter 6).

**Robert Galvin at Motorola**. Compare du Pont's involvement at General Motors to former CEO Robert Galvin's role at Motorola. A brilliant man with a huge stockholding, for many years provided the focus on shareholder value that is the goal of a governance structure. But this model has its own drawbacks, however. Galvin's son, who succeeded him as CEO, presided over a company with a muddled strategy and a dropping stock price, sparking questions about whether the family involvement benefitted other shareholders.

**Rosen at Compaq**. A model of ownership similar to du Pont's may be found in the venture capital industry. Venture capitalists provide start-up money to entrepreneurs with ideas for high-technology developments that may not come to the market for years.

Such companies as Apple Computer and Federal Express owed their success to venture capital. But venture capitalists provide more than money. They are involved and informed investors who closely monitor the company, generally hold a seat or two on the board, provide technical assistance, and help attract further capital, directors, managers and suppliers. As one entrepreneur said of his relationship with his venture capitalist: "Think of it as you would marriage."

Sevin Rosen Management, one of the most successful venture capital funds during the 1980s, invested $2.5 million in Compaq when the computer company was still little more than an idea. A few years later, that investment was worth over $40 million.

Sevin Rosen was closely involved with the running of Compaq. Indeed, the company's co-founder, Benjamin M. Rosen, served as the non-executive chairman of the board. Thus Compaq, like General Motors in the 1920s, was headed by a chairman with a significant ownership stake in the company. Rosen's presence proved to be vitally important when Compaq hit some hard times. In Rosen's words:

> From [Compaq's] start-up of operations in 1983, we enjoyed an unbroken eight-year run of rising sales, earnings and stock price. We went from start-up to $3 billion sales in record time, achieved Fortune 500 status in three years, an all-time record, and were flying high. We were recognized for producing PCs with the highest performance and quality, but also with the highest prices. No matter though, for the market clearly was willing to pay up for the best.
>
> And then in the second quarter of 1991, a funny thing happened on the way to prosperity. Our sales flattened, our earnings dropped and our stock price plummeted. In the third quarter, we faced our first-ever quarterly loss. What had happened was that competition was intensifying and product price was becoming much more important to customers. Yet we were locked in to a product line characterized by high costs and high prices.
>
> Over a period of several months, it became clear that management and the board disagreed sharply over whether the problems we were facing were a short-term perturbation (management's view) or a long-term structural mismatch between the company's product line and the marketplace (the board's view). After intensive study and discussion, the board concluded that only a management change and a corporate strategy revamping would restore the company's growth and profitability.
>
> We effected the changes in October 1991. We installed a new CEO and president, who in turn redirected the company's product strategy, marketing strategy, and, of critical importance, focused on a drastic cost-reduction strategy.

The results of these changes have been electric. As we reported to shareholders just this morning, sales and earnings for the March [1993] quarter were more than double those of a year ago and unit growth more than tripled. Our market share is up substantially, and our stock price has risen from the 20s into the 50s.

In April of 1999, Rosen attempted to repeat history by removing CEO Eckhard Pfeiffer and CFO Earl Mason. Observers were divided on whether this time it was the right decision. "We have re-energized this company before, and working together, we will do it again," Rosen said. In 2002, Compaq merged with Hewlett-Packard.

*Would Rosen have been so quick to force those changes if he didn't have $40 million at stake? See further discussion of this issue in chapter 3, and see discussion of Compaq's merger with HP earlier in this chapter.*

**Warren Buffett.** Some people think that a modern version of the ideal owner is Warren Buffett, the only person to reach the *Forbes* list of the country's wealthiest people through investments alone. Buffett is chief investment officer and principal owner (with a holding of 44 percent) of Berkshire Hathaway. Shareholders applauded Buffett's willingness to assume the position of chief executive officer in the disgraced banking firm Salomon Brothers (now Salomon Inc.). He served without salary. This signaled his dedication. He took on the challenge out of pride, in the best sense of that word; he wanted to demonstrate that a little straight thinking at the top could justify his original decision to invest in Salomon Brothers. Even with a 30 percent equity position, Buffett's involvement has given a "free ride" – or at least a discounted ride – to the rest of the shareholders.

But the ride is not always free, even with Buffett. It shouldn't be. In many corporate investments, Berkshire Hathaway insists on the purchase of a special class of convertible preferred stock, which guarantees a better return than ordinary common stock. In effect, Buffett is reducing the free-rider problem by charging a fee for his perceived – and, in the case of Salomon, proven – ability to add value to the company. This may be the ultimate example of the modern-day owner – big enough to make a difference, smart enough to make a valuable difference, and valuable enough to be paid for at least some portion of the difference that his contribution makes.

Buffett is one of the rare examples of a shareholder who is willing and able to intervene on behalf of the whole class of owners in return for some approximation of the value he confers on other shareholders. In his incarnation as holder of convertible preferred stock, Buffett is one model of an ideal modern owner. In July 1989, Buffett rescued Gillette Co. from a hostile takeover bid by Coniston Partners. Buffett paid $600 million for preferred shares paying a guaranteed dividend of 8.75 percent. In 1991, Buffett performed similar rescue missions at possible takeover candidates – USAir and Champion International. On the other hand, this kind of convertible preferred investment can be viewed as (or used as) an opportunistic entrenchment of existing management, as some of the "white knight" or "white squire" investors were in the 1980s. In 1999 and 2000, Buffett's performance tumbled by nearly half, and his troubled portfolio holdings included Coca-Cola and Disney. He serves on the board that replaced the CEO of Coca-Cola in 1999.

**Sunbeam.** CEO Al Dunlap was the most enthusiastic advocate director stock ownership ever had. He was brought into the company by its two largest shareholders, and he made sure that all of the directors held a significant amount of stock. But he was hoist by his own petard when his directors, spurred by their vital interest in the stock price, pressed him for more information about upcoming figures, and then, when he could not answer to their satisfaction, fired him.

**Relationship investing**. As discussed in greater detail in chapter 5, in other countries, "relationship investors" provide monitoring that many observers credit for making a substantial contribution to industrial competitiveness. The German Hausbank, with capacity to provide all manner of financing, places its own executives on the supervisory boards of corporations. The bank benefits from this relationship through the payment of fees and otherwise. The Japanese members of a *kereitsu* are financiers, customers, suppliers, and owners of each other. The ownership interest is an entrée to a more profound commercial relationship. Monitoring is not so much a function of ownership, but rather one of preserving a valuable commercial relationship.

Specialized investment firms with investment strategies that include shareholder activism performed very strongly through the 1990s and afterward. They include "Relational Investors," a fund established by Ralph Whitworth, the Hermes Focus Fund, Andrew Shapiro's Lawndale Capital Management, Active Value Investors, and others. All have shown that selecting firms with intrinsic value and pressing for changes in corporate governance to ensure that directors and managers had the appropriate ability and incentives could produce reliable above-market returns.

*What conflicts of interest do these owners have? How might the owners in the examples in this section, du Pont, Buffett, and the German and Japanese block holder, have at least a theoretical conflict of interest in their roles as officers of their principal employer and as "active owners" of a portfolio investment? Why did the courts stop Pierre du Pont's involvement in GM? If they had not, could GM have stopped him? In the case of Warren Buffett, will his obligation to his own shareholders at Berkshire Hathaway always align with his priorities as CEO of Salomon Brothers? Are these interests reconcilable? (One obvious conflict is which one gets his primary time and attention.) In Germany and Japan, is the interest of the bank consistent with the interest of the entity in whom it invests and with whom it does business?*

In order for this kind of involvement by owners to work, the owner's stake in the enterprise must align his interest with the interest of the shareholder more than his other organizational interests create conflicts.

*How can the relationship be structured to make sure this is the case? What are the alternatives for shareholders (or managers or boards of directors) if the alignment is insufficient? Are the inevitable conflicts preferable to the problems these relationships are designed to solve?*

*How can we encourage more activist owners? How can we make sure their activism will be appropriate and effective? Even the legendary Buffett is only human and cannot be expected to guide more than a dozen corporations at a time. Where do we find others who can play that role?*

The role of activist investor is unlikely to be assumed by any of the categories of institutional investor outlined in this chapter, because each of them faces commercial or political restrictions. Financial institutions are all subject to constraints against owning sufficiently large percentages of the outstanding stock of particular companies. With commercial banks, there is the prohibition of *Glass–Steagall* (though substantially rescinded in 1999); mutual fund holdings are limited by the Investment Company Act of 1940; insurance companies are limited by state law; private pension plans are required by ERISA to diversify as widely as possible; the federal system under FERSA is limited to equity investment through index funds. These provisions, enacted independently, have a cumulative impact of preventing the financial sector executives from being able to exercise control over commercial sector executives – to keep Main Street independent of Wall Street.

Like many barriers, the wall between Main Street and Wall Street was constructed out of mistrust and misunderstanding. It is probably based on what Columbia professor Mark Roe chronicled as the pervasive American distrust against centralized "money trust" power.[142] But this attitude may be based more in myth than reality. The reality is that Main Street needs Wall Street, and not just its money, more than ever. Unless finance executives can monitor portfolio companies, it is unlikely that a meaningful system of accountability based on institutional investors will be established.

*How would that work?* Look at the chief executive of the largest institutional investor, CalPERS. No one, inside CalPERS or inside corporate management, has ever suggested that it would be useful or even appropriate for the CEO of CalPERS to take a role in a portfolio company comparable to that taken by Buffett in Salomon Brothers. It is a question not of expertise but of culture; with public plan officials, one can only ask: *Is it possible to make an owner out of a bureaucrat?* An employee of a public pension system appears to have none of the characteristics of an owner. Although there is now some incentive compensation, the CEO bears none of the risk of loss if the value of the investment declines; his own career progress is only tangentially related to the performance of a particular company. He is unlikely to be invited to serve as a director of a portfolio company. Even if he is, and his trustees approve, he is likely to find the restrictions on insider transactions a practical obstacle that is insurmountable.

Despite this non-owner mindset, public plan officials, even those who preside over index funds, can be credible candidates for some kinds of investor activism. For one thing, they can be counted on to do their duty, in this case their fiduciary duty. To what extent is that duty compatible with the kind of focus and expertise required for meaningful monitoring of corporate performance? As we consider different models of shareholder involvement, we must keep in mind the strengths and the limits of the different categories of investor. Public plan officials face a set of conflicts and a set of impediments to obtaining information different from other institutional investors. This is, in a way, their greatest strength. Their inherent limitations may be what is needed to assure an elementary level of monitoring while protecting against undue interference. A public official, acting as trustee, can insist that a portfolio company perform at or above the level of its peer group. He can insist on a governance structure that will enable the board to do the closer monitoring that is beyond the capability of the shareholders. Indeed, that is what CalPERS and some of the other public pension funds have done over the past few years and – with the additional opportunities made available to them through the revised SEC shareholder communication rules and the increased oversight of pay/performance linkages – what they can be expected to do in the future.

*But is that enough, not from their perspective, or even their plan participants' perspective, but from the perspective of the economy as a whole?*

It is interesting to note that, although CalPERS had an early and visible role in raising issues of concern with James Robinson of American Express, they did not play a significant role in resolving the issues. The institutional shareholders who pushed Robinson to leave the company were not the public pension plans but the white-shoe Wall Street funds like Alliance Capital and J.P. Morgan. Two very different kinds of shareholder played two very different kinds of role, each one the other could not play (see the case study in chapter 6).

CalPERS could play a public role in identifying the problems, but could not follow through with something as specific and even radical as insisting that the CEO step down. This is because CalPERS' equity portfolio is almost entirely indexed, even with limited experimental forays into "relationship investing." In essence, indexed funds replicate the market. Their investment is not based on any particularized knowledge about the individual companies. If they select a target, based on poor performance, they must then invest the time and resources in trying to understand the company and its problems. When CalPERS' representatives speak with any CEO about their holdings in the company he heads (and this is rare, no more than a dozen or so each year of the more than 6,000 companies whose securities they hold), they recognize that they also own stock in all of that company's competitors, suppliers, corporate customers, potential takeover targets, or acquirers. Given these broad holdings, public pension funds cannot be sufficiently informed about their holdings to make recommendations about strategic issues (assuming they could do so without violating insider trading restrictions, triggering concerns about "pension fund socialism" or exceeding the limits of the legitimate shareholder agenda).

For these reasons, public pension plans can be visible, but they cannot be very specific. So they focus on issues of process – confidential voting, annual election of directors, executive pay, the independence of the directors on key committees, and similar issues.

The Wall Street investment firms are at the other end of the spectrum. They are stock-pickers. They buy into the company because of what they know about it, not because it happens to be on the index. Their "investment" in learning about the company is made already; it's a sunk cost. These institutional investors were not willing to take the commercial risks of making public statements or filing shareholder resolutions, but they were willing and able to meet with the new CEO of American Express to insist that James Robinson had to leave. They were rumored to be involved in the departures of CEOs at Borden and some other companies and in the search for a new CEO at IBM as well. This will increasingly be the pattern. After all, these same firms are very used to negotiating what are in essence governance issues on the bond side of the business. As governance is more unignorably translated into value, negotiations will become a part of the equity side as well.

On both sides of the institutional investor spectrum, then, there are potential plausible candidates for at least some forms of active monitoring. But the "carrot" of increased shareholder value is not enough to make it happen, in a world where the collective choice problem and political and economic reprisals present overwhelming obstacles. Neither the public pension funds nor the money managers will be willing or able to act as quickly, as publicly, or as meaningfully as is necessary for optimal monitoring. If ownership must provide more than the primary level of assuring honesty and minimal competency, both will have to follow. Others will have to lead.

## THE "IDEAL OWNER"

In the search for the ideal owner, it is useful to start with Harvard Business School professor Michael Porter's statement:

> Perhaps the most basic weakness in the American system is transient ownership, in which institutional agents are drawn to current earnings, unwilling to invest in understanding the fundamental prospects of companies, and unable and unwilling to work with companies to build long-term earning power . . . The natural instinct of many managers is to seek fragmented ownership to preserve their independence from owners in decision-

making . . . *The long-term interests of companies would be better served by having a smaller number of long-term or near permanent owners, whose goals are better aligned with those of the corporation* . . . Ideally, the controlling stake would be in the hands of a relatively few long-term owners . . . These long-term owners would commit to maintaining ownership for an extended period, and to becoming fully informed about the company. In return for a long-term ownership commitment, however, must come a restructuring of the role of owners in governance. Long-term owners must have insider status, full access to information, influence with management and seats on the board . . . Under the new structure, management will be judged on the basis of its ability to build long-term competitive position and earning power, not current earnings of stock price.[143]

Where are the "smaller number of long-term or near-permanent owners, whose goals are better aligned with those of the corporation?" Locating the ideal owner (or its closest approximation in our system) does not permit us to lose sight of the limits of ownership involvement. No one is suggesting that shareholders should second-guess corporate managers on "ordinary business" decisions. The contract between shareholders and the companies they invest in provides, in essence, that in exchange for limited liability shareholders will have a limited scope of authority and a limited agenda. Shareholders are not there to tell corporations how to run their business; they should be there, and they are beginning to be there, to tell corporations that they need to do a better job.

The ideal owner must be someone who has the information, the ability, and the alignment of interests with other corporate constituencies to provide the optimal level of monitoring. It is important to keep in mind, though, that the optimal level of monitoring is in part a function of the narrow range of appropriate issues for shareholder involvement.

The shareholder agenda should focus only on assuring that the interests of directors and management are aligned with those of the shareholder and that when a conflict of interest is presented, the shareholders make the decisions. As Ira Millstein, noted governance authority and advisor to outside directors, has said,

Where there is a "problem" company, an institution can ask for meetings with the board, pose the problem, and determine whether the board is dealing with it or ignoring it . . . In our system, if the shareholder satisfies itself that the board is knowledgeable, diligent, aware of the problems and attempting to deal with them, generally this should suffice.[144]

In order to make this possible, shareholders must be able to act when necessary to preserve the full integrity – and value – of ownership rights themselves. Any ideal shareholder must be vigilant about preventing dilution of the right to vote (by a classified board or by dual-class capitalization for example) and preserving the right to transfer the stock to a willing buyer at a mutually agreeable price (which could be abrogated by the adoption of a poison pill).

If any institutional investor is to be the ideal owner, the trustees must exercise their ownership rights with the "care, skill, prudence, and diligence" and "for the exclusive benefit" of the retirement plan participants (the employees), the people who are, after all, the real owners. That is the standard for ERISA fiduciaries (very similar to the common law and statutory standards applicable to other fiduciaries as well). This means that the "real owners" have their own obligation to monitor; they must not only delegate to their elected representatives (directors or trustees) the responsibility of safeguarding share value; they must assume part of it themselves. The trustees responsible for monitoring the accountability of corporate managers must themselves be genuinely accountable to their beneficiaries, whether they are elected officials, civil servants, or hired fund managers.

The system of accountability for those who manage institutional funds is not perfect. There are often efforts to dilute the accountability further, as with economically targeted investments. In general, however, it has worked well. New York State's Comptroller is sole fiduciary for the state fund. He is not only accountable as a fiduciary, he is accountable through the electoral process. The State Comptroller is one of four state-wide elected officials. While he does not have trustees, he has advisory councils made up of the representatives of beneficiaries and other groups. The CalPERS' CEO meets with his trustees (some of whom are elected by the beneficiaries directly, some appointed by state elected officials) for one week out of each month.

Former New York State Comptroller Edward V. Regan is not so sure that the present state is satisfactory. "This leaves us then exactly where we started. Shareholders, directors and the public react only after the economic damage has been done, to the detriment of the company and the nation. It leaves us with the activist pension systems presumably without the ability (and maybe the will) to stand up and oppose a company whose performance is deteriorating (not deteriorated), to force that company to turn around by attempting to fire, in a public manner, a prestigious board of directors."[145]

# Cases in point:
# A&P, Paramount, K-Mart

**A&P**. Regan announced in February of 1993 that his fund had selected an underperforming company to target with a shareholder initiative. He said his fund would solicit shareholders to withhold votes for the re-election of the board at his target company, A&P. Even if the target was not controlled by a single 52 percent shareholder, as this one is, it is impossible, as a matter of law, to prevent the election of a management-sponsored candidate unless someone is running against him.[146]

*Given Regan's then status as an elected official (and the only Republican elected to statewide office at the time), is it fair to say that this initiative was essentially symbolic?*

**Paramount**. Similarly, the Wisconsin Investment Board announced that it would urge other Paramount shareholders to join it in withholding votes for director candidates. The *Wall Street Journal* noted, "The effort by the pension fund, which owns 100,000 shares of Paramount's 118 million outstanding, is mainly designed to send a message to the movie and publishing company's management that it is unhappy with the company's stock performance, rather than to remove the four directors, since there are no alternate candidates for the board and the fund isn't putting up its own slate of directors.[147] In 2000, the New York City pension fund had a similar initiative at Great Lakes Chemical, with a record-breaking 30 percent withhold vote.

*What kind of a message did that send? How effective is this approach?*

**K-Mart**. In 1994 the Wisconsin state pension fund successfully blocked a proposed restructuring at K-Mart by conducting a campaign to solicit proxy votes against management's proposal.

*Do you agree that shareholders should have a say in major strategic decisions?*

What the New York and Wisconsin funds can do is put the pressure of publicity on the board. The board may very well react (as did the boards of IBM, GM, Westinghouse, and American Express). As Regan said, "The point is to alert board members that a significant number of shareholders do not believe they are doing their job." Perhaps the shareholder movement's most significant contribution is to make the world an uncomfortable place for a director of an under-performing company. As co-author of this book Nell Minow has said, "Boards of directors are like sub-atomic particles. They behave differently when they are observed."

And sometimes activism comes from less likely places. Gordon Crawford, the chief media stock-picker for Los Angeles-based money management firm Capital Research & Management Co., had a large holding in AOL Time-Warner that had lost $750 billion in value. He was reportedly a major factor in the decision of AOL founder Steve Case to resign as chairman of the board in early 2003. Another of his holdings, Disney, was also a disappointment. But there Crawford took the more traditional "Wall Street walk," and just sold his shares. *What might have been the factors that led to different decisions about activism vs. selling the stake in these holdings?*

# Case in point: Hermes

Hermes' corporate governance program is founded on a fundamental belief that companies with interested and involved shareholders are more likely to achieve superior long-term financial performance than those without. Tied closely with this is the belief that responsible pension fund investment requires investors to behave like owners rather than gamblers. In Hermes' view, exercising its stewardship rights in the companies in which it invests on behalf of clients is essential to ensure that managers and directors run companies in the best long-term interests of their shareholders. This is especially so when funds are managed on a passive or index-tracking basis, as is the case with the majority of funds managed by Hermes. Accordingly, Hermes has been actively voting at company meetings since 1990, when its first corporate governance policy was developed. Over time the policy has been revised and updated to reflect changes in best practice and, in March 1997, was published for the first time as a statement on voting and corporate governance. Since then, the policy has been republished twice, most recently in January 2001.

The Corporate Focus Department, in its current form, was established in January 1997. It is headed by Peter Butler, Corporate Focus Director, who also heads Hermes' specialist Focus Funds, so called because they focus on under-performing companies. Michelle Edkins, Corporate Governance Director, is responsible for voting and representing the interests of Hermes' clients in governance and voting matters through communication with external parties, and contributing to policy development on both a company and public level. She is supported in this by a team of three analysts. A commitment to vote at all company meetings in the UK means that Hermes submits votes on behalf of its clients at over 1,200 annual and extraordinary meetings a year. Hermes' pragmatic approach to applying its corporate governance policy involves regular communication with companies. Further, whenever votes are withheld from management Hermes will contact the company to explain its voting decision. As a result of this approach, the corporate governance team has built over the last ten years a detailed database of its voting history and correspondence with companies.

**Active Shareholder Programs**

Probably the first corporate governance issue on which Hermes took a highly public stance was three-year rolling contracts for directors. At the time these were the norm. Hermes' chief executive Alastair Ross-Goobey headed the highly successful campaign to have the notice period in executives' contracts reduced to two years; the issue was picked up by the Greenbury committee, which recommended contracts be reduced over time to one year. A campaign aimed at narrowing discounts suffered by investment trusts was started in 1997, led by Peter Butler, and will continue for the foreseeable future. Hermes encourages investment trusts to have only fully independent non-executive directors on their boards and to have one-year notice periods in their management contracts with fund managers. Hermes has also led or been involved in a considerable number of successful shareholder programs at individual companies.

Hermes differentiates its programs from those of the "raider activist" by adopting a relational approach on behalf of all shareholders, and is particularly critical of activist programs involving greenmail or micro-management of companies. Hermes' programs have generally been conducted in private and have not therefore been widely publicized. (Excerpted from <http://www.hermes.co.uk/corporate-governance/PDFs/activities.pdf>).

## PENSION FUNDS AS "IDEAL OWNERS"

*The Economist* sees the ideal owner in activist institutions, ranging from pension funds to brokerage firms:

> So everything now depends on financial institutions pressing even harder for reforms to make boards of directors behave more like overseers, and less like the chief executive's collection of puppets . . . Financial institutions must also fight to restore their rights as shareholders, lobbying for the dismantling of state takeover restrictions which have provided no protection to workers, only to top managers. Institutions should also demand that shareholder democracy be allowed to operate . . . But there is more to be done. In the age of the computer, access to shareholder lists should be cheap and simple, not jealously guarded by the boss; that would make it easier to solicit support from other shareholders. Institutions would then be able to use their clout in big firms to elect directors, who would be obliged to represent only their collective interest as owners. Chief executives would still run their firms; but, like any other employee, they would also have a boss. And when they failed at their jobs, they would face the sack.[148]

Public and private pension funds have many of the qualities necessary to play this kind of role. Their ownership, by virtue of their size and their time horizons, is as close to permanent as possible. And because of this near-permanent stake, their interest is far-sighted enough to incorporate the long-term interests of the corporation and (as an essential element of those interests) the interests of the employees, customers, suppliers, and the community.

Leadership cannot come only from the public plans. It must also come from the private (ERISA) plans. In addition to the benefits of size and long-term time horizons they share with public pension plans, they have the additional advantage of greater familiarity with business needs and the financial expertise of professionals whose qualifications price them out of the public plan market. In order for them to serve this role, the "non-neutral fiduciary" who administers the pension fund must recognize that involved ownership is essential to the healthy continuance of the capitalist system – and that it will make them money. And they must be willing to create and support a system with the resources and the insulation from reprisals to do the job.

Exercising ownership rights with regard to a limited agenda, and meeting the requirements of a strict fiduciary standard, means that a trustee voting proxies does not have to know how to make widgets, or even how to improve an under-performing company's widget-manufacturing operation or marketing strategy. The trustee must only be able to identify an under-performing company and determine, within the limited options available to the shareholder, which one is appropriate. A meeting with management? A nonbinding shareholder resolution? A vote against a compensation plan that does not provide the right incentives? A "withhold" vote for a board that is not doing its job? Limiting shareholders to a narrow range of substantive concerns and to a narrow range of procedural options is an important protection against abuse.

There is another important protection to limit any possible damage from a trustee who is wrong (whether through inaccuracy or political motivation) in identifying an under-performing company or in selecting a particular mechanism for making changes. Unless the trustee can persuade enough of the other shareholders to support the initiative, nothing will happen, and management will continue to move in the same direction, enhanced by the demonstration of support by a majority of the shareholders.

## IS THE "IDEAL OWNER" ENOUGH?

If we assume something more is needed, some entity that can initiate more than symbolic involvement, what model is appropriate?

One answer may be found in the communication made possible by getting representations of all sides together. Early 1990s efforts included the "Roots Group," a collection of pension fund and corporate attorneys that designed the "Compact for Owners and Directors." "New Foundations," a collection of many of the most thoughtful academics, institutional investors, and corporate executives working in this area, was convened by Harvard Law School in 1993. As described by the *New York Times*: "In an attempt to smooth the often contentious relationships between corporations and their shareholders, a group has been formed based at Harvard University, to create a road map for communication without confrontation."[149] This reflects the perspective of convener John Pound, of Harvard's John F. Kennedy School.

Unlike the Roots Group, which set out to achieve a consensus statement, New Foundations shared ideas without trying to get agreement. This is consistent with Pound's notion of the future CEO as more like a politician than a monarch, building consensus from the different parts of the corporate constituency. In "The Rise of the Political Model of Corporate Governance and Corporate Control," Pound suggests that consideration of governance issues should be removed from the static proscriptions of law and economics and cogently analyzes past development and future prospects from the dynamic perspective of the political process.[150] Though the promise of these two groups was never fulfilled, groups like these can improve communications and even develop new standards. One that shows great promise is the International Corporate Governance Network (<http://www.icgn.org>). Given the limits on even the most likely candidates for active monitoring, additional structures may be necessary. For example, new classes of special-purpose securities can encourage more effective involvement by pension funds. The kind of preferred shares issued for Warren Buffett in many of the companies in which he invests can also give institutional shareholders the incentive (and compensation) necessary to reduce the free-rider problem and make active monitoring worthwhile. Pension funds can take advantage of their size and their limited need for liquidity by insisting that the market present them with specialized instruments to meet their situation.

Another possibility is adding the "stick" of enforcement to the "carrot" of increased value. In 2002, at the direction of Senator Edward Kennedy, the General Accounting Office undertook an investigation into the Labor Department's past failure to bring a single enforcement action relating to the exercise (or lack of exercise) of share ownership rights. In addition to enforcement actions for those who do not, the Department of Labor could issue new regulations requiring ERISA trustees to demonstrate that they have acted "for the exclusive benefit of plan participants" in their voting and governance actions, including consideration of (and participation in) more active involvement in corporate governance. This would reduce the collective choice problem because many of any company's largest shareholders would be required to consider shareholder initiatives as an alternative to selling out. Furthermore it would spread to other institutional investors as well. Once a fiduciary standard is created and rigorously enforced for ERISA fiduciaries, other institutional investors tend to follow.[151] In addition to voluntary action and forced action from regulatory impetus, there are some options available to shareholders who want to strengthen their ability to respond to under-performing management and boards. Two options developed by the authors of this book were designed to bridge the gap created by the collective choice and free-rider problems – the gap between the level of activism that is optimal for individual shareholders (even large ones) and that which is optimal for maximum corporate performance.

The first of these options involves amending the corporation's bylaws to enable long-term shareholders to monitor the overall direction of the enterprise. It would require either the board or (in some states) the shareholders to enact this amendment. The bylaw is designed to permit "rational involvement" instead of "rational ignorance." The bylaw amendment would create a shareholder committee, made up of a class of "long-term shareholders" (defined in terms of the length and size of their ownership, perhaps $5 million-worth of common shares for three years, permitting groups to form in order to meet the minimum level). These long-term shareholders would be permitted to nominate candidates for a special committee. Those candidates would be submitted to a shareholder vote, on the same proxy as the board of directors.

The shareholder committee's primary task would be to exercise control over the board's priorities and composition. This will ensure that it spends its time on issues that are suitable, from the perspective of its members' abilities, resources, and interests.[152]

Rational apathy, the typical shareholder's attitude toward corporate governance, will not undermine shareholder committees. First, the committees need not participate in directing the company, they will only nominate directors to do the job. *The mere fact that the directors will know that they have been chosen by investors should make them more responsive to shareholder concerns.* Second, the committee should have access to corporate resources to obtain and generate information it needs; individual members need not spend much of their own money. Third, where individual expenses are incurred, they will be justified by investors' large holdings in the company and the utility of the expenses in performing the usual portfolio management functions. There are signs that institutions are willing to perform these tasks.[153]

The committee members would be compensated and have a budget to permit them to retain a lawyer, compensation consultant, accountant or banker to aid in their task of monitoring the board of directors. Most important, the committee would have access to the company proxy statement for a brief statement of its findings and recommendations, not annually, but possibly once every three years. The objective is to find a balance between allowing ownership to be effectively exercised when it is necessary and allowing it to interfere with "ordinary business." This would not mean that shareholders will start acting as another board of directors or as officers. It would be a mistake to create another self-perpetuating body: a new bureaucracy to monitor an old bureaucracy.

A second option is a new kind of institutional investor, one designed to be the "ideal owner," in partnership with the existing institutions. This would be a partnership organized for the purpose of capturing the profits available due to inefficiencies in the marketplace relating to governance. The partnership would buy shares in undervalued companies, push for governance reforms, and benefit from the value of those reforms. It is what Michael Porter described when he recommended that institutional investors increase the size of their stakes and create special funds to test these new (governance-based) investment approaches. The authors had such a partnership structure, named Lens. Our first efforts, at Sears and Eastman Kodak, are described in chapter 6.

> There are companies that perform poorly and are badly governed. Lens "focuses" on these companies, invests, negotiates and effects change. It is the agent of turnaround in the post-takeover era. It can act before the company is at the brink of disaster. The partnership's funding is provided by institutional investors with indexed or broadly diversified equity holdings; and its general partners are compensated only to the extent that they "turn around" focus companies sufficiently to outperform market indices. Lens is itself designed to minimize agency costs for its own investors. The General Partner of Lens receives a fee *only* to the extent that *value is added* to portfolio companies. This incentive fee arrangement is not legally available for trustees themselves. And the Lens principals have no affiliations with other commercial enterprises (thus, eliminating conflicting interests).[154]

Other investment firms have also focused on turning around under-performing companies, though their strategy has been a little different from that of Lens. They have selected mid-size to small companies, where an investment of $10 million or more buys a significant stake. And in general they have acted more like venture capitalists than mere shareholders, getting seats on the board and becoming involved in the company's operations, with little or no publicity, rather than using governance initiatives and working publicly with institutional shareholders. The United Companies Financial example in this chapter provides the most promising opportunity for effective shareholder oversight. The internet allows shareholders to locate and communicate with each other at almost no expense.

A third option is access to the company's proxy for shareholder nomination of candidates for the board, as proposed by SEC chairman William Donaldson.

Much of the focus of this chapter has been on the incentives, disincentives, and impediments shareholders have in fulfilling their "legendary monitoring role." In order to understand that issue more fully, however, we need to examine it from another perspective, the perspective of those who are "elected" by shareholders and owe the duties of care and loyalty to shareholders. So, in chapter 3, we turn to the board of directors.

## NOTES

1. Quoted in Milton Friedman, *Capitalism and Freedom* (University of Chicago Press, Chicago, 1962), p. 26.
2. "The holder of shares owns no part of the corporate property as such . . . He has, however, an equitable interest in the property, the extent of which interest is determined by the number of shares held." Arthur L. Helliwell, *Stock and Stockholders* (Keefe-Davidson, St Paul, MN, 1903), p. 3 (citations omitted). "It is incorporeal and intangible. The interest, thus being abstract, cannot, during the life of the corporation, be reduced to possession" (ibid., pp. 6–7, citations omitted).
3. Adam Smith, *An Inquiry into the Nature and Causes of the Wealth of Nations*, ed. Campbell and Skinner (1976), p. 709.
4. Mark 10: 24.
5. Adam Smith, *Wealth of Nations* (Modern Library, New York, 1937), p. 423.
6. For a discussion of Chile's privatization policies, see Rita Koselka, "A Better Way To Do It," *Forbes*, Oct. 28, 1991.
7. John J. Clancy, *The Invisible Powers: The Language of Business* (Lexington Books, Lexington, MA, 1989), p. 10.
8. John P. Davis, *Corporations: A Study of the Origin and Development of Great Business Combinations and of their Relation to the Authority of the State* (Capricorn, New York, 1961), p. 266.
9. Alfred F. Conard, *Corporations in Perspective* (Foundation Press, New York, 1976), p. 7.
10. 17 US 316.
11. Arthur M. Schlesinger, Jr., *The Age of Jackson* (Little, Brown, Boston, 1945), p. 75.
12. Harvey H. Segal, *Corporate Makeover: The Reshaping of the American Economy* (Viking, New York, 1989), pp. 5–6.
13. Ibid., p. 6.
14. Ibid., p. 7.
15. All information for this case study was taken from Alfred D. Chandler, *The Visible Hand: The Managerial Revolution in American Business* (Harvard University Press, Cambridge, MA, 1977).
16. David Halberstam, *The Reckoning* (William Morrow, New York, 1986), pp. 227–8 (emphasis in the original).
17. Ibid., p. 232.
18. Ibid., pp. 232–3.
19. Ibid., p. 234.
20. Frank H. Easterbrook and Daniel R. Fischel, "The Corporate Contract," *Columbia Law Review*, 89, 7, Nov. 1989, p. 1418.
21. Ibid., p. 1419.
22. Stephen Taub, "The Auto Wars," *Financial World*, Oct. 1, 1985, p. 12.
23. Jerry Flint, "Best Car Wins," *Fortune*, Jan. 27, 1990, p. 75.
24. See *ValueLine* for this information.
25. President Reagan, Detroit, 1980, in David Jernigan, *Restrictions on Japanese Auto Imports* (Kennedy School of Government, Boston, 1983), p. 45.
26. This information is available in the annual company reports of GM, Ford and Chrysler.
27. Paul H. Weaver, *The Suicidal Corporation* (Simon & Schuster, New York, 1988), pp. 88–9.
28. See Robert W. Crandall, "The Effects of US Trade Protection for Autos and Steel" Brookings Papers on Economic Activity (Washington, DC, 1987), pp. 271–88.
29. Rachel Dardis and Jia-Yeoung Lin, "Automobile Quotas Revisited: The Costs of Continued Protection," *Journal of Consumer Affairs*, 19, 2, Winter 1985, p. 290.

30. Ibid.
31. Davis, *Corporations*, at p. 273.
32. A.J. Chayes, quoted ibid., p. xviii.
33. See Edward J. Epstein, "Who Owns the Corporation?", a Twentieth Century Fund Paper (Priority Press Publications, New York, 1986).
34. Adolf A. Berle and Gardiner C. Means, *The Modern Corporation and Private Property* (Legal Classics Library, 1993 edn.), p. 338.
35. Berle and Means, *The Modern Corporation and Private Property* (Transaction Publishers, 1991 edn.), p. 8.
36. The effects of increasing the number of shares, and thus holders, has become increasingly limited due to the rise of institutional investors.
37. Ease of transferability is not a priority for Warren Buffett, whose Berkshire Hathaway trades in four figures per share. But he is a rare exception – most companies split their stock before it reaches $100 a share.
38. Melvin Aron Eisenberg, "The Structure of Corporation Law," *Columbia Law Review*, 89, 7, Nov. 1989, p. 1461.
39. Ibid., p. 1474.
40. Marlene Givant Star, "Paying for Approval", *Pension and Investment Age*, July 24, 1989, p. 1.
41. Eisenberg, "The Structure of Corporation Law," p. 1477.
42. Berle and Means, *The Modern Corporation and Private Property*, p. 64.
43. Ibid.
44. Ibid.
45. William Z. Ripley, *Main Street and Wall Street* (1926; reissued Scholars Book Company, Kansas, 1972), pp. 78–9. The quotation from Brandeis is not from his opinions on the Supreme Court, but rather from testimony before the Commission on Industrial Relations, Jan. 23, 1913, p. 7660.
46. See the R.P. Scherer case in point.
47. The Department of Labor in 1985 issued a release permitting incentive compensation in limited cases.
48. Daniel Fischel and John H. Langbein, "ERISA's Fundamental Contradiction: The Exclusive Benefit Rule," *University of Chicago Law Review*, Sept. 1988, 55/4, pp. 110560.
49. See, Lilli A. Gordon and John Pound, "Governance Matters: An Empirical Study of the Relationship Between Corporate Governance and Corporate Performance," the Corporate Voting Research Project, John F. Kennedy School of Government, Harvard University, June 1991; Stephen L. Nesbitt, "Study Links Shareholder Proposals and Improved Stock Performance," Wilshire Associates, Feb. 13, 1992; Stephen L. Nesbitt, "Long Term Rewards from Corporate Governance," Wilshire Associates, Jan. 5, 1994.
50. Bayless Manning, review of "The American Stockholder" by J.A. Livingston, *Yale Law Review*, 67, 1958, p. 1477.
51. See Henry G. Manne, "Some Theoretical Aspects of Share Voting," *Columbia Law Review*, 64, 8, 1964, pp. 1430–45; Andrei Shleifer and Robert W. Vishny, "Large Shareholders and Corporate Control," *Journal of Political Economy*, 1986, 94, 31, pp. 461–88.
52. Epstein, "Who Owns the Corporation?", pp. 24–5.
53. Albert O. Hirschman noted that deterioration in performance of an institution produces two options for its members and consumers: exit, "some customers stop buying the firm's products or some members leave the organization," and voice, "the firm's customers or the organization's members express their dissatisfaction directly to management or to some other authority to which management is subordinate or through general protest addressed to anyone who cares to listen." See *Exit, Voice, and Loyalty: Responses to Decline in Firms, Organizations, and States* (Harvard University Press, Cambridge, MA, 1970), p. 4.

54. Nathan Rosenberg and L.E. Birdsall Jr., *How the West Grew Rich: The Economic Transformation of the Industrial World* (Basic Books, New York, 1986), p. 229. Emphasis added.

55. Charles D. Ellis, *Investment Policy* (Dow Jones-Irwin, Homewood, IL, 1989), p. 5.

56. Dyan Machan, "Monkey Business," *Forbes*, Oct. 25, 1993, p. 184.

57. Jonathon Clements, "Don't Just Do Something, Sit There," *Forbes*, Dec. 26, 1988, p. 142.

58. Machan, "Monkey Business," p. 190.

59. Ibid., p. 188.

60. Ibid., p. 190.

61. The NYSE's one-share, one-vote rule was not made formal until 1940, and the sanction for violating the rule, delisting from the NYSE, was not added until 1957. In truth, the traditional requirement is not correctly termed one share, one vote, as there is nothing prohibiting some inequality in the voting rights allocated among security holders. What the rule did was limit the amount of voting power that could be attached to any class of stock. There was a flat prohibition on the listing of non-voting shares of common stock, and a prohibition against any non-common class of security holding more than 18.5 percent of all outstanding voting rights.

62. Sec. 3(a)(26) of the Exchange Act.

63. Testimony of John J. Phelan, Jr., Hearings before Subcommittee on Telecommunications and Finance of the Committee on Energy and Commerce of the House of Representatives, 100th Congress, First Session, on H.R. 2172 (Serial No. 10065), July 29, 1987, at pp. 538, 543, 544.

64. The American Stock Exchange later submitted a proposal permitting exchange offers with a vote by two-thirds of the outstanding shares or a majority of the shares unaffiliated with management or the controlling group. A multiple class company would have to have at least one-third of its board composed of independent directors, or provide that holders of the lesser voting class be entitled to elect at least 25 percent of the directors. The NYSE then came back with a second proposal that would allow companies to issue shares with disparate voting rights, or to change relative voting rights if: (1) the decision is approved by a majority of a committee of independent directors and a majority of the board as a whole; (2) in those cases following the implementation of the decision, management or a control group would have a majority of the voting power, the majority of the board is made up of independent directors; and (3) the transaction is approved by a majority of the outstanding shares and a majority of the affected class of shareholders, not including the vote of any "interested shareholder." The ASE defined an independent director as one who is not a current or former employee of the company.

65. Frank H. Easterbrook and Daniel R. Fischel, "Voting in Corporate Law," XXVI *Journal of Law and Economics*, 395, 410–11.

66. American Stock Exchange Chairman Arthur Levitt noted that, "One of the historical sources of the New York Stock Exchange rule against non-voting stock lay in the use of such shares in the public utility industry of the 1920s: non-voting stock was a key device that underlay the pyramiding of personal control in that industry and that ultimately led to collapse, to a tragic loss of public confidence in our capital markets, and to direct federal regulation in the form of the Public Utility Holding Company Act." Hearings before the Subcommittee on Securities of the Committee on Banking, Housing, and Urban Affairs of the United States Senate, 99th Cong., 1st Sess. 1171 (1985).

67. S. Doc. No. 92, 70th Congress, 1st Session, pt. 72-A , p. 64. (1935).

68. Hearings before the Subcommittee on Securities, supra, at 1171.

69.  *Guide to a Microfilm Edition of the Public Papers of Justice Louis Dembitz Brandeis*, in the Jacob and Bertha Goldfarb Library of Brandeis University, Document 128. Testimony before the Senate Committee on Interstate Commerce, 62nd Congress, 2nd Session, Hearings on Control of Corporations, Persons, and Firms Engaged in Interstate Commerce, 1(Pt. XVI) pp. 1146–91. (Dec. 14–16, 1911).

70.  See Stephen L. Nesbitt, "Study Links Shareholder Proposals and Improved Stock Performance"; id., "Long Term Rewards from Corporate Governance"; Lilli A. Gordon and John Pound, "Active Investing in the US Equity Market: Past Performance and Future Prospects," Gordon Group Inc., Dec. 2, 1992; Michael T. Jacobs, *Break the Wall Street Rule: Outperform the Stock Market by Investing as an Owner* (Addison-Wesley, Reading MA, 1993).

71.  Joseph Schumpeter, *Capitalism, Socialism and Democracy* (Harper & Row, New York, 1942), p. 142.

72.  Adolph A. Berle and Gardiner C. Means, *The Modern Corporation and Private Property* (Transaction Publishers, 1991), pp. 249, 250.

73.  Figures from the Federal Reserve's "Flow of Funds" report (3rd Quarter 2001)

74.  Includes both Private Trusteed funds and Private Insured funds.

75.  "Flow of Funds Report," ibid.

76.  "The Brancato Report on Institutional Investment," 1, 1, Dec. 1993, and Institutional Investment Report, "Turnover Investment Strategies, and Ownership Patterns," the Conference Board, 3, 2, Jan. 2000.

77.  PricewaterhouseCooper Management Barometer, 2002.

78.  Figures from The Corporate Library's Board Analyst database, Mar. 2003.

79.  Carolyn Kay Brancato, "Breakdown of Total Assets by Type of Institutional Investor, 1989," *Riverside Economic Research*, Feb. 21, 1991.

80.  Mark J. Roe, "Legal Restraints on Ownership and Control of Public Companies," paper presented at the Conference on the Structure and Governance of Enterprise, Harvard Business School, Mar. 29–31, p. 8.

81.  James E. Heard and Howard D. Sherman, "Conflicts of Interest in the Proxy Voting System," Investor Responsibility Research Center, 1987, p. 22.

82.  Larry Rohter, "Corporations Pass Alumni in Donations to Colleges," *New York Times*, Apr. 29, 1986, p. A16.

83.  Thomas A. Stewart, "The King is Dead", *Fortune*, Jan. 14, 1993, p. 35.

84.  Speech of David Ball to the Financial Executives Institute, Jan. 23, 1990.

85.  Ibid., p. 36.

86.  Named for Sir Thomas Gresham, the Gresham Law states that bad money will always drive out good.

87.  Peter Drucker, *The Unseen Revolution: How Pension Fund Socialism Came to America* (Harper & Row, New York, 1976), p. 1.

88.  Joseph Raphael Blasi and Douglas Lynn Kruse, *The New Owners: The Mass Emergence of Employee Ownership in Public Companies and what it Means to American Business* (HarperBusiness, New York, 1991), p. 3 (emphasis added).

89.  For a discussion of an index strategy, see Forbes, "Don't Just Do Something, Sit There."

90.  We are very grateful to David Wakelin for his help in pulling this discussion together.

91.  The NAPPA Report, 7, 4, Nov. 1993, p. 3.

92.  William M. O'Barr and John M. Conley, *Fortune and Folly: The Wealth and Power of Institutional Investing*, with economic analysis by Carolyn Kay Brancato (Business One Irwin, Homewood, IL, 1992).

93.  Ibid., p. 6.

94.  Ibid., p. 140.

95.  Ibid., p. 78.

96.  Ibid., p. 80.
97.  Ibid., p. 82. One of the public fund mangers interviewed for this book, describing the reason for the laws establishing the current system, said: "There was no formal account-ability mechanism (before these laws). At that time, there were more than a dozen funds and several hundred million dollars. And at one of the funds in particular, one of the treasurers did a lot of business with a particular broker. And it was a very easy thing to do. I'm not suggesting that this was a venal form of a scandal so much as it was just falling into what are normal political practices" (ibid., p. 83).
98.  Ibid., p. 85 (emphasis added). See also Pound's piece on balance in governance.
99.  Thomas A. Stewart, "The King is Dead," p. 36.
100.  Robert Reich, "Of Butchers and Bakers," address to the Council of Institutional Investors, Oct. 8, 1993.
101.  Mark J. Roe, "The Modern Corporation and Private Pensions," *UCLA Law Review*, 41, 1, Oct. 1993, p. 96.
102.  Edward Regan, "U.S. Competitiveness: Financial Markets and Corporate Governance," synopsis of remarks delivered at the Conference on Global Views on Performance Measurement, Financial Executives Research Fund, Dallas, December 16, 1991, pp. 2–3.
103.  Dale Hanson's speech to the Harvard Business School, Dec. 3, 1992.
104.  Paul Sweeney, "How CalPERS Can Ruin a CEO's Day", *Global Finance*, Feb. 1993.
105.  E.S. Browning, "Alabama Pension Chief Achieves a Rare Feat: He Stirs Controversy," *Wall Street Journal*, Feb. 4, 1994, p. 1.
106.  James A. White, "Divestment Proves Costly and Hard," *Wall Street Journal*, Feb. 22, 1989, p. Cl.
107.  For example, David Vise, "Va. Pension Fund Hires Too Many Advisers, Report Says," *Washington Post*, Dec. 14, 1993, p. D1; see also id., "DC Pension Plan Mishandled," *Washington Post*, Aug. 17, 1993, and "City Office Probes Pension Trustee," *Washington Post*, Aug. 16 1993, p. A1.
108.  Dr D. Jeanne Patterson, *The Use of Public Employee Retirement System Resources for Economic Development in the Great Lakes States* (Institute for Development Strategies, Indiana University, 1992), p. 114.
109.  Ibid., p. 118, emphasis in the original.
110.  Federal Employees' Retirement System Act of 1986, Section 8438(g).
111.  Editorial, "The Biggest Pension Scofflaw? Uncle Sam," *Business Week*, Dec. 6, 1993, p. 186.
112.  TIAA–CREF Policy Statement on Corporate Governance, Sept. 17, 1993.
113.  Leslie Scism, "Teacher's Pension Plan to Give Firms Tough Exams," *Wall Street Journal*, Oct. 6, 1993, p. C1.
114.  TIAA–CREF Policy Statement on Corporate Governance, Sept. 17, 1993.
115.  Scism, supra, p. C1.
116.  Roe, "The Modern Corporation and Private Pensions," p. 83.
117.  Ibid., p. 77.
118.  See Daniel Fischel and John H. Langbein, "ERISA's Fundamental Contradiction: The Exclusive Benefit Rule," *University of Chicago Law Review*, 55, 4, Sept. 1988, pp. 1105–60.
119.  Employees' Retirement Income Security Act (ERISA), 1974, Section 402(a)(2).
120.  ERISA, Section 3(16)(B).
121.  Money managers have an incentive to trade shares thanks to the "soft dollar" industry. Soft dollars or soft commissions are those arrangements whereby a fund manager agrees, whether formally or informally, to provide a broker with a certain commission flow each year in return for various financial services, such as analysts' research, portfolio val-uation or information systems. Some argue that soft dollar arrangements encourage money managers to trade shares regardless of the value to the ultimate beneficiary.

122.  The government seemed to agree – administration of ERISA was given to the Labor Department, not to the Treasury Department.

123.  Letter from J. Grills, chairman of CIEBA, to Linda Cane, director of the Division of Corporate Finance, SEC, Feb. 25, 1991. CIEBA is a committee of the Financial Executives Institute, a professional association of 13,500 senior financial executives.

124.  Leslie Scism and Albert R. Karr, "Retirees Share in Company Fortunes as Corporations Put Stock in Pensions," *Wall Street Journal*, Nov. 17, 1993, p. C1.

125.  Ibid., p. C22.

126.  Ibid.

127.  Olena Berg, Assistant Secretary of Labor for Pension and Welfare Benefits, speech to the AFL–CIO Asset Managers Conference, Sept. 2, 1993, p. 3.

128.  See Judge Kimba Wood's ruling in *Amalgamated Clothing and Textile Workers Union v. Wal-Mart Stores Inc.*

129.  Marlene Givant Star, "SEC Sued in Proxy Dispute," *Pensions and Investments*, Mar. 8, 1993, p. 2. In the Fall of 1993, Judge Kimba Wood of the US District Court for the Southern District of New York declared the SEC's decision improper. While its appeal is pending, the SEC must refrain from issuing any more no action letters under the proxy rule (14a-8(c)7).

130.  The authors were, at that time, President and General Counsel of Institutional Shareholder Services Inc.

131.  In 1993, the California Public Employees' Retirement Fund sponsored a similar shareholder advisory committee resolution at Pennzoil Co. The SEC, however, ruled that Pennzoil could exclude the proposal from its proxy because a provision calling for reimbursement of the committee's members contravened Delaware law, Pennzoil's state of incorporation. CalPERS offered to redraft the resolution, but the SEC still refused to demand that Pennzoil include the resolution in its proxy.

132.  Benjamin Graham and David L. Dodd, *Securities Analysis*, 1st edn. (McGraw-Hill, New York, 1934), pp. 51–511.

133.  Joseph A. Grundfest and Michael A. Perino, *Securities Litigation Reform: The First Year's Experience*, Release 97.1, A Statistical and Legal Analysis of Class Action Securities Fraud Litigation Under the Private Securities Litigation Reform Act of 1995, Stanford Law School, Feb. 27, 1997. Greg May, *Reality Check: A Report Card on the Private Securities Litigation Reform Act of 1995 after Twenty-Two Months of Practice* (Munsch Hardt Kopf & Harr, PC).

134.  NACD 1992 Corporate Governance Survey, National Association of Corporate Directors, Washington, DC, 1992, p. i.

135.  Many thanks to Aaron Brown for providing us with the case study from which this was adapted.

136.  Bernard S. Black, "Institutional Investors and Corporate Governance: the Case for Institutional Voice," *Journal of Applied Corporate Finance*, Fall 1992.

137.  Michael T. Jacobs, *Short-Term America: The Causes and Cures of our Business Myopia* (Harvard Business School Press, Cambridge, MA, 1991).

138.  Michael E. Porter, *Capital Choices: Changing the Way America Invests in Industry*, Research Report to the Council on Competitiveness, co-sponsored by Harvard Business School, June 1992.

139.  In Jan. 1994, Nesbitt completed a second study on CalPERS' activism, finding that 24 companies targeted by CalPERS had each lagged the S&P 500 Index by an average 86 percentage points in total for the five prior years. But for the four years subsequent to CalPERS' involvement, those same companies each exceeded the index by an average 109 percentage points. See Stephen L. Nesbitt, "Long Term Rewards from Corporate Governance."

140. Michael T. Jacobs, *Break the Wall Street Rule.*
141. Abram Chayes, in his Dec. 1960 introduction to John P. Davis, *Corporations* (1st pub. 1897; Capricorn Press, New York, 1961), pp. xvii–xviii.
142. Roe, "The Modern Corporation and Private Pensions," p. 77.
143. Porter, *Capital Choices*, p. 91 (emphasis added).
144. Ira Millstein, "The Evolving Role of Institutional Investors in Corporate Governance", prepared for American Bar Association Panel, Institutional Investors: Monolithic or Diverse?, Aug. 10, 1992, pp. 42–3.
145. Edward Regan, "US Competitiveness: Financial Markets and Corporate Governance," synopsis of remarks delivered at the conference on global views on performance measurement, Financial Executives Research Fund, Dallas, Dec. 16, 1992, pp. 4–5.
146. Susan Pulliam, "New York's Pension Fund Targets A&P," *Wall Street Journal*, Feb. 9, 1993.
147. Susan Pulliam, "Paramount is Targeted by Pension Fund due to Weak Stock Pricer, Executive Pay", *Wall Street Journal*, Mar. 4, 1993.
148. "Getting Rid of the Boss," *The Economist*, Feb. 6, 1993.
149. Leslie Wayne, "Assuaging Investor Discontent," *New York Times*, Feb. 3, 1993.
150. John Pound, "The Rise of the Political Model of Corporate Governance and Corporate Control", working paper prepared for the Subcouncil on Corporate Governance and Financial Markets of the Competitiveness Policy Council, Sept. 1992, p. 19.
151. In late 1993, the Supreme Court ruled that group annuities held by insurance companies were subject to ERISA. Previously, only state regulations applied to such investments. *John Hancock Mutual Life Insurance Co. v. Harris Trust & Savings Bank, as trustee of the Sperry Master Retirement Trust No. 2*, US Supreme Court, Dec. 13, 1993. See also Albert B. Crenshaw, "Court Backs Curbs on Pension Risks," *Washington Post*, Dec. 14, 1993, p. D1.
152. George W. Dent Jr., "Toward Unifying Ownership and Control in the Public Corporation," *Wisconsin Law Review*, 5, 1989, p. 881.
153. Ibid., p. 908, emphasis added.
154. Lens sales material, 1993.

# 3
# DIRECTORS: MONITORING

The board acts as a fulcrum between the owners and controllers of a corporation. They are the middlemen (and a very few middlewomen) who provide balance between a small group of key managers based in corporate headquarters and a vast group of shareholders spread all over the world. In theory, at least, the law imposes on the board a strict and absolute fiduciary duty to ensure that a company is run in the long-term interests of the owners, the shareholders. The reality, as we will see later in this chapter, is a little less certain.

Boards of directors are a crucial part of the corporate structure. They are the link between the people who provide capital (the shareholders) and the people who use that capital to create value (the managers). This means that boards are the overlap between the small, powerful group that runs the company and a huge, diffuse, and relatively powerless group that simply wishes to see the company run well.

The board's primary role is to monitor management on behalf of the shareholders. In this chapter, we will discuss the mechanisms and structures used to keep managers accountable to the board as well as the mechanisms and structures used to keep the directors accountable to the shareholders.

The strength – and indeed survival – of any corporation depends on a balance of two distinct powers: the power of those who own the corporation and the power of those who run it. A corporation depends on shareholders for capital, but reserves the day-to-day running of the enterprise for management. This creates opportunities for efficiencies far beyond what any one owner/manager, or even a group of owner/managers, could accomplish. It also creates opportunities for abuse.

This was the conundrum that almost stopped corporations before they began. Karl Marx and Adam Smith did not agree on much, but they both thought that the corporate form of organization was unworkable, and for remarkably similar reasons. They questioned whether it is possible to create a structure that will operate efficiently and fairly, despite the fact that there is a separation between ownership and control. Adam Smith criticized both those who invested in joint-stock companies and those who managed them. Of the investors he wrote that they "seldom pretend to understand anything of the business of the company," and of the directors he said: "Being the managers of other people's money rather than of their own, it cannot well be expected that they should watch over it with the same anxious vigilance with which the partners in a private co-partnery frequently watch over their own."[1]

*Put another way: is there any system to make a manager care as much about the company's performance as a shareholder does?*

Corporations cannot be run by consensus. Managers must be given the power to make decisions quickly and to take reasonable risks. If every managerial decision had to be communicated to the company's owners, much less ratified by them, industrial progress would be paralyzed, and everyone would lose.

Yet while shareholders delegate substantial powers to management, they need assurance that power will not be abused. *How do shareholders know that the assets they own are not being mismanaged, or even embezzled?*

The single major challenge addressed by corporate governance is how to grant managers enormous discretionary power over the conduct of the business while holding them accountable for the use of that power. Shareholders cannot possibly oversee the managers they hire. A company's owners may number in the tens of thousands, diffused worldwide. So shareholders are granted the right to elect representatives to oversee the management of the company on their behalf – the board of directors. Directors are representatives of owners (or, in closely held companies, the owners themselves), whose purpose under law is to safeguard the assets of the corporation.

---

# Case in point:
# Warren Buffett on boards

In his 2002 report to Berkshire Hathaway shareholders, the most successful investor of all time (and a director of several companies, including Coca-Cola and the *Washington Post*), wrote about the failures of corporate boards:

> In theory, corporate boards should have prevented this deterioration of conduct . . . [In 1993] I said that directors "should behave as if there was a single absentee owner, whose long-term interest they should try to further in all proper ways." This means that directors must get rid of a manager who is mediocre or worse, no matter how likable he may be. Directors must react as did the chorus-girl bride of an 85-year-old multimillionaire when he asked whether she would love him if he lost his money. "Of course," the young beauty replied, "I would miss you, but I would still love you." . . .
>
> Why have intelligent and decent directors failed so miserably? The answer lies not in inadequate laws – it's always been clear that directors are obligated to represent the interests of shareholders – but rather in what I'd call "boardroom atmosphere."
>
> Over a span of 40 years, I have been on 19 public-company boards (excluding Berkshire's) and have interacted with perhaps 250 directors. Most of them were "independent" as defined by today's rules. But the great majority of these directors lacked at least one of the three qualities I value. As a result, their contribution to shareholder well-being was minimal at best and, too often, negative. These people, decent and intelligent though they were, simply did not know enough about business and/or care enough about shareholders to question foolish acquisitions or egregious compensation. My own behavior, I must ruefully add, frequently fell short as well: Too often I was silent when management made proposals that I judged to be counter to the interests of shareholders. In those cases, collegiality trumped independence.

## A Brief History of Anglo-American Boards

US boards carried on a tradition that began with the earliest form of corporate organization, the joint stock companies. In the British colonies, as in Great Britain itself, the group of people who oversaw the company would meet regularly. Fine furniture was expensive in those days, and few people in trade had chairs or tables to contain the group. So the men sat on stools, around a long board placed across two sawhorses. The group was named "the board," after the makeshift table they worked at. And the leader of the group, who did not have to sit on a stool, by reason of his prestigious perch, was named the "chair-man."

The first commerce in America was conducted by two British enterprises, operating under royal charter: the Virginia Company of London and the Virginia Company of Plymouth. Two bodies governed these companies. The first was a local council – a management board of colonists responsible for day-to-day operations in the new land. This council was accountable to a second, more powerful, body in London. This "supervisory board" was answerable to the sovereign, and responsible for more general matters of policy and strategy.

Following the American Revolution, the new republic had to devise its own forms of governance. An early leader was one of the joint authors of the *Federalist Papers*, and the nation's first Secretary of the Treasury, Alexander Hamilton. In November 1791, the New Jersey Legislature passed a bill authorizing Hamilton's "Society for Establishing Useful Manufactures" (or SUM, as it was known). The society was allowed to produce goods ranging from sailcloth to women's shoes.

The governance of Hamilton's corporation was remarkably similar to that of today's largest companies. The Society's prospectus declared: "The affairs of the company [are] to be under the management of thirteen directors." Hamilton also created an early audit committee. He devised a committee of inspectors, separate from the board of directors, made up of five shareholders. They were generally chosen from among defeated directorship candidates, though shareholders could elect any five of their fellow stockholders. These inspectors were granted access to the company's books, and given power of review over all the company's affairs.[2]

## Today's Typical Board

The most important attribute of a corporate director is the ability to yawn with your mouth closed. *Tom Horton*

Hamilton would have no trouble recognizing the corporate board of today. The structure and composition of boardrooms have changed surprisingly little in 200 years. Average board size has remained at about 15, give or take a director or two. Audit committees remain an important force in board life. And most of today's directors come from the same segment of the population as the directors of SUM, the commercial elite.

None the less, organizations that have tracked shifts in board size, composition, and structure see significant changes.

## Size

Boards of directors "have made great strides in paring back to a more workable size," reported executive search firm Spencer Stuart in 1998. Spencer Stuart's 13th annual survey of board practices in large US companies found that average board size had shrunk from 15 in 1988 to 10.9 in 2002. One-quarter of S&P 500 boards have between eight and nine directors, as opposed to 16 percent five years earlier. As boards have grown smaller, there has been a net reduction in inside directors. The largest boards in the sample were Comerica (22), and SBC Communications and US Bancorp (21).

## Inside/Outside mix

Spencer Stuart's 2002 study found that, in nearly one-third of S&P 500 firms, the CEO is the only inside director. That was true of less than 10 percent in 1992. The year 2002 saw a 44 percent increase in the number of new outside directors, a record likely to be broken in 2003 and beyond. The most common job of the new directors is still CEO/chair/president of another public company; they make up 41 percent of the total.

## Diversity

Most corporate directors are still middle-aged white males. In 1973, just 11 percent of boards featured even one woman, and 9 percent had a director from an ethnic minority.[3] In 1998, Spencer Stuart offered the bold headline: "Boards Eager to Recruit More Women." They found that 16 percent of new outside directors were women (an improvement on the status quo, given that only 12 percent of all directors are women). But the 2002 survey showed a slight drop in the number of women on boards, with 18 percent of boards still all-male, compared with 15 percent five years ago.

The survey also found that 12 percent of new directors were academics or from non-profits, suggesting that companies are increasingly looking beyond the standard candidates (senior corporate executives) so that women may be recruited.

There is similar steady, if unspectacular, progress in the recruitment of directors from ethnic minorities. Spencer Stuart found that three-quarters of S&P 500 companies in 2002 had boards with African American directors, compared with only two-thirds in 1997. One-quarter have at least one Hispanic director, an increase of 20 percent since 1997. One tenth have an Asian director, an increase of 29 percent since 1997. And there is a significant over 50 percent increase in non-US directors, with one-third of responding boards having an international director.

## Meeting frequency

Standard practice is developing in the frequency with which boards meet. Spencer Stuart conclude that "there is little question that boards operate more efficiently than in past years." The average S&P 500 board met 7.5 times in 2002, down slightly from an average of 8.2 meetings in 2001.

The decline in the number of full board meetings is partly explained by the increased reliance on board committees. Though companies need only have an audit committee by law, most companies find the need for additional committees. Republic New York was unusual in requiring ten sub-committees; Nucor had only one.

In 2002, all but one board had compensation committees (Microsoft's entire board acts as its compensation committee); 75 percent had nominating/corporate governance committees; half had executive committees (many of these were being phased out as the emphasis on independent directors and the improvements in communications technology made it less essential to have a committee of insiders to rely on when the full board could not be reached); one-third had finance committees; 15 percent had social/corporate responsibility committees, and 10 percent had investment/pension committees.

## Ownership

In 1993, Spencer Stuart concluded that the idea of paying outside directors wholly in stock was a "non factor" in its board analysis. Five years later, their survey found that a small but significant body of 25 companies (just 5 percent of the S&P 500) were paying their directors wholly in stock. But 15 percent of companies now offer directors the choice to receive their retainer in stock or cash, up from zero in 1993. And more than half the S&P 500 offer outside directors stock options, up from 10 percent in 1993. Spencer Stuart concluded: "Presumably if directors do their jobs well, their efforts should be handsomely rewarded in the future."

## Governance

The 25th annual board survey by consultancy Korn/Ferry also found that governance standards in the boardroom had transformed over time. In Korn/Ferry's first survey in 1973, the words "corporate governance" did not appear in either the questionnaire sent to directors or the report that analyzed the results. "How times have changed!" commented the consultancy.

Korn/Ferry found that "generally accepted corporate governance practices are now solidly in place." For example, 75 percent of companies think that evaluation of individual directors should be done regularly (although only 19 percent of boards actually carry out such evaluations); 72 percent have a formal process to evaluate the CEO's performance; and 64 percent of companies have written guidelines on corporate governance.

Korn/Ferry asked directors for their views on what were the most important developments in board structure and practice during the last few years. Nearly half the respondents identified the increasing independence of audit, compensation and nominating committees.

Ten years ago, only the audit committee would have been made up entirely of outsiders, and five years ago the average nominating committee included an insider. Now it is considered best practice to have all three committees made up exclusively of outside directors, and that will be codified by the New York Stock Exchange listing standards that are a part of the post-Enron reforms.

But there are further reforms to come. More than a quarter of respondents felt that inside directors should be limited to one or two outside directorships, and more than 20 percent felt that retired CEOs should be required to resign from the board and that the board as a whole should appoint committee chairs and members.

Board meetings usually follow an agenda compiled by management, though directors can ask for items to be included. The agenda, plus relevant information, is typically sent to directors a couple of days before the meeting.

A meeting may feature a special presentation by a non-board insider, such as a divisional head. Alternatively, the company may schedule special board trips to foreign or regional headquarters.

Some companies schedule special meetings for the outside directors to meet alone, in order to evaluate the CEO and senior managers when they are not present. The New York Stock Exchange has proposed these meetings be required for listed companies.

## BOARD DUTIES: THE LEGAL FRAMEWORK

The responsibility of today's boards of directors is little different from what it was in Hamilton's day. Compare Hamilton's statement of the role of the board with today's General Corporation Law of the State of Delaware, which reads: "The business and affairs of every corporation organized under this chapter shall be managed by or under the direction of a board of directors."[4] Of course, since Hamilton's day, the legal implications of such statements have been examined and developed in enormous depth. Today, an enormously complex, ever-changing body of law governs the role of the corporate board of directors.

Legally, most jurisdictions describe the director as having two duties, the duty of care and the duty of loyalty. And directors' conduct will be judged according to the "business judgment rule."

*Duty of loyalty* means that a director must demonstrate unyielding loyalty to the company's shareholders. Thus, if a director sat on the boards of two companies with conflicting interests (both trying to buy a third business, for example), he would be forced to resign from one board because clearly he could not demonstrate loyalty to the shareholders of both companies at the same time.

*Duty of care* means that a director must exercise due diligence in making decisions. He must discover as much information as possible on the question at issue and be able to show that, in reaching a decision, he has considered all reasonable alternatives.

When a director can demonstrate that he has acted with all due loyalty and exercised all possible care, the courts will not second-guess his decision. In other words, the court will defer to his *business judgment*. Unless a decision made by directors and managers is clearly self-dealing or negligent, the court will not challenge it, whether or not it was a "good" decision in light of subsequent developments.

Of course, laws offer only a general definition of the director's role. The law, after all, must be sufficiently flexible to cope with ever-changing business developments that are forever challenging directors with new issues and questions to resolve. As we shall see later, the takeover era of the 1980s caused a fundamental re-evaluation of these concepts.

Many people have tried to step beyond the legal definitions of a board's duties and develop more specific descriptions of the responsibilities of the directors. The Business Roundtable, representing the largest US corporations, describes the duties of the board as follows:

The board of directors has five primary functions:

1. Select, regularly evaluate, and, if necessary, replace the chief executive officer. Determine management compensation. Review succession planning.
2. Review and, where appropriate, approve the financial objectives, major strategies, and plans of the corporation.
3. Provide advice and counsel to top management.
4. Select and recommend to shareholders for election an appropriate slate of candidates for the board of directors; evaluate board processes and performance.
5. Review the adequacy of the systems to comply with all applicable laws/regulations.[5]

Other groups have developed similar lists. The following, for instance, is the guide developed by the American Law Institute:

1.  Elect, evaluate, and, where appropriate, dismiss the principal senior executives.
2.  Oversee the conduct of the corporation's business, with a view to evaluation on an ongoing basis, whether the corporation's resources are being managed in a manner consistent with [enhancing shareholder gain, within the law, within ethical considerations, and while directing a reasonable amount of resources to public welfare and humanitarian purposes].
3.  Review and approve corporate plans and actions that the board and principal senior executives consider major and changes in accounting principles that the board consider material.

    Perform such other functions as are prescribed by law, or assigned to the board under a standard of the corporation.[6]

These lists, though they differ in emphasis, sum up the generally accepted duties of the board. Beneath such umbrella definitions stand the myriad details that the board might attend to: quarterly results and management's projections for the next quarter; the company's long-term strategic goals; its capital structure; debt financing; resource allocation; the need to buy or sell assets; dividend policy; research and development projects; the status of the corporation's competitors; or the company's global prospects.

Most commentators agree, however, that umbrella definitions do not adequately describe a job that has lofty – and nebulous – responsibilities. The difficulty lies in the fact that, although boards of directors are burdened with the responsibility of ensuring that management runs the enterprise efficiently, they are not permitted (as a practical or legal matter) to become intimately involved in the running of the company. The board is there to evaluate performance, and to respond promptly if it is not satisfactory.

The board is not sufficiently involved in the day-to-day decisions of the company to determine how the company should be managed – that is the job of the executives. As one academic comments: "Outside directors likely have the most difficult job of all – not running the store – but making sure that the individuals running the store run the store as well as possible."[7] As a result, many believe that the primary responsibility of directors is to see that they have the best management talent available – the best people to run the store – and to replace them promptly if performance slips.[8] Directors are responsible for the overall picture, not the daily business decisions, the forest, not the trees. Or, as one long-time observer likes to say, a director's position should be NIFO – "nose in, fingers out." In the past, the Delaware courts have bent over backwards to defer to the "business judgment" of the directors. Without compelling evidence of self-dealing, the court will not interfere with the board's decision. Occasionally, though, the courts will provide a warning. In the 1996 case *In re Caremark International Inc. Derivative Litig.*, Chancellor William T. Allen of the Delaware Chancery Court addressed the circumstances under which corporate directors may be held liable for breaching their duty of care by failing to adequately supervise the conduct of corporate employees accused of causing the corporation to violate the law. The case arose out of the 1994 indictment of Caremark International Inc., a provider of patient and managed health care services, and two of its officers and several mid-level employees for violations of federal health care reimbursement regulations under the Anti-Referral Payments Law (ARPL) prohibiting health care providers from paying any form of remuneration to induce the referral of Medicare or Medicaid patients.

Following the indictments, shareholder derivative complaints were filed in the Delaware Court of Chancery. Those complaints alleged that Caremark's directors breached their fiduciary duty of care by failing to monitor activities of the company's employees or to institute corrective measures that may have prevented the unlawful conduct, thereby exposing Caremark to substantial liability. No senior officers or directors were charged with wrong-doing in either the indictments or the government settlement agreements. Caremark and its directors then entered into a settlement with the shareholder plaintiffs. As part of this settlement, Caremark agreed, among other things, to establish a new compliance and ethics committee of the board of directors to monitor business segment compliance with the ARPL and report to the entire board semi-annually concerning compliance by each business segment.

The court, in ruling on a settlement agreement, addressed the issue of the standard to be applied. Because there was no evidence that the directors knew of the violations, the question was whether they should have known.

> A director's obligation includes a duty to attempt in good faith to assure that a corporate information and reporting system . . . exists, and that failure to do so under some circumstances may, in theory at least, render a director liable for losses caused by non-compliance with applicable legal standards . . . only a sustained or systematic failure of the board to exercise oversight – such as an utter failure to attempt to assure a reasonable information and reporting system exists – will establish the lack of good faith that is a necessary condition to liability.

Other descriptions of a board's responsibility are more general in their approach. Sir John Harvey Jones, the highly successful chief executive of Imperial Chemical Industries in the UK during the 1970s and 1980s, sums up the difficulty of defining the director's role:

> Management consultants are there for every conceivable part of the manager's job. But you try getting advice, guidance, a course, or a specialist book on the skills of being a good director of a company, and you will find almost nothing except a great deal of mystique.
>
> The job of the board is all to do with creating momentum, movement, improvement and direction. If the board is not taking the company purposely in the future, who is? It is because of boards' failure to create tomorrow's company out of today's that so many famous names in industry continue to disappear.[9]

From this description, one commentator who has served on many boards, describes his role as "creating tomorrow's corporation out of today's."[10]

## THE BOARD–MANAGEMENT RELATIONSHIP

The existence of boards, according to both the legal definitions of the board's role and Sir John's description, is based on the premise that they oversee management, select executives who will do the best job, and fire them when they don't. In theory, management serves at the pleasure of the board. The reality is the exact opposite. Directors are beholden to management for nomination, compensation, and information. Moreover, many directors are unable or unwilling to devote the time or energy necessary to oversee the operation of the company, or to make a financial commitment to its success.

As management guru Peter Drucker puts it, "Whenever an institution malfunctions as consistently as boards of directors have in nearly every major fiasco of the last 40 or 50 years, it is futile to blame men. It is the institution that malfunctions."[11] Allowing so many CEOs to receive gargantuan compensation for mediocre returns (as discussed in chapter 4) is just one symptom of the ineffectuality of boards over the past decade. The corporate failures of Enron, Adelphia, WorldCom, Heathsouth and others in 2002–3 are more than symptoms – they are an indictment.

What is wrong with the institution? Why does it malfunction? In this section we will draw on actual cases to show how various aspects of board organization serve to work against the representation of shareholders. As you read through this discussion, take a look at the DVD's Enron analysis and try to put it in the context of these issues.

## INFORMATION FLOW

Directors can never know as much about the operation of the company as management, so they are dependent on the CEO for being supplied with accurate, timely, and material information. But the CEO, who also acts as chairman of the board in the overwhelming majority of American companies, has a powerful incentive to organize the board meeting agenda and underlying information to emphasize his successes and avoid discussion of anything else. One sign of an ineffective board is a chairman who provides the wrong kind of information – too much, too little, or too late.

Furthermore, CEOs almost always play the dominant role in selecting and inviting board members (see discussion of nominating committees later in this chapter). CEOs always say they are looking for "consensus-builders," and that is wise – no one wants directors to be throwing things at each other or fighting for the chance to speak. But when you put eleven consensus-builders into a room with one visionary, dynamic leader who is used to being the boss, there is a real problem in making sure that the directors get the information they need to address the issues for which they are responsible.

Sarah A.B. Teslik, Executive Director of the Council of Institutional Investors, an association representing $650 billion in investment capital, described the problems a director might face in a newsletter to CII clients.

> What if some very clever record-keeping is occurring to mask problems that may or may not be detectable by auditors? Or what if a few big customers are angry about problems that could be fixed but haven't yet dropped their accounts (and the leader either doesn't know or doesn't want to reveal this)? Since the outside world can, by and large, detect many of the bigger, or later-stage problems without your help, it is presumably these kinds of nascent or potential problems that you [the director] are mostly there to detect, prevent or remedy.
>
> But how do you do this if the source of virtually all your information is the leader? The fact is, in too many cases, you don't. Because you can't. Because, under the circumstances, no one can.
>
> There isn't much point in fussing over the definition of an independent director, or the existence or makeup of board committees, or the procedures for electing directors if the information they get is inadequate. What can even the most brilliant and properly motivated director do if he or she lacks needed, accurate, or timely information?[12]

Unfortunately, the corporate history books are full of boards who knew too little too late.

# Cases in point: RJR Nabisco, Lone Star Industries, Tambrands, Enron

**RJR Nabisco**. CEO Tylee Wilson spent $68 million developing an ultimately disastrous "smokeless" cigarette without telling the board. As chronicled in *Barbarians at the Gate*, an epic of corporate excess, Wilson's directors were livid that he had far exceeded his spending limits without board approval.

> "Why didn't you tell us about this sooner?" Juanita Kreps demanded. "You trust hundreds of company people working on this project; you trust dozens of people at an ad agency you're working with: you trust outside suppliers and scientists, but you don't trust us" she said. "I, for one, absolutely resent that."[13]

Wilson's successor. F. Ross Johnson, behaved similarly. He handled his board with a combination of lavish perquisites and meager information. He arranged for his directors to rub shoulders with celebrities, use corporate planes and apartments, and he even endowed chairs at their alma maters with corporate funds. All this made it hard for directors to push him on tough questions.

Two *Wall Street Journal* reporters described the life of an RJR Nabisco board member: "A seat on RJR Nabisco's board was almost like Easy Street: lucrative directors' fees, fat consulting contracts and the constant loving care of the company's president and chief executive officer, F. Ross Johnson. 'I sometimes feel like the director of transportation' he once remarked, after ordering up a corporate jet for a board member. 'But if I'm there for them, they'll be there for me.'"[14] While he was dazzling his handpicked directors, who could expect them to complain about his jets and country clubs?

**Lone Star Industries**. The Lone Star board ordered a special inquiry into the expenses of CEO James Stewart, following a *Business Week* article that criticized his lifestyle at a time of company cutbacks. The inquiry alleged that Stewart billed the company $1.1 million for "purely personal expenses," including taking his personal music teacher on Lone Star trips to three continents. The nine-man board, including such luminaries as Robert L. Strauss, later ambassador to Russia, never scrutinized Stewart's expenses. "You make an assumption that the CEO is honest and prudent," said David Wallace, an outsider who succeeded Mr. Stewart. "We didn't know what he was doing." In 1990, Lone Star filed for bankruptcy protection.[15]

**Tambrands Inc.** On June 1, 1993, Martin F.C. Emmett was fired as the CEO of Tambrands Inc., the manufacturer of feminine hygiene products. Seemingly, his ouster was a routine affair, given the increasingly troubled operations of the company. Market share for Tampax, the company's leading product, had dropped 8 percent since mid-1992, and share value had declined by a third in less than six months. The board apparently fired Emmett after he failed to outline a satisfactory recovery strategy.

Ten weeks after the firing, the *Wall Street Journal* reported that Emmett's departure had opened a walk-in closet full of skeletons. The story demonstrates the extent to which an executive can keep his board in the dark. The *Wall Street Journal* commented that the story raises "murky ethical issues hinged on friendships, business relationships and, ultimately a board's role in policing corporate operations."[16] The scandal was based on Emmett's unusually close relationship with two principals in a consulting firm called Personnel Corp. of North America (PCA) – the firm that had originally landed Emmett his job at Tambrands. Immediately after Emmett's departure, Tambrands ended most of its contacts with PCA. PCA's two principals were long-time friends of Emmett's. During his tenure, he steered contracts worth $2 million to PCA, including compensation, pension administration, and outplacement. Not only did he retain the firm, but the two principals were placed on individual retainers that exceeded the salaries of most of Tambrands' officers.

Emmett's relationship with the PCA executives dated back to the mid-1970s, when PCA principals David R. Meredith and Jack L. Lederer conducted a compensation study for Standard Brands Inc., where Emmett was then an executive. When Standard Brands merged with Nabisco in 1981, Emmett referred PCA to Nabisco, and PCA was awarded a contract. When Emmett left Nabisco to chair the investment banking subsidiary of Security Pacific in New York, PCA followed also.

Even in those days, Emmett enjoyed the trappings of executive privilege. Emmett's boss in the Standard Brands days was the same Ross Johnson described above, who went on from Standard Brands to be CEO of both Nabisco and, following the merger with R.J. Reynolds, RJR Nabisco. *Barbarians at the Gate* describes Emmett's career at Standard Brands: "Johnson lavished gifts on Emmett, including a luxurious corporate apartment and an unlimited expense account." When Emmett was being hunted to head Tambrands, at least one executive search firm report commented on Emmett's apparent taste for the high life,

Lynn Salvage, a director who left the board in 1991, told the *Wall Street Journal* that, once PCA had been retained, the two partners "did everything in their power to get [Emmett] the most lucrative compensation scheme they could."[17] Pearl Meyer, a compensation consultant with her own firm, described the PCA consultants as "very capable and energetic advocates on [Emmett's] behalf."[18] Mr. Emmett's stock options and benefits were more appropriate for a company twice Tambrands' size. He received options to buy nearly 600,000 Tambrands shares over the years: in December of 1992 he exercised options for 150,000 shares, which he sold at a profit of over $5 million.[19] PCA also argued that the board was underpaid. Following this advice, the board voted to increase its annual retainer from $13,000 to $20,000, and to award themselves options on 1,100 shares annually.

Following his ouster, Emmett still had ten years to exercise his remaining 450,000 stock options – a severance package negotiated by PCA in 1992. Following his departure, he continued to work in an office provided by PCA in their Connecticut headquarters.

**Enron**. Look at these excerpts from the Powers Report on Enron:

> Beyond the financial statement consequences, the Chewco transaction raises substantial corporate governance and management oversight issues. Under Enron's Code of Conduct of Business Affairs, [Michael] Kopper was prohibited from having a financial or managerial role in Chewco unless the Chairman and CEO determined that his participation "does not adversely affect the best interests of the Company." Notwithstanding this requirement, we have seen no evidence that his participation was ever disclosed to, or approved by, either Kenneth Lay (who was Chairman and CEO) or the Board of Directors. . . .
> The Board approved Fastow's participation in the LJM partnerships with full knowledge and discussion of the obvious conflict of interest that would result. The Board apparently believed that the conflict, and the substantial risks associated with it, could be mitigated through certain controls (involving oversight by both the Board and Senior Management) to ensure that transactions were done on terms fair to

Enron. In taking this step, the Board thought that the LJM partnerships would offer business benefits to Enron that would outweigh the potential costs. The principal reason advanced by Management in favor of the relationship, in the case of LJM1, was that it would permit Enron to accomplish a particular transaction it could not otherwise accomplish. In the case of LJM2, Management advocated that it would provide Enron with an additional potential buyer of assets that Enron wanted to sell, and that Fastow's familiarity with the Company and the assets to be sold would permit Enron to move more quickly and incur fewer transaction costs. . . .

These controls as designed were not rigorous enough, and their implementation and oversight was inadequate at both the Management and Board levels. No one in Management accepted primary responsibility for oversight; the controls were not executed properly; and there were structural defects in those controls that became apparent over time. For instance, while neither the Chief Accounting Officer, Causey, nor the Chief Risk Officer, Buy, ignored his responsibilities, they interpreted their roles very narrowly and did not give the transactions the degree of review the Board believed was occurring. Skilling appears to have been almost entirely uninvolved in the process, notwithstanding representations made to the Board that he had undertaken a significant role. No one in Management stepped forward to address the issues as they arose, or to bring the apparent problems to the Board's attention.

Note also that the Enron board had a number of consulting fees and other related transactions involving directors, including charitable and political donations. Herbert S. Winokur Jr., who was on the committee that approved the special-purpose entities, was chairman of a water company set up with a $3 billion investment by Enron and whose board was made up of Enron directors. After it went public, Enron bought back the shares at more than double the market price. Furthermore, he was also a director of another company that did over $370,000 in business with Enron in 2000.

Of course, not many executives try to push the limits as far as the CEOs of RJR Nabisco, Lone Star, Tambrands or Enron. And not many boards allow themselves to be kept in the dark for so long. However, it is inevitable that executives will be more fully informed than the board, so there is inevitably an obvious problem deciding what information should be shared. See, for instance, the Polaroid case study. In that case, the board was unaware that employee groups opposed swapping various compensation benefits for an enlarged employee stock ownership plan (ESOP). Though a court ultimately determined that this information was immaterial, the example shows the kind of conflicts of interest present in management–board relationships. See also the Occidental Petroleum, WorldCom, and Adelphia case studies.

## The year of the corporate scandal

Behind each of the corporate scandals of 2002 was a board that complained that it had not been told what was going on. The outside directors of Adelphia and Tyco said that they had no idea that the executives were using corporate funds for personal expenses. The outside directors of Enron said they did not know that the Special Purpose Entities created to hide losses were based on fraudulent information.

*If directors have a duty of care and a duty of loyalty, how do they meet the duty of care in making sure that they get the information they need? When, if ever, is an "I didn't know" defense sufficient for a director?*

Who has the ultimate responsibility for the corporation? Who is genuinely responsible for a company? And who should have control – management or the board? Legally, the answer is clear; in the final analysis the board has the responsibility for the company and, is, therefore, the ultimate fountain of power. It is in practice, not in law, that the problems arise. Management has the expertise, infrastructure, and time to run and control the company. Given this degree of management domination, how can a board still exercise its responsibility? Can an entrepreneurial, energetic management run the company and at the same time reserve the ultimate control for the board? How do the board and management determine who should wear the "crown"? We believe the board carries more than *de jure* responsibility for the corporation. The paradox is how to allow both bodies to retain effective control without diminishing the initiative and motivation of either. The paradox creates tensions that are vexing for many corporations, causing friction at the top and considerable loss of energy . . . The complexity of the responsibility for corporate governance requires that management and the board find a comfortable, dynamic, balance of power between them. There will always be tension, but the tension that exists is not altogether bad. Like stress, a certain amount enhances creativity and productivity.[20]

# Director Information Checklist

What information should the board have? One veteran board member produced the following list.[21]

- Operating statements, balance sheets, and statements of cashflow that compare current period and year to date results to plan and last year. Management comments about the foregoing that explain the reasons for variations from plan and provide a revised forecast of results for the remainder of the year.
- Share of market information.
- Minutes of management committee meetings.
- Key media articles on the company and competition.
- Financial analysts' reports for the company and major competitors. Consumer preference surveys.
- Employee attitude surveys.

Robert K. Mueller, former outside chairman of A.D. Little and a veteran director, summed it up in his ninth book on boards of directors: "Ignorance is no excuse."[22]

There are ways to ensure that directors are well informed. Home Depot Inc., for instance, requires its directors to spend at least one full day a month at one of its stores, and to visit eight to ten stores a quarter, both in and out of the areas in which they live. Bernard Marcus, CEO of Home Depot, described the process:

They go in as a customer first, then they announce themselves and make themselves available to the employees of the company . . . It's a very, very good way for the board members to get a different feel for what's happening in the company. Typically, on a board, everything is filtered through the Chairman; everything you want the directors to know comes from him. Here we tell our board members to get out in the field. When they do this, they come back with recommendations. It's been very valuable for both sides – from our side as operators and for the board members for their knowledge of the company.[23]

## THE CEO/CHAIRMAN

According to data collected from the Corporate Library, 519 out of the largest 1,900 publicly traded companies have a separate CEO and chairman.[24] But even that tiny fraction is deceptive, because many of those chairmen are not truly independent; they are former CEOs, founders, former CEOs of acquired companies, or otherwise connected to the company beyond their service on the board. Only three out of the 202 UK companies in the database have the same person as chairman and CEO.[25] (Note, however, that UK boards have a higher percentage of inside directors as well.)

*What are the advantages and disadvantages of separating these two positions? Who is in the best position to determine whether it is worthwhile for a particular board? Does that person or group of people have the authority to impose that structure?*

These questions serve as a good way to look at the overall conflict between giving corporate management enough authority to do the job while maintaining sufficient accountability to make sure that the job is done for the benefit of shareholders.

We discussed earlier how the very existence of the board is based on the need for accountability. The board exists to keep management accountable for the vast discretionary power it wields. Thus, when the chairman of the board is also the CEO, it makes management accountable to a body led by management. It can mean that the CEO is put in the position of evaluating his own performance. For the same reason that we do not allow students to grade their own exams, that presents conflicts of interests in the corporate context as well.

According to Harold Geneen, former CEO and chairman of ITT Corp.,

If the board of directors is really there to represent the interests of the stockholders, what is the chief executive doing on the board? Doesn't he have a conflict of interest? He's the professional manager. He cannot represent the shareholders and impartially sit in judgment of himself.[26]

In its 1992 survey of company directors, Korn/Ferry found that just under 20 percent believed that separating the CEO and chairman positions would have a "very negative impact" on boardroom performance. A little more than 20 percent thought it would have a "very positive impact" and not quite 60 percent thought the impact of separating the roles would be neutral.[27] Those who thought separating the roles would have a negative impact thought it important that a company be led by one person. "You've got to have one boss," said one respondent to the Korn/Ferry survey. "Don't second guess him." Another said, "The CEO and the chairman need to be intimately involved in the business, so I believe they should be the same person. If they are not, the chairman would be a figurehead or would usurp the role of the CEO."

Those who were in favor of separating the roles believed it would lead to more objective evaluation of the CEO, and create an environment of greater accountability. One outside director commented that when the CEO is also the chairman there is "too great a temptation to 'tilt' things toward protecting CEO career interests."

The majority who believed that splitting the jobs was an unimportant issue typically commented that the chairman was simply the one who chaired the meetings, and that this was merely an argument about titles. While there has not been much empirical work done on this issue, at least one study found that companies with separate CEOs and chairmen consistently outperform those companies that combine the roles.[28] That may be, but resistance is predictably high. Combining the two positions does not mean that a CEO who is also chairman will inevitably manipulate his board, but it does give him that opportunity. Look at the American Express case study. It shows that board chairmanship can mean much more than parliamentary procedure. In the hands of a skilled power broker, the CEO/chairman can shift the locus of power to management and away from the board. Hugh Parker comments, in his book *The Company Chairman*,

> In the final analysis a board of directors can only be as effective as its chairman wants it to be. It is the chairman who, over time, is the main architect of the board – i.e. of its composition, agendas, priorities and procedures. The chairman chooses the directors he wants and uses them (or not) as he wishes. A chairman who wants a strong, independent and effective board will in time have such a board. But the reverse is equally true: a chairman who wants a passive and uninvolved board to rubber-stamp his own decisions can in time also achieve such a board.[29]

The single biggest issue that arises from combining the two roles is the issue of the agenda. As long as the CEO controls the quality, quantity, and timing of the information that is presented to the directors, they can never be assured of getting what they need for true independent oversight. Those boards who combine the two positions most successfully often find that it makes sense to have an independent outside director act as "lead director," an informal vice-chair, to review the agenda and make sure that it reflects the concerns of the rest of the outside directors. The 1999 Korn/Ferry board of directors study shows an increase in this area, with 30 percent of boards reporting that they have a lead director, up from 14 percent the year before. Of the directors surveyed, 53 percent thought it was a good idea. The National Association of Corporate Directors also recommends that boards that combine the two roles perform separate performance evaluations, as a way of keeping the goals and assessments clear and clearly communicated.

The corporate scandals of 2002 inspired a new look at this issue. While it was not unusual to hear the shareholder side call for splitting the two jobs, it was a surprise to hear that idea gain so much support on the business side. In January of 2003, a report was released by the Conference Board, the most highly regarded private think tank on business issues, called *The Conference Board Commission on Public Trust and Private Enterprise Findings and Recommendations*, part 2: *Corporate Governance* and part 3: *Audit and Accounting*.

A prestigious group that included Intel CEO Andrew Grove, CSX CEO (later Treasury Secretary) John Snow, TIAA–CREF CEO John Biggs, former SEC chairman Arthur Levitt, former Senator Warren Rudman, and former Secretary of Commerce Peter Peterson wrote the report. They had a thoughtful discussion on the potential conflicts that could arise from having the CEO serve as chairman of the board and concluded that boards had three options for addressing the issue. First, they could split the two functions, with an independent outside director serving as the chairman. Or, second, they could have a lead director or, third, a presiding director. A lead director serves as the liaison for the outside directors and conducts the executive session meetings. A presiding director is a lead director with some responsibilities for conducting meetings. Both would be expected to work with the chairman to "finalize information flow, meeting agendas, and meeting schedules." The group recommends that companies electing none of these options explain their reasoning to the shareholders.

## CATCH 22: THE ex-CEO AS DIRECTOR

In 1991, Institutional Shareholder Services (ISS), a consulting firm that advises institutional investors on corporate governance issues, found that 27 percent of S&P 500 companies had a former CEO as a board member.[30] Six companies even had two former CEOs on the board.

*Why might you object to an outgoing CEO remaining on the board?*

They could dominate the board agenda and decisions . . . many, if not all, inside directors may owe their jobs to the retiring CEO, and would be reluctant to contradict his views out of a sense of loyalty and/or fear: CEOs often continue to exercise enormous power even after their retirement. The same combination of fear and loyalty can appear to influence the non-executive directors recruited by the retiring CEO.[31]

But one current Fortune 500 CEO and chairman told ISS that most retired CEOs recognize the problem posed by their continuing presence and, to give the new CEO a chance to assert his own leadership, they stay silent on major policy questions.

*What do you think of this response? Is it enough? If they stay silent, are they doing their job? If they do not stay silent, do they risk improper interference? What kind of chilling effect might their presence have on boardroom discussions?*

The author of the ISS report, Howard D. Sherman, concluded, "In short, it is a Catch 22 for a retired CEO. Retired CEOs who care about their successor may not be effective directors. Retired CEOs who want to dominate the board should not be in the board at all."

But the ex-CEO has vast experience, and probably has more knowledge of the company than anyone else. How can shareholders make the best use of that knowledge? ISS recommended that the company should keep the CEO off the board, but keep him on as a consultant.

*What disadvantages does this pose? Look at the news reports surrounding CEO departures to determine how many are kept on as "consultants" and see if you can tell how often this is a bribe to get them to leave.*

Examples that appear to fit this category include Paul Lego at Westinghouse. Lego was forced by the board to resign as CEO and chairman of Westinghouse in January 1993. Despite the fact that Lego was, to all intents and purposes, fired, he received a two-year consulting contract at $600,000 a year (marginally less than the $700,000 salary he received as CEO). This was in addition to a severance payment of $800,000 and a lifetime annual pension of $910,000. If Lego's services were still useful to the company, why was he removed from his CEO post? And if he was fired for poor performance, why were the shareholders paying for his consulting services? The same analysis applies to the departures of Dean Buntrock from Waste Management (see case study) and Robert Annunziata at Global Crossing.

Interestingly, some CEOs told ISS that too much emphasis was put on keeping the ex-CEO around. Sir Adrian Cadbury, the esteemed former chairman of Cadbury Schweppes plc, said, "I personally favor CEOs making a clean break with their companies on retirement. I would like to see this become the accepted practice with the possibility of a consultancy as an exception . . . I am skeptical of the real value to a company of past experience, however vast."

Walter Wriston, ex-CEO of Citicorp and member of numerous boards as an outside director, made much the same point as Cadbury:

> One reason for mandatory retirement is to assure the corporation of fresh leadership to meet changing conditions. If the new leadership wants to consult the old, no corporate structure is necessary; if consultation is not desired no corporate arrangement will assure it. On the other hand, if the new CEO wants to get moving with his or her agenda, a board seat occupied by the retired CEO may be seen as an impediment to getting on with the job, particularly if new management feels that radical measures are called for.

One CEO who asked that he and his company remain anonymous said his company gave its outgoing chiefs an informal role:

> We strongly feel that "one should not look over the shoulder of a successor," for it could inhibit and restrict his freedom of action. We have always been fortunate that the retiring and incoming CEOs have had close and supportive relationships and that they could hold informal conversations on significant issues. Thus the new CEO could have the benefit of the counsel of the departed CEO if he sought it. The important consideration here is that the initiative in seeking such counsel must come from the new CEO. The retired CEO does not call or visit the incumbent CEO to offer advice unless it is requested.

The 1999 Korn/Ferry annual board of directors study reported that 54 percent of directors believe that the ex-CEO should not be on the board, but only 29 percent of companies have such a policy in place.

## CEO SUCCESSION

The biggest challenge for a board is often CEO succession planning, because it is there that the CEO/chairman's control of the agenda, information, and access to senior staff can provide an impenetrable barrier to independent oversight. In a 1988 book called *The Hero's Farewell*, Yale's Jeffrey Sonnenfeld brilliantly documents the various strategies CEOs have for conducting – and often undermining – the CEO succession planning process. He categorizes them as: Monarchs, who choose not to leave voluntarily but either die in office or are overthrown; Generals, who leave reluctantly and spend their retirement planning a comeback; Ambassadors, who retain close ties with their former firms; and Governors, who willingly serve a limited term and leave to pursue new interests.

A 2002 book by Harvard's Rakesh Khurana exploded the popular 1990s myth of the superstar CEO who justifies his high pay by comparing himself to Michael Jordan (the basketball star, not the former CEO of Westinghouse) or Harrison Ford. Khurana's title says it all: *Searching for a Corporate Savior: The Irrational Quest for Charismatic CEOs*. Khurana studied the hiring and firing of CEOs at over 850 of America's largest companies and found that, while boards tend to hire (and pay superstar salaries to) charismatic CEOs, they do not usually get what they (and the shareholders) pay for. He documents the changes to CEO searches over the past 20 years, particularly the increased tendency to retain a search firm and go outside the company. He concludes that this is not evidence of a robust and efficient market for CEO talent but a result of "the rise of investor capitalism and changing cultural conceptions of the role of the CEO." Boards tend to look for "leadership" and "vision" when they should be looking for strategic, political, and managerial skills – the ability to execute.

Boards of directors must understand that CEO succession planning is their responsibility, not the CEO's, and that it is a perpetual responsibility that begins right after the party celebrating a new hire for the top position. Boards must make sure they always have a name ready in case their CEO is suddenly incapacitated, makes a huge mistake, or takes another job. They should always be familiar enough with the senior staff to get a perspective on the CEO's performance and a sense of who should be cultivated as a candidate for the CEO position. And they should always have a sense of when they will be starting up the full-scale search and how it will be conducted.

## DIRECTOR NOMINATION

The fact that we speak of directors as "representing" or being "elected" by shareholders when the shareholders play no role in their nomination is evidence of the challenge we face in trying to understand corporate governance. In 95 percent of large US companies, candidates are recommended to the board by a nominating committee.[32] In many cases, however, the nominating committee receives the names from the CEO. One CEO told the authors of this book, "My nominating committee is very independent. Sometimes they turn down the names I send them." But when challenged to think of a time that the committee came up with its own names, he could not recall a single one. Once the nominating committee has decided on a candidate, it brings the name to the full board for its approval. Director candidates are usually interviewed by the full board (including the CEO), and then "elected" (actually ratified, since they almost always run unopposed) by a shareholder vote. In theory, this structure permits the board to evaluate director nominees independently, and to protect against management packing the board with its own allies. But Korn/Ferry found in 1991 that 82 percent of board vacancies were filled via recommendations from the chairman.

"Nominating committees all too often are a sham, pure and simple," said Dale Hanson, then CEO of the California Public Employees' Retirement System, before a House of Representatives Subcommittee.[33] In England, a 1992 ProNed survey found that 86 percent of directors were "dissatisfied with the amateur approach adopted by companies of appointing non-executive directors." Things are improving. In 1997, Korn/Ferry found that 42 percent of outside directors thought that the CEO did not play the dominant role in selecting new directors, and over 40 percent agreed that the nominating committee was taking over more of the responsibility. Many nominating committees are now turning to search firms to improve the independence and reach of the director nominating process.

# Case in point:
# A director's departure

A food service company made an ill-advised acquisition attempt for a restaurant group. The acquisition ended up costing the company over $680,000 – a large sum for a small-capitalization firm. One of the directors worried that the aborted acquisition might leave the company's directors liable for damages in a shareholder lawsuit charging that the directors had not acted with sufficient care or loyalty. He was particularly concerned because the CEO had canceled all board meetings for several months while he negotiated the ultimately unsuccessful deal.

After the CEO refused to schedule a board meeting, the director suggested to some of his fellow outside directors that they meet, separately from the insiders, to discuss their potential liability. For instance, he thought they should consider whether it might be wise for them to hire independent counsel.

None of the other outsiders accepted his invitation. Rather, they informed the CEO (who also served as chairman) of his suggestion. The director received a letter from the company's outside counsel accusing him of attempting to set up "clandestine" meetings. At the next full meeting of the board, the first held in over five months, the director was informed that he would not be re-nominated as a director at the company's next annual meeting. In other words, he was fired.

The director sent a letter to the CEO/chairman, requesting that his "resignation" be fully explained in the company proxy statement. He wrote:

> I believe that the number of board of directors' meetings has not been sufficient to keep the board members as informed as I feel they should be about the activities of the company . . .
>
> I am opposed to your having increased the compensation of officers of the Company without having come to the board, first. Not only was it contrary to the By Laws, but reflects our differences in philosophy as regards your view of the Board's functions . . .
>
> I thought the fact that my name was not set forth to be nominated as a director and to be voted upon at the next annual meeting because of "philosophical differences" with you was not in the company's or its shareholders' best interest. Although I may have views that are contrary to yours, even you have, in the past, indicated that it was good for the Company. This action (albeit with the concurrence of the rest of the Board) once again reflects your desire to have control over the Board . . .
>
> I feel that an independent compensation committee should be appointed and that it set up performance standards, evaluate achievements and judge corporate results.
>
> I would recommend that the positions of Board Chairman and Chief Executive Officer be separated, as you presently have too much control.

The company did not take his advice, and he no longer serves on that board.

*What is the basis on which a director should not be re-nominated? What information should the shareholders have in the event of such a decision? What do you think of the director's actions in this case? What, if anything, would you have done differently? What do you think of the result? What, if anything, would improve it?*

# Case in point: A director demands more from the board

A director at another company wrote this letter to a CEO who had been in place for about two years:

I have been thinking about the issues facing [our company], and I have become convinced that we have to come to grips with the mission and performance of the board. Everyone will agree that the board is responsible for strategic direction and management succession. But in my view, there is no single model of optimal board/management interrelationship. What this means, then, is that the board must constantly re-evaluate itself to make sure that it has the best possible structure for the company's present needs. The best results will obtain from recognition that change is always needed, that directors and management need to be committed to an ongoing process of self-examination and criticism, and that the balance will constantly be in flux. Until we have adopted an explicit "mission" for the board, we cannot adequately monitor our performance fairly, and if we cannot monitor ourselves, we cannot monitor the performance of the company or of you as CEO.

You inherited a board that was used to reacting to what was presented to us, and not used to asking for more. As a matter of personality and style, John [the former CEO] had little use for a board. For a long time the board acquiesced, as John produced superior results. During this period, the board was essentially limited to a consultative and oversight role (I refer to this later as a "watchdog" board). I believe that during at least part of this period, you served for him the role that a board often serves, providing feedback, support, and analysis.

The board has changed little, but the company you inherited is a very different one from the [company] of John's heyday. And you do not have a number two officer playing the same role for you as you played for John. In other words, the players are different, the challenges are different, and it is time for the board to be different, too. To go back to the two primary responsibilities of the board.

*Strategic direction* We have already established a goal: $5 of earnings per share within five (now three and a half) years; and $10/share within ten years. With our core business in worldwide recession, simply maintaining our position – approximately $100 million per year in cash flow – is a substantial accomplishment.

It should not, however, permit us to lose sight of our longer-term objectives. Do we have an industrial strategy as to how we are going to achieve these earnings targets? Is it going to be from internal growth? Or by acquisition? In what industrial sectors?

Do we have a financial strategy? If we are going to achieve our growth targets we will need substantial additional capital. My own sense is that the "cost" of equity capital is low. Our year-end closing price of 51 5/8 indicates a price/earnings multiple of 31. Have we decided to wait for a time when we can demonstrate an actual need for new capital or will we be opportunistic and go to the market place when capital is available on an historically attractive basis? These are the questions that the board should be considering right now. If we do not, I fear that we may be allowing a uniquely attractive time for raising additional capital to pass without adequate consideration.

*CEO selection, evaluation, succession* You have urged the board to evaluate your performance annually, and it is encouraging that we actually started this process in 1993. I find this to be a very constructive process.

But I am concerned about the issue of succession. When John was CEO, we knew we could turn to you. But I do not think any of the directors have a clear idea as to whom we would turn in the event that you were no longer able to serve. We need to make sure that you have a back-up. Any company is only as strong as its officer cadre. At present we are very "thin on the ground." The board must turn to this issue promptly.

These are the two most important responsibilities of a board of directors. It seems clear to me that our board needs to do more with regard to both. The fact that we have not done well enough in either of these areas demonstrates the importance of devoting time to examining ourselves to determine how we can improve our structure and composition to ensure that we function more effectively in the future.

It is very difficult – but absolutely essential – for our board to redefine itself to address our changing needs. This company needs a strong board.

Somebody needs to get this process started. I think it makes the most sense for you to take the initiative, to make sure that we develop a structure that accords with your sense of the company's needs today.

I found it useful to think of the possible roles of a board by keeping two matrices in mind. The first is a vertical matrix that illustrates a range of involvement – from a primarily reactive "watchdog" role on one end to a role as a fully participating partner with management to active participation, as boards often play in crisis situations like the board of General Motors a year ago or the board of Paramount right now. Second is a horizontal matrix that is a spectrum of modes of activity – ranging from exclusive focus on the strategic and succession issues that are always the core of the board's responsibility to setting policy, substantively analyzing tactical options, implementation, monitoring, and evaluation.

As far as I am concerned, a board could perfectly properly decide to locate itself anywhere on the graph emanating from these matrices. At the risk of redundancy, there is no "right" answer, but there is a "wrong" one. What is wrong is to have no defined role, no mission, no explicit benchmarks against which performance of the board can be evaluated. That is what I worry about here. In particular, I worry about the time we spend reviewing operating results instead of looking at the larger picture. None of us on the board have the time, the expertise, or the wish to become deeply enough involved in the day-to-day affairs of the company to evaluate these results in any meaningful way; even if that was an appropriate role for the board to play, this is not the group of people to play it.

In order to make sure that the board addresses the right issues, based on the right information, I think it might make sense for us to appoint an outside director as part-time chairman of the board. If that does not seem right to you, perhaps we could follow the advice of Marty Lipton and Jay Lorsch and appoint a "lead director" to help focus the outside directors on the agenda and other governance concerns. We should also have regular meetings of the outside directors in executive session at least twice a year. This is in no way a reflection on you and in no way intended to go behind your back. It is just the best way to make sure that the directors can talk to each other about what kinds of questions they want to ask. This is often mentioned by critics of boards as a key element in improving their performance.

Our board has really not "jelled." I think that is because we have not agreed on an explicit set of goals. Certainly, it is not lack of personal financial investment or personal commitment. What I am looking for is a shared sense of commitment, a sense that $5 per share within five years is more than just a slogan; that it represents a commitment by all of us to an extremely challenging and rewarding task: that we are each deeply personally committed to its achievement; that we discuss alternatives; that we see ourselves as successful or failures in terms of achieving the objective. I think having regular meetings of the outside directors would help a great deal.

In the absence of having a strong back-up within the company, it seems to me that you can make very good use of increased board involvement. I would like the board to be more of a resource for you than the rubber stamp with a micro perspective I feel that we have been. I am asking you to allow us to give you all that we can.

*How effective is this letter likely to be? What are the director's alternatives, if the CEO does not accept his recommendations? Once the structure has been created, what is the agenda? To find out more about this memo read the Tyco case study.*

Empowered shareholders should focus on the board of directors – its composition and its agenda. The job of effectively involved shareholders can be simply described as ensuring that the board of directors does its job. This means making sure that the right people are on the board, that they are focusing on the right issues, and that they operate under a structure that enables them to ask the right questions and reach the right answers. This is the answer to the agency costs issues, the most effective way for the ownership to exercise the appropriate level of control.

# Case in point:
# Two directors depart at Emap

Boards of directors, like cabinet governments, operate on the basis of collective responsibility. If an individual director disagrees with the majority decision of the board, he should of course express his views and seek to convince his colleagues by force of argument. But, in the end, majority opinion must prevail.

But what happens if collective responsibility breaks down? What if a significant minority of directors, say two or three, strongly disagrees with a decision? What if they believe the chairman has an overbearing influence on the rest of the board? And what if they believe that the decision is so fundamental to the well-being of the company that they cannot be bound by the overall decision?

The only choice, of course, is to resign. But does this benefit the shareholders? And, to the extent that the chairman is likely to replace the resigning directors with his own (more amenable) candidates, resignation merely reinforces the power at the head of the company.

These were some of the questions faced by shareholders of Emap, a rapidly growing UK broadcasting, magazines and communications company. Emap shareholders, reading their 1996 annual report, were asked to approve a series of amendments to the company's articles of incorporation. (Articles of incorporation are the UK equivalent of a company's bylaws.)

Two amendments were controversial. The first, if approved, deleted a provision in the articles that mandated a minimum number of non-executive directors. The second gave the board power to vote fellow directors off the board, given a 75 percent majority.

Emap shareholders were surprised to read in the annual report that these proposals were opposed by two outside directors – Professor Ken Simmonds and Joe Cooke. Collective responsibility had broken down.

The company argued that the amendments were "housekeeping" measures. The minimum outside director rule, it argued, didn't offer the flexibility that such a fast-growing company as Emap required. And, it was argued, several large UK companies had provisions for the board to rid itself of a troublesome minority. (Although, as research by UK governance watchdog PIRC showed, most companies had no such provision.)

The dissidents, in return, argued that the provisions were an important safeguard at a time of succession uncertainty and management tensions. The company's chief executive, Robin Miller, and his deputy, David Arculus, the group managing director, were known to have been at loggerheads for years. A boardroom memo of five years previously had identified difficulties between the pair.

According to press reports, the company chairman Sir John Hoskyns sought to designate Miller as his provisional successor as chairman, while forcing Arculus into early retirement. Emap denied that any such succession plan was made.

The dissidents argued that it was a mistake to weaken the company's provisions for a strong and independent non-executive presence at a time when just such a presence was needed to oversee fractious management.

As became clear, Messrs Simmonds and Cooke suspected Sir John Hoskyns, of trying to "roll" the board, and ensure that his preferred succession plan was carried out.

But, for the meantime, the debate took place in an amicable fashion. At the annual shareholders' meeting which followed three weeks later, the company chairman, Sir John Hoskyns, assured shareholders that the new articles were "a last resort and will not be used to restructure the board." He said, "there are no difficulties on the board."

In return, the dissidents were given the opportunity to put their side of the case. Professor Simmonds said he was opposed to the changes in principle, and he criticized the way that the board had put the proposal together, claiming that a "committee of two – namely the Chief Executive and Chairman" had met to decide on the new articles and that they were presented to a board meeting without sufficient notice or time to debate the full implications.

He asked the chairman to address the simple question "how is it in shareholders' interests to reduce the number of non-executives on the board and why should they relinquish the right to remove directors?" He argued that the current rules protect shareholders and removing them was akin to "removing the bolt from the door on the argument that we have never had a burglary and some others in the neighbourhood don't have bolts on their doors either."

Eighteen percent of shareholders voted against the changes, a significant signal of concern. But good governance seemed to have been observed: the non-executive directors had had their say, the issue had been debated openly by shareholders, the vote was cast.

Of course, the battle was far from over.

Having voiced their dissent, Messrs Simmonds and Cooke were now *personae non gratae* on the board. Some of their colleagues took great exception to the way the pair had washed the board's dirty linen in public.

The rump of the board felt that Simmonds and Cooke had given shareholders a false impression at the AGM, incorrectly suggesting that the chairman had behaved unethically and misled shareholders, and that the rest of the board had ignored their duties. More than one director demanded the dissidents' removal.

At the company's next board meeting, Simmonds and Cooke met in a separate room to the rest of the board, while David Arculus shuttled between the two groups trying to broker a deal. The two dissidents offered to resign, if Sir John Hoskyns and Robin Miller resigned likewise. Professor Simmonds told one newspaper: "The dispute stems from the chairman's behaviour. I cannot stand down unless I am first assured he would be standing down as well – without that I would not be discharging my responsibility to shareholders."

Ultimately, no deal could be reached. But Sir John had given assurances to shareholders at the annual meeting that the powers to remove directors enshrined in the freshly amended articles would not be used to oust Simmonds and Cooke.

Ironically, the board couldn't use its new powers to dismiss the two directors who had opposed the introduction of those powers. Instead, the company called an Extraordinary General Meeting – a non-routine meeting of all shareholders, usually called to consider a single issue. In this instance, that issue was the removal of Simmonds and Cooke from the board. In the end, therefore, the question of the pair's continued board service would be put to the people they represented – the shareholders.

The UK governance consultancy, PIRC, advised shareholders to oppose the measures. The US-based proxy advisors, Institutional Shareholder Services, did likewise.

At the EGM the company secured the support of nearly 90 percent of shareholders for the directors' removal, although several large institutions were said to have given support on certain conditions – that the non-executive directors be replaced and that the list of possible successors to the chairmanship not be limited to the current chief executive.

The EGM, however, provided a platform for the two dissidents to make a defense of good governance. Professor Simmonds explained to the meeting why he had not retired quietly when it was clear he no longer had the support of his colleagues: "All we could have delivered to shareholders by quiet retirement was complete capitulation."

He said that he had acted to protect Emap's future value, telling shareholders "You need to make sure that the board . . . does not fall under the effective control of any one person, and that internal self-policing is adequately provided for . . . The articles on corporate governance which we were keen to protect had been included specifically because of problems this company had experienced in the past when managing changes in board composition and responsibilities."

Professor Simmonds said that boards should actively encourage argument and minority views from non-executive directors, but that "to remove a minority for trying to ensure shareholders are fully informed is dangerous . . . It should not be viewed as a crime to inform shareholders properly. Non-executive directors have an overriding responsibility to speak out to shareholders when it is in the shareholders' and the company interest."

He concluded by offering a number of suggestions for protecting Emap's future value:

- Confront the succession issue speedily.
- Limit the board's power to remove directors to a 100 percent vote.
- Reinstate the article to have at least five non-executive directors.
- Expect full and clear reasons for all governance changes.
- Reject any private commitment to a sub-group of shareholders.

> • Welcome minority statements in good faith. They are not a crime.
> • Appoint some non-executive directors who are not also executives elsewhere.
>
> The *Financial Times*'s influential Lex column wrote that the vote was "a slap in the face to two courageous men" and that the EGM result sent "an unfortunate message to other companies tempted to ride roughshod over non-executives."
> The Emap dispute highlights the tensions inherent in a unitary board structure in which non-executives have a monitoring function. To keep that tension creative rather than destructive is the challenge for all sides.

*Is collegiality an essential boardroom virtue? More so than independence? How can the two virtues be reconciled?*

*What options does a non-executive have if he vehemently disagrees with the majority? What good does he do by resigning quietly? But does he harm the company by speaking out? (Bear in mind that by forcing Emap to call an EGM to remove them, the dissidents imposed considerable costs on the company, borne by shareholders.)*

*Should a director be sacked for opposing in good faith moves he or she considers not to be in shareholders' interests?*

*Would a company be hurt if a minority of non-executive directors spoke out publicly but amicably?*

*Do non-executive directors serve at shareholders' pleasure, or management's?*

*Is the Emap episode actually a good advertisement for corporate democracy? After all, the final decision was left to shareholders.*

*Political democracies have devised systems (such as the US Bill of Rights) to protect minority interests from the will of the majority. Can a board operate according to a similar constitution? If a company is indeed run by a tyrannous majority, is there any way of stopping it?*

It may be that there is no way that anyone invited on to a board by the CEO or even by the board itself can be considered "independent." This may be why, even though the idea of independence has a great deal of appeal, none of the empirical studies has ever documented a relationship between independence (as shown by an absence of disclosed financial relationships) and superior performance.

Although we use the term "election," in describing how directors join the board, it does not really apply. Management selects the candidates, they run unopposed, and management counts the votes. Shareholders cannot nominate directors without spending enormous amounts of money on a proxy contest, though this will change if SEC Chairman Donaldson's proposal to give shareholders the right to nominate director candidates using the company's proxy card becomes law. Having the right does not guarantee its use, however. The British investment institutions have so far not taken advantage of their ability to play a role in nominating directors, despite the strong recommendation of the Cadbury Report.

Increasingly, the board's nomination committee plays a more active role than the past rubber-stamping of management's candidates. But the critical appointment and any renewal depends on chairman/CEO agreement and is usually at their initiative, a process which falls far short of true independence. Non-executive directorships are generally prized, so how well can one hold one's benefactors to account? While current practice falls far short of original legal intention, its supporters claim that it avoids the potential disharmony of non-collegial boards. However, non-executives cannot fulfil their clear external accountability responsibilities if disagreement with CEOs or even a board majority is considered disloyal. In a rare case that became public, Sotheby's West Coast chief Andrea Van de Kamp wrote an explosive memo to her fellow Disney directors after she was told that she would not be re-nominated to the board. In it, she said that her ouster "gives the appearance that rubber-stamping [CEO] Michael [Eisner]'s decisions is an unwritten prerequisite for continued board membership." According to an article that appeared in *USA Today*, Van de Kamp accused Eisner of "threatening and bullying" her in the January 20 meeting at which he told her that she was out. She says he indicated that "he had a file" on her documenting how she had "demonstrated inappropriate behavior" on the board, and that he offered her a seat on the Disney Foundation board if she would make it seem that it was her idea to leave.

*What is needed for an "independent" director under pressure to act independently when required?*

Shareholder responsibility for board nominations is very clear in Britain. It is the obligation to ensure the services of an appropriate board of directors on a continuing basis, an obligation which is routinely delegated to chairmen/CEOs. But shareholders retain a powerful reserve power. The Companies Act permits the removal of directors by shareholders at a specially convened EGM. In America, while the theoretical obligation is the same, implementation is more difficult, particularly because of the chilling effect of disclosure requirements that are triggered by as few as 5 percent of the shareholders working together to influence management.

The end result in both countries is, then, that there is only ever one set of nominations for directors who are nearly always all but unanimously elected. Institutional investors usually give their consent in advance in the form of proxy votes, fairly described by Professor M.A. Eisenberg as "coerced ratification." The reality is thus of self-perpetuating boards without any ownership involvement. But chairmen/CEOs and their executive colleagues cannot fairly be blamed for a situation not of their making but due rather to legal restrictions in America and to apathy, acquiescence, and systemic fault in Britain. Hence the oft-repeated dictum that shareholders "appoint the directors" does not bear serious scrutiny.

Careful analysis of what boards do or can do in a crisis is needed. British boards, which have a non-executive chairman, with up to half the board comprising senior executives, are better informed than American boards, where typically the CEO is the only executive member. Non-executives typically devote 10–15 days a year to board duties (sometimes more in Britain), which may not match their growing responsibilities. Boards seem to work adequately only when the demands are predictable and slender.

Senator Carl Levin, as Chairman of the Permanent Subcommittee on Investigations, has recently provided perhaps the most authentic insight into the nature of US boards at a hearing with the five most senior directors of recently bankrupt Enron. These individuals are the flower of America's director culture; they had all served for seventeen years; they chaired the most important committees – executive, finance, compensation and audit; three had earned doctorates; all were paid a minimum of $350,000 a year. They appeared voluntarily and at substantial personal inconvenience and legal hazard in order to articulate plainly and repeatedly that individually and collectively as members of a board they were not responsible *in any way* for the collapse of Enron or for the loss of investments, pensions and jobs.

Chairman Levin issued a formal report in which he concluded that blame lay at the door of the board. Peter Drucker, as quoted above, provides the context: "Whenever an institution malfunctions as consistently as boards of directors have in nearly every major fiasco of the last 40 or 50 years it is futile to blame men. It is the institution that malfunctions." (The same comment applies to investment institutions and fund managers. It is all part of the systemic fault referred to earlier.) Is the experience of the Enron directors confirming Peter Drucker's conclusion – you can count on the board except when it is really needed? If so, there are major policy implications.

With hindsight, some characteristics of the Enron outside directors raise concerns. The unusually high pay, an average of 17 years' service, and no board self-evaluation or independent nominating committee all suggest too little rigorous scrutiny of management. Without an independent chairman, the information and agenda can become a closed loop. The few public statements by the directors indicate that they felt they were widely misled, but had no direct personal responsibility. When management set up the "independent" off-balance-sheet entity under the direction of the CFO – who had a personal financial interest – to which corporate assets and debts were "sold," the outside directors agreed to the waiver of the corporation's conflict of interest rules. They accepted the CEO's assurance that no harm would result.

The Enron case provides unique insight. As we turn to the very different situation in the United Kingdom, one question obtrudes – what were the lessons from the Marconi hearings? The losses, albeit absent fraud, were just as egregious as with Enron. Or what do we learn from the fact that there were no Marconi hearings or Railtrack hearings? Or any interest by regulators? Is it explained by the absence of any fraud? Or is it just a reflection of a more conformist culture?

Alan Greenspan's simple remark in his March 2002 speech at the Stern School in New York City that American corporations are essentially characterized by "CEO dominance" not only shocked the conventional wisdom but it directly challenged the American insistence on – at least – a vocabulary of democratic institutions in describing corporate functioning. The whole subject of corporate governance needs similar frankness if a system that lives up to the essentially sound principles of accountable shareholder capitalism is to be created.

In Britain the effectiveness and accountability of corporate boards – due in part to splitting the roles of chairman and CEO – are considerably better than in America while still falling well short of what is desirable. The CEO, however, is still the dominant figure. Boardroom revolts are still very rare, and resignations of even a single director on a matter of principle almost as rare. Further, seldom is any public statement made – they just go quietly in the traditional British manner, despite the Hampel Committee's call for a frank and public explanation.

## DIRECTOR COMPENSATION

A director serving on the board of a major corporation will normally have a retainer of over $40,000. According to the 1999 Spencer Stuart report, the highest director fees are at Travelers Group ($100,000, all in stock), Monsanto and Sears ($90,000, partially in stock), and Alcoa ($85,000). Microsoft is among the lowest, with $8,000. Other popular perquisites include matching education/charitable gifts (43 percent), life insurance (11 percent), and travel expenses for the spouse to accompany the director to board meetings (16 percent). And there is more. Many companies make stock grants in addition to the retainers. Most companies also give directors huge discounts on whatever they produce – not much value if they make ball-bearings, but invaluable if it is an airline. Retail company directors get free merchandise or discounts. See the General Motors case study: at that company, directors received a new car every 90 days. Some companies, particularly those in turn-around situations, are beginning to pay their directors entirely in stock. Those companies include: Apple Computers, Rite Aid, Campbell's Soup, Travelers, ITT, Tribune, and Colgate-Palmolive.

Still, for a job that seldom demands more than two weeks a year the compensation is generous, especially for those who serve on several boards in addition to having full-time jobs. President Clinton's transition team chief Vernon Jordan earned $504,000 in fees from nine of the boards on which he served in 1992, and, if he'd retired from all his board positions in 1993, he would have received $160,000 annually in retirement fees. Directors often get business from the companies for their law, consulting, or investment banking firms as well.

These pay schemes rarely relate to the performance of the company – or, of course, to the performance of the director. A director will receive his retainer and fees, no matter what. His compensation will not rise in good years, or fall in bad. Such a scheme provides no incentive. The stock component in some director's compensation packages is rarely significant enough to make the company's performance an issue. Thus, not only do most directors not hold a significant portion of their worth in the company's stock, but traditionally their pay has not been designed to align their interests with those of shareholders.

There have been two major changes in director compensation over the past decade, both in response to shareholder concerns. First, more directors are paid in stock or stock options, to more closely align their interests with the interests of the shareholders. Second, director retirement plans, which more than doubled from 1986 to 1991, have all but disappeared. A 1995 National Association of Corporate Directors report recommended that boards set a target for substantial stock ownership by directors and pay directors solely in stock (or stock options) and cash, dismantling benefit programs, eliminate any side payments (consulting, legal fees) to directors, and make comprehensive disclosure of the process and content of director compensation. Companies are slowly moving in that direction.

It is important to make sure, though, that directors' stock is not a gift or a substitute for some other perquisite like a pension. Otherwise, stock awards would merely be a way of exchanging one marginal compensation supplement for another. Programs "to facilitate share acquisition" are not meaningful unless the value of the incentives is directly and explicitly set off against current compensation levels. As Graef Crystal writes:

> Giving the directors more stock is not a bad idea *per se*. But I strongly suspect that the critics who were pushing for more stock had in mind some form of capital contribution by the directors, perhaps cutting the cash compensation of the outside directors and then substituting shares of stock with an equivalent economic value. I even more strongly suspect that the critics didn't have in mind letting the outside directors continue to receive their usual cash compensation and then giving them free shares of stock and stock options on top of that.[34]

Unless carefully designed, stock-related compensation (in the form of stock options and/or outright grants) for directors could encourage measures that attempt to engineer a short-term increase in the stock price at the sacrifice of long-term viability for the company (for example, drastically reducing R&D). This can be addressed by the use of awards of restricted stock vesting 12 to 36 months after the director retires from the board. A growing trend is deferral or conversion of retainer and fees for an up to 50 percent discount of the current stock price; however, these programs should be designed so that they do not interfere with the board's ability to limit the terms of directors they do not want to keep on the board. But the most important goal here is for directors to have enough of their own financial future at risk to think like shareholders. Lawrence Tucker of Brown Brothers Harriman was a director on one board in which the other outside directors' average investment in the company was nearly $1 million apiece. He said: "Believe me, that is a board that pays attention . . . I've never seen the pocket calculators come out so quickly in my life."[35]

Director compensation is one of the most sensitive and complex tasks facing the board and the company, because, by definition, no member of the board can view the issue without conflicts. For that reason, many observers, including the National Association of Corporate Directors' blue-ribbon commissions on Executive Compensation and on Performance Evaluation of Chief Executive Officers, Boards, and Directors recommend that boards should impose procedural safeguards to ensure credibility, including enhanced disclosure, review, and greater reliance on stock-based pay. Options for implementing these safeguards include full disclosure of director compensation in the proxy statement, with supporting data justifying the approach, and submitting the director compensation plan to a review by an independent expert (not the company's or the board's compensation consultants) from time to time, publishing a summary of that review in the proxy statement. But even that will not be enough unless shareholders review director pay disclosures carefully, and respond by withholding votes for directors who approve poor pay plans, and submitting resolutions to make sure that director pay plans are designed to align the interests of directors with shareholders.

*How can these improvements be achieved? What initiatives can shareholders, managers, or directors themselves take to better align director pay with corporate performance? With director performance?*

## Interlocks

As mentioned earlier, the most popular type of director is a top executive of another company. Eighty-six percent of billion-dollar company boards included at least one CEO/COO of another company.[36] This means that managers of one company oversee the managers of another. Though this may create something of the appearance of a generalized conflict of interests, that potential conflict is probably outweighed by the knowledge of trends and transactions that high-level corporate officers can bring to a board. What is troublesome, however, is the more specific set of conflicts arising from the number of managers who sit on each other's boards.[37] In 1993, the *New York Times* even found five pairs of companies where executives sat on each other's compensation committees.[38] In the words of Justice Louis Brandeis, "The practice of interlocking directorships is the root of many evils."[39] See, for example, the American Express case study for its discussion of the company's board members. CEO James Robinson relied particularly on the support of Drew Lewis, CEO of Union Pacific. Robinson sits not just on the board of that company, but also on the compensation committee. The case study describes a host of other relationships that helped to undermine the independence of AmEx's outside directors. See also the Carter Hawley Hale case study, which shows how Philip Hawley relied on the Bank of America for support in arranging a voting scheme for employee stock in the face of a takeover. Hawley sat on the executive committee of the Bank of America's board, and chaired its compensation committee.

## *Time and money*

Directors' ability to oversee management is further undermined by the fact that many directors are unable to devote sufficient time or resources to the job. The following comment was made by two of America's most astute observers of corporate boardrooms, Martin Lipton of Wachtell, Lipton, Rosen & Katz in New York and Jay Lorsch, senior associate dean of the Harvard Business School:

> Based on our experience, the most widely shared problem directors have is a lack of time to carry out their duties. The typical board meets less than eight times annually. Even with committee meetings and informal gatherings before or after the formal board meeting, directors rarely spend as much as a working day together in and around each meeting. Further, in many boardrooms too much of this limited time is occupied with reports from management and various formalities. In essence, the limited time outside directors have together is not used in a meaningful exchange of ideas among themselves or with management/inside directors.[40]

Lipton and Lorsch go on to say that, for a director to do his job properly, he or she needs to devote at least 100 hours annually to the job. But because so many directors serve on more than one board, in addition to a full-time job, they are quite unable to contribute that much time.

As mentioned earlier, according to Korn/Ferry's 1992 survey of Fortune 1000 directors, more than 20 percent of respondents served on four or more boards as an outside director. Consider a busy executive who has an important and demanding full-time job and who also sits on four boards. It is inconceivable that he will be able to devote 400 hours (or nearly seven 60-hour weeks) to his outside boards. In reality, that executive would devote far less than 100 hours to each of his outside boards, which is simply not enough time to do the job that, in theory, he is expected to do.

Though rare, there are "super-directors" who claim to be able to serve on numerous boards. One respondent to the Korn/Ferry 1992 survey served on 11 boards.[41] Former Secretary of Defense Frank Carlucci served on no less than 20 for-profit company boards, and on a dozen non-profits. This is in addition to a full-time job as chairman of the Carlyle Group. According to the *Washington Post*, Carlucci had a board meeting for one of his outside interests every single working day in 1992, including one that he attended by phone from his doctor's waiting-room.[42] It is our opinion that no one, however talented, can hope to sit on the boards of that many companies and effectively monitor the management of each.

As well as being unable to commit in terms of time, many directors are unable or unwilling to commit money. If directors are to be the representatives of shareholders then it is not too much to demand that they be shareholders. Yet all too often outside directors hold, at best, only small proportions of their net worth, and merely token holdings at worst. For example, at the 1993 Westinghouse annual meeting, Robert A.G. Monks (one of the authors of this book) was able to announce that his firm's $3 million holding represented more stock held by the entire board of directors put together, and nearly three times more than all the outside directors (including Frank Carlucci) put together. Carlucci had invested a total of $8,000 for each year he had served on the board. According to the director database at the Corporate Library's website, at least 850 directors had no stock at all in the companies on whose boards they serve.[43]

*Is this a sufficient contribution — of time or money — for a director to make? Who is in the best position to determine what a sufficient contribution is, and how can that determination be made effective?*

In cases like these, despite concerns about reputation and personal pride, directors may not have enough incentive to be aggressive in evaluating and overseeing management. One survey suggested that directors do not see a problem with an absence of stock holding. A 1989 polling of Fortune 1000 directors found that 69 percent of respondents agreed that "directors are likely to have the same commitment to representing shareholders' interests regardless of their equity holdings."[44]

## THE DIRECTOR'S ROLE IN CRISIS

Boards of directors receive attention only when faced with a crisis, such as disastrous performance or a hostile bid. Too often, it has seemed that they *only* pay attention when there is a crisis. There seems to be little concern with what a director is supposed to do, if anything, to *prevent* a corporate crisis. This seems to be one problem that directors' concern with their own reputation does not address; a survey of directors in 1989 showed that they themselves regarded the boards of IBM and General Motors as the most prestigious on which to serve.[45] It is no coincidence that both companies suffered precipitous decline with no apparent reaction by the board.

More recently, there has been some change as the General Motor's board's decision to replace the CEO was seen as something of a challenge and a grant of authority to other boards. As we described in chapter 2, the period from September 1992 through December 1993 appeared to be an open season on chief executives. The CEOs of General Motors, Westinghouse, American Express, IBM, Eastman Kodak, Scott Paper, and Borden were all pressured to resign in the face of their companies' long-term under-performance. These moves were heralded in the media as a breakthrough in boardroom activism.[46] Yet in all these instances the board took the necessary drastic action years too late. At IBM, John Akers resigned only after the company's market value had halved in six months, on the back of a $5 billion loss in 1992. At American Express, James Robinson was allowed to pursue a course of reckless financial expansion for 17 years. More recently, boards allowed the CEOs of Mattel, Waste Management, Occidental Petroleum, and Quaker Oats to stay on despite persistent poor results.

*Why does it take boards so long to respond to deep-seated competitive problems? And, if one of the leading responsibilities of directors is to evaluate the performance of the CEO, why do boards wait too long for proof of managerial incompetence before making a move?*

Judge William T. Allen, chancellor of the Delaware court, and leading expert on the judicial implications of corporate governance, described the "fire alarm" problem in a 1991 speech: "The view of the responsibilities of membership of the board of directors of public companies is, in my opinion badly deficient. It ignores a most basic responsibility: the duty to monitor the performance of senior management in an informed way. Outside directors should function as active monitors of corporate management, not just in crisis, but continually."

One of the most important reasons that boards have failed to fulfill their role as monitors is also the most intangible — the culture of the boardroom. By "culture" we refer to the psychology of belonging to a board – the collegiate atmosphere that prevents any one member speaking out against the prevailing view. It is the existence of this culture that leads to boards being accused of being "old boys' clubs."

The problem is that it is difficult to speak out against management when the CEO controls the board's agenda, information, compensation, and composition. In the "director's departure" case in point in this chapter, assume that some of the other outside directors were concerned about the CEO's decision to pursue the unsuccessful acquisition and cancel the board meetings. Once they saw their colleague removed from the board for raising these issues, they understood that they could not challenge the CEO on these or other matters without risking dismissal from the board. This works both ways – the board picks the new CEO when the time comes, and it therefore may be reluctant to find him incapable of performing.

A 1989 survey in the United Kingdom found that one-third of directors agreed that "don't rock the boat" was the unspoken credo of most boardrooms. The same survey reported that virtually all boardroom votes are unanimous; dissent, and a spirit of "we must agree to disagree", are strongly discouraged in today's boardrooms. As one CEO said, "I often say my directors can come in and vote one of two ways – either 'yes' or 'I resign.' "[47] The problem has been well summarized by New York lawyer Ira Millstein and former lawyer Winthrop Knowlton:

[Directors] appear, in theory, to have immense power and flexibility. They can help shape their corporations' missions in a great variety of ways, provided only that they create plausible evidence that they have taken their primary obligation to shareholders adequately into account. They can (and do) stimulate CEOs to formulate long-range plans. They can dismiss the CEO if they do not like these plans or the way he carries them out. They can urge management on to higher standards of performance through an arsenal of sophisticated incentives: salary increases, bonuses, options and a variety of grants. And yet, the gut feeling in their stomach is that their role is an exceedingly limited one. They feel they do not have time enough to know the company's products well and to know, especially, how truly competitive these products are. They do not have time enough to tour company plants, talk to middle managers, hear alternative points of view. While they can, in theory, criticize CEOs, punish them, and even remove them, there is immense reluctance to do so. This is an individual they themselves have selected. This is an individual who has far more information at his fingertips than they do, who is (surprising as it may seem to many corporate critics) usually devoting every waking hour to the firm's affairs, and who is in need of every bit of support the board can give. A number of outside directors who have managed or may still be managing companies of their own are particularly sensitive to this.[48]

Millstein and Knowlton comment further:

Whether [the board's] activities here take on an active or a passive coloration, whether boards respond only to crisis or to specific kinds of issues and the rest of the time restrict their activities to formal, even ritualistic review, depends in large measure on the kinds of people the directors are, the personality and operating style of the CEO, past board practice, and the challenges that the particular corporation faces.[49]

See the American Express, Carter Hawley Hale, Waste Management, and Polaroid case studies at the end of the book for further examples of these concerns.

# "INDEPENDENT" OUTSIDE DIRECTORS

One trend that has characterized boards of directors over the last 20 years has been the rise of the "independent" outside director. While definitions of "independence" vary, most agree that, in order to be "independent," a director must have no connection to the company other than the seat on the board. This excludes not just full-time employees of the company, but also family members of employees and the company's lawyer, banker, and consultant. Some include people with connections to the company's suppliers, customers, debtors or creditors, or interlocking directors. Some definitions include direct or indirect recipients of corporate charitable donations, like the heads of universities or foundations. In its report on the relationship between independent directors and corporate perform-ance, Faulk & Co. considered any director was not independent if he held 5 percent or more of the stock – a most unusual restriction, and one that, according to most lights, utterly skewed the results. Some definitions are so restrictive that they all but require that the CEO has never met the candidate. The theory is that if the director is a friend of the CEO, it is just as difficult for him to be objective as it would be if he was an employee.

A number of high-profile corporate crimes in the 1970s prompted a fresh look at the role of directors. The Watergate affair caused several illegal campaign contributions to come to light. On the international front, sleazy tales emerged of corporations bribing foreign officials to keep out competition. Observers wondered why boards of directors, whose job it was to prevent such transgressions, had failed in their duty.

Academics, investors, and others began to put more emphasis on the importance of inde-pendent directors – directors not primarily employed by the company. In theory, outsiders are not dependent on the chief executive for promotion, or for legal or consulting busi-ness. Thus, they are relatively free from conflicts of interest, and better able to protect the owners' interests. This philosophy prompted companies to raise the number of outside directors in America's boardrooms, and, more importantly, the ratio of outsiders to insid-ers on the typical board. Corporate apologists and critics alike agreed, at least in theory, that if outsiders command a powerful majority in the boardroom, they will be better able to check any tendency of those in top management to abuse their positions of power.[50] True or not, the notion of raising the ratio of outsiders to insiders on corporate boards proved extremely popular. Over the last two decades, America's boardrooms have wit-nessed a remarkable growth in the power of independent outside directors – in 1973, insid-ers occupied 38 percent of the seats in the average boardroom; today that ratio has dropped to 25 percent.[51] As we discuss later, however, these directors have not always been will-ing to use this power. "Independence" can also mean "indifference." More recent efforts have been directed not just at making sure that boards have independent directors but also at giving them a structure that makes it possible for them to monitor more effectively.

One early reform that had an enormous impact on the importance of the independent directors was a requirement by the New York Stock Exchange in 1978 that every listed company had to have an audit committee made up of a majority of outside directors. This forced companies to have at least two outsiders on their board. According to a Spencer Stuart boardroom survey in 1990: "The ratio of outside to inside directorships, which climbed steadily during the 1980s, reached a new high in 1990."

1980:   20 boards had an outside/inside ratio of 3:1 or greater.
1990:   51 boards did.

1980:    20 boards had an outside/inside ratio of 4:1 or greater.
1990:    40 boards reported such a ratio.

This increase has continued, as many corporate governance experts recommend that, other than the CEO, the board be made up entirely of independent outside directors. There are other indications that outside directors have become an increasingly dominant force on corporate boards:

1980:    seven boards had just one or two insiders, and 51 companies had six insiders or more.
1990:    27 companies had one or two insiders, and 24 had six or more.

Spencer Stuart concluded: "Since 1980 . . . the combined total number of inside directors for all the SSBI companies has fallen from 584 to 410. That's a decline of nearly 30 percent."[52] The number of affiliated outsiders has also declined.

1980:    32 percent of boards reported seating one of their own outside lawyers.
1990:    The incidence had dropped to 21 percent.[53]

The insider–outsider ratios continue to rise in the 1990s. Today, some boards (14 out of Spencer Stuart's sample of 100 in 1993[54]) report only one inside director, the CEO. Post-Enron reforms are likely to produce even higher percentages of outside directors.

What does all this really mean? "Independence" is impossible to discern from the limited information in the proxy. A director with no ties to the company can be indifferent. Although there is much theory and some data to recommend outside directors, their impact is still difficult to quantify, and research on this subject remains limited.[55]

## Case in point: Sears

The "independence" of independent directors selected by management was put into focus when Robert A.G. Monks, co-author of this book, ran a campaign to be an independent director of Sears in 1991. At Sears, where the CEO also served as chairman of the board, CEO of the largest operating division, and head of the board's nominating committee, outside directors not selected by management are so threatening that Sears budgeted $5.5 million (22 times Monks' budget) to defeat his candidacy. (See case study.)

In 1971, a Harvard Business School professor named Myles Mace conducted a landmark study of boards, and concluded that directors were "ornaments on a corporate Christmas tree." His description echoed one company chairman who once described directors as "the parsley on the fish."[56] Since Mace's day things have improved markedly, but directors still have a long way to go before they exercise their power on behalf of shareholders' interests.

Boards of directors, despite the much-ballyhooed rise of the independent outside director, have seldom succeeded in effectively overseeing management. Rather, the CEO/chairman wields the power in the boardroom, and directors mostly serve at his pleasure. This is not to say that directors do nothing, or that they cannot check managerial abuse. But it is true that boards are mostly reactive, not proactive.

Millstein and Knowlton put it this way:

> Directors are forced to spend a great deal of their time – in our view, most of it – going by "the numbers" and by "the book", endlessly reviewing financial results, making sure their tracks are covered, and helping their companies mostly, we feel, by the exercise of negative virtues: reducing risks, preventing egregious mistakes, making sure things are "in order."[57]

Not all boards fail in their duty to oversee management. It is worth looking at examples where a board has been proactive in solving a company's problems.

---

# Case in point:
# Compaq Computers

Ben Rosen, a venture capitalist with a significant stake in Compaq, served as the non-executive chairman of the company's board. After the stock price of the company plummeted, matched by Compaq's first-ever quarterly loss, a major disagreement developed between management and the board as to how the company should address the crisis. The board believed the company needed a fundamental shift in strategy, and the company's founder and CEO Rod Canion was forced to resign. The result was vastly increased earnings over the next year and a doubling of the stock price. In testimony to the House of Representatives, Rosen described the criteria for a strong board:

> (1) An outside, independent chairman; all directors, with the exception of the CEO, should be outsiders. (2) Board members who all have meaningful ownership in the company, making them natural allies of the shareholder owners. (3) Key committees that exclude the CEO. (4) Boards that are relatively small, to increase their effectiveness. In addition, reciprocal directorships should be discouraged, if not eliminated.

Compaq had such a board, which was vital as the company faced a difficult period:

> Compaq Computer, after a period of meteoric and profitable growth, ran into serious difficulties engendered by fundamental shifts in the marketplace. Our historical recipe for success was out of tune with the new needs of customers. For the first time, the board and management differed on the fundamental direction of the company. Because the board was composed of all-outside directors (except the CEO), had a non-CEO chairman, and was small (seven members), it was able to act dispassionately and entirely in the interests of the corporation. The board moved promptly, and the rest, as they say, is history.[58]

> *As noted earlier, ten years later Compaq faced the same problem and came up with the same solution – replacing the CEO. Is that evidence that the board is successful? Or is it evidence that it made mistakes in allowing the problems to get to that point?*

The same can be said for Sunbeam, where the board acted very promptly as soon as they discovered that there was a problem with the company's financial reporting. See the Eastman-Kodak, General Motors and Sears, Roebuck case studies.

> *Would those companies have suffered so badly for so long if the boards had followed Rosen's guidelines? What might have happened at those three companies if every director had a significant ownership stake, as Rosen did at Compaq?*

At Sunbeam, CEO Al Dunlap insisted that his directors hold a lot of stock. In the end, it worked just as he intended – the alignment of their interests with the interests of the shareholders led them to act quickly and decisively to throw him out.

We have seen in the previous section how the boardroom system conspires against genuine representation of owners' interests.

> *What can the shareholders do about it? What happens if the board fails to represent the owners? Who watches the watchers?*

The corporate structure has two provisions designed to ensure that directors are genuinely acting in the interests of the shareholders: the electoral process and the fiduciary standard.

## DIRECTOR ELECTION

In theory, directors, like politicians, are elected by their constituents. This system, like representative democracy, is predicated on the assumption that if shareholders don't approve of their representatives they will "throw the bums out."

As noted above, however, most observers will agree that the electoral process has not been an effective mechanism for assuring that directors represent the interests of the shareholders. Edward J. Epstein says that shareholder elections "are procedurally much more akin to the elections held by the Communist party of North Korea than those held in Western democracies."[59] The reality backs him up. Management picks the slate of candidates, no one runs against them, and management counts the votes. Managers even know how shareholders vote. As soon as the votes come in, they can call and try to persuade (or pressure) those who vote against them. And, of course, management has access to the corporate treasury to finance its search for candidates and solicit support for their election, while anyone running against them must put up their own money. (Successful dissident slates often get reimbursed, however, once they are in office.) Management has access to the shareholder list; a dissident shareholder faces significant obstacles (see the Sears case study), though fewer following the 1992 SEC rule changes.

In this section, we will look at how the electoral system can be manipulated to reduce the efficacy of shareholder voting rights. As mentioned above, in reality, it is more of a ratification than an election, because in more than 99 percent of the votes, the management candidates run without opposition. So the "election" is really just a formality. Except for the rare case of a proxy contest, where those trying for control of the company nominate (and finance) a competing slate of directors, there is no chance of the nominees not being elected. Shareholders cannot vote "no" to unopposed directors. They can only abstain by withholding their support. And their abstentions carry little weight; it only takes one yes vote from a single shareholder to get a slate of unopposed candidates elected, no matter how many shareholders refuse to support them.

Moreover, corporate managers often seek to limit shareholders' voting rights. They argue, correctly, that corporations cannot be run by referenda. However, there is a difference between governing a company as a "town hall" and allowing shareholders a voice in the governance of the corporation they own.

*How should we define this difference? Who should define it?*

## Staggered boards

Until the mid- to late 1980s it was the all but universal practice for all directors to be elected at each annual meeting of shareholders. Thus, a director would serve a succession of yearly terms either until retirement or until a decision was made by the nominating committee not to renominate him.

The takeover era, however, raised the possibility of raiders being able to take over a company by nominating a separate slate of directors and seeking votes from shareholders to vote for the dissident's slate over management's.

As a protective device, companies began to nominate directors for three staggered sets of three-year terms. Thus, the board would be divided into three sets, or classes, of directors who would each be nominated for re-election every three years. This way, an acquirer would have to run a dissident slate three years running to gain control of the board – an impossibly long time to maintain a hostile bid.

This practice became especially popular in the late 1980s. By 1991, 51 percent of sample companies elected directors to three-year terms, up from 33 percent in 1986.[60] And the Commonwealth of Massachusetts enacted a law *requiring* all companies incorporated there to adopt a staggered board structure, just to protect one local company from a prospective hostile acquirer.

In adopting a staggered (or classified) board structure, management argued that the moves assured the "continuity" of board service. This ignored the fact that it should be up to the shareholders whether they wish their directors to continue representing them or not.

Studies performed by SEC economists support the view that classified boards are contrary to shareholder interests. These studies demonstrate that adoption of a classified board can result in loss of share value.[61] There is the greater issue of accountability, however. Shareholder advocates believe that holders have the right to vote on all of their directors every year.[62] They believe that staggered boards, in protecting directors from raiders, also serve to "protect" the board from the company's shareholders. In making it more difficult for an outsider to present shareholders with an alternative, the staggered board structure makes it even more difficult for shareholders to play a meaningful role in the election of directors.

## Confidential voting

Conflicts of interest, both political and commercial, make confidential voting an important issue to many shareholders. These conflicts are inherent in any situation where management (or its agents) is counting the non-confidential votes. This is the practice that prevails in the vast (though shrinking) majority of corporations. Thus, corporate managers know as soon as the votes come in who has voted and how they voted. Since new proxies can be submitted at any time up to the moment votes are counted, intense pressure can be placed on shareholders who also happen to have a close business relationship with the company in question. It is common practice for companies to call dissident share-holders and persuade them to change their votes to support management[63] (see the discussion of conflicts of interest among institutional investors in chapter 2 and the case in point about the pressure Hewlett-Packard put on Deutsche Asset Management in the fight over the merger with Compaq, demonstrating the obstacles to effective shareholder oversight that result from a lack of confidential voting). But the beneficial holders, for example the individuals who are pension plan participants or investors in mutual funds, have no way of finding out how votes are cast on their behalf. For that reason, it is hard for institutional investors to resist pressure to vote with management.

Many companies have adopted some form of confidential voting policy, in part because the corporate community has decided that it costs it little and means a lot to shareholder activists. But some of these policies are written very narrowly. Many of them do not apply in case of a proxy contest, exactly the situation where confidential voting proponents argue they are most needed.

The Department of Labor has directed ERISA fiduciaries to monitor the way that proxies are voted by the money managers they retain,[64] which means that money managers must disclose their votes to the fiduciaries. There are two important aspects of full disclosure missing (or at least not explicit) in this requirement, however. First, the disclosure may apparently be in general or aggregate form. Unless the ERISA fiduciary insists on more detail, the information may be disclosed as "number of votes cast in favor of management-sponsored proxy issues relating to stock option plans" rather than "vote on the stock option plan proposed by Widget & Co." Second, the disclosure is made to the ERISA plan fiduciaries, and not to the beneficial holders, the plan participants, or to the public. Still, this requirement does provide information to at least some of those who make the decision about which money managers to use. And the State of California now requires institutional investors subject to state law to make public the record of their proxy votes in order to limit their liability for any failure to cast the votes appropriately.

*Should there be a requirement, along the lines of required disclosures for performance information, for institutional investors to disclose their proxy policies? Their proxy votes? To whom should the disclosures be made?*

In January of 2003, the SEC issued a new rule that will for the first time require money managers and mutual fund managers to disclose their proxy voting policies and any votes inconsistent with those policies. Despite these mandates, the electoral system still falls short of providing shareholders with any meaningful ability to make a change in the board. This raises the expectations for the fiduciary standard as the foundation for the corporate structure's legitimacy even higher. As discussed earlier, this standard means that a director is legally bound to an unwavering loyalty to the shareholders, and must pursue their interests with the greatest of care and diligence. To understand the operation of this standard in practice better, we will examine its greatest modern-day challenge: the takeover era.

## IMPACT OF THE TAKEOVER ERA ON THE ROLE OF THE BOARD

In the 1950s, corporate lawyers felt that their job had been done – they had no questions left to answer! As academic Bayless Manning put it in 1962: "Corporation law, as a field of intellectual effort, is dead in the United States."[65]

Twenty-five years later, however, the takeover era turned Manning's statement on its head. The creation of financial instruments to finance takeovers of any company, of virtually any size, presented directors with the most demanding challenges in corporate history.

Justifying decisions in terms of benefits to shareholders is one thing when the issues relate to marketing or research and development, and quite another when they relate to whether the entity will continue in its current state or be swallowed up by another company. And making a decision that affects the job security of the CEO who brought you on to the board (to say nothing of your own job security as a director) is of necessity less dispassionate than making a decision about ordinary business.

The early takeovers (and efforts to block takeovers) challenged in court produced judicial decisions reflecting concerns about the difficulty directors would have in acting on behalf of the shareholders when the interests of management, and perhaps the directors' own interests, could be in conflict.

The early challenges to takeover defenses produced case law that reflected traditional notions of the director's duty, and traditional concerns that corporate managers and directors would have a natural tendency to protect their own interests to the detriment of those of the shareholders. In the most important of the early cases, *Trans Union* (see *Smith v. Van Gorkom* discussed below), the court ruled against directors for agreeing to a sale of the company in a manner that seemed almost impetuous. Since the board had not taken enough steps to ensure that it was getting the best price, ruled the court, its members had not met their duty as fiduciaries. In *Trans Union*, the board gave in too easily.

In the next wave of cases, the courts objected when boards did not give in easily enough. Those cases, including *Revlon* and *Unocal*, concerned efforts by boards to block takeovers. When shareholders sued, the courts had to decide whether there was any limit to the defensive maneuvers a board could undertake in the face of an offer to buy the company.

## THE FIDUCIARY STANDARD AND THE DELAWARE FACTOR

The Delaware courts have decided most of the cases relating to takeovers, because most big companies are incorporated there. Some other courts have addressed the business judgment rule. The New York court ruled, for example, that issuing a block of stock to an ESOP and a wholly controlled subsidiary, just to avoid a takeover, violated the duty of loyalty.[66] But, in general, Delaware has a lock on the Fortune 500, and when it seemed that decisions limiting the protection of the business judgment rule might lead companies to incorporate elsewhere, the Delaware courts began to back off (see the "Delaware puts out" case in point in chapter 1).

## Case in point: Trans Union

In the landmark case of *Smith v. Van Gorkom*,[67] directors were found to have violated their fiduciary duty over the sale of Trans Union. The CEO of Trans Union, Jerome William Van Gorkom, suggested to potential buyer Jay Pritzker that $55 per share would be a good offer for his company, without consulting anyone on his board. When the board did meet to discuss the deal, Van Gorkom did not tell it that it was he who had suggested that figure to Pritzker, and he did not tell it how he had arrived at it. He did not ask the board whether it was the best price, just whether it was a fair price.

After about two hours, the board approved the deal, subject to two conditions: first, that the company could accept (though not solicit) another offer during a "market test" period, and second, to facilitate other offers, that the company could share proprietary information with other potential bidders.

The market test was a brief one. With the permission of his board, Van Gorkom signed the merger agreement that evening, although, the court found, at the time the agreement was executed neither Van Gorkom nor any director had read it.[68] Trans Union issued a press release announcing a "definitive" merger agreement, "subject to approval by stockholders."

The shareholders did approve the deal, but one shareholder sued. The lower court upheld the actions of the directors, but the Delaware Supreme Court reversed that finding, ruling that the Trans Union directors were "grossly negligent" in failing to make an independent determination of whether Van Gorkom did a complete job of evaluating the price and negotiating the terms of the merger agreement, and in failing to understand the transaction themselves.

The issue was not the substance of the decision; the court never said whether $55 per share was too low or too high. Instead, the issue was one of process. The court ruled that the directors had not taken adequate steps to be able to evaluate the offer. The substantial premium over the market price, the "market test" period for entertaining other offers, the advice of counsel that they might be violating their duty as fiduciaries if they failed to approve the merger, and the shareholder vote were not sufficient to make up for the board's failure to evaluate the deal independently. It should be noted that this was a close case – two justices dissented, finding the directors' actions reasonable. Controversy notwithstanding, however, *Van Gorkom* became the litmus test for director's duty.

The primary impact of the *Van Gorkom* case has been on the process for arriving at decisions, not on the substance of the decisions themselves. Courts have been very careful not to substitute their business judgment for that of boards. As long as a process is followed, the courts will defer to it. But the processes themselves have little substantive meaning. Law firms present boards with routine checklists of options which are then "considered" just to make a strong record in case of a challenge in court, rather than for any substantive purpose. And, sometimes, the record does not even need to be very strong, as in the Time Warner case study, where all the steps taken to establish due care and deliberation were taken in consideration of a deal that was different in every major respect (except management compensation) to the deal that went through.

# Cases in point: *Unocal* and Revlon

In *Unocal*,[69] the court expressed its concern with the "omnipresent specter" that a board would act to protect its own interests when faced with a takeover offer. For that reason, any action to protect the company from a contest for control would be reviewed with special care by a court reviewing a challenge, based on the assumption that the board and the top managers had a conflict of interest between what was best for them and what was best for the shareholders.

While the courts normally give directors' "business judgment" great deference, in takeover cases (as in other cases of possible conflicts of interest), directors would have what the law calls a "burden of proof" and therefore have to show "good faith and reasonable investigation" before the courts would defer to their decision. They also have to show that, unlike the actions of the Trans Union directors, their decisions were "informed." Directors' decisions must also meet another test: they must be "reasonably relationed to the threats posed."[70] Directors are not supposed to use an atom bomb to fight a squirt gun; if they do, it must be assumed that their primary interest is their own job security.

When Revlon adopted a poison pill[71] in reaction to Pantry Pride's offer of $45 a share, that was "reasonable in relation to the threat posed."[72] But when Pantry Pride increased its offer to $53, the defensive measures were no longer reasonable. At that point, according to the court, "it became apparent to all that the break-up of the company was inevitable"[73] and "the directors' role changed from defenders of the corporate bastion to auctioneers charged with getting the best price for the stockholders at a sale of the company."[74] The court lambasted the directors' decision to grant favorable treatment to a white knight[75] whose offer was only $1 per share more than Pantry Pride's, even though its offer provided more protection to note-holders. "[T]he directors cannot fulfill their enhanced *Unocal* duties by playing favorites with the contending factions. Market forces must be allowed to operate freely to bring the target's shareholders the best price available for their equity."[76] The court decided that once a company was "for sale," the only factor to be considered was the best price for shareholders; any other interest was a breach of the directors' fiduciary duty of loyalty.

The court specifically addressed the issue of "stakeholders." As discussed in chapter 2, the non-shareholder constituencies also have an interest in the company and have sought to advance these interests at the board level. The court said that, although boards may consider other interests, "there are fundamental limitations on that prerogative. A board may have regard for various constituencies in discharging its responsibilities, provided that there are rationally related benefits accruing to the stockholders . . . However, such concern for non-stockholder interests is inappropriate when an auction among active bidders is in progress, and the object is no longer to protect or maintain the corporate enterprise but to sell it to the highest bidder."[77]

## How did boards respond?

The takeover era of the 1980s demonstrated that the market for corporate control was more theoretical than real. Boards of directors and management joined to protect their companies from the threat of a hostile raid, but, ironically, they only distanced themselves from their own shareholders. By the end of the 1980s, most large companies bristled with a host of "anti-takeover" devices – collectively known as "shark repellents" – that only served to render management and the board still *less* accountable than they had been before. As we saw in chapter 2, these protective devices were one of the main reasons for the emergence of shareholder activists, and the dismantling of such devices was one of their main early aims.

## *Greenmail*

Possibly the most unconscionable way of avoiding takeover, greenmail forced shareholders to bear the cost of management's incumbency. There is a reason "greenmail" sounds a lot like "blackmail," though it is really more like extortion. Someone buys a large stake in the company and begins to make his presence known, perhaps by making noises about trying to take over the company. Management does not want him, so they offer to buy him out, at a substantial bonus over the market price of the stock. Raiders achieve huge profits without even having to make a bid for the company; managers are able to keep their jobs. But all other shareholders are left with the market trading price – which often goes down as a result of a large cash payment being made to silence a potential dissenting voice.

One of the earliest payments of greenmail was in 1984. The Bass brothers had acquired 9.9 percent of Texaco, and were known to be interested in purchasing the other 90.1 percent. Instead, Texaco's management paid the Bass brothers $1.3 billion for the stock, a $137 million premium over the market price. In other terms, the Bass brothers were able to sell their stock for $55 per share, while the vast majority of shareholders could only get $35. The payment so infuriated the then Treasurer of California, Jesse Unruh, that he formed the highly influential Council of Institutional Investors to lobby for improved shareholder rights.

Greenmail is evidence of board neglect. Directors should not permit managers to pay huge sums of shareholders' money merely to avoid possible loss of control. In all likelihood it was not in Texaco's interest to be taken over by the Bass brothers, but that is something for the market to decide. Moreover, the majority of shareholders should have been allowed to decide if selling their shares to the Basses was in their best interests. The Texaco board should have let the company's shareholders make that choice.

## *"Poison pills"*

In November 1985, in *Moran v. Household International, Inc.*, the Delaware Supreme Court upheld a company's right to adopt "shareholder rights plans," or "poison pills" as they are called by everyone apart from corporate management. Moreover, the Delaware court allowed a pill to be created without shareholder approval. The plans usually take the form of rights or warrants issued to shareholders that are worthless unless triggered by a hostile acquisition attempt. If triggered, pills give shareholders the ability to purchase shares from, or sell shares back to, the target company (the "flip-in" pill) and/or the potential acquirer (the "flip-over" pill). While a pill has the effect of entrenching a company from an unsolicited takeover, it also protects shareholders from such coercive practices as two-tier offers.

The widely used flip-over plan gives target shareholders the right to purchase shares of the potential acquirer's common stock at a steep discount, usually 50 percent, should the acquirer attempt a second-stage merger not approved by the target's board. Since the built-in discount would encourage all of the target shareholders to exercise their rights and purchase shares from the acquirer, and since the potential acquirer's shareholders would be prevented from participating, the result would be that the acquirer's pre-existing shareholders would find their own equity interests substantially diluted once the pill is triggered and the rights exercised. This is the "poison" in the pill.

The flip-in plan is often combined with a flip-over plan. Upon the triggering event, rights in a flip-in plan allow target shareholders to purchase shares of their own company at a steep discount, again usually 50 percent. The right is discriminatory in that the potential acquirer is excluded from participating if the pill is triggered by an action not approved by the target's board.

The pill is a "doomsday device" with such potent wealth-destroying characteristics that no bidder has ever dared proceed to the point of causing a pill actually to become operative.

A poison pill gives the board veto power over any bid for the company, no matter how beneficial to the shareholders. If the board opposes the bid, it can sit back and wait for the pill to be triggered – usually when an acquirer has purchased 15 or 20 percent. If the board is in favor of an acquisition, it can simply redeem the pill. The board can both create and redeem the pill without shareholder approval. Thus, while we have stated that shareholders have a basic right to sell their stock to whomever they please, "poison pills" showed that shareholders could only sell to people pre-approved by the board.

By the end of the 1980s, over 1,000 companies had implemented a poison pill. Meanwhile, academics studied the effects on shareholder value. The evidence has been inconclusive. One type of study has examined the price movement of company stock following the adoption of a pill. Some have suggested that adoption of a pill increases share value; some say the opposite. Another set of studies has focused on how pills are used in practice. Some of these suggest that companies with pills generally receive higher takeover premiums than companies without pills; others disagree.[78] As the takeover market has declined in recent years, so the need for protective devices such as pills lessened.[79] As described in chapter 2, shareholders have consistently sponsored resolutions calling for the redemption of pills, with considerable success.[80] There is some evidence that firms that abandon their pill experience short-term positive gains, as the market recognizes that the company has become more susceptible to the discipline of the takeover market.[81] Some companies, rather than canceling the pill outright, have modified the plan to create a "chewable" pill. This pill is not a "doomsday device" triggered by hostile interest, but a pill that sets certain conditions on an unsolicited bid. Thus, if a bid is fully financed, and is made for all shares, then a "chewable pill" generally won't be triggered. In many ways, such a device is beneficial to shareholders since it ensures that any bid made for the company is a fair one.

Other companies found ways to add more poison to the pill. Mentor Graphics Corporation launched a hostile cash tender offer for all the stock of Quickturn Design Systems Inc. in August of 1998. At the same time, Mentor announced that it would solicit proxies to replace all of the members of Quickturn's board at a special meeting of shareholders. Mentor proposed to solicit approvals from Quickturn's shareholders to call the special meeting under a provision in Quickturn's bylaws that allowed shareholders holding at least 10 percent of the outstanding shares to call a special meeting.

The Quickturn board soon decided that Mentor's offer was inadequate and adopted two defensive measures in response. First, the board amended Quickturn's bylaws to provide, among other things, that special meetings called by shareholders must take place not less than 90 days nor more than 100 days after the request has been received by Quickturn and determined to be valid. Second, Quickturn adopted the strongest pill defense it could create. Its pill had a "dead-hand" provision, meaning that it could not be amended or redeemed by anyone but the current board or directors they approved.

The practical effect of such a provision is that, even if an unwanted bidder succeeds in ousting a majority of the target's incumbent board members at an annual or special meeting or through action by consent, the newly elected board would be unable to redeem or amend the poison pill to allow the proposed acquisition to proceed. After the Delaware court invalidated the "dead-hand" pill in another case, Quickturn amended the pill to a "no-hand" or "slow-hand" provision. The rights plan could not be redeemed or amended for a specified period of time after a change in a majority of the directors or other similar event. While such a provision would not completely prevent a hostile acquisition, the delay might discourage would-be hostile bidders and might also allow additional time for alternatives to develop.

Mentor Graphics took Quickturn to court. The court invalidated the pill, on the grounds that it was disproportionate to the threat posed by Mentor.

## Other anti-takeover devices

There are other takeover defenses that also seek to prevent shareholders being coerced by such bids as two-tier offers. For instance, a "fair price provision" requires an acquirer to pay the same price for all shares bought, rather than only paying a premium for a sufficient number of shares to gain control.

Another popular strategy was the "white knight" defense. A "white knight" is a friendly third party who agrees to buy a significant portion of stock to keep it out of the acquirer's hands. This strategy was used successfully at both Polaroid and Carter Hawley Hale (see case studies). A similar strategy involves creating a new class of shareholder with unequal voting rights. Shares may be issued to friendly shareholders (usually management) with greater voting power than that which applies to common stock. Thus, friendly interests may control few of the shares but many of the votes (see the case in point "One share, one vote" in chapter 2).

Other takeover defenses are less shareholder-friendly, and give the impression that the target management would rather destroy the company than let it be taken over. For instance, a "crown jewel" strategy could result in a target company divesting itself of its most valuable assets. In this defense, the target company would sell or otherwise "lock up" the company's most valuable assets – its core business, for instance. Thus, the acquirer would be faced with undertaking an expensive takeover bid for a far less valuable company. Of course, this strategy only averts takeover at the cost of the dismemberment of the target company.

Still more risky was the "PacMan" defense, in which the target company made a bid for the acquirer. This "I'll eat you before you eat me" strategy was used most famously in the takeover battle between Bendix and Martin Marietta. In 1982, Bendix announced its intention to purchase Marietta; Marietta responded by making a tender offer for Bendix shares. Months later, United Technologies joined the battle by proposing to buy Bendix at a higher price than Marietta was offering. Ultimately, both companies were bought by Allied Corporation.

Perhaps the most bizarre strategy ever adopted was the so-called "Jewish dentist" defense, pioneered by leading takeover lawyer Joe Flom, in 1975. Sterndent, a manufacturer of dental equipment, was under attack from Magus Corp., a foreign-based conglomerate. Flom found that 10 percent of Magus was owned by the Kuwait Investment Company. Since Sterndent sold most of its products to dentists, many of whom were Jewish, Flom argued that an Arab-financed takeover would negatively affect Sterndent's operations as its customers would shop elsewhere. Flom was also able to find a white knight for Sterndent, and Magus backed off.[82] The causes and effects of takeovers, and whether management is justified in opposing a takeover without recourse to a shareholder vote, are still a matter of raging debate. Takeover lawyer Martin Lipton believes that the takeover era was disastrous for corporate America, and that such devices as poison pills are necessary to allow managers to run their companies without continually looking over their shoulders for a possible hostile bid. By contrast, raiders such as T. Boone Pickens believe the takeover era restored market accountability, by exposing poorly performing companies to the threat of correction. In many ways the debate has been rendered irrelevant by history – with the collapse of junk-bond financing in 1989, large-scale takeovers are now few and far between, a notable exception being the contest for Paramount Communications discussed in the Time Warner case study.[83] However, the years of increased takeover activity did raise a host of new questions regarding the role and responsibilities of the board. These questions remain as pertinent today as they did during the go-go takeover years.

> *Should a board have the right to "just say no" to a hostile bid without offering shareholders any alternative transaction? Should shareholders have the right to sell their shares to a raider under any circumstances? Did the increasing use of more sophisticated and more bizarre anti-takeover devices render managers more or less accountable? Should a board let a company be either dismembered or destroyed rather than let it be taken over? Is it right for a board of directors to entrench a company against a possible hostile bid? Read the Carter Hawley Hale and Polaroid case studies. Should the directors of those companies allow themselves to be taken over? Should the shareholders of those companies have been allowed to chose for themselves?*

In a 2001 paper, "Corporate Governance and Equity Prices," Paul Gompers, Joy L. Ishii, and Andrew Metrick reviewed the performance of 1,500 firms with single classes of stock from 1990 to 1999 and found that the firms with fewer than five anti-takeover provisions significantly outperformed the ones with 14 or more. More work needs to be done on these data – for example, the authors gave all of the provisions they looked at equal weight, and they acknowledge that there are some cause and effect questions about the way adoption of entrenching provisions reflects management's level of comfort with risk. But even this preliminary work suggests that fiduciary shareholders should look carefully at this information when making investment or proxy voting decisions.

## RECOMMENDATIONS FOR THE FUTURE

Boards have an extraordinary range of responsibilities (see figure 3.1). Academics, judges, legislators, shareholders, managers, board advisers, and even directors themselves have made a number of recommendations for improving their ability to perform. The General Motors and American Express case studies show how boards overcame the obstacles of the current structure to respond to crises. In this section we will discuss some of these proposals to improve the performance of boards of directors that might allow – or even encourage – boards to pre-empt crises.

The post-takeover era has resulted in a new focus on independent directors as a group separate from the other directors. Increasingly, shareholders are looking to outsiders to take the lead on board issues. They are also asking for more of a role in setting the criteria for board service, if not involvement in the selection of the candidates themselves.

### *Improving director compensation*

As noted above, boards have already made a lot of progress in this direction, with increasing proportions of director compensation in the form of stock or stock options.

## Increasing the authority of independent directors

The scandals of 2002 led to calls for more independent boards of directors. The New York Stock Exchange's new listing standards will require listed companies to have a majority of independent outside directors and to have all of the key committees composed exclusively of independent outsiders. The Investor Responsibility Research Center's analysis showed that 13 percent of NYSE-listed companies did not have a majority of independent outside directors. Boards will have two years to comply after the NYSE rules are approved by the SEC. With the new requirements to disclose whether there is a "financial expert" on the audit committee, and increased sensitivity to the issue of independence from investors, director and officer liability insurers, and rating agencies, we can expect to see more turnover on boards in that two-year period than in as many as five years previously.

It intuitively seems a good rule of thumb to have a majority of the directors be independent, and many authorities recommend that the CEO should be the only insider on the board. Shareholders have submitted proposals asking that companies have a majority of outside directors, or that crucial committees like nominating, audit, and compensation be made up exclusively of outside directors. Some companies, including General Motors in 1991 (which already had a majority of outside directors, and even adopted a bylaw making it formal), agreed to the terms of the proposals, so they never went to a vote.[84]

Proposals to split the positions of chairman and CEO fall into this category as well. In 1992, a shareholder resolution advising that Sears, Roebuck separate the two positions won 27 percent of the vote. The following year, the proposal was resubmitted and won 32 percent. The sponsor of the resolution at Sears explained the reasons for recommending a split:

> I believe a person in the position of Chairman/CEO is subject to an inherent conflict of interest that the shareholders of Sears can no longer afford. This conflict, in my opinion, results from the obvious concentration of power and lack of accountability that results from combining the two positions. The CEO is the company's most senior manager, responsible for executing corporate strategy. When the same individual is chairman of the board of directors, which is charged with the duty of monitoring management on behalf of shareholders, it can create an untenable situation.[85]

Sears has so far resisted the pressure, but other companies, also targeted by shareholders, have not. At General Motors, Westinghouse, Waste Management, and American Express – companies where the chief executive was forced to resign – the board took the opportunity to separate the roles of CEO and chairman, at least for a transitional period.

Many governance activists have backed the moves to separate the roles. Jamie Heard, then president of Institutional Shareholder Services, said: "The goal here is really not to emasculate CEOs, the goal is to empower the board."[86] Jay W. Lorsch of the Harvard Business School called such a separation "the single most significant thing to do" by a company's board.[87] John Nash of the National Association of Corporate Directors said that CEOs' attitude is that: " 'It's my company and it's my board.' They don't get it that it's not."[88] True independence will always be an issue as long as the CEO plays a dominant role in selecting directors. An independent nominating committee, working on the basis of a thoughtful board evaluation and in conjunction with a search firm, is the only way to achieve real independence of thought and action.

## *"A market for independent directors"*

A widely circulated proposal by Stanford's Ronald J. Gilson and Harvard's Reinier Kraakman suggests that institutional investors create "a market for independent directors" by "recruiting a class of outside directors who actively monitor public corporations, much as LBO sponsors or universal banks in Japan and Germany actively monitor their own companies."[89] They suggest that the institutions, perhaps through some coordinating entity like the CII or ISS, develop a cadre of full-time directors whose entire professional obligation would be to serve as director of five or six companies. Gilson and Kraakman point out that the institutions have the votes to make this possible. They suggest that compliance with SEC rules should not be too burdensome, as control is not at issue (though they recognize that reform of the proxy rules would be a significant help). And they suggest that a director of five companies is unlikely to become co-opted by any one of them.

The National Association of Corporate Directors (NACD) is a trade association based in Washington. NACD provides courses, studies, surveys, and materials, hosts conferences, convenes working groups on topics like executive compensation and CEO and director evaluation, and tracks and comments on legislation. Its publications include *Director's Monthly*. NACD also evaluates boards, provides training courses for directors, and maintains a database of director candidates. It has the potential for developing along the lines of the Gilson–Kraakman proposal.

In 1982, a group of British financial and industrial institutions, including the Bank of England, the Institutional Shareholders Committee, and the Confederation of British Industry, established "PRO NED," a clearinghouse/headhunting firm to provide boards with qualified independent ("non-executive" in the UK) directors. PRO NED stands for the Promotion of Non-Executive Directors. Sir Adrian Cadbury, chairman of PRO NED, described the group as having three main tasks:

1. To promote the wider use of non-executive directors through publicity and other means; to provide general guidance for non-executive directors on the discharge of their duties; and to contribute to current thinking on the structure of company boards, the role of non-executive directors, and legislative and other developments (including prospective developments in the EEC) concerning these matters. PRO NED holds seminars and discussions on aspects of the non-executive director's role and work.
2. To maintain an extensive register of names of actual and/or potential non-executive directors, of high quality and of a wide range of business experience and qualifications.
3. To provide companies on request with the names of suitable candidates for their boards, of the right quality and background, from which a choice may be made; and to give help on the assessment of the overall capabilities of individual candidates and of their suitability for particular appointments.

PRO NED was ultimately purchased by an international search and consulting firm.

*Would a PRO NED work in the US? What are the advantages and disadvantages of the kind of full-time director Gilson and Kraakman envision? Would this process ensure that the directors felt beholden to the shareholders rather than to management for their job? Gilson and Kraakman suggest that these directors would not worry about opposing management when necessary because the possible loss of one director position (out of five) would not be too great a financial risk. Do you agree?*

## "Designated director"

An interesting legislative initiative in Michigan permitted companies incorporated there to designate an independent director, meeting certain criteria, for special compensation, rights (including communication with shareholders at company expense), and responsibilities (including determinations on indemnification, transactions that raise conflicts questions, and derivative litigation). This designation is limited to a three-year term. Significantly, companies who exercise this option have more limited liability. An organization called the Independent Director Foundation was created to encourage companies to take advantage of the new Michigan law and gather information on the way that independent directors are used. This idea, ahead of its time, never went anywhere, but it could serve as a model for reform in the post-Enron era.

*Compare this to the "lead director" proposal of Lipton and Lorsch discussed below. What are the advantages and disadvantages of both proposals?*

## Splitting the chairman and CEO positions

There is growing support for splitting the positions of CEO and board chairman, as described in chapter 2. One of the core challenges for a board is making sure that it gets the information it needs and the opportunity to deal with the most pressing issues, even if they are not the issues the CEO wants scrutinized at the moment. Splitting the two positions and giving an independent outsider the authority over the agenda and information could be the most powerful option for increasing effective, independent oversight. There is an exceptionally thoughtful discussion of the benefits of this approach in Sir Adrian Cadbury's book, *Corporate Governance and Chairmanship: A Personal View* (Oxford University Press, 2002).

## "Just vote no"

In November of 1990, former SEC Commissioner Joseph Grundfest urged members of the CII to "just vote no" – to withhold votes for directors as a way of sending a strong message of concern to management and boards of under-performing companies.[90] The members of the Council were receptive. According to a scholarly and painstakingly documented follow-up by Grundfest himself, institutional investors representing more than $269 billion in equities have used this mechanism.

His article gets right to the point: "The takeover wars are over. Management won." To the extent that the market for corporate control was effective in disciplining and removing inefficient managers in the 1980s, it is no longer available.

Grundfest recommends "just vote no" as an alternative. He argues that the withhold vote's symbolic nature (it cannot prevent the election of unopposed candidates) is its strength. It will not leave a vacuum at the top or upset the company's governance structure. But it will send an embarrassingly public "vote of no confidence" to the board, thus providing an incentive for improved performance. That could mean making the hard decision to get rid of the CEO, a decision that recently increased value by more than $2.7 billion at just four companies examined in the article. Grundfest also does a cost-benefit analysis of a "just vote no" strategy and concludes that the costs (mechanics, information, coordination, publicity – good and bad) and the conflicts (with money manager's clients or other commercial relationships) are more than outweighed by the benefits: "Symbols . . . have consequences. A successful 'just vote no' campaign can reduce internal reforms as a result of social pressures that lead board members to engage in more effective monitoring. Alternatively, a substantial 'just vote no' turnout can increase the probability of a hostile proxy contest or tender offer that will be treated more kindly by the courts precisely because it follows a significant 'just vote no' turnout."

Grundfest's approach has been supported by some CEOs. H. Brewster (Bruce) Atwater, CEO of General Mills and then chairman of the Business Roundtable's Special Task Force on Corporate Governance, has encouraged disgruntled institutions to "just vote no." In a 1991 Senate hearing on shareholder rights, Atwater testified: "I know of no board that would not be moved dramatically by as little as 20 percent of the shareholder votes being withheld for the election of directors. The board would perceive itself as being vulnerable and would do everything in its power to attempt to correct the situation which led to this shareholder vote of no confidence."[91]

It is important to note that even a 99 percent withhold vote cannot keep anyone off the board. State law reasonably provides that shareholders cannot prevent someone from being elected unless there is an opposing candidate who is elected instead. But, as Grundfest points out, this is one of the advantages of "just vote no." Shareholders can send a strong message of concern, not only to the company's directors and management, but also to anyone considering running a dissident slate. This response by shareholders strikes a good balance between the need for oversight by shareholders and the need for stability and continuity in the management of corporations. Some shareholders have had some success with this approach. An effort led by the New York City Pension Fund in 2000 resulted in a 30 percent withhold vote at Great Lakes Chemical. There were also majority votes in favor of shareholder proposals on annual election of directors and submitting the poison pill to a shareholder vote.

## Audit committees

The SEC proclaimed 1999 "the year of the accountant," following audit scandals at Cendant, Green Tree, Mercury Finance, Waste Management, and Sunbeam. The Cendant proxy issued just before the fraud was uncovered revealed that, in the previous year, the audit committee had met twice, while the compensation committee met eight times. There were reports of audit committees whose meetings were brief and whose duties consisted of signing the signature block of documents they had not reviewed. And there were reports of CEOs who put their least experienced or financially literate directors on the audit committee as a way of keeping them from asking too many questions. The National Association of Corporate Directors, a blue-ribbon commission convened by the SEC, and several accounting and law firms, issued reports in 1999 setting new standards of care and practice for audit committees. And the post-Enron reforms put additional focus on the audit committee. Sarbanes–Oxley imposed new duties and required the committee to disclose whether it includes a "financial expert," strictly defined.

## Board evaluation

The NACD published a report on the performance evaluation of CEOs, boards, and directors in 1994. Prepared by a blue-ribbon commission of directors, shareholders, academics, and corporate officers, the report urged boards to develop a system for setting goals and evaluating the performance of individual directors, board committees and the board as a whole. One key recommendation was a separate evaluation of the CEO in his capacity as chairman, if the CEO serves in both positions. NACD's subsequent reports on director professionalism, CEO succession, and strategic planning, and audit committees have been influential in promoting policies like director stock ownership and executive session meetings for outside directors, and in making sure that directors are independent and have core competence in matters of finance.

### Executive session meetings

One of the key advances of the past decade has been the regular scheduling of executive session meetings of the outside directors, without any of the management team present. As one executive put it, "Having the meetings on the schedule following every board meeting means that no one ever has to ask that awkward question." The 1999 Korn/Ferry study reported that 69 percent of the directors surveyed meet in executive session an average of three times a year. The proposed New York Stock Exchange listing standards will require all boards to schedule executive session meetings of outside directors.

### Succession planning and strategic planning

Boards are becoming more involved in both succession planning and strategic planning, which, of course, are closely related. Both, in the past, have often been controlled by the CEO. The 1999 Korn/Ferry report showed that over 60 percent of the number of directors say that they control the CEO succession process.

### Lipton/Lorsch's "Modest Proposal"

Academic Jay Lorsch and corporate lawyer Marty Lipton co-wrote an article entitled "A Modest Proposal for Improved Corporate Governance." They described their ideas as modest, not because they were modest in scope, but because (unlike Lipton's Quinquennium idea) their implementation would not require the involvement of Congress, the SEC, or the stock exchanges. Rather, the authors argued, their proposals could be implemented simply via the willingness of boards of directors and management.

Lipton and Lorsch offer some basic structural changes – such as shrinking the size of the board, increasing the time spent by directors on board service, and limiting the number of boards that a director serves – and some reforms that they believe would encourage director independence. For example, they suggest that boards chaired by the CEO should identify a "lead director," taken from one of the independent outsiders.

What this person is called is not important, but his or her duties are important. We believe that the CEO/chairman should consult with this lead director on the following matters: the selection of board committee members and chairpersons; the board's meeting agendas; the adequacy of information directors receive; and the effectiveness of the board meeting process.

Furthermore, Lipton and Lorsch argue that a board with a designated lead director would be able to establish a better system of CEO evaluation, and thus deal more effectively with the possibility that the only person to judge the CEO's performance would be the CEO himself. While arguing that specific rules cannot suit every company, the authors produce detailed guidelines for evaluating the CEO.

THE BOARD'S RELATIONSHIP TO THE MANAGEMENT PROCESS

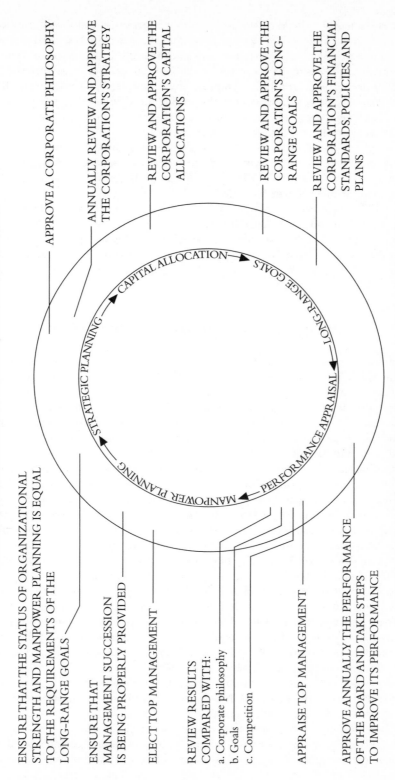

— APPROVE A CORPORATE PHILOSOPHY

— ANNUALLY REVIEW AND APPROVE
THE CORPORATION'S STRATEGY

— REVIEW AND APPROVE THE
CORPORATION'S CAPITAL
ALLOCATIONS

— REVIEW AND APPROVE THE
CORPORATION'S LONG-
RANGE GOALS

— REVIEW AND APPROVE THE
CORPORATION'S FINANCIAL
STANDARDS, POLICIES, AND
PLANS

ENSURE THAT THE STATUS OF ORGANIZATIONAL
STRENGTH AND MANPOWER PLANNING IS EQUAL
TO THE REQUIREMENTS OF THE
LONG-RANGE GOALS

ENSURE THAT
MANAGEMENT SUCCESSION
IS BEING PROPERLY PROVIDED

ELECT TOP MANAGEMENT

REVIEW RESULTS
COMPARED WITH:
a. Corporate philosophy
b. Goals
c. Competition

APPRAISE TOP MANAGEMENT

APPROVE ANNUALLY THE PERFORMANCE
OF THE BOARD AND TAKE STEPS
TO IMPROVE ITS PERFORMANCE

STRATEGIC PLANNING
CAPITAL ALLOCATION
LONG-RANGE GOALS
PERFORMANCE APPRAISAL
MANPOWER PLANNING

**Figure 3.1**   The board oversees the full cycle of management activities

1. The assessment should be based on company performance, and the progress the CEO has made toward his or her personal long- and short-range goals. Such personal goals would constitute the major extraordinary initiatives the CEO wanted to achieve, e.g., developing and selecting a successor; expanding into markets internationally; making a major acquisition; creating a significant joint venture. We contemplate that short-term goals will be agreed upon annually among the CEO and the independent directors. The longer-term goals might have a three- to five-year horizon, but would be reviewed annually and changed as necessary.

2. Each director would make an individual assessment of the CEO's performance. These assessments then would be synthesized to reveal the tendency, as well as any range of views. This synthesis could be done by the lead director, or by a small group or committee of independent directors.

3. The CEO would receive this synthesized feedback in a confidential manner with which both he or she and the independent directors were comfortable.

4. After the CEO had time to reflect on it and to develop a response, he or she would then discuss his or her reactions to the assessment with all the independent directors. This discussion also should focus on any changes in goals for the company or the CEO which seem appropriate.

## Making directors genuinely "independent"

The primary conclusion of this chapter is that America's boards of directors have, more often than not, failed to protect shareholders' interests. In one respect, this was inevitable. We demand too much of corporate boards. We expect directors to accept usually less than $50,000 a year, devote less than two weeks' work a year, and still be able to monitor a company that may generate billions in sales with hundreds of thousands of employees in dozens of countries. There is the theory of the fiduciary standard holding them accountable, and the reality of not actually being able to.

Independent directors were meant to be a means to an end. It was thought that informed, intelligent, and wise directors, of proven integrity, bound by a fiduciary standard, would effectively oversee management. Being outsiders, they wouldn't face the conflicts that, say, the chief operating officer might face, reluctant to criticize his boss and in no position to call for his ouster. The idea proved to be a mirage. Independence is an intangible concept. Outsiders cannot be guaranteed to be independent, any more than insiders can be assumed to be deferential. Personality plays a strong role, so that the CEO's brother may be able to evaluate the boss's performance while an outsider may not.

Directors do not become independent just because they have no economic ties to the company beyond their job as a director. Disinterested outsiders can mean uninterested outsiders. The key is not "independence," arbitrarily defined, but whether a director's interests are aligned with those of the shareholders. If a director is to represent the interests of the shareholders, he must share those interests. More, he must be intimately familiar with those interests. Put simply, he must be a shareholder.

One key to a good board is ownership. Each director's personal worth should be closely tied to the fortunes of the company. No director is going to remain passive if a quarter, or even a tenth, of his net worth is at stake.

Ultimately, though, it may also be necessary to level the playing field for nomination of directors to remove control by the CEO to ensure genuine independence. Even then, the dangers of co-option through control of the information and agenda mean that eternal vigilance by each individual and regular board-wide self-evaluation will be required.

---

# Case in point: Compaq and Salomon Inc.

See the Ben Rosen/Compaq case in point in chapter 2.

*Would the chairman of Compaq, Ben Rosen, have acted so promptly if he did not have a $40 million investment in the company?*

A CEO of Wall Street securities house Salomon Inc. described that company's criteria for board membership. The first such criterion was: "Be owner oriented – usually best demonstrated by an investment in Salomon's stock that is significant in relation to the individual's net worth."[92]

---

## Involvement by the federal government

Ira Millstein and John C. Whitehead, co-chairs of the blue-ribbon Committee on Improving the Effectiveness of Corporate Audit Committees, proposed that Congress enact legislation to:

1. create and federally fund a Corporate Governance Conduct Board (or some such denominated entity):
   (a) with a chairman selected by the SEC, with the consent of the Senate, who is charged with selecting eight other members in consultation with the SEC
   (b) members of which would be representative of the corporate governance constituency: shareholders, corporate directors, corporate management, investment banks and institutions, the New York Stock Exchange and NASDAQ
   (c) charged with developing, through outreach and discussion, issuing and updating, as appropriate, a voluntary corporate governance code of conduct ("the Code")
2. direct (and, if necessary, empower) the SEC to require that reporting companies disclose on an annual basis whether they comply with each element of the voluntary code and explain any areas of non-compliance ("comply or explain"), and
3. direct the Corporate Governance Conduct Board and the SEC to regularly survey and report to Congress and the public on the degree of compliance.

## Involvement by shareholders

Whether it is the Exxon Committee or a Lens-like special-purpose monitoring organization, there are a number of proposals for shareholders to assert and exercise control over the selection and ordering of priorities of the board through some kind of collective action vehicle.[93] One such vehicle is the shareholder committee described in chapter 2. As we emphasized there, "*The mere fact that the directors will know that they have been chosen by investors should make them more responsive to shareholder concerns.*"[94]

# THE SARBANES–OXLEY LEGISLATION

The U.S. Congress, under enormous pressure to respond to the domino-like toppling of American corporations amid allegations of corruption of unprecedented scope, adopted the Sarbanes–Oxley (S–Ox) legislation in 2002. It was named for its sponsors in the House and Senate. Originally, just after the Enron bankruptcy filing, it appeared that the less pre-scriptive House version proposed by Congressman Michael Oxley (R–Ohio) would be passed. But when other companies followed, especially Tyco, with the details of the CEO's use of shareholder funds to finance a lifestyle of pasha-like opulence, and WorldCom, with its allegations of accounting fraud at the most basic level (see case studies), the stricter Senate version sponsored by Senator Paul Sarbanes (D–Maryland) gained momentum. Its most significant provisions include:

1.  Attestation: chief executives and chief financial officers must personally attest that the company's financial reports meet securities law requirements.
2.  Real-time disclosure of material events.
3.  Stricter independence standards for board audit committee members and for auditors, including a requirement for regular rotation of audit partners (but not, as some re-formers urged, of audit firms).
4.  Prohibition of loans to employees and executives.
5.  Increased criminal and civil liability for securities violations.
6.  Obligation of counsel to report violations (the interpretation of this provision is, at this writing, still a matter of some concern, given the privilege of attorney–client communication).
7.  The creation of a private/public entity to oversee the accounting profession.

S–Ox was very much the result of political expedience and uneasy compromise, hardly the ingredients for thoughtful public policy. Even long, thoughtful consideration, how-ever, would have been unlikely to make much of a difference. As already noted in the section above on the "Delaware Factor," by history and policy, corporate governance in the United States is still the province of state law, with the federal government's role very limited and mostly concerned with disclosure and process rather than substance. In effect, that means that the legislature of Delaware, the second-smallest state, sets the rules for the majority of public corporations and their directors, officers, and shareholders. This has been a good situation for corporations, who trade filing fees and tax money for highly protect-ive laws and judicial rulings. It has not been as good for shareholders, but since most of them do not live in Delaware, they have had no recourse.

While S–Ox does present the greatest incursion ever into the state control of corpor-ate governance, it still just nibbles at it around the edges. For example, it does not add anything new to say that audit committees have the right to select the auditors and to retain consultants; it is merely a reminder of rights they already had under state law.

Then there are "locking the barn door" provisions – new requirements that would prob-ably have become standard practice through market demand. These include the "attestation" provision (requiring executives to "attest" that they have read and believe the numbers in the financial reports), the requirement of auditor rotation, the reduction of organizational and incentive compensation conflicts of interest for security analysts (this was further resolved in the settlement of litigation brought by New York State Attorney General Eliot Spitzer, the SEC, and the Justice Department against the Wall Street firms), and the prohibition of auditor consulting services.

Some reforms are so over-broad that they almost qualify as shrill. The prohibition of loans to executives is so broadly drafted that there is concern it may even preclude travel advances in some cases. The "noisy withdrawal" requirement that attorneys who resign due to concerns about violation of securities rules must make a public disclosure of the basis for their withdrawal may be counter-productive. Corporate officers could become more reluctant to consult counsel in sensitive situations if they believe that the traditional attorney–client privilege has been curtailed and that they might be subjected to disclosure without their participation and permission. It is not certain that going from a two-year sentencing guideline in prison for low-level securities fraud a few years ago to a 15-year one now is particularly beneficial.

Potentially, the most significant and far-reaching provision of S–Ox is the creation of the Public Accounting Oversight Board, the first independently funded authority with the ability not just to set but also to enforce standards on the accounting and auditing professions. However, it is just getting started (with some sense of irony, it has moved into the office space vacated by the now closed Arthur Andersen). Its import and effect will not be known for years.

The key point to remember about S–Ox is that under it, the role for regulation by government or by the quasi-governmental self-regulatory organizations is really quite limited. The corporate abuses of Enron, Global Crossing, WorldCom, Tyco, and the others were primarily a market problem and the role of the government should be to remove impediments to market-like conflicts of interest and then let the market do what it does best – respond to information with precision and efficiency. That is why the most significant change has been, appropriately, on the market side. The primary impact of S–Ox in the first year after it was enacted was the all but instant appearance of literally dozens of firms, seminars, consultants, and publications, all providing assurances that they will solve – for a healthy fee – all worries associated with S–Ox compliance. But even full compliance with S–Ox, with or without the help of outsiders, is likely to have more form than substance.

The S–Ox requirements will take time to implement and understand, so it would be unfair to make any attempt to measure their effectiveness at this point. But it is likely that the response from the market in recognizing and evaluating what is now understood to be "governance risk" will surpass the impact of the legislation.

## NOTES

1.  Adam Smith, *The Wealth of Nations* (New York: Random House, 1937), pp. 699–700.
2.  For more on the governance of SUM, see Stanley C. Vance, *Corporate Leadership: Boards, Directors, and Strategy* (McGraw-Hill, New York, 1983), pp. 3–6.
3.  Korn/Ferry International, *Boards of Directors, Twentieth Annual Study* (1993).
4.  Delaware General Corporation Law Annotated Franchise Tax Law Uniform Limited Partnership Act. As of Feb. 2, 1988.
5.  The Business Roundtable, *Corporate Governance and American Competitiveness*, Mar. 1990, p. 7.
6.  American Law Institute, *Principles of Corporate Governance: Analysis and Recommendation*, Draft 2, 1984, pp. 66–7.
7.  Wayne Mart, "Do Independent Outside Directors Improve Corporate Performance?", research paper, Clemson University, College of Commerce and Industry, July 1991, p. 1.

8. Attorney Ira M. Millstein of Weil, Gotschal & Manges in New York, says that, in addition to hiring, monitoring, and firing CEOs, directors are there to "certify" them. This means that when corporate performance *suffers*, directors need to judge whether this is because of or despite CEO performance. If it is the former, they must replace the CEO. If it is the latter, they can provide support in the form of "certification." See Ira M. Millstein, "The Evolution of the Certifying Board," *The Business Lawyer*, 48, 4 (Aug. 1993), pp. 1485–97. Also see "Corporate Governance Headed in the Right Direction," *Director's Monthly*, 18, 1 (Jan. 1994), p. 1. Note, however, that the ability to make this distinction requires a level of independence and commitment from directors that has been difficult to find in the past, as the examples in this chapter show.

9. John Harvey Jones, *Making It Happen* (Collins, London, 1988), p. 147. For more on ICI, see the case in point in chapter 1.

10. Hugh Parker, "The Company Chairman – His Role and Responsibilities," *Long Range Planning*, 23, 4, 1990, pp. 35–43.

11. Peter Drucker, "The Bored Board," in *Toward the Next Economics and Other Essays* (Harper & Row, New York, 1981), p. 110.

12. "The Governance of Oozcskblnya," CII Central, Newsletter for Members of the Council of Institutional Investors, 6, 8 (Aug. 1993).

13. Bryan Burrough and John Helyar, *Barbarians at the Gate* (Harper & Row, New York, 1990), p. 75.

14. Bryan Burrough and John Helyar, "RJR Nabisco Board Asserts Independence in Buy Out Decisions," *Wall Street Journal*, Nov. 10, 1988, p. A1.

15. Joann S. Lublin, "More Chief Executives are being Forced Out by Tougher Boards," *Wall Street Journal*, June 6, 1991, p. A1.

16. Suein L. Hwang, "Fired Tambrands CEO was Unusually Close to a Consulting Firm," *Wall Street Journal*, Aug. 23, 1993, p. A1.

17. Ibid.

18. Ibid.

19. Ibid.

20. Ada Demb and F. Friedrich Neubauer, *The Corporate Board: Confronting the Paradoxes* (Oxford University Press, Oxford, 1992), pp. 70, 97.

21. Walter Salmon, "Crisis Prevention: How To Gear Up Your Board," *Harvard Business Review*, Jan.–Feb. 1993, p. 69.

22. Robert K. Mueller, *Building a Power Partnership: CEOs and their Boards of Directors* (Amacom, New York, 1993). Of Mueller's 17 books, nine have concerned boards.

23. Bernard Marcus, "How Directors Mind the Store at Home Depot," *Directorship Magazine*, 17, 10 (Oct. 1992), p. 1.

24. The Corporate Library's Board Analyst Database, 2003.

25. Ibid.

26. Egon Zehnder International, *Corporate Issues Monitor*, USA, IV, 1 (1989).

27. See also the 1992 NACD survey, supra, for a similar result.

28. P.L. Rechner and D.R. Dalton, "CEO Duality and Organizational Performance: A Longitudinal Analysis," *Strategic Management Journal*, 12, 1991, pp. 155–60.

29. Hugh Parker, *The Company Chairman: His Role and Responsibility* (Pergamon Press, Oxford, 1990).

30. The figure is bigger for larger companies. In 1994, Boardroom Consultants of New York found that 38.6 percent of the 300 largest public companies retained the former CEO as a board member. However, that figure was down from previous years. See Marlene Givant Star, "Few CEOs Stay with the Board," *Pensions and Investments*, Jan. 24, 1994, p. 11.

31. Howard D. Sherman, "Catch 22: The Retired CEO as Company Director," Institutional Shareholder Services, July 15, 1991.

32. Korn/Ferry Organizational Consulting, "Reinventing Corporate Governance: Directors Prepare for the 21st Century. Results of *Fortune* Company Directors," Jan. 1993.
33. Dale Hanson, Hearing before the Subcommittee on Telecommunications and Finance of the Committee on Energy and Commerce, House of Representatives, Aug. 2, 1989.
34. Graef Crystal, *In Search of Excess* (W.W. Norton, New York, 1991), p. 229.
35. Lawrence Tucker, *Investor's Business Daily*, July 7, 1993, Finance, p. 4.
36. Korn/Ferry International, 1989 annual study of boards. The study found the following make-up at billion-dollar companies: 86 percent included at least one CEO/COO of another company, and 74 percent included at least one retired executive from another company.
37. The interlocking compensation committee practice may not be widespread, but it is common enough to have prompted a new SEC disclosure requirement in 1992. The amendments to executive compensation disclosure mentioned earlier include a requirement that companies disclose compensation committee interlocks.
38. Alison Leigh Cowan, "Board Room Back Scratching?", *New York Times*, June 2, 1993, p. D1.
39. Louis Brandeis, Pujo Committee: House Committee on Banking and Currency, "Investigation of Concentration of Control of Money and Credit," House Report No. 1593, Feb. 28, 1913.
40. Martin Lipton and Jay W. Lorsch, "A Modest Proposal for Improved Corporate Governance," *The Business Lawyer*, 48, 1, Nov. 1992, p. 64.
41. Korn/Ferry Organizational Consulting, "Reinventing Corporate Governance."
42. Kathleen Day, "Frank Carlucci and the Corporate Whirl," *Washington Post*, Feb. 7, 1993, p. H1.
43. See <http://www.thecorporatelibrary.com>.
44. See Egon Zehnder International, *Corporate Issues Monitor* USA, IV, 1 (1989).
45. Ibid.
46. Dana Wechlser and Nancy Rotenier, "Goodbye to Berle & Means," *Forbes*, Jan. 3, 1993, p. 100.
47. Barbara Lyne, "The Executive Life," *New York Times*, Jan. 2, 1992.
48. Ira M. Millstein and Winthrop Knowlton, "Can the Board of Directors Help the American Corporation Earn the Immortality it Holds So Dear? An Examination of our System of Corporate Governance with Recommendations for Change," research paper, Center for Business and Government, John F. Kennedy School of Government, Harvard University, Jan. 1988.
49. Ibid.
50. Stanley C. Vance, *Corporate Leadership: Boards, Directors and Strategy* (McGraw-Hill, New York, 1983), p. 50.
51. Korn/Ferry International, Board of Directors Twentieth Annual Study, 1993. According to Vance, *Corporate Leadership*, a sampling of over 1,000 directors in 1963 found that 59.3 percent were insiders.
52. Spencer Stuart Board Index, 1991.
53. Ibid.
54. Spencer Stuart Board Index, 1993.
55. See, for example, Elmer W. Johnson, "An Insider's Call for Outside Direction," *Harvard Business Review*, Mar.–Apr. 1990, pp. 46–55; Sir Adrian Cadbury, *The Company Chairman* (Fitzwilliam, London, 1990).
56. Arthur Fleischer, Geoffrey C. Hazard, and Miriam Z. Kipper, *Board Games* (Little, Brown, Boston, 1988), p. 3.
57. Millstein and Knowlton, "Can the Board of Directors Help the American Corporation?".
58. Testimony of Benjamin M. Rosen before the Subcommittee on Telecommunications and Finance, Committee on Energy and Commerce, United States House of Representatives, Apr. 21, 1993.

59.  Edward J. Epstein, "Who Owns the Corporation?", a Twentieth Century Fund Paper (Priority Press, New York, 1986), p. 13.
60.  Spencer Stuart Board Index, 1991.
61.  Securities and Exchange Commission, "Shark Repellents and Stock Prices: The Effects of Antitakeover Amendments since 1980," Office of the Chief Economist, Washington, DC, July 1985, p. 5.
62.  See the resolution sponsored by John J. Gilbert at the Sears, Roebuck & Co. annual meeting, 1993.
63.  See Dale Hanson's testimony to the Subcommittee on Telecommunications and Finance of the Committee on Energy and Commerce, House of Representatives, Aug. 2, 1989. Hanson testified that, following a CalPERS-sponsored shareholder resolution at USAir, "The representative from USAir said, 'Gee, you guys had us worried. We had to call many shareholders back 3 or 4 times to get them to change the vote because it looked like you were going to win.'"
64.  See the "Avon Letter," US Department of Labor, Feb. 23, 1988: "Finally the Department notes that section 404(a)(1)(B) requires the named fiduciary appointing the investment manager to periodically monitor the activities of the investment manager with respect to the management of plan assets. In general, this duty would encompass the monitoring of decisions made and actions taken by investment managers with regard to proxy voting."
65.  Bayless Manning, "The Shareholder Appraisal Remedy: An Essay for Frank Coker," 72 *Yale Law Journal*, 223, 245 (1962).
66.  *Norlin Corp. v. Rooney, Pace Inc.*, 744 F.2d 255 (2d Cir. 1984), applying New York law. See also discussion of the use of ESOPs to defend against takeovers at the end of this chapter.
67.  *Smith v. Van Gorkom* 488 A.2d 858 (Del. 1985). For a summary of *Van Gorkom* and other landmark legal case summaries, see Stanley Foster Reed and Alexandra Reed Lajoux, *The Art of M&A: A Merger/Acquisition/Buyout Guide* (Business One Irwin, 1995), pp. 805–23.
68.  Ibid., p. 869.
69.  *Unocal Corp. v. Mesa Petroleum Co.*, 493 A.2d 946 (Del. 1985).
70.  Ibid., p. 956.
71.  For a discussion of "poison pills" see later in this chapter.
72.  *Revlon, Inc. v. MacAndrews & Forbes Holdings, Inc.*, 506 A.2d 173, 181 (Del. 1986).
73.  Ibid., p. 182.
74.  Ibid.
75.  For a definition of "white knights" see later in this chapter.
76.  Ibid., p. 184.
77.  506 A.2d 173, 182 (Del. 1986).
78.  See, for example: Analysis Group, Inc., "The Effects of Poison Pills on Shareholders: A Synthesis of Recent Evidence," Belmont, MA, Nov. 4, 1988; Office of the Chief Economist, Securities and Exchange Commission, "The Economics of Poison Pills," Mar. 5, 1986; Office of the Chief Economist, Securities and Exchange Commission, "The Effects of Poison Pills on the Wealth of Target Shareholders," Oct. 26, 1986; Michael Ryngaert, "The Effect of Poison Pill Securities on Shareholder Wealth," *Journal of Financial Economics*, 20 (1988), pp. 377–417; Nancy Sheridan, "Impact of Stockholder Rights Plan on Stock Price," Kidder, Peabody & Co., New York, June 15, 1986; Richard Wines, "Poison Pill Impact Study," Georgeson & Co., New York, Mar. 31, 1988; and Richard Wines "Poison Pill Impact Study II," Georgeson & Co., New York, Oct. 31, 1988.
79.  Note, however, that in Jan. 1994, Time Warner reinstated the poison pill that it had eliminated three years previously. The company brought back the pill after Seagram, the Canadian spirits company, purchased over 11 percent of Time Warner on the open

market. Time Warner defended the reinstatement of the pill, saying it wished to prevent Seagram exercising "creeping control" over the company. See Laura Landro and Eben Shapiro, "Time Warner Protects Itself Against Seagram," *Wall Street Journal*, Jan. 21, 1994, p. A3.

80. At Hartmarx, a majority of shareholders voted to redeem a poison pill two years in a row, but the company still refused to do so.
81. Michael Ryngaert, "The Effect of Poison Pill Securities on Shareholder Wealth," *Journal of Financial Economics*, 20 (1988).
82. Robert Slater, *The Titans of Takeover* (Prentice-Hall, Englewood Cliffs, NJ, 1987), p. 155.
83. See Robert Comment and G. William Schwert, "Poison or Placebo? Evidence on the Deterrent and Wealth Effects of Modern Anti-Takeover Measures," Bradley Policy Research Center, William E. Simon Graduate School of Business Administration, University of Rochester, Mar. 11, 1993. Their figures show that takeover activity tripled between 1975 and 1988, but that by 1990 takeover rates were back to 1975 levels. However, in 1993, a very 1980s-style takeover battle developed as Paramount Communications Inc. was forced to auction itself following a friendly offer from Viacom Inc., and a competing, hostile offer from QVC Inc.
84. Support for independent directors as a legitimating force comes from other sources as well. The controversial one-share, one-vote proposal submitted for SEC approval by AMEX in 1976 provides that dual-class recapitalizations through exchange offers (which can be coercive) will only be permitted if one-third of the directors are independent, or if holders of low-voting stock have the exclusive right to elect 25 percent of the directors.
85. Sears, Roebuck & Co. 1992 proxy statement, pp. 16–17.
86. Editorial Roundtable, "Chair and CEO: Should the Jobs be Split?" *The Corporate Governance Advisor*, Apr.–May 1993.
87. Judith H. Dobrzynski, "Chairman and CEO: One Hat Too Many," *Business Week*, Nov. 18, 1991, p. 124.
88. Ibid.
89. Ronald J. Gilson and Reinier Kraakman, "Reinventing the Outside Director: An Agenda for Institutional Investors," presented at the Salomon Brothers Center and Rutgers Centers Conference on *The Fiduciary Responsibilities of Institutional Investors*, June 14–15, 1990.
90. Joseph A. Grundfest, "Just Vote No: A Minimalist Strategy for Dealing with Barbarians Inside the Gates," 45 *Stanford Law Review*, 4, Apr. 1993.
91. H. Brewster Atwater, Senate Testimony, Subcommittee on Securities, Oct. 17, 1991.
92. Robert E. Denham, "Envisioning New Relationships Between Corporations and Intelligent Investors," speech to the Institutional Investor Project of the Columbia University School of Law conference on "Relational Investing," May 7, 1993.
93. George W. Dent Jr., "Toward Unifying Ownership and Control in the Public Corporation," *Wisconsin Law Review*, 5, 1989, p. 881.
94. Ibid., p. 908, emphasis added.

# 4
# MANAGEMENT: PERFORMANCE

In 2002, a cartoon by Mark Magee had a mother trying to break up a fight between two children. "Mommy!" one of them said, in tears, "Billy just called me a CEO!"

A year earlier, CEOs were up there with rock stars as figures of glamour and magic. For decades, *Time* magazine's men of the year were figures from politics and international affairs. In the 1990s, however, three were from business: CNN's Ted Turner, Intel's Andy Grove and Amazon.com's Jeff Bezos. When longtime General Electric CEO Jack Welch retired, he was lauded as the greatest business leader of the twentieth century.

But by the end of 2002 the CEOs with household names were the ones audiences watched refusing to testify before Congress. And Welch is known for his messy divorce and his post-retirement goodies.

CEOs like to think of themselves as leaders who communicate and inspire. But the business community has shown little leadership when it comes to speaking out on the failures at Tyco, WorldCom, Enron, Qwest, Adelphia and Global Crossing. Mismanagement at those companies cost investors hundreds of billions of dollars and thousands of employees their jobs. Business leaders blame the victims by describing the declining market as a crisis of investor confidence when it is more accurately a crisis of management credibility.

The 1990s saw one of the greatest wealth transfers in history, as CEO pay skyrocketed both in absolute terms and as a multiple of what the average worker took home. The average CEO makes 411 times more than the average worker. If the minimum wage had risen at the same rate as executive pay since 1990, it would be $21.41 an hour as opposed to $5.15. CEOs reaped windfall profits from mega-grants of stock options, made possible in part by accounting quirks that did not require the value of the options to be subtracted from the balance sheet at the time of the award. CEOs also overdid the perks. Investors and employees believe that executives who are paid tens of millions of dollars should pay for their own cars and plane tickets.

In the 1990s, the cult of the CEO was based on the idea that vision and the ability to inspire were what made the CEOs worth the hundreds of millions of dollars they were paid. But a book by Harvard Business School professor Rakesh Khurana, *Searching for a Corporate Savior: The Irrational Quest for Charismatic CEOs*, makes a compelling case that corporate boards err seriously when they pick chief executives based on "leadership" and "vision." Bringing in a CEO with a great record at another company may give the stock price a short-term boost. But with high-profile transplants such as Al Dunlap at Sunbeam (now in bankruptcy) and Gary Wendt at Conseco (now in bankruptcy), CEOs should have to make the same disclaimers that money managers do: "Past performance is no guarantee of future performance."

Corporate board meetings are more often pep rallies than meaningful exchanges. In almost all companies, the CEO also acts as chairman, setting the agenda and determining the quantity, quality, and timing of the information. There have been encouraging reports that boards are asking more questions and insisting on meeting without management present. But there also have been discouraging reports that CEOs are responding by drowning board members in the minutiae of the financial reports. The board is supposed to pay attention to the big picture. It may be time to adopt the British approach and have an independent outside director serve as the chairman to keep the board focused on the forest, not the bark.

CEOs have also not set a good example of responsible shareholdership. The largest investors in the world are America's corporate pension plans. The trustees of those plans are the very CEOs who run public companies. CEOs entrust their employees' retirement money to fund managers who have too often neglected early signs of problems at companies such as Global Crossing and Enron because they were dazzled by short-term returns. CEOs should have made sure that, before fund managers invest employee retirement money in the stock of a company, they look carefully at its corporate-governance practices. While they hold the stock, CEOs should have insisted that fund managers continue to monitor the boards of the companies they invest in on behalf of America's working families.

Management of the modern corporation involves a series of Herculean challenges. Many of the corporate governance issues concerning corporate management have been raised earlier, in the discussions of the corporation, the role of shareholders, and the CEO's relationship with directors. In this section, we will examine some of these issues from the perspective of management.

In January 1993, a *Fortune* magazine cover story had a provocative headline echoing the Declaration of Independence: "The King is Dead." It went on: "Booted bosses, ornery owners, and beefed-up boards reflect a historic shift in corporate power. The imperial CEO has had his day – long live the shareholders." The article ran down a list of deposed CEOs, 13 from the Fortune 500 in just 18 months. How did this happen? Veteran journalist Thomas Stewart saw the events in Shakespearean terms:

> And in the encircling tents, their armor glittering, their coffers brimming with gold, the Bolingbrokes of the piece: institutional investors, activist shareholders, and even the boards of directors themselves, the king's own court, to whom he gave preferment, now demanding his obeisance – if not his head . . . What's manifest here is large, basic, and historic.[1]

Stewart explained where the idea of the "CEO-King" began:

> The passing of generations had attenuated the power of founding families, (noted Adolf Berle and Gardiner Means), while the rise of the public corporation had spread ownership among tens of thousands of individual share-holders, none of whom could cast a meaningful vote in the governance of their companies. The result, Berle and Means showed, was a new class of professional managers who owned little of the corporation they nevertheless controlled. The merest whim of the imperial executive echoed like thunder down a valley. The CEO has to be careful, ran an old joke at General Electric; if he asks for a cup of coffee, somebody might run out and buy Brazil.[2]

But Stewart went on to say that, "paradoxically, executive leadership is becoming more indispensable than ever. Only the executive can mediate among the multitude of constituencies vying to influence every corporation: investors and lenders, communities, employees (who may be big investors), customers. The CEO may be on a shorter leash, but he's a more valuable dog."[3] Harvard's John Pound predicted that in the future CEOs will be more like politicians than monarchs, negotiating agreement with all of the different parts of the corporate constituency. Long-time counsel to CEOs and directors Ira Millstein advises CEOs to adjust to a more consensus-based corporate governance structure. He wrote, in an article addressed to CEOs, "I ask you . . . to determine to what extent the board procedures at your companies encourage independence and hence suggest credibility. After all, if you don't, shareholders, plaintiffs, and the government may."[4]

In any relationship, especially one as intertwined as that of the CEO, board, and shareholders, any change in one party has an impact on the others. As shareholders and directors have become more active, the imperial CEO in the General Electric joke has begun to seem like a quaint cartoon figure.

But it was only a very short time ago that CEOs (and their lawyers) were quite comfortable with the idea that the CEO was, if not a king, then a benevolent dictator. Just three years before the "King is Dead" cover story, *Fortune* magazine ran a cover story about the "Pharaonic CEO," noting: "Pharaoh in all his glory would have envied today's CEOs their perquisites and ever-sweetening pay. Too busy living the cosseted life, America's managerial elite have lost touch with the humble employee. Workers' faith in top management is collapsing. CEOs who don't come down from the heights are in for trouble."[5] The article predicted that CEOs could not expect the support of employees who consider them out of touch. "Hourly workers and supervisors indeed agree that 'we're all in this together,' but what 'we're in' turns out to be a frame of mind that mistrusts senior management's intentions, doubts its competence, and resents its self-congratulatory pay."

Interestingly, the insistence on change came not from employees, but from elements never mentioned in the article: the shareholders and the board. The CEOs of the early twenty-first century may resemble the pharaonic model in some respects, particularly in the level of pay. But the "King is Dead" syndrome still prevails. A 1998 report by Tom Neff and Dayton Ogden of consulting and search firm Spencer Stuart identified "several trends that make the job of today's CEO more like 'The Perils of Pauline' than the 'Triumph of Succession.' The principal pressure comes from a demand for performance and board control of succession. Independent directors have made a CEO's seat much less secure and open to external benchmarking – not just within the industry where a company competes, but across industries." In addition, they noted the impact of mergers and acquisitions, pressure to perform, and another kind of pressure – from potential successors – as factors in reducing tenure. They found that 60 percent of the CEOs in the Fortune 200 served only five years or less.

Still, the idea of the CEO as benevolent dictator has some support. In a 2002 speech at the Stern School of Business, Federal Reserve chairman Alan Greenspan said that "it has increasingly fallen to corporate officers, especially the chief executive officer, to guide the business, hopefully in what he or she perceives to be in the best interest of shareholders." He admits that there is no such thing as an "independent" director, as long as management decides who gets to be on the board. What if the CEO doesn't pay enough attention to shareholder value? Greenspan is sanguine. "When companies do run into trouble, the *carte blanche* granted CEOs by shareholders is withdrawn." He is content to rely on "existing shareholders or successful hostile bidders." But there is an inconsistency in his position, because he then says that only a handful of investors have the capacity to make these judgments.

And, as noted in chapter 3, Rakesh Khurana's *Searching for a Corporate Savior* documents the mistakes made by boards of directors in selecting "superstar" CEOs who can dazzle the analysts and investors, but who may not have what it takes to run a company. Khurana makes it clear that the top priority should be managerial skills, not "leadership." Indeed, the kind of show-boating that leads to magazine covers and paying for sports stadiums should be a sell signal, or even an indicator to go short.

## WHAT DO WE WANT FROM THE CEO?

The one certainty in business, as in life, is change. If it were possible, we all – investors, lenders, communities, employees, and customers – would want a CEO who could predict the future and guide the company accordingly. Since that is impossible, what we want is a CEO who is able, by virtue of ability, expertise, resources, motivation, and authority, to keep the company not just ready for change but ready to benefit from changes, ideally to lead them. The CEO must be powerful enough to do the job, but accountable enough to make sure it is done correctly. The challenge for all of the participants in corporate governance is to make sure that there is enough of a balance between the two so that, overall, the decisions made by the CEO are in the long-term interests of the shareholders (and thus by definition all other constituencies) rather than in his own interests.

One of the key areas for achieving and evaluating this balance is executive compensation, discussed later in this chapter. The essential conflict between the goals of shareholders and management is not over the amount of pay but over its variability and risk. Shareholders want a compensation plan with maximum variability based on corporate performance, and management's natural tendency is to want a compensation plan with maximum security. Before we can understand how to best link management compensation to corporate performance, however, we must take a look at how we measure corporate performance.

All methods of evaluating a company's value and performance are useful for evaluating the CEO. But perhaps one of the clearest indications of CEO quality is the structure of the organization itself. In general, the more diversified and conglomerated the company, the more likely it is to reflect the CEO's empire-building and the less likely it is to demonstrate focus and commitment to shareholder value (see the Sears and American Express case studies). As one management consultant put it, "The design trick is to be small where small is beautiful and then be big where big is beautiful."[6]

## Cases in point: AT&T and NCR

In the years after the end of the go-go years of the takeover era, there was only one genuinely hostile takeover, and it was not by a raider like Carl Icahn or Donald Trump; it was AT&T's purchase of NCR. When NCR, a very entrepreneurial enterprise, made the classic argument of the target, that its special culture

and constituencies required its independence (indeed, it was a pioneer of the constituency concept), it fell on deaf ears, ironically the ears of a board of directors that included several CEO veterans who had fought off their would-be hostile acquirers, characterizing them as all but in league with the devil. Under their direction, AT&T, the giant bureaucracy, was willing to go forward at (literally) almost any cost. And the shareholders were hard pressed to refuse. "As a stockholder, I have to say, 'Take the money and run . . .' It's a major premium on the market by a qualified buyer. I don't see how they can say 'no.'"[7]
The acquisition was a disaster, destroying almost all of the value of NCR.

*What was the logic of this deal? Why would an AT&T want an NCR? Why would an NCR resist? Keep in mind that such deals are generally supported by advice from lawyers and investment bankers who receive fees from the company, and evaluation by directors who have every reason to support management (and who get some satisfaction from presiding over an empire), and shareholders who say "take the money and run." So who is going to stop the bad deals and develop the good ones? More recent examples of disastrous acquisitions include Snapple at Quaker, the Learning Company at Mattel, and Telerate at Dow Jones. What happened to the CEOs who made these acquisitions?*

If, as one thoughtful consultant argues, in order to master change, the primary requirement for organizational health over the long term is a continual sense of renewal, then what investors and other corporate constituents most want from the CEO is someone who will create a "culture of questions."

If you look at the history of companies, there's an irony in that, the more successful they become, the more convinced they become of their knowledge and the rightness of their view of the world, and the more arrogant and insular they become. Whatever helped them become successful in the past becomes institutionalized. The more successful, the more institutionalized, and the more this is a danger. It's not surprising that the problems at GM or IBM or Sears developed while the companies were clearly their industry leaders.[8]

## THE BIGGEST CHALLENGE

Unquestionably, the biggest challenge a company faces is not failure, but success. If we look at the most spectacular meltdowns of the last thirty years, all were at one time almost as spectacular successes. The giants of the 1960s – Xerox, Kodak, Sears, Waste Management, General Motors, and others – became the problems of the 1980s and 1990s. Enron, Tyco, Global Crossing, Qwest, Adelphia, WorldCom, and others that set records in the 1990s saw their names become synonyms for corruption and mismanagement in the early years of the twenty-first century. When a company is failing, it will try almost anything. But when a company is successful, it generally does not know why it is successful, and so, like an athlete on a lucky streak who won't change his socks, it will fall into an almost superstitious pattern of not changing anything. See the General Motors and Sears case studies for more details.

# Cases in point: Exxon, AT&T, and General Electric

**Exxon**. The world market for oil has been such that Exxon has not been required to alter radically its strategy to stay ahead. Exxon, unlike Sears, IBM, or General Motors, has not been the victim of a dramatically shifting marketplace – yet. But it has been affected by consolidation in the industry, which included the BP–Amoco merger; the refining and marketing consolidation of Shell, Texaco and Star; Tosco's acquisition of Unocal's California refineries; Ultramar Diamond Shamrock's acquisition of Total's refining and marketing operations; and the Marathon–Ashland consolidation. Exxon merged with former rival Mobil in 1999.

**AT&T**. Ironically, AT&T has survived because, unlike IBM, it lost an antitrust case and was required to break itself up into seven "Baby Bell" companies. The breakup forced a rigorous redefinition of the company's mission. IBM, by contrast, emerged from the antitrust suit victorious, but floundered as a result of its failure to undertake just such a review.[9] Exxon, of course, had its own experience with antitrust a century earlier, and there is some irony in the merger with Mobil, the reuniting of two of the divisions split up by one of the first major antitrust enforcement actions.

Similarly, the "Baby Bells" are coming together again in a reverse Balkanization. It will be interesting to see which direction Microsoft takes following the resolution of its antitrust suit.

**General Electric**. In 1980, General Electric (GE) was a huge and sprawling conglomerate, though in rock-solid financial condition – AAA bond rating, and a handsome 19.5 percent return on equity.[10] The company was the eleventh largest corporation in *Fortune*'s list of the most highly valued companies in the US. In December 1980, the company announced the appointment of a new CEO and chairman, John (known as Jack) F. Welch. Welch did not believe that GE's respectable results reflected the true value that the company could generate. Over the succeeding decades he shook up the conglomerate from top to bottom. It is arguable whether, without him, GE would still feature in *Fortune*'s list of the world's largest companies.

Welch insisted that each of GE's divisions be the number 1 or number 2 business of its kind in the world. Any business that failed to meet this test would be sold. Over the next decade, GE sold or closed almost $10 billion-worth of businesses and product lines, and over $18 billion was spent on acquiring further businesses to boost those that remained. Notable acquisitions included Kidder Peabody in 1986 to join GE Financial Services, and NBC to join GE's broadcasting operations.

But Welch was not satisfied with merely buying and selling businesses. His aim was to drive change through every part of GE's massive operation. He wanted the company to be as lean and responsive as the smallest startup. Partly, he did this by downsizing the company, and stretching middle management to the limit. Welch's notion was that, if employees were overworked, they would spend less time in committee meetings or on other bureaucratic procedures that inhibited the company's ability to respond.[11] The effects of these changes were far-reaching – GE shed over 100,000 employees through the 1980s. While Welch was criticized for these cuts, and while many managers complained that the changes undermined security and loyalty, evidence of their worth was made plain in ever-improving financial results.

20 largest companies worldwide, by stock market valuation, in billions

| 1972 | | 1982 | | 1992 | | 2000 | |
|---|---|---|---|---|---|---|---|
| 1 IBM | 46.8 | 1 IBM | 57 | 1 Exxon | 75.8 | 1 General Electric | 520.25 |
| 2 AT&T | 29.2 | 2 AT&T | 52.2 | 2 General Electric | 73.9 | 2 Intel | 416.71 |
| 3 Eastman Kodak | 23.9 | 3 Exxon | 25.7 | 3 Wal-Mart | 73.5 | 3 Cisco Systems | 395.01 |
| 4 General Motors | 23.2 | 4 General Electric | 21.6 | 4 Royal Dutch/Shell | 71.8 | 4 Microsoft | 322.82 |
| 5 Exxon | 19.6 | 5 General Motors | 19 | 5 Nippon Tel. & Tel. | 71.4 | 5 Exxon Mobil | 289.92 |
| 6 Sears Roebuck | 18.2 | 6 Royal Dutch/Shell | 16.9 | 6 Philip Morris | 69.3 | 6 Vodafone Airtouch | 277.95 |
| 7 General Electric | 13.3 | 7 Eastman Kodak | 14.2 | 7 AT&T | 68 | 7 Wal-Mart Stores | 256.66 |
| 8 Xerox | 11.8 | 8 Schlumberger | 13.4 | 8 Coca-Cola | 55.7 | 8 NTT Docomo | 247.24 |
| 9 Texaco | 10.2 | 9 Toyota Motor | 12.6 | 9 Mitsubishi Bank | 53.5 | 9 Nokia | 242.19 |
| 10 Minnesota Mining & Mfg. | 9.7 | 10 Amoco | 11.7 | 10 Merck | 50.3 | 10 Royal Dutch/Shell | 213.54 |
| 11 Procter & Gamble | 9.1 | 11 Chevron | 10.9 | 11 Indus. Bank of Japan | 46.5 | 11 Citigroup | 209.86 |
| 12 Royal Dutch/Shell | 9.1 | 12 Mobil | 10.7 | 12 Sumitomo Bank | 45.6 | 12 BP Amoco | 207.51 |
| 13 Coca-Cola | 8.9 | 13 Sears Roebuck | 10.3 | 13 Toyota Motor | 44.1 | 13 Oracle | 204.01 |
| 14 Dupont | 8.4 | 14 Atlantic Richfield | 10.2 | 14 Fuji Bank | 41.8 | 14 IBM | 192.49 |
| 15 Ford Motor | 8 | 15 Hitachi | 9.9 | 15 Daiichi Kangyo Bank | 41.8 | 15 Nippon Telegraph & Telephone | 189.16 |
| 16 Avon Products | 7.9 | 16 Procter & Gamble | 9.8 | 16 Sanwa Bank | 37.9 | 16 Deutsche Telekom | 187.25 |
| 17 Mobil | 7.5 | 17 Matushita Electric Ind. | 9.6 | 17 British Telecom. | 37.8 | 17 Lucent Technologies | 183.34 |
| 18 Johnson & Johnson | 7.4 | 18 General Electric Co. (U.K.) | 9.3 | 18 Procter & Gamble | 36.4 | 18 American International Group | 173.50 |
| 19 Chevron | 6.8 | 19 Johnson & Johnson | 9.3 | 19 Glaxo Holdings | 36.1 | 19 Merck | 172.87 |
| 20 Merck | 6.6 | 20 British Petroleum | 8.7 | 20 Bristol-Myers Squibb | 35.1 | 20 Pfizer | 171.52 |

**Figure 4.1**  Some leaders in market value do a disappearing act

Note: 2000 figures taken from Business Week, July 10, 2000, p. 49.

Welch wished to reinvigorate every employee, from the bottom up. Welch wanted full-scale cultural change at GE, and that meant shaking up the entire workforce. He introduced a concept called "workout," a practice similar to German methods of employee relations. Workout introduced sessions in which 50–100 employees, generally chosen to represent a cross-section in terms of rank and tenure, would meet for two days to discuss their work. The lowliest employees were encouraged to make suggestions as to how their job could be made easier or more efficient, and how ingrained bad habits could be eliminated. In its first two years, more than 2,000 workout sessions were held, some including suppliers and customers.

Though some have criticized Welch's "empowerment" approach as futile,[12] there can be no doubting the impact that his changes have had on the bottom line. According to a 1999 *Forbes* story called "The Jack Factor,"

> Consensus has it that General Electric is the best-run company in the world. Yet this giant is an eclectic collection of seemingly unrelated pieces – jet engines and light-bulbs, synthetic polymers and *Friends* sitcoms. ITT, Westinghouse and other conglomerates failed to make sense of their disparate mishmash of businesses, but GE has made it all work, in the sense that it carries a very rich multiple on Wall Street (44 times trailing earnings) . . . Under Welch's leadership, GE defies the conventional logic that the sum of the parts is worth more than the whole. Other corporate grab bags traded at a cheaper value than the sum of their parts, yet GE (priced lately at $137 a share for a market value of $450 billion) gets a premium of 40% to 70% over its bust-up value.

*What did GE do that GM failed to do? What happened after Welch retired?*

As far as the "dinosaurs" are concerned, there can be no doubt that the failure of IBM, GM and Sears was at least partly a failure of governance. It is not surprising, for instance, that the problems at Sears developed when the same person held the jobs of CEO, chairman of the board, CEO of the largest (and worst-performing) operating division, chairman of the nominating committee of the board, and trustee of the 25 percent of the company's stock that was held on behalf of the employees (see Sears case study). The company had circumvented all of the systems set up to ensure that the right questions would be asked by putting the same person in all of the positions that were supposed to monitor each other. It is impossible to identify what Albert O. Hirschman calls "repairable lapses"[13] when the same person is both making the decisions and evaluating them.

The best way to make sure that the right questions are asked of the right people is to create a structure that aligns the interests of the CEO with the long-term interests of the shareholders as much as possible. Indeed, it is just this alignment that gives managers the expertise and the credibility to do their job effectively.

> Although managers are self-interested, this interest can be aligned with that of investors through automatic devices, devices that are useless when those in control are "disinterested;" hence the apparent contradiction that self-interested managers have more freedom than disinterested regulators.[14]

"It is often better to have a great deal of harm happen to one than a little; a great deal may rouse you to remove what a little will only accustom you to endure."
*Sir Fulke Greville*

# EXECUTIVE COMPENSATION

It took the abuses of the takeover era to wake up the institutional investors, and almost before they got started, the takeover era ended. But by that time, there was a new issue to provoke outrage: excessive CEO compensation. In some ways, this was an ideal corporate governance issue for the new activists. Complaints about compensation could be made in a sound bite, with political and economic appeal, to say nothing of the gossip value. This was the first corporate governance issue to go from the financial pages to the front pages to the editorial pages to the comic pages – even "Doonesbury" got in a few digs. And this was not just some Capra-esque populist movement. No one complained about the money Bill Gates made at Microsoft. But when pay was not related to performance, the business press was just as outraged as the shareholders. Even *Forbes*'s cover story on executive pay bore a banner headline: "It doesn't make sense."[15]

It was also an issue uniquely suited to being addressed by shareholders. Compensation for performance is the perfect issue; no shareholder initiative could have a more direct impact on shareholder value. If compensation is connected to performance, all other shareholder initiatives become secondary. If compensation is unrelated to performance, however, all the shareholder resolutions in the world won't make a difference.

The role of the shareholders with regard to compensation starts with one simple point: compensation presents an investment opportunity. The compensation plan is a clear indicator of the company's value as an investment. It reveals what the CEO's incentives are. If homeowners are deciding between two realtors who want to sell their house – one who charges a flat fee and one who charges a percentage of the sale price – they know they are likely to do better with the one whose compensation is tied to the money they themselves will eventually receive. Similarly, a shareholder should want to invest in a CEO whose compensation depends on the money the shareholder will receive. Compensation plans also reveal what the company's goals are and how confident the CEO and board are of the company's future.

Graef Crystal, in his book on executive compensation, *In Search of Excess*,[16] discusses the impact that compensation plans should have on stock-picking by sophisticated investors. His conclusion that restricted stock grants are made by boards who do not think the stock will go up is supported by his data on companies that have made these awards. If his analysis is correct, selling short on companies that make restricted stock grants should be a highly profitable investment strategy.

Furthermore, compensation issues present shareholders with some of their most cost-effective (highly leveraged) opportunities for "investing" in shareholder initiatives. A shareholder can submit a shareholder proposal about executive compensation for little more than the cost of a stamp. Shareholders can distribute information about their views to other shareholders under the enormously simplified revised proxy rules for little more than the cost of a couple of dozen letters or phone calls. With a high likelihood of improving returns through this visible focus, and negligible, if any, downside risk, this is an "investment" that shareholders, especially fiduciary shareholders, will find increasingly appealing.

Shareholder initiatives on compensation have special appeal. CEOs get paid a lot for one reason – because they take risks. Their compensation should provide the appropriate incentives for those risks. To the extent that a shareholder initiative can better align these incentives, it is an investment with substantial returns.

The question, then, is not whether there will be increased activism by shareholders on the subject of compensation; the question is what form it will take. With the exception of a few extremists, shareholders have not objected to chief executives earning a lot of money, as long as they created a lot of value for shareholders first. The late Roberto Goizueta's $81 million stock grant got four standing ovations from the Coca-Cola shareholders, who were delighted with the 38.2 percent annual returns during his tenure. What shareholders have objected to is chief executives being paid a lot of money without earning it; their focus has been on strengthening the link between pay and performance.

It is a very small group at the top of the compensation scale: rock stars, movie stars, athletes, investment bankers, and CEOs. All but CEOs are compensated for performance. And it is not coincidental that, of that group, CEOs are the only ones who pick the people who set their compensation. In all of the other categories, pay and performance are closely linked. And that means financial performance. Meryl Streep can get a record number of Oscar nominations, but she doesn't sell a lot of tickets. So, she gets an average of $7–$9 million for a movie, while Arnold Schwarzenegger, unlikely to get anywhere near an Oscar, got a record $30 million for making *Terminator 3*. Investment bankers who earned bonuses in the millions in the 1990s were laid off when deals disappeared. But statistics show that CEOs do well regardless of performance, and the publicity for those numbers provided much of the momentum for the reforms on compensation disclosure.[17]

Of course, some of the fuss missed the point. Despite the headlines, in many, perhaps even most cases, compensation is not outrageous. The problem is that the extreme cases point up the failure of the system as a whole. If shareholders, as the consumers of executive compensation, cannot act when it is out of control, the system simply isn't working. Executive compensation unrelated to performance is just one symptom of a corporate governance system that fails to ensure management accountability.

The issue is not only matching compensation to performance. There is almost always some standard that can be used to support a bonus, and compensation consultants are good at providing a mix of "performance plans" that ensure that at least one of them will pay off. Crystal's book devotes an entire chapter to document in devastating detail the compensation package of Time Warner's late chairman, Steve Ross, dubbed by Crystal the "Prince of Pay." Ross's seven different long-term incentive plans included $21.1 million in stock options, $69.6 million in bonus units (plus $3.8 million in dividend equivalent payments) and another set of units that would pay out based on the stock's highest average price over an eight-week period over the previous two years.[18] There was also another set of units tied to the Warner stock price that paid him $58.7 million because the stock was valued at the time of the acquisition by Time. According to Crystal, "[h]is total take from all seven plans was $236 million over a period of effectively 17 years or about $14 million a year."[19] And it is worth noting that Ross' employment contracts were voted on by a board that included five officers of his company, without whom the contract would not have been approved.

Ross' performance at Warner may have been terrific. The problem was that the high compensation was almost coincidental; the compensation plan did not link compensation to performance. The issue shareholders should focus on is not just tying compensation to performance, but really improving performance.

*What kinds of plans, in which kinds of circumstances, motivate what kinds of managers to guide a company to maximum total shareholder returns over the long run? Which plans have consistently led to the best long-term performance? What are the indicators of a good plan, and, maybe more important, what are the indicators of a bad one?*

In 1999, Graef Crystal named Linda Wachner of Warnaco his "pay anti-hero," based on the following excerpt from the Crystal Report (April 19):

- Base salary of $2.7 million – 299% above the market. And that doesn't count further salary of $1.1 million she received for running a smaller public company, Authentic Fitness [Given the company's performance, it is particularly striking that her board allowed her to have another full-time job. Perhaps this is why they voted to buy Authentic Fitness from her in 1999, a deal in which she and several of her directors were on both sides of the table.]
- Total Current Compensation of $8.7 million – 638% above the market
- Total Direct Compensation of $73.8 million – 1,818% above the market
- That 1,818% market overage was higher than that for any of the 857 CEOs in our 1998 pay study. The next overage was a mere [*sic!*] 893%
- The options granted in 1998 had an estimated present value of $58.2 million
- In addition, she exercised options in 1998 for a gain of $75.6 million

Crystal noted, "Her board is also excessively paid – large fees and extra-large option grants."

Wachner took over Warnaco in 1986 in a hostile takeover and built the apparel maker into a $1.4 billion company, responsible for manufacturing and distributing more than a third of all the bras sold in the US.

In June of 2001, Warnaco filed for bankruptcy, its stock trading at 39 cents a share, down from $44 a share in 1998. The press release about the bankruptcy blamed a soft retail market and insufficient support of the retailers. The fault was entirely the board's, once described by *Fortune* as "notoriously ineffectual," for not just enabling but rewarding a CEO whose self-dealing and bad decisions all but destroyed the company.

Wachner was fired shortly after the bankruptcy filing. It should be noted that she submitted notice to the bankruptcy court that, since she had been terminated without cause, she was entitled to have her $25 million severance payment classified as an "administrative expense" and thus given top priority among the creditors. She later settled for $452,000, promising to donate $200,000 of that to charity.

Warnaco emerged from bankruptcy in February of 2003.

It is all very well to talk about incentive plans, but all the incentives in the world cannot work if there are other impediments to getting the job done. Some so-called "incentive plans" can be manipulated. Targets can be hit by divesting a subsidiary instead of increasing product sales. More important, there is no incentive plan that can make a weekend athlete into an Olympic gold medallist. And no incentive plan will make a CEO who is in over his head suddenly able to turn the company around.

As mentioned at the beginning of this section, there is an inherent conflict of interest between shareholders and management with regard to compensation. It is important to note, however, that the conflict is not over the amount of compensation, but over the variability of the compensation. Shareholders want compensation to vary with performance as much as possible, while managers understandably want as much certainty as possible; even those who want a lot of variability on the upside are less willing to allow it on the downside.

This inherent conflict did not become obvious until the early 1990s, when executive compensation became the subject of magazine cover stories, *Nightline* and *Crossfire* debates on television, and hearings before the US Congress. In 1991, CalPERS called for shareholders to withhold their votes from the board of directors of ITT, where CEO Rand Araskog's compensation more than doubled as the stock sank. The 1 percent of "withhold" votes cast led to a massive overhaul of the company's compensation plan. At Fairchild, an overpaying company that merited an entire chapter in Crystal's book, the board approved substantial revisions to the company's compensation plan, including a $250,000 cut in CEO Jeffrey Steiner's cash compensation, cancellation of 50,000 options, and agreement to no new options until 1993 and no raises until 1996. This was in settlement of a shareholder lawsuit, worth noting because courts are very reluctant to permit challenges to executive compensation.

General Dynamics reacted to the sobriquet "Generous Dynamics," accorded it by *Business Week* for a compensation package that gave its executives double their salary for a ten-day rise in stock prices. The company called a special meeting to get shareholder approval for substantial changes after pressure from shareholders – and a visit from "60 Minutes." United Airlines executives agreed to increased disclosure of their compensation in the proxy statement, after negotiations with the United Shareholders Association. Many companies announced cuts: at USAir, the directors took a 20 percent compensation cut to mirror the cuts they were asking of employees.

In 1992, the focus on compensation continued, as the SEC reversed its long-time policy and allowed advisory (non-binding) shareholder resolutions on compensation. (For further discussion of shareholder proposals, see chapter 2.) Later, they reversed another policy to allow votes on proposals that would require companies to obtain shareholder approval before re-pricing stock options.

The media and the politicians emphasized the size of certain executive compensation packages. Shareholders focused, as Michael Jensen and Kevin Murphy put it, not on "how much," but on "how."[20] Two crucial elements of the "how" are stock options and restricted stock grants, and shareholders began to make some important distinctions.

Compensation consultants Towers Perrin found that the average face value of stock options to CEOs had doubled from the mid-1980s to the mid-1990s, to more than twice the value of annual compensation. According to one study, in 1992, 53.92 percent of firms included stock options as a part of a compensation package. By 1997, it had risen to 71.85 percent.[21]

In the late 1990s, a "how you gonna keep 'em down on the farm" attitude caused the CEOs of established companies to insist on pay to match that of the new economy high-tech entrepreneurs. Most of their boards complied, even in the absence of any evidence that there was any risk that they might accept – or get – a competing offer. The new economy executives received superstar pay for lackluster performance. AOL's Steve Case grossed $303.3 million from 1996 to 1999, while average return on equity was −119 percent. The old economy executives did the same. Disney's Michael Eisner, once the poster boy for good pay due to his premium-priced options, came in last in the annual *Business Week* pay-performance survey, with three-year pay of $636.9 million for a three-year performance of 28 percent. Metro-Goldwyn-Mayer re-priced the options of a retired CEO, from $24 to $14.90 per share. Philip Morris decided to pay dividends on stock options, so that even if the options were under water, the executives would still get an income stream. Sears, Roebuck reacted to the news that its employees did not meet the performance goals that would have triggered bonuses by extending the deadline, subverting the pay-performance link. The sheer number of options granted became staggering. George Sheehan of Webvan received, in addition to the 1,250,000 unrestricted shares, 15 million options. Joseph Galli was recruited to Amazon with a promise that, if his options were not worth at least $20 million by 2003, he would get that amount in cash.

*What does this tell us about the board of directors?*

"The salary of the chief executive of the large corporation is not a market award for achievement. It is frequently in the nature of a warm personal gesture by the individual to himself." *John Kenneth Galbraith*

# Case in point:
# ICGN on compensation

In 2002, the International Corporate Governance Network (ICGN) adopted a statement on executive compensation. These excerpts give some sense of its take on the issues:

> The subject of executive remuneration, a word with which even native English-speakers have difficulty, dominates discussions of corporate governance. There are two reasons for this: nothing fascinates the average reader more than the "how much?" question. At a more sophisticated level, boards awarding themselves money from their shareholders' assets potentially creates a direct conflict of interest between the owner and the agent that is not present in almost all other areas of managerial activity. Unfortunately, because there is little consensus between company managers and their owners' other agents, the institutional investment managers, about this area, the debate drowns the perfectly sensible discussions about other areas of governance that may have a more direct effect on the long-term success of the companies concerned. It also consumes large amounts of time, for company managers and investors alike, with limited effect. . . .
>
> The fundamental requirement for executive remuneration reporting is TRANSPARENCY. The base salary, short-term and long-term incentives, as well as other payments and benefits for all main-board directors, should be published. Remuneration committees should publish statements on the expected OUTCOMES of the remuneration structures, in terms of ratios between base salaries, short-term bonuses and long-term rewards, making both "high" and "low" assumptions as well as the "central" case. . . .
>
> The Committee recommends that a remuneration report be presented as a separate voting item at every annual meeting.

## STOCK OPTIONS

Stock options, of course, are supposed to be the ultimate example of compensation for performance. The company gives the option recipient the right to purchase a block of the company's stock at some specified point in the future at a "strike price" set at the time of award, often the current trading price. So if the stock rises between the time of award and the time the option is exercised, the executive will get the benefit of the gain, without having had to make the capital expenditure to buy the stock. (For information about the controversy on valuing and expensing stock options, see the discussion in chapter 1.)

Theoretically, at least, the person granted the options will not make any money unless the stock goes up. A typical description of a stock option plan notes, "The company's stock option program is designed to focus attention on stock values, and to develop Company ownership, promote employee loyalty, reward long-term business success and develop a parallel interest between key employees and shareholders." But as one compensation consultant argues, market and industry factors (over which company management has no control) account for about two-thirds of the stock price's movement.[22] Warren Buffett noted in one of his annual reports that stock options do not tie individual performance to individual compensation:

Of course, stock options often go to talented, value-adding managers and sometimes deliver them rewards that are perfectly appropriate. (Indeed, managers who are really exceptional almost always get far less than they should.) But when the result is equitable, it is accidental. Once granted, the option is blind to individual performance. Because it is irrevocable and unconditional (so long as a manager stays in the company), the sluggard receives rewards from his options precisely as does the star. A managerial Rip Van Winkle, ready to doze for ten years, could not wish for a better "incentive" system . . .

Ironically, the rhetoric about options frequently describes them as desirable because they put owners and managers in the same financial boat. In reality, the boats are far different. No owner has ever escaped the burden of capital costs, whereas a holder of a fixed-price option bears no capital costs at all. An owner must weigh upside potential against downside risk; an option holder has no downside. In fact, the business project in which you would wish to have an option frequently is a project in which you would reject ownership. (I'll be happy to accept a lottery ticket as a gift – but I'll never buy one.)[23]

Fans of options say that they are effective in motivating long-term performance. But Philip Morris gave CEO Hamish Maxwell options on 500,000 shares on his retirement, when motivation and performance were scarcely relevant.

The most troubling aspect of stock option awards is "re-pricing," reissuing stock options when the stock price is below the option price. Companies that have re-priced executive options included Apple Computers, Salomon Brothers, and Occidental Petroleum.[24] This removes all of the risks to management (and all of the benefits to shareholders) of a stock option grant. For the purpose of incentives, it is just like giving the managers cash. One of the most beneficial aspects of shareholder involvement is that re-pricing of stock options has been widely discredited.

But at the same time another kind of option award with almost no relation to performance is gaining in popularity. That is the awarding of huge option grants, so that even an increase of one dollar a share will lead to a million-dollar payoff even if the gain is at or even less than the rest of the market. Like re-pricing, enormous option grants remove any downside from the compensation plan. Leon Hirsch, CEO of US Surgical, was awarded so many options that his compensation risk was all but removed. Four years'-worth of grants gave him nearly 6 million shares on option. If the stock climbed by as little as one dollar he would make $5.9 million. As then SEC chairman Richard Breeden noted, "Mega-grants of options are an increasing and quite disturbing trend. Some mega options make mini sense for shareholders . . . shareholders are entitled to expect the directors who make those awards to have an affirmative reason for every award and its pricing."[25]

# Case in point: The chairman speaks

Some thoughtful comments on stock options from chairman of the Federal Reserve Alan Greenspan, in a speech delivered at the 2002 Financial Markets Conference of the Federal Reserve Bank of Atlanta, Sea Island, Georgia (May 3, 2002):

> The seemingly narrow accounting matter of option expensing is, in fact, critically important for the accurate representation of corporate performance. And accurate accounting, in turn, is central to the functioning of free-market capitalism – the system that has brought such a high level of prosperity to our country . . .

I fear that the failure to expense stock option grants has introduced a significant distortion in reported earnings – and one that has grown with the increasing prevalence of this form of compensation . . .

Stock option grants, properly constructed, can be highly effective in aligning the interests of corporate officers with those of shareholders. Such an alignment is an essential condition for maximizing the long-term market value of the firm.

Regrettably, some current issuance practices have not created the alignment of incentives that encourages desired corporate behavior. One problem is that stock options, as currently structured, often provide only a loose link between compensation and successful management. A company's share price, and hence the value of related options, is heavily influenced by economy-wide forces – that is, by changes in interest rates, inflation, and myriad other forces wholly unrelated to the success or failure of a particular corporate strategy.

There have been more than a few dismaying examples of CEOs who nearly drove their companies to the wall and presided over a significant fall in the price of the companies' stock relative to that of their competitors and the stock market overall. They, nonetheless, reaped large rewards because the strong performance of the stock market as a whole dragged the prices of the forlorn companies' stocks along with it.

Stock or options policy should require that rewards reflect the success or failure of managements' decisions. Grants of stock or options in lieu of cash could be used more effectively by tying such grants through time to some measure of the firm's performance relative to a carefully chosen benchmark. Many corporations do tie the value of stock and option grants to relative performance, but most do not. To be sure, an untied option grant can be thought of as an option whose value moves with the performance of the corporation relative to the competition, coupled with a call option on, for example, the S&P 500 stock index. It can be argued that the latter is merely another form of compensation that helps firms retain valued employees. I am sure that is right, but does a compensation system tied to the overall stock market serve a company well?

To assume that option grants are not an expense is to assume that the real resources that contributed to the creation of the value of the output were free. Surely the existing shareholders who granted options to employees do not consider the potential dilution of their share in the market capitalization of their corporation as having no cost to them.

The particular instrument that is used to transfer value in return for labor services is irrelevant. Its value is not. Abstracting from tax considerations, one must assume that the value is the same for the employer irrespective of the nature of the instrument that conveys it – which could be cash or its value equivalent in the form of stock, free rent, a college annuity for one's children, or an option grant.

The ability of options to substitute for cash obviously rests on an expectation by an employee that the price of the company's stock will rise. Expectations of stock price movements, in turn, appear to be significantly influenced by recent stock price behavior. Thus, there is little surprise that stock options gained considerable favor as a form of compensation with the steep rise in stock prices in the late 1990s. Similarly, one might reasonably expect that in an environment with slower stock price gains, option grants would no longer be so favorably viewed by employees as a substitute for cash. As a consequence, more cash or its equivalent might then be required to fund labor services.

One may argue that, because option grants are fully disclosed and their effect on earnings can, with some effort, be estimated reasonably well, financial markets in their collective wisdom see through the nature of any bookkeeping transactions. Hence, how expenses and profits are reported is of no significance, because nothing in the real world is altered. Cash flows, for example, are unaffected. The upshot of this reasoning is that stock prices should be unaffected by whether option grants are expensed or not. Clearly, most high-tech executives believe otherwise. How else does one explain their vociferous negative reaction to expensing if its only effect were to change the book profit reported to shareholders?

I fear they may be right. Indeed, most American businesspeople must believe expensing is more than bookkeeping. Current accounting rules encourage firms to expense option grants. However, only two of the S&P 500 firms reportedly chose to do so in the year 2000. If expensing does indeed matter, at least some of the unsustainable euphoria that surrounded dot-com investing at its peak may have been exacerbated by questionable reported earnings.

The measure of diluted earnings per share currently reported by corporations partially reflects the number of shares that employees could obtain with vested but, as yet, unexercised options. Some have maintained that this is all that is required to capture the effects of option grants. Clearly, this adjustment corrects only the denominator of the earnings per share ratio. It is the estimation of the numerator that the accounting dispute is all about.

Some have argued against option expensing on the grounds that the Black–Scholes formula, the prevailing means of estimating option expense, is approximate. It is. But, as I indicated earlier, so is a good deal of all other earnings estimation. Moreover, every corporation already implicitly reports an estimate of option expense on its income statement. That number for most companies, of course, is exactly zero. Are option grants truly without value?

As I noted earlier, critics of option expensing have also argued that expensing will make raising capital more difficult. But we need to remember that expensing is only a bookkeeping transaction. To repeat, nothing real is changed in the actual operations or cash flow of the corporation. If investors are dissuaded by lower reported earnings as a result of expensing, it means only that they were less informed than they should have been about the true input cost of creating corporate revenues. Capital employed on the basis of misinformation is likely to be capital misused.

Critics of expensing also argue that the availability of options enables corporations to attract more productive employees. I am sure that is true. But option expensing in no way precludes the issuance of options. To be sure, lower reported earnings as a result of expensing, should it temper stock price increases, could inhibit option issuance. But, again, that inhibition would be appropriate because it would reflect the correction of misinformation.

It is no more valid, in my judgment, to assume that option grant expense is zero than to arbitrarily assume depreciation charges are zero. Both assumptions, excluding interest, increase reported pretax earnings. Both imply that the inputs that produce valued corporate outputs are free.

# Case in point: Borden

At Borden, just after the proxy statement explained that the CEO did not get a bonus because the company had not met its performance goals, the board awarded the CEO options to purchase 100,000 shares of the company's common stock at a price to be set in the future, subject to shareholder approval at the next annual meeting. Furthermore, according to the employment contract, "In the event that the Stock Option Plan is not approved by shareholders at the Corporation's next annual meeting of shareholders, the Corporation shall provide the executive with compensation of equivalent value as determined by the

Compensation Committee." In other words, if the shareholders decided that the CEO should not get the new stock options, the CEO would get the equivalent in the form of cash.

*What connection is there between pay and performance in this arrangement? What does this show about the directors' representation of the shareholders who "elected" them?*

Note: this plan also provided that the company would pay for two residences for the CEO, along with all applicable taxes. Note further that, despite the contract's provision that the CEO could not be removed for any reason other than commission of a felony, he was removed within six months of signing this contract. While he no longer had the job, this did not affect his salary. He received the present value of the full five years of pay.

What shareholders look for in options is some way to make sure that they tie returns to the particular company's performance rather than to the performance of the market as a whole. One way to do this is to index the options, so that the "strike price" rises with the stock market. That way, the compensation reflects the performance of the particular company's stock. Another option is to grant the options at a price greater than the current stock price. Compensation consultant Ira Kay, of Hay Group management consultants, says that committees should build downside risk into their plans by *selling* jumbo stock option grants, paying bonuses for executives who retain option shares and granting premium options. Shareholders are becoming more sophisticated about compensation. According to the Investor Responsibility Research Center, the percentage of shareholders voting against option plans was 3.5 percent in 1988, and 12 percent in 1991. In 1998, 15 proposals were defeated by shareholders and 270 had at least 30 percent opposition.

## RESTRICTED STOCK

Instead of stock options, some companies make "restricted stock grants," awarding stock with limits on its transferability for a set time, usually two or three years, but sometimes for the executive's tenure with the company. Some restricted stock grants have performance requirements as well, as at FleetBoston, where the stock will vest only if executives meet "aggressive financial targets." Restricted stock becomes more appealing in a down market (or when executives think the stock is not going to increase in value) because, unlike an option, restricted stock has value unless the stock goes down to zero. Crystal is leery of restricted stock grants, arguing that they should be a signal to the market that even management does not think that the stock price will go up. They are low in risk. An executive granted restricted stock will always make money, unless the stock goes down to zero. Compare Lee Iacocca's compensation plans at the beginning of his time at Chrysler with the plan at the end. He once ran Chrysler for a dollar a year, but with some "monster (very large) options" that paid out $43 million in six years. On the other hand, between 1983 and 1987, Iacocca received 455,000 shares of restricted stock. By the end of the 1980s, Chrysler stock had halved. In 1991, Chrysler's bonus-eligible executives received grants of restricted stock, with restrictions that lapsed within months. Since they paid nothing for these grants, this was additional compensation that was all upside and little downside.

In 2002, the board of Bank of America Corporation granted chief executive Kenneth Lewis an $11.3 million restricted stock award in addition to 750,000 stock options. We expect to see more awards of restricted stock instead of, or, as here, in addition to stock options as market pressure or changes in accounting rules force options grants to be expensed, thus removing the balance-sheet advantage of options over stock, and as CEOs hedge their bets in an uncertain market.

# SHAREHOLDER CONCERNS: SEVERAL WAYS TO PAY DAY

Some other issues of recent shareholder concern include the following abusive compensation practices:

## The "guaranteed bonus" – the ultimate oxymoron

Compaq CEO Michael Capellas was brought in as CEO of WorldCom after it entered bankruptcy following the disclosure of accounting fraud. His proposed pay included an annual salary of $1.5 million, a $2 million signing bonus and a $1.5 million guaranteed bonus in 2003. Lucent's Pat Russo had a base salary of $1.2 million and a guaranteed bonus of $1.8 million. Jim Adamson, the new chief executive of K-Mart, also in bankruptcy, got a $2.5 million singing bonus just for agreeing to be the new CEO; his salary is to be a minimum of $1 million a year, he gets a contingency payment of $4 million next year, and he gets a guaranteed bonus of more than $1 million a year. That's at least $8.5 million in only his first year. Guaranteed. The whole purpose of a bonus is to adjust pay up or down on the basis of performance. To give a CEO a guaranteed bonus in any circumstances is to make the term itself meaningless. But it is particularly difficult to justify in a turnaround situation, where shareholders want someone who is willing to bet on himself. Gary Wendt insisted on a $45 million cash signing bonus (showing up money) when he went to the troubled Conseco. This was a clear signal that he was not sure the turnaround would work, but he was sure he would do fine either way. Under his leadership, the company went into bankruptcy.

## Deliberate obfuscation

New executive compensation disclosure rules promulgated by the SEC in 1992 (discussed in greater detail below) were designed to prevent companies disguising compensation awards in pages of numbing legal narrative. As soon as the new rules were issued, however, lawyers and compensation consultants began designing ways to make compensation less clear to shareholders.

In part, increased attempts to evade disclosure have been thwarted by the revisions to the shareholder communication rules. The SEC's express exemption of proxy analysis services from the pre-clearance provisions of the proxy rules gives more latitude to the firms that are in the business of dissecting and revealing compensation plans. Smart corporate management, concerned about good investor relations, will not seek to evade the new requirements, but rather will see them as an opportunity for effective communication of corporate objectives and their relationship to performance.

A 1993 amendment to the tax laws eliminated the deductibility of most compensation over $1 million, except for performance-based compensation meeting specified criteria. At least some compensation consultants thought that this rule would merely provide a new test of their ingenuity. The *Wall Street Journal* reported: "Few, if any, companies intend to respond to the law by cutting big compensation packages."[26] Favorite gimmicks include: deferring more pay until after retirement, creating a two-tier bonus arrangement, and altering stock option plans by setting a maximum number of possible options that may be awarded. One compensation consultant told the *Journal*: "The professional fees generated by this piece of legislation will far outweigh the tax revenue it generates."[27] The unintended consequence of this rule turned out to be the award of unprecedented levels of stock options that brought executive compensation to $100 million-dollar levels during the roaring 1990s. With the post-2001 down market and the pressure to expense option grants, pay began to move away from options to restricted stock and other forms of pay not tied to the stock price.

### The Christmas tree

Many compensation plans contain elements that are in themselves admirable, but which in combination with a host of other plans add up to a package that has no sensitivity to performance. For example, stock options and performance unit plans are all too often an addition to compensation packages, not a substitute for something else.

### Compensation plans that are all upside and no downside

These plans include any grants of stock or stock options that fail to discount for overall market gains, or that are cushioned against loss of value through compensatory bonuses or re-pricing. Management will face increased opposition to these kinds of plans. Increasingly, investors are likely to push for option grants that are indexed to the company's peer group as more directly tied to performance.

### Loans

The corporate scandals of 2002 included extraordinary abuses of corporate loans, including "non-recourse" loans which do not have to be repaid. The board of WorldCom authorized an astounding $408 million loan to CEO Bernie Ebbers, and the Rigas family got $3.1 billion in loans that the board now says it did not authorize (see case studies). Tyco's Dennis Kozlowski got $88 million in loans, and Conseco's Stephen Hilbert got $162 million in loans.

While the origins of insider loans may have been legitimate, like almost every other element of executive compensation they have been distorted and abused. They are also widespread. In fiscal 2002, a third of the largest 1,500 companies in the US had outstanding loans to one or more executives. Only 362 of the 508 companies disclosing loans actually indicated in any detail whether loans were interest-bearing or not and whether they would be required to be paid back. Of these 362 companies, 102 had forgiven or were forgiving loans. Many companies even paid the taxes for the executive when the loans were forgiven.

There is little justification for using corporate assets to make loans to people who can get loans from any commercial lending facility. Loans to executives are prohibited by Sarbanes–Oxley (see chapter 3 above), so investors must watch closely to make sure that "non-recourse" loans do not become outright grants.

## Phony cuts

In a down market, no one wants to be in the top quartile any more. Some companies made highly publicized "cuts," but again, all too often, these "cuts" are more than made up for by mega stock options, restricted stock grants, plain old cash, or other awards. In 2003, then-Citigroup CEO Sandy Weill said that he would not accept a cash or stock bonus because the company's stock fell 30 percent. (In 2001, Weill took $25.7 million in bonus and restricted stock and $27.5 million the year before.) Weill also had 4 million underwater options that expired. But the forgone bonus was overshadowed by a new option grant three times greater than his previous grants. Since Weill currently holds just under 23 million shares of Citigroup, it is hard to imagine that additional option grants provide significant additional incentives.

## Golden hellos

Sometimes called joining bonuses, compensation for income opportunities forgone, or reimbursement for benefits forfeited from a former employer, these "golden hellos" are now almost ubiquitous in executive recruitment. The range of terms used to describe golden hellos is only exceeded by the range in the size of such payments, from a high of $45 million paid to Gary Wendt by Conseco, to a low of $150,000 for Steve Odland of Autozone. In one case that attracted a lot of attention, Ron LeMay was recruited from Sprint to be the CEO of Waste Management (see case study). His pay package included Sprint options, on the theory that Waste Management shareholders should make sure he was able to benefit (apparently without having to buy any stock) from the work he had done at Sprint. Those who thought this continuing interest in Sprint was a bad sign about his commitment to Waste Management were proven right when he returned to Sprint after less than five months. LeMay and his boss, CEO William Esrey, were removed from their positions at Sprint in 2003 after disclosure of a tax avoidance scheme that allowed them to shelter $288 million in stock option profits.

## Transaction bonuses

The golden parachutes for Sprint executives were triggered not by completion of a merger with MCI, but by a vote in favor of the merger by the board. Thus, when the merger was not approved by federal regulators, the shareholders got the worst of both worlds — a failed deal for which they had to pay out bonuses to the executives. Some CEOs also get "transaction bonuses" for acquisitions, regardless of subsequent performance by any measure. To give a bonus for a transaction is to create a perverse incentive, especially if the executive can get another transaction bonus for selling or spinning off the acquisition when it does not work out.

## Retirement benefits

Post-employment compensation for CEOs is not subject to the same rigorous disclosure standards as pay while the CEO is still in his job. It took an ugly divorce proceeding to make public the lavish benefits given to former GE CEO Jack Welch. The public filing simply said that he would have "continued lifetime access" to company facilities. Companies that make a clear statement about what is – and is not – covered after retirement will benefit from enhanced credibility as shareholders learn to be more skeptical, and more inquisitive, about this category of compensation.

## FUTURE DIRECTIONS FOR EXECUTIVE COMPENSATION

In October 1992, the SEC promulgated two sets of rule changes that had important consequences on shareholders' ability to ensure that executive pay is performance-related.

First, the SEC demanded that companies reveal and display compensation information in the proxy statement in a clear and comprehensible manner. From the 1993 proxy season forward, companies were required to publish a summary compensation table for the five highest-paid executives, giving separate disclosure of salary, bonuses, and other annual compensation. Stock options, stock appreciation rights, and other long-term incentive payouts also had to be disclosed. Two tables were also required under the new rules. The first table lists all stock option grants, and their estimated value given a range of possible stock price increases. A second table required companies to include a chart comparing a corporation's total five-year return to shareholders to a broad market index (such as the S&P 500) and an industry peer group. Thus, shareholders can, at a glance, gauge the performance of their company and decide if the compensation they are paying executives is justified.[28]

A second rule change freed shareholders from burdensome disclosure requirements in communicating with each other on these issues. (For a further discussion of this issue, see chapter 2.)

All indications are that shareholders will continue to use the improved disclosure about compensation required by the new rules to make decisions about "just voting no" for directors, and the increased flexibility of the SEC's new Section 14 communication rules to share information about their analyses, their compensation-related proposals, and their voting decisions. The SEC has also confirmed the validity of executive compensation as a subject for shareholder proposals. In 2003 it was the number 1 topic for shareholder proposals, with 275 proposals, 44 percent of all governance proposals filed, covering topics like expensing of stock options and tying pay to performance. This was an increase in number and proportion; only 19 percent of proposals in 2002 related to compensation.

The fact sheet accompanying these two SEC rule-making changes notes that the SEC's intention is not to create new causes of action for shareholder litigation, but to give shareholders a better basis on which to evaluate the directors. The requirement that the names of the compensation committee members appear below the committee's statements on the compensation plan[29] will help shareholders connect the plans to the individuals responsible for adopting them. The requirement that interlocks be disclosed will enable shareholders to withhold votes for those directors who appear to have conflicts of interest. (For a discussion of withheld votes, see "Just vote no" in chapter 3.)

Improved disclosure is also important to investors because it will enable them to make an informed investment decision, whether it is voting proxies or deciding to buy or sell a company's stock. Nothing is of greater interest to an investor considering whether to buy or sell than whether the company has an incentive scheme that aligns the interests of management and shareholders. Nothing is of more interest to a shareholder who is considering candidates for election to the board (including members of the compensation committee) than the priorities reflected in the compensation plan they approve and the independence of the members of the committee. Shareholders will use the increased clarity and consistency of the information available to them to make decisions about when to buy and sell, and about when to submit or support a shareholder initiative. Directors and management will no longer have the luxury of the SEC pre-clearance rules to track shareholder communication on these issues. Smart managers will want to seize the initiative to reach out to the shareholders and address their concerns.

Compensation should be seen as one item – and an important one – on the board's report card. How does a board balance conflicting interests of managers (who want less variability in pay) and shareholders (who want more)? The way the board reconciles these interests is a crucial indicator of their focus, independence, and ability. Bad compensation schemes are not the disease; they are the symptom. The disease is bad boards, and shareholders must now be persuaded that bad boards must be fixed.

This does not mean that CEOs will be paid less; it means that they will be paid better. Shareholders have learned that if they do not make sure they get what they pay for, they will certainly pay too much for what they get. In the words of then SEC chairman Richard Breeden, echoing his predecessor from the Carter administration in the late 1970s, Harold Williams, "The best protection against abuses in executive compensation is a simple weapon – the cleansing power of sunlight and the power of an informed shareholder base."[30]

## CEO EMPLOYMENT CONTRACTS

The CEO's annual salary is just the tip of an iceberg. To get the full story, you need to move past the proxy statements and look at CEO employment contracts, which are theoretically public, but in reality very hard to find. They are filed as an attachment to the company's 10K, but not sent out to shareholders. Since there is no way to know when they were signed or amended, it can take a search through years of filings before finding the contract. The authors of this book have created a website at <http://www.thecorporatelibrary.com> to make them accessible in reality as well as in theory.

These contracts are thoroughly massaged by lawyers, compensation consultants, and headhunters. Because the same consultants and advisors work on so many of them there is a "lowest common denominator" aspect – one bad idea (like having the company pay the fees of the lawyer who represented the CEO in the negotiation) gets picked up by others, so that they tend to have a numbing sameness to them. But there are a few outliers – good and bad – worth mentioning.

In 2000 Robert Annunziata announced his departure from Global Crossing just a week after the Corporate Library selected his contract as the worst. Annunziata created tremendous shareholder value during his one-year tenure at the company. But his contract's pay–performance link was weak. As the company's performance leveled off, Annunziata's compensation did not diminish commensurately. Just for showing up, Annunziata got a $10 million signing bonus and 2 million stock options at $10 a share below market. He got a "guaranteed bonus" of not less than half a million dollars a year. The make and model of the Mercedes the company had to buy for him and his wife was spelled out in the contract. He got use of the corporate jet for commuting until such time as he might find it appropriate to move. And to keep him from getting homesick, his family got first-class airfare to come see him once a month, including his mother.

It is likely that the board and even its shareholders would argue that the cost of the family's first-class airfare and the "brand-new 1999 model Mercedes-Benz SL 500" for the use of the CEO and his wife were trivial in light of the importance of the job and the value the company has created. But it seems to us that anyone who gets the equivalent of $30 million just for showing up can pay for his own airfare and Mercedes. And, much more important, anyone who is willing to make a real commitment to the company can take options at or above market. Shareholders like to bet on people who are willing to bet on themselves. By filling Annunziata's contract with a series of ridiculous perks, Global Crossing was sending the wrong message to employees, customers, and investors.

Annunziata's departure shows that while it may be necessary to include provisions like these to attract certain executives, that does not mean that those are the executives a board should want to attract. The contract succeeded in getting him on board, but it did not succeed in keeping him. Annunziata was one of three Global Crossing CEOs in less than two years. The company filed for bankruptcy in 2002 amid charges of self-dealing and suspicious accounting.

In 2000, the Corporate Library picked the contract of GE's Jack Welch as an exemplar of good corporate governance. On the face of it, it was short, simple, and with that rarest of provisions, the right of the board to fire the CEO for failure to perform. Unlikely as it was given Welch's reputation as the greatest CEO of the century, it was still a classy touch. But an acrimonious divorce case led to revelations in 2002 that Welch had undisclosed post-retirement perquisites including lifetime use of the corporate jet, apartment, and Knicks tickets. After being paid over $900 million, his retirement benefits included having the company pay for his dry-cleaning, caterer, and postage stamps. Welch quickly gave up these benefits, which he valued at about $2 million a year, saying that, while they were proper when he entered into them, the climate had changed and they were no longer acceptable.

More interesting than the extremes is standard operating procedure. There are three routine provisions worth special mention.

## Gross-ups

Just about all CEOs at this level of pay end up owing some extra income taxes, in particular a special "excise tax." Most of the contracts have a provision requiring the company to pay it. There may have been some justification for these payments to prevent unequal treatment during a transition period just after the excise tax rules were adopted, but it is harder and harder to justify as time goes on. This is the Leona Helmsley "only little people pay taxes" approach. These people are getting paid a lot. They should be able to pay their own taxes, just like the rest of us.

## "Deemed" years of service

When the CSX Corporation calculates pension benefits for its chief executive, John W. Snow, later Treasury Secretary in the second Bush administration, it includes credit for 44 years of service to the company, though he worked there for just 25. Moreover, Snow's benefits will be based not just on his salary, or even his salary and bonus, but also the value of 250,000 shares of stock the CSX board gave him. This is a recent trend in compensation, basing pension benefits on "imputed" (basically, made-up) years of service.

## Cause

CEOs who are terminated for cause do not receive the full package of termination benefits that they would if they were terminated without cause. This makes sense. Anyone terminated without cause should be entitled to some financial arrangement as compensation.

The problem is that, in the world of CEO employment contracts, terms like "cause" are redefined. The contracts whittle away at the definition to make it impossible to terminate employment on the basis of poor performance without substantial expense. "Cause" is most often defined as felony, fraud, embezzlement, gross negligence, or moral turpitude. At Toys "Я" Us, the contract for former CEO Michael Goldstein provided that he could not be fired for cause without "a felony involving moral turpitude." Newmont Mining's Ronald C. Cambre has a contract that requires three-quarters of the board to find that he acted in bad faith in order to support termination for cause. Richard J. Kogan's contract at ScheringPlough provides that if he challenges a for "cause" termination, his own determination of good faith prevails unless there is a final and non-appealable judgment to the contrary by a court. The most outrageous of these provisions was surely the now notorious contract for Dennis Kozlowski of Tyco, which provided that conviction of a felony was not grounds for termination unless it was directly injurious to the company. He had no contract for the first four years he served as CEO, so it now seems clear that he only asked for it after he knew he was under investigation for sales tax evasion. Apparently, his board did not consider the timing or language to be of concern.

Very few contracts even mention poor performance as the basis for termination for cause, though some contracts do include willful refusal to follow the direction of the board. Some of those that do refer to performance require a showing of bad faith to make it clear that failure to perform alone is not sufficient for "cause."

The recent push to make termination without cause payments equal those for termination in connection with a change in control is particularly troubling. Change of control payments are intended to align the interests of the CEO with those of the shareholders in evaluating a business combination. Payments for termination without "cause" are intended to ease a non-performing CEO out the door. They can also provide an incentive for a bored CEO to trigger his own parachute with a buy-out deal that may be contrary to the long-term interests of the shareholders.

The cost of these provisions may be small in comparison to the peace of mind that comes from being able to fire an unsatisfactory CEO without worrying about litigation. But we think that boards can do better than this. One of the justifications often claimed for astronomical amounts of CEO pay is the element of risk. But provisions like this can make the position risk-free or even provide an incentive to leave, as the departures of CEOs at ATT, Mattel, Disney, and Global Crossing demonstrate.

*Any other employee at any other level has some accountability for poor performance. What can boards do to make performance a factor in these contracts?*

## Change of control

As with "cause," there is a through-the-looking-glass quality to the definition of "change of control." Summit Bank is one company that requires acquisition of 51 percent of the stock. But other boards do not make any effort to require a CEO to work with substantial block holders of stock, even though studies show that block holders can be effective monitors of shareholder value, especially when they have representation on the board. Many contracts define change of control that can trigger a parachute as low as 20 and even 15 percent.

We believe that it can be in the shareholders' interests to ensure that a CEO must make every effort to work co-operatively with a substantial block holder. Making departure so painless can be a disincentive for those considering the purchase of a block of stock. This can discourage the involvement of substantial investors, who will not want to buy in knowing that the CEO can just walk out the door, taking a hefty sum from the corporate coffers on the way out.

Furthermore, these low triggers can create perverse incentives. The motivation for the Time Warner/AOL merger became clearer when Graef Crystal revealed in his newsletter that the deal paid out at least $1.8 billion in option profits for Time Warner executives, and that this was triggered not by completion of the deal but merely by the vote of the directors in its favor.[31] Similarly, as noted above, the Sprint executives received their golden parachutes for the merger with MCI, even though regulators refused to approve the deal, so that it was never completed. A 2003 settlement of a shareholder lawsuit against Sprint included a precedent-setting 50 governance improvements, including a commitment not to trigger future parachutes unless the transaction was completed.

## Half now, half later

An ideal contract for a chief executive should provide incentives and protections solely designed for tying compensation to the creation of shareholder value. Anything that distracts from or contradicts that goal is an indication that a company's board is not sending a clear message to the CEO, the officers and employees, or to the investment community about its priorities.

These contracts are most important not because of what they show us about the CEO, but for what they show us about corporate boards. Shareholders want CEOs to be aggressive and even a little greedy. But shareholders depend on directors to make sure that those qualities are directed at shareholder value. It is fine for the CEO to ask for the moon. But it is the job of the directors to say, "Sure! You can have half of the moon now, and the other half when the stock price doubles." And when the board fails to do so, it is the job of the shareholders to remind it that we demand accountability.

## EMPLOYEES: COMPENSATION AND OWNERSHIP

"The employer puts his money into . . . business and the workman his life. The one has as much right as the other to regulate that business." *Clarence Darrow*

*What role should employees have in the setting of corporate policies and direction? Should employees be owners? What is the role of the employees in corporate governance? Or, to be more specific, what is the best way to align their interests with the long-term growth of the company?*

Scholars from law and economics, and, more recently, from management theory, have shown that giving employees more authority over their work and more of an ownership interest makes companies stronger and more productive. Some even suggest that employment itself creates a form of ownership, echoing the sentiments of Clarence Darrow quoted above.[32] The role of the employees in corporate governance is another area where it is particularly useful to examine models from different countries. As the examples in this section show, a number of different approaches have worked very well.

Many times each day, every employee is faced with a choice between performing the job to maximize benefit for the company or performing it to benefit himself. *What is the best way to make sure that the employee will be likely to make the right decision?* Let's look at one such choice: business travel. Once the employee leaves the office, he has a number of opportunities to affect the returns to the firm from the trip. He can fly first-class, with very little, if any, benefit to the company. He can schedule the trip to make the time or the place more congenial for him. He can pad his expense vouchers and keep the difference. Most companies address this "agency cost" issue by imposing rules. Employees below a certain level, for example, must fly coach. They must get extra approval for travel that includes a Friday or Monday, to make sure the trips are not designed to give the employee a free weekend away from home. A few rare companies take the opposite approach. Their view is that if they trust the employee to conduct their business in their interests, they trust him to arrange travel in their interests as well.

Trust alone is not enough, however. What makes this approach possible is that it is just one part of a system of involvement, ownership, information, and authority that minimizes agency costs. Development of prescriptive rules can divert employees' attention from the company's objectives, provide a false sense of security for executives, create work for bean counters, and "teach[es] men to stone dinosaurs and start fires with sticks."[33] Rules of this kind are more likely to be used to shield someone from accountability ("I was following the rule!") than to create accountability.

*How do we create a governance and ownership structure that gives employees the optimal role, from the perspective of fairness (to recognize their past contributions) and productivity (to maximize their future contributions)?*

If we accept that the advantage of the corporate structure is that it enables different groups to combine capital and labor for the benefit of all of them, we must recognize that one of the core issues is how those benefits are divided.

Indeed, the debate over this issue goes back to Plato, who wrote extensively on the subject of property in virtually all of his works. Karl Marx argued that "ownership" ultimately belonged to those whose labor created a "product." The capitalist employer enjoys what Marx called "surplus value." He meant that all value is the result of work. The capitalist employer pays the worker less than the value he produces and keeps the surplus for himself as profit. Marx predicted that in future socialist economies workers may receive "from the social supply of [the] means of consumption a share corresponding to their labor time."[34]

Shann Turnbull, an Australian scholar and businessman, considers the question of "surplus value" from a modem perspective. His perspective is that of an investor in a resource-rich but capital-poor country trying to induce foreign investment to create jobs and wealth. In that context, "[i]t does not make good business or macro economic sense to pay foreign investors more than they require to attract their investment. It is simply not a good deal to export surplus profits. It should be considered economically subversive to use corporate concepts which provide external interests with unknown, uncontrolled and unlimited financial claims on a host community."[35]

Turnbull analyzes the factors involved in making a decision to invest: "it is the time horizon rather than the rate of return which becomes the overriding factor for investment decisions" by large institutions.[36] Each sets a rate of return that must be yielded if the investment is to be accepted; this can be translated into the number of years necessary to pay back the original investment. And this in turn relates to risk – the shorter the time period for payback, the less the risk. In balancing risk and return, investors traded off maximization of potential profit to secure protection against risk. Turnbull hazards as a rule of thumb: "We may conclude from the above analysis, that as a rule, all cash received from an investment after ten years represents surplus profits or incentives."[37] This leads to his most important conclusion: "[I]t is evident that investors do not require perpetual property rights to provide them with the incentive to invest."[38] After the investor has recovered sufficient cash to compensate him (or, to look at it another way, to provide optimal incentives) for risking the initial investment, ownership entitlement may be directed to other corporate constituencies – pre-eminently, the employees.

   Go back to our original questions: *What decisions must be made? Who is in the best position to make each decision? Does that person have the authority to make it?* Over the long term, the employees may be the ones who are in the best position to decide many aspects of corporate direction, based on their superior access to information and their minimal conflicts of interest. After all, no one has a longer-term commitment to the company or a more closely aligned interest in the company's long-term vitality. The employees do not just represent members of the community; they *are* the members of the community. When it comes to questions of factoring in the long term and allocating externalities, they may have the fewest agency costs or conflicts of interest.

# Four reasons for employee ownership

1. Owners are the only party affected by corporations who are able to monitor its activities at the micro and macro levels. Put another way, they have minimal agency costs.
2. Ownership is a responsibility as well as a right. As the party with the ultimate interest in enterprise, owners not only can, they should be responsible for its impact on society. Because of their ability to represent the interests of the suppliers of work and capital and the interests of the community, employees are well suited to this role.
3. Ownership requires a level of vigilance that is hard to obtain from a holder of securities, a rather indirect form of "ownership" at best.
4. In order for the ownership function to be discharged within the corporate structure, there must be "owners" who are:

   - rationally informed and involved;
   - unrestricted by laws and regulations in the exercise of their ownership; and
   - free from the "morbidity" arising out of removal from active involvement in the venture.

This concept is also very relevant to the macro perspective, going back to the discussion of the basis for establishing the corporate structure. From the earliest times, the law has created barriers to limiting the use of property or removing it from commerce for an indefinite period of time. These "mortmain" statutes were referred to in the passage by justice Louis Brandeis quoted in chapter 1 when he referred to the early laws of incorporation imposing a time limit to a corporation's existence. The most famous example of the law's concern over mortmain (literally "dead hand") is the Rule against Perpetuities in trust and estate law, which prohibits holding inherited property in trust – and, therefore, removing it from commerce – for longer than 21 years beyond the life term of those in existence at the time the trust is created. In other words, though the rule is somewhat arcane and peculiar in its application, in essence it is intended to prevent someone from limiting the use of his property far into the future according to the judgment of his time. This rule reflected the concern that making it more difficult for assets to meet contemporary needs would have the effect of a "dead hand" on society.

This characterization of share capital in perpetual ventures acting as a permanent drain on productivity recalls the view of capital in the Middle Ages.[39] It is not difficult to make an analogous argument about the provider of capital. While the "ownership" changes continuously, as shares are bought and sold, the uses of capital are still limited by the "dead hands" that established the structure.

Many observers argue that giving the passive shareholder perpetual rights to the ultimate fruits of enterprise promotes economic inequality and perpetuates a dead hand element at the heart of the national economy. Their position is that whatever value the provider of capital contributed has long since been rewarded, and the continued siphoning of the fruit of enterprise must diminish the opportunity, and therefore the incentive and the morale, of others who must make a living from the enterprise. They conclude that thus, even if a venture has perpetual existence, the entitlement of "owners" can be appropriately limited to a set term. The theory is that the corporation evolves from a structure that best benefits from widely dispersed public ownership (with the inducements of limited liability and easy transferability to attract capital) to a structure that is ultimately hampered by it. As the company matures, the best guarantee of continuous renewal is ownership by a group more vitally connected to the enterprise.

There is a lot of appeal in the notion that those who provide the labor have an "ownership" right to the economic value of a corporation. One of the great business leaders of the years between the two world wars was Owen D. Young, for many years the CEO of the General Electric and a genuine "industrial statesman." In a 1927 speech at the dedication of the George P. Baker building at the Harvard Business School, he shared a vision of ownership of corporations by their employees seldom before or since articulated by business leaders.

> Perhaps some day we may be able to organize the human beings engaged in a particular undertaking so that they truly will be the employer buying capital as a commodity in the market at the lowest price. It will be necessary for them to provide an adequate guarantee fund in order to buy their capital at all. If that is realized, the human beings will then be entitled to all the profits over the cost of capital. I hope the day may come when these great business organizations will truly belong to the men who are giving their lives and their efforts to them, I care not in what capacity. Then they will use capital truly as a tool and they will be all interested in working it to the highest economic advantage. Then an idle machine will mean to every man in the plant who sees it an unproductive charge against himself. Then every piece of material not in motion will mean to the man who sees it an unproductive charge against himself. Then we shall have zest in labor, provided the leadership is competent and the division fair. Then we shall dispose, once and for all, of the charge that in industry organizations are autocratic and not democratic. Then we shall have all the opportunities for a cultural wage which the business can provide. Then, in a word, men will be as free in co-operative undertakings and subject only to the same limitations and chances as men in individual businesses. Then we shall have no hired men.[40]

This same theme – the ultimate ownership of an enterprise by its employees – is prevalent in modern-day Japan. "For instance, when asked about who owns the company, in theory most Japanese reply the shareholders, but when asked who in fact owns the company, they reply the employees."[41] The author of those words, Ben Makihara, is the American-educated CEO of a Japanese company, Mitsubishi. A second-generation career Mitsubishi employee, he is married to the daughter of the company's founder, whose family was divested of substantially all of its ownership in the Mitsubishi group following World War II. Makihara, thus, is connected to his company in a way few employees are.

In the half-century since Hiroshima, Japan has been single-minded about creating an exporting industrial colossus. Executives work without holiday and for pay levels very much lower than their counterparts in the West; employees hold themselves to standards of diligence that are viewed with awe all over the world, and the government has supported and encouraged this effort. The results have been extraordinary: in one generation Japan went from total destruction to ascendancy over the world's economy.[42]

Robert Ozaki, in *Human Capitalism*,[43] describes this essentially Japanese creation first by contrasting it with the conventional Western prototype and then by carefully evoking a structure based on mutual concern that is capable of moral judgments:

> Contemporary capitalists typically are not insiders involved in the affairs of the firm they "own." *They* are interested in the company only to the extent that it serves their own interest. At a sign of unprofitability, they have the option of selling their shares and investing their money in another firm. Understandably, they are interested in short-run maximization of the firm's profit; the executives who opt for long-term growth at the expense of short-term profits run the risk of losing their positions . . .
>
> An individual will predictably be motivated when he assumes rights and responsibilities for his conduct. The contemporary firm is a grouping of many individuals. For it to behave like a highly motivated individual, it must, freely and independently of outside interference, be able to make its own decisions toward maximization of its own gains, and at the same time it must take responsibility for the consequences of its failure.
>
> There are different ways to construct a firm so that it can control its own destiny and in effect become a well-motivated quasi-person. A worker-owned and -managed producer-co-operative type firm is one alternative . . .
>
> The humanistic firm has enabled itself to behave like a motivated individual by separating ownership from control through mutual stockholding, an extensive reliance on debt financing, and (more recently) the use of accumulated earnings.
>
> Management and workers form one group, exercising joint sovereignty and sharing a common interest. The firm's gain is their gain. Given the internalized nature of the human resources market, they must pay a high price if their firm fails.
>
> The ethos of the humanistic firm requires new thinking about the very concept of ownership and control. Ownership of the humanistic firm is clearly not public in the socialist sense, nor is it purely private in the capitalist sense. It is not somewhere in between, either, and cannot be well articulated under the dichotomy of public versus private ownership. The members of the humanistic firm do not perceive their firm to be owned by stockholders. They may not legally own it, yet it belongs to them, as they occupy the firm and operate its facilities. One may argue that this is an instance of usufruct and that they are usufructuaries. These terms are not satisfactory, however, since usufruct implies that the property one is authorized to use is privately owned by someone else, whereas the members of the humanistic firm do not consider themselves to be leasing their firm from capitalists. In the absence of the appropriate expression, we might say that they are the quasi-private owners of the firm.

Shann Turnbull proposes a specific mechanism for transferring ownership from shareholders to others. "A dynamic tenure system transfers property rights from investors to operational stakeholders after the investors' time horizon. This would encourage those people who are operationally involved in the creation of surplus profits to promote further profits. In this way, the inefficiency and inequity of surplus profits being returned to investors is replaced with improved efficiency and equity arising from stakeholder control and ownership."[44]

## EMPLOYEE STOCK OWNERSHIP PLANS

The United States has another approach that, at least partially, transfers ownership from outside shareholders to employees, the employee stock ownership plan (ESOP). ESOPs were created in 1974 by two forces: the legislative efforts of legendary Louisiana Democrat and longtime Senate Finance Committee chairman Russell Long and the philosophical evangelicalism of Louis Kelso, who dedicated his career to advancing employee ownership. Kelso wrote:

> The problem with conventional financing techniques is that they address only the productive power of enterprise and the enhancement of the earning power of the rich minority. Sustaining or increasing the earning power of the majority of consumers who are dependent entirely upon the earnings of their labor, or upon welfare, is left to government or governmentally assisted redistribution of income and to chance.[45]

In Kelso's view, there are no developed mechanisms through which an individual – no matter how talented or hard-working – can secure "capital" in exchange for his work. Kelso has promoted "self-financeability" by which employees "earn" a capital position as a result of their labor. This requires tax incentives and credit arrangements. "Thus, the logic of a market economy itself, that legitimate income must be earned by participation in production, requires a form of capital credit for the acquisition of capital ownership by individuals who will use its income to support their consumption of goods and services."[46]

The ESOP is the modern American effort to enable employees to acquire meaningful ownership interests in the firms in which they work. Conceptually, ESOPs work rather as Turnbull has urged. The government provides a substantial tax incentive for companies to borrow in order to be able to acquire their own stock in the ESOP trust, which is then distributed to employees over a long period of years corresponding with their continued employment – or in Turnbull's terms, when the ownership entitlement of the original investor expires. ESOPs, like the one at Polaroid, which are "stockholder neutral," are funded by the deferral of raises and bonuses by employees.[47] Over a relatively short period of time, employees can acquire a significant block of their company's stock. Indeed, it is not uncommon that the employee benefit plan is substantially the largest owner of large modern corporations – for example, Sears, Roebuck and Westinghouse. Lockheed corporation carried this a logical step further: the company intended its ESOP to become the majority holder of its equity securities.

Note, however, that in some cases corporate management has used the ESOP form to protect itself from prospective hostile acquirers (see the Polaroid and Carter Hawley Hale case studies). In these cases, employee ownership is arguably only the extension of management's desire to maintain its incumbency. See the Stone and Webster case study for another example of an ESOP that insulated management from market forces.

Some substantial questions remain as to whether ESOPs will carry out their authors' intention of making owners out of employees. Their status as "trusts" under ERISA and their use as financing devices for the fundamental benefit of management or outside entrepreneurs have severely restricted their utility as ownership vehicles for employees.

> In 1985 concern about the role of workers in worker ownership surfaced from an un-expected quarter. In proposals that stunned traditional supporters of ESOPs, the Reagan administration, acting through the Treasury Department, called for fundamental changes in the ESOP as part of the giant tax reform package. The administration said that em-ployees must have all the rights of direct ownership, including voting rights and in some circumstances dividend rights, if employee ownership were to merit the tax expendi-tures it demanded. It questioned whether ESOPs that restrict the "traditional incidence of ownership" could really improve profitability or employee motivation. The adminis-tration proposed to remove ESOPs from retirement law and continue to encourage them with tax incentives as a socially desirable goal. It called the bluff of ESOP apologists by saying plainly that, if ESOPs were not retirement plans, they should be vehicles of real ownership.[48]

In 1986, after 12 years of active ESOP advocacy, Senator Long made a last effort before his retirement to make sure that ESOP legislation would be seen primarily as intending to enable employee ownership:

> The Congress has made clear its interest in encouraging employee ownership plans as a bold and innovative technique of corporate finance for strengthening the free enterprise system. The Congress intends that such plans be used in a wide variety of corporate financing transactions as a means of encouraging employers to include their employees as beneficiaries of such transactions. The Congress is deeply concerned that the object-ives sought by this series of laws will be made unattainable by regulations and rulings which treat employee stock ownership plans as conventional retirement plans, which reduce the freedom of employee stock ownership trusts and employers to take the necessary steps to utilize ESOPs in a wide variety of corporate transactions, and which otherwise impede the establishment and success of these plans.[49]

# Case in point: United Airlines and employee ownership

In late 1992, the employees of United Airlines agreed to buy 53 percent of the company (63 percent, if the stock price hit certain levels in the plan's first year), in exchange for about $5 billion in wage and work-rule concessions over the next six years. This is the biggest and most dramatic example of a growing trend toward employee ownership. The objective of the employees in designing this deal was to save their jobs. To stay employed, they were willing to take pay cuts of 10 to 17 percent. In addition, there were other concessions, like unpaid lunch breaks and reduced pension plan contributions. It is unlikely that they would have been willing to make these concessions without majority ownership to guarantee the manage-ment of their choice. Interestingly, however, the 13-member board of directors has seats for only four employee representatives, one from each of the three unions and one to represent non-union employees.

*Can employees think like owners? What structures are likely to encourage them to make decisions for the long-term value of the shareholders, as well as (and possibly instead of) the employees? Compare the employee ownership plans at other companies. At Wierton Steel, the company did extremely well at first, ahead of its peers. But the board replaced the CEO, a favorite of employees, with an outsider, a mutual-fund executive. A worker group filed a shareholder suit accusing the officers and directors of mismanagement. The board's efforts to raise capital (and dilute the workers' share) by issuing new stock led to a major battle.*

Following severe setbacks, including the post-September 11 increase in expenses and decrease in air travel, United filed for bankruptcy in late 2002. United indicated it would be seeking deep cuts from its pilots, mechanics, flight attendants and other employees, the "owners" of the company. And, as noted in chapter 2, the employees sued the money managers for holding on to the United stock.

# Case in point:
# The "temping" of the workplace

In contrast to the notion of employees as partners, or even owners, is the increased reliance on temporary employees. As companies save storage and other carrying costs with "just in time" inventory, they are increasingly taking advantage of the benefits of "just in time" employees. In 1993, the largest single private employer in the United States was a temp agency, Manpower Inc., with roughly 600,000 people on its payroll. By some calculations, one in four employees in the US are now members of the "contingency work force." Once thought of as a place to call if the receptionist was out sick or on vacation, these agencies are now relied on for "outsourcing" facilities for photocopying, word processing, accounting, and other technical operations. Some companies even go to temp firms for higher-level employees. Many hospitals outsource their emergency rooms to independent groups of physicians. Matthew Harrison works for Imcor, a firm that supplies high-level temporary employees. Reflecting on his experience as a high-level employee at four companies in seven years, he said, "There can be a real value in having a throwaway executive, who can come in and do unpleasant, nasty things like kill off a few sacred cows."[50] British consultant Charles Handy says, "Instead of being a castle, a home for life for its defenders, an organization will be more like an apartment block, an association of temporary residents gathered together for mutual convenience . . . [Corporations will still conduct business] but to do so they will no longer need to employ."[51]

Manpower CEO Mitchell Fromstein says that outsourcing is a good choice when there is high turnover (with high training costs) and when work is highly cyclical. Unquestionably, temping has made some companies more productive, and it has provided flexibility for workers like parents of young children and others who do not want the demands of a full-time career. But it has also been used as a tax dodge, at least in the view of the US Internal Revenue Service, which has insisted on recategorizing some 439,000 workers as employees (and therefore subject to withholding requirements). And it has been used as a way to avoid the cost of benefits. Microsoft uses temp employees because it does not have to share its lucrative stock options with them. Temp agencies do not give the employees they send out to other companies comprehensive health and pension benefits.

*What is the impact on the corporation when a substantial portion of its work-force receives a paycheck from someone else? How does the "contingency work-force" fit in to corporate governance? How do we permit employees to contribute to corporate direction if, as Handy says, corporations will "no longer need to employ"?*

## MONDRAGÓN AND SYMMETRY: INTEGRATION OF EMPLOYEES, OWNERS, AND DIRECTORS

Governance is ultimately concerned with the alignment of information, incentive and capacity to act. The challenge is aligning the responsibilities and authorities of all of the various constituencies to achieve the optimal conditions for growth and renewal. One of the most dramatic examples is the employee-owned enterprise, essentially taking the ESOP to its final conclusion. In this model, the two constituencies with the largest interest in the success of the venture are identical. It is not perfect; there are problems with the dual nature of the workers' interest, for example. In the short run, they want to maximize their compensation for work performed, but as owners they have a long-term interest in maximizing the value of the enterprise. Overall, however, this model probably does the best job of minimizing agency costs.

# Case in point: Mondragón and "co-operative entrepreneurship" or "co-operation instead of competition"

The Mondragón co-operatives were founded as a training facility for apprentices by a priest and some students in a small Basque city in the north of Spain. It has grown from 23 employees in one co-operative in 1956 to 19,500 employees in more than 100 enterprises in 1986. In 1987 sales were $1.6 billion, including $310 million in exports. Mondragón includes a large bank, a chain of department stores, schools, clinics, high-tech firms, appliance manufacturers, and machine shops. The individual co-operatives range in size from six employees to 2,000, from one location to 180. Mondragón is almost like a living organism, with each enterprise like a cell that divides when it grows too large. (In this way, it is similar to Semco, which compares itself to an amoeba.) There is no set limit, but practice has shown that 400–500 members is the maximum, since "beyond that size bureaucracy almost unavoidably intrudes and attenuates co-operative intimacy and solidarity."[52] Its achievement is not just in its growth, but in the success rate of the enterprises: there have been only three failures. Perhaps its greatest strengths are the commitment of its members (based in part on their role in its governance) and the co-operatives' ability to respond to change (based in part on the system for communication and the flexibility of the structure).

Its organization is designed to match entitlement and responsibility. Every employee has one vote. The companies operate according to ten co-operative principles:

1.  Admission is open to anyone who agrees with the basic co-operative principles.
2.  All workers must be members. All members have one vote, and all governing structures are democratically elected and are responsible to the general assembly.
3.  Labor is sovereign; the workers make the decisions.
4.  Everyone must make a capital contribution (generally equal to one year's salary of the lowest-paid member). Members get a set return on capital, not tied to losses or surpluses of the co-operative.
5.  Co-operation requires both individual effort and individual responsibility. This means information on which to make an informed decision must be available and all those who are affected by a decision must be consulted.
6.  The difference between the lowest- and highest-paid member of a co-operative may not be more than 1:6. And compensation must be comparable to local markets.
7.  "Co-operation exists on three levels: among individual co-operatives organized into groups; among co-op groups; and between the Mondragón and other movements."[53]
8.  Mondragón is committed to "social transformation." "The co-operatives invest the major portion of their surpluses in the Basque community. A significant portion goes toward new job development, to community development (through the use of social funds), to a social security system based on mutual solidarity and responsibility, to co-operation with other institutions (such as unions) advancing the cause of Basque workers, and to collaborative efforts to develop Basque language and culture."[54]
9.  The members are committed to solidarity with everyone who works for economic democracy, peace, justice, human dignity, and development in Europe and elsewhere, especially in the Third World.
10. They are dedicated to education for young people and workers.

Neither members (employees) nor outsiders own stock in any Mondragón co-operative. Instead, a co-operative is financed by members' contributions and entry fees at levels specified by the Governing Council and approved by the members. It is as if members are lending money to the firm. So each member thus has a capital account with the firm in his or her name. Capital accounts involve paper transactions between the members and the firm. Real money is, of course, involved because management is obligated to manage the co-operative with sufficient skill and prudence so that the firm can meet its financial obligations to members if they leave the firm or retire.

Ultimate power resides in the General Assembly, in which all members not only have the right, but the obligation to vote. The General Assembly meets at least annually. The Governing Council is the top policy-making body of the firm, which is elected on the basis of one vote per worker. It includes only worker-members. Key executives may attend council meetings, but they are not members of the council.

Members of the Governing Council are elected every two years for four-year terms. Members are not specially compensated for their council responsibilities but continue to be paid their regular salaries. The council has overall responsibility for management policies and programs. It selects the manager, who serves a four-year term unless he is deposed by the council. There is an audit committee consisting of three persons elected by the members.

There is also a Management Council, which consists of the manager and chief department heads. Finally, there is a Social Council, which has the right to advise the governing council on matters such as safety and health on the job, social security, systems of compensation, and social work activities or projects.

Mondragón is thus a structure of interested parties. No one is permitted access to the governance structure who has not made a material contribution of personal resources to the enterprise. No one is permitted the speculative profits that arise out of public ownership. Thus, a level of alignment is possible, because only interested parties are involved in setting values. The vagaries of the outside world are not permitted to upset the careful economic equilibrium of a Mondragón co-operative. In a sense, Mondragón is saying that jobs and the continuity of the enterprise are too important to permit the involvement of speculative money interests.

Figures 4.2, 4.3, and 4.4 show the contrast between Mondragón and traditional Anglo-American governance structures.

The Mondragón model, like any other model, should not and cannot be applied in all cases. But it does raise the question as to what extent "capital" is pre-eminently a commodity of use to the market speculators and to the expensive providers of financial advice. And it does provide one example of a system that minimizes conflicts of interest and maximizes information.

The record shows that a worker co-operative is likely to find itself in a Catch-22 situation: It disappears if it goes bankrupt or it is highly successful. When stock provides the basis of ownership, a successful firm must deal with the problem we call collective selfishness. As new workers are needed so that the firm can expand or replace those who leave, the original worker-owners recognize that they can increase the value of their investment if they resort to hiring labor . . . [examples of successful co-operatives leading to going public or selling out to a major competitor] . . . Unless the problem of collective selfishness is prevented in the way the firm is initially structured, we can expect this scenario to occur in financially successful co-operatives; the worker-owners will be reluctant to include new workers as owners; when they retire, they will be glad to sell to co-workers, but the value of the stock will make this impractical. The structure and financial policies of Mondragón prevent this problem from occurring. No stock is issued, and the constitution and by-laws of the individual co-operatives impose a 10 percent hiring limit on non-members. Because their capital accounts are non-transferable and no stock is issued, members cannot profit from selling shares to outsiders. There remains just one theoretical possibility for collective selfishness. The original members of a growing co-operative could vote to change their constitution and by-laws to allow more than 10 percent of their employees. In that case, the value of the individual member's share in profits would increase. This has never happened in Mondragón.[55]

For more information about Mondragón, please see
<http://www.Mondragón.mcc.es/ingles/menuing.html>,
<http:/www.sfworlds.com/linkworld/Mondragón.html>, and
<http://www.ping.be/jvwit/Mondragón.html>.

One especially interesting aspect of the Mondragón structure is the separate governing bodies for social and financial purposes. Compare this to the dual board system in Germany (see chapter 5). Here is one other idea about this approach:

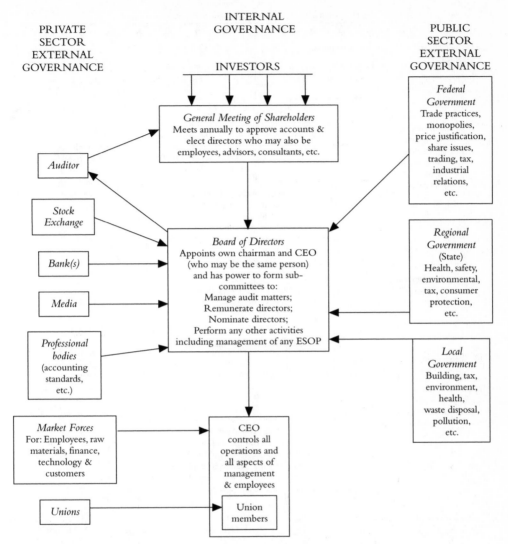

**Figure 4.2** Anglo-Saxon corporate governance (Courtesy Shann Turnbull)

Professor Bayless Manning has sketched the outlines of an idea which has intriguing implications and merits further exploration. His suggestion is addressed primarily to the issue of accountability, rather than to the problem of providing with a more tangible mandate. His article proposes to consider the large, publicly held corporation as if it were in law what it often is in fact, a kind of voting trust, where the stockholder delegates all his rights save that of collecting his dividend to the directors – that is, to management. Viewing the corporation in the light of this theory of itself, he points out, immediately brings certain problems into the foreground, and indicates certain possibilities for remedial action. In order to establish more effective procedures for visitation and control, he has in mind the development of a new device, public or private, which could carry out certain functions presently neglected, or relatively neglected. He seems to visualize this device as

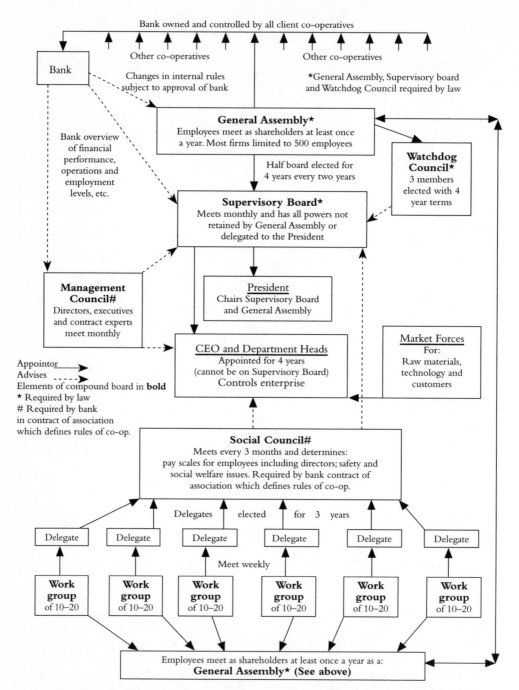

**Figure 4.3** Information and control architecture of Mondragón cooperatives
*Sources*: Based on information from: D.P. Ellerman, *The Socialization of Entrepreneurship: The Empresarial Division of the Caja Laboral Popular,* Industrial Co-operative Association, Sommerville, MA, 1982; W.F. Whyte and K.K. Whyte, *Making Mondragón: The Growth and Dynamics of the Worker Co-operative Complex,* ILR Press, Ithaca, NY, 1988; R. Morrison, *We Build the Road as we Travel,* New Society Press, Philadelphia, 1991.

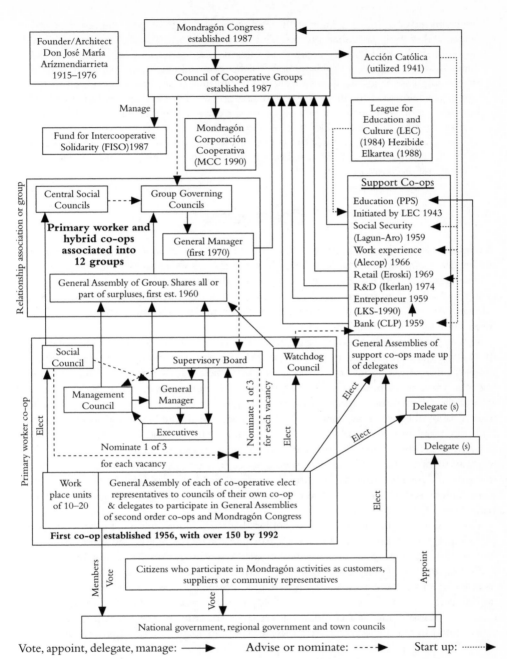

**Figure 4.4**   Mondragón cooperative system, with dates of establishment
*Sources*: Based on information from:
CLP, *Annual Report*, Caja Laboral Popular, Euskadiko Kusxa, Spain, 1992;
MCC, *Annual Report*, Mondragón Corporacion Cooperativa, Mondragón, Spain,
1992; T. Mollner, *The Prophets of the Pyrenees: The Search for the Relationship Age*,
Trustee Institute, Northampton, MA, 1991; R. Morrison, *We Build the Road as we
Travel*, New Society Press, Philadelphia, 1991; W.F. Whyte and K.K. Whyte,
*Making Mondragón: The Growth and Dynamics of the Worker Co-operative Complex*,
ILR Press, Ithaca, NY, 1988.

preferably private, and as a kind of "second chamber," distinct from the board of directors, and with more limited powers. This "extrinsic" body would presumably review decisions of the board where conflicts of interest arise, particularly with regard to the compensation of officers; it could also pass on other board and managerial decisions, notably where corporate funds are spent for charitable contributions not directly related to the company's business. It might well have broader powers, in enforcing a full disclosure of the corporation's financial and business affairs, for example. In a corporate world organized in this way, the stockholder would hold in effect certificates in a voting trust. He would "own" his stock, and not the equity of the corporation, save for such problems as the determination of creditors' rights, where Professor Manning would not alter the existing law of contractual priority.[56]

## CONCLUSION

We return to our original questions: *Who is in the best position to make a given decision about the direction of a corporation, and does that person or group have the necessary authority?* The material we have covered has given us a context for developing the answers. The person or group in the best position to make any decision about the corporation's direction is determined by two factors: conflicts of interest, and information. Decisions should be made by those with the fewest conflicts and the most information.

This applies from the smallest decision to the largest. Who should decide what color the walls should be painted in the workroom? The people who work in that room have the best information about which color suits them best. Furthermore, looking at them as a group, there is no possible conflict of interests because there are no agency costs; they are deciding something that affects them. The question of how often the walls should be painted is another question, however. Workers are not in the best position to determine how often the money should be spent to repaint. They would be acting as agents for management if they made this decision, and the agency costs would be considerable. There is a way to minimize these agency costs, if so desired by any of the parties, of course. If the workers are meaningfully responsible for budget allocation (which is a system with some benefits), they will "feel" the impact of the decision enough to align their interests with those of management.

The corporate structure has been so robust that it has outgrown most of the structures, including the political structures, designed to control it. Accountability must come from within, and that requires an effective governance system that is itself accountable. All three major players in corporate governance, the board, the shareholders, and the management, must be able to act and must be motivated and informed enough to act correctly. There is no one perfect corporate governance model, just as there is no one perfect financial structure. The ultimate aim of a corporate governance structure must be that it is continually re-evaluated so that the governance structure itself can adapt to changing times and needs.

## NOTES

1. Thomas A. Stewart, "The King is Dead," *Fortune*, Jan. 14, 1993, p. 34.
2. Ibid., p. 35.
3. Ibid., p. 40.
4. Ira M. Millstein, "Advising a CEO on Boardroom Relations," *American Lawyer*, Nov. 1993, p. 87.

5. "The Pharaonic CEO," *Fortune*, Dec. 4, 1989.

6. "It Could Happen To Us," interview with David A. Nadler, in *Across the Board*, Oct. 1993, p. 28.

7. Randall Smith, John J. Kelle, and John R. Wilke, "AT&T Launches $6.12 Billion Cash Offer for NCR after Rejection of its Stock Bid," *Wall Street Journal*, Dec. 6, 1990, p. A3.

8. Interview with David A. Nadler, in *Across the Board*, p. 28.

9. See James B. Stewart, "Whales and Sharks," *New Yorker*, Feb. 15, 1993.

10. "General Electric, Strategic Position – 1981," Harvard Business School Case Study 9381-174, Mar. 24, 1993, p. 1.

11. See "General Electric: Jack Welch's Second Wave (A)", Harvard Business School Case Study 9-391-248, Apr. 2, 1993.

12. Ibid.

13. Albert O. Hirschman, *Exit, Voice, and Loyalty: Responses to Decline in Firms, Organizations, and States* (Harvard University Press, Cambridge, MA, 1970).

14. Frank H. Easterbrook and Daniel R. Fischel, "The Corporate Contract," 89 *Columbia Law Review*, 7, Nov. 1989, p. 1418.

15. *Forbes*, May 27, 1991.

16. Graef Crystal, *In Search of Excess* (W.W. Norton, New York, 1991).

17. See Graef Crystal's study for the United Shareholders Association, "Executive Compensation in Corporate America 1991," and Graef Crystal, "The Compensation 500: What America's Top CEOs Should Be Paid This Year," *Financial World*, Oct. 29, 1991. For press coverage, see Michelle Osborne, "Author's Recipe for CEO Pay," *USA Today*, Oct. 9, 1991; Robert J. McCartney, "Quoth the Maven, Cut Some More," *Washington Post*, Jan. 29, 1992; Alison Leigh Cowan, "The Gadfly CEOs Want To Swat," *New York Times*, Feb. 2, 1992.

18. Graef Crystal, *In Search of Excess*, pp. 51–85.

19. Ibid., p. 75.

20. Michael C. Jensen and Kevin J. Murphy, "CEO Incentives: It's Not *How Much* You Pay, It's *How*," *Harvard Business Review*, May/June 1990, p. 138.

21. Stephen Bryan, LeeSeok Hwang, and Steven Lilien, "CEO Stock-Based Compensation: An Empirical Analysis of Incentive-Intensity, Relative Mix and Economic Determinants," *The Journal of Business*, 73, 4, Oct. 2000.

22. See Towers Perrin, "XYZ Company: Weaknesses of Conventional Stock Option Plans and a Proposed Solution: An Indexed Stock Option Plan" (New York, 1991).

23. Berkshire Hathaway, Inc., *Annual Report to Shareholders* (1985), p. 12.

24. Crystal, *In Search of Excess*, p. 134.

25. Statement of Richard Breeden, chairman of SEC, at open meeting of the Commission, Oct. 15, 1992.

26. Joann Lublin, "Companies Seek Loopholes for Executive Pay Deduction," *Wall Street Journal*, Nov. 19, 1993, p. B1.

27. Ibid.

28. See Jamie E. Heard, "How New SEC Rules Impact '93 Proxy Season," *ISSue Alert*, Nov. 1992, VII, 11.

29. See *The Federal Register*, 57, 204, Oct. 21, 1992, p. 48138.

30. "Shareholder Communication and Executive Compensation," opening statement of Richard C. Breeden, chairman of the Securities and Exchange Commission at the open meeting of the Commission, Oct. 15, 1992.

31. We particularly appreciated Crystal's pointing out the unique provision in the Time Warner options – they became exercisable not when the deal was concluded, but as soon as the board voted to approve it.

32. See, for example, Joseph W. Singer, "Reliance Interest in Property," 40 *Stanford Law Review* 611, 1988, and "Jobs and Justice: Rethinking the Stakeholder Debate," 43 *University of Toronto Law Journal* 475, 1993, and materials cited therein.

33. Ricardo Semler, *Maverick: The Success Story Behind the World's Most Unusual Workplace* (Warner Books, New York, 1993), p. 97.

34. Ivan Alexander, *Foundations of Business* (Basil Blackwell, Oxford, 1990), p. 93.

35. Shann Turnbull, *Reinventing Corporations* (IOS, 1991), p. 176.

36. Ibid., p. 177.

37. Ibid.

38. Ibid., p. 179.

39. Morbid capital is a graphic name for a phenomenon that is explicitly articulated in the British common law of property, which became part of the American common law of property with the adoption of the US Constitution in 1789. It relates to two limitations on the rights that a person possesses with respect to a thing he or she owns. Specifically, a private property owner may not (1) use that property to cause injury to the property or person of another, or (2) use that property in ways that injure the public interest or the public welfare. "Morbid capital . . . beggars others by depriving them of the economic opportunity to increase their earnings as capital workers." Louis O. Kelso and Patricia Hetter Kelso, *Democracy and Economic Power* (Ballinger, Cambridge, MA, 1986).

40. Owen D. Young, Dedication Address, June 4, 1927, published in *Harvard Business Review*, 4, pp. 385, 392.

41. Private letter from Ben Makihara to Robert A.G. Monks.

42. A complete discussion of the political, cultural, strategic and financial reasons for Japan's economic growth is beyond the scope of this book. We will therefore consider only one aspect, the role of the employee as owner.

43. Robert S. Ozaki, *Human Capitalism* (Penguin Books, London, 1991), p. 18.

44. Shann Turnbull, "Democratic Capitalism; Self-Financing Local Ownership and Control," prepared for the *Symposium on the Interplay of Economics and Politics in Economic Transformations in Russia and Central Europe*, Mar. 27, 1993, p. 7.

45. Kelso and Kelso, *Democracy and Economic Power*, p. 47.

46. Ibid., p. 45.

47. They are "stockholder neutral" because the formation of the ESOP does not require the creation of any new shares that would dilute existing shareholders' equity.

48. Joseph R. Blasi, *Employee Ownership: Revolution or Ripoff?* (Ballinger, Cambridge, MA, 1988), p. 154.

49. *The Congressional Record*, Sept. 18, 1986, H7744–46.

50. Jaclyn Fierman, "The Contingency Work Force," *Fortune*, Jan. 24, 1994, p. 31.

51. Ibid.

52. Roy Morrison, *We Build the Road As We Travel* (New Society Publishers, 1991), p. 13.

53. Ibid., p. 12.

54. Ibid.

55. William Foote Whyte and Kathleen Kind Whyte, *Making Mondragón: The Growth and Dynamics of the Worker Cooperative Complex*, 2nd edn. (Cornell, 1988), pp. 288, 289.

56. Eugene V. Rostow, "To Whom and For What Ends is Corporate Management Responsible?" in Edward S. Mason (ed.), *The Corporation in Modern Society* (Harvard University Press, Cambridge, MA, 1959), pp. 57–8.

# 5

# INTERNATIONAL GOVERNANCE

## CORPORATE GOVERNANCE HAS GONE GLOBAL

When the first edition of this book was published in 1995, it included analysis on the different approaches that individual markets took to corporate governance. It is now more fitting to analyze the ways in which local market practices are converging.

Of course national culture remains a powerful force, and it would be wrong to exaggerate the degree of governance harmony that exists. Even in markets such as those of the US and UK, whose language and legal systems are closely aligned, there remain considerable differences in style, structure and emphasis. Furthermore, the accounting systems are completely different in approach and result, and as transparency is a key aspect of any governance system and a key responsibility of the board, that makes the similarities of the two systems more an illusion than a reality.

In the last few years, there has been a remarkable acceleration in governance activity, in both mature and developing markets. If it is still far from convergence, there is at least widespread agreement on the core principles of independence, transparency, and accountability as the cornerstone of a credible capitalist system that can attract investment from outsiders – those outside the business and especially those outside the country. The acceleration has its roots in the emergence of the global economy, which has transformed both the corporate and investment landscape and created fertile ground for governance development. Vital trends include the following.

### The triumph of the corporation

A new economic orthodoxy has taken root worldwide – that the corporation, as opposed to the government, is the principal driver of economic growth and improved living standards. In developed markets (particularly the UK and France) and emerging ones (eastern Europe, the former Soviet Union, Asia and South America), the triumph of the corporation has been expressed in the form of widespread privatizations, as the government seeks to minimize its role in the economy. One UK observer wrote: "Private business has rarely been as celebrated and lauded as today. It is hailed not only as the source of wealth creation and job generation; it is the driver of technological innovation and the very idea of modernity."[1]

## The global company

Large companies can no longer afford to compete solely in their domestic markets. In sectors such as banking, telecoms, pharmaceuticals or automobiles (see the DaimlerChrysler case in point), there has been widespread cross-border consolidation. Partly, this is due to changes highlighted in the paragraph above – governments are less willing to protect "national champions" from takeover. Other contributing factors include the rise of companies that are global in scope and the breakdown of import tariffs and other trade restrictions that protected domestic companies from competition. It is also a response to the rise of the global investor – see the next section.

## The global investor

Information technology allows investors to gain critical information about distant companies and make trades at the click of a mouse. Research on foreign companies has been facilitated by the wider use of internationally recognized accounting standards by companies worldwide. Investment institutions have themselves been deregulated, allowing them a far greater range of investment opportunities. Country-wide economic slumps have been a powerful reminder that only global diversification can provide the protection of diversification. The collapse of the Soviet bloc, the integration of Europe and the opening of other national borders have created new markets; and the privatization programs mentioned above have created new companies and sectors.

The result, over the past 20 years, has been to make investment a truly global phenomenon.

Until 1985, equity investment by US pension funds was a largely domestic activity. UK and Dutch investors had a wider horizon, given the relatively large amount of capital compared to the relatively small number of publicly traded companies. But between 1985 and 1994, US investors began looking overseas. There were hiccups – particularly following the 1987 market crash and the Gulf War.

By 1994, foreign investors accounted for more than 1 percent of total world stock market capitalizations. This figure has not since been exceeded, although the flow of funds across national borders has shown a consistent rise.[2]

In 1988, just 2 percent of US pension fund assets were invested in non-domestic equities. Ten years later, that figure stood at 12 percent. In dollar terms this means that some $800 billion of US pension fund assets were invested overseas, up from just $48 billion in 1988.[3]

"Globalization of equity markets looks unstoppable as trade and capital flows are increasingly liberalized and multinational companies continue to dominate the marketplace," wrote one commentator. "The corporate world's drive for the cheapest capital options is leveling all sorts of playing fields. At the same time, investors' learning is accelerated by the IT revolution. Under these twin thrusts, the investment world is shrinking and becoming more uniform."[4]

A few examples make the case. The foreign holdings of the world's largest pension fund, the teachers' retirement system TIAA–CREF, amount to more than $23 billion in 32 different markets. In 2002, CalPERS, the largest US public pension fund, held $25 billion (18.7 percent of its portfolio) in non-US equities. Hermes, a leading UK fund held more than $20 billion abroad in 1999.

## The demands of capital

Global companies (or companies wishing to become global) are thirsty for capital. The hugely wealthy institutional investors of the UK, US and Holland are more than willing to give it to them. At a price.

Investors are interested primarily in the growth of their investments, but they also need to be confident that that growth rests on secure foundations. Confidence is established by the presence of such basic building blocks as:

- an effective legal and regulatory system that minimizes the chances that their capital will be squandered or stolen (especially if they are minority shareholders);
- a board of directors who are genuinely vigilant protectors of shareholder interests and value;
- properly audited accounts that give a real view of the company's performance;
- a fair voting process that allows them to be consulted before major corporate decisions are taken;
- corporate reporting that offers a real-world view of the company's future prospects;
- the freedom to sell their shares to the highest bidder.

In short, investors demand transparency and accountability in return for their capital. They would be foolish to demand anything less. Countries and companies round the world have found that the best way to attract much-needed global capital is to meet those demands.

The substance of this chapter is about how individual markets and companies – with vastly different histories and investment cultures – have adapted to attract global capital. And how that capital, in turn, has responded to governance progress or failures in numerous markets.

## The triumph of the code

A respected observer of the international governance scene, Stephen Davis, commented that if corporate governance codes appeared in trade figures, Britain would have a far healthier balance of payments.[5]

His comment reflected the fact that the first corporate governance code of the modern era – that instituted in the UK by the Bank of England and London Stock Exchange in 1992, and chaired by ex-chocolate chief, Sir Adrian Cadbury – spawned so many imitators.

By the close of the century, there were more than 60 governance codes in 30 markets, as well as numerous international codes. This is not to mention the vast number of individual governance or voting guidelines produced by individual investment institutions.

The Cadbury Committee latched on to a formula for governance progress that has become the industry standard – it developed a list of "best practice" governance standards to which companies were encouraged to aspire. Companies were then required to disclose how they measured up to the code, giving explanations for any areas of non-compliance.

The formula was neat – it avoided burdensome regulation or inflexible legislation; allowed for the fact that companies should be free to develop their own governance practices; and, via disclosure, put the onus for improvement on investors. This method of combining an advisory code with a disclosure regime has been adopted by dozens of codes worldwide.

In the UK alone, there have been three major governance committees – Cadbury (1992), Greenbury (on executive pay, led by Marks & Spencer chief, Sir Richard Greenbury), and Hampel (chaired by ICI chairman, Sir Ronnie Hampel). In addition, a committee chaired by Rank finance director Nigel Turnbull offered advice on how companies should manage their internal controls. And the Myners Committee report on the ways that investors and managers could work together focused on improving the communication between institutions and their portfolio companies, particularly in sharing goals and strategies.

Other countries have produced thoughtful and comprehensive codes. South Africa's King Report on Corporate Governance was produced in 1994 by a committee chaired by former High Court judge Mervyn King. It was updated in 2002 to emphasize the role of the board and the importance of structures for transparency and accountability. It encourages a focus on the "triple bottom line," concluding that:

> successful governance in the world in the 21st century requires companies to adopt an inclusive and not exclusive approach. The company must be open to institutional activism and there must be greater emphasis on the sustainable or non-financial aspects of its performance. Boards must apply the test of fairness, accountability, responsibility and transparency to all acts or omissions and be accountable to the company but also responsive and responsible towards the company's identified stakeholders. The correct balance between conformance with governance principles and performance in an entrepreneurial market economy must be found, but this will be specific to each company.

The US, notably among major markets, lacks an overarching code of best practice. As of this writing, the authors have posted 54 countries' codes on the Corporate Library's website at <http://www.thecorporatelibrary.com/international/index.asp>. Codes have been developed by OECD countries like the United Kingdom, Japan, Poland, Portugal, the Czech Republic, Sweden, and Spain, and by emerging markets like Peru, Egypt, Venezuela, and Kenya.

While these advisory codes vary widely in terms of standards and authority – the Corporate Governance Forum of Japan code, for example, is purely advisory and has no regulatory clout – the aim of each code is the same: to raise governance standards in a market as a means of attracting (and reducing the cost of) capital.

## *Universal codes*

As individual markets have sought to raise their internal governance standards, so there have been efforts to develop universal governance codes that can apply worldwide.

All commentators agree that there can be no "one size fits all" standard. Other countries' practices cannot be transplanted or imposed any more than their cultures and legal systems can, and individual companies and markets will always be subject to local cultures, pressures and practices.

But it is possible to identify and promote a set of guiding principles to which companies should aspire.

The first effort to offer a global set of principles was by the Paris-based international agency, the Organization for Economic Cooperation and Development (OECD). It faced a knotty problem in attempting to harmonize practices across its 29-country member base, ranging from the US to South Korea. A task force was established. Finding common ground proved tricky, and the debate was sometimes contentious. The OECD offered guidelines under five headings:[6]

1.   the rights of shareholders
2.   the responsibilities of shareholders
3.   the rights of stakeholders
4.   disclosure and transparency
5.   the role and structure of the board.

## *An investor perspective*

The OECD code proved useful, as far as it went. As a statement of the basic virtues of accountability and transparency it can hardly be faulted, and for the success with which it navigated tricky political waters it is a remarkable achievement.

But it is not particularly visionary, and not especially substantive. The OECD has no power to implement the code, and no there is no requirement on individual companies to take notice or even disclose how much of it they have adopted. The OECD code acts rather as a reference point for companies that wish to amend their governance practices.

A more forceful statement of global principles was made by the International Corporate Governance Network (ICGN), an investor-led body representing more than $10 trillion in assets. The ICGN Principles equal a statement of investors' expectations. And investors have the power to effect real change.

The ICGN Principles thus represent not just a statement of minimum best practice standards, applicable worldwide, but one that is backed by a body with the power to implement change.

For this reason, it is worth reproducing the ICGN Principles in full.

### ICGN STATEMENT ON CORPORATE GOVERNANCE PRINCIPLES

*Adopted at the annual meeting on July 9, 1999, Frankfurt, Germany*

The International Corporate Governance Network (ICGN), founded in 1995 at the instigation of major institutional investors, represents investors, companies, financial intermediaries, academics and other parties interested in the development of global corporate governance practices. Its objective is to facilitate international dialogue on the issues concerned. Through this process, the ICGN holds, companies can compete more effectively and economies can best prosper. The organization's charter empowers it to adopt guidelines when it feels they can contribute to achieving this objective.

### STATEMENT ON THE OECD PRINCIPLES

In May 1999 ministers representing the 29 governments which comprise the Organization for Economic Co-operation and Development (OECD) voted unanimously to endorse the *OECD Principles of Corporate Governance*. These principles were negotiated over the course of a year in consultation with key players in the market, including the ICGN.

They constitute the chief response by governments to the G7 Summit Leaders' recognition of corporate governance as an important pillar in the architecture of the 21st century global economy. The Principles were welcomed by the G7 leaders at the Cologne summit in June 1999 and are likely to act as signposts for activity in this area by the International Monetary Fund, the World Bank, the United Nations and other international organizations.

The ICGN applauds the OECD Principles as a declaration of minimum acceptable standards for companies and investors around the world. Much of the document reflects perspectives promoted by ICGN representatives serving on the OECD's Ad Hoc Task Force on Corporate Governance, relying on the draft principles under discussion at the ICGN. The ICGN welcomes the OECD Principles as a remarkable convergence on corporate governance common ground among diverse interests, practices and cultures.

The ICGN affirms – with the OECD Principles – that along with traditional financial criteria, the governance profile of a corporation is now an essential factor that investors take into consideration when deciding how to allocate their investment capital. The Principles highlight elements that ICGN investing members already take into account when making asset allocation and investment decisions.

While the ICGN considers the OECD Principles the necessary bedrock of good corporate governance, it holds that amplifications are required to give them sufficient force. In particular, the ICGN believes that companies around the world deserve clear, concrete guidance on how the OECD Principles can best be implemented. Practical guidance can help boards meet real-world expectations so that they may operate most efficiently and, in particular, compete for scarce investment capital effectively. The ICGN contends that if investors and managers succeed in establishing productive communication on issues, they will have enhanced prospects for economic prosperity, fuller employment, better wages, and greater shareholder wealth.

The ICGN therefore advocates that companies adopt the OECD Principles as amplified in the attached statements. First, to offer more concise guidance, the ICGN distills the most significant points in its statement on the OECD Principles into a short-form roster of corporate governance tenets – a "Working Kit" – that reflects the viewpoints of ICGN members. Then the ICGN statement amplifying the OECD Principles tracks that document's format, underscoring or interpreting as appropriate.

It is the ICGN's view that it is in companies' best interests to adhere to these recommendations even in the absence of any domestic legal requirements for their implementation.

## ICGN APPROACH TO THE OECD PRINCIPLES

A "Working Kit" Statement of Corporate Governance Criteria

### 1. Corporate Objective
The overriding objective of the corporation should be to optimize over time the returns to its shareholders. Where other considerations affect this objective, they should be clearly stated and disclosed. To achieve this objective, the corporation should endeavor to ensure the long-term viability of its business, and to manage effectively its relationships with stakeholders.

### 2. Communications and Reporting
Corporations should disclose accurate, adequate and timely information, in particular meeting market guidelines where they exist, so as to allow investors to make informed decisions about the acquisition, ownership obligations and rights, and sale of shares.

### 3. Voting Rights

Corporations' ordinary shares should feature one vote for each share. Corporations should act to ensure the owners' rights to vote. Fiduciary investors have a responsibility to vote. Regulators and law should facilitate voting rights and timely disclosure of the levels of voting.

### 4. Corporate Boards

The board of directors, or supervisory board, as an entity, and each of its members, as an individual, is a fiduciary for all shareholders, and should be accountable to the shareholder body as a whole. Each member should stand for election on a regular basis.

Corporations should disclose upon appointment to the board and thereafter in each annual report or proxy statement information on the identities, core competencies, professional or other backgrounds, factors affecting independence, and overall qualifications of board members and nominees so as to enable investors to weigh the value they add to the company. Information on the appointment procedure should also be disclosed annually.

Boards should include a sufficient number of independent non-executive members with appropriate competencies.

Responsibilities should include monitoring and contributing effectively to the strategy and performance of management, staffing key committees of the board, and influencing the conduct of the board as a whole. Accordingly, independent non-executives should comprise no fewer than three members and as much as a substantial majority.

Audit, remuneration and nomination board committees should be composed wholly or predominantly of independent non-executives.

### 5. Corporate Remuneration Policies

Remuneration of corporate directors or supervisory board members and key executives should be aligned with the interests of shareholders.

Corporations should disclose in each annual report or proxy statement the board's policies on remuneration – and, preferably, the remuneration break up of individual board members and top executives – so that investors can judge whether corporate pay policies and practices meet that standard.

Broad-based employee share ownership plans or other profit-sharing programs are effective market mechanisms that promote employee participation.

### 6. Strategic Focus

Major strategic modifications to the core business(es) of a corporation should not be made without prior shareholder approval of the proposed modification. Equally, major corporate changes which in substance or effect materially dilute the equity or erode the economic interests or share ownership rights of existing shareholders should not be made without prior shareholder approval of the proposed change.

Shareholders should be given sufficient information about any such proposal, sufficiently early, to allow them to make an informed judgment and exercise their voting rights.

### 7. Operating Performance

Corporate governance practices should focus board attention on optimizing over time the company's operating performance. In particular, the company should strive to excel in specific sector peer group comparisons.

### 8. Shareholder Returns

Corporate governance practices should also focus board attention on optimizing over time the returns to shareholders. In particular, the company should strive to excel in comparison with the specific equity sector peer group benchmark.

### 9. Corporate Citizenship

Corporations should adhere to all applicable laws of the jurisdictions in which they operate.

Boards that strive for active co-operation between corporations and stakeholders will be most likely to create wealth, employment and sustainable economies. They should disclose their policies on issues involving stakeholders, for example workplace and environmental matters.

### 10. Corporate Governance Implementation

Where codes of best corporate governance practice exist, they should be applied pragmatically. Where they do not yet exist, investors and others should endeavor to develop them.

Corporate governance issues between shareholders, the board and management should be pursued by dialogue and, where appropriate, with government and regulatory representatives as well as other concerned bodies, so as to resolve disputes, if possible, through negotiation, mediation or arbitration. Where those means fail, more forceful actions should be possible. For instance, investors should have the right to sponsor resolutions or convene extraordinary meetings.

## OECD PRINCIPLES AS AMPLIFIED

### Preamble

The ICGN affirms that, to be effective, corporate governance practices should focus board attention on optimizing over time the returns to shareholders with a view to excel in comparison with the company's equity sector peer group.

To achieve this objective, the board is expected to manage successfully its relationships with other stakeholders, i.e. those with a legitimate interest in the operation of the business, such as employees, customers, suppliers, creditors, and the communities in which the company operates.

### I. The Rights of Shareholders

*Overall Strategy.* Major strategic modifications to the core business(es) of a corporation should not be made without prior shareholder approval of the proposed modification. Equally, major corporate changes which in substance or effect materially dilute the equity or erode the economic interests or share ownership rights of existing shareholders should not be made without prior shareholder approval of the proposed change. Shareholders should be given sufficient information about any such proposal, sufficiently early, to allow them to make an informed judgment and exercise their voting rights.

*Access to the Vote.* The right and opportunity to vote at shareholder meetings hinges in part on the adequacy of the voting system. The ICGN believes that markets and companies can facilitate access to the ballot by following the ICGN's *Global Share Voting Principles,* adopted at the July 10, 1998 annual meeting in San Francisco. In particular, the ICGN supports initiatives to expand voting options to include the secure use of telecommunication and other electronic channels.

*Disclosing Results.* The ICGN underlines both the OECD assertion that "equal effect should be given to votes whether cast in person or in absentia" and the Annotation's statement that "as a matter of transparency, meeting procedures should ensure that votes are properly counted and recorded, and that a timely announcement of the outcome be made." To implement this recommendation, the ICGN believes that corporations should disclose voting levels for each resolution in a timely manner.

*Unequal Voting.* The ICGN affirms that divergence from a "one-share, one-vote" standard which gives certain shareholders power disproportionate to their equity ownership is undesirable. Any such divergence should be both disclosed and justified.

*Duty to Vote.* The ICGN believes that institutional investors have a fiduciary obligation to vote their shares, subject to considerations of excessive cost and obstacles.

## II. The Equitable Treatment of Shareholders

*One-Share, One-Vote.* The ICGN affirms the OECD's recognition that "many institutional investors and shareholder associations support . . . the concept of one-share, one-vote." The ICGN holds that national capital markets can grow best over the long-term if they move toward the "one-share, one-vote" principle. Conversely, capital markets that retain inequities are likely to be disadvantaged compared with markets that embrace fair voting procedures.

*Protections.* As the OECD declares, boards should treat all the corporation's shareholders equitably and should ensure that the rights of all investors, "including minority and foreign shareholders," are protected.

## III. The Role of Stakeholders in Corporate Governance

*Board Member Duties.* The ICGN is of the view that the board should be accountable to shareholders and responsible for managing successful and productive relationships with the corporation's stakeholders. The ICGN concurs with the OECD Principle that "active co-operation between corporations and stakeholders" is essential in creating wealth, employment and financially-sound enterprises over time.

*Stakeholder Participation.* The ICGN affirms that performance-enhancing mechanisms promote employee participation and align shareholder and stakeholder interests. These include broad-based employee share ownership plans or other profit-sharing programs.

## IV. Disclosure and Transparency

*Objective.* The ICGN holds that corporations should disclose accurate, adequate and timely information, in particular meeting market guidelines where they exist, so as to allow investors to make informed decisions about the acquisition, ownership obligations and rights, and sale of shares.

*Ownership and Voting Rights.* In addition to financial and operating results, company objectives, risk factors, stakeholder issues and governance structures, the information enumerated in the OECD Annotations is needed. These are "data on major shareholders and others that control or may control the company, including information on special voting rights, shareholder agreements, the beneficial ownership of controlling or large blocks of shares, significant cross-shareholding relationships and cross-guarantees" as well as information on differential voting rights and related party transactions.

*Board Member Information.* The ICGN further asserts that corporations should disclose upon appointment to the board and thereafter in each annual report or proxy statement sufficient information on the identities, core competencies, professional backgrounds, other board memberships, factors affecting independence, and overall qualifications of board members and nominees so as to enable the assessment of the value they add to the company. Information on the appointment procedure should also be disclosed annually.

*Remuneration.* Remuneration of corporate directors or supervisory board members and key executives should be aligned with the interests of shareholders. Corporations should disclose in each annual report or proxy statement the board's policies on remuneration – and, preferably, the remuneration break up of individual directors and top executives – so that it can be judged whether corporate pay policies and practices meet that standard.

*Audit.* The ICGN advocates annual audits of corporations by independent, outside auditors, together with measures that enhance confidence in the quality and independence of the audit. The ICGN itself has voted support for the development of the highest-quality international accounting standards, and would encourage corporations to apply those or other standards of comparable quality. The ICGN also backs active, independent board audit committees and, to limit the risks of possible conflicts of interest, disclosure of the fees paid to auditors for non-audit services.

### V. The Responsibilities of the Board
The ICGN agrees with the OECD's enumeration of board duties and responsibilities.

*Independent Board Members.* It endorses the assertion that "the board should be able to exercise objective judgment on corporate affairs independent, in particular, from management." To meet this challenge, the ICGN holds that each company should take the following steps. First, it should acknowledge that the board of directors, or supervisory board, as an entity, and each of its members, as an individual, is a fiduciary for all shareholders, and should be accountable to the shareholder body as a whole. Each elected member should stand for election on a regular basis. Second, each board should include sufficient independent non-executive members with appropriate competencies. Responsibilities should include monitoring and contributing effectively to the strategy and performance of management, staffing key committees of the board, and influencing the conduct of the board as a whole. Accordingly, independent non-executives should comprise no fewer than three members and as much as a substantial majority.

*Independent Committees.* To further strengthen the professionalism of boards, the ICGN endorses earlier language considered by the OECD. "Certain key responsibilities of the board such as audit, nomination and executive remuneration, require the attention of independent, non-executive members of the board. Boards should consider establishing committees containing a sufficient number of independent non-executive board members in these areas where there is a potential for conflict of interest or where independent business judgment is advisable." The ICGN considers that to meet this challenge audit, remuneration and nomination board committees should be composed wholly or pre-dominantly of independent non-executives.

Since adopting these principles, the ICGN has gone on to support a number of initiatives both at the public- and private-sector levels: uniform global accounting standards; equitable shareholder voting procedures for all investors, whatever their country of origin; and sharper focus on corporate governance matters by company managements. The ICGN is currently working on a number of fronts to address and resolve cross-border proxy voting problems.

## LIMITS TO CONVERGENCE

There are still fundamental differences in underlying assumptions that limit structural convergence. Some countries, including the US, base their systems on an agent-principal approach, with creation of shareholder value as the primary focus of a company's strategy. Others take a stakeholder approach, concerned with the entire network of relations, including employees, customers, suppliers, and the community. Another way of looking at this is "insider control" vs. "outsider" control of management by investors and the more arm's-length, quantitative measure of performance. A more technical but equally pervasive dichotomy exists between the "principles-based" accounting of the EU vs. "rules-based" accounting principles in the US.

## THE ASIAN FINANCIAL CRISIS, THE WORLD BANK AND GOVERNANCE IN EMERGING MARKETS

A major initiative was launched by the World Bank in 1999 to promote global governance reform, with a particular focus on emerging markets.

The roots of the initiative can be found in the financial crisis that swept the world in the summer of 1998. Triggered by a massive default on loans by the Russian government, the crisis raised fears of a complete meltdown of the Western financial system epitomized by the failure of the poorly named New York hedge fund, Long Term Capital Management (LTCM). The fund was bailed out by its investors to the tune of $3.5 billion.

The bailout of LTCM demonstrated that the Western financial system had the capacity to withstand sudden rude shocks – largely by passing the costs on to shareholders and beneficiaries of those finance houses that had invested in LTCM. But, at the same time, the lack of stability of other markets was ruthlessly exposed.

The 1998 financial crisis demonstrated that the vital institutional architecture that underpins investor confidence simply did not exist in emerging markets. These markets offered no security to investors, who were quick to cut their losses and run. The whole house of cards was quick to tumble.

The crisis spread like a forest fire to Central and South America and, with disastrous force, to Asia. Currency, bond and equity markets collapsed, and hundreds if not thousands of companies were rendered bankrupt. In Indonesia, nearly one-third of listed companies folded.

A key aspect of the crisis was the flight to relative safety of Western capital. The flow of equity into emerging markets which averaged nearly $40 billion a year in the mid-1990s, according to the OECD, dived virtually to zero in 1998.

The capital flight carried enormous costs, not just for the investors who suffered substantial losses, but to the emerging markets themselves. It was the equivalent of a small business having its bank loans recalled at its time of greatest difficulty.

The harsh lessons of the 1998 financial crisis at least had the benefit of kick-starting substantial efforts to improve governance standards in developing economies.

The crisis exposed how shallow were the foundations on which the Asian economic miracle was based. Firms were hopelessly indebted, accounts presented a barely recognizable picture of companies' financial status, directors lacked training, regulators and courts lacked power, managers were unaccountable, and, in many markets, the whole corporate edifice was riddled with government interference, corruption and kickbacks.

Governance reform in emerging markets has been all about restoring investor confidence by providing a secure institutional platform on which to build an investment market.

## World Bank and G7 response

Preventing a 1998-style market crisis from occurring again was an issue of critical economic, social and moral responsibility for the political and financial world. Improved corporate governance was seen as a cornerstone of that process.

At its October 1998 annual meeting, the World Bank announced a raft of measures to improve governance worldwide, including expert and technical assistance, knowledge-sharing, and loans tied to governance reform. Shortly thereafter, the Bank opened an internet site offering a catalogue of governance codes, research, and links.

UK Chancellor Gordon Brown, speaking to the meeting, called for the Bank to endorse the OECD's governance principles, and for the Bank's individual country reports to list how each market was implementing them.

Brown made similar calls at a Commonwealth summit and at a meeting of the finance ministers of the G7 group of leading industrial nations. The G7 called for "international principles and codes of best practice . . . on corporate governance and accounting" as part of efforts to stabilize the global economy.

The seriousness with which the World Bank took governance reform was highlighted at the end of 1998 when Bank chief James Wolfensohn endorsed governance reform in the *Economist*'s late 1998 forecast of the coming year. "Strong corporate governance produces good social progress," he asserted. "Good corporate governance can make a difference by broadening ownership and reducing concentration of power within societies. It bolsters capital markets and stimulates innovation. It fosters longer-term foreign direct investment, reduces volatility and deters capital flight."

Wolfensohn demanded "tough rules of transparency and disclosure" and said that in South-East Asia, the Bank will lay down "strict requirements for financial and corporate restructuring" in return for financial assistance.

The Bank's crisis loans to Korea ($2 billion), Indonesia ($1 billion), Thailand ($400 million) and Malaysia ($300 million) depend partly on corporate governance reforms being made by those countries.

The reforms were underpinned by research conducted by the Bank's own chief economist, who found that countries that pursue privatizations without putting good governance structures in place experience worse economic growth. The results reflected frequently voiced criticism of the International Monetary Fund for promoting free market policies without securing meaningful securities law, regulation, and disclosure practices, etc.

# Cases in point: Institutional reform in emerging markets[7]

The World Bank, OECD and G7's work had an effect. Markets that had previously paid little attention to governance concerns began to implement the kinds of architectural and institutional reforms that provided investors with a modicum of security, and allowed them to invest with more confidence.

Of course, not all these reforms were appreciated by business concerns.

**Korea**. In September 1998, the OECD's annual survey on the South Korea economy recommended in its annual survey that "all company boards should include outside directors."

In early 1999, the Korea Stock Exchange announced a Cadbury-style committee.

In November 1998, the Federation of Korean Industry, the representative body of large Korean companies, sought to dampen enthusiasm for governance reform. The FKI responded to the OECD's draft governance principles (see above) by arguing that the agency should "not deal with internal governance issues such as the composition of the board of directors." It also argued that the costs of meeting internationally accepted accounting standards outweighed the benefits.

In 1998, leading South Korean company SK Telecom added three independent directors, to shareholders' delight. But a year later, over the independents' opposition, the company offered a rights issue that unfairly favored the SK group crossholding conglomerate. The minority shareholder activist group People's Solidarity for Participatory Democracy (PSPD) and US hedge fund Tiger Management called a resolution to oust the executives. The stock plunged. Later in 1999, SK Telecom made a deal with the dissidents. PSPD won the right for minority investors to elect independent board directors, and brought forward the use of cumulative voting. The company wouldn't give up a takeover defense, however, that was opposed by half of the votes of foreign holders.

In early 1999, PSPD and two US-based investment companies filed a dissident shareholder resolution at Samsung. The measure required an annual board review of any transactions over 10 billion *won* (about $10 million). The purpose was to prevent the widely practiced habit of diverting profits into poorly performing subsidiaries.

The Ministry of Finance-sponsored Corporate Governance Reform Committee published a detailed code in September 1999. It demanded that large companies (over $800 million) should feature 50 percent independent directors, which would apply to about one-fifth of listed companies. The Federation of Korean Industries, representing companies, wanted the rule to apply only to companies of twice that size.

In early 2000, the number 2 telecoms firm Dacom reached a settlement with PSPD – at least half the board would be independent, including an independent chairman, and a fully independent audit committee. The key to reform? Dacom wanted to list on the NASDAQ.

Also in 2000, a report by Stanford law professor Bernard Black, Coudert Brothers lawyers Barry Metzger and Timothy O'Brien and Korean lawyer Young Moo Shin to the Ministry of Justice of the Republic of Korea recommended legal reforms to improve Korean corporate governance and protect against a repeat of Korea's governance-related financial crisis of 1997–8. The report's principal recommendations include enhancing the role of public company boards of directors, strengthening independent director and non-interested shareholder review of related party transactions, and requiring cumulative voting and pre-emptive rights for public companies.

**Asia/Pacific Rim**. At a May 1999 meeting of the Asia-Pacific Economic Cooperation group, the region's finance ministers endorsed radical new governance measures, including:

- easing proxy voting processes;
- requiring disclosure of insider transactions;
- creating "investor protection agencies especially for minority shareholders";
- increasing the number of outside directors;

- requiring board committees to be chaired and made up largely of outsiders;
- requiring each country to form an Institute of Directors;
- measures "encouraging shareholder activism", including training programs and shareholder agencies;
- the rapid adoption of high-quality, internationally acceptable accounting and auditing standards.[8]

**Hong Kong**. In May 1998, the Stock Exchange of Hong Kong mandated board audit committees to oversee each company's outside audit. At the time of the reform, only 12 of 600 listed HK companies had such a committee, The Exchange proposed a structure that almost – but not quite – matched Western best-practice standards – that the committee should be chaired by an outsider, but may include executives.

In February 2000, the Pacific Economic Co-operation Council announced a corporate governance work program. According to Alan Lung's May 2, 2001 "Financial Reforms for Hong Kong," "Hong Kong is certainly not a 'paragon' of corporate governance at present; it may be better than other Asian jurisdictions, but some of these are catching up, and in such areas as protection of minorities, insider dealing, manipulation, Hong Kong's record is not good. This will seriously impact Hong Kong's competitiveness if not addressed."

**Kyrgyz Republic**. This ex-Soviet state attempted to become an emerging market leader. With World Bank help it developed a governance code as an early part of its economic development. The code and its company law statutes were launched on the internet. At the moment, however, privatization is not complete and significant blocks of stock are still held by the state, and a recent report was frank in admitting that they have not been able to gain the confidence of many investors in other countries.

**Thailand**. In a 1999 paper called *The Importance of Corporate Governance Reforms in the Recovery from Financial Crisis: Viewpoints from Thailand* Dr. Prasarn Trairatvorakul, Commission Member and Deputy Secretary-General, Thailand SEC, said, "A significant cause of this [economic] crisis is the massive capital inflows into the economy without effective management mechanisms. Some examples of the weak initial conditions are ineffective corporate governance, inadequate supervision and regulation, and insufficient or in some cases inaccurate disclosure which resulted in lax credit policies in banks and other financial institutions and misuses of funds in the corporate sector." He promised that "Regulations in the area of corporate governance will be set up in accordance with four main principles namely, fairness, accountability, transparency and responsibility." But these rules are not very powerful. They require only two independent outside directors and provide that the board owes its loyalty not just to shareholders but also to other stakeholders. Furthermore, even these provisions are voluntary.

The Stock Exchange of Thailand, the Bank of Thailand, and the Thai SEC announced the launch of an Institute of Directors in September 1999, intended to train directors in corporate governance.

**Malaysia**. At the beginning of 1999, the Kuala Lumpur Stock Exchange proposed a limit on the number of board seats any single director could have – the measure was opposed by Malaysian corporate interest groups.

Three months later, Malaysia unveiled a 70-point governance code, the work of a committee chaired by the Finance Ministry. The code called for one-third of the board to be independent – or more, if there is a controlling shareholder. Companies were also advised to designate a lead non-executive director, and to set out individual compensation. The Kuala Lumpur Stock Exchange proposed a Cadbury-style comply-or-explain model. The Finance Ministry aimed to back the code up with legal reforms – notably to bar controlling shareholders from voting when there is a conflict of interest, and to facilitate proxy voting by mail. The committee also proposed an Institutional Shareholder Watchdog Committee to police companies for violations of minority shareholder rights. "Good governance is no longer a luxury; it has become a basic ingredient in the recipe for long-term and sustainable growth," declared one Finance Ministry official.

The country's top ten institutional investors responded to the call for a watchdog group, which was formed in August, 1999. The body said it would examine ways of enhancing shareholder activism.[9]

Malaysia has also undertaken a three-year program with the anti-corruption group Transparency International. It will develop an ongoing education effort to build private sector awareness of corporate governance and relevant expertise by developing a regional code of ethics which promotes greater transparency and accountability in corporate life, in conformity with a universally agreed set of standards. The program will include surveys to gauge corporate views and attitudes towards corruption, as well as regular talks and conferences involving heads of major corporations and chambers of commerce from Asian countries, as well as academics, lawyers and other experts. Existing company laws and codes of conduct which promote transparency and accountability, such as Transparency International's proposed Integrity Quality Standard and the OECD's Principles of Corporate Governance, will be also used to help develop a workable regional code of ethics. A working committee will look into the mechanisms needed to develop and implement such a code, which will cover:

- a code of conduct with clear guidelines for disclosure, tender process, conflict of interest, compliance, payment to suppliers, internal auditors, an audit committee, and the safeguard of whistle blowers, as well as sanctions against bribes;
- an annual report which provides adequate information over and above what is required by law;
- a salary structure which is clear, open and transparent with no room for favoritism

The program will also include an annual corporate governance award designed to motivate private sector companies operating in East Asia to improve their levels of corporate transparency as well as publicize and educate business about the value, financial and in public relations terms, of corporate transparency.

## Russia

We must confront the reality in Russia of Original Sin. The Original Sin in Russia was that Privatization was artificial. It was ordered by a distant and incomprehensible Power and forced on an uncomprehending and usually unwilling People. It is no great insight to look back on the past ten years in Russia and to make this statement. But the consequences of that Original Sin naturally color all perception in Russian business and society on the full spectrum of questions concerning corporate governance. *Ruben Vardanian, President and CEO of Troika Dialog, "Corporate Governance in Russia", World Economic Forum, Davos, Switzerland, February 2001*

Russia adopted a corporate governance code (again, suggestions, not requirements) in 2002, but it acknowledged frankly that "Russian law already incorporates the majority of the fundamental principles of corporate governance; however, in practice, their use, especially in court, and corporate governance traditions, is still at the formative stage."

Sibneft, Russia's seventh largest company, has adopted a governance charter, with the help of Western experts. And a new National Council for Corporate Governance was created with the support of the Russian Institute for Directors in 2003 to try to get the support of government and CEOs for governance reform.

## GLOBAL CORPORATE GOVERNANCE FORUM

In late 1998/early 1999, the World Bank and OECD joined forces to create a formal program of governance assistance – the Global Corporate Governance Forum.

The two agencies jointly asserted that governance reform was an "important element in strengthening the foundation for individual countries' long-term economic performance and contributing to a strengthened international financial system."

As Sir Adrian Cadbury wrote in the launch document, the initiative put "corporate governance firmly on the world stage."

As with the 1998 OECD Principles, the Forum avoided imposing a set of prescriptive standards, but sought to work with banks active in developing countries, professional standard-setting bodies, and international organizations. Better governance, said the Forum, is "fundamentally a process in which the government and the private sector join hands."

The Forum attracted some vital support. It was assisted by a Private Sector Advisory Group, which includes investors, directors, managers, and bank and union representatives from across the world, chaired by New York attorney and governance veteran Ira Millstein.

The Private Sector Advisory Group will advise the Forum on its program and provide a link to the private sectors of the major economic regions. The Forum argued that "the very senior level of the PSAG members will enable the group to mobilize support among private sector players worldwide and carry weight with senior officials from the government/regulatory side."

Ira Millstein described the private sector's job as creating a "demand pull" for improved governance, so that companies in emerging markets feel an incentive to improve governance to attract capital, and investors feel secure about their commitment. The Advisory Group's work is aimed at "creating a climate for investment," said Mr. Millstein.

In addition to the PSAG, the Forum is backed by a powerful Investor Responsibility Taskforce, which plans to bring $3 trillion-worth of muscle to the business of improving governance standards in emerging markets.

The taskforce was, at its inception, jointly chaired by Mark Mobius, Templeton Emerging Markets Fund Manager, and Peter Clapman, chief counsel of TIAA–CREF. It included Bill Crist, chairman of the board of trustees of CalPERS, and Hermes chief Alastair Ross-Goobey.

The taskforce's aim, according to the World Bank, is to "use its leadership role in the capital markets to ensure that countries and companies are properly rewarded by the markets if they make governance reforms . . . Its objective is to encourage investors to pay more attention to corporate governance issues so as to speed up the flow of funds to those countries and companies that make progress on the reform agenda."

Its first step was to write to equity research firms that cover emerging markets, calling on them to include governance considerations alongside their traditional financial analysis. They will also lobby emerging market indexers to include governance benchmarks (shareholder rights, board structure, audit process, etc.) in company ratings. Ira Millstein said: "That's a pretty powerful tool. You've got many trillions of dollars talking to the people who advise them on investments in emerging markets and saying to them: put corporate governance into the matrix of advice that we get."

The Forum's first effort was to create an inventory of governance activity worldwide. Using a survey form on its web page, the Forum developed a digest, several hundred strong, of shareholder and director organizations around the world.[10]

The Forum's initial program of activities included:

- Establishing "Centers of Excellence" across Africa in partnership with the Commonwealth Association of Corporate Governance.
- Sponsoring a project to support and promote the role of the media in governance, to assist its role as an effective watchdog. The plans include drawing in private sector players such as Reuters and the *Financial Times*.
- Regional roundtables. The plan is to bring together lead players from the private and public sectors. By January 2000, roundtables had already been held in Russia and Korea, and were scheduled for Brazil and Africa.
- Forming partnerships with regional and local private sector groups, such as the Asia Corporate Governance Committee, to promote best practice on the ground through practical projects.

The Forum's first practical project is to co-operate with the Confederation of Indian Industry in its bid to bring 50 Indian companies into compliance with New York Stock Exchange standards of disclosure and accountability.

---

## Case in point: Indian governance

An example of the World Bank working together with the governments and private sector bodies of international markets is found in India.

India has some of the oldest stock exchanges in the developing world, and has approximately 7,000 listed companies, fractionally more than there are in the UK. Yet, only a small proportion of the world's $300 billion in annual capital flow reaches the country. The challenge facing Indian industry was to attract some of that capital to Indian shores.

Even before the Asian financial crisis, the Confederation of Indian Industry (CII) took steps to answer this question via a code of best practice. Issued before the Asian financial crisis in May 1998, this is a self-regulatory effort by business leaders, but one that includes some tough recommendations. The CII called for boards to be made up of at least 30 percent of outsiders, for attendance records to be disclosed, and for no director to have more than ten board seats. Critically, Indian companies listing abroad should disclose to domestic shareholders the same information as they do abroad. Some of the CII's provisions were tougher than those prevailing in supposedly governance-mature markets, such as the UK.

In quick order, 17 companies, representing 14 or so percent of the market, signed up to the CII code.

The CII expressed higher ambitions. Its aim was to create not just a local code devised for its own purposes, but a group of companies up to international standards. The first goal was to get Indian companies a listing on the New York NASDAQ.

Nor did governance reform end with the CII. In late 1999, the Securities and Exchange Board of India (SERI) issued a second code, in draft. It was tougher than the CII code and aimed to make compliance (or disclosure of compliance) part of the listing rules. "If we can champion this group of corporations, and they do list on NASDAQ and raise money, I think we've got a very practical way of showing how the Forum can promote investment on the ground and really bring some benefits," said the Forum's, leader, Anne Simpson.

Note that a 1999 study by researchers from the Indira Gandhi Institute of Development Research (IGIDR) looked at the role of monitors in India, whose corporate governance system is a hybrid of the outsider-dominated market-based systems of the UK and the US and the insider-dominated bank-based systems of Germany and Japan. They found mixed results. While block holdings by directors and other insiders decrease company value for low levels of holdings and increase it thereafter, they found no evidence that institutional investors are active in governance. The results suggested that lending institutions start monitoring the company effectively once they have substantial equity holdings in the company and that this monitoring is reinforced by the extent of debt holdings by these institutions. They found that foreign equity ownership has a beneficial effect on company value and that the identity of large shareholders matters in corporate governance.

## THE DEVELOPED WORLD

While there has been significant reform in emerging markets, the established economies have also been making progress, especially after the corporate scandals of 2002. The demands of capital, so forcefully applied in Asia, have been just as strongly put in leading markets such as Japan, Germany, the United States, and France.

These countries each developed sophisticated and effective governance structures that suited the country and its business culture. But, as we shall see, they were structures that favored introspection, parochialism and opacity. In some or all of these markets, the government's role was strong, debt financing was preferred to equity, stock market capitalizations were low, systems of cross-holding made ownership illiquid, a few giant shareholders predominated, takeovers were rare, and disclosure was poor.

This kind of system can continue indefinitely as long as returns are good and there is no need for outside investment. In an era of global capital, however, Japanese, German, French, and, more recently, US companies found themselves increasingly unable to compete.

These markets needed global capital, and that meant they needed to adopt standards of governance that global capital understood.

## THE EUROPEAN UNION

In October of 2002, the foreign ministers of the EU agreed that they would work together to prevent Enron-style scandals from happening under their jurisdiction. Among top priorities of the group, chaired by Dutchman Jaap Winter, was corporate executive pay, as well as the role of auditing committees and non-executive directors. Germany announced plans to beef up the regulatory powers of its financial sector watchdog, BAFin, turning it into a sort of "accounting police" along the lines of the US Securities and Exchange Commission in the fight against balance-sheet fraud. "The view that deregulated financial markets would themselves be the best placed to serve as a monitoring body . . . has turned out to be a mistake," said Finance Minister Hans Eichel.

## JAPAN

"The governance structure of Japanese corporations is often characterized as 'contingent governance' in which company insiders retain effective control of management as long as the firm performs well, but once performance deteriorates, the control is taken away and they are subject to severe sanctions such as forced liquidation of the corporation." *Takahiro Yasui, "Corporate Governance in Asia: A Comparative Perspective," March 1999*

As Japan rebuilt its economy in the years following World War II, it developed a unique corporate governance structure. Given the success of the Japanese economy since 1945, many in the West felt that the Japanese system must be worth imitating. After all, the Japanese model seemed to have developed a highly effective form of "relationship investing." Indeed, US reformers of the early 1990s suggested lifting the long-established ban on US banks holding shares in US corporations as a means of fostering the kinds of long-term relationships that had served Japan and Germany so well.

Notable features of the symbiotic Japanese system include:

- Powerful government intervention, dominated by the Japanese Ministry of Finance (MOF). MOF has maintained strong regulatory control of all Japan's business, supervising every aspect of industrial activity, including capital flows.
- A pattern of cross-shareholdings by affiliated companies, often including customers and suppliers. There is often a dominant shareholder, such as a "main" bank or a *keiretsu* partner. (The *keiretsu* system roughly translates to what in the West would be called "relationship investing.")
- The existence of very close relationships between the corporate and government sectors, that has often bordered on corruption.
- Corporate priorities are focused on growth and market share, not shareholder returns (except through share price appreciation).
- An all but non-existent market for corporate control with minimal takeover activity.

Such was the situation in 1992, when the US labored in a recession and the "Japanese miracle" showed few signs of coming to an end. By the end of the decade, the picture had reversed dramatically. As the US economy boomed, so Japanese finance and industry stumbled from crisis to calamity.

Before looking at the ways in which the Japanese structure is reforming, however, we should examine the fundamentals of the Japanese model as it developed from 1945 to the mid-1990s.

In an excellent introduction to the Japanese system, *Evolution of Keiretsu and their Different Forms*, Martin G. Evans of the University of Toronto explains that Japan before the war was dominated by four large Zaibatsus: Mitsubishi, Mitsui, Sumitomo, and Yasuda.

> These were involved in steel, international trading, banking and other key sectors in the economy and controlled by a holding company which established financial links between the different members. Large, influential banks were part of these conglomerates, providing necessary funds.
>
> At the end of the war the occupational forces decided that these structures had to be broken up, since they constituted powerful monopolies that helped the former government to execute the war. As a result it was planned to sell shares to the public, to remove executives from their positions and so forth. In 1947 a law was enacted to dissolve large companies and enhance competition.
>
> However, in 1948 the allied forces realized that they needed a strong Japan to fight the Korean War and communism in general. Therefore they stopped weakening the Japanese economy and conversely, pumped substantial aid into it.

Thus, the banks became the center of a system of cross-holdings and conglomerates called *keiretsu*.

According to Evans, "Different forms emerged, where the most important ones are the 'financial Keiretsus' (Big Six) with horizontal relationships across industries. The ex-Zaibatsus – Mitsui, Mitsubishi and Sumitomo – belong to this grouping with close-knit relationships among group members. Sanwa, Fuyo and Ikkan are new formed groups with a bank at their core. Usually they only have one enterprise in each business sector to enjoy economies of scale and avoid competition within the group. Another form is represented by the 'distribution' Keiretsu with vertical relationships, controlling this way the flow of products, services, prices etc. from the factory to the consumer."

Evans notes that *keiretsu* "behave as if they were one company: giving loans, technology, development costs, long-term supply agreements etc. from customers higher up in the pyramid to subcontractors. The latter even absorb losses occurring in other sectors and pursue set prices. The result is a conformist structure producing high quality while shutting out foreign suppliers. Many other forms of cartels and groupings are common in Japan. The Japanese believe that they ensure full employment, the security of the nation and distribute risks, it is their version of capitalism."

While in general the Western model is based on the assumption that the primary loyalty of managers and directors should be to the providers of capital, in Japan the system was set up to promote the interests of the company and its employees rather than the outside shareholders. Almost all directors are insiders, and those that are outside are usually associated with the company's lenders. Pay is tied to growth, not profits. Shareholders are passive; they have very few rights if they are not happy with management, and what rights they do have are seldom exercised. An extensive system of cross-holdings provides stability, but it does not provide much by way of market pressure to respond to poor performance. The government also acts almost as another participant in the cross-holdings. A report by Oxford Analytica, *Board Directors and Corporate Governance*, said, "The government sees itself not so much as an impartial regulator, but as a promoter and protector of domestic industry." The system is designed to work very co-operatively, but that means that the mechanisms for accountability through markets: hostile takeovers, proxy contests, other uses of shareholder rights – or through government: antitrust enforcement, disclosure requirements, are very weak.

# Case in point: Ripplewood Holdings

The following is an internal memorandum, dated November 1999, written by one of this book's authors, Robert A.G. Monks, to Hermes.

The financial disaster of the decade of the nineties has intensified the traditional Japanese habit of introspection and mode of self-criticism. So much has gone wrong that virtually everything can be changed. Using the terminology of Mao Tse Tung in a different decade – "let a thousand flowers bloom" – could well be the epitaph for this decade of Japanese history. After all, it is very rare in human history for a defeated people in a destroyed country to adopt plans and faithfully assure their implementation over a half-century to the point where Japan was the envy of the world. It should not be surprising that a new plan is plainly needed. We will have to detect its outlines from the steps that Japan's government and principal industries take. It should not be surprising if the new plan is very successful.

The "secret" of Japanese competitiveness in the world is only partly hard work and industrial cleverness. It is in large measure attributable to a huge and low-cost source of capital. At the end of World War II, the private sector's wealth had been destroyed in Japan. As the painful period of reconstruction progressed, symbolized by the public re-establishment of the Mitsubishi *keiretsu* on 1 July 1954, two patterns developed. Each of the *keiretsu* companies would own stock in each of the others providing protection against takeovers and, in effect, double counting the group's wealth. The government created a banking system that would loan virtually limitless sums of money to companies that were considered loyal to the national interest. For fifty years. Japan has been characterized by these enterprises with very small equity capital, confused by interlocking shareholdings, and huge amounts of debt capital abundantly available to those providing employment, generating export sales and co-operating with the detailed plans of the all powerful government bureaucracies – pre-eminent among them the Ministry of Finance (MOF) and the Ministry of International Trade and Industry (MITI). There were exceptions like Toyota, but that is another story.

The great asset inflation occurred in the late 1980s when it was calculated that the aggregated value of Japanese golf club shares was larger than the entire Australian stock market and the appraised value of the Imperial Palace was greater than all of California. Unhappily, the banking system believed these values to the extent of making loans against their inflated values as collateral. When the bank bust occurred in the nineties, Westerners were critical of Japanese authorities for not more quickly and decisively writing down the losses and getting about the business of the future. This criticism was particularly pointed from the United States that had seamlessly socialized the debts of the S&Ls [savings and loans], locked up a token few malefactors, and proceeded into the rest of the roaring nineties. There were several points of comparison in the two banking crises – most importantly, political figures of all parties were involved up to their armpits so there was not the usual partisan political wrangling that ultimately produces a kind of solution. The difference is that the level of non-performing debts in the Japanese crises was not some large percentage of their capital or net worth, it was a multiple of both. As a practical matter, both the banks and the economy simply had no strategy beyond survival. No longer would Japanese companies be able to rely on the availability of quantities of loan capital at attractive rates. They would have to find other modes of financing.

This raised the critical question underlying all talk of corporate governance reform. Does the country and do the companies of Japan require foreign capital in order to develop their businesses optimally? Japan is a country so rich in savings and so wealthy in assets – a substantial percentage of the US national debt was incurred to finance Japanese exports, for example – that it seems highly unlikely that domestic sources will not be available to meet business's needs. The source of the seemingly inexhaustible bank credit was the savings habit of the hard-working Japanese, and more particularly their continuing willingness to "invest" their savings at rates of return that would have been considered ridiculous and confiscatory in more open societies. The usual mode was a seven-year Postal Money Certificate yielding 3 percent. The really important question facing Japan today is whether the financial industries will be deregulated and foreign competition admitted so as to provide alternative vehicles for Japan's inveterate savers. If Fidelity, for example, with its massive presence in Japan, is allowed to compete aggressively and sell "money market funds" with an indicated yield twice that of the postal money order, it is apparent that the extraordinary competitive advantage of "free capital" enjoyed over the last half-century by Japanese companies will cease to exist. At the beginning of the twenty-first century, there is increasing evidence that Japanese savers are turning to American-style mutual fund products.

The Japanese are very critical of their own management failings. They are enthusiastic about the concept of corporate governance as it may enable them to run their enterprises in a more efficient way. Japanese managers set very high standards for themselves, but there are respects in which the system plainly deviates from focus on shareholder benefit. If one seeks an answer to the question – Who are the owners of Japanese companies? – the answer would likely be "the cadre of senior managers". Competitively selected from a brutally competitive academic system, the executives of the *keiretsu* companies are a privileged cadre. While they are not greedy in the Western sense, their insulation against being fired and the certainty of being well cared for in any event continues to be protected. Governance principles will permeate the core of these companies only to the extent that owners' requirements for a competitive return on their investment prevails. Their adoption of the principles will, however, surely be modified for domestic consumption. It is difficult to imagine two concepts more antithetical to Japanese life than the fundamental precepts of Western governance – transparency and accountability. Several years ago, I was introduced to the senior Minister in many postwar cabinets – Miyazawa (to everyone's surprise this gentleman was chosen in his late seventies to be Finance Minister in the Obuchi cabinet). In those days, he had time. He was a reflective and experienced man who listened well. When I had finished describing the concept of governance, he said with the pleasant tones of one comfortable with English "You must understand that you are a dangerous man in Japan." He was referring to the dislike of Japanese leaders of exposing more information about their functioning than absolutely necessary and to the cultural horror at a group being accountable to outsiders. As virtually everyone today assures you of his or her enthusiasm for "corporate governance," Miyazawa's words echo in my skull. Japanese society is largely self-referential. There is a consciousness of being apart from other people – the apotheosis of being insular. No one is ignorant of the extraordinary accomplishments of the last fifty years; no one feels that *all* of the practices of the past need be jettisoned.

The question remains – Do you need foreign capital? A fair answer is that nobody knows. We do know that in the unwinding of the *keiretsu* companies, many will use portions of their investment portfolio to fund fully new defined benefit pensions.

This, in turn, will provide new institutions with liquid capital available to invest in the future needs of corporate Japan. At the very least, it seems clear that Japan will want to be in the position where they can have access to foreign capital if that turns out to be the best choice for industry. Already, many Japanese companies – largely those outside of the traditional *keiretsu* arrangements – Kyocera,

Sony, Toyota, for example – have substantial foreign shareholdings and have been able to accommodate their functioning to the demands of investors. The way is open, others will follow.

The driving force will be the requirement of shareholders, domestic and foreign. Locally, individual Japanese buying Fidelity mutual funds will expect higher yields. If they are to be available, higher rates will have to be charged to business. The much discussed "demographic problem" of inverting the ratio of savers to retirees will require that the funds standing as collateral for the pension promises yield returns sufficient to pay the pension promises. This pressure – what Peter Drucker calls the Middle Class Revolution – is new. Formerly, when companies performed badly and stock prices declined, a relatively small percentage of the population was affected – the more affluent portion. When owners are pensioners, bad performance affects critically half the population. This makes government intervention in the event of bad management a certainty. It is incumbent on companies to govern themselves sufficiently well to forestall that eventuality that the history of this century has demonstrated to be disastrous.

Japan is not the homogenous family often fantasized in the West. There are determined people who are willing to take large chances. This is an environment of chaos and change that encourages such individuals. There will be suitable Japanese individuals and institutions willing to undertake corporate governance and shareholder activism. The country needs to appear to be a part of the OECD world as a manager of business and – with the new pension funds in the *keiretsu* companies, liberalization of investment restrictions for private company pensions and the reforming of the public pension into huge newly governed entities like the proposed federal Health and Welfare Fund with a projected size of ¥160 trillion – roughly the size of CalPERS – Japan will be a substantial owner of foreign companies, along with Hermes, CREF and the other Global Shareowners. Indeed, Japan's pension assets are second only to those of the United States.

Late in 1999, an unusual event occurred – a hostile takeover involving a foreign winner, Britain's Cable & Wireless, a highly prestigious loser NTT, and a traditional investment banker, Schroeders. The firm IDD is less important than its role in the evolving of modern Japanese commercial practice. This event signaled an important change in evaluating Japanese attitudes. No longer listen to what they say, watch what they do.

On December 24, 1999 Japan's financial reconstruction commission announced that it had reached a basic accord with Ripplewood Holdings LLC of the United States on the sale of the nationalized Long Term Credit Bank of Japan (LTCB). LTCB collapsed under the weight of heavy non-performing loans in October 1998 and was placed under temporary state control of its eventual sale to the private sector. The choice of Ripplewood, a special purpose partnership put together by the enterprising Timothy Collins, a former Lazard partner, is the clearest possible indication of Japan's determination to be a participant in the global economy. Not only was LTCB one of the "crown jewels" of Japan's long commercial expansion, but its revitalization will involve the payment of substantial subsidies and a continuing willingness of the government to be responsible for what will turn out to be unacceptable credits. In one stroke, Japan permitted one of its core financing assets to be taken over by foreigners and indicated a willingness to use Japanese taxpayer assets to effect the transaction. As they would say in Hollywood – you can't get much realer than that!

Ripplewood Holdings is a consortium consisting of the top talents in particular financial specialties from the United States and Europe – GE Capital Corp, Deutsche Bank AG, ABN-Amro, Mellon Bank and Paine Webber Group. Ripplewood plans to introduce Anglo-American corporate practices into LTCB. The bank will have a 15-member board of directors, about half of whom will be outside directors, including Paul Volcker, a former US Federal Reserve chairman, and Takashi Imai, head of the Keidanren business group. This is believed to be the first time that a foreign group has purchased a Japanese bank, the first time a Japanese company has functioned with so many external directors, and the first time that staff are to be incentivized with a large-scale US-style stock option program. "It's a plus for the entire banking industry," Nozumu Kunishige, banking analyst at Lehman Brothers, said. "Foreign management will bring a clear focus and a direction [to LTCB] and improve its operational efficiency. That will prompt Japanese banks to accelerate their own restructuring efforts."[11]

## Corporate Governance Forum of Japan

Japan, like markets in the rest of the world, produced a corporate governance code. In May 1998, the Corporate Governance Forum of Japan issued its final guidelines. The Forum was made up of executives, academics, lawyers and shareholder representatives who clearly identified the need for improved governance of Japanese governance: "the practice of good governance has become a necessary prerequisite for any corporation to manage effectively in the globalized marketplace."

The Code accepted that Japanese corporate culture took a more "holistic" view than in the West. It agreed that companies are made up of many constituencies, but argued that "shareholders, the providers of equity capital, are given a special position." At the same time, it advised that "a sense of corporate solidarity with social harmony is expected."

The Forum made several recommendations that would require major change in Japan. For example, it called for more outside directors – who then accounted for just 4 percent of board seats in Japan. The Forum also called for independent audit, pay, and nomination board committees; almost no Japanese company has any board committees. The Forum itself monitors progress and has urged the Tokyo Stock Exchange to incorporate the Code into its Listing Rules.

The recommendations also achieved international recognition – CalPERS put the Forum's code at the heart of its Japanese voting guidelines.

## Cases in point: Aspects of Japanese governance reform

- In 1997, Sony cut its board from 38 to 10 in a clear attempt to change the board from an honorific body to a genuine decision-making body offering strategic input and oversight. In 1998, Long Term Credit Bank slashed its 28-member board down to 6, largely due to pressure from Swiss Bank Corp., which was entering a series of joint ventures with LTCB. It will also include non-executives among the six. Another motivation was to get its hands on some of the $100 billion that the Japanese government had earmarked for rebuilding the banking sector. In 1999, 37 companies, including Sumitomo Bank and Nissan, sought shareholder approval to shrink their boards – from as big as 40 down to a manageable 10–15. This follows over 100 companies which acted similarly in 1998.

- In 1999, People Co. – a small start-up with just 47 staff that had been public for less than two years – instituted Western-style governance practices. Three of the four director nominees were independent, the annual report disclosed individual salaries, and the company introduced shareholder value-related incentive pay.
- In the same year, Nomura Asset Management announced that it would vote against management-sponsored resolutions for the first time.
- Sumitomo Trust & Banking in the spring of 1999 formed a Focus Club for Japanese executives fearful of global shareholder activism. The idea was to help companies manage relations with global shareholders better.
- In March 1999, the Association of Japanese Corporate Pension Funds expanded its governance guidelines, building on its earlier, groundbreaking assertion that pension funds had a duty to monitor governance. The Association called on funds to vote against managements that were not pursuing shareholder value strategies.
- The OECD's 1998 Economic Survey on Japan made tough governance demands, against the background of Japan's worsening recession. The recommendations focused on more independent directors serving smaller boards. The OECD called on the Tokyo Stock Exchange to recognize the value of boards capable of a meaningful oversight role by making them of a workable size (Japanese companies can have up to 60 directors) and by recruiting outsiders. Other recommendations included the wider use of independent audits and incentive pay – options were legalized in 1997, but only 141 of the top 2,000 firms adopted them.
- Hermes Pensions Management, one of the largest UK fund managers and among the most active, announced in March 2000 that it was appointing a resident Japanese corporate governance adviser. Mr. Ariyoshi Okumura's first job was to translate Hermes' international governance principles and communicate them to the 450 Japanese companies in which Hermes has holdings. "Our new Japanese program is designed to ensure we can vote more intelligently on key issues and take proper account of local laws and business culture," said Michelle Edkins, Hermes' corporate governance executive. "We see this as a two way learning process which over time will encourage more Japanese companies to implement generally accepted corporate governance principles."

In early 2000, a fund called M&A Consulting launched Japan's first hostile takeover bid, for ailing property developer Shoei. M&A was led by Yoshiaki Muakami, a former official at the Ministry of International Trade and Industry. He was defeated, but the venture was widely applauded.

He followed up the takeover bid with two shareholder proposals at the company's March 2000 annual meeting. The resolutions called for the dividend to be more than doubled, and for some of the company's ¥66 billion to be returned to shareholders. Muakami also proposed himself for the board.

M&A offers a three-point program for continued shareholders in Japan:

- management under "effective control" of shareholders;
- non-performing assets to be spun off;
- mergers and acquisitions are the "perfect tool" to restructure companies and focus them on realizing value.

M&A was not alone. In early 2000, German pharmaceuticals firm Boehringer Ingelheim made a $190 million bid for Japanese over-the-counter drugs firm SSP. The German firm already owned nearly 20 percent of SSP, but made the bid to get full control. "This is the first time a tender offer has been launched in the Japanese pharmaceuticals industry and the population is not used to it yet. We wanted to make an offer which got their attention," said Boehringer vice-chairman Roll Krebs.[12]

In 2002, the Japan Corporate Governance Index Research Group (JCGIRG) surveyed Tokyo Stock Exchange First Section firms (1,504 firms as of March 11, 2002) on their corporate governance practices. They received 159 valid responses, which they used to develop the "JCG Index," which measures how closely a firm adheres to a model of corporate governance based on the "Revised Corporate Governance Principles" of the Japan Corporate Governance Forum. The average rating of these self-selected companies was 36.3 points out of a possible 100, though the range was from 13 to 73. In general, the greatest gap between current structure and the JCGF principles was in the structure and make-up of the board of directors. JCGIRG compared the returns of the top and bottom 25 responding companies and found that ROA, ROE, and stock returns were higher for the top-ranking firms, so that firms with the highest index "had superior capital efficiency and delivered greater returns to shareholders." Furthermore, contrary to fears about a more accountable system of corporate governance, the top-ranked firms were adding employees, while the low-ranked firms were decreasing the number of employees.

One commentator noted that the *keiretsu* system was unwinding, and investors were becoming intolerant of under-performing assets. He suggested that, while the larger Japanese banks have close ties to big business that would probably prevent them acting for raiders, smaller banks might sniff an opportunity. "A successful hostile takeover would be the most exciting event to have hit corporate Japan since the transistor," he wrote.[13]

Miyauchi Yoshihiko, chairman and CEO of Orix Corporation and chairman of the Japan Association of Corporate Directors, gave a speech about corporate governance at a RIETI (Research Institute of Economy, Trade and Industry) policy center conference on March 3, 2003. He said, "society tolerates the existence of companies because they fulfill the function of utilizing the limited resources in society in the most effective way possible and provide society with wealth." In that context, corporate governance is simply about creating the best system to achieve that result.

While he supports the idea of international coordination on fundamental principles of corporate governance and even says that "some fundamentals of corporate governance are, in a sense, held in common internationally," he also says that these fundamentals must be implemented according to the cultures and legal systems of individual companies. "For example, the role of an independent board member within the executive board can be highly universal within the corporate governance framework. However, when it comes to the issue of whether independent members should comprise the majority of the board, there is sufficient basis for the argument that this is not necessary. For example, when we think of Japanese culture, it is very possible for corporate governance to be effective even where there is only one independent board member, if that person is highly respected." As corporate governance evolves in Japan, he notes that the one thing it needs most is more effective oversight by shareholders. "Japan's institutional investors have not yet reached the stage where they place weight on corporate governance when making investment decisions, or use it as a means to ensure the safety of their investments. Company management is gradually beginning to deal with the issue of corporate governance. If institutional and other investors show greater awareness, corporate governance in Japan has the potential to progress in leaps and bounds."

One significant indicator that this potential may be realized is the creation of the Japan Independent Directors Network (JIDN). According to Stephen Davis, "Not long ago, independent directors were so rare in Japan that newspapers using the term had to supply a lengthy definition." But Japan now sees US-style independent boards and a focus on shareholder value as a key element in attracting capital. Sony, Konica-Minolta, Hitachi, Toshiba, Orix, and others have already announced that they will switch to smaller, more independent boards. But the people who serve on those boards will need training. JIDN will provide monthly seminars, lunch briefings, an annual symposium, and research.

## GERMANY

"The purpose of corporate governance is to achieve a responsible, value-oriented management and control of companies. Corporate governance rules promote and reinforce the confidence of current and future shareholders, lenders, employees, business partners and the general public in national and international markets. The supervisory board, management board and executive staff of the company identify themselves with these rules and are contractually bound by them. They are part of the general obligation to observe other interests related to the corporate activity." *German Panel on Corporate Governance, Corporate Governance Rules for German-Quoted Companies, July 2000*

Germany has a governance system that resembles the Japanese structure in some respects, yet is very different in others. A similar pattern of reform also emerges – Germany, like Japan, was forced to rebuild its economy from scratch following World War II, and developed a highly interdependent structure, based on co-operation and long-term stability.

For a long time the German defense of its corporate system was that it worked. When short-termism was the UK/US bugbear, the German system was held up as a shining example of the effectiveness of long-term relationship investing.

But the system ultimately could not provide German companies with the capital they needed to compete in a global marketplace. And, as we have seen, international institutional investors became increasingly intolerant of parochial governance practices that obstruct shareholders' rights.

In early 1997, leading representatives of the German financial community, including delegates from industry, financial services, investment and politics, founded Finanzplatz, a task-force devoted to promoting Germany as a financial center. Finanzplatz's aim was simple: to attract foreign capital to Germany. By the end of 1998, foreign ownership of German equity had reached 20 percent.

Finanzplatz led a high-energy program of seminars and discussions in London and New York to persuade investors of the merits of the German market, and that share voting was a great deal easier than it appeared.

The government came to Finanzplatz's assistance with its mid-1998 Control and Transparency Law (KonTraG), which exposed German companies to takeover for the first time and freed up the voting system. Voting caps and multiple voting rights were virtually abolished, cross-held shares were barred from voting for supervisory board candidates, and banks' voting powers were reduced. Disclosure of supervisory board members' other board positions was made mandatory for the first time.

## German governance code

In January 2000, Germany finally bowed to international pressure and produced its first corporate governance code.[14] A panel consisting of representatives of large, mid-cap., and small companies, lawyers, and individual and institutional investors produced a code focusing on improved disclosure, ease of voting, pay for performance and enhanced professionalism of the supervisory board.

The last point is perhaps the most important. Until recently, a supervisory board seat was a largely honorary position. Long-time managers could expect to be automatically promoted; it was normal for German companies simply to list supervisory board members, with no information about their background or experience; a few big names had a considerable number of supervisory board positions; and there were examples of supervisory boards manifestly failing to supervise – see the Holzmann case in point below.

The German Corporate Governance Panel was clear that the supervisory board had to be transformed into a genuinely authoritative body, professionally organized and accountable to shareholders. The Code proposed that outgoing CEOs should not, as a matter of course, be promoted to the supervisory board.

The recommendation was a clear recognition of the fact that in an era of internationalization and fast-moving markets, a greater breadth of strategic input was needed at board level.

A second recommendation sought to embarrass supervisory board members into improved performance – directors failing to attend more than half the board meetings in a given year should be identified in the annual report.

Christian Strenger, managing director of mutual fund manager DWS and architect of the Panel, said "there is quite an awakening among supervisory board members."

The Panel was criticized in some quarters for failing to confront some of the major structural features of the German system – it sought to improve governance within the German system as it existed, rather than trying to change the system wholesale. For example, the presence of union representatives on the supervisory board remains a major sticking point for international investors, but the Panel did not engage the question of whether, and if so how, this employee role should be abolished. Christian Strenger argued that progress was more likely to be achieved via a gradual "ratcheting up" of standards, rather than a radical reform that failed to carry German corporations with it.

# Case in point: Comments on the governance code

One of the authors of the present book, Robert A.G. Monks, responded to the request of the authors of the German Governance Code in a letter to Christian Strenger dated February 15, 2000.

Corporate Governance in my terminology refers to two separate, but not unrelated, conditions: accountability to the public for the impact of corporate functioning on society and accountability to the owners for the effective management of assets. The second usage is the most common and I will refer to it in this paper. Evaluation of different systems can be simplified into a single question – is the management meaningfully accountable to the owners?

Is this the right question to ask about German company law? About the Code? If not, what other standards would be appropriate?

It is not immediately apparent from reading the German Code how an outside shareholder – even one with a very large holding, say 15 percent – would effectively communicate its concerns to a reluctant management. One presumes that the right to vote for Board Members at Annual Meetings in Germany is like the United States – shareholders are free to vote, not to vote, to abstain, even to write in their own candidates, but those elected are inevitably those whose names were placed on the ballot by the incumbent management It appears that the Code contemplates the continuance of a system of self-perpetuating management. Shareholders from the outside will not be able to have direct impact. Therefore, protection of shareholder rights will have to be found in the internal functioning of the corporate organs.

In this regard, the Code seems altogether praiseworthy. There is a wealth of careful and thoughtful suggestion in the Code so as to enhance the internal integrity of the organization. The effort to make the interrelationship of the boards transparent and to address the problem of issues falling between their jurisdictions seems largely successful.

It requires a more subtle understanding of the language and culture than I possess to know whether and the extent to which the "Corporate interest, Company policy" is understood as placing on management the unequivocal obligation to optimize shareholder profits. At best, the terminology is not straightforward. Those who – like me – advocate optimization of long-term ownership values as the corporate purpose insist that this includes the appropriate costs of "best practice" with respect to employees, customers, suppliers and affected communities. We use the word "optimize" rather than "maximize" in order to put people on notice that the words are used as terms of art. What I mean by all of this is that the words quoted above from the Code might need be understood with a "gloss" not unlike that which we employ in the US and UK.

The question of the appropriate scope of disclosure by corporations of the impact of their functioning on society needs more attention. Germany is perceived by its evaluators – Deminor puts it at the bottom of the European league table – as being guarded in its attitude towards a public entitlement to information Possibly, Americans can understand this as a cultural difference in that the informing energy of the federal laws concerning corporations is "full disclosure" and little regulation.

For a variety of reasons corporations in the US and UK are not usually tasked with responsibilities beyond optimizing their own value. It is clear that German corporations are far more tied in with German society – illustrated by the obligation to be the source of many pensions and the legal and cultural commitment to participate with work councils – and that these responsibilities will necessarily shape their policies on corporate governance. I will conclude with the only statement in which I have complete confidence – do not repeat our mistakes.

# Case in point: Metallgesellschaft and Holzmann

For a long period, the success of the German economy seemed to offer proof that its governance system was effective. Did it not foster long-term relations between owners and managers? Were not German companies able to make strategy backed by long-term patient capital? Did not the watchful eyes of bank and corporate representatives on the supervisory board ensure that the monitoring of management was effectively carried out? And, as a result, was not Germany free of the large-scale and sudden corporate collapses that seemed to be part and parcel of the US/UK landscape?

To this last question, at least, the answer was no. In December 1993, the management of Metallgesellschaft, Germany's fourteenth largest company, announced the firm was close to collapse. Metall's US subsidiary, MG Corp., had racked up losses requiring a $2.15 billion rescue package.

Metall's shareholders included some of the biggest names in German finance – Deutsche Bank, Dresdner Bank, and Allianz Insurance. They, and other large shareholders, owned 60 percent of the company between them, reflected in seats on the supervisory board.

Nor was Metallgesellschaft an isolated incident. In late 1999, the argument in favor of continued governance reform was dramatically strengthened by the failure of Holzmann, a leading German building company.

Expressing amazement that the company's creditors were willing to see it fail, Chancellor Gerhard Schröder arranged a €130 million rescue package.

Both incidents demonstrated that the German system was as prone to failure as its Anglo-Saxon counterpart, and that the presence of the supervisory board merely raised the question: what supervises the supervisors?

And the Holzmann rescue underlined the fact that the owner–manager relationship in German companies is complicated by the close attentions of the state.

## Earthquake

Germany was not content with feeling its way to improved governance, via encouragement and a best-practice code.

In late 1999/early 2000 two remarkable events set the scene for a fundamental restructuring of the German corporate landscape. The first was the takeover by a foreign firm of a large German company; the second was a proposed tax change that would facilitate the unwinding of the German cross-holding structure.

### Mannesmann

In 1999, the German company Mannesmann, a conglomerate incorporating fixed and mobile telecom services as well as automotive and engineering units, took over the UK mobile phones provider, Orange.

The merger was seen as a kick in the teeth for the leading UK mobile telephone company, Vodafone Airtouch – itself the result of an international merger of the UK's Vodafone and Airtouch of the US. The Mannesmann deal presented Vodafone with a dilemma: the European mobile phones sector was consolidating, and it wasn't taking part.

Vodafone's choices were either to suffer this strategic threat in silence, or to make a bold bid for European dominance by taking over Mannesmann.

There was an obvious objection to this second strategy – there had never been a successful takeover of a large German company. Nevertheless, Vodafone made a €130 billion bid for its rival, then the largest takeover in history.

At first, the offer suggested that governance convergence and European consolidation was a myth. German Chancellor Gerhard Schröder dismissed Vodafone's effort, saying "hostile takeovers are always negative." One German newspaper, *Bild Zeitung*, asked "Will greed triumph?" Not to be outdone, the UK's *Daily Telegraph* responded with: "Takeover? Was ist das?"

In time, however, it became apparent that governance nationalism was a far inferior force to the international market.

Finanzplatz's CEO, Stefan Seip, was more reasonable than his Chancellor. The bid, he said, is "a big lesson for Germany and for our corporate governance culture. A lot of German politicians do not really fit into the thinking of modern German capital markets. They are not familiar with what is normal in other parts of the world." Their response, he said, demonstrates that Germany's markets are "still emerging."

Shervin Setareh of Deminor, Europe's leading governance consultants, agreed that Germany has taken radical steps toward meeting investor expectations of shareholder value. He said it had become "shockingly apparent" to German companies and market players that a DAX 30 company would be taken over sooner or later. The bid caused "a big shake up among the German investment audience. It shows it can happen to any company." This, he said was "a new taste for the German consciousness," and one which was "not easy to digest." But the bitter mouthful was necessary, he argued, if Germany was to develop as it wished. Germany anticipated the development of a pan-European stock market, he said, "and it wants to be a leader. If that's where you want to go, you have to take the good with the bad." Setareh said that there was "a strong move towards an Anglo-American corporate governance framework for Germany." The market was "very much trying to adopt good practice."

The key to Vodafone's bid was that up to two-thirds of Mannesmann was held by non-German investors. The success or failure of the bid would come down to a reasoned analysis of the competing strategies offered by the two companies, not to local market nationalism.

Vodafone pitched aggressively in London and New York. The Mannesmann defense, in the prevailing view of analysts and journalists, was by contrast disappointing.

In January 2000, Mannesmann conceded. "The shareholders have decided," said Mannesmann chief, Klaus Esser. Such a remark by a leading German corporate boss would have been inconceivable even a couple of years before.

### Tax reform

Against the background of the Mannesmann–Vodafone tussle, the German government announced that it would seek to abolish the punitive rate of capital gains tax on equity sales. The implications for corporate Germany of this announcement were profound.

The dominant feature of the current German corporate system is the web of cross-holdings that bind German companies and banks tightly together. German companies long called for the chance to unravel these holdings and manage their assets more aggressively. They were prevented from doing so by a punitive capital gains tax of 50 percent on any sale of equity. The Finance Ministry said the proposed abolition of this tax "will give an important impulse for the necessary modernization and restructuring of business."

While a rushed, bulk sale seems unlikely – most of the stakes are too big to be disposed of quickly without driving down the price – the government's move sets the scene for a gradual unwinding of the structure. For example, in 2000, when the Allianz insurance company made a friendly $23 billion takeover offer to Germany's third-largest bank, the

Dresdner Bank, Charles E. Boyle noted in *Insurance Journal* magazine that "It portends the opening of Germany's 'closed shop' which has been in place since the end of WWII, and signals a sea change in the country's business structures."

Banks and companies, having demanded just such a reform for years, can hardly now fail to act. Deutsche Bank called the change "a remarkable move," and said "the removal of the paralyzing tax regulations will unleash a major wave of corporate restructuring and a significant reduction in cross-holdings in corporate Germany which may help to ease foreign concern over corporate governance in Germany."

Stefan Seip called it a "revolutionary step." He said that "no one dared hope that the government would make such a move. It really wanted to show German companies and the world that they are willing to reform."

Dirk Schlotermeyer, director of market policy at Deutsche Borse, was equally enthusiastic. "I am optimistic," he said, "that this will lead to a restructuring of the whole economy."

The market responded positively to the news, sending the DAX 30 index of leading shares up 4 percent in a single day.

The cross-holdings were intended to provide German-led investment, long-term stability, and a sense of "all for one" solidarity in the business community. But in an era of global capital and demanding shareholders, the structure has calcified, leaving companies with vast stakes that they don't want but can't sell.

For example, insurance group Allianz and reinsurer Munich Re own 25 percent of each other. Allianz further owns 21 percent of Dresdner Bank, which in turn owns 10 percent of Allianz. Between them, they own nearly 35 percent of Münchener Ruck, with Deutsche Bank (whose non-bank assets weigh in at more than $20 billion) owning a further 10 percent. Just to confuse things, Deutsche owns about 10 percent of Munich Re and 7 percent of Allianz.

Altogether, German companies own an estimated $100 billion in each other.

Both German companies and shareholders complain that these holdings turn leading corporations into *de facto* passive management investment trusts. Critics of the system argue that German companies should be free to invest these assets in core business areas, or return the cash to shareholders.

The proposed reform, once passed, is expected to unleash a flurry of M&A and takeover activity in Germany.

Companies will be under immense pressure from investors to respond to the strategic opportunity that restructuring would bring. "National and international investors will measure management against this new opportunity," said Seip.

German companies, previously immune to takeover, thanks to the presence of friendly controlling owners, will suddenly become vulnerable.

Dirk Schlotermeyer stresses that international institutional investors will also play a part in forcing the restructuring of the German corporate system, as an array of combinations and consolidations now becomes possible. "They will have a new shopping window to look into," he says.

## Future perfect?

Where does this leave Germany's peculiar brand of home-grown governance? Certainly, Germany's highly inward-looking economy is a thing of the past. As equity floods to German markets – and the high-tech Neuer Markt has expanded rapidly – the demands of international capital will increasingly hold sway.

But the German communitarian spirit remains a powerful force, and it will not disappear overnight. Under the republic's constitution, German companies owe a duty to society in general, a duty that is taken seriously and that could not be removed without considerable resistance.

The structural forms by which this social duty is expressed, however, will likely change, particularly the presence of employee representatives on the supervisory board.

Dr. Maria Chetcuti Cauchi's thoughtful paper, "Corporate Governance Under the Proposed European Company Statute" (May 2001) noted, "With its management codetermination, Works Councils and institutional representation on the Supervisory Board, German company law has been classified as the system which best offers protection to the employee, a system which is 'at the ultra-red end of the comparative spectrum on industrial democracy.' The argument in favor of the two-tier system claims that only non-executive directors, who are separate and independent from the board, can exert effective control on the management. Critics of this system state that this procedure slows down the decision–making process and the supervisory board remains too detached from the work carried out by the management" (footnotes omitted).

Germany's DVFA (Deutsche Vereinigung für Finanzanalyse und Asset Management, or Union for Financial Analysis and Asset Management), including 1,100 professionals from some 400 investment firms, banks, asset management firms, and investment advisors, has developed a quantitative score for evaluating the corporate governance of German companies. Criteria include corporate governance "commitment," transparency, management, and auditing. Some of the items considered in these categories are: corporate governance principles, equal treatment of all shareholders, availability of online access to proxy voting, and a commitment to communication between the supervisory and management boards. DVFA has also published a code of best practice for corporate managers and directors making more specific to German law and corporations the corporate governance principles published by the OECD. As this "demand–side" analysis of corporate governance from the investor side becomes institutionalized, there will be increased pressure for more focus on shareholder value and less of the traditional emphasis on the priority of job security that Dr. Cauchi describes.

# Case in point: DaimlerChrysler and the perils of globalization

The conflict of differing governance styles is nowhere better highlighted than in the merger of the German and US auto firms, Daimler-Benz and Chrysler in May 1998.

The strategy behind the merger was entirely logical – neither firm on its own was large enough to compete in the increasingly global car market, but each had a solid, if not leading, position in the key US and European markets. *Business Week* called it "a marriage made in automotive heaven."

But even if the industrial logic was sound, could the merger overcome the inevitable problems of uniting two companies with very different cultures, histories and styles?

After all, Chrysler was still suffused with the brash "lead, follow or get out of the way" spirit of Lee Iacocca, who had rescued the company in the early 1980s. Iacocca's compensation at that time had been a salary of $1 a year, backed by a raft of stock options. German law, by contrast, does not even recognize option plans.

The *Financial Times* reported that "much attention has focused on how far the car producer can successfully blend a rigid, technically sophisticated German culture with American mass-market orientation and flair."[15]

The cultural differences were perhaps most notable at board level. The merger terms meant that DaimlerChrysler would be incorporated under German law. Thus, the new company would have a two-tier board system with half the supervisory board seats taken up by employee representatives. In the 1960s, Chrysler had once experimented with a union delegate serving as a director, but the plan had not worked out. Chrysler, like any other US company, was exclusively dedicated to the maximization of shareholder value. In time, a member of the US United Auto Workers union would join the DaimlerChrysler board.

Daimler-Benz's largest shareholders – Deutsche Bank, Commerzbank and Dresdner Bank – had three Daimler supervisory board seats between them. Chrysler's board, by contrast, was 75 percent made up of outsiders.

The contrast in board styles was neatly personified. Chrysler's largest shareholder, and board director, was Kirk Kerkorian, an octogenarian billionaire who had made his fortune investing in the gaming tables of Las Vegas. Kirk Kerkorian had kept Chrysler focused on the share price via a series of threatening takeover bids, calls for share buybacks and dividend raises.

Daimler's chairman was Hilmar Kopper, chairman of Deutsche Bank, and the very image of a serious German banker. "The bare-knuckle fighter and the discreet corporate politician" commented the *Financial Times*, "the two men's styles sum up the starkly different styles of capitalism that have developed in the US and Germany."[16]

In fact, Daimler was unusual among German companies for the degree to which it favored shareholder value. Daimler managing director Jurgen Schrempp, for example, had pushed through an incentive pay package that mirrored an option plan in many respects. "It has made me unpopular in Germany," he said.

Nevertheless, Daimler's definition of a shareholder value approach would hardly meet that of Kerkorian, who would find his influence greatly diminished on a board which met only six times a year, and where his aggressive shareholder-value message would likely be opposed by half those present.

Shortly after the merger was complete, Christoph Walther, senior vice-president, corporate communications of Daimler-Benz in Stuttgart, wrote to the *Financial Times* to point out how a shareholder value approach was being incorporated into the new company. "DaimlerChrysler is bringing together parts from the Anglo-Saxon and German corporate governance by establishing a shareholders' committee that includes shareholder representatives, and outside directors, as well as the two chairmen."[17]

But he took issue with what he saw as the *FT*'s critical remarks about German governance: "Your comment could also be interpreted as implying that the Anglo-Saxon system of corporate governance is superior to others. To the best of our knowledge, there is no evidence that the Anglo-Saxon system is better set to avoid mismanagement or corporate failure."

Another potentially fractious issue concerned disclosure – German investor relations practices and accounting standards are far less transparent than in the US. Sure enough, the company's first annual report caused palpitations in America. The annual report (*sans* proxy statement) contained no details on executive pay, director stock ownership or information on largest owners. Moreover, the company refused to accept any votes received electronically. And the deadline for receiving votes by mail was four days before the meeting, not the day of the meeting as is standard in the US. "Some investors will doubtless claim disenfranchisement," said international governance commentator Stephen Davis.

A third critical issue was pay. As discussed, Germany's consensual, egalitarian corporate culture meant that German executive pay was modest compared to that of their US counterparts. In the year before the merger, the ten members of Daimler-Benz's management board earned about $11 million between them. Jurgen Schrempp himself took home about $1.5–$2 million of this sum.

Bob Eaton, in the same year, received salary and bonus of about $4.6 million, but cashed in share options worth more than $5 million. Bob Lutz, Chrysler's out-going vice-president, did even better, cashing in more than $13 million of share options.

In sum, the top five Chrysler managers took home more than three times what their ten Daimler counterparts made.

The two companies reached a compromise on pay. Both agreed that, in principle, low fixed incomes should be paid coupled with high performance-related incentive pay. But, equally, they agreed that pay levels in the respective companies would remain unchanged for two years.

Other thorny problems concerned seemingly small issues, not least the name of the merged firm. US negotiators held out for ChryslerDaimler; the German party demanded Daimler-Benz Chrysler.

Lastly, although Daimler was clearly the senior partner in the deal, English was adopted as the merged corporation's official language.

DaimlerChrysler is on track to deliver $3 billion of "synergies" and cost cuts within three years, although a mixed investor relations performance has left the share price stagnant.

The initial unwieldy management board of 17 has been trimmed, mostly at the expense of Chrysler executives. And, in another signal that the deal was less a "merger of equals" than a Daimler takeover of Chrysler, Bob Eaton stepped down as joint chairman earlier than planned.

A final statistic serves as a warning of the dangers of cross-border mergers. In early 1999, Standard & Poors decided not to include DaimlerChrysler in its S&P 500 index, causing numerous US tracker funds to drop the stock from their port-folios. When the merger was complete in November 1998, 44 percent of the company was in US hands. Within six months, that had dropped to 25 percent.

*Is there such a thing as a "global corporation," or do national values always hold sway? And, if so, how do you merge different national values that aren't always compatible?*

**Update**. Kirk Kerkorian, once the holder of 14 percent of the stock of Chrysler, filed a lawsuit for $8 billion in damages, saying that he would never have supported the merger with Daimler if the company had been honest with him about its intentions. He alleged that the deal was presented to him and to the other share-holders as a merger of equals when Daimler-Benz intended it only as an acquisition and planned to treat Chrysler as a division of Daimler. Clearly, the real underlying basis for the suit was the poor performance of the merged company. But just as clearly, the significance of the multi-national lawsuit (an evidentiary ruling in early 2003 was issued by a court neither in the US nor Germany but in the UK) is the questions it raises about the ability of shareholders to raise questions and create meaningful accountability in a company with global operations.

# Case in point:
# Awkward options for SAP

The governance implications of globalization in the high-tech sector were vividly demonstrated by SAP, a German company that was the biggest software company in Europe.

SAP became the first German company to introduce a share option plan for executives. Controversially, SAP chose to adopt a US model, whereby options are granted with no performance conditions attached, rather than a UK model, where several hurdles are usually set.

SAP's explanation for the scheme was that in an international sector like software, the company had to compete for talent. The company said that a "brain drain" had hit the US workforce.

Hasso Plattner, co-chief executive, told the company's annual meeting: "We are in competition for customers but also for workers, and we must at least make sure that we can compete with Oracle and Microsoft in this market."

The scheme was overwhelmingly approved by shareholders at the annual meeting, "yet the gulf between the two countries' corporate cultures was plainly apparent" according to the *Financial Times*.[18]

In 2002, Germany adopted a new code, noting that its purpose was:

> to make Germany's corporate governance rules transparent for both national and international investors, thus strengthening confidence in the management of German corporations. The Code addresses all major criticisms – especially from the international community – leveled against German corporate governance, namely

- inadequate focus on shareholder interests;
- the two-tier system of executive board and supervisory board;
- inadequate transparency of German corporate governance;
- inadequate independence of German supervisory boards;
- limited independence of financial statement auditors.

The release also noted that "the Government Commission on the German Corporate Governance Code will remain in existence after the Code has been handed over. It will observe the development of corporate governance in legislation and practice and will review the Code at least once a year for possible adaptation.

According to Ministerial Counsellor Dr. Ulrich Seibert, Federal Ministry of Justice, the new (voluntary) rules for Control and Transparency in Business (KonTraG) are as follows:

## 1. Board

- Risk management: boards of public limited companies are obliged to ensure that adequate risk management and internal revision systems exist in their own companies.
- Reporting obligations of the board of directors to the supervisory board over future corporate planning are increased.

## 2. Supervisory board

- "Old boy network": The maximum number of supervisory board seats permitted per person, which is currently 10, is reduced (chairman's seats count as two).
- Candidate recommendation: in the recommendation to shareholders on the election of new supervisory board members, details of their other board memberships and their main occupations are to be given, so as to avoid conflicts of interest and overload situations in advance.
- Frequency of board meetings: the annual number of compulsory supervisory board meetings is increased for quoted companies from two to at least four (not counting committee meetings).
- Contracts with auditors are no longer awarded by the board of directors, but by the supervisory board. This is intended to ensure a greater distance between auditors and management. The report has to be passed directly to the supervisory board, for the attention of the chairman.
- It will be obligatory for the auditor to be present at meetings of the supervisory board held to approve the annual report and accounts, or at a financial audit committee meeting.
- Distribution of the auditor's report to all supervisory board members or members of the financial audit committee will be mandatory.
- In its report to shareholders, the supervisory board must state how often it has met over the year, and how many committees have been formed.
- Enforcement of compensation claims against members of one of the boards, particularly of supervisory boards, is eased by lowering the minimum quorum (5 percent or a nominal DM1 million) where there has been serious neglect of responsibilities.
- In an appendix to the annual report and accounts, quoted companies must list for each board member all their other supervisory board seats and memberships of similar controlling bodies.

## 3. Annual general meeting and shares

- Exercise of proxy voting rights of banks is more strongly oriented towards the interests of the shareholders represented. A bank must name a member of the management who will have to ensure that the statutory obligations involved are being observed.
- Banks and companies must advise shareholders of alternative ways of taking part in ballots (through transferring their vote to a proxy, or shareholders' groups, etc.).
- The banks' reporting obligations to their depositors will be stricter, where there are possible conflicts of interest: they must make it known when bank employees are on the supervisory board of the company concerned, and give details of stockholdings in the company concerned.
- The annual general meeting is authorized to provide rules of procedure for the conduct of the annual general meeting. This should create an opportunity for streamlining and revitalizing annual general meetings.
- Plural voting rights are no longer allowed.
- Existing plural voting rights are to cease after five years, in exchange for a fair equalization of their value. An annual general meeting may also, at any time, with a simple capital majority, cancel existing plural voting rights.
- Maximum voting rights are no longer permissible in quoted companies. Existing maximum voting rights will cease after two years.

- Where there are cross-holdings between companies, the possibility of the second company exercising voting rights in the first is excluded in the election of supervisory board members. This is intended to limit the risk of the administration controlling itself.
- Listed Companies must also make public in an appendix to the annual report and accounts all stakes of more than 5 percent in large limited companies.
- Stock buy-back is generally allowed. This should give more flexibility and provide more price growth potential in the German stock markets.
- The management should gear itself to increasing the value of the company. For that reason, provision of stock options as part of remuneration for top management has been made easier. Abuse must be excluded, however. The annual general meeting has to regulate the major details of these programs.

### 4. Banks as stakeholders

- Limitation of exercise of voting rights: banks may not exercise voting rights stemming from proxy voting rights at an annual general meeting if, at that meeting, they are also exercising votes of their own holdings in the company of more than 5 percent. This regulation is targeted at dealing with criticism of the banks' accumulation of influence through holding equity stakes and exercising proxy votes.
- Increased obligation for bank transparency in connection with annual report and accounts: banks (of whatever legal constitution) are to make public all the mandates held by members of their boards and by other employees; any holdings of more than 5 percent must also be stated.

### 5. Audit

- Income dependency: to ensure the independence of the auditor, the auditor is excluded from performing the audit if more than 30 percent (previously 50 percent) of his total revenue over the previous five years stems from that company.
- Change of auditor: when the same auditor is contracted to a company over a period of years, it can give an impression of dependency. However, as a switch of the auditing company generally is not expedient, a change at the level of the individual who signs the audit certificate must take place if the same person has signed the certificate more than six times in the past ten years.
- The audit report should be geared more to problems.
- The interests of the supervisory board are to be taken into greater consideration in the preparation of the audit report.
- Accountability of auditor: liability will be increased. Instead of the current limitation of liability to DM500,000, a higher liability limit has been fixed: for audits of non-quoted companies DM2 million, for quoted companies DM8 million.
- Segmentation and cashflow statements are now a mandatory part of the consolidated financial statement for quoted companies.
- The legal requirements for the acceptance of a privately organized standard-setting body are introduced (in the UK: ASB; in the USA: FASB). This private body is supposed in particular to develop proposals for application of the basic principles of group accounting and to represent Germany in international bodies (IASC).

# FRANCE

The defining characteristic of the French governance system is the absence of a diverse investment community. Rather, the state, banks, and corporate management hold the controlling interests in the French governance structure. In this respect, the French system departs from the Anglo-American model, though it also departs significantly from the German model.

## French ownership

Companies in France are controlled by the state, management, or by families. The top 50 industrial, commercial, and service companies of France break down as follows:

- 12 state-controlled;
- 17 management-controlled;
- 14 family-controlled and managed;
- 3 family-controlled (but with outside management);
- 4 subsidiaries.

In no other modern industrialized country, save Japan, does the state play as powerful a role as it does in France. This is, in part, due to the long French tradition of encouraging the nation's finest minds into the civil service, via the educational system of the Grandes Écoles. Since World War II, when the state stepped in to rebuild France's economy, the French intellectual elite – represented by both civil servants and industrial managers – has been intimately involved in the formation of industry.

Thus serving industry and serving the state have become almost one and the same thing in France. The managers who run the largest companies, the bankers who provide them with capital, and the government officials who oversee them are all drawn from the same educational background and all share the same goal of keeping French industry in French hands.

The state's strong role in the economy, known as *dirigisme*, is perhaps the main factor affecting governance in France. Though the state is becoming less *dirigiste*, it has been active in forcing mergers and restructurings in state-owned industries for policy purposes, and keeping key industries firmly under government control. The results have been mixed. While France has enjoyed some notable successes (nuclear power, aerospace), it has not been without failures (computers, consumer electronics). The government has substantial holdings in cars, steel, insurance, and banking and has a monopoly in most public utilities, rail, coal, tobacco, radio, and television.

The state's control over private companies also extends indirectly through the banking system. France's financial institutions (banks and insurance companies) are leading providers of capital to French industry, and now account for one-twentieth of the Bourse's capitalization. However, many of the banks are state-owned, or heavily state-influenced – for instance even the largest private banks are usually run by ex-government officials. Banks are informed, long-term shareholders who have played a strong role in protecting French companies from takeover.

France has developed a complex system of cross-shareholding, not unlike the Japanese *keiretsu*. The *verrouillage* system, in which shares are "parked" with friendly companies, accounts for an estimated two-thirds of the shares traded on the Bourse. By other mechanisms, companies can effectively hold their own shares. This system plays a strong role in defeating unsolicited takeovers.

## Management and boards: Non-state-owned companies

Managements at French companies are extremely powerful. The *président directeur-général* (PDG) wields almost unchecked control over the enterprise. Indeed the PDG of one French company told the consulting group Oxford Analytica that France is the only Western country where one man determines the strategy of the company, executes it, and controls it, without the counter-power of the board of directors.[19]

The PDG has virtual control over the board of directors. He or she controls their selection and may dictate the subjects on which they become involved. Indeed, it is regarded as "bad manners" for the board to take a vote on a management decision, since it shows that the PDG has lost the confidence of the board. The PDG is responsible not just for day-to-day operations, but also for the long-term strategic direction of the company. Indeed, if the PDG seeks advice on a major strategic move, he is as likely to go to the state (the company would probably require the help of the state banks) as he would to the board.

Because even privately owned companies tend to be in the hands of controlling blocks director selection usually takes the interests of the few large shareholders into account. Though the PDG has absolute power over the board and its selection, he would invariably pay close attention to the wishes of his owners in choosing new board members. Indeed, the largest banks are represented on the boards of most sizeable companies.

There are complex legal rules governing the structure and composition of French boards. For a start, French companies may choose between two methods of board governance. They may adopt either a unitary boardroom structure (as in the Anglo-American model) or a two-tier structure (as in German companies). Most companies opt for the single-tier system.

The most striking fact about French directors is the extent to which they interlock. In 1989, 57 people accounted for one-quarter of all the board seats of the 100 largest companies, and 20 people accounted for 11 percent, more than 120 seats.

## Viénot I and II

France, in line with the rest of the world, has promoted corporate governance reform via codes of best practice. They were issued in 1995 and 1999, and both were chaired by ex-Société Générale chief Marc Viénot.

The first Viénot code prompted some far-reaching governance reforms. By 1999, executive search firm Korn/Ferry was able to report the following:

- 92 percent of companies were applying Viénot recommendations;
- 30 percent of directors were independent;
- 90 percent of boards have audit, remuneration and nomination committees, which were playing an increasingly important role;
- the presence of foreign board members increased from 10 to 20 percent between 1994 and 1999.[20]

In other areas, however, the Viénot recommendations either did not go far enough or went unheeded. In particular, the concentration of power in the PDG remained strong, companies were reticent about pay, and a handful of directors continued to occupy numerous board seats – Korn/Ferry found that 10 percent of directors occupied 35 percent of board positions in 1999. "Inbreeding is still rife," concluded the report.

The second Viénot report took steps to correct some of these governance shortfalls.

### Board structure

Under French law, companies could either opt for a single-tier board with combined chairman and chief executive officer, or a two-tier structure of supervisory board and separate chairman.

Companies complained that this denied them flexibility. Should they choose to have a separate chairman and chief executive, they are also required to adopt the more cumbersome supervisory board structure. Viénot II gave companies the right to opt for a single-tier board with separated leadership roles.

The new position of chief executive officer (as separate from the PDG) will take the title *directeur général exécutif.*

Viénot II also proposed some significant reforms to the operation of the board, promoting increased transparency and accountability at board level.

At the time of the first Viénot report, non-executive directors were a largely unheard-of phenomenon. As Korn/Ferry found, there had been progress, although Anglo-American investors might argue with French definitions of independence. Viénot II sought to cement this progress – the report recommended that independent directors account for at least one-third of the board, and make up at least one-third of the audit and nominations committee. The compensation committee should consist of a majority of independent directors.

The annual report should also disclose the number of meetings of the board and committees and should provide the shareholders "with appropriate information regarding the directors' attendance at such meetings."

French directors were able to serve (once elected) for up to six years without seeking re-election by shareholders. Viénot proposed that French companies limit the term of office to four years, "in order to enable the shareholders to rule upon their appointment with sufficient frequency." This may not seem like an immense step to investors in the UK and US (in the latter market, annual election of the full board is increasingly accepted as best practice), but it represented progress.

Viénot also proposed that "the terms of office should be staggered so as to avoid renewal as a whole and to make the replacement of directors smoother." The dates of each director's term should be disclosed.

Also, the annual report should disclose each director's age, major executive position, directorships in other listed companies, and shares held. This information can currently be obtained under French law, but, thanks to Viénot, is now more readily available.

The annual report should also disclose the make-up of each board committee – a fresh disclosure for French shareholders.

Proxinvest, the leading French governance advisers, called these recommendations "positive governance improvements."

However, as Korn/Ferry found, French companies had moved only slowly in seeking a wider pool of director candidates. Viénot felt compelled to repeat his earlier guidance: "The committee stresses the recommendation in the 1995 report that a director performing executive duties in a listed corporation should limit the number of outside directorships, and in any event hold no more than five positions."

*Pay disclosure*

Viénot II recommended that annual reports should include a chapter disclosing the compensation of corporate officers. The chapter should include:

- a detailed description of the policy for determining executive pay, the principles for the allocation of the fixed and variable portions, criteria for determination of the basis for variable portions, and rules for the awards of bonuses;
- the aggregate amount of compensation of all kinds collected by executives, broken down between the fixed and variable portions;
- the individual amounts of attendance fees paid to directors.

This proposal disappointed many French governance activists and international investors, who were hoping to see individual director packages disclosed. French executives proved distinctly reluctant to reveal levels of individual pay and the Viénot committee, largely made up of leading executives, has maintained this status quo. The report described the attention paid to executive pay as "voyeuristic."

But voyeurism won the day. Just months after Viénot II, a group representing large companies, Medef, recommended that individual pay packages be set out in full.

Medef acted in anticipation of the government forcing improved disclosure by law, a response to growing public disquiet over the use of share options. In 1999, the French government initiated an enquiry into the so-called "Jaffré Affaire" in which Elf Aquitaine boss Philippe Jaffré had made nearly $30 million in stock option gains following the company's takeover by TotalFina.

# Case in point: Rhône-Poulenc

Europe's only pan-Continental corporate governance fund flexed its muscles at Rhône-Poulenc, the French pharmaceutical company.

ABF Euro AV, a fund which weights investments according to corporate governance criteria, intervened at the May 1999 annual meeting to protest against the company's implementation of a voting cap.

Rhône-Poulenc had been mired in a messy agreed merger with its German rival, Hoechst. Progress towards a final merger agreement was slow, as shareholders in both companies questioned the wisdom and terms of the deal. Doubts about the price raised the possibility of a third party making a bid for either of the companies.

Rhône-Poulenc, eager to protect its tie-up with Hoechst, sought shareholder approval for an anti-takeover device that would limit any predator's voting rights to 8 percent. The proposal required a two-thirds majority to be passed.

Ahead of its annual meeting, Rhône-Poulenc proposed a number of changes to articles. Most of them were minor in scope, save the voting cap. The proposed new articles were released on Christmas Eve, suggesting that the company had something to hide.

In 1992, the food group Danone implemented a voting restriction similar to that proposed by Rhône-Poulenc. Eight percent of shareholders opposed the move, a then unheard-of level of dissent. Among those protesting the cap was the ubiquitous US activist fund, CalPERS.

Scheider introduced a similar cap, although shareholder opposition ran less high, perhaps because the cap was introduced as one of 78 resolutions.

In 1995, Elf Aquitaine put forward a resolution to limit voting rights – a record 17 percent of shareholders rejected it.

The tide of opinion flowing against voting limitations was accelerated by the French association of fund managers, which introduced governance guidelines in 1998. While stopping short of endorsing one share one vote, the guidelines were against limited voting rights. The association has recommended that its members "question the resolution" at Rhône-Poulenc.

In the end, the measure squeezed through by 1 percent, but only after Rhône-Poulenc pledged to drop the cap once the merger with Hoechst was complete. A second takeover defense, that would allow the sale of equity following a bid, was quashed by shareholders.

# Case in point: Eramet

The danger to minority shareholders of mixing politics and business was highlighted in the case of Eramet, the French metals group.

Eramet was privatized by the French government in 1994, but the state held on to a 55 percent share. The government guaranteed that Eramet would be run "independent of state control and political interference."

In February 1997, the government announced that the company would be forced to give up rights to a nickel mine in the South Pacific country of New Caledonia. The handover was an attempt to quell a nascent independence movement in that territory. Eramet's stock hit a two-year low.

International Investors – who owned more than 20 percent of the company – were outraged that their assets (which represented up to 25 percent of the company) were being given away without compensation. Their anger was shared by Eramet PDG Yves Rambaud, who opposed the government's move.

The world's largest pension fund, TIAA–CREF, which owned 1.3 percent of the firm, filed no fewer than nine shareholder resolutions. Fidelity, Franklin Templeton, Mercury Asset Management, and Capital International were other big holders.

A change of French government prompted a reversal. The incoming Jospin administration abandoned efforts to give away rights to the mine. The new prime minister endorsed Rambaud as PDG, appointed New Caledonia nationalists to the Eramet board, and put together a commission charged with finding a solution to the case.

In return, the big investors abstained on the dissident proposals.

A deal was eventually reached that awarded Eramet a more limited concession to the mine than before, while compensating investors for their loss. The company's stock leapt at the news.

According to *The Transformation of Corporate Governance in France* by MIT's Michel Goyer, corporate governance first appeared as a topic of conversation in France in the mid-1990s in the wake of two quasi-simultaneous developments: the growing importance of foreign ownership (i.e. Anglo-Saxon institutional investors) and the succession of spectacular financial losses resulting from unmonitored managerial initiatives (e.g., Crédit Lyonnais, Michelin, Paribas, Suez, Union des Assurances de Paris). But the French were skeptical at best of efforts to push them to adopt a more rigorous system of corporate governance, associating terms like "shareholder value" with lay-offs and focus on quarterly results.

But France recognized that it needed a more credible system of corporate governance if it was to attract non-French capital. Goyer notes that, after Enron and other US scandals, the French pointed with pride to the opposition of management at Suez (utilities group) to adopt Enron-style off-balance-sheet accounting in order to dress up its financial ratios despite the pressures of its auditors, as well as to the refusal of the Commission des Opérations de Bourse (the French securities regulator) to give into Vivendi Universal's demands on the use of questionable methods for reporting financial results as examples of the success of the French system in curbing corporate greed.

Nevertheless, French firms are changing the way they do business at home and abroad. Goyer says that its transformation is most prominent in three areas. First, the ownership structure of companies has undergone a major transition in recent years from concentrated cross-shareholdings in the hands of friendly fellow domestic companies to high levels of foreign ownership. Foreign investors – composed primarily of Anglo-American mutual and pension funds – now own a little over 40 percent of the equity capital of blue-chip CAC 40 firms. This was a result, in large part, of the deliberate strategy of firms to sell their cross-shareholdings in an effort to convince foreign investors that they would be responsive to shareholder concerns. Second, large French firms have reversed their strategy of corporate diversification in many business areas and have dismantled their conglomerate structure. Blue-chip companies, with the notable exception of some traditional family-owned firms, are currently focusing on a limited set of core competencies. As a result, employees of French companies can no longer enjoy the employment protection offered by the internal labor market of conglomerates and the cross-subsidization from fast-growing units to poorer-performing counterparts. Their employment tenure is increasingly dependent on the financial performance of the firm. Third, French firms have adopted managerial performance incentives. A little over half of the total remuneration of French CEOs and top managers now comes in the form of variable pay based on some performance measure as opposed to a fixed salary. As a result, large French firms now pay out the biggest stock options packages among Continental European companies.

## CORPORATE GOVERNANCE AND FOREIGN POLICY

In 2002, the Council on Foreign Relations produced an excellent report by James Shinn and Peter Gourevitch called *How Shareholder Reforms Can Pay Foreign Policy Dividends*. They found that:

> International capital flows are creating incentives for countries to adopt greater shareholder protections, or "corporate governance reforms." When adopted, these protections reorient the priorities of both industrial firms and banks in ways that can defuse many trade disputes and reduce the likelihood of destabilizing financial meltdowns. Corporate governance reforms abroad can also buffer the US domestic securities regulatory model from some contagion risks caused by tighter integration with foreign capital markets.

They recommend that the US become more involved in promoting high standards for corporate governance (including setting a good example) as a low-cost, high-gain strategy. In particular, they recommend:

- more US support for the OECD principles of corporate governance (see above);
- SEC support for merging GAAP with IASB rules to create a higher consolidated standard for accounting and audit rigor and independence;
- more US support for international standards to open all companies up to contests for control;
- disclosure by institutional investors of proxy voting policies and other principles of exercising ownership rights;
- corporate governance standards for global financial institutions;
- independent, third-party governance indices; and
- senior policy coordination on these issues.

## A RACE TO THE BOTTOM?

In 2000, a staff analyst of the Corporate Library called Los Angeles-based Global Crossing and asked for the names of their board of directors. "We don't have to give it to you," she was told. "We're a Bermuda company."

She was able to persuade them that this was information they should be willing to share. But that experience showed that a company with headquarters, operations, employees, customers, and shareholders in the United States could, by paying a nominal fee and renting a mailbox, avoid some of the basic obligations of American corporations – including paying income taxes on income earned outside the US.

This shows the absurd results of allowing the fiction of corporate "citizenship" to permit big business to get the benefits of an American domicile without paying taxes. Non-citizens living in the US have to pay income taxes. American citizens must pay income taxes no matter where they live. Or, if they choose to relinquish their citizenship, they relinquish its benefits. But American corporations can literally get the best of both worlds by becoming "citizens" of Bermuda and getting out of paying income taxes. They don't have to move out of their American facilities or stop using taxpayer-funded amenities. They can continue to lobby Congress and they can continue to obtain lucrative government contracts. They can continue to enjoy all of the benefits of doing business in America while American citizens pay for them.

Corporate managers argue that moving to Bermuda benefits their shareholders. After all, what shareholder would not want to keep the $400 million that New Hampshire-based Tyco would otherwise have had to pay to the IRS in 2001? The answer is that shareholders, mostly American citizens who will have to make up that $400 million shortfall when their own tax bills come in, can lose more than they gain. Tyco shareholders would be glad to pay $400 million to save some of the more than $2 billion that the company lost in just one quarter last year due to poor management. And it is easy to make the case that Tyco could not have deteriorated as quickly as it did if it had remained an American company.

Just as important as the savings on income tax, from the corporate executive's perspective, are the advantages of moving to a less rigorous legal system. Bermuda insulates corporate executives and directors from the kind of liability they would be subject to under American law. Under Bermuda law, the directors are obligated to do what is best for the company; under American law they are obligated to do what is best for shareholders. This is a crucial distinction. For example, Bermuda does not restrict directors from engaging in self-dealing transactions that would be prohibited under US law. Shareholders are not entitled to put resolutions to a vote. And it limits the ability of shareholders to bring class action lawsuits for damages. Even lawsuits that are permitted are difficult to bring. Bermuda's judicial system does not have an official court reporter for its court decisions, so no one really knows what the basis for a complaint should be. Even if a case is brought in the US, there is no guarantee that a judgment can be enforced in Bermuda – the US does not have a treaty about court judgments with Bermuda. So it should not surprise us when the directors of these newly Bermudan corporate "citizens" become a little neglectful.

Bermuda reincorporation has become very popular. Ingersoll-Rand, Foster Wheeler, Cooper Industries, and Nabors Industries have all become Bermudan "citizens." Their shareholders, persuaded by the tax savings or just not willing to oppose management, approved the move.

But the scandals at Tyco and Global Crossing have demonstrated how much shareholders give up when companies reincorporate offshore. In 2002, when Stanley Works announced that it was changing its incorporation to Bermuda, shareholder objections forced it to drop the plan. Bills that would require taxes from companies reincorporating outside the US or limiting federal contracts to non-US companies were considered in the last session of Congress, and more are likely to be introduced.

Shareholders have now made this issue a top priority. The pension fund of the American Federation of State, County, and Municipal Employees (AFSCME) submitted a shareholder proposal at Tyco calling for reincorporation back in the United States. Although fewer than 30 percent of the shareholders voted in favour, Tyco's CEO agreed to investigate the option of reincorporating back in the US and issued a report to the shareholders. AFSCME president Gerald W. McEntee said, "We cannot feel confident about the credibility of the new Tyco board unless they subject themselves to the strictest legal standards. As long as they remain in Bermuda, they are telling investors that they are not willing to be fully transparent and accountable." Four similar proposals from union and state employee pension funds are pending at other US companies with Bermuda incorporations.

It is likely that place of incorporation and company-specific governance provisions will increasingly be factored into investment decisions and risk assessments.

## CONVERGENCE?

The alternative to a "race to the bottom" system predicated on a fictional notion of corporate "domicile" is some core minimum global standards. These are less likely to be imposed by law than by market forces. Whoever has the most credible and transparent system of corporate governance will win the race for the cheapest cost of capital. A 2002 McKinsey study found that investors would be willing to pay as much as an 18 percent premium for companies they believe have superior corporate governance.

We have seen in this chapter how the need of global corporations for capital and the ability of shareholders to invest with ease worldwide has led to a remarkably effective dialog concerning governance reform.

But, as we warned at the beginning of this chapter, local practice remains a powerful force. No company likes to be told what to do (especially by foreign shareholders!), and each company and market is able to argue that its local practices have developed for a reason. Moreover, good governance involves powerful people either giving up that power or being held accountable for it, and human beings rarely cede power willingly or graciously.

Frequently in this book we have referred to Anglo-Saxon or US/UK governance practices. Indeed, those two countries have similar investment markets and share a broadly common approach to governance issues. And yet, looking more closely, we find that local practice in the UK and US markets remains utterly different on some fundamental points:

- *Board structure*. That independent outside directors make up a majority of the board is a truth universally acknowledged in the US; in the UK, such a board make-up remains rare. Executives still remain dominant on UK boards – see the Mirror Group case study. This structural difference derives from a different view of what the board is there to do. The notion that the board is there to oversee executive management is constantly challenged in the UK. The board is seen as a genuine unitary body with responsibility for driving the company forward. Hence, executive and non-executive directors are not accorded different roles and the oversight function remains secondary.
- *Chairman/chief executive*. In the UK, the positions of chairman and chief executive are almost always separated, the exact opposite of the US position. Again, the difference reflects a difference in philosophy. The qualities sought after in a UK non-executive chairman – aloof, wise, unassuming, well-connected, and dispassionate – reflect a very British set of values. Americans, by contrast, tend to prefer heroes – visible, dominant, and powerful. US companies prefer a joint chairman/chief executive because they like the company to be led by a single "supreme commander" figure. However, as discussed in chapter 3, that may be the area most likely to change in the US over the next decade.
- *Executive pay*. For philosophical reasons similar to those just mentioned, the British have an antipathy to high pay. Well-paid executives are dubbed "fat cats" and each windfall options gain is reported in the press with glee. In the US, executive pay has reached a staggering level, with $100 million fortunes no longer rare. Americans, unlike the British, have always believed that successful people should get rich – and successful chief executives now get very, very rich indeed.
- *Takeover defenses*. US companies bristle with "poison pills" and other obstacles to takeover. None of these defenses is legal in the UK.

If such fundamental differences are apparent in such seemingly similar markets as the US and UK, what chance is there for convergence among markets that are wildly different? Between the bank-dominated market of Germany and the family-firm Italian model? Between the conglomerate-dominated South Korean markets and the Japanese *keiretsu*? Between mature and emerging markets?

*Which aspects of a country's local governance practices are likely to change? And which will prove resistant?*

*What kinds of changes are investors most likely to insist upon?*

*Is convergence of governance practices necessarily a positive development? Does governance practice reflect wider national characteristics or society models that should be left free of interference?*

## NOTES

1. Will Hutton, chief executive of the UK's Industrial Society, in *Society Bites Back, The Industrial Society*, <Feb.2000.www.indsoc.co.uk>.
2. Jeffrey Brown, "From Slow Start to Relentless Build Up," *Financial Times* Survey – Markets 2000, Jan. 11, 2000.
3. Ibid.

4. Ibid.

5. Stephen Davis, "Malaysia and Italy: Developing a Taste for Cadbury," *Governance*, 67, Apr./May 1999, p. 8.

6. The Principles can be found at <www.oecd.org>.

7. Examples are taken from *Global Proxy Watch*, the weekly newsletter of international corporate governance and shareowner value. See <www.davisglobal.com>.

8. See <www.apecsec.org.sg>.

9. See <www.sc.com.my>.

10. See <www.gcgf.org>.

11. Jonathan Watts, "US Firm Buys LTCB for a Song: Foreign Takeover Signals Reform in Japan," *Guardian*, Sept. 29, 1999.

12. "Boehringer Move Could Set Trend," *Financial Times*, Jan. 18, 2000.

13. Paul Abrahams, "Why Japan Needs Raiders," *Financial Times*, Jan. 17, 2000.

14. See <www.corgov.de>.

15. *Financial Times*, July 30, 1998.

16. *Financial Times*, May 8, 1998.

17. Letter to the *Financial Times*, Nov. 10, 1998.

18. Bertrand Benoit, "SAP Option Scheme Backed by Investors," *Financial Times*, Jan. 19, 2000.

19. *Board Directors and Corporate Governance: Trends in the G7 Countries Over the Next Ten Years* (Oxford Analytica, UK, Sept. 1992), p. 96.

20. "Gouvernement d'entreprises 1999: Les Sociétés du CAC 40 et le rapport Viénot 2," Korn/Ferry International, Oct. 1999.

# 6
# CASE STUDIES:
# CORPORATIONS IN CRISIS

# General Motors

## GENERAL MOTORS AND PIERRE DU PONT

In 1915, the Treasurer of the DuPont Company, Jacob J. Raskob, persuaded Pierre S. du Pont to buy 2,000 shares of a fledgling company called General Motors (GM). Raskob had been interested in the motor vehicle industry for some years, believing that it would enjoy enormous growth when life settled down after the war.

General Motors at this time was a motley grab-bag of small companies including Buick, Cadillac, Oldsmobile, and Oakland, which later became Pontiac. The companies were joined only by the fact that they had been bought by GM's founder, the visionary but unpredictable William Crapo Durant. Durant, at one time a highly successful carriage engineer, had been acquiring small motor companies and parts manufacturers since 1904. By 1914, GM was the second largest automaker in the country, though admittedly a very distant second to the mighty Ford.

Pierre du Pont's personal investment of 2,000 shares proved bountiful. By December 1915, the shares that du Pont had bought for $82 had shot up to $558. The rise did not reflect GM's growth so much as the massive industrial expansion generated by the war effort. However, the rapid increase in value was enough to persuade du Pont that he had stumbled on a very promising business. In 1915, Pierre du Pont joined GM's board, unofficially as chairman. (In line with convention, we will refer to the company as DuPont, and the person as du Pont.)

In fact, GM was dogged by uncertainty: mismanagement constantly threatened to throw the company into bankruptcy. Durant was regarded by contemporaries as too much of a genius to be a successful businessman. GM's headquarters consisted only of Durant, a few assistants and a handful of secretaries, so that Durant had neither the time nor the resources to exert central control. Moreover, he planned only on the basis of ever-increasing sales producing consistently improving cashflow so that even the slightest recession could leave Durant unable to pay his workers or suppliers. In 1910, such a drop had left GM close to collapse. The company was only rescued by the infusion of a $15 million loan from Durant's bankers, who assumed control of the company as collateral. In 1915, with GM's stock price booming once again, Durant set out to reclaim his company from the banks. By April 1915, Durant had been able to buy 50 percent of General Motors stock via a series of hastily constructed deals. Durant claimed that he had the support of du Pont – an assertion that Pierre read with astonishment in his Delaware newspaper.

Pierre du Pont agreed to serve as chairman because he wished to protect his investment. While he admired Durant's drive and imagination, he believed him to be financially haphazard and without discipline. He wished to impose some of the rigorous financial controls and committee structures that characterized Pierre's own DuPont Company. Durant had other ideas; he wanted du Pont's financial backing, but not his advice. In the words of business historian Alfred Chandler, Durant "had no intention of working with his board. He considered it merely a paper organization that he had to have to meet legal requirement and accepted business practices. The founder, who had regained his company, was going to run it by himself."[1]

Durant contemplated a five-man board, a three-man executive committee, and no finance committee. Raskob and du Pont refused, believing that strict financial control was the only thing that could prevent Durant from running amok. They insisted on a large board, with both financial and executive committees. Not that this rendered Durant accountable. As Chandler writes, "The meetings of the board itself were called only on the shortest notice and then at the initiation of the president, not the chairman."[2] The result was constant friction between du Pont and Durant. Pierre demanded monthly balance sheets to be presented to the finance committee, but often didn't receive them. He insisted that Chevrolet be merged with the GM parent to sort out some of the financial tangle that existed between the two companies and to create an ordered, single corporation. Durant gave in reluctantly.

Ultimately, du Pont gained the upper hand in the relationship because he had the money. Increasingly, Durant relied on du Pont to help out his cash-starved company. After rising at the beginning of the war, auto stocks collapsed as the market recognized that people wouldn't be buying cars for a while. In late 1917, it became apparent that GM would not survive without the kind of investment that only the DuPont Company could provide.

DuPont at this time was rich, with $90 million earmarked for investment. Of that, only $40 million was to be spent on the chemical industry, leaving $50 million for outside projects. Pierre du Pont thought a stake in a business that was sure to expand postwar made perfect sense. After long negotiations with the DuPont board, the company bought $25 million of GM common stock in January 1918. This was equal to a 23.8 percent stake.

A crucial part of the deal was that, in exchange for its cash, DuPont would gain control. Pierre insisted that the finance committee be comprised of a majority of du Ponts, and be chaired by Raskob. Pierre's idea was that if DuPont could exert strict financial control, Durant could take charge of operations. Pierre wished to exploit Durant's drive and imagination but to keep it under his own disciplined oversight.

GM, meanwhile, was engaged on an ill-advised program of expansion, as the company set out to integrate its operations vertically by buying a major supplier, dramatically increasing production capacity. It also bought Fisher Body Corp. for nearly $28 million, and GM's workforce increased exponentially. As the expansion continued, DuPont was required to add fresh infusions of capital. By the end of 1919, DuPont had increased its investment in GM to $49 million, equal to a 28.7 percent stake.

The strategy did not survive the onslaught of the postwar recession. As demand collapsed still further in the ravaged American economy, Ford slashed prices, knowing that GM would have a hard time doing likewise. Ford took an even greater slice of market share, capturing 60 percent in 1921, up from 45 percent in 1920. GM's market share fell from 17 to 12 percent over the same period. GM was capturing a diminishing share of a diminishing market. The company's sales declined by three-quarters between the summer and winter of 1920, and in January 1921 the company recorded an all-time low in the production of vehicles.

The combination of the expansion and the recession was disastrous. Worse, Durant made a desperate single-handed effort to prop up GM's collapsing stock price. Borrowing money from whatever sources he could, he bought up GM stock as it was dumped by the market. In November 1920, Durant's debt amounted to some $38 million as GM neared financial collapse.

Pierre du Pont was faced with a choice. He could abandon the troubled company and cut his losses on the investment, or he could stand by his initial belief that GM represented a potential high-growth company and take steps to ensure its survival. He opted for the second choice, bringing his financial credibility to bear in persuading J.P. Morgan to refinance GM. At the same time, DuPont contributed still more money, raising its stake to 36 percent.

Having restored the company's ability to operate, Pierre du Pont took a huge step in ensuring that GM wouldn't run into such problems again. In December 1921, Durant was forced to resign and Pierre took over the presidency of the company himself. He set about reorganizing and revitalizing GM, making DuPont's investment spectacularly profitable. By 1928, when Pierre retired as chairman of GM, the company had surpassed the once unassailable Ford as the nation's number 1 automaker. GM still holds that distinction today.

Part of the reason for du Pont's success at GM was his recognition of the management genius of Alfred Sloan, who would continue to be involved at GM until after World War II. Pierre stayed on as president until 1923 – just long enough to ensure GM had sound financial foundations – before handing over to Sloan. Sloan, in turn, was responsible for the reinvention of the motor car as a work of style and design, in contrast to Ford's one-type-only Model T.

Sloan's leadership also transformed GM's operations, creating the multidivisional structure that still characterizes the company today. Since the 1920s, GM has remained divided into five automaking divisions: Chevrolet, Pontiac, Oldsmobile, Buick, and Cadillac. The five represented very different automobiles aimed at very different markets. GM operated under what Sloan called a "price pyramid,"[3] so that Cadillac, at the top, had the highest price and the lowest volume and Chevrolet, at the base of the pyramid, had the lowest price and the highest volume. The aim, as Sloan put it, was to manufacture "a car for every purse and purpose."

Pierre du Pont also succeeded because he was much more than an idle investor. For instance, in 1923, du Pont committed more than a quarter of his GM shares to fund a stock purchase plan for senior GM managers. In Sloan's words, du Pont was fixed "on creating a partnership relationship between General Motors' management and itself." Possibly it was the close relationship between DuPont and GM that prompted antitrust regulators to intervene. In 1957, the Supreme Court forced DuPont to dispose of its stake in GM. The court did not find that DuPont had violated the law; it merely concluded that the potential for abuse existed.

William Taylor, associate editor of the *Harvard Business Review*, identifies three critical factors in du Pont's involvement:

> First, the size of the investment created a real stake for both sides. Will Durant could not afford to ignore the opinions of a 25 percent owner, and du Pont could not ignore problems with his company's largest outside investment. Second, there was commitment. Du Pont did not own shares in Ford or in any of GM's other competitors, so GM could provide him with confidential plans and information without worrying that they would be misused or end up in the hands of rivals. Finally, there was expertise. Pierre du Pont

was named chairman of GM's finance committee in 1917; by 1920, he had a good sense of the company's operations, people, and strategic blind spots – the hard and soft data that are invisible to most outsiders but are the essence of why big companies function poorly or well.[4]

A second author, Columbia Law School's Louis Lowenstein, comments on why the DuPont–General Motors relationship was so unusual.

> DuPont's power at GM was impressive, but there was also a remarkable sense of its responsibilities. Unless GM grew and prospered, there would be no profit . . . At times the only sensible course, and the one du Pont followed was to commit further resources . . . In the troubled days after WWI there was pressure to dismember GM and to recoup DuPont's investment, as part of what now would be called a "restructuring." DuPont was able to extend itself, partly because it had the wherewithal to do so but more profoundly because from the outset its decision about GM had been as particular and deliberate as it was significant. DuPont understood why it invested in GM, and neither the dramatic downturn of 1920, the predatory pricing by Ford, nor the failures of GM's management shook that faith. And somehow neither the initial losses nor the later profits ever blurred the separate identity of the two companies. DuPont never contemplated merger, but neither was GM just part of a portfolio that could be dumped at the first hint of a quarterly downturn.[5]

Both these commentators regard the DuPont–GM relationship as a model of "relationship investing," in which the providers and managers of capital work together to achieve their mutual goals. Indeed, Lowenstein comments dolefully, "It is tempting to think about whether GM would have stumbled so badly in the 1970s and 1980s if the DuPont company had still been there."

## GENERAL MOTORS: WHAT WENT WRONG?

### *The postwar period*

In the dazzling firmament of America's postwar industrial success, there was no brighter star than General Motors. Along with Ford and Chrysler – the "Big Three" – GM rode the coat-tails of the United States' spectacular journey to worldwide commercial dominance. The American middle class grew in size and wealth; a network of highways opened up the continent; gas prices remained absurdly low; Americans developed a romance with the road and a love of driving. Under these blissful conditions, Detroit's automakers captured nearly 90 percent of the North American market, with GM itself responsible for nearly half of all cars bought in the US.

Thanks to Sloan's legacy, GM was organized to match a person's progression in car buying. A 16-year-old would pick up a cheap but trusty Chevrolet; married with no children, he might trade in for a classier, racier Pontiac; when the kids arrived, he'd need a bigger car to pack in the crew and would aim for maybe an Oldsmobile; when he'd aged a bit, he'd plump for the nice, safe Buick; and if he was old and rich he'd cruise to the country club in a Cadillac. In other words, if a customer bought a Chevy and liked it, he remained locked into buying GM for life.

In 1952, GM's president, Charlie Wilson, testified to the Armed Services Committee that: "What's good for the country is good for General Motors, and what's good for General Motors is good for the country." His statement captured the arrogance of the largest corporation on earth. Indeed, GM's greatest concern in the 1950s and 1960s was to keep its market share *down* so as to avoid a possible antitrust suit from the federal government.

Its dominance continued into the 1970s. In 1972, GM was the fourth largest company on earth with a stock market valuation of over $23 billion – nearly four times the value of Ford.

In two short decades, this bright picture dimmed. In 1992, GM was the fortieth largest company in the world, its stock market valuation only $22 billion – less than it had been 20 years earlier. Its market share had plummeted to less than 35 percent, causing GM's core North American operations to lose $7 billion in 1992 alone.

The scale of GM's decline became obvious in December 1991, when CEO Robert Stempel announced a huge downsizing. Six assembly plants were earmarked for closure, with 15 other plants to follow by 1995. A total of 74,000 jobs would be lost as a result of the cuts – reducing the GM workforce to half its 1985 size. The layoffs merely worsened GM's already testy relationship with the United Auto Workers (UAW) union.

At the time of this announcement, GM's stock traded at a four-year low, about half what the stock was worth in 1965, though the S&P 500 had quadrupled in that period.

In October 1992, the GM board did what no GM board had done since 1921. It pressed for the resignation of the chairman and CEO, Robert Stempel. Stempel, who had only had the helm of GM since August 1990, was pushed out for moving too slowly on down-sizing the company, streamlining operations and improving efficiency. A new breed of managers took over, their mission to fix General Motors.

In 20 years GM had gone from being a golden corporate success to being what *Fortune* magazine called a corporate "dinosaur." What went wrong?

The history of GM is an instructive story in how success can breed failure; how being the biggest and the best can lead to arrogance and an inability to adapt. GM was the pre-mier car company in the world for so long that it failed to see the need for change. The company was so used to being leader that it couldn't contemplate following others. It was this mindset, this overwhelming belief that it was GM's divine right to be the most successful automobile company on earth, that condemned the company to two decades of disaster. When GM did finally see the need to adapt, it did so with wild ineptitude, spending tens of billions in the 1980s for little reward.

As we review what went wrong at GM, and why, keep in mind our corporate "tripod" of shareholders, directors, and management.

- *Which group should have been responsible for seeing that GM adapted to a new competitive environment? All three?*
- *Or some other group, less intimately involved in GM and less beholden to its culture: suppliers, consumers, employees, the government?*
- *Given that it is in none of these groups' interests to see GM fail, and given the company's enorm-ous resources to compete, why did no one (or at least no one in a position to do anything about it) see GM's decline coming?*
- *And why couldn't anyone head the crisis off before billions of dollars were wasted and tens of thousands of jobs lost?*

GM was not alone in its failure to reposition itself for a new competitive environment. Ford displayed equal hubris in the face of the Japanese and suffered just as badly; Chrysler was only saved from bankruptcy by the intervention of billions of dollars in federal loan guarantees. However, both companies, being smaller, were able to respond to their respective crises with more rapidity. GM, by contrast, became living proof of the old boxing maxim: the bigger they are, the harder they fall.

## The GM "culture"

GM was such a powerful, dominant company that its cars, and its name, were an American institution. The trouble was, the company was managed like an institution. It was highly risk-averse, chronically slow to change, endlessly bureaucratic, and contemptuous of competition.

GM employees were expected to display unwavering loyalty to the GM organization, subsuming their personality to that of the corporate giant. Employees were expected to be "team players," meaning that they never questioned a decision, never contradicted the boss, and conformed with the corporate stereotype. One author describes a GM employee driving 40 miles each morning to pick up his superior's newspaper, and saying he didn't mind the chore because one day he would be promoted and have someone perform the task for him.[6] A second writer tells the story of a GM executive who required his morning orange juice to be a certain temperature, so each day an underling would check the glass of juice with a thermometer.[7] Risk and creativity were not in the GM lexicon. A memo circulated by a senior GM executive in 1988 said, "Our culture discourages frank and open debate. The rank and file of GM personnel perceive that management does not receive bad news well."[8] Automotive analyst and author Maryann Keller quotes one executive who told her, "If you raised a problem, you got labeled as 'negative,' not a team player. If you wanted to rise in the company, you kept your mouth shut and said yes to everything." Keller asserts that the guiding principle of GM corporate life was, "Above all, be loyal to your superior's agenda."[9] This culture was matched by the decision-making process. Decisions were shuttled higher and higher up a hierarchy of committees so that if anything went wrong, nobody would ever take the blame. Orders flowed from the top down; ideas seldom percolated up. It was a system in which no one took responsibility for any decision, so no one had any need to be accountable for one. The same 1988 memo pointed out that fewer than 100 salaried workers (out of over 100,000) were dismissed annually for poor performance between 1977 and 1983.[10] Keller points to a 1980s study by the McKinsey management consulting firm that highlighted the accountability problem. The study detailed how an engineer, faced with a defect, couldn't simply offer a solution to the manufacturer. Rather, "you have to produce 50,000 studies to show that it's a better solution, then you have to go through 10 different committees to have it approved."[11] The stultifying bureaucracy resulted from the fact that GM concentrated more on "making the numbers" than on making cars. This derived from the dominance of the financial wing of the company.

From 1958 and the appointment of Frederick G. Donner as chairman, GM was headed by a succession of finance men – "bean counters" as opposed to "car guys." The understanding was that an engineer, left to his own devices, would spend limitless amounts of money in pursuit of the ultimate car, and it was important for the financial people to keep the engineers in check.

The rule of the finance department was that no idea was worth introducing if it didn't directly boost the bottom line. In the 1950s, GM couldn't afford to raise its sales – to do so would be to arouse the ire of federal antitrust regulators. Instead, GM sought to increase earnings from the same level of sales by cutting costs and thus raising the profit margin per car. Corporate heroes were those who could shave a dollar from a manufacturing process. GM never chased grand new ideas because there was no need. When existing car lines were capturing half of the US car market, what was the point of spending millions of dollars developing a different model that might not sell? What was the point of offering seat belts when customers were perfectly ready to buy GM's cars without them? As one observer notes, "It was much easier for GM to add a $20 piece of chrome or a $5 sports stripe and call the car a 'new model' than take a chance with costly new technologies, such as antilock brakes or multivalve engines."[12]

## GM and quality

GM sold so many cars that there was no reason to slow up assembly lines to improve quality – after all, dealers only complained that they weren't receiving enough cars, not that the cars being delivered were defective. Again, the pressure was to "make the numbers" and produce the required number of cars. GM's only worry was whether it could produce enough vehicles to serve its massive market, so cars were subjected only to routine inspections. If a customer bought a dud, he could always send it back.

Shoddy quality was never fixed because bad news never traveled far in the corporation. If too great a percentage of GM cars failed their quality inspection, the standards were simply lowered so that more cars could pass. Keller interviewed one truck executive who learned the hard way. In the late 1960s he reported to the executive committee that few GM trucks lasted even a single year without a breakdown, so poor was manufacturing quality. After the meeting, the boss approached him and said, "We don't talk about things like that in administrative meetings."[13] This combination of factors meant that Detroit continued to make much the same cars in much the same way year after year. The lack of innovation was startling. This didn't escape the notice of some GM executives, notably John DeLorean.

> My concern was that there hadn't been an important product innovation in the industry since the automatic transmission and power steering in 1949. That was almost a quarter century of technical hibernation. In the place of product innovation the automobile industry went on a two-decade marketing binge which generally offered up the same old product under the guise of something new and useful. There really was nothing essentially new.[14]

## The "fourteenth floor"

The fourteenth floor of General Motors' Detroit headquarters became the living symbol of GM's size and dominance. Here was Executive Row, housing the offices of GM's most senior officers, people who almost invariably had spent their whole working life at GM. Behind two sets of locked glass doors, near the private executive elevator (that ran down to the heated executive garages), and close to the private executive dining rooms, the most vital issues concerning the corporation were decided.

John DeLorean, who quit shortly after being promoted to the fourteenth floor, describes how he found himself buried in paperwork, wrapped up in endless committee meetings, and cut off from the business of building automobiles. DeLorean describes one executive meeting (which he says often put a third of attendees to sleep) in which a minor point of compensation was being discussed. Suddenly the chairman, Richard C. Gersternberg, barked out some orders:

> "We can't make a decision on this now . . . I think we ought to form a task force to look into this and come back with a report in 90 to 120 days. Then we can make a decision." He then rattled off the members of the task force he was appointing. There was an eerie silence after the chairman spoke. It lasted for what seemed like half a day. The whole room was bewildered but no one had the courage to say why. Finally, Harold G. Warner, the snow-white-haired, kindly executive vice president, who was soon to retire, broke the silence. "Dick this presentation is the result of the task force that you appointed some time ago. Most of the people you just appointed to the new task force are on the old one."[15]

### Governance at GM: Corvair, Nader, and "Campaign GM"

One episode sums up most of what was wrong with GM. The story concerns the Chevrolet Corvair, built in 1959. Even in the testing stage, Chevrolet's engineers noted some alarming safety defects, particularly the car's tendency to spin out of control when taking turns at speed. The president of Chevrolet wished to add a stabilizer bar to the vehicle, at a cost of $15 per car. He was overruled by the finance department, which claimed that the bar was an unnecessary cost. The Corvair rapidly gained a reputation as a lethal vehicle, but rather than admitting to the Corvair's faults and making changes, GM continued to market the dangerous car. In a sop to the critics, GM spent $1 million on safety studies.

General Motors was subjected to embarrassing congressional hearings led by Senators Abraham Ribicoff and Edward Kennedy. Chairman Frederick Donner was unable to recall GM's earnings from the year before, and had to ask an aide to come up with the $1.7 billion figure. Kennedy said that $1 million spent on safety out of such enormous profits was a meaningless gesture.

The main source of GM's nemesis turned out to be a young consumer advocate named Ralph Nader. Nader exposed the safety defects of the Corvair in a book entitled *Unsafe At Any Speed*. Instead of responding to the allegations, GM assailed Nader. The company hired private investigators to tail Nader, and produce whatever dirt they could. Rumors were spread that the consumer advocate was a homosexual and anti-Semitic. Ultimately, GM's president James Roche publicly apologized to Nader and admitted the defects in the Corvair. A stabilizer bar was finally added to the car in 1964, but by then Corvair's name was already damaged beyond repair.

Nader wasn't finished with GM, however. In 1970 he, along with three other public-interest lawyers, set up the "Project on Corporate Responsibility" to raise public consciousness about corporate behavior. GM was their first target, not only because of Nader's experience with the company, but because GM was such an obvious epitome of the giant American public corporation.

Originally, "Campaign GM" called for Nader to run as a candidate for the board, but Nader declined the offer. Instead, the project submitted shareholder proposals for GM's 1970 annual shareholders meeting, calling for three reforms: an amendment to the corporate charter stating that GM's operations would be consistent with "public health, safety and welfare"; the establishment of a shareholder committee on corporate responsibility; and the expansion of the board to allow for three public-interest representatives. Within three weeks, six more proposals were added concerning auto safety, pollution control, mass transit, and minority hiring, but the Securities and Exchange Commission (SEC) ultimately permitted all but two to be excluded from the proxy. The remaining two – concerning a shareholder committee and the expansion of the board – were enough to make the 1970 annual meeting a spectacle. Three thousand people attended the May meeting, which turned into a lengthy question-and-answer session regarding GM's commitment to social issues. Although neither proposal gained 3 percent of the vote, meaning that Campaign GM could not resubmit the proposals the next year, GM did make changes in response to the public pressure. It went on to create a public policy committee and a special committee of scientists to monitor the corporation's effect on the environment. It also appointed an air pollution expert and its first black director to the board.

In the end, as Campaign GM showed, the company could be moved. The disaster of the Corvair, and the weight of public pressure, were enough to force GM to make a few, mostly token gestures. But Campaign GM took place 11 years after the introduction of the Corvair and seven years after Nader's book detailing its defects. In the rarefied, conservative atmosphere of the fourteenth floor, it took that long for the company to see the need to change. GM refused to be accountable either to a congressional investigation or to a consumer advocate, and it took years for GM to see the need to be accountable to the market. In the 1980s, as we shall see, this mindset was critical in causing GM's decline.

The point is well made by automotive journalist and author Doron Levin, in his account of the Corvair episode:

> The company had failed to appreciate its impact on, and its duties to, society. Instead of perceiving Nader's activism as a symbolic warning to heed public sensibilities, GM was confident he was an isolated nuisance. GM clung to the outdated notion that it was powerful enough to create its own social and economic landscape.[16]

## New trends: efficiency, quality, safety, the Japanese

At the peak of GM's power – in the 1950s and 1960s – Americans liked their cars big and showy. Power was vital, fuel efficiency irrelevant. When the Japanese showed up in the late 1960s and early 1970s, with their small, non-gas-guzzling vehicles – "shitboxes," as they were known in Detroit – GM paid no attention. If there was a market in America for small cars, ran the reasoning, GM would already have cornered it. Rather, the company pledged to continue the lines that had always made money, the big, wide and heavy cars that could carry a family in comfort and the rich in luxury.

General Motors could be forgiven for its lack of vision in 1970. It was quite true that small cars did not sell in America, and the Japanese competition at this time was terrible, producing badly designed, badly made cars. But by 1980, Japan was making good small cars and Americans were buying them. GM's market share dwindled year after year as a result. This was not just a failure to guess where the new markets might be, it was a failure to adapt to a current market that was right before GM's eyes.

In retrospect, we can identify the 1970s as the decade when the American car industry should have changed its ways. Three factors combined to reshape the competitive environment:

1. ever-improving Japanese quality and design;
2. two oil crises that drove up the price of gas; and
3. federal regulations demanding better fuel efficiency and safety standards.

Of course these factors were related. It was the oil crises that awoke the federal government to the need for fuel efficiency; and it was Detroit's reluctance to treat quality and reliability as important issues that allowed the Japanese a huge head-start in that field.

In 1973, in response to America's support for Israel in the Yom Kippur war, the Organization of Petroleum Exporting Countries (OPEC) agreed to impose an oil embargo on the West. As America and Europe scrambled to step up the search for oil in the North Sea, Alaska, and the Gulf of Mexico, Western leaders also looked for ways to avoid being put at the mercy of OPEC again. One solution was to use less oil.

The oil crisis of 1973 – or the energy crisis as it came to be called – came as a particular shock to Americans, who were used to paying about 30 cents a gallon for gas. Overnight, it was a dollar. People found themselves lining up all day for a commodity that had been almost as readily available as water. Suddenly, driving a car that only ran ten miles to the gallon was no longer affordable. The move to smaller, lighter, more efficient cars was lightning fast. There was one group in a position to respond: the Japanese.

At the time of the 1973 oil crisis, Japanese cars accounted for about 10 percent of the car market, compared with the 80 percent share commanded by the Big Three. Japanese automakers were still finding their feet in the early 1970s; they were not proficient in body design or engine production. Moreover, they had little idea about the market, producing cars in designs and colors that failed to appeal to Americans.

But the Japanese response time was incredibly quick. Sensing a massive market for smaller, cheaper cars, Toyota and Honda worked at producing just that. They focused on quality, efficiency, and reliability – issues that Detroit, with its massive guaranteed market share, had ignored.

Japanese management practices, in contrast to GM's bureaucracy, were lean and highly flexible. They had none of the burdensome committee structures that crippled Detroit, none of the rigid hierarchies, and none of the acrimonious labor relations. The result was an altogether more efficient operation. As late as 1981, a GM internal study found that the Japanese could build a car for $1,800 less than it cost GM.

The Japanese were not burdened by GM's institutional culture. Rather, the Japanese stressed innovation and customer service. Manufacturers and designers, labor and management, worked in teams with the lowliest assembly-line workers, all seeking ways to make jobs easier and products better. At the same time, Japanese firms guaranteed their workers employment for life, engendering a loyalty to the company that was matched only by a loyalty to the customer. As a result, quality was built into the system. In Detroit, cars were pulled from the assembly line to correct defects or were sent to the market on the basis that discontented customers could send them back. In Japan, cars were built right first time. Even in 1993, Japanese companies manufactured nine out of the top ten quality-ranked vehicles, according to one survey.[17] Japan was able to respond to consumer trends in a fraction of the time that it took the Big Three. As Americans moved toward smaller cars, the Japanese were there. As customers increasingly sought quality and reliability, the Japanese were there again. Even today, Japanese automakers are able to get a new model to the market a year quicker than their American counterparts. In the 1970s, this meant that Japan was able to get a massive head start in the race to build small, efficient cars.

A second oil crisis in 1979, prompted by the overthrow of the Shah of Iran, merely accelerated the Japanese invasion. By 1980, the Japanese had raised their market share to 20 percent, double what it had been in 1970. In less than a decade, the Japanese had made quantum leaps in design and styling, and the small car market had become far more than a niche.

But GM continued to underestimate the threat. As Keller comments, "GM never under-stood their foreign competitors. They were viewed as opportunists who got lucky during the oil crises."[18] As Detroit continued to ignore the Japanese, so too did it ignore the trends that were making the Japanese successful. Partly, the problem lay with the federal government. Following the 1973 oil shock, the government initiated a host of regulations concerning fuel efficiency, clean air standards, and safety. Detroit's designers found them-selves trying to develop cars that matched these standards. The Japanese, already ahead in the efficiency game, concentrated on quality and customer satisfaction.

The Big Three's response to new federal regulations was to lobby for loopholes. In 1975, Congress passed the Corporate Average Fuel Economy (CAFE) law, which estab-lished increasingly stringent fuel efficiency standards for US cars. The intention was to double car mileage by 1985. The law encouraged smaller cars, since automakers were bound only by the average that their fleet recorded – larger cars could under-perform the CAFE standard as long as smaller cars could make up the difference. The CAFE law grew pro-gressively weaker as Congress approved loophole after loophole. By 1986, GM had failed to meet the standards for four years in a row, but had paid no fines thanks to laws lower-ing the mileage requirements, or approving new methods of measurement that allowed GM to record higher fuel efficiency. In 1986, an attorney for Ralph Nader's Public Citizen consumer group told the *Wall Street Journal*, "If all the [CAFE] statute is designed to do is ratify what GM and Ford want to do on their own, there isn't much point to the statute."[19] Detroit also resisted efforts to improve safety standards. In April 1971, listening devices in the White House (made famous by the Watergate scandal) recorded Ford executive Lee Iacocca telling Richard Nixon that a federal law mandating airbags would cost US automakers crippling sums of money. He told Nixon that airbags represented a possible $4 billion annual cost to Ford, "and you can see that safety has really killed all of our business." Iacocca's pitch was successful – Nixon delayed federal laws mandating airbags.

Safety features such as airbags actually represented a competitive advantage for the Big Three – they were way ahead of the Japanese on safety technology. But they failed to anticipate increasing consumer demand for safety features, stressing the paramount import-ance of protecting the earnings column.[20]

Detroit responded to new CAFE and safety standards by arguing that efficiency and safety standards were low among consumers' priorities compared to comfort and reliabil-ity. The automakers argued that they would provide more efficient engines and safety features just as soon as buyers demanded them. As we shall see in our discussion of the import restraints of the 1980s, the Big Three were very quick to abandon this free market position.

As small cars became increasingly popular, GM tried half-heartedly to compete. In 1970, it introduced its "import buster," the Vega. The car was a lemon. It failed to meet any of its projections for weight, length, or price, and arrived at the market costing $300 more than the VW Bug. It was also riddled with mechanical defects. The car was outsold by the Ford Pinto in its first year, and was cancelled the next in the wake of a violent strike at the Vega plant. GM didn't mind. Executives resisted the opportunity to improve the Vega, believing that its failure merely proved that the small car market was ephemeral and a distraction.

By the late 1970s, when it was clear that small cars had arrived to stay, GM was still confident of its leadership. In a momentous high-cost decision, the company planned to shift away from heavy, gas-guzzling rear-wheel-drive cars to more efficient front-wheel versions. The generation of "X-cars", due to hit the streets in 1980, would show that GM's engineering was still the best there was.

The X-cars were disastrous. GM underestimated the huge changes that were necessary to switch from rear-wheel to front-wheel drives, and failed fully to re-engineer engines and transmissions. The result was that X-cars achieved a reputation for being shoddily made and unreliable. In 1981, GM unveiled the J-car project, another car series that was meant to send the Japanese packing – GM president F. James McDonald called the J-Cars a $5 billion "roll of the dice."[21] The J-cars suffered from the same cost-cutting problems as the X-cars, borrowing unsuitable engine and transmission designs from earlier models. The result was that the J-cars, like the X-cars, were panned both by the automotive press and the buying public. Indeed in 1981–2, GM recalled more cars than it produced.[22] The X-cars also looked bad – hardly surprising since GM didn't bother with consumer market research until 1985. By contrast, the Japanese had made huge strides in styling, creating glossy paints and friendly interiors with appealing trim. They had developed features like internal trunk and gas cap releases, things that appealed to the driver as a "user." Detroit was still relying on decorative gimmicks like a chrome strip.[23]

## *The 1980s*

The X-cars were meant to show the world that GM still led in automotive engineering, but they only showed how out of touch the automaker had become. In 1980, GM lost over $700 million, its first loss since 1921, as its sales dropped 26 percent. But the scale of GM's problems was overshadowed by the crises threatening Ford and Chrysler.

In 1979, Ford recorded a $1.5 billion loss, followed by losses totaling a further $1.75 billion over the next two years. This volume of red ink was almost enough to leave Ford bankrupt. 1979 was an even worse year for Chrysler. Iacocca, traveling to Washington as Chrysler's new CEO, told the federal government that without a massive loan guarantee, the company would fold with the loss of tens of thousands of jobs. The next year, 1980, the government approved $1.5 billion in loan guarantees. The loans covered Chrysler's $1.7 billion loss, and allowed the company to survive.

It wasn't just Chrysler that received help from the government. All three members of the Detroit trio joined to lobby for protection from the Japanese. In other words, Detroit sought to keep the Japanese out of the United States rather than compete with them.

In 1981, after months of negotiation with both the UAW and the federal government, Japan agreed voluntarily to limit the number of cars it would ship to the US each year. The first year's limit was set at 1.68 million vehicles – significantly reducing the Japanese threat. Detroit had negotiated itself a breathing space; indeed the uncompetitive market allowed the Big Three to enjoy record profits over the next few years. It was a golden opportunity to take charge of the auto market, improve efficiency and quality to Japanese levels, and compete fairly and squarely with the Japanese. But the hard-won lull proved brief – especially for GM.

Ford and Chrysler's perilously close journey to the brink of collapse forced them to rethink. Clearly, they could no longer run their companies as they once had – the world had moved on, and they had to move on too if they were to survive. As a result, the two automakers showed some brave developments through the decade: Chrysler with the reintroduction of the convertible and in the production of minivans, Ford with a new aerodynamic design. As a result, Ford and Chrysler made it through the 1980s. Both companies had mixed results through the decade, but both were vastly better positioned to compete in 1990 than they had been ten years earlier.

GM was not driven to change by the same fiscal crises that beset its Detroit counterparts. In 1980, GM was still a massively wealthy corporation, protected by its size and its financial strength. Not that GM went untouched by the changes made at Ford and Chrysler; it too saw the need to upgrade and compete. In 1981, GM appointed a new chairman and CEO who was determined to drag GM into the twenty-first century – Roger Bonham Smith.

## The Smith era

Roger Smith had a consuming vision of the GM of the future. He saw the car as not just a mechanical object, but an electromechanical one, in which on-board computers and circuitry were as important as the actual engine. He saw cars manufactured in "lights out" factories, where the only employees were people supervising the robots and computers. Smith also envisioned a world in which high-tech smoothed the process of buying a car. The customer would reel off his order – tinted glass, automatic transmission, color blue, power windows – to a salesman who would tap the particulars into a computer. The information would be relayed to factory robots that could custom-build every vehicle. The consumer would no longer be forced to choose between competing models, since every car could be tailor-made.

Clearly, Smith was thinking long, long term. He had a vision of the industry as it might develop in the twenty-first century. But he was determined to put GM on the fast track toward that future, and to block the Japanese from using their superiority in microelectronics to dominate the car market as they had the consumer electronics market. With a cast-iron balance sheet and mountains of cash, Smith was determined to remake GM into the world's strongest automaker.

Over the next decade, GM spent nearly $90 billion reforming itself. By most accounts, this money was all but wasted. GM lost market share throughout the 1980s, and became a high-cost, inefficient producer. The company's continued decline set the scene for the massive downsizing of 1991, and the ouster of Robert Stempel in 1992.

Why did the 1980s prove so disastrous for GM? An examination of Smith's strategy reveals three main themes:

1. reforming GM's bureaucracy;
2. purchasing advanced technology;
3. attempting to instill an entrepreneurial spirit in the company.

### Organizational reform

The CEO, Roger Smith, was acutely aware of GM's bloated, blundering organization. He knew that GM would have to become leaner and meaner if it wished to compete. In 1984, Smith set out to reorganize totally the outdated GM structure.

Through the 1960s, as the men from finance had increased their control over the separate divisions, GM had become more centralized. Alfred Sloan's rule of "centralized policy and decentralized administration" was being eroded by the demands from the fourteenth floor. This problem was compounded in the 1970s by the onslaught of federal efficiency and safety regulations that limited design possibilities.

Also, all car bodies were made by a single division – Fisher Body – and assembled by another – GM Assembly. These two divisions were able to impose their own authority over the designers and engineers at Chevy and Pontiac, etc. The result was that Sloan's structure of five semi-autonomous divisions had become an anachronism. The extent of the problem became apparent during the 1970s, when GM experimented with "badge engineering." Under this scheme, divisions shared as many parts as possible to keep costs down, while small stylistic changes were meant to identify a particular car as a Pontiac or an Oldsmobile. "Badge engineering" was not a success since it resulted in cars that looked too much alike.

But although GM was becoming increasingly centralized, each division maintained its own design and marketing operations, so that resources were duplicated across GM. The company was organized the wrong way round – several design centers produced a range of similar cars.

Smith wished to accomplish two goals: decentralize authority back to the manufacturing divisions and streamline the company's resources so that the divisions didn't duplicate each other's work.

Smith reorganized GM into two main groups. Chevrolet-Pontiac-Canada (CPC) would design, manufacture, and market small cars. Buick-Oldsmobile-Cadillac (BOC) would take charge of the big ones. The regrouping eliminated two whole divisions – Fisher Body and GM Assembly – in a move that eliminated thousands of jobs and created thousands of others. It was a wholesale shift of personnel in which reporting structures were realigned and channels of communication redirected. The reorganization might have been a good idea in theory, but in practice it created chaos. As *Fortune* put it, "The shakeup froze GM in its tracks for 18 months."[24] The problem was that while the old structure had been dismantled, a new structure had not been constructed in its place. The result was an organization in which no one knew who was responsible for what. Suppliers complained that they could never find the right representative, or when they did, he or she soon changed jobs. In the mêlée, new layers of management were created to try and sort out the mess. Indeed, CPC wound up adding 8,000 people following the restructuring.

In 1985, CPC produced 3.5 million cars a year – roughly the same as Toyota. But CPC employed 160,000 people in contrast to Toyota's 60,000.

General Motors became more, not less, inefficient, causing more people to be hired. In 1983, the total GM workforce was 691,000. By 1985, it had climbed to 811,000.

The confusion led to chaos in GM's basic manufacturing. In one absurd instance, it became efficient for a Chevrolet plant to build Cadillacs, while Buick assembled Pontiacs. One GM observer told *Fortune* that GM started producing 17 ignition systems where three would have been enough, and 40 types of catalytic converter instead of four.[25] Even as late as 1992, GM produced more than a dozen separate caps for windshield washer fluid bottles![26] Smith's reorganization seemed to have exactly the wrong effect. Rather than chasing the Japanese dream of leanness and efficiency, the plan had made GM more confused and cumbersome.

### GM-10

The failure of the reorganization was most acutely felt in Smith's other big shake-up, the GM-10 program. One academic called GM-10 "the biggest catastrophe in American industrial history."[27]

GM-10's aim, like that of the 1984 reorganization, was to streamline the resources of the five divisions to create a consistent, non-duplicative car line. Starting in 1982, GM set out to replace all existing midsize cars produced by Chevrolet, Pontiac, Oldsmobile, and Buick. Under GM-10, each division would manufacture a coupé, a sedan, and a station wagon. The plan called for seven plants, each to assemble a quarter of a million of the new cars, which would account for 21 percent of the US car market – a bigger market share than Ford's. According to *Fortune*, "It would be the largest new-model program ever, the ultimate expression of GM's ability to capitalize on its enormous economies of scale. But GM couldn't pull it off. The world's largest corporation choked."[28] The 1984 reorganization played havoc with the management of GM-10: people working on the project were moved; responsibilities shifted or were left undefined; the program manager in charge of GM-10 was replaced, as was his successor; responsibility for the program was moved to CPC; finally, and most gallingly, GM was forced to change the styling of GM-10 cars so they didn't appear to be replicas of the Ford Taurus, introduced in 1986.[29] As GM-10 suffered setback after setback, GM pulled back from the grand vision that had initiated the program. First, GM downsized the project, dropping the station wagon and cutting back the plants involved from seven to four. Then GM found it couldn't afford to produce all eight GM-10 cars simultaneously, so it rolled the cars out to market over two years, two-doors before four-doors. But even in this, GM guessed wrong. Baby boomers who wanted coupés in 1980 now wanted family-size sedans. Ford, for instance, never introduced a two-door Taurus, yet in 1988, GM was rolling out four brand-new two-door coupés.[30] In 1990, eight years after the GM-10 program was launched, the final cars hit the showrooms. They were a disaster. In 1989, GM lost over $2,000 on every GM-10 car it produced. In 1979, Oldsmobile had sold 518,000 models of a car, scheduled for replacement under the GM-10 program. Twelve years later, in 1991, Oldsmobile sold only 87,500 models of the new GM-10 version.[31] When asked by *Fortune* why GM-10 was such a catastrophe, Roger Smith replied, "I don't know. It's a mysterious thing."[32]

### Look-alikes

Other errors compounded the manufacturing problems. In attempting to unify the disparate sections of the five divisions, GM endeavored to create a corporate "look" so that consumers could identify a GM vehicle at a glance. GM took this plan too far and created a line of identical-looking cars. GM shrank its luxury cars to such an extent that they no longer looked different from their cheaper counterparts – a $9,000 Pontiac ended up looking similar to $25,000 Cadillac.

The results were disastrous for GM's luxury end, traditionally the company's most profitable business. GM resorted to cosmetic changes, such as adding a three-inch fender extension to one Cadillac model to make it appear longer. The irony was plain to all. Once, GM had cornered the large car market. Indeed, during the 1970s it seemed that those were the only cars GM made well; now the company couldn't even seem to do that right.

### Purchase of new technology

If there is one characteristic of Roger Smith that came to dominate his tenure as chairman, it was his love of technology. To Smith, GM's future lay with high-tech, and he was determined that GM should be the leader. In his ten-year tenure as CEO, Smith spent over $50 billion on technology projects. As Bob Eaton, chief of GM's advanced engineering, put it, "When you told Roger about new technology, he'd get excited and ask, 'Where do I sign?'"[33]

The list of GM's high-technology projects through the 1980s is a long one:

- When Roger Smith was appointed chairman, GM had 300 robots. Smith made a pledge to acquire 14,000 by 1990.[34] To fulfill this promise, Smith engaged in a 1981 joint venture with the Japanese robot manufacturer, Fujitsu-Fanuc. GMF Robotics would build robots for the US market, with 70 percent of the output earmarked for GM. Via this joint venture, GM became the largest manufacturer of robots in the world.

- Detroit also poured money into an acquisition binge of small-time European car manufacturers. GM bought 48 percent of Lotus for $20 million and half of Saab for $600 million. The hope was that GM could exploit the advanced engineering of these companies.

- In 1983, Smith unveiled Saturn, the "car of the future." The plan was to reinvent the way GM made small and mid-sized cars. Saturn would be built in new plants, employing the newest technology and the most productive management practices, and sold in standalone showrooms. Quality would be the watchword of the new vehicles. Saturn held out the promise that GM could manufacture small cars as well as the Japanese.

- Smith also spent money to learn directly from the Japanese. In 1983 he formed New United Motor Manufacturing Inc. (NUMMI), a joint venture with Toyota. NUMMI was set up in an idle GM factory in Fremont, California, and set out to build Chevy Novas, using American labor and Japanese management.

- In 1985, GM offered $5.2 billion to purchase Hughes Aircraft, an aerospace manufacturer. Smith hoped that Hughes's space-age engineering could be used to juice up GM's cars.

- In 1984, GM bought Electronic Data Systems (EDS) for $2.55 billion. The Texas concern, headed by Ross Perot, was fully bought out by GM, yet remained independent within the company, trading under a separate GM "E" stock. Smith hoped that EDS would speed up GM's huge data-processing operation, and put GM on the cutting edge of information technology. The purchase of EDS made GM the world's largest data-processing company.

Smith didn't just pursue high-tech. GM bought two major mortgage companies that overnight turned GM into America's largest home-mortgage holder.

Smith's plan was to use technology to make GM responsive to niche markets. Rather than employing a blanket strategy, in which GM produced "a car for every purse and purpose," Smith intended GM to cover niches as they appeared. As consumer trends developed, GM would respond, bringing the right car rapidly to the market.

The high-technology dream never materialized; nor did Smith's "rapid response" to niche markets. GM was so big that scale economies didn't kick in until large numbers of cars were sold. GM needed to sell over 100,000 cars of a new model to make its development profitable. The Japanese made money selling models in volumes of 40,000 or less.

Nor could GM speed up its production time. The C-car line, due to hit the showrooms in the Fall of 1984, wasn't ready until December 1985. Other lines failed to satisfy their target markets. A good example concerns the Pontiac Fiero, a zippy two-door sports car, aimed particularly at young females. GM spotted the market and dominated it, selling over 100,000 Fieros in both 1984 and 1985. Encouraged by initial sales, GM continued to manufacture and market the car as if there were no tomorrow – and no threat of competition. Both came, and GM was not ready to face either. For instance, during Fiero's development, to keep costs down, GM had eliminated power steering. As it turned out, however, power steering became a popular feature with women since it makes a car so much easier to park. The Japanese picked up on the trend, GM didn't. Toyota shipped its MR-2 with retrofitted power steering, and ate into the Fiero's market. As Fiero's sales sunk, so GM found it couldn't afford to compete in the market. The MR-2, and Mazda's Miata, are still on sale today, unlike the Fiero, canceled in 1988. General Motors found that the new technology created more problems than it solved. Typical of the problems were those experienced by the Hamtranck plant in Michigan. The plant was opened in 1985–6 at a cost of $600 million, and was to be a showcase for GM's brave new manufacturing world. Hamtranck boasted nearly 2,000 computers on its assembly line, requiring 400 workers to be trained for a year before the plant opened. Doron Levin tells of the travails experienced at the plant when it finally began operations:

> GM engineers were having a devil of a time de-bugging the hundreds of advanced machines and laser-guided devices. No sooner did the robots in the body shop weld sheet metal properly than the new modular painting robots commenced spraying one another . . . If GM had tried to introduce one or two glitzy automation projects instead of dozens and dozens, the [Hamtranck] plant might have opened smoothly. GM's software and engineering expertise, under extreme deadline pressure, just wasn't sufficient for the job.[35]

Despite the advanced machinery, Hamtranck never operated at more than 50 percent capacity. The *Wall Street Journal* commented in 1986 that the plant "instead of a showcase, looks more like a basket case." Just 25 miles away, Mazda opened its own plant for a quarter of the cost of Hamtranck. With 1,500 fewer employees, the Mazda plant made just as many cars, of better quality.

The results of the technology improvements did not justify their huge cost. In a 1986 management conference report, executive vice-president of finance F. Alan Smith pointed out that GM projected to spend $34.7 billion between 1986 and 1989. That sum, he argued, was equal to the total market capitalization of Nissan and Toyota combined. Theoretically, GM could buy out both companies, increasing its worldwide market share to 40 percent. What was GM's $34 billion going to buy them that would generate that kind of sales increase?

### Deteriorating results

In actual fact, GM became only less competitive as the spending continued. Alan Smith's report pointed out the nasty numbers. In 1983, GM had the highest operating margins in the game – it earned 2 percent more on sales than either Ford or Chrysler. By 1985, those two companies were both 3 percent more efficient.[36] Over the same two-year period, GM's sales increased 22 percent, though earnings declined 35 percent. And whereas, in 1980, GM could produce a car for $300 less than it cost Ford or Chrysler, by 1986, GM's costs were $300 more than both.[37]

GM lagged its crosstown rivals by other measures.

- In 1985, GM's profit margin was 4.1 percent, compared to 7.7 percent for Chrysler.
- An investment in GM during 1983–5 returned 16.2 percent, compared to 22.9 percent in Ford over the same period.
- According to GM's calculations it took the company 35 hours to assemble the average GM-10 car, compared with the 18 hours it took Ford workers to build a Taurus.[38]
- In 1985, GM recorded 12 vehicles produced per employee, compared with 18 for both Ford and Chrysler.
- In 1986, GM achieved an annual revenue of $100 billion. Yet in the same year, the company earned less money than its smaller rival, Ford.
- In 1986, in a booming economy that produced record auto sales, GM lost money.

Market share continued its depressing downward spiral: from 44.6 percent in 1984 to 42.7 percent in 1985 to 41.2 percent in 1986. Each lost percentage point represented about $1 billion in annual revenue, and 6,000 jobs at GM and its suppliers.

In 1986, the chairman of the Chrysler Motors unit of Chrysler told the *Wall Street Journal*, "There was a day when the gorilla said 'jump' and you jumped, because GM was the pricing leader and the styling leader. They've lost that. They aren't the low-cost producer. The industry no longer marches to their tune."[39] GM said that the poor results could be expected as a result of its reorganization, and predicted rapid recovery. In 1987 there could be no such complacency.

- Market share plummeted nearly five points to 36.6 percent.
- Oldsmobile alone sold nearly 400,000 fewer cars in 1987 than it had the year before.

The skid resulted from a combination of problems:

- GM's costs were still huge. GM's production cost of the 1985 S-car line was twice that of Isuzu for a similar model.
- Those who had bought GM in 1981–2 and had been disappointed by the quality and reliability of the X-cars had not come back to GM next time round.
- GM's shrunken Cadillacs, and the "look-alike" problem damaged the higher-end divisions.
- GM's smaller line of A-cars came to the market in 1985 just as gas prices headed downwards again, revitalizing the large-car market. GM continued to market its older models, damaging sales of the new models and causing confusion among customers.
- GM lagged the competition in styling. The 1985 Ford Taurus revolutionized the sales of "aero"-look cars, even as GM was still producing boxy, square-shouldered vehicles. Meanwhile, Chrysler took a huge head start in the minivan market.
- Smith wanted GM to develop cars more quickly, but in the effort to rush new models to the market, it failed to concentrate on quality. Most GM models produced through the 1980s were not as good as the vehicles they replaced.
- GM still retained the production capacity to serve a 50 percent share of the US market, despite the fact that its share was less than 40 percent and slipping. The result was that GM operated fearfully under capacity, with six-car factories even running at half-capacity. The fixed costs of running auto plants at anything less than full capacity were huge.
- GM remained stuck in the past in other ways, as discussed in a 1986 *Wall Street Journal* report. The article discussed a 53-year-old GM plant in Ohio that turned out 19,000 car brakes daily, shipping the parts for inclusion in every GM car from Chevy to Cadillac. The plant typified the massive vertical integration that had once made GM the most powerful company on earth. But in 1986, GM spent 15 percent more on manufacturing its own brake parts than it would cost to buy them from an outside supplier. Ford and Chrysler, by contrast, purchased their brakes from suppliers as far away as Brazil, and saved money.[40]

### Saturn

Like Smith's other projects, Saturn was hugely ambitious. Saturn had to sell 500,000 cars a year over the long haul to be profitable, as much as Nissan sold in the US each year. A *Wall Street Journal* article explained how Saturn's ambition might be its downfall:

Everything at Saturn is new: the car, the plant, the workforce, the dealer network and the manufacturing process. Not even Toyota Motor Corp., everyone's candidate for the world's best automaker, tackles more than two new items on any single project.[41]

The very size of the undertaking meant that GM was unable to complete it cheaply. Moreover, it did not get as much "bang for the buck" as did its chief competitor, Honda.[42]

- Honda's US factories cost $600 million, employed 3,000 workers, and turned out 300,000 cars a year.
- GM's new Saturn plant cost $5 billion, employed 6,000 workers and would turn out, at most, 500,000 cars a year.[43]

Saturn was launched in the Fall of 1990 in a $100 million blitz of advertising and publicity. The opening months proved far from auspicious . . .

- GM hoped Saturn would sell 150,000 in its first year. In the first nine months of production, Saturn built 24,000 cars and sold 15,000 of them.
- Six months after opening, Saturn was operating at half-speed, and selling only half of what it produced. One manager told the *Wall Street Journal* that the plant made cars at full speed for maybe a few hours, "then we run into a snag."[44]
- Despite its emphasis on quality, the division has not delivered. In Saturn's first months, some 35–40 percent of the car's plastic panels were sent back with defects.[45]

Despite the glitches, Saturn was very popular with its buyers, the only problem being there weren't very many of them. Saturn opened just as the US was slipping into a recession – inhospitable circumstances for the launching of a new car line. Saturn also proved to be cannibalistic – 41 percent of Saturn owners already owned a GM vehicle.

### Japan roars back

Just as GM was making a terrible mess of reinventing itself, the Japanese were plotting their return. Anyone who thought that the import restriction would hold Japan at bay for long was sorely mistaken.

Japan adopted a two-pronged strategy. In the first place, it circumvented the import restrictions by building plants in mainland America rather than shipping them from Japan. In this respect, the voluntary restraint helped the United States – Honda, Toyota, and Nissan invested billions of dollars and created tens of thousands of jobs – but it didn't help Detroit. The Japanese, more than ever before, were competing in the Big Three's back yard.

- In 1980, Honda announced that it would open its first US assembly plant in Ohio.
- In 1986, Toyota opened a factory in Kentucky.
- In 1989, Honda opened a second plant, and Subaru and Isuzu announced that they too would open US-based operations.

By 1990, there would be eight Japanese manufacturing plants in the United States. The investments paid off. By 1992, Japan would by assembling 1.4 million cars and trucks on the American mainland. Their lines would include two of the three best-selling vehicles, and five of the top 12. By contrast, GM produced only the fifth best-selling vehicle and could only manage four in the top 12.

Second, the Japanese targeted the luxury car market. Since they were limited to a number of vehicles they could export, it made sense for the Japanese to export higher-priced vehicles that carried a greater profit margin per car. Hence the arrival of Acura in 1986 and Lexus and Infiniti in 1989. In 1992, these three divisions sold over $3.5 billion-worth of automobiles. While this was money made partly at the expense of the leading European luxury car makers – Mercedes, Volvo, BMW, and Jaguar – it also heavily dented Cadillac's performance.

General Motors found it was not merely being outclassed in the small car market, but in the expensive, classier range as well. GM remained dominant in the luxury car market – Cadillac was positioned at first, fourth and seventh in the ten top-selling luxury cars in 1992 – but the Japanese had nabbed spots three and six. Japan did not dominate the big-car market as it did the small, but it was a serious competitor in a market GM had once owned. All of this contributed to GM's ever-dropping market share.

It was not technology that made the Japanese better competitors, it was superior, participatory management.

- Japan's automakers made do with five levels of management; GM had 14.
- NUMMI, run with GM labor under Toyota managers, produced the lowest-cost, best-quality cars in GM. Yen for dollar, it spent less but received more.
- GM's own quality audit found that the Honda and Nissan plants in the American South produced cars with one-fifth as many defects as did GM's.[46] In other words, the difference between Japanese and American quality was not labor. The Japanese could beat the United States in the United States.

The Japanese success was encouraged partly by the US automakers. The voluntary restraint agreement forced the Japanese to raise their prices by as much as $2,000 a vehicle. It presented a perfect opportunity for Detroit to exploit their price advantage and recapture market share. Instead, the Big Three raised their own prices, creating a short-term boom in profits. The VRA merely raised the cost of cars for consumers, and did nothing to restore American competitiveness.

### Labor relations

Labor relations had never been good at GM, dating back to violent strikes in Flint, Michigan, in the 1930s. But even as the Japanese showed the way in creating a friendly working environment, relations between GM management and labor grew ever worse.

Seeing the need to cut costs, GM signed a new contract with the UAW in 1982. Management stressed "shared sacrifice" to get through difficult times, and wrung a $2.5 billion concession out of the union, in the form of a freeze of the cost of living adjustment (COLA). The very same day, GM's proxy statement was mailed to shareholders. One of the items under consideration was a new bonus scheme, awarding 5 million shares to 600 senior executives. In the firestorm of criticism that resulted, Smith cut his own pay, and that of other bonus-eligible executives, by $135 a month – the same deduction as the UAW had agreed to take. The notion that millionaire Roger Smith (who had taken an 18.8 percent rise in base pay the year before) and a $12-an-hour machinist taking the same pay cut entailed "shared sacrifice" was, of course, nonsensical. Smith only fanned the flames of the controversy.

To develop better relations with the UAW, GM began a profit-sharing program for blue-collar workers. In 1985, GM workers were paid $384 as part of the program, compared with the $1,200 Ford workers were paid under a similar scheme.

Roger Smith regarded labor as opposition, to be replaced by machines wherever possible. In negotiations with the UAW, Smith said, "Every time you ask for another dollar in wages, a thousand more robots start looking more practical."[47] In 1986, Smith initiated an aggressive cost-cutting drive, which included the closure of 13 plants and 25,000 white-collar layoffs. The next year he promised to cut a further $10 billion out of GM's costs.

## The 1980s: A difficult decade

Clearly, Smith's strategy failed. GM ended up spending tens of billions of dollars for little or no reward. Despite the high technology, GM became less, not more, efficient. Its cars found no favor with the public. Its market share dropped. When its competitors burgeoned in a booming auto market, GM lost money.

General Motors suffered throughout the 1980s because it failed to address its basic problems with sufficient alacrity or aggression. The Chrysler and Ford crises, and the relentless Japanese onslaught, should have shown GM that it needed to *compete*, that it could not take a 50 percent market share for granted any longer. The massive vertical integration that had served GM so well for so long was out of date.

At the time of the voluntary restraint agreement in 1981, the Japanese had shown that they could produce high-quality cars in a fraction of the time it took GM. To stay in step, GM needed to show that it too could efficiently produce a well-made car. Given the breathing space afforded by the import restraint, GM could have committed itself to streamlining operations, and cutting away the layers of the organization that stood between the makers of the automobile and their customers.

The import agreement brought record profits to the Big Three. But the windfall was wasted. GM didn't put the money back into its core operations, upgrading their operations to Japanese standards. GM didn't reinvest the money in ways that would lower the cost, and improve the quality of cars that went to the showrooms. GM failed in the 1980s because it tried to solve problems without addressing their fundamental, underlying causes. As Keller comments, "Acquiring EDS and Hughes was like the four-hundred-pound woman coloring her hair and doing her nails. It wasn't tackling the real problem."[48] Its problem was not that it was short of technology; it was that it was a badly organized, insular, backward-looking, and inefficient producer of motor vehicles. Smith's obsession with technology made no impact on GM's ability to compete.

Its failure was also a failure of leadership. Smith failed to realize that GM's most important commodity was its people. GM could not become a twenty-first-century automaker without the company's employees – its engineers, machinists, and assembly-line workers – coming along for the ride. But Smith treated labor as a problem to be limited, not as a resource to be nurtured. Indeed, with all his talk of a "lights out" factory and robot automation, one could be forgiven for thinking that Smith wanted to dispose of labor altogether. How could Smith hope that GM's employees would pursue his vision, if all it promised them was the sack?

## And the board played on . . .

Where was the GM board of directors when Smith's strategy started to come apart at the seams in 1986? The answer to this question is important because the ultimate problem

– and solution – for GM lay in the realm of corporate governance. It is a truism of the corporate system that management must have sufficient freedom to take risks and experiment. Inevitably, not every risk-taking venture succeeds. Plenty of companies adopt strategies that ultimately prove to be costly mistakes. It is at this point that governance becomes important. It is the board's job to see that management has adopted a sound strategy and executes it competently; and it is the board's responsibility to replace management when it fails in these duties. In turn, the board is beholden directly to shareholders, and indirectly to stakeholders such as consumers, suppliers, and employees.

As we saw earlier in the discussion of the Corvair episode, GM did not appreciate outside critics. This same view dominated board–management relations through the 1980s. As *Fortune* put it:

> Roger Smith kept the board on a very short leash. He withheld key financial data and budget allocation proposals until the day before meetings and sometimes distributed them minutes before the participants convened. The monthly sessions were rigidly structured and Smith adjourned them promptly at five minutes to noon, leaving little room for discussion. Circumstances and personality enabled Roger Smith to exercise his iron control. Quick to anger, he was intolerant of criticism. Few directors had the ability or desire to take him on.[49]

One outside director told the *Wall Street Journal* that board meetings "were like ceremonial events, with no real information."[50]

Smith was able to exert control via the board committees. Increasingly, the full board became just a ratifying council for the work of the various committees. This allowed Smith to keep loyalists on key committees. The make-up of the board allowed Smith to exercise such control. In 1989, three members of the board (not including Smith) were GM executives who reported directly to Smith. Among the 11 non-executive directors, four had little or no business experience – Anne Armstrong, former ambassador to the Court of St James; Thomas E. Everhart and Marvin L. Goldberger, both academics; and the Reverend Leon H. Sullivan. Of the eight remaining directors, two were retired and a third ran GM's chief Detroit bank.

The non-executive directors were paid average fees of $45,000 a year and received a new GM car for their own use every quarter. But these material benefits paled in comparison to the prestige conveyed by sitting on the board of General Motors. Doron Levin speculates on the motivations of one outside director, Edmund T. Pratt, chairman emeritus of Pfizer Inc.:

> Ed Pratt had served on numerous corporate boards of directors. None of the posts, including his chairmanship of Pfizer, one of the nation's leading pharmaceutical firms, carried as much prestige or clout as his GM director's seat. In Pratt's eyes, GM was an American institution, the country's dominant single business force. Hell, GM was America! For a businessman such as himself . . . association with the nation's premier corporation was an immense honor.[51]

But the honor he felt belonging to the GM board did not inspire Pratt to commit much personal wealth to the company. In 1988, Pratt owned 100 GM shares, despite having been on the board for 11 years. In other words, he had purchased about nine shares each year he was a director. Pratt was not alone. Five other outside directors owned 500 shares, and three owned 200 shares.

This was the group responsible for probing, challenging, and, if necessary, changing Smith's strategy. Yet, for many critical years it did nothing of the sort. GM's directors let themselves be browbeaten by the CEO's personality, and blinded by the honor of serving on the board. They had too much to gain – and too little to lose – from the status quo to shake it up. Thus, the GM story is one not just of management failure, but also one of the failure of the board.

In the rarefied atmosphere of the fourteenth floor, GM executives were cut off not only from the vast body of GM's employees but also from the board of directors and the shareholders the board was meant to represent. Management was accountable to no one. The truth of this statement will be made clear when we examine the courtship, brief marriage, and messy divorce between GM and Texas billionaire, and later presidential candidate, Ross Perot. The Perot episode shows how completely the governance structure had collapsed at GM, and how unwilling the board was to challenge management, no matter what the circumstances.

## GENERAL MOTORS AND ROSS PEROT

No one was more frustrated by GM's hidebound culture than Roger Smith. He was frustrated and confused at his company's inability to turn its operations around. He felt burdened by GM's insular, backward-looking culture, and he tried hard to break it. Smith liked to explain his vision in the form of an allegory: a GM manager clinging to a tree stump, unwilling to swim across a fast-moving river. Smith's job, as he saw it, was to convince the manager to let go and swim hard, aiming for some unknown spot on the other side. The tree stump was GM's old way of doing business, the river was the fast-moving marketplace, the unknown place on the opposite shore where the swimmer ended up was GM in the next century. In Smith's view, GM could no longer cling to the past – it had to swim for it. The question was, how could he persuade GM to let go of the stump?

Smith did not believe incremental, evolutionary changes would work. Rather, GM would need to be revolutionized. Programs such as Saturn, NUMMI, and the purchase of Hughes were ways of wrenching GM dramatically from the past and forcing it into the future. Ross Perot and his company, Electronic Data Systems (EDS), seemed to present an ideal opportunity. On the one hand, GM was held back by outmoded data-processing and computing methods – how could GM be lean and responsive without modernizing its paper-driven bureaucracy? – and on the other hand, EDS was headed by a feisty, no-nonsense Texan entrepreneur who could lend some zip to GM's stodgy style. Smith liked successful entrepreneurs; they represented everything that GM wasn't. That was why Smith wasn't content just to hire EDS, but wanted rather to buy it and make it part of GM. Smith hoped that some of what had made EDS successful would rub off on the GM giant.

Roger Smith and Ross Perot were perfect for each other. Smith sought an aggressive entrepreneur, not beholden to GM and ready to speak his mind. Perot was lured by the challenge of lending his services to such a giant corporation, and, born with a strong patriotic streak, he liked the idea of helping out America's most established company.

General Motors was assiduous in its pursuit of EDS, seeking to overcome Perot's reluctance to sell the company he had spent his life building. The essence of the agreement appeared paradoxical: GM would pay $2.55 billion to buy EDS, yet EDS would remain independent inside the parent company, managed by EDS executives, setting its own compensation practices, and answerable only to Roger Smith and the GM board. In other words, within the button–down establishment of GM would exist a group of autonomous, non–conformist, Texan rebels.

The deal worked as follows:

- GM issued promissory notes to EDS executives that their new ownership in "E" stock would not be worth less than $125 in seven years – that is, if, in seven years, "E" traded at only $100, GM would make up the $25 difference. It was a way of guaranteeing EDS officers a wonderful return on their holdings in EDS as well as creating an incentive for them to stay for seven years.
- Ross Perot would receive $1 billion for his interest in EDS and 43 percent of the newly created "E" stock. Perot instantly became GM's largest individual shareholder, and one of the largest overall, owning 0.8 percent of the stock, or 11 million Class E shares. By contrast, Smith had acquired 26,500 GM shares in a 36–year career.
- EDS was guaranteed long-term, fixed-price contracts for its work on GM. The contracts guaranteed EDS $2.6 billion of new business, a sum that was 33 times EDS's current earnings.
- To merge EDS with GM's own data-processing operation, 10,000 GM employees would be transferred to EDS.

No sooner had the vows been exchanged than the problems began. The new couple started fighting before the honeymoon had even started. As EDS's senior executives arrived in Detroit, they were given a glacial reception – indeed, many GM-ers seemed not to have been briefed about EDS's arrival at all. One account of the merger tells how some senior EDS executives were introduced to Alex Cunningham, executive vice-president of North American operations. Cunningham uttered not a word to his visitors before showing them out of his office with the words, "It will be a cold day in hell before I'm going to help pad the pockets of a bunch of rich Texans."[52]

General Motors executives were not the only ones to oppose the arrival of EDS. For the 10,000 GM data-processors who would be transferred to EDS, the move meant an end to the strict hierarchy and chain of command they were used to. Instead, they were told to accept lower pay, lower benefits, and more job risk under EDS management. GM employees wondered how EDS could be owned by GM and yet be in charge. Some of the data workers applied to the UAW for affiliation, a move that upset EDS's traditionally union-free labor relations.

Meanwhile, Ken Riedlinger, EDS's most senior officer in Detroit, was receiving hate mail and obscene phone calls, and was finding his car tires slashed almost daily. Ultimately, he quit.

Perot himself received a cold shoulder. On arriving for his first meeting of the board of directors, he found that he had been placed on the public policy committee, the least influential of any of the board committees. Perot believed that the holder of 11 million shares should be closer to the beating heart of GM's decision-making, on the finance or executive committees. Perot's irritation, however, was minor compared to the fundamental difficulties of getting GM and EDS to work together.

The agreement that EDS would have a monopoly over GM's data-processing business soon broke down. GM, because of its size, was used to being able to bully its suppliers. EDS, by contrast, charged premium prices for the vast numbers of computers and processors it wished GM to purchase. The data-processing department felt it should be receiving discounts. EDS replied that if GM wanted a twenty-first-century computer system, then it needed to pay what it cost. Anyway, advanced systems would help lower costs for GM in the long term. By the same token, EDS was astonished by examples of spectacular inefficiency and money-wasting inside GM, but felt they weren't given the opportunity to cure them. EDS felt its efforts were being sabotaged by their own client. The result was constant bickering over pricing and contract terms, so that it was not until April 1986, nearly two years after the merger, that GM and EDS finalized a pricing agreement for EDS's services. The compromise settled little – just months later, Perot considered suing GM for its failure to sign long-term contracts with EDS.[53] Increasingly, EDS-ers found themselves appealing to Perot, and GM-ers to Smith for help in defending their turf. The two chief executives found that their main role in the merger was as peacemakers.

Another increasingly bitter bone of contention concerned compensation. GM employees were used to climbing up an utterly predictable career ladder, with guaranteed annual salary increases, regular bonuses, a generous package of benefits, and a secure retirement. Compensation at GM was utterly risk-free and never spectacular. Roger Smith certainly made a lot of money – more than most executives in the country – but even Smith's pay paled in comparison to the fortunes amassed by EDS's senior officers. EDS was a place where spectacular fortunes could be made in a relatively short time. Base salaries and benefits were small – far smaller than GM's – but the possible rewards via stock options and performance grants were the stuff of dreams. Perot loved incentives: if his people performed, he rewarded them lavishly. For instance, his number two, Mort Myerson, was promised a salary equal to 1 percent of EDS's 1984 profits – the sky was the limit. Perot believed that this motivated not just his top employees, but everyone in the company, since even the lowliest worker could see that hard work and success were rewarded with wealth. Perot believed that such a system was essential to the success of EDS.

Compensation soon became a thorny problem. The nature of the original merger agreement meant that, even as relations between the two companies grew worse and worse, EDS-ers continued to expect huge rewards. But GM dragged its feet on the lavish stock bonuses promised in the merger agreement. Under EDS's pre-merger stock incentive plan, shares were due to have been distributed late in 1984. Following the merger, the award was postponed until early 1985. By midsummer no decision had been reached, despite Perot's frequent reminders to Smith. Perot became annoyed. Not only did he regard the stock awards as his prime means of employee motivation, but they had been categorically guaranteed in the GM–EDS merger agreement.

The cause of delay was Roger Smith. He was insulted by how much wealth was already being transferred to EDS employees and the proposed grants were far richer than the grants made to any GM executive, including Smith. GM had already made EDS's top executives multimillionaires – Perot was worth nearly a billion, Myerson a hundred million – and Smith couldn't justify any extra largesse. By GM's calculations, the award would cost GM a further $300 million – paid to people already vastly wealthy thanks to GM. In Smith's view, the payouts were obscene. In Perot's view, that was the way EDS had always worked and, under the merger agreement, would continue to work.

Finally, Smith told Perot that he was vetoing the grants, and he traveled to Dallas to explain why to the top EDS officers. The meeting was not a success. According to Levin's account, Tom Walter, EDS's CFO, told Smith that he was overstating the cost to GM of the stock grants because he was working from a false set of numbers. Levin writes:

> Walter didn't get a chance to finish his point.
> People in the room later would remember Smith's angry explosion as being wondrous and terrifying at the same time: wondrous for the extreme colors and sounds it brought to the room, terrifying because none of them had ever seen someone lose his temper so completely in a business meeting . . .

"Don't tell me my numbers aren't correct," Smith sputtered. His already ruddy expression flushed a furious scarlet. His voice rose almost to choking, and he slammed his briefing book on the table.

Inadvertently, Walter had delivered the most humiliating insult possible to a GM financial executive. Smith might have endured accusations of being a poor marketer or manager. Telling a GM finance man he had "bad numbers" was invitation to a brawl.

"I didn't come here to be insulted," Smith shouted. By this time flecks of saliva had formed at the corners of his mouth. The EDS officers stared in disbelief as the chairman of the world's biggest and most powerful company lost it.[54]

The outburst was the first step down a slippery slope that led to Perot's separation from GM. Despite all the problems involved with integrating EDS into GM, and despite all the petty rows and disagreements and frustrations, Perot had always believed that the merger would work. He had expected difficulties, and he had expected it to be hard to merge a small, lean, entrepreneurial company with a vast, old, and bureaucratic one. But ultimately, Perot had believed it could be done. He felt that he and EDS had something that could help GM. Following Smith's outburst, he began to doubt it. He began to doubt that Roger Smith was a man with whom he could do business or that GM could overcome its culture. Perot thought he had been brought on board to shake GM up a little. Now he wasn't so sure it could be done. Was Smith really ready to do what it would take? Was he going to talk about revitalizing GM, or was he actually going to do it?

But Perot was more than just the man who had created EDS. He was also GM's largest shareholder, with tens of millions of dollars tied up in the company's performance. And as grave as EDS's problems with its new corporate parent might be, Perot was first and foremost a member of the GM board of directors.

Perot was concerned that even as GM's massive capital spending program was failing to solve the company's fundamental problems, Smith was intent on spending big bucks to acquire Hughes Aircraft. To Perot, the purchase was simply money down the drain at a time when GM was taking bigger and bigger hits to its market share.

Perot's increasing dissatisfaction at GM and its management reached a climax at a board meeting held in November 1985. One of the items of the agenda was for final board approval to buy Hughes Aircraft for $5.2 billion. To Perot, the planned purchase represented everything that was wrong with the way GM was being run – big, thoughtless spending with no regard for the company's most basic problems.

In a dramatic speech to the board, Perot explained his opposition. First, he outlined where he thought GM had gone wrong. He explained that the company was "procedures oriented, not results oriented" and that business matters that should be decided in minutes took days or weeks shuttling up the hierarchy in a series of unproductive meetings. "Senior management is too isolated from the people," Perot concluded.[55] Perot told the board that he had attended a Cadillac dealers' conference where the common complaint had been that it was impossible to sell Cadillacs when they were riddled with defects. Perot had asked the dealers why the problems were so pervasive: "The answer was 'GM doesn't give people the responsibility and authority to get things done – and the GM system avoids individual accountability.' "[56]

Perot asked the directors why they should approve a $5 billion purchase for space-age engineering when GM couldn't even build a reliable car. He argued that throwing money at the problem was not going to solve it: "The experiences of our successful competitors demonstrate that people – plus the intelligent application of capital – are the keys."[57] Whether Perot meant it to be or not, this was a sharp dig at Smith's entire strategy.

Perot did not just attack management, he also went after the board. He called for the board to become a genuine decision-making body, not a silent ratifying counsel: "We must change the format of board meetings from passive sessions with little two-way communication to active participatory sessions that allow us to discuss real issues and resolve real problems."[58] Months earlier, Perot had sought approval from Smith for meetings of the outside directors alone. He felt the board would be better able to assert its independence if it was freed from the counterweight of the executive board members. Smith refused Perot's request.

Perot reminded the directors of their duty to represent the stockholders:

> They own this company. We must make it clear that the management serves at the pleasure of the shareholders . . . The managers of mature corporations with no concentration of owners have gotten themselves into the position of effectively selecting the board members who will represent the stockholders.[59]

When it came to a vote on the Hughes purchase, Perot's was the lone dissenting vote. It was the first such dissension in the GM boardroom since the 1920s.

Relations could not but deteriorate. Perot and Smith continued to haggle over compensation and bonus formulas, an issue that Perot believed was none of GM's business. Meanwhile, Perot forbade GM to audit EDS's books. In a series of increasingly combative letters to Smith, Perot demanded that EDS be left to run its business independently – the way the merger agreement intended. In a letter of May 19, 1986, Perot accused the automaker of trying to "GM-ize EDS."[60] Of course, the entire point of the merger had been to "EDS-ize GM."

In background interviews with the *Wall Street Journal* in the spring and early summer of 1986, Perot explained where the EDS–GM merger had gone wrong. He went far beyond the difficulties of combining the two companies; instead, he discussed why GM was failing in the marketplace. "Until we nuke the GM system," he said, "we'll never tap the full potential of our people."[61] He was even more critical of Roger Smith than before, saying that "he talks a good game" about turning GM around but that he failed to understand how to do it.[62] Perot criticized management for its obsessive attention to executive perks and bonuses – and even demanded that GM scrap its executive dining rooms! Perot believed the trappings of power interfered with management's ability to see the company in an honest light.

Perot reserved further ire for the board: "Is the board a rubber stamp for Roger? Hell, no! We'd have to upgrade it to be a rubber stamp."[63] Perot believed that the board knew nothing of GM's fundamental problems. Each outside director received the latest GM model every three months – what would they know about reliability? Perot bought his own cars, and sometimes visited showrooms incognito, trying to discern problems. He came across GM dealers who were now selling Japanese cars to stay competitive. How could the directors, receiving a new car every 90 days, hope to know anything about problems like these?

The *Wall Street Journal* published Perot's comments – much watered down – in an article entitled "Groping Giant." The article showed how GM, despite its pricey automation drive, was more inefficient than its rivals and losing market share as a result. "Poised for the 21st Century?" asked the *Journal*, the first paper to criticize Smith's highly lauded strategy.[64] The criticisms were backed by the poor performance of the year. The rest of the financial media pricked up its ears, and Perot was willing to talk. In a series of interviews, Perot continued to assail GM, telling *Business Week* that "revitalizing General Motors is like teaching an elephant to tap dance."[65]

As the battle between Perot and Smith became ever more public, so the chances of reaching an understanding became ever more slim. Smith was infuriated by Perot's public ridicule of GM; senior executives were distressed by the lack of respect Perot showed for what had for so long been the most respected company in the world. The marriage between GM and EDS had broken down irreparably, and divorce became the only option.

Perot's lieutenants and GM counsel negotiated a buyout of Perot's holding in GM. On December 1, 1986, the board agreed to pay Perot $742.8 million for his stake in GM. The buyout offered $61.90 for shares that were then trading at about $33. In return, both GM and Perot agreed that neither side would criticize the other, on penalty of $7.5 million. In other words, if Perot continued his attacks on GM, he would have to return $7.5 million to GM. The buyout was so preferential to Perot that he could not believe the board approved it. He thought the price was so great that the directors could not but oppose Smith. Perot was dumbstruck that not one director dissented from the decision to send him packing with so much of GM shareholders' money. In court testimony two years later, Perot said, "My attitude all the way was no one will ever sign this agreement on the GM side, it's not businesslike. I underestimated the desire on the GM board to get rid of me."[66] Perot was concerned the press would report that he had bribed GM, that he had offered the deal as the price of his silence. He was determined to show that GM had initiated the deal. So he offered the money back. He put the money in escrow and gave the GM board two weeks to rethink the decision to buy him out. If, after two weeks, the board of directors thought that ridding GM of Ross Perot was in the shareholders' best interest, he would take the money. If not, Perot would pay the money back and continue to work at GM. In a press conference held immediately after he signed the buyout agreement, Perot told reporters, "Is spending all this money the highest and best use of GM's capital? . . . I want to give the directors a chance to do the right thing. It is incomprehensible to me that they would want to spend $750 million on this. I am hopeful that people will suddenly get a laserlike focus on what needs to be done and do it."[67] Following the announcement of the buyout, and Perot's press conference, GM stock declined $3, and EDS stock lost $4.50.

Ross Perot's involvement in GM caused almost immeasurable bad publicity for GM. Roger Smith and his fellow board members were painted as corporate villains. One group particularly incensed was, unsurprisingly, the shareholders. One sizeable shareholder, the State of Wisconsin Investment Board (SWIB), wrote a letter to GM directors saying the buyout "severely undermines the confidence we have in the board and in the officials of General Motors." SWIB was prepared to back up its letter with a shareholder resolution or a lawsuit, but one phone call from GM to the governor of Wisconsin threatening to shut down some planned developments in the state, quickly put an end to the protest.

This last story is, if nothing else, indicative of the governance structure at GM. Roger Smith ran his company unchallenged by either the board or the shareholders the board was meant to represent. Smith wanted to revitalize the company, but it had to be done his way.

*Was this mode of operation in the best interests of GM's shareholders?*

## GENERAL MOTORS AFTER PEROT: SMITH AND STEMPEL

From 1984 to 1986 Smith garnered universal praise for his effort to push GM into the future, and won just about every business award going. In 1985, the *New York Times Magazine* featured him in an enthusiastic cover story. In 1986, he was named 1986 Executive of the Year by both *Financial World* and *Chief Executive*. But the tide turned that same year.

Not only did the Perot affair leave Smith with egg all over his face, but the company's performance demonstrated that Smith's strategy, now five years old, was not achieving results. Instead, Smith's drive for automation had merely turned GM from the lowest-cost producer among the Big Three to the highest.

The combination of these results and the devastating adverse publicity of the Perot episode changed many perceptions of GM. Suddenly, Smith was no longer seen as a corporate wizard, but as a bully who could not take criticism.

Roger Smith certainly wasn't to preside over an upturn in GM's fortunes over the last years of his tenure. In his last four years at GM, Smith found himself under pressure from all sides as GM's results continued to deteriorate. The company still suffered from excess capacity, bearing huge fixed costs. Smith was faced with either raising sales, and thus productivity, or downsizing the company in line with GM's diminishing market share.

On the eve of Smith's retirement, GM's results were worse than ever.

- By 1989, GM was recording a market share of 34.4 percent. This was down from 44.1 percent in 1979. This decline meant nearly $10 billion per year in lost revenue to GM.
- Between 1980 and 1990, the S&P 500 rose 227 percent, and it appreciated 27.3 percent in 1989 alone. GM, by comparison, had achieved 69 percent and 1.2 percent respectively.[68]
- Harbour & Associates, an automotive consultancy based in Troy, Michigan, found that over the 1980s, GM's assembly efficiency had improved 5 percent compared with 17 percent at Chrysler and 31 percent at Ford.

## The post-Perot board

The Perot affair had some impact on the board. The *Wall Street Journal* reported years later that directors such as John G. Smale, then CEO of Procter & Gamble, and former ambassador Armstrong were afraid their personal reputations would suffer if they didn't do something about the "pet rock" image that they had acquired as a result of Perot's media barnstorming. The *Journal* quoted one source as saying, "There's a feeling that perhaps [the board] wasn't as involved in some past decisions as it should have been."[69] They were backed by GM's outside counsel, Ira Millstein, a partner at the New York firm of Weil, Gotshal & Manges, who was a vocal governance advocate. Millstein counseled the outside directors to assert more independence in the face of some of Smith's requests.

There were other signs of increasing discontent among board members. In 1988, GM's general counsel, Elmer Johnson, quit. Johnson had been brought in from outside – a rare move for GM – as part of Smith's plan to nudge the GM system. Johnson had been motivated by the hope that he might achieve the presidency, but he soon became disillusioned at his lack of ability to change the GM establishment. Shortly after, James D. Robinson, chairman of American Express, resigned from the board after a short tenure. Even he, a stern ruler of his own fiefdom, was frustrated by the lack of power board members possessed in the face of Smith's determination to manage his way.

The board got its chance to assert its independence in 1988. Smith proposed to add three further GM officers to the board. The move would have meant that insiders made up 40 percent of the board. Smith was rebuffed. It was the first time anyone could remember a GM chairman not getting his way with the board.[70] Another factor in the board's new independence could have been the growing activism of some of GM's shareholders. GM's owners were becoming increasingly uneasy about the company's management and the stock's continued stagnation. The year before Smith retired, GM's board voted to raise executive pensions. Smith himself would see his pension rise from around $700,000 to $1.25 million. The raised pensions would affect 3,350 managers and cost $41.6 million annually. GM said such a move was necessary to attract top talent. Many shareholder groups, including Institutional Shareholder Services, agreed, saying the increase was needed to bring GM's executive pensions up to par with those offered by GM's competitors.

Though the board had the sole power to approve the increased pensions, it decided to seek shareholder ratification none the less. In doing this, GM was attempting to rid itself of the shareholder-unfriendly image it had acquired thanks to Ross Perot. In the 1990 proxy, the board sought a shareholder vote on the move. Though the measure ended up being overwhelmingly approved – by 87 percent in favor – the size of the increase caused a blaze of criticism for management and the board. For instance, the local public employee pension fund, the Michigan State Retirement System, voted to oppose the moves. Smith described the idea to permit a shareholder vote on the raise as a "corporate governance experiment gone astray"[71] and said that he regretted involving the shareholders in the decision to raise pensions.

As Smith's retirement neared, shareholders made their presence known once again. Traditionally, the leadership transition at GM was uncontroversial. The outgoing CEO generally tapped his successor long before any retirement date. The result was a smooth succession of GM loyalists. Since 1958, the baton had always been passed to a finance chief. It was also customary for the outgoing CEO to retain a seat on the board.

The succession process was worrisome to two of GM's largest owners, the California Public Employees Retirement System (CalPERS) and the New York State Retirement System (NYS). Both were pension funds serving the public employees of their respective states, and both were vocal governance activists. The two groups were worried that the clone-like succession process at GM was contributing directly to GM's decline. It was particularly nettlesome to these investors that the retired CEO could continue to exert influence over his successor via his seat on the board. There was no room for an outsider, someone who might have fresh ideas or a new approach. The process, like everything at GM, seemed geared to conservatism, making sure the company continued to be run in the same way it always had – clearly not a good idea at this point in GM's history.

Ned Regan, the New York State Comptroller at the time, asked what "processes and criteria" the GM board would use to select Smith's successor. Regan cited some of GM's dismal results, saying, "presumably these figures point to a management problem."

CalPERS wrote a similar letter to GM's directors, adding a specific recommendation: that Smith not be retained on the board.

The directors never even responded to the shareholders' concerns, preferring to leave their answer to a corporate spokesman, who replied huffily, "Corporate governance, which includes the selection of officers, is the board's responsibility." According to one report, Roger Smith even called the governor of California to complain about CalPERS' unsolicited advice.

CalPERS and other shareholders lost that round, but they went on to win others. In 1990, at shareholders' urging, GM adopted a provision against greenmail, prohibiting the company from buying shares at above-market prices from anyone who had held more than 3 percent of the company's voting stock for less than two years. In 1991, GM adopted CalPERS' proposal to have a bylaw-mandated majority of outsiders on the board.

Of course, both of these victories were symbolic only. There was no chance that any raider was looking to be paid greenmail by GM, though the clause would prevent anything like the Perot buyout from ever occurring again. Also, GM had had a majority of outsiders for years and wasn't looking to change such a make-up. The bylaw merely confirmed what had been the case for many years.

In April 1990, GM picked a new CEO, Robert Stempel. Stempel had spent his GM career as an engineer, and his appointment constituted a significant departure from the run of finance men who had headed GM since 1958. One person overjoyed at the news was Ross Perot, who told the *Washington Post*, "This is too good to be true. This is an all car-maker team. It's a terrific day for General Motors."[72] Stempel took over from Roger Smith on August 1, 1990. But Smith continued to hold his seat on the board.

Even during the succession process, the board failed to impose its authority. Stempel wished to have Lloyd Reuss as president, in charge of North American Operations. The board vacillated. It didn't have much faith in Reuss' abilities, but it capitulated in the face of Stempel's demand that he pick his own management team. As a signal of displeasure, the board withheld the title of chief operating officer from Reuss.

Stempel had a great first day as CEO. On his second day, Iraq invaded Kuwait, setting off a period of unease in America and a worldwide recession. GM, Stempel would later reflect, headed into a "kamikaze dive."[73] The fundamental premise behind doing business in as cyclical an industry as that of cars is to make money hand over fist in good times, and try to retrench and curb losses in bad. The excellence of the good years should make up for the depressed conditions of the bad. But GM lost money in the boom market of 1986–7; now it had no brake shoes to slow its own drive downward as the economy skidded into recession. The reality of Smith's failure became vividly and shockingly clear during the next two years.

Before 1990, GM had never recorded back-to-back yearly losses. During 1990–2, it suffered three. As the 1990s wore on, it became ever more apparent that GM was suffering more than a downturn; it had struck a full-scale crisis. The root of the problem was the disastrous state of GM's North American operations, which suffered from being the highest-cost producer in the flattest auto market since 1982.

- 1990 ushered in the worst yearly loss in GM's history.
- In the final quarter of 1990, GM recorded its worst-ever quarterly loss, $1.6 billion.
- Between June 1990 and September 1991, GM recorded five straight quarterly losses totaling $5.8 billion.
- North American Operations lost approximately $10 a share in 1990.[74]
- In 1991, North American Operations lost $7.1 billion. That is, $1,700 on every car and truck it sold in North America.[75]
- During 1990–2, North American Operations racked up losses of almost $15 billion.[76]
- A 1992 Harbour & Associates study showed that GM spent $795 more to assemble a car than did Ford. This translated into a $4 billion a year disadvantage.

Stempel continued the downsizing that Smith had begun in 1986. In October 1990, GM announced the closure of seven plants, requiring a charge to earnings of $2.1 billion. Months later, in February 1991, GM announced it would cut a further 15,000 white-collar jobs from the workforce by 1993, with 6,000 employees being pared in 1991 alone.

The aim of the downsizing was to reduce GM's huge capacity in line with its diminished market share. GM hoped to become competitive by running fewer factories faster. Smith's $90 billion spending had failed to achieve this simple aim.

The closing of plants, and the layoffs they involved, usually evoked a storm of protest from the UAW. This time around, however, the union stayed silent. That was because of a contract, signed between GM and the UAW in March 1990, in which GM guaranteed to keep paying its 300,000-plus blue-collar workers up to 95 percent of their salary for as long as three years if they were laid off. From GM's point of view, the contract bought peace, enabling the company to downsize quietly and quickly.

In practice, the contract only damaged GM's ability to compete during the recession. By paying even those workers it laid off GM turned what was normally a modest variable cost into a gigantic fixed one. Generally, automakers lower costs during times of slow production by laying off workers who are not needed. The company can then rehire them when sales pick up. In this instance, however, GM was struggling through a recession with a payroll better suited to boom times, paying as many as 80,000 workers to stay at home.

The contract destroyed GM's ability to control the cost of its workforce. It cost GM $500 million within a few months of its signing. GM had pledged $4 billion to the job security fund, to last through 1993. Now, some GM officials felt that might not be enough.

General Motors' competitors were having a field day. In 1990, Japanese automakers acquired four points of market share in one year, for a total of 29 percent.

General Motors needed new infusions of capital to repair its balance sheet. In 1991, it was able to raise $2.4 billion via new common and preferred stock issues, but this equity was matched by increased debt. GM's long-term debt nearly doubled between 1985 and 1991, to 35 percent of equity – not a crippling ratio by the standards of the time but an alarming contrast to GM's traditionally rock-solid balance sheet. Given the terrible state of the auto market, the heavy debt load threatened GM's ability to borrow further. The company took steps to conserve cash.

- Early in 1991, GM nearly halved its annual dividend, slashing it to $1.60 from $3. The cut saved it over $840 million a year.
- GM slashed its capital spending by $1.1 billion for the years 1992–3.[77]

As GM ran low on cash to support its operating expenses and stock obligations, the credit rating agencies threatened to downgrade. In November 1991, Standard & Poors announced that it was putting GM on a credit watch, with potentially disastrous consequences for GM. *Fortune* wrote, "For a company that once routinely luxuriated in triple-A ratings, the prospect of a downgrading was not only an embarrassment but a financial menace. Borrowing costs for GMAC, which is GM's finance arm, could increase by $200 million or more annually." By the end of the third quarter of 1991, GM had $3.5 billion in cash – half the amount it usually kept to meet payroll demands and pay suppliers, and less than half the amount of cash kept on hand by Ford.[78]

Another element of GM's shaky finances was the under-funding of GM's pension fund by nearly $17 billion in late 1993.[79] From 1989 onward, to make up for its cash shortage, GM began diverting money earmarked for the pension fund to operations. To keep the pension fund looking healthy, GM made generous assumptions about the rate of return it would achieve. For 1992, GM had targeted an 11 percent rate of return, but only achieved 6.4 percent.

While Stempel denied that the cash squeeze would harm GM's ability to develop new models, analysts remained skeptical. One plant due to produce a new model of a successful Chevrolet truck was forced to stand idle until 1994.[80] Given these problems, the board could not stay stuck in neutral. By late 1991, it became obvious that GM had to undergo a massive overhaul to survive. Moreover, GM could no longer resort to the Roger Smith solution of throwing money at the company's problems. The GM board finally pressed

Stempel to take the necessary, savage, steps to put North American Operations back on the road to profitability.

In December 1991, Stempel announced the most sizeable cuts to date. GM would close 21 plants over a three-year period, cutting 74,000 jobs in the process. The aim was to reduce GM's capacity by one-fifth so it could operate profitably on a 35 percent market share. It appeared likely that at least some of the plants scheduled for closure were ones that had been renovated and modernized in the 1980s at a cost of billions. *Fortune* called it "the greatest upheaval in [GM's] modern history."

The board was still not satisfied. It wanted Stempel to drive a sense of urgency through every part of GM, instilling the kind of cultural change that Smith had so longed for. It was becoming apparent to the board that nothing short of a revolution at GM could cure its ills. But Stempel was a reluctant revolutionary, insisting to the board and shareholders alike that the company would pick up with the economy.

On April 6, 1992, the board put Stempel on notice. He was demoted from his post as chairman of the executive committee (a group created in 1989, but seldom convened). At the same time, Lloyd Reuss, Stempel's right-hand man, lost his job running North American Operations and was removed from the board. In a candid press release, the board said, "Regaining profitability requires a more aggressive management approach to remove excess costs."

The *Wall Street Journal* put Stempel's "wing clipping" into its corporate governance context: "He became the first GM chief executive in more than 70 years to lose control of his board."[81] It also reported the comment of one outside director: "[Stempel's] heart is in the right place, but bold moves aren't in his nature. He needs to be prodded. That's where the board comes in."[82] The new-found boardroom activism put GM's stock up $1.25 in a heavily down market.

Reuss was replaced at North American Operations by John "Jack" Smith, who had previously run GM's profitable European operations in the mid-1980s and turned a big loss-maker into GM's most profitable operation.

The media engaged in a frenzy of speculation as to which directors had demanded the move and how the decision to scold Stempel publicly had been reached. The *Wall Street Journal* reported that Roger Smith, who was still a board member, had not been invited to some of the key meetings. Smith apparently thought the board had acted hastily, just as GM's fortunes were on the upturn. According to the *Journal*, Smith told friends that if the board had held off for six months, it would not have acted at all.[83]

The energy behind the announcement of April 6 was apparently Millstein, GM's outside counsel. Millstein had been doing a busy job as go-between, meeting not just with GM board members but with big, angry investors such as Ca1PERS. In the January 1992 board meeting, when Stempel was accompanying Bush to Japan, the outside directors met alone with Millstein – a rebellion that would have been unthinkable under Roger Smith.

The media also speculated that Stempel's demotion would undermine his leadership, leaving him looking over his shoulder, uncertain if he had the confidence of the board. From April onwards many were simply awaiting the moment at which Stempel would be replaced. In October 1992, as rumors flew, the GM directors issued a statement saying that the board "continues to reflect upon the wisest course for assuring the most effective leadership for the corporation." This was hardly a vote of confidence.

As the pressure to remove Stempel became overwhelming, other changes seemed to be waiting in the wings. Analysts contemplated the possibility of another dividend cut; shareholder activists waited to see if Roger Smith would be forced off the board, or if GM would separate the roles of CEO and chairman.

The end, when it came, was almost anticlimactic. On October 26, 1992, Stempel resigned as chairman and chief executive officer. On November 2, the board approved the appointment of Jack Smith as CEO, and John Smale as chairman of the board. Thus, Smith would be in charge of day-to-day operations but would have to report to Smale as chairman. Roger Smith resigned from the board, and three new directors were named. GM also slashed its quarterly dividend to 20 cents a share.

In an interview with *Time*, one outside director commented nostalgically on the seismic shake-up that had taken place at GM. "This is not the company it once was," he said.[84]

## Lessons for the board

Following Stempel's ouster, the GM board was hailed for its activism. Trumpeting "The High Energy Boardroom," the *New York Times* hailed "the outside directors that shook GM."[85] The *Wall Street Journal* responded similarly, with an op-ed that declared, "Board Reform Replaces the LBO."[86]

In fact, the board deserved as much criticism as either Roger Smith or Robert Stempel. The directors took hold of their duties years too late. After Stempel's departure, one outside director told *Time*, "There is going to have to be special oversight by the board for the next three years."[87] Why had there been no special oversight in the 12 preceding years?

The GM board learned something between the buyout of Ross Perot in 1986 and the edging out of Robert Stempel in 1992. It learned that no company can remain unaccountable to the market for ever. For years, GM's size and wealth protected the company from the competitive forces that caused change at Ford and Chrysler. But, ultimately, GM could not escape from its own failed strategy. Having spent itself into financial peril, with no commensurate increase in quality productivity or sales growth, GM was brought to the brink of collapse. There was even speculation that GM, once the defining symbol of American industrial success, would file for Chapter 11 bankruptcy protection.

It was only at this point that the board got a grip. It took the bold step of opposing Smith in 1988, and the departure of Robinson and Johnson sent another strong signal of frustration. But the board continued to play a waiting game. Smith's tenure would soon be over, and change could be effected through the succession process. But in all the time the board waited, GM's results grew worse and worse, and the company's basic flaws went ignored.

In 1990, the board rejected the idea of appointing an outsider as CEO, though it considered that possibility. It believed that Stempel, a car guy, could tackle GM's problems with sufficient aggression. But as the recession sent GM into a nosedive, the board became convinced it had been mistaken. Stempel was not the right man for the top job. Barely 18 months after his appointment, Stempel was put on public notice to do better. Six months later, he was fired. Eventually, finally, tragically late, the board did the right thing.

In the five years that the board took to summon up the courage to do its duty, GM dug itself into a hole of such proportions that it could take even longer for the company to climb out. The price has been paid by GM's shareholders, its suppliers, its employees, and most everyone with an interest in the economy of the Midwest.

The GM board is now determined that the same mistakes will not be made again. GM's current bosses have a new commitment to corporate governance. In a November 1993

*Fortune* article, GM's chairman, John Smale, outlined eight rules for building a better board, which reflected principles being adopted in the GM boardroom.

- There should be a majority of outside directors.
- The independent members of the board should select a lead director.
- The independent directors should meet alone in executive session on a regularly scheduled basis.
- The independent directors should take responsibility for all board procedures.
- The board should have the basic responsibility for selection of its own members.
- The board should conduct regularly scheduled performance reviews of the CEO and key executives.
- The board must understand and fully endorse the company's long-term strategies.
- The board must give an adequate amount of attention to its most important responsibility: the selection of the CEO.

## GENERAL MOTORS: A POSTSCRIPT

Ross Perot liked to say that getting GM moving again was like teaching an elephant to dance.

So, how are things in Jack Smith's *salon*? Is the elephant turning elegant wheels round the ballroom? Or is it still treading on everyone's toes?

*Fortune* magazine took an in-depth look in 1997 and found that, unfortunately, this monster company was proving as difficult as ever to shift.

On the good side, GM's famously rock-solid finances have largely been restored – the company ended 1996 with $14 billion in reserve – thanks to a considerable consolidation of assets. In 1996, for example, GM's defense electronics business was offloaded to Raytheon for $9 billion. A 20 percent stake in the Delphi parts-making business was also offered to the public.

International operations continued to perform strongly, as did the GMAC finance arm. And, in the core domestic market, GM makes money on trucks.

But, in its own back yard, the company still can't turn a decent profit making cars.

In 1996, North American Operations returned just 1.2 percent on sales. If you exclude the contribution from the parts-making subsidiary (according to GM's own accounting policy), NAO's return does even worse – a mere 0.8 percent return. This does not compare well with the company's target of 5 percent. NAO, said *Fortune*, "remains burdened by its past."

*Fortune* asked "Why is it so hard to get this monster moving?" And then answered its own question by suggesting that "GM dithers over almost everything."

The magazine pointed the finger at many of the problems that we saw in the Roger Smith era – confusion and rivalry between the six vehicle divisions, and infighting between powerful groups of suppliers, dealers, and unions. Labor relations, *Fortune* commented, hit a "postwar low." In 1996, UAW strikes prevented GM building 300,000 cars at a cost of $1.2 billion after tax.

The chairman and CEO, Jack Smith, told *Fortune* that his task is to get GM to "run common." This sounds like an uncomfortable echo of what Roger Smith was trying to achieve nearly two decades previously.

GM has long been identified as a sprawling, cumbersome beast. But even when it streamlines operations, the company is still left playing catch-up. *Fortune* outlines how duplicative and wasteful is the simple process of metal stamping. GM spent $850 million to standardize the die production at 13 plants and reduce the number of press line set-ups from 57 to 6. But when the reform is complete, GM will still be spending 20 percent more on metal stamping than Toyota.

This competitive disadvantage is mirrored in other key areas. GM takes 29 hours to assemble a Pontiac; Toyota assembles a Camry in 20. GM's domestic plants spend an average 3.5 months getting production of a new car up and running at full speed in an assembly line. Honda does it in a weekend.

Nor is GM any better positioned in the contemporary domestic market. For example, the demand for trucks, sports utilities and minivans has grown at such a pace that they now account for 50 percent of the total US auto market. But three of GM's six divisions continue only to make cars.

The result? GM continues to be seen as old-fashioned and backward-looking – a view that is reflected in sales. At Oldsmobile, sales went from 1.1 million in 1986 to 331,287 in 1996. *Fortune* comments: "If GM had decided to kill Olds in 1992, it would have been euthanasia." Ultimately, that decision came in 2000.

As a whole, GM's market share for the first two months of 1997 was 30.3 percent, down from 32.5 percent for the same period a year before.

*Fortune*'s conclusion: "Fixing GM has turned into a decade-long project that few people – investors, analysts, or company executives – can have foreseen."

*How differently might GM's fortunes have turned out if Smale's rules had been in place, and obeyed, at GM from 1980 onwards? Or from 1960 onwards?*

*Was Roger Smith right to chose revolutionary change over evolutionary change? Why did Smith fail? Did he have the wrong strategy, or was the strategy poorly executed? Was GM's problem one of managerial incompetence or board neglect? Did Smith do anything more than just to throw money at problems? How did he use his capital? How should he have used it?*

*To what extent was GM's problem one of "culture" or bureaucracy? Was the company so poorly organized that it was capable of swallowing any amount of money with no constructive result? Could GM's culture have been changed from the top – i.e. by a new type of CEO?*

*Is Smith characteristic of American CEOs today? Can you identify companies with a Roger Smith at the helm?*

*To what extent are the changes in GM attributable to competition from outside the US? Why couldn't competition from within the US have been more effective? To what extent was the absence of strong domestic competition the result of GM's influence with the government?*

*Does it appear that GM's problems are uniquely American? Or will Daimler-Benz, Mitsubishi Heavy Industries, and ICI have similar histories? Is there such a thing as "large company disease"? How can it be treated?*

*What is the definition of boardroom negligence? Is there a standard of corporate poor performance which suggests that the board is guilty of negligence? Should boards of directors, and more particularly board nominating committees, insist that any search for top officers, especially the CEO, includes candidates from outside the company? What are the benefits and dangers of promotion from within?*

*Since World War II, all the largest US institutional investors have held GM stock. They continued to hold it through the 1980s and 1990s. To what extent were those investors negligent in failing to demand better performance? What should, or could, the shareholders have done?*

*The narrative arguably demonstrates the failure of management, the board, and the shareholders to prevent GM's decline. Does this suggest a basic failure in the governance structure? What other structure might work better?*

*What might have happened in the 1970s and 1980s if an investor such as the DuPont Company had owned 30 percent of GM's stock?*

*At what point in the narrative should the directors have intervened?*

*Ross Perot owned less than 1 percent of GM's shares. Was his stake too small to ensure his continued involvement in the company? To what extent can Perot be accused of "selling out"? If he had owned 5 percent, or 10 percent, would he have agreed to the buyout?*

*What might have happened if each of GM's outside directors had held 25 percent of their own net worth in GM stock?*

## NOTES

1. Alfred D. Chandler and Stephen Salsbury, *Pierre S. du Pont and the Making of the Modern Corporation* (Harper & Row, New York, 1971), p. 443.
2. Ibid., p. 444.
3. Ibid., p. 460.
4. William Taylor, "Can Big Owners Make a Difference?", *Harvard Business Review*, Sept.–Oct., 1990, p. 74.
5. Ibid.
6. Ibid.
7. Maryann Keller, *Rude Awakening: The Rise, Fall and Struggle for Recovery of General Motors* (William Morrow, New York, 1989), p. 33.
8. Alex Taylor, "Can GM Remodel Itself?", *Fortune*, Jan. 13, 1992, p. 32.
9. Keller, *Rude Awakening*, p. 65.
10. Alex Taylor, "Can GM Remodel Itself?", p. 32.
11. Keller, *Rude Awakening*, p. 106.
12. Doron P. Levin, *Irreconcilable Differences* (Little Brown, Boston, 1989), p. 152.
13. Keller, *Rude Awakening*, p. 50.
14. J. Patrick Wright, *On a Clear Day You Can See General Motors: John Z. DeLorean's Look Inside the Automotive Giant* (Wright Enterprises, Grosse Pointe, Michigan, 1979), p. 4.
15. Ibid., p. 27.
16. Levin, *Irreconcilable Differences*, p. 149.
17. Survey by J.D. Power Associates, cited in William McWhirter, "Back on the Fast Track," *Time*, Dec. 13, 1993, p. 70.
18. Keller, *Rude Awakening*, p. 22.
19. Jacob M. Schlesinger, "Auto Companies' Lobbying Drive Aims to Poke Widest Loophole Yet in US Fuel-Economy Law," *Wall Street Journal*, Oct. 1, 1986, p. 68.
20. It took a long time for US automakers to exploit their advantage on safety features, though by the 1990s, Lee Iacocca was appearing in Chrysler commercials stressing that more Chrysler cars came equipped with airbags than did those of Japanese competitors. "Who says you can't teach an old dog new tricks?" said Iacocca in a 1988 advertising campaign.
21. Levin, *Irreconcilable Differences*, p. 156.
22. Albert Lee, *Call Me Roger* (Contemporary Books, New York), p. 20.
23. Levin, *Irreconcilable Differences*, p. 155.
24. Alex Taylor, "Cars Come Back," *Fortune*, Nov. 16, 1992, p. 59.
25. Ibid.
26. Paul Ingrassia and Joseph B. White, "Major Overhaul: Determined to Change, General Motors is Said to Pick New Chairman," *Wall Street Journal*, Oct. 23, 1992, p. A1.
27. Alex Taylor, "Cars Come Back," p. 78.
28. Ibid.
29. Ibid.

30. Ibid.
31. Ibid.
32. Ibid.
33. Lee, *Call Me Roger*, p. 24.
34. Ibid., p. 99.
35. Levin, *Irreconcilable Differences*, p. 267.
36. Lee, *Call Me Roger*, p. 129.
37. Ibid., p. 175.
38. Alex Taylor, "Cars Come Back," p. 78.
39. Doron P. Levin, "Groping Giant: In a High-Tech Drive, GM Falls Below Rivals in Auto Profit Margins," *Wall Street Journal*, July 22, 1986, p. A1.
40. Ibid.
41. Joseph B. White, "Low Orbit: GM Struggles to Get Saturn Car on Track after Rough Launch," *Wall Street Journal*, May 24, 1991, p. A1.
42. Lee, *Call Me Roger*, p. 20.
43. Levin, *Irreconcilable Differences*, p. 258.
44. White, "Low Orbit," p. A1.
45. Ibid.
46. Lee, *Call Me Roger*, p. 67.
47. Ibid., p. 25.
48. Keller, *Rude Awakening*, p. 248.
49. Alex Taylor, "What's Ahead for GM's New Team," *Fortune*, Nov. 30, 1992, p. 59.
50. Paul Ingrassia, "Board Reform Replaces the LBO," *Wall Street Journal*, Oct. 30, 1992, p. A10.
51. Levin, *Irreconcilable Differences*, p. 108.
52. Ibid., p. 178.
53. Joseph B. White, "Perot, EDS Bare Claws over Clause, In Court and Out," *Wall Street Journal*, Oct. 20, 1988, p. A3.
54. Levin, *Irreconcilable Differences*, p. 238.
55. Ibid., p. 258.
56. Ibid.
57. Ibid., p. 259.
58. Ibid.
59. Ibid., p. 260.
60. Ibid., p. 276.
61. Ibid., p. 284.
62. Ibid., p. 285.
63. Ibid.
64. Levin, "Groping Giant," p. A1.
65. Levin, *Irreconcilable Differences*, p. 297.
66. White, "Perot, EDS Bare Claws."
67. Levin, *Irreconcilable Differences*, p. 326.
68. James B. Treece, "Can GM's Big Investors Get It to Change Lanes?" *Business Week*, Jan. 22, 1990, p. 30.
69. Jacob B. Schlesinger and Paul Ingrassia, "GM's Outside Directors are Ending their Passive Role," *Wall Street Journal*, Aug. 17, 1988, p. 6.
70. Ibid.
71. Marcia Parker, "GM's Smith Still Uneasy with Holders," *Pensions and Investments*, June 11, 1990, p. 14.
72. Warren Brown, "Top Production Manager Picked to Head GM," *Washington*, Apr. 4, 1990, p. C1.

73. Joseph B. White and Paul Ingrassia, "Eminence Grise: Behind Revolt at GM, Ira Millstein Helped Call the Shots," *Wall Street Journal*, Apr. 13, 1992, p. A1.
74. *ValueLine*, Mar. 22, 1991.
75. John Greenwald, "What Went Wrong," *Time*, Nov. 9, 1992, p. 44.
76. Alex Taylor, "What's Ahead for GM's New Team," p. 58.
77. Alex Taylor, "Can GM Remodel Itself?", p. 32.
78. Ibid., p. 29.
79. Barry B. Burr, "GM Finding Proposal Hits E Shares," *Pensions and Investments*, Nov. 29, 1993. p. 1.
80. Alex Taylor, "Can GM Remodel Itself?", p. 32.
81. White and Ingrassia, "Eminence Grise."
82. Ibid.
83. Ibid.
84. Greenwald, "What Went Wrong."
85. Alison Cowan, "The High Energy Board Room," *New York Times*, Oct. 28, 1992, p. D1.
86. Ingrassia, "Board Reform Replaces the LBO."
87. Greenwald, "What Went Wrong," p. 44.

# American Express

At the spring annual meeting of shareholders in 1977, James D. Robinson III was elected chairman of American Express, the New York-based financial services company known for its travelers' checks and its unique "charge now, pay now" credit card. His ambition was to take the splendid cashflow that the card and checks business generated and use it to create a giant "financial supermarket." According to *Business Week*, Robinson "set about transforming American Express into a financial empire of unequaled proportions."[1] Financial diversification was all the fashion in the early 1980s (witness Sears, Roebuck's acquisition of Dean Witter, or General Electric's of Kidder Peabody), and Robinson was determined that American Express would be the biggest, the best, and the brightest. As reporter and author Bryan Burrough notes:

> Jim Robinson outlined a vision of a financial empire that would offer all things to all people: charge cards, insurance brokerage services, money management, private banking. It would be unlike any other company ever formed, offering cradle-to-grave financial care for anyone in the world, anywhere in the world. The potential synergies were awe-inspiring: Shearson mutual funds and Fireman's Fund insurance offered to American Express card holders; American Express travel planning offered to Shearson's Wall St clients. The combinations seemed endless.[2]

To this end, American Express acquired:

- in 1981, Shearson, at a cost of nearly $1 billion – "Era of Financial Conglomerate May Dawn on Wall St." said the *Wall Street Journal* headline;
- in 1981, The Boston Company;[3]
- by early 1982, regional brokerages Foster & Marshall and Robinson Humphries;
- in 1983, Edmond Safra's Trade Development Bank;
- in 1984, Investors Diversified Services;
- in 1984, Lehman Brothers Kuhn Loeb; and
- in 1987, E.F. Hutton & Co.

Robinson pursued other targets with less success.

- In September 1977, he tried to buy Philadelphia Life, which was already the subject of a takeover bid from its largest shareholder, Tenneco Inc. When American Express launched an unsolicited $230 million bid, Tenneco upped its offer and swept AmEx aside.

• In 1987–8, Robinson wooed Disney and the Book of the Month Club, but these overtures were rejected out of hand.

• Then came McGraw-Hill in January 1979, when AmEx launched a "friendly" $830 million bid. The ensuing fight was far from friendly. McGraw-Hill responded with a series of aggressive newspaper articles, letters to shareholders, even a libel suit. At a press conference, Harold McGraw told of a letter he had sent to Robinson accusing him of a lack of integrity and corporate morality.[4] AmEx withdrew. Bryan Burrough comments, "It was the low mark of Robinson's career."[5]

• Later in 1979, AmEx engaged in a joint venture with Warner Communications to form a cable TV company called Warner-AmEx. The operation continued to lose money until Robinson sold out in 1985, shortly before the business became spectacularly profitable.

## Robinson's travails

Aborted mergers weren't Robinson's only headaches. Other events damaged AmEx's bottom line, as well as the company's prized image and integrity.

• In 1983, an AmEx-owned insurance firm called the Fireman's Fund posted a $242 million pre-tax loss for the year, dragging AmEx's overall earnings to barely $30 million. The crisis came as a big surprise to AmEx executives. The loss also spelled an end to AmEx's cherished 36-year record of annual profit increases. "With virtually no warning, the myth of American Express's financial supremacy had ended."[6]

• Also in 1983, Robinson merged the troubled American Express Bank with the Trade Development Bank owned by Edmond Safra. Lebanese by birth and one of the world's richest men, Safra was the embodiment of exclusive, private banking. Robinson envied his franchise, and felt that Safra's name could boost AmEx's reputation. The relationship between Safra and AmEx was a disaster. Safra withdrew from the company in 1985 and later resigned from the board. In 1989 he accused AmEx of leading a smear campaign against him. Robinson made a public apology, and agreed to pay $8 million to Safra's chosen charities. Robinson ended up selling Trade Development Bank in 1990.

• In December 1988, the Boston Company admitted "accounting errors." The president confessed to overstating 1988 pre-tax earnings by $30 million. He was fired, and two other senior executives promptly retired.

• In 1988, Shearson became embroiled in the battle for control of RJR Nabisco on the management side, which eventually lost the high-publicity battle to Kohlberg, Kravis & Roberts. Shearson's role was savaged in a best-selling 1990 book about the contest.[7]

• In 1991, Boston restaurateurs cut up their American Express cards, and declined to accept the card at their establishments, in a highly public campaign against AmEx's high merchant charges. The incident became known as "the Boston Fee Party."

• In 1987, AmEx introduced its own credit card called "Optima." Known as "Pessima" in financial circles, the charge card cost the company $112 million.

• In March 1988, Shearson's Mergers & Acquisition department figured it could merge Koppers, a Pittsburgh chemicals manufacturer, with Beazer plc, a British construction firm. Shearson would kick in $50 million, and provide a $200 million bridge loan. Koppers launched a fierce public campaign against both Shearson and AmEx, accusing them of siding with a British firm at the expense of American jobs. Pennsylvania Senator John Heinz threatened to introduce legislation in Congress to block the takeover, while the mayor of Pittsburgh joined in a public cutting-up of AmEx cards. The negative publicity for American Express was devastating.

The biggest headache of them all, however, was Shearson.

- The company had been in a slide ever since its record year in 1986. 1989 profits were running 88 percent lower than at their peak. The stock was trading at roughly half the $34 high it had reached in April 1987.
- By 1989, Shearson's president, Peter Cohen, was pleading with AmEx to infuse more capital. In late 1989, Moody's placed Shearson on credit watch.
- By the start of 1990, Shearson shares had fallen to as low as $10, one-third of their high.
- Talks in 1990, to merge Shearson with Primerica, run by former AmEx president Sandy Weill, deadlocked. Weeks later, Cohen was fired. When a second round of talks with Weill failed, as did a new issue of Shearson equity, AmEx announced it was going to purchase the remaining shares in Shearson that it didn't already hold at a cost of $1 billion. Howard Clark Jr., the son of Robinson's predecessor as CEO, was named the new Shearson boss.

By 1992, Robinson had served as chairman and CEO for 16 years, one of the longest tenures of any American corporate chief. The year was not a good one for American Express. The company was on its way to posting a $243 million profit, but that was down 39 percent from the previous year. Shearson lost $116 million for the year, while other Wall Street firms were showing record profits. These results set the stage for a battle inside the American Express boardroom.

### Inside the boardroom, 1992–3

In late 1991, American Express director Rawleigh Warner asked CEO James Robinson to allow a new boardroom procedure: as a matter of regular policy, the outside directors should meet alone once or twice a year. Warner had joined the board in 1972, along with Richard Furlaud. They were the two most senior members of the 19-person board, and were the only ones elected before Robinson's appointment as CEO in 1977.

Warner requested the meeting of outside directors "to protect ourselves against a charge that all we did was sit around and play patty-cake for Jimmy."[8] Robinson agreed and scheduled two such meetings for February and September 1992.

Before leaving the room to the outside directors at the February meeting, Robinson raised the question of his successor. Robinson said he wished to remain at AmEx for about two more years, until age 60. He identified Harvey Golub, AmEx president and the chief of the core Travel Related Services (TRS) division, as a replacement. The timing, he added, was perfect. Golub was relatively new to American Express and was unfamiliar with many parts of the sprawling AmEx empire. Golub was a man of prodigious talent, Robinson said, but he would make a better CEO given a couple more years' seasoning.

The succession issue was raised more forcefully at the September meeting. As the outside directors gathered prior to an informal supper meeting of the board, Warner asked if he could make a statement. What followed was a biting 20-minute critique of Robinson's tenure as CEO. He read out a detailed list of setbacks that had befallen AmEx under

Robinson's leadership, going back to the attempted takeover of Philadelphia Life Insurance Co. in 1977. He described the aborted mergers, the problems at Shearson, the embarrassing episodes involving Safra and RJR Nabisco, the losses from Optima, and the erosion of the card's market share. Terrible mistakes had been made, he argued, mistakes that had cost shareholders billions of dollars. Worse, the future was not looking any brighter. American Express was in a mess, he concluded, and James Robinson was not the man to bring it out. His proposal: Robinson should be asked to retire immediately, and a successor found forthwith.

The board's reaction was mixed. Some were shocked by the sheer volume of evidence Warner had brought to bear against Robinson. At least one director was angry at Warner's tactics, saying that Robinson was being made the victim of a boardroom cabal. Drew Lewis, CEO of Union Pacific, defended Robinson, saying that many of the problems that Warner had described were the result of industry-wide downturns and were not attributable to poor management. Henry Kissinger, the former Secretary of State, said the issue of Robinson's ouster was difficult for him because Robinson was "a good friend of mine."[9] But the weight of Warner's argument was compelling. *Fortune* wrote, "Says one source close to the proceedings: 'Jimmy was cooked.' "[10] A compromise was reached. Robinson would be asked to retire, but not immediately. A committee would be set up to search for his successor and report its findings to the board; when the board had made its choice, Robinson would relinquish his post.

Robinson was informed of the decision. At the meeting of the full board the next day, the search committee was appointed. Five directors, including Robinson, were named to the committee, with Furlaud appointed as its chair. In a retrospective story covering American Express, the *Washington Post* wrote, "Both the Robinson loyalists and the Warner-led insurgents wanted to prevent the other side from seizing control of the search committee, sources said."[11]

The board's decision was not made public, though in any company as closely watched as AmEx, secrets seldom stay secret for long. *Fortune* reported in December that Robinson had been pushed out by the board. The company responded by announcing that Robinson had decided to retire, but that he would only step down when the search committee had reached a decision. The suggestion that Robinson was the victim of a boardroom putsch was strongly denied. Warner said in a statement, "This is an orderly succession process initiated by and managed by Jim Robinson. To characterize it in any other way is totally inaccurate. Clearly, this is not a coup."[12] Richard Furlaud commented, "Prompted by Jim Robinson's discussion of his own plan for retirement before age 60 . . . the board at its September meeting asked Jim to lead an orderly process to identify a successor CEO."[13] Robinson himself said, "I did not feel any pressure on the succession issue coming up to the September meeting. I told them that the time was right. The momentum was there." When asked whether the board had pressured him to leave, Robinson said: "I think that would be a gross exaggeration."[14] The semantic difference between "coup" and "orderly succession process" was lost on investors. The news that AmEx was to have a new CEO gave a 6 percent bounce to the stock. Shares rose $1.38 to $24.75 on the news of the succession plan, raising American Express's market value by $667 million.

The media speculated as to possible candidates to succeed Robinson. An obvious frontrunner was AmEx's own Harvey Golub. Golub had moved to TRS after a spell as chief of IDS, the Minneapolis-based fund management group bought by AmEx in 1984. He achieved stellar performance at IDS and was a lead figure in TRS's renaissance, responsible for a $1 billion cost-cutting plan and a more flexible approach to merchant charges. He was known to be Robinson's first choice. The press suggested that possible outsiders included Sir Colin Marshall, president of British Airways, and Frito-Lay chairman Roger Enrico.

As the search committee continued its deliberations, it became apparent that the Golub-versus-outsider issue had become a bone of mighty contention. "Outsider Gains in American Express Search" reported the *Wall Street Journal* in January 1993.[15] Three days later, it carried a different headline: "Decision Nears on American Express Search, Clash Looms as Robinson Seeks Support on Golub, Others Back an Outsider." The story continued:

> According to one person close to the situation, Mr. Robinson believes he has enough support on the board to make Mr. Golub chief executive under an arrangement that would let Mr. Robinson remain chairman for an indefinite period. "Jimmy thinks he has between 12 and 14 votes and all he needs is 10 votes," the individual said. "Throughout the [search] process, he has been working like hell to line up [board] votes" for Mr. Golub. Mr. Robinson's goal has been "to make sure that it isn't an outsider" who succeeds him as chief executive, the individual added.

The same story reported that Enrico had issued an internal staff memo denying any interest in the job at American Express. Pundits also suggested that a recent scandal at British Airways – in which the airline had admitted a "dirty tricks" campaign against Richard Branson's rival Virgin group – had harmed Sir Colin Marshall's chances. There was no indication that Marshall had been involved in the misdeeds, but it was thought that AmEx, still smarting from the Safra affair, would want to avoid even the whiff of scandal to restore its image of cast-iron integrity.

But while no clear outside candidate emerged, doubts also circulated about Golub. They were not questions about his ability, but about his lack of experience as a senior AmEx executive and his unfamiliarity with large parts of the sprawling AmEx empire. The *Wall Street Journal* reported:

> An alternative to Mr. Golub is being sought, the person close to the committee said, because "Harvey is like the sophomore at West Point who is getting all As. But such a great company as American Express needs a general who has already fought a few wars."[16]

Another difficulty was the need to cater to Golub's own ambitions. Having been groomed for the top job, he would be unwilling to remain at AmEx under another CEO. The company did not want to lose Golub's talents, but if American Express did not offer Golub the top job, another company surely would.

On January 21, the search committee met to make its choice. Robinson brought two advisers with him – investment banker Felix Rohatyn of Lazard Frères and lawyer Joseph Flom. Both men advised the appointment of Golub as CEO but suggested that, given his lack of experience, and for the sake of continuity of leadership, Robinson should be kept on indefinitely as chairman. Flom and Rohatyn argued that it was no use waiting for the perfect candidate to arrive. A decision had to be made, and made quickly; the continuing speculation over the succession was harming morale and damaging the company's reputation.

According to accounts of the meeting, members of the search committee were reluctant to accept this advice, knowing that a recommendation for Robinson as chairman would be rejected out of hand by some members of the board. The argument was persuasive, however. There was no outside candidate better suited than Golub, and there was no point running the risk of losing Golub to another company by appointing an outsider just for the sake of it. Furthermore, there was the concern that Golub, while exceptionally talented, had little experience in AmEx's global operations and was unfamiliar with AmEx's problem child, Shearson Lehman Brothers. Keeping Robinson on as chairman, ran the argument, would give Golub the chance to grow into the job under Robinson's experienced supervision.

A Robinson–Golub team appeared to solve all problems, except one: the outright opposition of three to four members of the board to Robinson's continued presence at the top of the company. No one believed, however, that they would carry a majority of the 19-member board. The search committee voted unanimously to recommend Golub as CEO and keep Robinson as chairman.

But the committee did not end its decision-making there. It also addressed the question of who should lead the company's troubled Shearson operation. Since the departure of Cohen in 1990, Shearson's CEO had been Howard Clark Jr., the son of legendary AmEx chairman Howard Clark Sr. The elder Clark had been Robinson's predecessor and was primarily responsible for Robinson's rapid progress to the executive suite. But having groomed Robinson for the corner office, Clark had become increasingly disturbed by his protégé's performance. By 1992, he was one of Warner's closest allies in the bid to replace Robinson. Clark Sr., while not officially a member of the board, attended virtually every board meeting as a non-voting participant.

But while Clark Sr. had become disenchanted with Robinson, so Robinson had become disenchanted with Clark Jr.'s performance as CEO of Shearson. Nor was Robinson alone. Senior director Furlaud told *The Economist* that Clark Jr. "seems to have got lost a little bit."[17] Clark's tenure at Shearson had not been auspicious. In the first two years of the 1990s, Shearson was the only business of its kind that wasn't turning out record profits. Hamstrung with bad debts and high costs, the once promising unit lost money hand over fist. In 1990 alone, Shearson reported a loss of $996 million, the largest ever for a US brokerage firm. The picture did not improve. Shearson lost $166 million in the last quarter of 1992 alone. The continued losses contributed to downgrading from the credit rating agencies.

AmEx had attacked Shearson's problems in a number of ways. It had "deconsolidated" the firm, reducing AmEx's holdings to 51 percent in 1988. Later, Robinson engaged in talks with Sandy Weill, Shearson's ex-boss, to sell the operation to Weill's Primerica Co. The talks broke down twice before they were abandoned. Finally, in 1990, AmEx had bought back all the shares to inject further capital into the brokerage firm.

Robinson did not want to leave a troubled Shearson as his legacy. Shearson, perhaps more than any of the other businesses AmEx had bought under his tenure, represented Robinson's pursuit of financial diversification. It epitomized Robinson's entire acquisition strategy. If Shearson continued to drag on the earnings of its parent, nay-sayers would continue to criticize Robinson's empire-building. On the other hand, if Shearson started to reap the kinds of profits that Merrill Lynch and Goldman Sachs were making, Robinson could be credited with making the "financial supermarket" work.

Robinson told the search committee that he wished to head Shearson. Not only did he feel personally responsible for the firm's success, but he believed Shearson had the kinds of problems that he, with his experience as an investment banker and undoubted might in the Wall Street ring, could solve. As it stood, Howard Clark Jr. was out of his depth. *Business Week* quoted a source close to the situation: "Jim feels a personal obligation to get this done. He is in a do-or-die situation with Shearson."[18] All told, Robinson's pitch was a bold one. He wished to remain as chairman in order to provide stability and leadership to his hand-picked successor and protégé, Harvey Golub, and he would take over day-to-day running of Shearson Lehman Brothers, replacing the son of a fierce Robinson critic. Such a resolution would leave an awkward hierarchy. Robinson, as Shearson's chief, would report to Golub as CEO. Yet Golub would be accountable to the board, chaired by Robinson. Both Robinson and Golub said they were happy with the set up, and agreed to share an "office of the chief executive," which would be the senior management decision-making body.

If the other members of the search committee were uncomfortable with this prescription, they weren't for long. They resolved to offer such a solution to the board when it met four days later.

Robinson further strengthened his hand by informing Clark Sr. – who, as a board advisor, customarily attended board meetings – that he would not be welcome at this one. Clark was told by Robinson subordinates that his presence would be inappropriate since his son's performance would be one of the topics under review. Clark was incensed. He believed he was being kept away for one reason: that he would oppose Robinson as chairman.

The question remained: would the board accept the recommendation of the search committee? There was no doubt that Robinson's opponents, now numbering three – possibly four – and led by Warner, would vehemently oppose both Robinson's continued chairmanship and his appointment to Shearson. They believed that, after 16 years as CEO, Robinson had served his time and now should leave. They would settle for nothing less.

It was harder to predict the reaction of the remaining members of the board. Would they reject Robinson's gutsy power play, or would they side with the man who appointed them to the board in the first place?

With 19 members, American Express had a big board by Fortune 500 standards. Of these, only three were employees of the company: Robinson, Golub, and Aldo Papone, a senior adviser to the company. But the presence of a large majority of outside directors did not free American Express from charges that its board was management's patsy.

The board of AmEx had a reputation as one of the least independent-minded around. In the words of one board member: "The general belief was that the board was in Jimmy's pocket because he'd appointed 15 of the 17 outside directors."[19]

As well as 19 regular directors, AmEx board meetings were regularly attended by four advisory members, selected by Robinson. Rawleigh Warner says the advisers "engaged in the dialogue, argued points, and made proposals just as if they were board members. The only thing they could not do was vote, and sometimes they forgot this caveat."[20] Christopher Bryon wrote in *New York* magazine, "In a sense, Robinson had created American Express's board for just this emergency. Since every board member except Furlaud and Warner had been hand-picked over the years by Robinson himself, there was no question as to where its allegiance lay: the American Express chairman had instant rapport with – and could count on the support of – virtually every director ringed around him at the table."[21] AmEx was attacked for "stunt casting" in the boardroom. Henry Kissinger, the former Secretary of State, had served as a director since 1984. And President Gerald Ford was a special adviser.

Moreover, American Express paid nearly $500,000 in consulting fees to Kissinger's foreign affairs advisory firm in 1991. Ford received a further $100,000. Both Ford and Kissinger were known to be close personal friends of Robinson's, as was F. Ross Johnson, the impetuous ex-CEO of RJR Nabisco, and Vernon Jordan, the civil rights lawyer who sat on the board of Revlon with Robinson's wife.

Other directors received substantial consulting fees for advice to Shearson and other AmEx units. Rawleigh Warner commented that these directors "seemed to me to be clearly under Mr. Robinson's wing."[22]

Byron describes a network of interlocks that added to a sense of "clubbiness." Furlaud sat on the board of American Express, and Robinson sat on the board of Bristol Myers Squibb, Furlaud's old company, where Furlaud was still a director. And, at meetings of the Business Roundtable, Robinson would often bump into Drew Lewis, Frank Popoff and Joseph Williams, all directors of AmEx.[23] Lewis, former secretary of the Department of Transportation, was now the CEO of Union Pacific Corp. He is described in media accounts as one of Robinson's staunchest defenders in the whole succession affair. Not only did Robinson serve on the board of Union Pacific, he also served on the compensation committee, directly responsible for setting Lewis's pay. Kissinger also sat on the board of Union Pacific.[24]

Other interlocks existed. Kissinger served on the International Advisory Committee of Chase Manhattan Bank, along with Furlaud. And the Council on Foreign Relations featured not just Kissinger and Furlaud, but Robinson and Charles Duncan as well. Kissinger also sat with Beverly Sills on the board of Macy's, and with Anne Armstrong at the Center for Strategic and International Studies. Byron concludes, "The effect of all these interlocks was to develop a cozy sense of belonging to a kind of corporate in-crowd – an arrangement that no one who was already 'in' would want to disrupt with something so unseemly as a vote to oust one of the insiders."[25] Rawleigh Warner later wrote, "It's quite obvious that most of the American Express directors were under Jimmy Robinson's thumb.[26] The board met on January 25, four days after the search committee had reached its final decision. News of its likely recommendation filtered out to directors over the weekend, and as the board met at 10 on Monday morning, Robinson's opponents knew that they had failed in their bid to bring new management to American Express.[27] Before the meeting had even been formally opened, Warner asked Robinson to leave so that discussion of his future would not be compromised. Robinson, with Lewis coming to his defense, said that he was a voting member of the board and would therefore stay.

Furlaud announced the decision of the search committee: Golub would assume the role of CEO; Robinson would remain chairman as well as taking over the top job at Shearson from Clark Jr. Joseph Williams said that the board had manifestly failed in its duty and that the directors had lacked independence in the face of Robinson's determination not to leave.

Kissinger spoke in favor of the motion, noting that the proposal had been supported unanimously by the search committee. Others, including James Byrne and William Bowen, were troubled by the bundled nature of the proposal. They were happy with Golub as CEO, but did not want to see Robinson remain as chairman. A vote to separate the issues was defeated.

Golub was brought into the room for a final vote. Fifteen directors voted in favor of the search committee's recommendation. Three directors – Warner, Williams and Armstrong – voted against. Bowen abstained on the basis that he could support Golub but not Robinson. Warner immediately announced his resignation in light of his fierce opposition to the result. "I fought the good fight," he told a *Wall Street Journal* writer, "and I lost."[28] The next day two other directors resigned.

One director told the *Washington Post* that the would-be insurgents had underestimated Robinson: "We had been arrogant. We thought the facts were so much on our side that we turned our backs while Robinson was lobbying the rest of the board constantly. That's how he beat us."[29] Another source, quoted by Byron, said, "What everyone missed in this situation is that Jim's job was never really in jeopardy at all."[30] Another said, "In October not one director was ready to support Harvey. But in January they were. There had been a very, very well run campaign, a PR campaign, with Harvey leading dinner meetings with key directors. I realized, and other directors did too, that we were being spun by Robinson. He is an absolute master."[31]

Robinson responded to the charge: "There was a campaign to make sure that the directors had full knowledge of the strategy in place and Harvey's grasp of it . . . If that is a PR campaign, I accept full responsibility."[32]

The new management structure might have been approved by the board, but it did not sit well with the market. "American Express Lineup Strikes Out with Investors," reported the *Wall Street Journal*. On the day following the news, AmEx stock dropped 5 percent on five times normal trading. The stock slid $1.25 to $23.87 in the first full day's trading, and the company's market value dropped $835 million in two days.

The dissatisfaction stemmed from a belief that AmEx was badly in need of a radical shift in strategy, and that Robinson's "counter-coup" meant that no such shift was likely. Wilson Davis, analyst at Gerard Klauer Mattison & Co., told the *Wall Street Journal*, "Arrogance and self-absorption won out over the interests of shareholders. Mr. Robinson is a big negative. Whatever the P/E ratio is, it's less with Jim Robinson in the company. Period."[33] Observers doubted that the shake-up represented much of a power loss for Robinson at all. Indeed, some thought Robinson had actually increased his influence by taking over day-to-day responsibility of Shearson. "Curiouser and Curiouser at AmEx," said a *Business Week* headline. "The newly drawn lines of power seem to be at cross purposes." A graphic accompanying the story showed how Golub and Robinson would report to each other under the new structure, and asked the question: "Who's Really in Charge?"[34]

Other investors criticized the board for not being more aggressive in its stance towards Robinson. Paul Ehrlichman, partner in Brandywine Asset Management, told the *Wall Street Journal* that his group planned to sell its million-share stake in American Express. "This was very disappointing," he said. "When you see politics win out over shareholders, once again it makes you think that Mr. Robinson is unique in his disregard for shareholders and control over the company."[35] In the same vein, *The Economist* carried a cartoon of Jim Robinson with the AmEx board wrapped around his little finger. "It's incredible," said one of AmEx's largest institutional investors to Byron. "Think of just how out of touch that company's board really was. Here was all of Wall Street expecting Robinson to be tossed out on his ear, then suddenly here was the board of directors saying he wouldn't be going after all – and expecting investors to feel as if nothing had happened."[36]

There was trouble inside the company as well. On the day following the announcement, Robinson addressed a group of about 400 Shearson branch managers. He was not greeted favorably. "The reception was glacial," one attendee told the *Wall Street Journal*. Another account reported that Robinson had walked out of the meeting early after some hostile remarks from the audience. The *Journal* also reported that Lehman Brothers bankers were complaining that winning clients had become harder because Robinson gave the firm a credibility problem.[37] The *Washington Post* described another meeting on January 28, in which Robinson discussed some of his ideas for Shearson with the firm's executives. The meeting ended in turmoil according to a source when one of the Shearson managers stormed out of the room having threatened to physically assault Robinson.[38]

Golub, meanwhile, faced some difficult meetings of his own. On January 28, he attended a breakfast meeting with a dozen of AmEx's largest institutional investors. The shareholders were not interested in Golub's plan for the future – they just wanted to know how Robinson had managed to cling to, even increase, his power. Investors mostly approved of Golub's assumption of the CEO post; it was just that with Robinson holding positions both above and below, it was doubtful how much power Golub would actually be wielding. As a plan for forging a bold new strategy at American Express, it looked like a non-starter.

In an unprecedented display of concern, even the traditionally least active Wall Street funds registered their displeasure. Funds such as Alliance Capital Management, Putnam

Management Co., and J.P. Morgan Investment Management pointed out the decline in share value since the announcement, and expressed reservations about Robinson's continued tenure at the company.

In just over a week since the search committee had made its decision, American Express's value had dropped 13 percent. It was clear to members of the board that more needed to be done. Robinson's counter-coup was damaging American Express in the marketplace, harming the company's valuable reputation, and causing a collapse of employee morale. Three senior directors, the chairmen of various board committees, gathered to discuss what should be done. Later, Furlaud told Golub that Robinson should consider stepping down. Golub later discussed the issue with Robinson and Joe Flom over dinner. Golub suggested that Robinson step aside for the good of the company. In an interview with the *Post*, Robinson insisted that he was still undecided about leaving. He considered giving up the chairman role, but remaining CEO of Shearson, an idea that received short shrift from Golub. Robinson continued to vacillate through Thursday night and Friday: "I went through a whole series of permutations in my own mind about what would be most helpful to Harvey and the company," he told one journalist. A source close to Robinson told the *Post*: "Jim's mood was on again, off again, sometimes bitter and mad, sometimes concil-iatory and realistic."[39]

Finally, on January 29, Robinson concluded that his position was untenable. He would resign from all positions at American Express. In a statement he denied that pressure from the board had forced his hand: "A combination of things led me to the conclusion that it's nuts to leave confusion over whether Harvey is really boss; so I decided to pull up stakes and get out of town."[40]

Robinson's withdrawal gave the AmEx board the opportunity to appoint a non-executive chairman, a measure designed to salve the discontent of the company's largest shareholders. Richard Furlaud was selected. Mindful of his aggressive turnaround of Squibb Co., observers believed that Furlaud would be forceful in advancing a clear strat-egy for American Express. "The company's mission," said a Morgan Stanley analyst to the *Wall Street Journal*, "has become a bit muddled. The mission needs to be made clear. Maybe someone of [Furlaud's] stature can do that."[41]

But Robinson's ouster still rankled with certain members of the board. At a board meet-ing, held by telephone, to appoint Furlaud as chairman, a motion was made and seconded for Robinson to rescind his resignation, since he had been pushed out by outsiders. As Warner comments, "The outsiders, in this instance, only happened to be shareholders."[42] The motion never went to a vote.

American Express stock rose $1.37 in the two trading days following Robinson's resignation and Furlaud's appointment.

Later in 1993, Rawleigh Warner was elected "Director of the Year" by the National Association of Corporate Directors. Warner shared the lessons he had learned from the AmEx experience:

> The size of the board does make a difference. The American Express Board had 19 members and four advisors to the board. That large a board, I believe, makes for an unwieldy number and prevents an opportunity for each member to speak freely.
>
> It is extraordinarily difficult to mount an attack on a CEO who has been in the job for a long time and who has appointed a majority of a board's directors.
>
> A small group of dissenting directors with a split board has very little capability to do battle with a CEO who is determined to hold on and has access to the full apparatus of the corporate public relations department.

It is imperative to have directors who are not only independent but who can tell the difference between a company that is having some difficulties but moving to correct them with a reasonable chance of success, and a company that is in serious and potentially harmful trouble and under attack from the shareholders, media, and analysts for extended poor performance.

Directors unable to distinguish between such different situations tend to circle the wagons around the embattled CEO rather than represent the owner shareholders. This, I believe, was the case with Mr. Robinson and the majority of American Express directors.[43]

*What does this case tell you about the relationship between management and the board?*

"In the final analysis a board of directors can only be as effective as its chairman wants it to be" (Hugh Parker). *Do you agree with this comment?*

In an interview with the *Washington Post*, Robinson commented on Warner's damning indictment of Robinson's leadership: "I am amused at Rawleigh listing all this," he said, "since he was on the board during all of this."[44] *Who should we blame for long-term under-performance – management or the board? Should Warner have acted sooner? Could he have done?*

Most shareholders did not register their discontent with Robinson's tenure until after the board elected to keep him on as chairman. *Should they have acted sooner?*

Compare the roles played by the public pension funds and the other institutional investors. *How and why did they differ?*

In 1993, at the annual meeting, shareholders re-elected a board of directors whose rearrangement of executive functions had five months earlier been utterly repudiated by these same shareholders. What does this tell you about the ultimate significance of the board? *What does it tell you about the board's accountability to the shareholders? How meaningful is the electoral process?*

## NOTES

1.  John Mehan and Jon Friedman, "The Failed Vision," *Business Week*, Mar. 19, 1990, pp. 109–13.
2.  Bryan Burrough, *Vendetta* (HarperCollins, New York, 1992), p. 75.
3.  One of the authors of this book, Robert A.G. Monks, was the chairman of the Boston company at the time of its purchase by American Express. He can attest to both Robinson's competence and integrity.
4.  Robert Slater, *The Titans of Takeover* (Prentice-Hall, Englewood Cliffs, NJ, 1987), p. 156.
5.  Burrough, *Vendetta*, p. 74.
6.  Ibid., p. 103.
7.  Bryan Burrough and John Helyar, *Barbarians at the Gate* (Harper & Row, New York, 1990).
8.  Brett D. Fromson, "American Express: Anatomy of a Coup," *Washington Post*, Feb. 11, 1993, p. A1.
9.  Ibid.
10.  Bill Saporito, "The Toppling of King James III," *Fortune*, Jan. 11, 1993, p. 42.
11.  Fromson, "American Express," p. A1.
12.  Steven Lipin, Peter Pae, and Fred R. Bleakley, "Robinson to Resign at American Express, Denies Receiving Pressure from Board," *Wall Street Journal*, Dec. 7, 1992, p. A3.
13.  Ibid.

14. Ibid.
15. Fred R. Bleakley, "Outsider Gains in American Express Search," *Wall Street Journal*, Jan. 18, 1993, p. A3.
16. Ibid.
17. Editorial, "Don't Leave Home Without Me," *The Economist*, Jan. 30, 1993, p. 67.
18. Leah Nathan Spire, "Curiouser and Curiouser at AmEx," *Business Week*, Feb. 4, 1993, p. 109.
19. Fromson, "American Express," p. A1.
20. Rawleigh Warner, "'Always Do Right' − Observations from a Retired Director," *Director's Monthly*, 17, 12, Dec. 1993, p. 1.
21. Christopher Byron, "House of Cards," *New York*, Feb. 15, 1993, p. 28.
22. Warner, "Always Do Right," p. 1.
23. Byron, "House of Cards," p. 28.
24. Ibid.
25. Ibid.
26. Rawleigh Warner, "A Lead Director . . . the Practice," Speech to conference on "CEO and Board Relationships: Towards Common Ground" sponsored by Booz, Allen & Hamilton, J.L. Kellogg Graduate School of Management, and Spencer Stuart, Northwestern University, Apr. 28−9, 1993.
27. Fromson, "American Express."
28. Steven Lipin, "Three Directors at American Express Resign after Failing to Oust Chairman," *Wall Street Journal*, Jan. 28, 1993, p. B8.
29. Fromson, "American Express."
30. Byron, "House of Cards."
31. Fromson, "American Express."
32. Ibid.
33. Steven Lipin and Craig Torres, "American Express Lineup Strikes Out With Investors," *Wall Street Journal*, Jan. 27, 1993, p. C1.
34. Spire, "Curiouser and Curiouser at AmEx," p. 109.
35. Lipin and Torres, "American Express Lineup Strikes Out."
36. Byron, "House of Cards."
37. Fred R. Bleakley, Peter Pae, and Michael Siconolfi, "Robinson Quits at American Express Co.," *Wall Street Journal*, Feb. 1, 1993, p. A3.
38. Fromson, "American Express."
39. Ibid.
40. Bleakley, Pae, and Siconolfi, "Robinson Quits."
41. Peter Pae and Michael Waldholz, "Furlaud is Likely to Play Pivotal Role in Shaping American Express Strategy," *Wall Street Journal*, Feb. 3, 1993, p. B10.
42. Warner, "Always Do Right," p. 1.
43. Ibid.
44. Fromson, "American Express."

# Time Warner

Just about everything the courts said about the duty of directors to shareholders in the early takeover cases was reversed in the case involving the Time Warner merger. That case represents probably the greatest incursion in United States business history into the rights of shareholders. The Delaware Court allowed the directors of Time to redesign completely its proposed business combination with Warner, just to keep the decision away from the shareholders.

This is the chronology: Time Inc. and Warner Communications Inc. originally negotiated a stock-for-stock merger in which the shareholders of Time would have the chance to vote whether to exchange their Time shares for new pieces of paper worth about $125 per share. Paramount entered the situation with a cash bid of $175 per Time share, later raised to $200. According to most commentators, Paramount was prepared to raise this sum still further, to $225 a share. Time and Warner, concerned that shareholders would not support their merger, revised their deal so that it would no longer require shareholder approval. When the contest reached the Delaware Supreme Court, the court examined the history of the Time Warner merger as initially proposed, and concluded that because it had been under discussion for more than two years, it was proper to proceed with it, even as radically revised in a very short time, and even in the face of a legitimate alternative.

This approach is consistent in process but not in substance with the factors that the Delaware courts consider in evaluating maneuvers which may be characterized as defensive. It is appropriate to consider the motives of directors to determine whether such actions are taken in good faith, and therefore deserve the broad protection of the business judgment rule. But it is not appropriate to give weight to an action just because it has been considered for a long time. First, it has nothing to do with an obligation to respond to something like the Paramount offer, which could not be predicted. Second, it creates a very perverse incentive for boards to have their lawyers read aloud a list of every possible defensive action and every possible business combination at each board meeting, just to make sure that it is on the record as having considered it, but leaving entirely open the question of whether that consideration has been at all meaningful.

The *Time v. Paramount* case presents a clear question. The court put it this way: "Did Time's board, having developed a strategic plan of global expansion to be launched through a business combination with Warner, come under a fiduciary duty to jettison its plan and put the corporation's future in the hands of its shareholders?"[1] The Delaware courts answered, "No," a result that must be viewed against an offering price of $200 in cash versus a price on August 23, 1990, little more than a year later, of $76$^7/8. When the authors of this book wrote a letter objecting to the deal (reproduced on pages 399–400), Michael Dingman, an outside director of Time, responded. Monks asked Dingman whether he didn't think that there was a problem in giving managers such broad discretion in a deal where their own compensation played such an important role. Mike was characteristically direct: "To put it bluntly, I believe that the directors of Time did an extraordinary job of preventing the shareholders from getting screwed."

In the litigation over the merger, a great deal of financial data was introduced to the court with various extrapolations of projected long-term value. The Warner transaction valued Time stock at $125, compared to the Paramount offer of $200 per share. It is hard to imagine a way that a shareholder could not do better with $200 cash, which he would be free to invest in any venture of his choice, than with a $125 investment in Time Warner, even with the most competent management ever known. How could any fact-finder ignore the simple fact that starting with 60 percent more capital is virtually certain to make more money? What this suggests is that the case is not about money; that the Delaware courts have devised a language to resolve disputes that does not include a vocabulary for maximizing owners' value.

What are owners left with after *Time*? Michael Klein, who argued as special counsel for the Bass Brothers in this case put it: "When the marketplace has put a 25-percent or 30-percent premium on one answer as opposed to another, why should the legal system be constructed so as to deny institutional and other shareholders the opportunity to accept that premium? What's heinous about this case is the manipulation of the corporate machinery by the directors of Time to accomplish an avoidance of the shareholder franchise."[2] In this case, as in *Moran v. Household International*, management deliberately structured the transaction to avoid having to seek shareholder approval. The issue here was not merely the difference between anti-takeover provisions; it was the very essence of the transaction. Time conceived of the deal as providing a capital base which would give it the capacity to be an aggressive worldwide competitor. As the Supreme Court of Delaware found:

> The Time representatives lauded the lack of debt to the United States Senate and to the President of the United States. Public reaction to the announcement of the merger was positive. Time Warner would be a media colossus with international scope.[3]

Following Paramount's initial $175-a-share offer, however:

> [C]ertain Time directors expressed their concern that Time stockholders would not comprehend the long-term benefits of the Warner merger. Large quantities of Time shares were held by institutional investors. The board feared that even though there appeared to be wide support of the Warner transaction, Paramount's cash premium would be a tempting prospect to these investors. In mid-June, Time sought permission from the New York Stock Exchange to alter its rules and allow the Time Warner merger to proceed without shareholder approval. Time did so at Warner's insistence. The New York Stock Exchange rejected Time's request . . .[4]

Thereafter, "Time's board decided to recast its consolidation with Warner into an outright cash and securities acquisition . . . [t]o provide the funds required for its outright acquisition of Warner, Time would assume 7–10 billion dollars worth of debt, thus eliminating one of the principal transaction-related benefits of the original merger agreement."[5] The decision utterly to alter the capital structure of the surviving company to heavy leverage was made in a matter of days and appeared to undercut the purported rationale of the entire transaction.

Furthermore, Time's commitment to the merger with Warner was less than its commitment to making sure Mr. Ross had a fixed retirement date. Negotiations were broken off for several months, until Mr. Ross was induced "to re-evaluate his position and to agree upon a date when he would step down as co-CEO."[6] The agreement reached was that Ross would retire five years after the merger and that Nicholas would then become the sole CEO of Time Warner. (So much for the role of shareholders and boards in selecting management.) The decision finds that "other aspects of the agreement came easily."[7] Despite the evidence about the importance of compensation and succession (these parts of the deal remained as the rest of it was completely restructured), somehow Chancellor Allen found that "there is insufficient basis to suppose at this juncture that such concerns have caused the directors to sacrifice or ignore their duty to seek to maximize in the long run financial returns to the corporation and its stockholders." The concerns he referred to as "corporate culture" seemed to be focused only on compensation.

An enterprise and its equity securities are a function of two components – their businesses and their capitalization. There is an enormous difference between an equity-funded worldwide communications colossus and a debt-ridden venture. That the courts would base a decision on the long-standing plan respecting the businesses and ignore the quickly cobbled together complete change with respect to capitalization suggests that Delaware courts will endorse any action of management, even if self-interested. "Finally, we note that although Time was required, as a result of Paramount's hostile offer, to incur a heavy debt to finance its acquisition of Warner, that fact alone does not render the board's decision unreasonable so long as the directors could reasonably perceive the debt load not to be so injurious to the corporation as to jeopardize its well being."[8] Rarely has the irrelevance of shareholder significance been so clearly articulated. Why pretend that there is such a thing as shareholder rights?

In the lower court decision, the Chancellor stated his position with a double negative: "I am not persuaded that there may not be an instance in which the law might recognize as valid a perceived threat to a 'corporate culture' that is shown to be palpable (for lack of a better word), distinctive and advantageous." Of course there is an instance in which the law recognizes the validity of a "corporate culture." The instance is in the value that corporate culture provides to shareholders. Time shareholders want the company to be able to reap the benefits of its culture, whether alone, or in a productive synergy with another company. But it is difficult for Time to claim that its culture and editorial independence could not have been preserved with Paramount, since they did not even meet with Paramount to discuss it.

Chancellor Allen was correct in saying that "Directors may operate on the theory that the stock market valuation is 'wrong' in some sense without breaching faith with shareholders." But they may only operate on that theory if they base it on fact. Let them demonstrate to the shareholders that they can do better. Without that, we abandon any pretense of a market test, in favor of "expert opinion," paid for by management, usually with a contingent "success factor." Even Chancellor Allen was appalled at the company's estimated valuation of $208–$402 for Time Warner stock in 1993, calling it "a range that a Texan might feel at home on."[9]

In 2001 Time Warner merged with AOL, a company that barely existed at the time of the Time Warner–Paramount battle. Whatever the synergies created by the merger of two old-economy companies, the shareholder value they created was dwarfed by that created by an online newcomer.

*Are there any limits, short of explicit fraud or corruption, to the deference that the court will give to management's determination of value? Is there any level to justify, even require, judicial intervention?*

The obvious reluctance of courts to involve themselves in second-guessing the management of enterprises is understandable, even justifiable. But the result denied owners both the right to vote on the merger of Time with Warner and the right to sell their shares to a willing buyer at a mutually agreeable price.

The Time board did not fulfill in an objective, independent manner its critical role coordinating the restructuring for the benefit of those to whom it owes the most scrupulous fiduciary duty, the shareholders. The court did not object. As Michael Klein pointed out, the Time Warner decision theoretically allows companies to "create a high threshold of risk, and then do everything deliberately to deprive shareholders of any alternative. The Time Warner directors did not even need to confront, evaluate or compare alternatives."[10] The "Revlon mode" (requiring directors to preside over an auction) should be triggered whenever a conflict of interests between shareholders and management arises, because that is the key issue, not some formal notion of whether the company is "for sale." At that point, the board must step back and preside over an orderly evaluation of all alternatives, to decide which will provide the best long-term return for the shareholders.

Within three years, Paramount switched sides, and again found itself losing in the Delaware courts. This time it was Paramount, headed by Martin S. Davis, that wanted to preserve a business combination, over the objections of another would-be bidder. Paramount, a producer and distributor of entertainment, including movies, records, television programs, and books, agreed to a merger with Viacom, an entertainment and communications company whose core businesses include cable networks like MTV and Nickelodeon. Viacom is controlled by Sumner M. Redstone. QVC, a retailer that operates a home-shopping cable channel, run by Barry Diller, sought to acquire Paramount instead.

In announcing the merger, Redstone and Davis made it clear that Paramount was for sale only to Viacom, and other bids were not welcome. Redstone called Diller and John Malone, a large block holder in QVC, to discourage them from making a bid. The agreement with Viacom had several provisions specifically designed to discourage other bidders. One was a $100 million "termination fee" to be paid to Viacom if for some reason the deal would not go through. Another was a stock option agreement that gave Viacom the right to buy 19.9 percent of Paramount's stock for $1 a share in cash and seven-year subordinated notes for the remainder (about $1.6 billion). If triggered, both of these provisions would have a significant adverse impact on the Paramount's value.

Nevertheless, Diller wrote to Davis, proposing that QVC acquire Paramount. Both potential acquirers escalated their offers. The board continued to support the Viacom deal, and QVC and a shareholder group brought the issue to court.

The Delaware Chancery court granted QVC's motion for a preliminary injunction, and sent the issue back to the board. The Delaware Supreme Court agreed. Both found significant differences making it impossible to give the board the broad deference to "business judgment" they granted in the Time Warner case. It is important to remember that the Delaware courts apply different levels of scrutiny to board decisions, based on what is at stake. The most significant factor in the courts' decision to apply a stricter level of review was the fact that the Paramount–Viacom deal was a change of control, not from Paramount management to Viacom management, but from the outside shareholders to inside management. When a group loses control, it is entitled to a control premium. While the Viacom deal had such a premium, it was less than that offered by QVC.

Paramount tried to argue, as Time did successfully in blocking its bid, that the Viacom merger would carry out a pre-existing strategy, afford higher value to long-term holders, and be in the corporation's best long-run interests; therefore they were not obligated to forgo these returns for short-term profit. The Chancery court said, "What is at risk here is the adequacy of the protection of the property interest of shareholders who are involuntarily being made dependent upon the directors to protect that interest. In such circumstances fairness and our law require that the directors' conduct be made subject to the enhanced judicial scrutiny . . ."

When that scrutiny was applied, the court found it was clear the directors had not had sufficient information. The court said the directors had to make their decision based on "a body of reliable evidence." It did not have to be an auction or a market canvass, but it had to be as reliable as those options. The court noted, "Even if the board did not intend to deter bidding (with the lock up and stock option provisions), it had no informed basis upon which to grant an option with these Draconian features . . ."

## Correspondence between Robert A.G. Monks and Time director Mike Dingman

*July 21, 1989*
Dear [Shareholders]:

Delaware's Chancellor William Allen, in his decision to permit the merger of Time and Warner, has not just missed the forest for the trees; he has missed the forest for the bark.

As the Delaware Supreme Court prepares to hear oral argument in the challenge to the *Time* decision he issued last Friday, we wanted to let you know how we see the issues. We believe that Chancellor Allen missed the central issue, which is this: Can we justify a transaction that presents directors with a conflict of interest, by protecting their employment and compensation, but denies shareholders the opportunity to express their views?

As you know, Time and Warner negotiated a stock-for-stock merger in which the shareholders of Time would end up with new pieces of paper worth approximately $125 per share. Paramount entered the situation with a cash bid of $175 per Time share, later raised to $200. Time and Warner, concerned that shareholders would not support their merger, revised their deal so that it would no longer require shareholder approval. The revision also meant that the new company – and its shareholders – would have an enormous debt burden, at least $7 billion of new debt and possibly more than $10 billion. Reported earning will be essentially eliminated, because $9 billion of goodwill will have to be amortized. The equity deal was based on both industrial and financial logic. The debt was justified by the same industrial logic, but there was no longer any financial justification for the deal.

What this means is that Time's management (1) devised and began to put into place a plan that was at least $50–75 per share under the market's evaluation of the stock; (2) refused to meet with Paramount to discuss its offer, and (3) completely restructured the deal, along lines considered and rejected in favor of the original merger, to prevent shareholder involvement. Their utter disregard for the rights of shareholders was demonstrated even further by the line of succession they locked in for directing the company. This is one of the most important rights reserved to shareholders. All of this was permitted by Chancellor Allen's decision.

He also concluded that because the merger had been under discussion for more than two years, it was proper to proceed with it. But the deal he allowed to go forward was not the one they designed during that period of deliberation; it was one they rejected and then put together quickly to obstruct Paramount. Furthermore, the original deal was developed without reference to Paramount's offer. At the very least, that offer should have forced the board to determine why it was so much higher than the share value realized in their merger. Chancellor Allen said, in one of a series of double negatives, "I am not persuaded that there may not be instances in which the law might recognize as valid a perceived threat to a 'corporate culture' that is shown to be palpable (for a lack of a better word), distinctive, and advantageous." The facts suggest that it was not the "corporate culture" that Time management was planning to preserve but the extremely favorable employment and compensation schemes they had negotiated with Warner. Chancellor Allen notes that the "Time culture" issue was of concern in setting the compensation for Time executives, but that this was resolved by paying them at a higher level, though still on the same basis, rather than revising it along the formula used at Warner.

The Time board has not fulfilled its critical role in coordinating the restructuring in an objective, independent manner, for the benefit of those to whom it owes the most scrupulous fiduciary duty, the shareholders. The court has not objected. The issue is the same one as that presented by management buyouts, a question of conflict of interests. The "Revlon mode" should be triggered whenever such a conflict arises, because that is the key issue, not some formal notion of whether the company is "for sale." At that point, the board must step back and preside over an orderly evaluation of all alternatives to decide which will provide the best long-term return for the shareholders.

When directors, due to the impact various alternatives will have on their compensation and employment, have a conflict of interest that prevents their fulfilling their obligation as fiduciaries to protect the interests of the shareholders, then the decision should be made by the shareholders. That is the critical issue ignored by the court. We hope that the Supreme Court will reverse this decision. If not, shareholders have the choice of seeking legislative change, either in Delaware or at the federal level, or using their ownership rights to reincorporate the companies they hold in states with more respect for the interests of shareholders.

We will continue to keep you posted. In the meantime, if you have any comments or questions, please do not hesitate to call.

Sincerely,

R.A.G. Monks

*August 15, 1989*
Dear Bob,

Your letter of July 21st has been brought to my attention.

As you know, when it comes to shareholder value, I've believed, espoused, and supported many of the same things as you. In fact, in cases like Santa Fe, I've earned a reputation as an opponent of poison pills and entrenched management. But with the Time Warner merger, we part company. In the main, I find your opinions to be ill-informed and off target.

Paramount's highly conditional offer of $175 or $200 per share was not only ludicrously low but transparently cynical. In making it, Mr. Davis [Chairman and CEO of Paramount Communications Inc.] had two motives. The first was tactical. He wanted to sabotage Time Inc.'s carefully considered merger with Warner and thereby destroy or weaken a competitor that would dwarf his own newly created media/entertainment company. The second was opportunistic. If his public relations campaign succeeded, Mr. Davis saw a chance to panic the board into letting him pick up Time Inc. for a song.

He wasn't that lucky. Unlike the role played by Paramount's board in ratifying the tender offer to Time Inc., we weren't about to rubber-stamp a managerial *fait accompli*. That's not the way the Time board works. We had been looking at the merger with Warner for over two years and had considered the long-range payoff for shareholders, as well as the strategic and financial implications.

In the media coverage surrounding Paramount's tender offer, it was the universal consensus that the Time board was composed of eight outside directors with reputations as hard-nosed individualists, men and women equally unwilling to do the bidding of either Time Inc.'s management or Mr. Davis. In this, at least, the media were on the money.

As a participant in the board's deliberations, I was a witness to the demanding independence of the other seven outside directors. They lived up to their reputations as mavericks, asking all the tough questions and looking without sentiment or illusion at the offers on the table. In the end, all of us, without a single dissent, voted to proceed with the Time Warner deal.

I have no regrets about that decision. *None*. We've created the strongest and potentially most profitable media/entertainment company in the world. And if Mr. Davis succeeded in changing the terms of the original deal, nothing he said or did changed its rationale. It remains an extraordinary opportunity to improve dramatically the value of Time Inc. stock.

Frankly, I find it more ridiculous than insulting for you to accuse me and the other outside directors of a "conflict of interest." No one − not even Paramount's lawyers − raised this as an issue. In fact, if you really think I'm worried about my "employment" [*sic*] as a Time director or depend in any way on the compensation it entails, then you are probably beyond the reach of rational argument.

The ultimate outcome of the Time Warner situation will be decided in the near future as the managements come together to build what they set out to. Despite whatever speculative losses some investors may have incurred in betting on Paramount's bid, I do hope you and others try to make an honest appraisal of the values represented by this new company.

There's no question in my mind that the eventual outcome will resemble what happened at Disney after Saul Steinberg was paid his greenmail of $19.25 per share. Michael Eisner and his management team left the employ of Martin Davis and Paramount and brought a whole new energy and direction to Disney. At some point you may wish to examine for yourself why Eisner and other creative managers left Paramount, but this much is already certain: They have revived the company's fortunes. Disney stock is now selling at $120 per share.

Dick Munro, Steve Ross, and Nick Nicholas have proven records of attracting and holding the best talent in the media/entertainment business. They have shown that they can create substantial value for shareholders, and now that the fight with Paramount is over, they will make an immense success out of their new venture.

I don't mean to oversimplify all the issues that surrounded the Time Warner deal. It was a complex transaction that required some very tough judgments. And, in my opinion, the press did such a miserable job of covering the facts and issues involved that I can't really blame you and your colleagues − never mind the ordinary shareholder − for being confused.

To put it bluntly, I believe the directors of Time did an extraordinary job of preventing the shareholders from getting screwed. And except for a few major shareholders like Capital Research − who understood the real values at stake and stood by their beliefs − they did it alone.

I look forward to seeing you in the future and discussing this at greater length. In the meantime, I felt it necessary to express my personal opinion concerning your previous letters.

Sincerely,

Mike Dingman

*August 23, 1989*
Dear Mike,

I very much appreciate your thoughtful response of August 15, to my letter about the Time/Warner decision issued by Chancellor Allen, and since then upheld by the Delaware Supreme Court. Although you described my "opinions to be ill-informed and off target", I think we agree more than we disagree. I can support many of the points you made, and still think that the courts (and the board of Time) were wrong to disregard the rights of the shareholders. And I suspect that both of our positions lead to the same ultimate diagnosis, even the same solution.

I agree with you that the directors of corporations should have the power to consummate mergers; however this must be done in a way that recognizes the clear conflicts of interest that exist for top management in such situations. Even though it imposes an additional burden on the "outside" director, I see no alternative to their taking over the merger process, much in the same way and for the same reason that they have been required by this same Delaware court to take over the "auction" process, as in RJR and McMillan. The chief advantage of outside directors is that they can bring some objectivity and discipline to the process. (I agree with your characterization of the Time Board. Indeed, I have frequently cited *your* involvement as conclusive evidence that the problem is systemic and not personal.)

Here is where I think we disagree. To my way of thinking there is a world of difference between "outside" and "inside" directors. The Time Board apparently chose to conduct the merger (acquisition) negotiations without limiting the participation of the "inside" directors. That the "outside" acquiesced in and supported direction of the transactions by "insiders" – and not that I am "beyond the reach of rational argument" – is why I refer to a conflict of interest by the Board.

Corporate reorganizations ultimately devolve into a question of who gets how much. There is no objective standard – no Mosaic decalogue – that proscribes how much shareholders, how much management and how much of the total consideration should be allocated to other corporate constituencies. When, as I am sure you will agree was the case with Time, the consideration to be paid the principal executives is not immaterial, isn't it better practice to limit their role in leading the negotiations? Should anybody be in the position of being the ultimate arbiter of their own entitlement? Should those with the largest personal stake continue to select and direct the professional advisers and thus the information reaching the Board? I think of the transaction as one where the top management took the top dollar for themselves, whether or not it was in the long-term best interest of the company and the shareholders as parties whose interest is far more genuinely long term than that of the people who put this transaction together.

Let's look at the transaction for a moment. It is ironic that the original proposal required shareholder approval, under the rules of the New York Stock Exchange, while the revised plan, far worse from the shareholders' perspective because of the debt burden, did not. Time was easily able to take the choice away from the shareholders, by redesigning the deal to make it much worse for them, and the shareholders did not have any way to get it back.

The court gave great deference to the fact that the merger with Warner was negotiated over a period of two years. However, the business combination that was actually executed was put together in days, in response to the Paramount offer, on terms that were explicitly considered and rejected during that two-year period of deliberation, terms that left the company with a gigantic burden of debt. The fact that the record showed compensation and succession of the top management to be the most contentious issues (apparently the only contentious issues) did not suggest to the court that perhaps self-interest might have been the primary factor in setting the terms of the merger. It does suggest it to me.

You could very well be right that the merger between Time and Warner makes more sense than a merger between Time and Paramount. The question is who makes that decision. You suggest that it should not be shareholders, because they are uninformed and only look to the short term. I suggest that it should not be top management, acting without meaningful accountability, because they have a fundamental conflict of interest. I have the same problem with MBOs. There simply cannot be a level playing field when one party has all of the resources and all of the information. In this case, Time's management also had all of the power.

I do not think that institutional shareholders are irretrievably short term in their orientation. If they take short-term gains, they then have to find another place to invest them, and that is a real problem. Furthermore, most institutions have highly diversified portfolios, with major investments in thousands of companies. Many of our clients were investors not only in Time, but also in Warner and Paramount, not only in stocks, but also in bonds. They must look to the net impact of any proposed transaction, as fiduciaries and as prudent investors. This militates against a short-term orientation.

I agree that the institutional shareholders have a way to go before they can persuade those, like you, who are convinced that they look no further than the quarterly returns. In this regard, it is important to note the escalating portion of institutional investments that today are *de facto* or *de jure* indexed. Over the last few years, the index funds have performed better than the managed funds, which makes them hard for any "prudent and diligent" asset manager to ignore. I am enclosing testimony that I gave earlier in the year before the Markey subcommittee, where I recommended that indexed investments be deemed *per se* prudent under ERISA. It is essential to take some step to encourage (possibly, even, to ensure) that the largest class of institutional investor — one for whom liquidity serves no private or public objective — to be a genuine "long-term" holder and source of "patient capital," and, therefore, begin to function as a permanent shareholder. I recognize that a gap exists today between my desired world of a solid core of long term institutional shareholders and the arbitrageur driven world of contemporary takeovers.

If the arbs were the only institutions, I would find it difficult to argue that a governance system be organized for their benefit; on the other hand, I see no reason to disqualify ownership as the fundamental object of governance just because arbs are involved. No one has suggested that newly elected CEOs have any the less authority because of the brevity of their tenure, nor are directors required to serve an apprenticeship period.

I suggest that to the extent that the institutions have a short-term orientation, it is in large part attributable to the failure of the governance system. If you were an investment manager with a large holding in Time, your alternatives would be quite limited, even under the terms of the original deal with Warner. But if you had a real voice, a real relationship with management based on real accountability, to give you confidence in the long term, there would be no incentive to go for a short-term gain.

Under the current system, managers and boards and shareholders face real impediments to making the best long-term decisions on these issues. But the obstacles to shareholders can be removed, while the essential conflicts presented to managers and boards will always be there. As Professor Roberta Romano has noted, "We focus on enhancing shareholder value because when looking at a corporation, it is difficult to conceive of who else's interests would be appropriate for determining the efficient allocation of resources in the economy." That is why it makes more sense to entrust these decisions to shareholders than to the people whose employment and income is at stake.

I am not at all convinced that the Delaware Courts consider these issues fairly. (You and I have been in agreement on this point in times past!) I am certain that the "Delaware interest" factor played an important role in the Time decision, as it did in Polaroid and many others. Delaware risks losing its title as champion of the race to the bottom. The Pillsbury and McMillan decisions led to Marty Lipton's call to reincorporate elsewhere, and the Supreme Court's CTS decision gave the domicile states' authority a boost. Pennsylvania and other states are moving quickly to pass laws even more accommodating than Delaware's, with the "stakeholder" laws the latest fad.[11] I testified before the Delaware state legislature, arguing against adoption of the anti-takeover law, along with every other shareholder representative. When the parade of CEOs came in, saying that they sure would hate to have to reincorporate elsewhere, it was no contest.

In order to protect Delaware's economic interest in accommodating the Fortune 500, the courts have created a special language of takeovers that has no base in law or economics, and they make that language go through all kinds of acrobatics to make precedent appear to apply. This gives us the "Revlon" and "Unocal" modes. And it gives us the contortions that Chancellor Allen went through to keep Time out of those modes.

Another element of Delaware's special language is the "business judgment" rule. Certainly, managements need and deserve the widest indulgence of courts in deferring to their "business judgment." No one thinks that they should second-guess these decisions. But the courts should be there to make sure there is a process in place that promotes fair treatment – or at least one that does not impede it. Shareholders deserve a level playing field, too. The original Time/Warner proposed transaction can and should be supported. This represents a determination by management that ownership values can be maximized within the framework of a merger company, virtually debt free, that can be the aggressive competitor in a multinational world. The Time management has made three judgments for its owners: (i) the business of Time can best be carried out in tandem with Warner; (ii) the merged businesses can best be conducted with a solid equity base, permitting capital investment and acquisitions on a global basis; and (iii) that this merger is the best way to bridge the "value gap" for Time shareholders. At this point, the Paramount offer gave some public indication of the exact size of the "value gap." Paramount offered $200 per share and was willing to offer more; Time management dismissed this as inadequate notwithstanding that the market valued common stock in its proposed merger at $120 per share. Time then decided to buy Warner. While this preserved the face of the "business logic" of the merger, clearly a debt-encumbered survivor is not going to be able to pursue the course of multinational aggressive dominance that was the apparent keystone of the original merger. Management thus has turned 180 degrees from an equity-heavy company to one drowning in debt.

Should there not be some common sense limit to the extent of deference paid to "business judgment" when deference is paid to a business strategy based on all equity and then it is paid again to a strategy based on all debt? Conceivably, one of these is correct. Both cannot be, and yet deference is paid to both. And, can the courts ignore arithmetic? How many years, and at what implicit rate of return, does a holder of Time common have to wait until his stock will achieve the levels that Paramount offered in 1989 in cash? Should there be any limit to this, or should deference extend indefinitely? Chancellor Allen conjures up only the most unsatisfactory "red herring" of limits based on fraud.

What is to be done? The Time/Warner decisions represents a real failure of the system of governance. America cannot simply give over the assets and power of the private corporate system to managers who are not meaningfully accountable to anyone. I personally have little appetite for the federalization of corporate law, and yet I recognize that "Delaware interest" decisions like Time/Warner will tend to make federal pre-emption more appealing.

What I have been interested in for the past several years is fortuity of large fiduciary ownership. What seems to me to be a beginning point is to require that institutional owners act as such; that those with long-term interests be required to be long-term investors; that we stop regulating institutional fiduciaries in the interest of service providers and that we elevate the interests of the beneficiaries, who constitute an adequate proxy for the national interest.

Of one thing do I feel certain, had Michael Dingman been a large shareholder of Time, the transaction would not have been consummated without the meaningful involvement of owners.

I look forward very much to the opportunity to spend a few hours together to talk of this and so many other things of mutual interest.

With respect,
Your Friend,

R.A.G. Monks

*August 31, 1989*
Dear Bob,

Thank you for your letter of August 23, 1989. If we keep this up, we'll be able to publish a book – *The Monks–Dingman Correspondence!*

You're right. We agree on more than we disagree. But not on everything. For example, you believe that once a corporate merger comes under consideration, management and the inside directors should at some point turn the process over to the outside directors. (In your words, "Even though it imposes an additional burden on the 'outside' director, I see no alternative to their taking over the merger process . . .") Then, at some later point – again unspecified – the outside directors should step aside and let the shareholders decide.

I believe this would turn corporate governance into a muddle. More to the point, it has little bearing on the case of the Time Warner merger. The outside directors were in charge. Every step was reviewed and approved by us, and we weren't the empty vessels you seem to believe we were, filled with whatever ideas and information management cared to pour in our ears. We challenged management every step of the way. We asked the kind of questions that we would ask of our own employees, and we didn't settle for stock answers. In the end, we agreed that the merger was a magnificent opportunity that should be pursued.

You use the word "acquiesce," i.e. "to accept quietly or passively." We did a lot of things in the unfolding of the merger. Argued. Probed. Questioned. Inquired. Cross-examined. It went on and on until we were satisfied. But we never acquiesced.

One final thing. The central issue in the Time Warner deal was neither debt, nor compensation. Paramount would have loaded on more debt than Time's acquisition of Warner, and provided a far less significant cash flow with which to service it. And Michael Eisner and Frank Wells were offered an extraordinary package by Disney, and they've proved themselves worth every dime. If Steve Ross can deliver the same return to Time Warner that he has for Warner, a company he built from scratch, his compensation will be more than justified.

The board wanted to build Time Inc. so it could provide the very best return for shareholders. I think we did.

You raise a number of interesting points in your letter and, if I had the time, I'd like to look at them all. But I don't. The reality of creating shareholder value doesn't leave much space for dwelling on theories. Sometime in the future, when we can manage it, I look forward to sitting down and discussing the whole matter of Time Warner, as well as its wider implications. I hope that we'll both learn something.

There is one thing I am absolutely against and that is the federalization of corporations and/or the establishment of more government rules concerning how businesses, managements, shareholders, *et al.* interact. I hope we agree on this point as well, and please stay away from Mr. Metzenbaum.

Again, thank you for your thoughtful response to my letter.

Sincerely,

Mike

## NOTES

1. *Paramount v. Time*, 571 A.2d 1140, 1149, 1150 (Del. Sup. 1990).
2. *Directors & Boards*, 14, 2, Winter 1990, p. 35.
3. *Paramount v. Time*, p. 1147.
4. Ibid., p. 1148.
5. Ibid.
6. Fed. Sec. Law Reporter, pp. 94, 514, 93, 269.
7. Ibid., pp. 93, 269.
8. *Paramount v. Time*, 571 A.2d 1140, 1155.
9. Fed. Sec. Law Reporter, pp. 93, 273.
10. Interview with Michael Klein, July 6, 1990.
11. This is a standard to which one cannot be held accountable. He who is responsible to many, is responsible to none.

# Sears, Roebuck & Co.

Sears, Roebuck & Company is one of the great success stories in American commerce. The company had its roots in 1886 when Richard Sears started selling watches in rural areas. Later, he developed the idea of selling goods by mail order, taking a host of new products to populations cut off from big city stores. The famous Sears catalog became a byword for Sears' reliability and quality. In the 1920s, the company began opening stores to back up the catalog business. The stores proved every bit as successful.

By the 1950s, you could buy a prefabricated house from Sears, not to mention clothes for your family and a kitchen table for them to eat at. Single-handedly, the company set out to raise the standard of living of the great American middle class.

By the 1970s, Sears accounted for a whole 1 percent of the gross national product. Two in three Americans shopped at Sears within any three months of 1972. Almost 900 stores covered the American continent.[1]

## DIVERSIFICATION STRATEGY: THE FATE OF RETAIL

In the early 1980s, Sears built on the success of its insurance subsidiary, Allstate, by adding real estate and brokerage services as well – Coldwell Banker and Dean Witter, both purchased in 1981. This diversification was the brainchild of CEO Ed Telling and was initially successful. From 1984 to 1990 the earnings of the financial side improved 55 percent. But nobody was minding the store. The vast chain of over 850 outlets, the flagship division of the Sears, Roebuck empire, was failing fast. In the seven years up to 1990 the retail group's earnings declined at an annual rate of 7.7 percent. By the late 1980s, Sears was set to lose its century-old position as the largest American retailer. The decline was reflected in the stock which, between January 1984 and November 1990, offered investors a total average return of as little as 0.1 percent.[2]

This lethargy was in part a function of the corporate culture at Sears. Its style was inward-looking and change-resistant; in many ways, that had been Sears' strength. Consumers liked the consistency and reliability of its products and employees liked the commitment to promotion from the inside. Sears' rock-steady reputation allowed the company the ability to weather most economic downturns. Sears had always been a shopping chain that people could trust; a place selling quality goods at reasonable prices, all under one roof. It became more than just a store. It was a venerable American institution, and Sears rightly traded on that reputation.

But Sears' venerability became a liability when it failed to respond to changing times. Retail changed dramatically, and the ancient, lumbering Sears was last in the race for the new markets. Trendy national chains like The Gap or The Limited captured a vast market of people wanting reasonably priced clothes that look stylish. Wal-Mart and K-Mart attracted people who liked their clothes cheap. Specialty stores undercut Sears on almost every other front. People who wanted a hi-fi ten years earlier might have gone to Sears knowing that they would find one of good quality at a reasonable price; now they would probably go to Circuit City knowing they could find the same model cheaper.

Sears has a dated image. Joe Cappo described a New York store in *Crain's Chicago Business*: "It was like being time-warped 30–40 years back into history. This wasn't a store. It was the Metropolitan Museum of Outdated Kitsch. Remember the ugly lamp your grandmother had in her parlor? Sears still has that lamp."[3] Another shopper said: "I still think of it as a place where you go to buy a ladies Size 18," and *USA Today* asked: "Will anyone believe Sears stands for fashion as well as bowling balls?"[4] Lean and efficient discounters like Wal-Mart and K-Mart were catching up and were soon to overtake Sears' sales volume. Sears was stuck with locations and properties that were selected years before; newer competition could create stores for today's market. Sears had always boasted that it was the place where America shopped, the definition of solid middle-class values, the purveyor of the American dream. According to *Crain's Chicago Business*: "If Sears is ever to turn the tide of the last decade, it will need new thinking and new people. This doesn't mean Sears is a bad company. In fact, it is a very good, solid 1950s company. And it will need something better than 1950s thinking to move it into the 1990s."[5] But with the money from the financial divisions coming in, it was easy to ignore the tumbling profits and shrinking markets.

Edward Brennan, the corporation's chairman, CEO, and chief executive of the retail division was an undeniably capable man. He had led the retail division in the early 1980s and made a brilliant job of it. He was the man behind the "Store of the Future" that made a successful early attack against Sears' competitors. He became CEO in 1984. But it was under his tenure that, somehow, the Store of the Future had become the Store of the Past in the minds of so many Americans. Brennan was a "Searsman" to his marrow. He had worked in retail all his life, and at Sears since he was 26. His father, mother, brother, uncle all worked at Sears. Brennan was dressed only in Sears clothes for the first ten years of his life. He had never owned a pair of jeans because his father was a dress-slacks buyer. According to Donald R. Katz in *The Big Store*, "No one in Ed Brennan's family ever managed to leave Sears . . . the Brennans ranked among those special families so bred to the romance of the place that it was hard to tell company and family apart. Even by Sears, Roebuck's unusually emotional standards, Eddie Brennan took it all quite personally."[6] Carol Farmer, a retail consultant from Chicago said: "The trouble with Ed Brennan is that he's in love with Sears the institution. And it's the institution that needs to be debunked."[7]

The problem was obvious; the cure, less so. In November 1988, CEO Ed Brennan launched a new strategic plan to revive the ailing merchandise division. The plan was the product of "an intensive strategic examination of our corporation" that would usher in "a period of unprecedented growth." Sears committed itself to "everyday low prices" in an effort to compete with thriving discount stores, and launched "power formats" to sell brand-names alongside Sears' traditional house labels. The board also voted to spend $1.6 billion buying back Sears stock and resolved to sell the Sears Tower, the tallest building in the world, much touted as a symbol of pre-eminence, but considered by critics to be just the company's largest white elephant.

Wall Street was disappointed by this strategy. Many observers had hoped for much more. Sears' stock had risen on the back of a hope that a major restructuring was in the pipeline. Analysts predicted that Sears, Roebuck stock could possibly double in value if the successful financial divisions were spun off and management's resources and energy were devoted to making the retail operation efficient. Analysts thought it was misguided to use the money raised from selling valuable assets to buy back shares rather than build up business. "From the point of view of gaining long-term strategic advantage," said Louis W. Stern of Kellogg Business School, "it's madness."[8] One analyst predicted that the changes would not satisfy the increasingly hostile shareholders: "Institutional investors will be disappointed by today's announcement," said Robert Raiff the Sears analyst at C.J. Lawrence & Co. "They were expecting more and I hope they get more."[9] Others were dismayed by the failure of merger talks with Montgomery Ward, run by Brennan's brother.

Despite the criticism, the corporation went ahead with its restructuring. But, in two years, this strategy failed to stimulate business. The competitive pricing policy failed to halt the sweeping invasion of Sears' retail markets by discounters and the "power formats" campaign had resulted in only Brand Central being rolled out to all stores. Meanwhile, the cash generated by the financial divisions of the company – Dean Witter, Allstate and Coldwell Banker – were used to buttress the corporation's flagging fortunes. The retail division continued to wilt; Wal-Mart and K-Mart continued to catch up.

From 1984 to 1990 Sears had a total annual return, including dividends, of a mere 0.7 percent. For ten years in a row, the company promised a 15 percent return on equity, and for ten years in a row it failed to deliver. And things were looking worse: 1990 was a disastrous year for the company with earnings and stock prices at 1983 levels, a return on equity of 6.8 percent, and a loss in the first nine months of $119 million.

## *Where was the board?*

What about the board of directors? A board, after all, is responsible for overseeing the overall strategic direction of the company. If Brennan's program continued to fail in its bid to raise sales; if Wall Street continued to advise more fundamental treatment for the problem; if Sears' stock continued to sag at somewhere under half its intrinsic value; if the financial services continued to have their profits swamped by retail's losses; if Sears' reputation continued to sink under the weight of accusations that it was out of date – shouldn't the board do something? In theory, of course, the answer is "yes." At Sears, in practice, the answer was silence. Like management, the board of Sears had grown up as an inward-looking, self-perpetuating dynasty.

Another extract from *The Big Store* details how board meetings worked a decade earlier under Telling. The view expressed is that of Charlie Bacon, a senior manager in the Merchant division:

> Charlie believed that the board of directors under Telling had become one of the least animated decision-making bodies imaginable. He knew that reports to the board were all checked over by [chief financial officer] Dick Jones, and scripts were so rigidly followed that no deviation from approved texts was tolerated . . . The outsiders on the Sears board were by and large people who owned few shares of Sears stock and who collected $40,000 a year for attending occasional meetings. What they knew of the company came largely from the company.[10]

## *Shareholder unrest*

In July 1990, the first rumblings of the coming shareholder storm were heard. At a breakfast meeting with Sears, Roebuck's largest 12 investors, Ed Brennan and retail chief Michael Bozic gave an upbeat assessment of the corporation's plans. Investors exploded. They cited a grim share performance – value had dropped 15 points since 1989 – and gave Brennan one year to achieve marked improvement in retail, or look for another job. Russell Thompson, a money manager with Waddell & Reed, who was present at the meeting, said: "We told them 'somebody could raise $25 billion and easily take you guys out tomorrow.' "[11] Or, in the words of one board member, Albert Casey: "It was time to fish or cut bait."[12]

Brennan's first step was to take control. Michael Bozic lost his job as head of the retail division and was replaced by Brennan himself. The CEO then committed himself to an acceleration of the power-formats campaign, and to a savage, across-the-board cost-cutting program. Brennan announced that 21,000 jobs would be pared within the year, and numerous stores were closed or remodeled. In interviews with the press, Brennan got tough; no part of the Sears empire was safe. "If it doesn't pay its way, it goes," he said, raising the possibility that the century-old catalog business could come under the knife.[13]

But, as with the 1988 announcements, Brennan found that few people were convinced. In early December, the California Public Employees Retirement System, holder of 2.2 million shares, voiced its concern about Sears' performance, citing depressed stock and the failure of retailing strategies. The message, said CalPERS then chief Dale Hanson, was simple: "From 1984 on, Sears went to hell in a handbag."[14] In an open letter to Brennan, Hanson proposed the creation of a shareholders' advisory group. Such a group would give the board non-binding advice on matters such as major restructurings, acquisitions, mergers, and executive compensation. Hanson hinted that he favored a major restructuring, thus joining the growing school of thought that argued that Sears' value could only be realized when the successful financial divisions were spun off from the plunging retail division.

In February 1991, some four months after launching the idea of a shareholder advisory group, CalPERS agreed not to press for its creation at the May annual meeting on condition that Sears executives meet with CalPERS at least twice a year. But performance continued to decline, and investors continued to seethe. Fourth-quarter earnings revealed in early February showed a 37 percent decline in earnings, before a $155 million charge for the retail division restructure. Including the charge, earnings declined 74 percent.

Public confidence in Sears hit a new low. Business leaders surveyed by *Fortune* magazine rated Sears at 487th out of 500 companies for the reputation of their management. Wall Street analysts said that Sears required $1 billion in cuts to make it competitive, substantially more than the $600 million that Brennan said the cost-cutting program would achieve. Standard & Poors reduced its credit rating on Sears to single A. *Asset Analysis Focus* commented that: "Sears, Roebuck & Co. has one of the greatest price to intrinsic value disparities of any large publicly traded company."[15] In February 1991, Sears traded at between $25 and $30 a share, while analysts speculated it had a breakup value of up to $90 a share.[16]

George Regan of the Teacher Retirement Fund of Texas said: "Obviously whatever management is doing isn't working. Either you can change the management or you can change the system. And sometimes the only choice is to change the management."[17] *Business Week* speculated that "a power shift may be in the works" and that P.J. Purcell, chief of Dean Witter, might be poised to take over.[18]

In May of 1991, Robert A.G. Monks (co-author of this book) stepped in. He engaged in a proxy contest for one seat on the board of a public company, something no one had ever done before at any company. And his target was Sears.

Monks had submitted his name to the board the previous fall, along with the names and numbers of six CEOs on whose boards he had served, as references. The directors did not discuss his candidacy at the November meeting, they said, because they did not have enough information, though at no time did they contact the references provided. They did discuss his candidacy at the February meeting. It wasn't that they used the extra time to gather more information; they didn't. They explained later that they decided that additional information was not necessary since Monks' record, already well known to them, clearly qualified him for the job.

The board turned him down. However, Sears' own bylaws provide that a shareholder may nominate a candidate for the board. Apparently, the corporate leaders think this is a fine system, as long as no one tries to use it. Monks was nominated by an old friend, also a Sears shareholder, and he sought election as a dissident candidate.

Monks had been looking for a company that would allow him to raise some of his general concerns about corporate governance and corporate performance. Sears met all of his criteria. First, the issues were suitable for shareholder involvement: they concerned the overall structure and direction of the company. Second, the obstacles to realizing shareholder value were those that could be addressed by shareholder activism. Third, success was achievable: the level of institutional ownership, the vacancy on the board due to the retirement of a director, and the cumulative voting in director elections made it possible to be elected with only 16 percent of the vote, with five seats up for election. Monks wrote about their response to his decision:

> It threw Sears into such a tizzy that they hired [renowned takeover lawyer] Marty Lipton, brought a lawsuit to stop me and budgeted $5.5 million dollars over and above Sears' usual solicitation expenses, just to defeat me (as *Crain's Chicago Business* pointed out, one out of every seven dollars made by the retail operation last year). Sears also assigned 30 of its employees to spend their time working to defeat my candidacy.
>
> The real outrage was that they got rid of three of their own directors, just to prevent me from winning one seat, what I refer to as "Honey, I Shrunk the Board."[19] With cumulative voting and five directors up for election, I could get a seat with only 16 percent of the vote, not impossible for someone with strong connections to large institutional holders. But Sears shrunk its board by eliminating three director seats, which meant that I needed 21 percent of the vote to win a seat; virtually impossible to obtain, because 25 percent of the vote was held by Sears employees (and voted by Sears trustees) and the rest was held by individuals that it was impossible for me to solicit, without spending millions of dollars. The myth is that the officers of the company report to the board. The reality is that the board reports to the CEO, at least at Sears. When the CEO (who is also Chairman of the Board and head of the board's nominating committee) tells three directors they are off, they are off, especially, as in this case, when they are inside directors, full-time employees of the corporation.

Jay Lorsch, Harvard Business School professor and expert on boards of directors, wrote in the *New York Times*: "This bothers me. I like to see American managers take boards seriously and use them as a check and balance against the abuse of management. When you play with boards in this way, you undermine their legitimacy."[20]

*Crain's Chicago Business* cited Sears' "abysmal performance" and criticized Brennan for having "led the company's flagship retail division down one strategic dead end after another."

The newspaper fully praised Monks' attempt to let some fresh air into the Sears board-room: "Sears is scared and with good reason. For years, its shareholders have been lapdogs. Now they're showing some teeth . . . Why doesn't Mr. Brennan let his record speak for itself? Then again, maybe that's what he's afraid of."[21] *Pension and Investments* ran an article criticizing both Chrysler (which shrank its board to get rid of a genuinely independent outsider) and Sears for shrinking its board to keep out Monks: "The moves were virtually admissions by the two companies that they prefer to maintain tame boards that will go along with whims and wishes of strong chief executives. Given the poor performance of both companies the desire for tame boards is understandable. And nothing so demonstrates the need for more independent voices on each board as their board's acquiescence in these moves."[22] Monks wrote:

> There was never any question about who had more money. Sears spent half of what it budgeted, and still outspent me 10 to 1. Sears brought suit against me to prevent me from getting a shareholder list, claiming I wanted it for an "improper purpose." The "improper purpose" they alleged was promoting my new book. I would have to be Kitty Kelley to make enough money on a book to pay for a proxy contest, but I would have to be Sears in order to finance both a proxy contest and a lawsuit to make that point. So the lawsuit effectively stopped me from communicating with smaller shareholders. Even if it had not, though, the expense would probably have been prohibitive.
>
> Following approval and mailing of their proxy statement, Sears was free to have press conferences and to comment to the press on my candidacy, including mischaracterizations of my positions, but I was not permitted to respond. The weird world of SEC regulation prevented me from making any public statement for two crucial weeks, because of the risk that some shareholder might see my remarks before the SEC had approved my solicitation materials. [Note: this rule was later changed, partly as the result of Monks' situation.] This problem persisted right up to the annual meeting, as I could not afford the roughly $1.5 million necessary to send the approved material to every shareholder.
>
> It was not my intention to displace anyone. One of the reasons I picked Sears was that there was an opening on the board, with the retirement of former CEO Edward Telling. Therefore, I wanted to put the Sears candidates on my proxy card, so that a shareholder who did not want to cumulate votes could vote for me and for two of the incumbent directors. SEC rules do not allow that. [Note: this rule was also later changed, as a result of Monks' situation.] If there had not been cumulative voting, this would have been an even more devastating blow, as a fiduciary voting proxies would have to throw away two votes to give me one.

It was on this basis alone that Monks lost substantial votes. One of the other candidates, a black woman university professor, had a good deal of support from investors who were unwilling to throw away two of their votes to give one to Monks. Monks also lost votes from institutional investors who had (or hoped to have) commercial relationships with the company and felt pressured to vote with management. And he lost the votes of at least one long-time supporter in the institutional investor community because a proxy contest for one board seat was not covered by their proxy guidelines, and the bureaucracy did not provide for a timely way to develop new ones. Monks continued:

> But perhaps the biggest frustration was that I could not reach the largest group of shareholders, Sears' own employees. Sears offered to mail my materials to them, if I would pay $300,000 in costs (more than my entire budget for the solicitation). But more serious was that the trustees (four out of five of whom were past and present members

of the Sears board) would have voted the stock without even considering my candidacy, if not for the intervention of the Labor Department. That resulted in a pro forma meeting with the trustees, who proceeded to vote for their board colleagues. Many Sears employees called me to say that they were unable to get any information about my candidacy, or that they wanted their stock voted for me, but could not direct it. Sears refused my request for confidential voting, which would at least have allowed employees who held stock in their own names to vote for me without fear of reprisal.

In theory, of course, the directors are there to represent the shareholders, evaluate the performance of the chief executive officer (CEO), and oversee the overall direction of the company. If they have one obligation, it seems to me, it is to ask hard questions. But the current rules not only fail to ensure that directors ask questions, they prevent others from asking them as well.

Let's look at Sears. Edward Brennan holds four different jobs. He is CEO of the company as a whole, chairman of the board, and head of the company's flagship division, the retail operation. Part of the job description for those jobs is that the people in them are supposed to communicate with each other, measure each other, ask questions of each other. One person simply can't do them all. On top of that, Brennan is head of the board's nominating committee. He gets to pick his own bosses, and, as my experience shows, when he is faced with someone he didn't pick, he brought all of the corporate resources to bear to stop me.

Where was the board in all of this? The answer lies in another question – Who are the directors? "Independent director" is something of an oxymoron in today's companies. The directors are selected by the CEO. The candidates run unopposed, and management counts the votes. In the rare case of an opposing slate, management gets to use the shareholders' money to pay for their side of the contest, without regard for the interests of shareholders, while the dissidents must use their own. The CEO determines the directors' pay, and the directors set the CEO's pay. It's a very cozy relationship, and one that has been most profitable for both parties, as CEO pay and director pay have skyrocketed over the past decade, at many times the rate of increase in pay for employees. This system does not promote accountability, or even the questions that are a necessary predicate for a climate of accountability.

At the annual meeting, after the votes were cast, I said that Sears had changed, as a result of my contest. Brennan said, "Baloney." Time will tell. But I can think of three important changes already. First, my arguments about the ability of Sears' investment banker to give an objective opinion about the value of remaining a conglomerate led to the disclosure that Goldman Sachs had indeed advised them that they could realize more value – as much as three times more – by spinning off the other entities. This may not have changed Sears – yet – but it certainly changed the perception of Sears in the investor community. Second, possibly as a result, there has been some evidence that Sears is "in play." If Sears wants to continue as a conglomerate, it will have to find a way to produce that value for shareholders. Finally, ironically, Sears is now left with a board with a higher percentage of outside directors, directors who can expect extra focus on their election next year. Brennan may just find that at least some of the extra accountability I was seeking may be the result of the actions he took to stop me.[23]

Monks was right, but it took another year. While he was not elected to the board, Monks received more votes than any other director from the shareholders who received his proxy card. Sears responded to this strong indicator of shareholder concern by making some changes, including reducing the number of Brennan's jobs to three (and later to two when a new CEO was found for the retail division). Brennan was removed from the board's nominating committee, and independent trustees (not directors) were appointed for the employee stock plan.

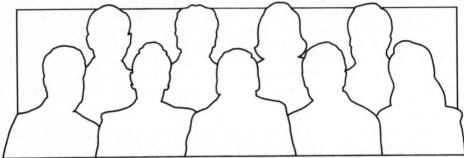
**Figure 6.1** The *Wall Street Journal* advertisement

In 1992, Sears "shrank the board" again, again making it virtually impossible for Monks to get enough votes to be elected. Instead, he devoted his resources to supporting five shareholder proposals submitted by others. This included an SEC–cleared mailing (note: this would not be required under the revised rules) and a full-page ad in the *Wall Street Journal* calling the Sears board "non-performing assets" (see figure 6.1).

The five resolutions came from a wide variety of sponsors, almost a "who's who" of shareholder activism: a public pension fund, a Sears employee, a member of the United Shareholders Association, an individual investor, and one of the Gilbert brothers, who started the whole shareholder crusade more than 50 years ago. They proposed: to restore annual election of all directors (as was the practice for more than a hundred years, until staggered elections were adopted as an anti-takeover move in 1988); to separate the positions of CEO and chairman of the board, to allow confidential voting by shareholders (to prevent pressure on shareholders who vote against management); to study the benefits of divesting one or more of the financial services divisions; and to impose minimum stock ownership requirements for directors.

The annual meeting, held in Atlanta on May 14, was a catalog of protest. The *Chicago Tribune* wrote: "For more than two hours . . . Brennan was forced to stand by as speaker after speaker told him his company's performance had been poor in the last year."[24] *USA Today* agreed, describing the mood of shareholders as "rebellious."[25] Hazard Bentley, the Allstate employee who sponsored the divestment resolution, said "there are grave problems in the company to which I have dedicated my working life," and Cari Christian of the United Shareholders Association asked, "How can the board effectively serve shareholders as the overseer of management, when it is led and dominated by the company's senior manager?" Other shareholders were even more blunt: "Your retail stores are lousy," said a 70-year-old veteran Sears customer.

At the meeting, Monks made a statement that concluded:

> We are the owners of Sears, Roebuck and Company and we are asking for the most basic elements of accountability. We are asking for the most basic and the most essential attribute of ownership: true confidential voting, the right to express opinion free of the possibility of coercion or reprisal. This is the right guaranteed to all citizens of the United States in the exercise of political rights; it is accorded to the shareholders of Exxon, IBM, General Motors and other leading corporations in the exercise of their shareholder rights. I have looked shareholders in the eye as they told me they could not vote with me due to fear of coercion. As the former chairman of a major fiduciary bank, I have felt it myself. Even the most conscientious and courageous shareholder cannot risk the commercial suicide of opposing a substantial potential customer. No vote can be meaningful as long as the company can retaliate. Why won't Sears give its shareholders the dignity and full protection of true confidentiality? A more difficult question is why our management would advertise that it has adopted a policy of confidentiality, when the fine print says that it doesn't apply in a proxy contest, the one situation where it makes a difference?
>
> What does it mean when management announces an objective and then fails to achieve it for every one of ten years? In the interest of honesty, should the objectives be lowered? Should there be some consequences for this failure to meet their own goals, some increased accountability? Two of the shareholder proposals, the proposal to separate the Chairman and the CEO and the proposal for annual election of all directors, will make a difference. These are changes that make questions more likely.
>
> Should there be a change in the corporate strategy? What does it mean when the board opposes an independent study, by a firm of their own choosing? To me, it demonstrates yet again that they just don't want to respond to any questions.

Who are the directors? Won't it make a difference in their attitude toward shareholders if they have some minimal shareholding themselves, not the 100 shares a year they are given but shares purchased with their own money? That is the purpose of the last of the resolutions.

Sears has a slogan: "You can count on us." We want to hear the board say that to the shareholders. We want to see the board earn that trust. The resolutions currently presented by five different and diverse shareholders and groups demonstrate a high level of concern, even dissatisfaction. We want better. We are tired of waiting. And until we see some change, we will keep reminding you – you can count on us.

Two of the resolutions (confidential voting and annual election of directors) got votes of over 40 percent. The proposal to separate the CEO and chairman positions captured 27 percent. The proposal for a study of the benefits of divestment received a 23 percent vote. And nearly 6 percent of the shareholders withheld approval of the candidates for the board of directors, then a record vote of no confidence for a public company board.

Things continued to worsen for Sears. The Sears auto repair facilities were charged with fraud by the Attorneys General of California and New Jersey, who complained about the "company culture." A law suit was filed in connection with Arthur C. Martinez' appointment as CEO of the merchandise group. Dean Witter partnerships had "roll up" problems. Allstate fared worse than its competitors in the liabilities incurred by Hurricane Andrew.

The company announced the appointment of two new outside directors, Michael Miles, chairman of Philip Morris, and William LaMothe, former CEO of Kellogg.

On September 29, 1992, Sears announced a massive divestment plan. Sears would no longer offer its "socks and stocks" policy, and would focus more directly on the retail division. Coldwell Banker would be sold in its entirety. Twenty percent of Dean Witter would be sold, and the rest spun off to shareholders. Sears would also put 20 percent of Allstate on the block.

The reaction of the market was positive. In a single day the stock rose $3^7/8$ in a market that slid nine points. Over $1 billion was added to Sears' market value in that day alone.

One year later, it was clear that the restructuring helped Sears turn itself around. For stockholders, the shakeup proved bountiful. A year after the restructuring, the stock traded at around $56, down from a 52-week high of $57.75. On the day Sears announced its restructuring, the stock opened at $41. Thus, shareholders saw each of their shares appreciate about $15 in a single year. This increased Sears' market value by over $5 billion.

Sears shareholders garnered other values as well, via the spinoff of Dean Witter, Sears' brokerage arm. Twenty percent of Dean Witter was sold in March 1993, ahead of schedule. The remaining 80 percent was spun off to shareholders. Sears holders received a special stock dividend of four-tenths of a share of Dean Witter for each Sears share they owned.

The Sears example demonstrates the role that focus by active shareholders can and should play in under-performing companies. What is more, it shows the crucial link between activism and value. As a result of shareholder involvement, Sears became a better run, more open, more accountable, and more valuable company.

## SEARS: A POSTSCRIPT

It was *Fortune* magazine that first identified Sears, Roebuck as a "dinosaur" but, in recent years, the famous retailer has shrugged off its carapace and evolved into something that can survive and thrive.

Looking at Sears four years later, *Fortune* commented that "the 'dinosaur' . . . turned into a cash cow."[26]

The company took a fresh approach, and was finally able to rid itself of its fusty, out-moded image. In 1997, Sears was voted *Fortune*'s most innovative general merchandise retailer, and the company gained market share in almost all categories of merchandise.

What was the key to the turnaround? *Fortune* identified a change in culture, a change that required Sears to free itself of its glorious past and concentrate instead on the future: "the main reason Martinez has been able to change Sears is that he changed the people . . . 'We used to be so inbred, it's a wonder we didn't have one eye in the middle of our foreheads' says executive vice president Bill Salter, a 32 year old Sears veteran."

## NOTES

1. Donald R. Katz, *The Big Store* (Viking, New York, 1987), p. vii.
2. Editorial, "The Need for Activism," *Pensions and Investments*, Dec. 24, 1990, p. 12.
3. Joe Cappo, "Big Store Masters Art of the Big Store," *Crain's Chicago Business*, May 20, 1991, p. 9.
4. Ellen Neuborne, "CEO Pitching New Vision for Retailer," *USA Today*, Apr. 10, 1991.
5. Cappo, "Big Store Masters Art of the Big Store."
6. Katz, *The Big Store*, p. 164.
7. Bill Inman, "Boss Bros," *Business*, Feb. 1991, p. 55.
8. Diana B. Henriques, "Covert Action against Sears," *Daily Journal*, May 7, 1991.
9. Eric N. Berg, "Sears To Cut More Jobs: Profit Falls," *New York Times*, Feb. 12, 1991.
10. Katz, *The Big Store*, p. 520.
11. Inman, "Boss Bros."
12. Ibid.
13. Ibid.
14. Julia Flynn Silver, with Laura Zinn and John Finotta, "Are the Lights Dimming for Ed Brennan?" *Business Week*, Feb. 11, 1991, p. 56.
15. "Update: Sears, Roebuck & Co." *Asset Analysis Focus*, XVII, II, Feb. 28, 1991.
16. Associated Press, May 8, 1991. See "Maverick Pursuing Seat on Sears Board," *Bridgeport Post*, May 9, 1991.
17. Silver, Zinn, and Finotta, "Are the Lights Dimming?"
18. Ibid.
19. While Sears asserted that the primary purpose was to raise the proportion of outside directors (all three shifted directors were employees), it also admitted that the step was taken as a mechanism to keep Monks off the board. One Sears executive, insisting on anonymity, said: "That's the real motivation of today's announcement – to keep Monks out."
20. Leslie Wayne, "Boards Shifts Called Manipulative," *New York Times*, Mar. 18, 1991.
21. Editorial, "Let Brennan's Record Speak for Itself," *Crain's Chicago Business*, Apr. 8, 1991.
22. Editorial, "Independent Boards," *Pensions and Investments*, Apr. 1, 1991.
23. Robert A.G. Monks, "My Run for the Sears Board," *Legal Times*, Aug. 12, 1991.
24. John Schmeltzer and Charles Storch, "Sears Shareholders Fire 'Warning Shot' at Execs," *Chicago Tribune*, May 15, 1992, p. 1.
25. Ellen Neuborne and Michael Osborn, "Mutual Funds, Pensions Lead the Charge," *USA Today*, May 15, 1992.
26. Patricia Sellers, "Sears: The Turnaround is Ending: The Revolution has Begun," *Fortune*, Apr. 28, 1997, pp. 106–18.

# Armand Hammer and Occidental Petroleum

In 1989, the proxy statement of the Occidental Petroleum Company informed shareholders that the company intended to spend tens of millions of corporate dollars to build a museum to house the art collection of Occidental's founder, CEO, and chairman, Dr Armand Hammer. Furthermore, a much smaller sum would be spent on a book detailing two years in the life of Armand Hammer. The story provides an excellent study of boardroom neglect in the face of a powerful and domineering chief executive.

Occidental's proxy revealed that the company had undertaken to finance the cost of a biography of Hammer, detailing his life from 1987 to 1989. The proxy stated that costs had run to $255,000 already, with another $120,000 committed for further expenses. Occidental would have its costs reimbursed from the proceeds of the book. The publication was expected to be successful since Hammer's first volume of biography, published two years before, had been a bestseller. Any remaining profits from the book would be donated to the Armand Hammer United World College of the American West, in Montezuma, New Mexico.

The volume of Hammer-ography was a small endeavor compared to the second project described in the proxy. Occidental pledged to finance the Armand Hammer Museum of Art and Cultural Center, to be located in a building next to Occidental's Los Angeles headquarters. The proxy stated that, "Occidental's board of directors believes that the financial support of the Museum will promote the continuation of goodwill which has inured to Occidental from its long-standing past association with and support of the [Armand Hammer's] collections."

Occidental would bear the cost of constructing the new museum, and renovating four floors of the Occidental HQ building for use by the museum under a 30-year rent-free lease. These construction costs were estimated at $50 million.

Occidental was the subject of several shareholder suits charging that the museum represented improper use of corporate assets. During discovery, more facts emerged that further illustrated the careless use of shareholder money that the board had allowed. For instance, in 1980, Hammer had purchased a Leonardo da Vinci notebook called the Leicester Codex for $5.3 million. Hammer renamed it Codex Hammer. It later transpired that the notebook had been bought with Occidental's funds. In other words, Hammer had spent the Occidental shareholders' money on a work of art that he named after himself. More outrageously, the board let him do it.

Further, Occidental would contribute funds to the museum for 30 years at a cost of $24 million. At the end of the 30-year lease, the museum would have the option to buy the museum building and the Occidental HQ building from Occidental for $55 million, its "currently estimated fair market value at that time." Occidental would then lease its HQ building back from the museum at a fair market rent.

The issue here is not whether corporate charitable giving is of benefit to shareholders. Some level of charity by corporations is not only acceptable; it should be encouraged. Companies should recognize their obligations to the community through charitable contributions. And these contributions provide important benefits to long-term shareholders, both directly and indirectly. Directly, shareholders benefit from the favorable tax treatment of charitable contributions. Indirectly, they benefit from the goodwill, support, and name recognition they inspire. But did the museum and book projects constitute corporate charity, or were they gifts to Armand Hammer?

Consider the book. Unarguably, Hammer has led a fascinating life, and his first volume of biography had sold superbly, appearing for 18 weeks on the *New York Times* bestseller list. However, the very success of the first book should have made it possible for Dr. Hammer to negotiate a contract for a sequel with a commercial publisher. Instead, Hammer borrowed the money from Occidental's till and gave it to someone to follow him round the world for two years. If the book made money, Occidental would be reimbursed, but why should the shareholders bear that risk? Why should a publicly held company be in the business of making interest-free loans to the CEO? Especially given the fact that the CEO was a billionaire and could easily afford to bear the risk of publication himself.

Of course, the book's cost represented a fraction of the costs of the museum, which soon crept way above the $86 million mentioned in the proxy. One shareholder court filing in October 1990 alleged the total cost to be closer to $157 million. What was Occidental paying for?

The company argued that it "expects to receive appropriate public acknowledgment of its role in forming the Museum." This was a highly tendentious claim. Hammer had originally promised his collection to the Los Angeles County Museum of Art (LACMA), but reneged on his promise when the museum refused certain of Hammer's demands. Among these demands was that his collection must be housed only in rooms bearing his name (and his name only), and should be housed together, separate from other works. Further he insisted that the entry way to his collection contain a life-size portrait of not just Hammer, but also his wife. Lastly, he demanded that the collection have its own curator, answerable to the Armand Hammer Foundation rather than LACMA. Hammer was insulted by LACMA's failure to accede promptly to his demands and promised that he would house his collection in his own museum. Los Angelenos felt betrayed by this abrupt U-turn.

Occidental's claim that it would gain recognition via its association with the museum failed on a second count. Art critics and historians believed that Hammer's collection was not sufficiently good to merit its own museum. As the *New York Times* put it, for each of the good works, "there are a dozen Victorian pot-boilers, saccharine nudes and other losers."[1] *Time* magazine was harsher: "Most of it [the collection] is junk: a mishmash of second- or third-rate work by famous names."[2] In other words, Occidental's shareholders weren't merely stumping up $95 million for a private museum, they were doing so for a *second-rate* museum.

*Should shareholders bear the cost of a museum memorializing the company's founder? Especially when various works of art in the museum don't belong to him anyway? Should shareholders pay for Hammer to acquire a reputation as an art-lover, charitable donor, and philanthropist? Should Occidental's shareholders pay tens of millions of dollars to divert the collection from a superior facility at LACMA in order to assuage Hammer's bruised ego?*

It was also dubious whether the museum counted as legitimate charitable giving. Under Delaware law (Occidental was incorporated in Delaware) charitable contributions in excess of the amount deductible for Internal Revenue Code purposes may be considered unreasonable. Occidental's taxable revenue in 1988 was $111 million; and charitable giving was deductible only up to 10 percent of that sum. However, Occidental was planning to spend $86 million on the museum, rather more than the $11 million that could be deemed "reasonable."

Where was the board in all of this? Let's begin with the chairman of the board, the legendary Dr. Armand Hammer himself. His career is the subject of hundreds of articles and several books. His career as an industrialist, philanthropist, and unofficial diplomat spanned the twentieth century. He was one of the first Westerners to do business with the Soviet Union and with many Third World countries. He was the friend of world leaders. He was also a convicted felon, due to his violation of federal campaign contributions in 1976. (He was later pardoned by President George Bush.) At the sentencing proceeding, held in Los Angeles because Hammer was too weak to travel to Washington, he appeared in a wheelchair, his heart hooked up to monitoring machines checked by a team of cardiologists in the next room. His lawyer told the court that Hammer was "a sick old man [who] lives four blocks from the office, goes in late, goes home for lunch and takes a nap in the afternoon."

Despite being too old and sick to work, Hammer was paid over $6 million in compensation from 1985 to 1988. Furthermore, his employment contract, which provided for nearly $2 million in annual pay (including a "guaranteed minimum bonus" of $420,000), was written to remunerate him for his services until February 1998, when Hammer (had he lived) would have been 99 years old. One feature of the contract was that it would be paid in full whether Hammer lived or not. Thus, following Hammer's death, Occidental's shareholders coughed up a further $18.3 million to the Armand Hammer Foundation. The *Los Angeles Times* labeled this compensation gimmick a "Golden Coffin."

However old and sick Hammer was alleged to be, there was no doubt that he was an energetic and highly "hands-on" CEO who ran the company in many ways as though it was his own kingdom. Wall Street recognized his deep (and sometimes eccentric) involvement in every aspect of the company with sharp increases in the stock price every time he got sick. (Indeed, on the day Hammer died, Occidental's stock appreciated by over $500 million.)

Hammer picked his board members carefully. More than half the directors were insiders, or outsiders with ties to the company. Louis Nizer was a partner, and Arthur B. Krim was a counsel to a law firm that received $5 million from Occidental the year the board approved the museum. Another "outsider" was Rosemary Tomich, who was also a director of an Occidental subsidiary. Arthur Groman, also an Oxy director, was a partner in a law firm that received fees of $1.8 million from Occidental in 1987, and Groman performed legal fees for Hammer and was a paid consultant to Occidental. George O. Nolley was the founder of the Permian Corporation, which had been bought by Occidental.

There was a widespread rumor that Hammer had signed, undated letters of resignation from each of his directors. True or not, Occidental's board was ready to respond to every whim of the company's domineering chairman.

Occidental had a staggered board, divided into three classes. The stated reason for the staggering was to ensure the "continuity" of board service. Such "continuity" seemed unlikely given the average age of Occidental's directors. Hammer himself was 91 years of age; Nizer was 87, Gore was 82, and Krim 79. More than half of the board was over the age of 72. The "continuity" of this board was not something over which the company had much control.

It seems that Hammer went ahead with the museum plan even without full board approval. He had presented his proposal to the executive committee of the board, but the plan was not approved by the special committee (made up of outside directors) until long after construction had actually begun on the site.

One shareholder suit charged that the special committee had lacked sufficient information to appraise the museum proposal thoroughly. For instance, the committee received its legal advice from the firm of Dilworth Paxson – Hammer had chosen the firm to advise the committee, despite the fact that Dilworth Paxson was at that time representing Hammer in a personal legal matter. The committee was never advised of this conflict of interest. The committee also accepted, without investigation, the $55 million option price – the price the museum would pay if it wished to buy the complex after 30 years – on the basis of a report by an appraiser selected by Hammer. It accepted this report despite its startling conclusion that a building that cost $50 million to build would be worth only $55 million 30 years later. (Rockefeller Plaza, for instance, is 60 years old and is still the most valuable commercial property in New York.)

When the committee approved the museum proposal it did not know:

- that Hammer had promised the collection to LACMA, and the public disapproval that resulted when Hammer reneged on this promise;
- whether the museum building would be owned by Occidental or the museum itself;
- the value of the art to be contributed by Hammer and the Hammer Foundation;
- what portion of the art had been purchased with Occidental money;
- whether Hammer would provide any financial support for the museum;
- the cost to Occidental of the museum's rent-free use of space in the company's headquarters building;
- the tax aspects of the proposal – the committee didn't even know if Occidental's payment for construction of the museum complex would be tax-deductible;
- even where Occidental would get the funds to pay for the museum.

Senator Albert Gore Sr., at his deposition, showed that he understood few aspects of the museum proposal he had approved. The defendants suggested that Senator Gore, at 82 years of age, should not be expected to recollect corporate matters between board meetings. The obvious question is: what was he doing on the board at all? But that question can equally be asked of every board member.

A shareholder lawsuit challenging the museum was settled – over the objections of the large institutional investors – because the court found it likely that the contribution would be protected by the business judgment rule.

*Who, then, is in the best position to establish accountability here? How?*

## NOTES

1. Michael Kimmelman, "Unintended Legacy of Armand Hammer is a Museum Dispute," *New York Times*, Jan. 9, 1991. p. B1.
2. Robert Hughes, "America's Vainest Museum," *Time*, Jan. 28, 1991, p. 98.

# Polaroid[1]

In the spring of 1988, Shamrock Holdings, an investment group headed by Roy Disney, bought a position of roughly 5 percent in Polaroid Corp. The stock of the imaging company was then trading at $30–$35 a share.

This trading range was low, considering Polaroid's distinguished history. Since its formation in 1937, the company can rightly claim to have been one of America's most innovative. Under the leadership of Edwin Land – who had more patents to his name than any other American inventor save Thomas Edison – Polaroid developed many leading-edge technological products, most notably its signature instant camera.

But such stellar achievements did not guarantee commercial success. Though Polaroid is credited with developing and advancing instant-imaging technology, the company suffered heavy competition from increasingly cheap, high-quality, 35 mm cameras and film. By the late 1980s, Polaroid was seen as a ripe candidate for takeover, for the following reasons:

- The company's profits were relatively low.
- It carried a small amount of debt.
- It owned a potentially enormous, though unliquidated, asset in the form of a patent infringement suit against Eastman Kodak. It was anticipated that Polaroid would obtain a very substantial damage award against Kodak, possibly up to $6 billion.

Polaroid already had significant anti-takeover defenses in its charter, including:

- a shareholder rights plan, or "poison pill";
- a prohibition on shareholder action by written consent;
- a prohibition on shareholders' ability to call special meetings;
- authorized issue of "blank check" preferred stock.

Shamrock was known as a potential acquirer. There was no question but that it intended to use its 5 percent stake as a springboard for a Polaroid bid. On June 16, Roy Disney and Stanley Gold of Shamrock Holdings tried to reach Polaroid CEO I. MacAllister Booth by phone to request a meeting. Booth, then out of town, instructed his secretary to tell Shamrock that he would be unavailable for a meeting in the near future. Booth, however, cut short his trip and returned to Boston the next day to meet with representatives of Shearson Lehman Brothers, Polaroid's investment bank.

Disney, unable to reach Booth by phone, wrote a letter on June 17, reiterating his interest in a meeting. The letter stated that the purpose of such a meeting would be "to establish the ground work for a good relationship with the company." Though Shamrock gave no indication that it intended a hostile bid – indeed, Booth later testified that the letter "had no threatening aspect to it"[2] – there could be no doubt that Shamrock was determined to take Polaroid over. Shamrock was a takeover vehicle; Polaroid was a prime target.

Polaroid management finally agreed to meet with Shamrock, and set a date for July 13. Polaroid insisted on certain conditions, including a demand that Shamrock not exceed a 5 percent holding by the time of the meeting. Shamrock agreed, and reversed some commitments it had made to continue buying the stock. Shamrock later charged that it cost $500,000 to reverse these commitments and stay below a 5 percent holding. In return, Shamrock sought assurance that Polaroid was not merely trying to buy time to erect antitakeover barriers. In later court testimony, representatives of both sides directly disagreed. A Shamrock associate said that he received an assurance from Polaroid that the company had no plans to alter the status quo. A Polaroid representative, by contrast, said that the company merely promised not to sell itself to a third party before the July 13 meeting.[3]

The meeting between Booth and Shamrock never took place. On July 12, one day before the scheduled meeting, a special meeting of the Polaroid board was convened to approve a "comprehensive plan" for the reorganization and redirection of the company. Included in the scheme was a proposal for an employee stock ownership plan (ESOP) that would account for 14 percent of Polaroid's shares. Other details of the "comprehensive plan" included a commitment to enter the worldwide market for 35 mm film, and various streamlining and cost-cutting measures.

The board approved the strategy, and issued a press release announcing the formation of the 14 percent ESOP. At the same time, Shamrock was informed that the meeting scheduled for the next day was canceled.

Under Delaware law, a hostile acquirer must gain 85 percent of a company's shares to consummate a merger within three years. If the ESOP shares remained beholden to incumbent management, this would all but destroy Shamrock's chances of taking Polaroid over.

Shamrock bitterly protested the decision of Polaroid's board. Gold wrote to Booth, saying, "Contrary to your assertion that the so-called 'comprehensive plan' will improve shareholder value . . . I believe some of the actions planned will have a significant adverse impact on such value." At the same time, Shamrock announced that it would seek to have the ESOP invalidated in the Delaware courts, on the grounds that the Polaroid directors had breached their fiduciary duty in hastily adopting the ESOP in the face of a presumed threat.

Before the case reached the hallowed chambers of Wilmington, however, Shamrock launched its long-expected bid for the company. In September 1988, Shamrock bid $42 in cash for all of Polaroid's shares, conditional upon 90 percent of outstanding shares being tendered and the ESOP being declared invalid in court. Later, Shamrock raised its bid to $45, and declared it would raise it to $47 if the ESOP were struck down. Polaroid's board of directors ruled that the Shamrock bid was "inadequate" and announced its opposition, citing:

- an insufficient price;
- the highly conditional financing of the Shamrock bid;
- the extent of Polaroid's leverage if Shamrock succeeded;
- Polaroid's bright future prospects;

- the prospect that a takeover by Shamrock might jeopardize the expected return from the Kodak litigation. On this last point, directors claimed that Shamrock would be forced to settle early for less than the possible award, or that Shamrock would not be viewed as the "victim" of the patent infringement and would therefore receive a lesser reward.

In a September 20 press release confirming the rejection of the offer, MacAllister Booth said, "The board also considered several factors including Polaroid's excellent initial progress in implementing its comprehensive strategic plan, announced July 12."

Shamrock's interest in Polaroid had now become a fully fledged takeover battle. Shamrock had to persuade Polaroid shareholders to tender their shares despite the strong recommendation from Polaroid management that they not do so. Of course, Shamrock's bid depended wholly on the ESOP. If the Delaware court ruled the ESOP invalid, Shamrock had a far better chance of succeeding in its bid. If the ESOP was upheld, Shamrock's chances were next to non-existent.

The case was heard before Vice-Chancellor Carolyn Berger in December and January 1988–9.

The case went into great detail about the timing of the ESOP and the effects it was intended to have. The following questions were raised:

- When directors approved the 14 percent ESOP, were they fully informed about the terms of the plan? For instance, did the board consider the effect the ESOP would have on productivity or on the independence of the company? Did the board know how the company's employees felt about the plan?
- Did the board have a fiduciary duty to study such issues?
- Did Polaroid adopt the ESOP primarily as a device to thwart Shamrock, or did the plan serve a fundamental business purpose?

On January 6, 1989, Berger delivered her opinion, upholding the Polaroid ESOP. Before we weigh the merits of the opinion, let us consider the facts.

## POLAROID'S ESOP: DELAWARE SITS IN JUDGMENT

An ESOP of sorts had been under consideration at Polaroid since 1985. In that year management floated a proposal that would allocate 4 million shares over ten years. At the time, management noted that one of the benefits of such a scheme, aside from the intrinsic merits, was that it would help deter a hostile acquirer.

In 1987, the company approached the issue in greater depth. Management decided that the ESOP would have to be funded by the employees, who would exchange various benefits in exchange for their shares in the plan. Various meetings were held with employee representatives to see what employee benefits could be exchanged to pay for the plan and the size of plan that could be created from such exchanges.

At a meeting in March 1988, Polaroid's corporate benefits committee debated and approved an ESOP of "up to 5 percent" of the company's stock. Their proposal was put to Polaroid's board of directors four days later on March 29, 1988. The board approved in principle, though the size of such a plan was not discussed. Minutes of the meeting noted, "[T]he plan should also serve to introduce a note of stability at this time of increased corporate takeover activity."[4] The board approved the idea of an ESOP, but stipulated that it would be funded by an exchange of employee benefits, and that the shares would be purchased in the open market to avoid a dilutive effect on shareholders.

At the presentation to the board, chief financial officer Harvey Thayer showed that the costs of the employee 401(k) plan and the profit-sharing retirement contributions could be exchanged for an ESOP somewhat less than 5 percent. Several directors recommended an ESOP of larger than 5 percent as long as the plan remained shareholder-neutral.

Polaroid issued a press release after the meeting, announcing the formation of a smaller ESOP. The release said, "The ESOP as currently envisioned will own somewhat less than 5 percent of the outstanding shares in the company."

Defending this plan later before Judge Berger, Polaroid's chairman and former CEO William J. McCune testified that he had no recollection of an ESOP in excess of 5 percent being discussed during this period.

Judge Berger concluded, "In short, I am satisfied that the press release was accurate – the board approved, in principle, an ESOP of approximately 5 percent of the outstanding stock."[5] Such was the situation when Shamrock principals confirmed in a letter to Polaroid that they were substantial holders of Polaroid's stock, and interested in a meeting with management. Booth would later testify that the letter was "a jolt of reality." Norwood said that it was received like a "cold shower."[6]

On June 26, nine days after receiving the "good relationship" letter from Shamrock, the management executive committee (MEC), consisting of Polaroid's senior managers, met in a special Sunday morning meeting to discuss its response to Shamrock's overture. Judge Berger wrote, "As Booth explained, there was 'no question' but that everyone wanted to put together the ESOP quickly because of the Shamrock letter."[7]

However, there also seemed to be no question that an ESOP accounting for 5 percent of the stock was inadequate. In Judge Berger's words:

> Booth announced that he wanted a larger ESOP funded in part by the five year seniority increase (this was an automatic 5 percent pay raise granted to all employees after they had served five years). Booth apparently was surprised that the MEC (which in April had been unable to agree upon even a 2 percent pay cut to fund the ESOP) was aggressively pushing a larger ESOP. Booth even got to the point where he had to play "devil's advocate" and point out to his senior people that the pay cuts would not be an easy thing to sell to the employees . . . During the course of the discussion, the committee members were advised that an ESOP greater than 18.5 percent would require stockholder approval. Although the committee members were pushing for an ESOP of 20 percent or larger at this meeting, when they learned of this additional requirement, they agreed that 18.5 percent would be the cap on the ESOP.[8]

On June 29, Booth met with two employee representatives. He told them he had decided on funding a $300 million ESOP with an across-the-board 5 percent pay cut, the 401(k) matching funds, a delayed pay-scale change, and the profit-sharing retirement contribution. The employees did not cheer the news, as the Berger court later noted: "The two employee representatives argued against the 5 percent pay cut and pointed out the severe financial impact that [it] would have on employees."[9]

Having decided on the enlarged ESOP and the means of funding, Booth wished to implement the plan before the next scheduled board meeting on July 26. His motive, he testified, was that the last two weeks of July coincided with Polaroid's annual "summer shutdown," and he didn't want employees to read of the new ESOP and pay cuts (if approved by the board) in their holiday newspaper. Booth therefore called a special meeting of the board for the earliest convenient date, which was July 12 – one day before the scheduled meeting with Shamrock.

Due to the short notice of the special meeting, three directors were unable to attend and a fourth had to leave before any votes were taken.

At least one Polaroid executive managed to attend in spirit, however. Judge Berger commented, "The minutes are not a model of accuracy . . . [they] refer to two proposals made by [vice president of corporate personnel, John] Harlot, who did not even attend the meeting."[10] At the meeting, Booth explained the "comprehensive plan" to the board and sought approval of the enlarged ESOP.

The ESOP was discussed for two hours. Berger wrote, "Although the directors had approved the concept of an ESOP on March 29 . . . they had never considered an ESOP as large as $300 million and they had never considered funding an ESOP (regardless of size) with employee pay cuts . . . The directors did not question the ESOP size chosen by management and they did not ask about or discuss alternative funding sources."[11] Directors also failed to discuss two other important points. Judge Berger noted:

- that employee representative groups strongly opposed the use of a pay cut and had proposed alternative funding sources;
- that a 14 percent ESOP would make a hostile takeover of Polaroid almost impossible.

One of the chief issues before the Berger court was whether Polaroid directors would be protected by the business judgment rule.

Under Delaware law, directors are "charged with an unyielding fiduciary duty to the corporation and its shareholders" (*Smith v. Van Gorkom*). Normally, their decisions will be protected by the business judgment rule, "a presumption that in making a business decision the directors . . . acted on an informed basis, in good faith and in the honest belief that the action taken was in the best interests of the company" (*Aronson v. Lewis*). The protection of the business judgment rule will not be afforded to directors who fail "to inform themselves, prior to making a business decision, of all material information reasonably available to them" (*Aronson v. Lewis*).

The business judgment rule is available to directors even when they are facing a takeover threat. In such circumstances, however, there is "an omnipresent specter that a board may be acting primarily in its own interests" (*Unocal v. Mesa Petroleum*). Thus, the Delaware courts have established a more burdensome business judgment standard for takeover situations. Directors must show that they had "reasonable grounds for believing that a danger to corporate policy and effectiveness existed" and that the measures taken to oppose takeover were "reasonable in relation to the threat posed" (*Unocal v. Mesa Petroleum*). The board must make such a determination, referred to as a "*Unocal* analysis," if they are to be afforded the protection of the business judgment rule when faced with a takeover threat.

Shamrock's argument was simple. The decision of Polaroid's board could not be protected by the business judgment rule because, in approving the ESOP, the directors had breached their fiduciary duties.

The directors, charged Shamrock, were both uninformed and misinformed. They had not fulfilled their duty to consider "all material information reasonably available to them" (*Aronson v. Lewis*). In particular, the board approved a massive alteration of Polaroid's capital structure without questioning management's conclusion that the ESOP would enhance productivity. The board simply accepted this argument as valid, without subjecting it to any independent or expert examination. Also, the board was uninformed – or rather misinformed by Booth – with regard to the opposition of the employees to the pay cut.

Shamrock, in its pretrial memorandum, wrote, "We believe that the directors' virtually unquestioning reliance on management's conclusory recommendation to triple the size of the ESOP reflects a self-interested motivation to protect the corporate 'fiefdom' they have shared with management for many years."[12] Shamrock also argued that the board had approved the ESOP as a defensive measure yet failed to apply a *Unocal* analysis. Shamrock asserted, "Polaroid's board cannot establish, as it must, (i) that the defensively oriented Lock-up ESOP was the product of a reasonable investigation into any perceived threat and (ii) that the Lock-up ESOP was itself a reasonable response to any such threat."[13] Polaroid's actions, concluded Shamrock, "were certainly an unwarranted and unreasonable response to a request by a substantial shareholder to meet with management – a request conceded by Booth to be non-threatening and which in any event could not reasonably be perceived by anyone as any sort of threat at all."[14]

For these reasons, argued Shamrock, the decision to approve the ESOP could not be protected by the business judgment rule. The directors had breached their fiduciary duties in reaching their decision, so the ESOP should be invalidated by the court.

Polaroid argued, in Judge Berger's words, that, "The ESOP can withstand even the highest level of judicial scrutiny. That being so, it becomes irrelevant whether the 'process' was tainted, since the result is a plan that is entirely fair."[15] In other words, Polaroid asserted that the court should not worry about the means, given that the end result was a workable, effective ESOP.

### Judge Berger's ruling

The judge first considered the question of the business judgment rule. Were the directors informed of "all material information?" Judge Berger concluded that the board did indeed act hastily, deciding to implement the ESOP in only two hours' discussion in a meeting called at short notice, with no materials distributed beforehand, and from which three directors were absent: "There is no question but that the directors did not know all of the relevant facts."[16]

Judge Berger, however, sided here with the defendants, agreeing with them that "a board's failure to become fully informed does not take its decision outside of the protection of the business judgment rule unless its lack of information was so extreme as to reflect gross negligence on the part of the directors."[17] Polaroid admitted that the directors were unaware of the opposition of the employee groups to the pay cuts, but said this was not crucial to the decision to enlarge the ESOP. The directors, after all, were hardly to assume that the employees would *welcome* a pay cut. Thus, the failure of the board to become informed on this point did not render them "grossly negligent."

Next, Judge Berger considered whether Polaroid had responded inappropriately to the takeover threat, if indeed Shamrock's advance constituted such a threat. Her opinion discussed some of the previous cases that had come to Delaware in which would-be acquirers had charged their targets with unfair defenses. She wrote: "However, none of those cases address the issue, arguably presented here, of whether a board, largely composed of disinterested directors, should be deemed to be acting from the same motives as the members of management who proposed the transaction."[18] In other words, what if management had enlarged the ESOP as an anti-takeover device, but the board had approved it for very different reasons, such as to enhance productivity?

In the end, Judge Berger decided that all these questions were irrelevant. "Neither a board's failure to become adequately informed nor its failure to apply a *Unocal* analysis, where such an approach is required, will automatically invalidate the corporate transaction. Under either circumstance, the business judgment rule will not be applied and the transaction at issue will be scrutinized to determine whether it is entirely fair."[19] Thus Berger put aside the issue of whether the board's decision-making process was tainted. She deemed that question secondary to that of whether the approved ESOP was one that would benefit the company and its shareholders.

The judge addressed this latter question along three lines:

1. Would the ESOP impair productivity?
2. Would it unduly discourage takeovers?
3. Would it unfairly dilute share value?

She answered "no" to all three questions. On the first question, Berger concluded that even if the 14 percent ESOP was not very popular with employees, it would be unlikely to impair productivity. Moreover, the costs of the ESOP would not be damaging to the company's ability to operate.

As to the second question, the judge agreed that ESOP shares were more likely to be voted for incumbent management, but she pointed out that employees retained the right to vote their ESOP shares confidentially, and so were open to solicitation by an acquirer. She observed:

> I find that the anti-takeover aspect of the ESOP does not make it less than fair. Given its confidentiality provisions, it cannot be said that management controls the [ESOP share block, or] that the leg up it gives management in any way harms the company or its public stockholders. The ESOP may mean that a potential acquirer will have to gain the employees' confidence and support in order to be successful in its takeover effort. However, there has been no showing that such support is or would be impossible to obtain.[20]

Lastly, she found dilution but dismissed its unfairness. Because the ESOP shares were issued by the company and not purchased on the open market, the interests of public stockholders were diluted. But that, in her view, did not render the ESOP unfair. Berger decided that there was no hard evidence that the dilution would adversely affect Polaroid's non-employee shareholders. Indeed, she added that if the ESOP resulted (as hoped) in increased productivity, such dilution would be more than made up for by improved earnings.

Judge Berger wrapped up her opinion as follows:

> After considering all of the evidence, including the timing of the ESOP's establishment, its structure and operation, its purposes and likely impact (both as a motivational device and an anti-takeover device) I am satisfied that the Polaroid ESOP is fundamentally fair. It is essentially stockholder neutral although it does have some dilutive effect. It is structurally fair in its voting and tendering provisions and I do not find either the timing of its implementation or its possible anti-takeover effect objectionable under the facts of this case . . .[21]

> Defendants rushed to put this ESOP in place before Shamrock took any other steps to express its interest in Polaroid. The timing of the meeting, change in allocation provisions and decision to issue treasury shares all had to have been motivated, at least in part, by a desire to add one more obstacle to Shamrock's potential acquisition bid. The fact that the ESOP was partly defensive, however, does not make it unfair. This is a

defensive device (assuming it is one) that is designed to and appears likely to add value to the company and all of its stockholders. It does not prevent the stockholders from receiving or considering alternatives. In sum, the plan adopted by the directors, whether adequately considered or not, is fair and should not be invalidated.[22]

Shamrock did not abandon its bid. Rather, it appealed Berger's decision.

Let us look at Judge Berger's decision in a broader context. What does this case tell us about the interrelationship of managers, the board of directors, shareholders and employees? Who is entrusted with what, on behalf of whom?

It is universally accepted that the shareholders entrust the board to oversee management. Directors are entrusted with seeing that the corporation is managed in its own long-term interests.

*Did Judge Berger lose sight of this truism?*

The court accepted that the board was uninformed. Judge Berger wrote, "There is no question but that the directors did not know all of the relevant facts."

*As a shareholder, would you expect the board that you elected to consider the reallocation of 14 percent of a company's capital in a two-hour meeting, at which four directors were not present?*

*When Polaroid's stockholders bought their shares, did they trust the company's board to have a more thorough oversight of management than that?*

Judge Berger even concluded that the board accepted management's recommendation for a 14 percent ESOP while approaching the question with a different set of assumptions. The judge wrote: "The evidence establishes that management was responding to a takeover threat. It is not as clear that the outside directors were operating in a defensive mode."[23] In other words, judge Berger validated the board's decision to approve the ESOP, even though that approval was granted without a full understanding of management's motives for recommending the ESOP in the first place.

*Given the admitted failure of the board to inform itself of all the facts, or to inform itself as to management's motives, would you, as a Polaroid shareholder, continue to entrust those directors with the oversight of the company?*

Judge Berger decided that these questions did not need to be answered. Though she accepted that the board was uninformed, she did not believe that its lack of information was so extensive as to constitute gross negligence. Berger said that the information withheld from the board was relatively unimportant, and, while the board's decision-making was hasty, it had ended up, by hook or by crook, in approving a plan that was fundamentally fair.

Let us look a little more closely at the judge's reasoning. On the one hand, the courts had to ensure that managers were accountable to shareholders; on the other, they did not wish to chill management's incentives for risk-taking and innovation. The result was the business judgment rule's emphasis on *process*. As long as directors made informed decisions with care and attention, the *results* would not be second-guessed.

In this case, however, Berger completely reversed this accepted principle. She judged that, although the process was suspect, the end result was fair. In other words, if the process is fair but the end result is not, directors have the protection of the business judgment rule. And, if the process is not fair, but the end result is, the courts won't oppose that decision-making either.

*Who can lose, apart from the shareholders?*

There can be no doubt that Polaroid management and the board of directors faced a conflict of interest. A successful Shamrock bid, after all, would mean unemployment for the incumbents. As the judge in *Unocal* stated, there is the "omnipresent specter" that management and the board will act in their own interests when facing a possible takeover. According to many of the depositions in the case, at least one of the motives for the ESOP was to render the company less susceptible to takeover. It may not have been the leading motive (indeed, if it had been, the court would have no choice but to invalidate the ESOP, since Delaware directors aren't allowed to issue new stock for defense purposes), but both Polaroid executives and directors admit that protection was among their motives for creating and enlarging the ESOP.

*Given this fact, shouldn't we subject their decision-making to closer examination? Shouldn't we require that the directors be even more rigorous in their analysis of the ESOP? Or should we agree with Judge Berger that it really doesn't matter whether the board's approval of the ESOP was hasty and uninformed, as long as the end result is fair?*

This line of questioning leads to another: *Who gets the ultimate say over what constitutes fairness?* Shareholders own the corporation, and they hire managers to run it for them. But because shareholders are numerous and diverse, they elect a board of directors to oversee management on their behalf. The question is: *Who should protect the shareholders if the board is derelict in its duty?* In this instance, Judge Berger decided she should. She argued that the directors had failed to exercise "business judgment," and thus "the transaction at issue will be scrutinized to determine whether it is entirely fair." Judge Berger did such scrutinizing herself and decided to approve the transaction on behalf of the shareholders. *Couldn't the shareholders decide that for themselves?* It would be a simple matter to explain the 14 percent ESOP in the proxy statement, and put it to a vote at the annual meeting. We already know that one issue management discussed when they enlarged the ESOP was avoiding the 18.5 percent threshold that would need shareholder approval.

*Why was management afraid of seeking such approval? Can't shareholders be trusted to act in their own best interests? Should crucial decisions relating to a company's capital structure be left to a judge?*

*What do you believe was the motivation behind the formation of the 14 percent Employee Stock Ownership Plan? Do you believe the decision to move from a 5 percent ESOP to a 14 percent ESOP was the result of Shamrock's interest in the company? Do you believe the ESOP was created primarily in the employees' interests, or to fend off a possible hostile bid?*

Before the case reached the Delaware court of appeal, Polaroid pulled more tricks from out of the corporate sleeve. On January 29, the company announced a sweeping recapitalization. Polaroid said it would spend up to $1.1 billion to buy back up to 22 percent of its stock at $50 a share, and that a special issue of preferred stock would be issued to Corporate Partners, an investment concern run by the Wall Street firm Lazard Frères. The issue, for which Corporate Partners would pay $300 million, would be convertible into 10 percent of the common stock.

Polaroid argued that the recapitalization plan represented a better means of realizing shareholder value than the Shamrock offer. Shearson issued an opinion to this effect, based on an estimated $1.2 billion recovery in the Kodak litigation and on management's financial projections, which assumed growth of about 10 percent over historical results. If such sales growth was achieved, Polaroid would be close to the top of the Fortune 500 list.

In a press release, Booth described the recapitalization as "a program designed to deliver directly to shareholders a portion of the company's current value while enhancing Polaroid's prospects for future growth in shareholder value."

Shamrock put a rather different spin on the announcement. Gold described the recapitalization as "irresponsible and another indication of management entrenchment at any cost . . . [The moves serve] no discernible business purpose." Gold continued:

> The placement of preferred stock, together with the proposed stock buy-back program, is clearly a defensive action designed to park even more Polaroid shares in "friendly hands" at the expense of Polaroid's public shareholders . . . Polaroid's thinly veiled effort to "stuff" the ballot box in anticipation of its annual meeting vividly demonstrates that Polaroid management is more interested in preserving its position than allowing Polaroid shareholders an opportunity to receive at least $45 per share in cash for all their shares, pursuant to Shamrock's offer.

In a reprise of the ongoing legal battle over the ESOP, Shamrock announced that it would sue Polaroid and Corporate Partners in the Delaware courts, asserting that the recapitalization plan was adopted to thwart Shamrock's takeover, and not with any valid business purpose in mind. This case has come to be known as "Polaroid II" – the sequel to the case settled by Judge Berger discussed above.

Days later, Shamrock announced that it would seek control of the company via a proxy fight. That is, Shamrock would nominate its own slate of directors and seek to have them elected in the place of management's slate at the annual meeting. Even this looked like a vain bid by the California-based acquirer. The effect of the ESOP, the buyback, and the Corporate Partners deal was to put about 30 percent of Polaroid's stock in management-friendly hands – almost overwhelming opposition.

The viability of Shamrock's bid now rested with the Delaware Supreme Court, which was reviewing Berger's judgment on appeal. On March 23, the court upheld Berger and let Polaroid's ESOP stand. Four days later, Shamrock announced that it was abandoning its nearly year-long interest in Polaroid, and was calling off its proxy fight. "We are disappointed and frustrated by the Delaware Courts," said Gold.[24] In a settlement deal between Shamrock and Polaroid, the photographic company agreed to repay Shamrock's expenses to the tune of $20 million, as well as buy $5 million in advertising time on Shamrock's radio and TV stations. In return, Shamrock agreed not to seek control of the company for a period of ten years.

## NOTES

1. All the information for this case study has, unless cited otherwise, been drawn from relevant court documents. See *Shamrock Holdings v. Polaroid Corp.*, Del. Ch., Civil Action Nos. 10,075 and 10,079, Berger, V.C. (Jan. 6, 1989). Also see "Polaroid II," a complaint by Shamrock and a purported class of Polaroid stockholders against Polaroid, its directors and Corporate Partners, L.P.
2. See Plaintiff's pretrial memorandum, p. 35.

3.  *Shamrock Holdings v. Polaroid Corp.*, p. 19.
4.  Ibid., p. 11.
5.  Ibid., p. 13.
6.  Plaintiff's pretrial memorandum, p. 35.
7.  Ibid., p. 20.
8.  Ibid.
9.  Ibid., p. 21.
10. Ibid., p. 24.
11. Ibid., p. 26.
12. Ibid., p. 96.
13. Ibid.
14. Ibid., p. 6.
15. *Shamrock Holdings v. Polaroid Corp.*, p. 30.
16. Ibid., p. 33.
17. Ibid.
18. Ibid., p. 35.
19. Ibid., p. 36.
20. Ibid., p. 44.
21. Ibid., p. 48.
22. Ibid., p. 49.
23. Ibid., p. 35.
24. Dana Kennedy, "Shamrock Holdings Abandons 8-Month Fight for Polaroid," *Washington Post*, Mar. 28, 1989, p. E8.

# Carter Hawley Hale

In 1984, Carter Hawley Hale stores (CHH) was the largest retailing chain on the west coast, and sixth largest in the country. Based in Los Angeles, its nationwide empire stretched from trendy LA bargain basements to tiny Fifth Avenue boutiques, with a bookstore chain in between. Operating under the CHH flag were Bergdorf-Goodman, The Broadway, Contempo Casuals, Emporium-Capwell, Hole Renfrew, Neiman-Marcus, Thalimers, Walden Books, John Wanamaker, and Weinstock's.

Philip M. Hawley had been chief executive of this diverse conglomerate since 1973. He had led the company on an ambitious acquisition drive, increasing revenue threefold.

Despite the strength of the company's franchise, however, there was a widespread belief that weak management was dragging down the company's earnings, reflected in Wall Street's favorite saying about the company: "God gave them Southern California and they blew it." Hawley's acquisition program had resulted in enormous growth in sales, but not in profits. The company's net earnings had barely grown in the ten years of Hawley's stewardship.

Not all was wrong in the Hawley empire. The specialty stores division, especially its Contempo Casuals, was performing superbly. The big department stores, however, including The Broadway and Emporium-Capwell, continued to show marginal returns.

The company's sluggish growth was reflected in its stock price. CHH did not keep pace with the explosive growth of the rest of the market during the early 1980s and hovered around $20–$25 a share. However, the stock carried a healthy dividend of $1.22, prompting *Barron's* writer Benjamin J. Stein to comment: "Some investors viewed CHH common as a sort of bond with no redemption date and carrying no say in the affairs of the company."[1]

## HOSTILE TAKEOVER

On April 3, 1984, CHH's management received an unsolicited bid to take over the company. The would-be buyer was The Limited Inc., an aggressive Ohio-based retailer led by billionaire Leslie Wexner. The Limited offered $30 a share (a premium of nearly 50 percent over the pre-bid price) for 56 percent of CHH's shares, and then a package of Limited shares worth about $30 per CHH share for the remainder.

CHH responded with vigorous defiance. Management wasn't giving up without a fight.

The first step taken by CHH was a rapid repurchase of its own stock. The admitted aim was to buy up sufficient shares to prevent The Limited from acquiring a dominant position. CHH's stock climbed higher and higher as the company repurchased nearly 18 million shares within a week.

The second part of the strategy was to bring in a so-called "white knight." By persuading a friendly third party to buy a large position, CHH could keep stock out of The Limited's hands. General Cinema, one of CHH's largest shareholders and headed by Richard A. Smith, agreed to buy a special issue of preferred stock for $300 million. The shares carried preferential voting rights, giving Smith 37 percent of the voting power for a much smaller fraction of the stock. The stock paid a guaranteed dividend of 13 percent, at a post-tax cost to CHH of about $39 million a year. Lastly, Smith was offered an option to buy Walden Books (probably CHH's most profitable asset) at a discount. In exchange for this deal, Smith agreed to vote his stock in line with the recommendations of a majority of the CHH board of directors.

The Limited responded to CHH's defensive measures by raising its offer to $35 a share, roughly a 75 percent increase on CHH's pre-bid trading price.

The General Cinema deal did not guarantee CHH its independence, however. The crucial chunk of stock – which could decide the takeover battle one way or the other – was in the hands of the employees.

For some years, CHH had run an employees' profit-sharing plan, structured as a 401(k). While most 401(k) plans allow employees to choose between a variety of investment options, the CHH plan purchased only the company's stock. On retirement, employees could claim the stock they had collected over the years or the cash equivalent. Thus, employees who saved under the plan relied entirely on the good performance of the company's stock for the growth of their savings. The plan involved over 20 percent of the company's 56,000 employees, and some 6.5 million CHH shares. Prior to The Limited's bid, these shares accounted for 18 percent of CHH's outstanding shares. Following the repurchase effort, this figure rose to 39 percent of the total, though the plan's shares represented only 23 percent of the voting power owing to the issue of the preferred stock to General Cinema. The size of the plan gave it a virtually decisive say in the takeover battle. If The Limited could persuade CHH employees to vote against incumbent management, its bid would almost certainly succeed.

This left a possible divergence of interests between the members of the plan and the senior managers of the company. Employees stood to make an instant 75 percent gain on their 401(k) savings if they tendered their shares to The Limited and the bid succeeded. From the executives' point of view, however, a successful Limited bid meant losing their jobs – Wexner would certainly replace top management if he won control of the company. Thus, while it might be in the employees' interests to tender their shares, it was in the interests of CHH executives to see that they didn't.

## *The role of Bank of America*

The duty of resolving this dichotomy was left to the trustee of the profit-sharing plan, Bank of America. Under the Employees' Retirement Income Security Act (ERISA), the trustees of such a plan must see that the plan's assets are managed "solely in the interest of the participants and beneficiaries" and with "complete and undivided loyalty" to them.

To this end, a trustee must not have any conflict of interest in administering the plan, or act in any transaction involving a conflict of interest.

*Did Bank of America have a conflict of interest in dealing with the stock of the profit-sharing plan?*

- The bank agreed to be the lead lender to the CHH takeover defense. It arranged a $900 million line of credit to CHH, pledging the largest single share of $90 million. Much of this money was used to repurchase CHH shares. For this service, Bank of America received an initial fee of $500,000.
- Before The Limited announced that CHH was the target of its tender offer, Bank of America had agreed to commit $75 million to The Limited for use in an unspecified acquisition. When it became known that CHH was the target, it withdrew from this arrangement.
- Hawley sat on the Bank of America's board of directors, was a member of the executive committee, and chairman of the compensation committee. He had held those positions for nearly a decade.
- For years, the bank had been CHH's most important lender. At the time of The Limited's bid, it had loans outstanding of over $57 million and lines of credit of $15 million.
- Following the announcement of The Limited's bid, the Bank of America revised these loan agreements so that if a majority of CHH's board of directors was replaced, the loans would automatically be in default. Were The Limited's bid to succeed, the bank could, at least theoretically, step in and instantly repossess CHH assets.

Stein wrote in *Barron's*: "Bank of America was supposed to administer the plan according to the sole interests of the stockholder-employees. But it was simultaneously in the active, highly paid service of CHH management with a life or death interest in seeing that the shares of the plan were voted against the tender offer."[2]

*Do you agree with this comment?*

The possibility of a conflict of interest between the company's management and the plan's trustees at the bank had been addressed when the CHH profit-sharing plan was first created. The trust agreement, signed in 1971, included a "pass-through" provision that would come into effect if CHH were ever subject to an unsolicited takeover bid. In that situation, Bank of America would inform the plan participants of the terms of the offer, and allow them to vote their shares in confidence.

Despite the terms of the pass-through, the bank still had two responsibilities under ERISA. First, it had to explain fully to employees the terms of the offer, to ensure that they made an informed choice. Second, it had a duty to ensure that employees made an independent choice, free from any coercion from management to vote their way.

The pass-through was designed to achieve both these ends in a hostile bid situation. Under the terms of the provision, the bank would inform employees of the terms of the bid and individuals would then instruct the bank how to vote the shares in their accounts. If employees representing more than 50 percent of the plan's stock instructed the bank to sell the stock in their accounts, then it was to tender all the stock held by the plan. Otherwise, none of the stock was to be tendered.

The pass-through received its first test when The Limited made its bid. No sooner had the offer been made, however, than the terms of the provision were radically changed. Under the new terms, CHH's employee-shareholders were given four choices:

1. to tender all the shares in their account but only if plan participants representing a majority of the plan's shares chose to tender;
2. not to tender their shares unless the majority voted to tender;
3. not to tender their shares, the votes of the majority notwithstanding; and
4. to tender their shares, the votes of the majority notwithstanding.

Letters were sent to employees explaining these choices. The letter stated that if plan participants chose either of the last two options, the bank would be unable to preserve the confidentiality of that vote. In other words, if a CHH employee voted to tender to The Limited (essentially a vote against management), CHH management would know that he or she had done so. This was because the plan participants' account records were maintained by CHH, not by the bank.

The bank's instructions added that, under the new provisions, any shares for which no voting instructions were received would automatically be voted according to the second option – not to tender unless a majority did so.

All of the plan's assets were ultimately distributed to individual accounts maintained for participants. At any given time, however, the plan owned a big chunk of unallocated stock because shares acquired during the course of a year were not distributed to individual accounts until the year's end. At the time of The Limited's bid there were 800,000 such shares, or 11.4 percent of the total plan. The bank announced that these shares would be voted in line with the voting instructions received from a majority of the plan's shares.

> *Did the bank act in the interests of CHH senior management, or the plan participants? Did the bank fulfill its ERISA requirement to act with "complete and undivided loyalty" to the beneficiaries? Did the fact that management knew how an employee voted constitute coercion?*

## The Department of Labor takes note

These were some of the questions raised by the federal agency charged with overseeing ERISA funds, the Pension and Welfare Benefits Administration (PWBA), a branch of the Department of Labor (DOL). The PWBA was then headed by one of the authors of this book, Robert A.G. Monks. On April 30, 1984, Monks wrote to the law firm representing Bank of America to inform them of PWBA's interest in the case. The letter strongly suggested that if Bank of America did not alter some of the terms of the pass-through (such as the provision to vote all unallocated shares against the tender if a majority so voted), then the bank would be in violation of its fiduciary duties under ERISA.

The DOL's warning was just one of several regulatory and legal challenges filed against CHH and Bank of America.

- A single employee of CHH launched a suit against Bank of America charging misadministration of the profit plan.
- The SEC sued CHH, on the basis that the giant buyback of stock constituted an illegal tender offer.
- The New York Stock Exchange (NYSE) threatened CHH with delisting because the issue of preferred stock to General Cinema, and the massive dilution that resulted, had been consummated without shareholder approval.

The DOL concluded that the amended pass-through was insufficient in protecting employees' independence, and prepared a suit charging violations of ERISA. The *New*

*York Times* commented: "Analysts yesterday said they found it remarkable that Carter Hawley had managed to run afoul of the SEC, the stock exchange and possibly the Labor Department, considering the caliber of its legal and investment advisers."[3] CHH had hired the New York firm Skadden, Arps, Meagher & Flom as counsel, and Morgan Stanley as investment adviser.

One by one, CHH dodged the bullets. The NYSE reached an agreement with the company under which CHH shareholders would get their chance to vote on the General Cinema issue in the summer. Soon after that settlement, a Los Angeles court ruled that the SEC's case was without merit. Less than a week later, a second LA court dismissed the employee's suit. The judge agreed with Bank of America's argument that there was no connection between the bank's trust department that administered the plan and the commercial department that arranged loans to CHH for its takeover defense.

The DOL, however, broke ranks. In a draft complaint prepared by PWBA, the DOL charged that, under ERISA, "participants must be given a free choice, monitored by an entirely neutral trustee."[4] The complaint argued that Bank of America had broken this guideline in two respects:

1. The pass-through provision, as amended, did not leave employees with an uncoerced, free choice.
2. Bank of America had a conflict of interest in connection with the outcome of the tender offer that precluded it from acting as an impartial plan trustee.

In connection with the second argument, the DOL demanded that the court appoint an independent fiduciary to oversee the tendering process of the plan's stock.

Several aspects of the new pass-through worried the DOL. First, DOL officials decried the fact that non-responses, and the 18,000 unallocated shares, would be treated as votes not to tender, unless a majority voted in favor of tendering. Second, they objected to the option that allowed employees' votes to be reversed depending on the choice of the majority. Third, they noted with concern that Bank of America had not guaranteed the confidentiality of employees' votes.

ERISA imposes onerous fiduciary duties on plan trustees, who must manage the plan's assets with "care, skill, prudence and diligence." This includes voting the plan's shares. Where Bank of America had received no direction from individuals as to how to vote the shares – whether because the shares were unallocated, or because the individual concerned had not responded – the bank, argued the DOL, had a fiduciary duty to make a reasoned, independent decision about how to vote. The bank could not simply abrogate this fiduciary duty by lumping all the shares together under a decision not to tender. The complaint argued, "The trustee must reach an independent fiduciary decision as to whether to tender shares for which proper directions are not received."[5]

The complaint also contended that there was an ERISA violation in the option that allowed employees to vote a certain way, depending on the decision of the majority. Under ERISA, there were only two groups that could lawfully make investment decisions about the shares in the CHH profit-sharing plan – Bank of America, as the plan trustee with a fiduciary responsibility to the participants, and the participants themselves, as the "named fiduciary." However, two of the options on the voting card allowed for the possibility of an employee's vote being reversed if his or her choice was in the minority. Thus, the responsibility for the outcome of the vote lay with "the majority" of the employee shareholders, a group with no fiduciary responsibility to either the plan or its participants.

The DOL's brief also challenged the lack of confidentiality in the voting procedure, particularly the fact that an employee who wished to tender his shares could not do so without management knowing: "A trustee could not be considered to have fully discharged its responsibility to make sure that participants' directions are proper unless it takes all available steps to preserve the confidentiality of their choices and makes reasonable efforts to assure that the directions are not the result of pressure or coercion."[6]

The DOL's case included a broader criticism. Given that the pass-through, in the DOL's opinion, was insufficiently protective of employees' independence, the fiduciary responsibility for the CHH plan remained with Bank of America. As the plan trustee, the bank was ultimately responsible for seeing that the administration of the plan conformed with ERISA. The DOL alleged that the bank, due to multiple conflicts of interest, was incapable of fulfilling this role. The bank could not possibly act with complete objectivity to the tender offer, given its intimate connections with one of the parties concerned: "Rather than serving as a fiduciary protector of the participants, the Bank here has already aligned itself with CHH as the lead lender to the CHH takeover defense, thus presenting not only a conflict of interest in fact and law, but a necessary perception in the minds of the participants that the trustee is acting in league with their employer."[7]

The DOL argued that there were numerous legal precedents for a plan trustee to step aside. The complaint referred to one Supreme Court opinion that said the chief purpose of ERISA's fiduciary provisions is "to prevent a trustee from being put in a position where he has dual loyalties, and, therefore . . . cannot act exclusively for the benefit of a plan's participants and beneficiaries."[8]

The DOL's complaint cited a case argued before the US Court of Appeals in which the court stated: "As a practical matter we view favorably the suggestion . . . that the preferred course of action for a fiduciary of a plan holding or acquiring stock of a target, who is also an officer, director or employee of a party-in-interest seeking to acquire or retain control, is to resign and clear the way for the appointment of a genuinely neutral trustee to manage the assets involved in the control contest."[9]

The DOL complaint never got beyond its draft stage. The DOL was instructed by the Department of Justice (DOJ) to drop its suit. It was government policy that any suit brought by any part of the federal government had to be approved by the DOJ. And the DOJ put an end to this one.

Why was the DOJ so concerned? In a statement to Stein, Michael Horowitz, general counsel at the department, said the matter was purely one of government intervention: "We were concerned that a part of the government seemed to be expanding its role through litigation and we did not want any part of the government making policy through litigation. Our feeling was in no way related to the personalities involved or even the dollars involved."[10]

Stein questioned whether the decision was a little more political than that. The US Attorney General at this time was William French Smith, a California lawyer and a long-time friend of Phil Hawley. Smith had served on various corporate and non-profit boards alongside Hawley.[11] Stein also noted that Smith's office, along with the White House and Federal Trade Commission, had been lobbied hard by the Californian congressional delegation. Over three-fifths of California's representatives had gathered at a press conference, pledging their support for an independent CHH. They were joined by Tom Bradley, mayor of Los Angeles, and many other Californian public officials.[12] Stein verified that Bradley, among other CHH supporters, had received contributions from the CHH political action committee.[13]

The DOL dropped its suit, as ordered. Each of the three legal suits, as well as NYSE's threatened delisting, had now collapsed. Within days of the May 1984 dismissal of the employee's suit, The Limited dropped its tender offer. Wexner stated that he would seek other ways to gain control of CHH.

The CHH stock, which had been run up into the $30 range by arbitrageurs and speculators, quickly dropped back to the low twenties.

1984 was not a great year for CHH. Depressed by the cost of defending itself against The Limited, earnings fell to half their 1983 figure. CHH struggled to pay the guaranteed 13 percent dividend to General Cinema for its preferred stock, while finding enough left over to pay dividends on the common. Despite slightly better performance in 1985, Standard & Poors placed CHH on credit watch in March 1986.

## *The Limited attacks again*

In November 1986, The Limited formed a special acquiring group called Retail Partners with real estate developer Edward J. DeBartolo. Together, they made a second bid for CHH, offering $55 a share. The pre-bid trading price of CHH was $35–$40. Stein notes that The Limited had doubled in size since its 1984 bid and reported earnings were about four times those of CHH on 40 percent less sales.[14]

It faced up to the second battle in much the same shape as it had fought the first. General Cinema held more stock than it had before, but its voting rights were limited to 39 percent. The employee profit-sharing plan owned about 20 percent of CHH. Again, these would be the two crucial elements of CHH's defense.

Richard Smith, head of General Cinema, announced that he was not adamantly against the idea of tendering his shares to The Limited, but that he considered $55 too low. Believing that Smith could be persuaded to tender at a higher price, Retail Partners raised their offer to $60 a share.

Meanwhile, Bank of America had put new procedures in place in the event of a tender offer.

- Employees could request information about the tender and, if they wished to vote, could apply for their share certificates and vote the shares themselves, rather than issuing instructions for the trustee to vote for them.
- If an employee didn't request his or her certificates, however, the shares would automatically be voted against the tender.

The new procedures were hardly a step in the direction of confidentiality, since the only reason an employee would apply for his share certificates would be in order to vote for the tender. The records of employee shareholding were still at CHH headquarters, so management would know exactly which employees had requested their shares and might be considering a vote for Wexner.

Not only were the new Bank of America voting procedures transparent, they were moot. Even if an employee decided to tender his shares, it was impossible to do so. Employees were informed that it would take six to eight weeks for their certificates to arrive, if requested. Retail Partners' offer expired in five weeks.

On December 8, 1986, CHH announced that it was rejecting the $60 bid in the light of a widespread restructuring of the company. Morgan Stanley issued a fairness opinion, saying that the restructuring was a much better choice for shareholders than the inadequate

Limited offer. It was later asserted that such a restructuring had been under consideration since October 1986, just before The Limited's second bid.

The restructuring, if approved, would split CHH into two new companies. Each would carry a separate stock. One company, still called Carter Hawley Hale, would consist of department-store operations including Broadway, Thalimers, and Weinstock's. The second company, called the Neiman-Marcus Group Inc., would consist of the specialty stores: Contempo Casuals, Neiman-Marcus, and Bergdorf Goodman.

Stockholders, including employee-shareholders, would receive the following for every share of CHH they owned:

- one share of the department store company;
- one share of the Neiman-Marcus Group;
- a one-time payout of $17, which could be converted into further shares of CHH and Neiman-Marcus.

Under the restructuring, General Cinema would end up with a huge interest in the Neiman-Marcus Group, while CHH would be owned by its employees. Top management would convert its $17 a share payout, and its outstanding stock options into a 22 percent holding of the department store company – a massive holding compared to the less than 1 percent that management owned of the unrestructured CHH. The employee plan would own a further 23 percent.

The net effect was to insulate CHH from any hostile takeover attempt and to give the employees a huge stake in the company. In Phil Hawley's words to *Women's Wear Daily*: "The big story, and you can forget all this other stuff – the big story is that we are the first major retailer owned by the people who work for it . . . All of a sudden we have 12,000 entrepreneurs."[15] The restructuring was announced to shareholders in the form of a 400-page proxy statement and prospectus. The proxy stated that the board had unanimously approved the restructuring, and asked shareholders to ratify it. The restructuring contained some amendments to CHH's certificate of incorporation. These included:

- the division of the CHH board into three classes;
- elimination of directors' liability in future damages if claimed as a result of any breach of their fiduciary duty of care;
- elimination of the ability of stockholders to call a special meeting of stockholders, or to take any action by less than unanimous written consent;
- a shareholder rights plan, or "poison pill", that would kick into effect if any person acquired 20 percent of the company's shares.

The proxy admitted, "Certain of the amendments to the Company's certificate of incorporation . . . may make more difficult or discourage the removal of company management . . . and may make more difficult, if not impossible, certain mergers, tender offers or other future takeover attempts."

The proxy warned that the restructuring would "include an immediate change in the Department Store Company's capitalization to one that is highly leveraged," since the department store half of CHH would assume the debt burden of the entire company. The proxy disclosed the fact that shareholders faced "the prospect that no dividends will be paid to holders of the Department Shares for the foreseeable future." Finally, the proxy said that paying for the $17-per-share distribution, and financing the restructuring, would cost over $1 billion.

The proxy predicted a bright financial future for the department store company. Sales were expected to rise from $2.7 billion in 1988 to $3.2 billion in 1991. Earnings per share were expected to rise from $1.41 in 1988, to $3.2 in 1990, and to $4.51 in 1991. As Stein comments, "These projections were provided, with the straight face that only a financial document can offer, as 'in line with recent results' . . . results had never shown such dramatic improvement, except over periods of less than three quarters."[16] Stein also pointed out the fantastic fees that would be paid to Morgan Stanley for its part in the restructuring. The investment banking firm received a basic fee of $24.375 million, though its involvement in the placement of the securities associated with the restructuring would take the overall fee to over $43 million.[17] This figure is substantially greater than CHH's own estimate of its 1988 earnings of $32 million.

Shortly after the announcement of the restructuring, The Limited and Edward DeBartolo withdrew their offer. The ownership structures of the two companies under the restructuring made a takeover impossible without the cooperation of either management or the board of CHH. It was clear to Retail Partners that neither would be forthcoming.

## AFTER THE RESTRUCTURING

How did Hawley's "12,000 entrepreneurs" fare as a result of this shake-up? At first, the employee-shareholders appeared to have made out like bandits. CHH stock reached a peak of nearly $80 during the period following The Limited's bid, and continued to trade at roughly the $60 price Wexner had offered. Stein, in his May 1987 article, concluded: "Considering the current share prices, the CHH story could have come out a lot worse than it did."[18]

*Barron's* later admitted it was wrong[19] – as far as the shareholders were concerned the CHH story came out just about as badly as it possibly could have. In the months following their approval of the restructuring, CHH's shareholders witnessed the freefall of their shares.

By the end of 1987, CHH's stock had plunged to around $10.

Moreover, over the next four years the company manifestly failed to live up to the projections provided in the 1987 restructuring prospectus. That prospectus had predicted that net earnings would reach $85 million for the year ended July 31, 1990. Instead, the company reported a $26 million loss in that year. In other words, the company lost $1.03 a share, compared to its 1987 prediction that it would earn $3.25 per share in 1990. Meanwhile, the stock continued on its downward spiral, reaching a low of less than $5 a share in late 1990. The company filed for Chapter 11 bankruptcy protection on February 11, 1991.

Employee-shareholders went down with the ship. Because the CHH plan was a profit-sharing plan, not an employees' retirement fund, the plan trustee was not obliged by ERISA to diversify employee holdings. That is, Bank of America was merely charged with acquiring CHH stock on behalf of the plan, not ensuring that it had a diversified, less risky portfolio. The result was that Bank of America had continued to buy CHH stock on behalf of the plan, even up to a week before the Chapter 11 filing.

Employee-shareholders experienced a devastating reduction in the value of their plan accounts. *Barron's* described one employer, Bill Fiore, who had contributed $8,000 to the plan over 13 years. His contribution was now worth less than $2,000.[20] The *Wall Street Journal* interviewed Shirley J. Miner, an employee of 26 years' standing, who had expected her contributions to have grown to $80,000. On retirement, she found that her account was worth just $15,000.[21] What did the 12,000 employee-shareholders now own?

- One CHH share, trading at about $2 in the months following the Chapter 11 filing.
- One Neiman-Marcus share, received at the time of the restructuring. Following the spinoff, Neiman-Marcus stock traded at highs of up to $45. By the time of CHH's bankruptcy filing, it had dropped to around $17.
- The $17-a-share special payout.

So the shares in the plan, for which Wexner had offered $60 in 1986, were worth about $36 four years later.

This loss in value did not go unnoticed in the press. Rising to his company's defense, Hawley told the *Journal* that the plan accounts were not "retirement savings."[22] Strictly speaking, this was true – CHH's 401(k) scheme merely allowed employees to share in the company's profits. As such, employees could decide whether to contribute up to 12 percent of salary for the purchase of CHH stock, or keep the extra cash and make their own investment decisions. CHH employees, however, charged that the choice was not that simple. Employees told the press that they were pressured into contributing a full 12 percent to the plan, for fear of seeming uncommitted to the welfare of the company. Bill Fiore told *Barron's*, "It was common knowledge that if you were thinking of going into management, you'd better have your 12 percent in or you weren't going anywhere."[23] Ms. Miner told the *Journal* that she felt she had "no choice" but to convert her $17-per-share payout at the time of the restructuring (worth $23,000) into further CHH and Neiman-Marcus shares: "I feared being labeled as disloyal."[24]

Employees must have wondered why they hadn't realized an instant 75 percent gain on their shares by tendering to Wexner in 1984 or accepted $60 dollars a share in 1986. Of course, if either of those bids had been successful, Hawley and his management team would have lost their jobs.

*Whom did the profit-sharing plan serve?*

*To what lengths should incumbent managers be allowed to go to protect their company from takeover? Did Phil Hawley go too far?*

*Does this case study present a "free market" for corporate control? Should takeovers be encouraged or discouraged? Would your answer change if you knew that The Limited also suffered from years of poor performance following its attempted takeover of CHH?*

*Were the employee-shareholders of CHH genuine shareholders? Were they genuine stakeholders? How might their interests be protected?*

*Is employee ownership in the best interests of good corporate performance?*

*What role did Bank of America play in fending off The Limited? What role should it have played?*

## NOTES

1. Benjamin J. Stein, "A Saga of Shareholder Neglect," *Barron's*, May 4, 1987, pp. 8–75.
2. Ibid.
3. Isadore Barmash, "Carter Faces Suit by SEC," *New York Times*, May 2, 1984, p. D1.
4. *Raymond J. Donovan, Secretary of the United States Department of Labor v. The Bank of America*, Unfiled Memorandum in Support of Plaintiff's Motion for Preliminary Injunction, Appointment of Independent Fiduciary, and Ancillary Orders, p. 4.
5. Ibid., p. 26.
6. Ibid., pp. 25–6.
7. Ibid., p. 4.

8. *NLRB v. Amax Coal Co.*, 453 US at 334 (1981).
9. *Leigh v. Engle*, 727 F.2d 113, 7th Circuit (1984).
10. Stein, "A Saga of Shareholder Neglect."
11. Ibid.
12. Ibid.
13. Ibid.
14. Ibid.
15. Quoted in Maggie Mahar, "Cracked Nest Egg: A Double Whammy for Employees of Carter Hawley Hale," *Barron's*, Apr. 8, 1991, p. 15.
16. Stein, "A Saga of Shareholder Neglect."
17. Ibid.
18. Ibid.
19. Mahar, "Cracked Nest Egg," p. 14.
20. Ibid.
21. Francine Schwadel, "Carter Hawley 401(k)'s Yield Falls Short," *Wall Street Journal*, June.
22. Ibid.
23. Mahar, "Cracked Nest Egg," p. 24.
24. Schwadel, "Carter Hawley 401(k)'s Yield Falls Short," p. C1.

# Eastman Kodak

*The following report is a study prepared by Lens Inc., an investment management firm in which both authors of this book are Principals. This study shows how informed and involved shareholders may add value to their target companies.*

## July 1992 (stock price, 7/1/92 – $40.50)

Eastman Kodak was first selected as a Lens "focus" company. Kodak was unnecessarily diversified into non-value-adding businesses, with a record of long-term under-performance. Kodak's problems included:

- *Debt.* Kodak's balance sheet has deteriorated seriously over the last ten years. As of late 1992, Kodak's total debt stood at $10.3 billion, having doubled since 1988. The ratio of debt to total capital was nearly 60 percent.
- *Unrelated diversification.* The $5.1 billion acquisition of Sterling Drug in 1988 has never produced the anticipated returns. Analysts speculated that the money-losing copier division could also be sold.
- *Long-term under-performance in its core businesses.* According to *Business Week*, "The company angered Wall Street by assuming that the slowdown in its core photographic market in the 1980s was only temporary. Its cost structure was predicated on a return to growth that never materialized." Contrary to analysts' predictions, Kodak assumed growth in its core photo business of 6–8 percent. Actual growth was nearer 2–4 percent.
- *Poor long-term strategy.* Since 1982 Eastman Kodak has undertaken four separate restructurings, including billions of dollars in write-offs. Yet (according to a PaineWebber market analyst) the company has under-performed the S&P 500 Index by 200 percent since 1982. During the last decade sales growth has been at an annual rate of 6.7 percent, but earnings, which in former times were running around $3 per share, had dropped to virtually break-even in 1991. Over the last four years Kodak has spent $5.2 billion on R&D, and has made $8.2 billion of capital expenditures. Long-term debt increased by $5.2 billion, total debt by $6.1 billion, and shareholders' equity rose by less than $100 million. Management has not been able to convert massive expenditures into additional value for shareholders, despite several restructurings.

## *August 1992* (stock price, 8/3/92 – $43.37)

Lens Principal, Robert A.G. Monks, wrote to Kodak's CEO, Kay R. Whitmore, identifying Kodak as a company where the involvement of credible shareholders could add value. Monks wrote:

In Eastman Kodak's 1991 Annual Report you [Mr. Whitmore] describe the company's underlying precepts: "We will not participate in a market or enter into a business simply because we possess the technical competence to do so. Our goal is the number one or number two positions in markets where rates of return consistently exceed the cost of capital." It is not apparent that Eastman Kodak's position in chemicals, drugs, or copying is at the top of their respective industries; nor is there indication of progress towards that goal in the performance of recent years; it is clear however that the rates of return achieved are not among the leaders . . . Kodak still has the dominant position in photographic markets throughout the world, but competition is growing. Is it better able to confront its formidable competitors in that field as a diversified conglomerate or through the focused creation of a competitive corporate culture?

## *November 1992* (stock price, 11/2/92 – $41.37)

Three Lens Principals met with CEO Kay Whitmore and other senior managers to discuss Kodak's competitive position. Both sides agreed that the meeting was frank and constructive. In a letter following the meeting, Lens outlined its specific concerns with the company's strategic direction:

The financial results of Eastman Kodak in recent years could objectively indicate to an outsider that management has:

• followed a policy of building an empire measured only by gross size;
• thrown larger and larger amounts of money at Kodak's core problem – competition for market share – seemingly without a strategy;
• invested heavily in diversification in an attempt to sustain corporate growth and restore shrinking margins; and
• allowed the development of a vast bureaucracy.

Kodak's diversification efforts have been generally unsuccessful to date. Cost of acquisitions, and of the huge research programs and capital budgets, have been financed by a nearly five-fold increase in debt, while shareholders' equity has remained flat. Growth has remained slow, and margins have fallen drastically, Management has taken six special write-offs, totaling $4.7 billion, in less than eight years, with little or no improvement in margins.

The letter was accompanied by a detailed financial plan (available on request) outlining a six-point plan for improved shareholder value:

1.  increasing the realization on assets and sales;
2.  resuming earnings growth;
3.  shifting the usage of cashflow to reduce debt and allow dividend increases as soon as prudently possible;

4.  restoring the company's financial strength by reducing debt;
5.  focusing the attention and energies of the board and the management on Kodak's core business; and
6.  distributing unrelated assets to Kodak shareholders.

The plan also recommended some "governance reforms" to create a constructive relationship between the managers and owners of Eastman Kodak. The recommendations were to:

*   introduce confidential voting;
*   end the system of staggered board elections to provide for the annual election of all directors;
*   improve the ratio of insiders to outsiders to provide for a genuinely independent board; and
*   separate the positions of chairman and CEO.

Finally, the letter said that Lens would be filing a shareholder resolution at the Eastman Kodak 1993 annual meeting. The resolution proposed a bylaw amendment to create an advisory committee of the company's largest long-term shareholders.

## *January 1993* (stock price, 12/31/92 – $40.50)

Kodak's management took a series of steps that demonstrated a new commitment to the company's owners. *Business Week* wrote: "Insiders say Kodak Chairman Kay R. Whitmore has concluded that only radical surgery can rescue the company . . . 'Shareholders have been the most underserved of our constituents' he confesses.'" The new measures included:

*   *The appointment of a new chief financial officer, Christopher J. Steffen.* Steffen came to Kodak in January 1993, having helped create successful turnarounds at Chrysler and Honeywell. Significantly, Kodak broke its traditional rule of promoting insiders, Steffen being the highest-ranking outsider appointed since 1912. His recruitment was greeted enthusiastically – Kodak's stock improved 17 percent in a matter of days. *Business Week* dubbed Steffen the "$2 billion man" for his contribution to the company's market value.
*   *An overhaul of the core imaging business.* In a letter to Monks, Whitmore described the strategy as "an aggressive action plan . . . which is quite consistent with much of what we discussed when you visited with us last November here in Rochester." The strategy was based on an admission that growth in Imaging would be a sluggish 2–4 percent, and that cashflow would have to be increased in other ways. To this end, Kodak announced it was cutting R&D spending, revamping overseas operations, and paring some 2,000 employees from its Rochester headquarters. These measures were expected to lower net costs by over $200 million a year. The plan received widespread approval: "It's a belated recognition that Kodak is no longer growing its core business," said Eugene Glazer of Dean Witter. "This is a business strategy that really fits with reality," said PaineWebber's Kimberly Retrievi.[1]
*   *A new compensation plan for senior executives.* The plan requires 40 top managers to buy stock in the company equal to 1–4 times their current salary. Whitmore personally pledged himself to achieving holdings of four times his current salary, or $3.8 million, within five years. The plan was applauded by investors across the board. "There's nothing

that gets management thinking like a shareholder than being a shareholder," said Lens principal Nell Minow.[2]

- *A new corporate directions committee.* The committee will consist solely of outside directors, and has a straightforward charter: "to assess Kodak's competitive position and develop plans to increase shareowner value."

- *A new long-term strategy.* Two weeks after his appointment as CFO, Steffen said that he expected to have a business plan ready in about six months. He intends to cut the debt-capital ratio from its current 59 percent to around 30–40 percent, and he said he would not rule out asset sales to achieve that goal. The stock jumped a further $2.63 on the news.

The response of the investment community to Kodak's measures was very positive. By the end of January 1993, the company's stock had risen to $49.88.

## *February 1993* (stock price, 2/26/93 – $53.62)

As a result of the giant steps Kodak's management took to gear the company to improved performance, coupled with the company's genuine desire to address shareholder concerns, Lens agreed on February 26 to withdraw its shareholder proposal calling for a shareholder advisory committee.

Kodak was not long out of the news, however. On April 28, just 11 weeks after his arrival in Rochester, Chris Steffen resigned as Kodak's CFO. Mr. Steffen found that his ideas were perceived as too "revolutionary" when others wanted a more "evolutionary" approach. When Steffen abruptly resigned (causing Kodak's stock to lose over $5 in a single day), Kodak shareholders questioned the company's commitment to change.

During the two-week period between Steffen's departure and the company's annual meeting, investors demanded that Kodak explain why Steffen had resigned, and why they should trust incumbent management to lead the company to success. Ultimately, many institutional holders recognized that CEO Whitmore had not sought Steffen's departure, and that his commitment to change had not weakened. At the annual meeting, Whitmore spoke to shareholders about the "constructive" and "helpful" role Lens and other investors had played over the previous year. He said, "It provides us an external point of view that we have to listen to with care."

Ultimately, the independent directors at Kodak were not convinced that Mr. Whitmore would be able to fulfill the commitment made to shareholders to improve Kodak's performance significantly. On August 6, 1993, the independent directors announced that Mr. Whitmore would step down upon the naming of a successor, and on October 27, 1993, they announced the appointment of Motorola CEO George Fisher as Kodak's new CEO. On the day of the announcement, Kodak's stock rose $4.87 to $63.62.

### NOTES

1. Joan E. Rigdon, "Kodak Expects Slow Growth in Core Business," *Wall Street Journal*, Jan. 20, 1993, p. A4.
2. Marlene Givant Star, "Investors Give Nod to Kodak Stock Buy Rule," *Pensions and Investments*, Jan. 25, 1993, p. 74.

# WASTE MANAGEMENT CORP.

Waste Management was a star stock of the 1970s and early 1980s. Its founders, Dean Buntrock and Wayne Huizenga (who went on to launch the worldwide Blockbuster video rental chain) understood that domestic trash collection could be a national business. Until then, garbage collection was the preserve of thousands of small, regional companies dealing only with a local area. Waste Management saw that vast economies of scale could be achieved if these companies could be folded into a single company with nationwide reach.

Waste Management moved aggressively, and its growth was phenomenal. Founded in 1971, it grew by acquisition (at one point it was performing 200 mergers and acquisitions a year) to become the largest waste haulage company in the country. In doing so, it acquired more than 2,000 companies.

The result was a fiendishly complex corporate organization. At the peak of Waste's expansion, the company featured about 250 local divisions, 40 regional offices, and 9 area offices not to mention headquarters.

Initially, the market did not mind these convolutions. Adjusted for splits, the stock rose from $1.84 in 1980 to the mid-forties in the early 1990s.

But growth at this speed could not last. As the company grew, so it had to acquire even more companies to maintain that growth. Its size impeded its continued acceleration. Furthermore, the market settled down. Other companies followed Waste's lead and consolidated their own regions. Over a period of 15–20 years, the domestic trash-hauling business matured.

But Waste was not done. Its managers continued to insist it was a growth company. The company diversified into international waste hauling, recycling, environmental cleanup, hazardous waste disposal, and home services. By 1990, WMX had become a complex conglomerate that owned or part-owned companies ranging from a UK water utility to lawn-care contracting.

Some idea of the sprawl that was WMX is provided by the company's 1996 10-K filing with the SEC. The company listed more than 700 direct subsidiaries, which in turn owned a further 600 sub-subsidiaries.

The *Wall Street Journal* argued that Buntrock "saw the company as a kind of mutual fund of environmental business, setting up as many as four publicly traded units."

WMX Technologies consisted of Waste Management, which concentrated on North American residential and industrial solid waste disposal. A publicly traded subsidiary (until 1995), Chemical Waste Management, dealt with hazardous waste, and a 60 percent-owned subsidiary, Advanced Environmental Technical Services, provided hazardous waste services. A further wholly owned subsidiary, Chem-Nuclear Systems, dealt with radioactive waste management.

The company's international operations were provided through Waste Management International, which was owned 56 percent by WMX and 12 percent each by the company's Rust International and Wheelabrator Technologies subsidiaries. Waste Management International offered services in ten countries in Europe as well as Australia, South America, Asia and the Middle East. It also owned 20 percent of Wessex Water, a publicly traded water utility in the UK.

Wheelabrator Technologies (58 percent owned by the company) was a public company primarily providing clean air and water to municipalities and industry. Rust International, also a public company until WMX bought back its stock in 1995, was part-owned by WMX and Wheelabrator. It offered environmental and infrastructure engineering and consulting, ranging from hazardous waste cleanup to scaffolding provision. Rust had international operations in 35 countries.

Rust owned 41 percent of NSC Corp., a publicly traded provider of asbestos abatement, and a 37 percent interest in OHM Corp., a publicly traded provider of environmental remediation services. Finally, Rust owned a 19 percent interest in ServiceMaster, a provider of management services including management of health care, education and commercial facilities, lawn care, pest control and other consumer services.

In 1993 Waste Management renamed itself WMX to reflect its modern, all-encompassing presence. Buntrock boasted that WMX had become "one of the most important companies in the world."

The trouble was that, almost without exception, they lost money in these non-core areas. For example, in the 1980s, there was a sudden fear that the US was running out of landfills. Waste Management spent wildly to develop more landfill facilities only to suffer from vast over-capacity. Meanwhile, Americans produced less waste as producers emphasized "source reduction," creating less packaging in the first place.

At the same time, a vast market was projected for recycling. Waste Management, like others, moved to attack this market, only to find that the expected development never happened. The market for treating hazardous chemical waste proved similarly elusive.

*One of the authors of this book, Nell Minow, told the press: "They were successful for so long that they didn't realize that they stopped being successful . . . They were successful in their core business and made the fatal mistake of trying to go beyond that." Whose job is it to ensure this doesn't happen?*

## GOLD INTO GARBAGE

By the mid-1990s, WMX's star had tarnished. The *Washington Post* commented: "In the 1980s, when investors looked at the company named Waste Management Inc., they saw gold. But in recent years, the company now known as WMX Technologies has looked more like garbage."[1]

In 1994, the picture darkened considerably – profits fell by 50 percent, and the company failed to meet earnings projections. Meanwhile, the stock headed south – ticking over at over $46 in February 1992, it slipped to less than $23 in April 1994.

If one looks back at the company's ten-year performance from 1996, it is apparent that it had experienced a sharp downturn in its fortunes.

If you had invested $100 in WMX in 1986, it would have been worth $318 in 1991. The same sum invested in the S&P 500 index and the Smith Barney Solid Waste index would have returned $204 and $222 respectively. In other words, from 1986 to 1991 WMX was outperforming both the market and its sector.

By 1996, the story is less sunny. That same $100 invested in 1986 would now have been worth $269, about one-sixth less than five years previously. The same sum invested in the S&P 500 would have been worth $415, and an investment in the index would have been worth $215. So WMX was still doing a bit better than its competitors, but the company was failing to keep up with the bull market. And, worse, the return over five years was actually negative.

In fact, WMX continued to report profits, but these were all but wiped out by year after year of special charges. Such special charges are meant to be exactly that – special. They reflect extraordinary one-time losses. Unfortunately, at Waste, they became all too familiar.

From 1990, these charges read as follows:

1991    $260 million pre-tax charge to boost reserves for cleaning up old dumps

1992    $159.7 million pre-tax charge to write down value of medical waste business and incinerators $23.4 million after-tax charge to write down value of asbestos-cleaning business

1993    $550 million pre-tax charge to write down value of hazardous waste business

1994    $9.2 million pre-tax charge to get out of marine construction and dredging

1995    $140.6 million pre-tax charge, mostly further write-down of value of hazardous waste business

         $194.6 million pre-tax charge to write down value of international waste business

1996    $88 million after-tax charge on sale of Wessex stake.

*In a 1996 meeting with the authors, Dean Buntrock said: "The trouble is, no one believes our numbers." What warning bells does this ring?*

*What do the special charges tell you about the company's attempts to diversify?*

But the company appeared unfazed by the charges or the stock's downward trajectory and continued to pour capital into projects. The *Wall Street Journal* quoted Steve Binder, analyst at Bear, Steams who said: "They continue to allocate resources as if they were still participating in a growth industry."[2]

Indeed, Buntrock told the 1994 annual meeting: "We are a growth company."

*Was it? If not, whose job was it to find an alternative strategy?*

## LENS AND SOROS

In the mid-1990s, Lens Inc., an investment fund of which the two authors were principals, invested several million dollars in WMX.

Lens's first concern was to call for fresh talent on the board. When the fund first invested, the board was made up as follows:[3]

- **H. Jesse Arnelle**, 61, director since 1992. A corporate lawyer, and holder of five other non-executive director positions.

- **Jerry E. Dempsey**, 62, director since 1984. A former employee of the company – he served as senior vice-president from 1988 to 1993. Since retiring from Waste, he had acted as chairman and CEO of a glass, coatings, and chemicals company.
- **Dr. James B. Edwards**, 67, since 1995. Former United States Secretary of Energy, dentist, former governor of South Carolina, president of the Medical University of South Carolina. He held eight other non-executive director positions.
- **Alexander B. Trowbridge**, 65, since 1995. Former Secretary of Commerce. He had served as consultant to the company since 1990, an arrangement which in 1995 was worth $30,000. He held nine non-executive director positions.
- **Dr. Pastora San Juan Cafferty**, 54, since 1994. Professor at the University of Chicago School of Social Service Administration.
- **Donald F. Flynn**, 55, since 1981. He had served as senior vice-president of the company from 1975 to 1991. He had been CFO from 1972 to 1989 and the treasurer from 1989 to 1996. He was also a director of two WMX subsidiaries. Until the end of 1994, Flynn was making $300,000 p.a. in consultancy fees. The consulting arrangement included a retirement benefit that was due to pay out for the rest of his life.
- **James R. Peterson**, 67, since 1980. The CEO of the Parker Pen company.
- **Phillip B. Rooney**, 50, since 1981. He had been an employee of the company since 1969.
- **Dean L. Buntrock**, 63, chairman and CEO since 1968.
- **Howard H. Baker**, 69, since 1989. Lawyer, Reagan's chief of staff, three terms as US Senator. He was a partner in a law firm retained by the company.
- **Peter H. Huizenga**, 56, since 1968. Nephew of the founder, consultant to the company from 1989 to 1993. Served as vice-president and secretary of the company from 1975 and 1968 respectively until he resigned from those positions in 1988.
- **Peer Pedersen**, 70, since 1979. Lawyer, and Dean Buntrock's personal attorney. He was chairman of a law firm retained by the company.

It is noteworthy that non-executive directors also took part in a Phantom Stock Plan and stock option plans – they had a vested interest in the performance of the stock rather than the performance of the company. This was, as we shall see, highly significant.

Pedersen, an affiliated director, chaired the compensation committee. Baker, also connected, served on this committee. In 1995, the audit committee featured as many affiliated outside directors as independent ones. The five-member Nominations Committee contained four affiliated outsiders.

So, of the 12-member board, two were full-time insiders, three were former employees, three were affiliated due to consultancy arrangements, and four were independent outsiders. As Nell Minow told the press: "Two-thirds of the board is on the payroll."

The one, indeed the most important, area in which the board did demonstrate best practice was in stock ownership. James B. Edwards owned over 1,700 shares on joining the company. H. Jesse Arnelle owned over 9,000, and Trowbridge over 20,000. But even these shareholdings, given the numerous other connections that tied the directors to the incumbent management, failed to create the right environment of tough-speaking independence.

There was one director with a considerable stake – Peter Huizenga, nephew of Waste's co-founder Wayne Huizenga. He owned over 8 million shares. But, like management, his stake in the company was intimately bound up in its past. Peter Huizenga showed little aptitude or appetite for the tough choices required in a turnaround.

## First feelers

Lens sought and was granted a meeting with management. The Lens principals came away with the view that the executives did not perceive a problem. They were confident that their strategy was the right one, and that the magical growth of earlier years would return.

Lens concluded that the very success of the company's early years – a success that the present managers had helped create – was inhibiting an honest view of the current situation. Having established a great company, the founding team could not view the company any other way.

Lens came away with three conclusions:

1. that Dean Buntrock was a dominant CEO who stifled debate;
2. that there was a need to clean up the numbers;
3. that the board required more aggressive outside talent.

Related to the need to clear up the numbers was a need for a new CFO. James E. Koenig, with the company since 1987 and CFO since 1989, was the incumbent and had hence overseen several years of the restructuring charges. If, as Dean Buntrock said, "no one believes our numbers," the problem was clearly partly Koenig's. It was an early demand of Lens and other investors that Koenig be replaced.

In May 1996, the company had a rude shock. George Soros, the tycoon speculator who became famous for making $1 billion betting against the Bank of England in the September 1992 sterling crisis, announced that he had acquired more than 5 percent of the company. His stake was worth $750 million.

The investment was made by a Soros affiliate, Duquesne Capital Management, and was a clear signal of intent. Soros was not a takeover predator in the traditional mode – he had no plans to launch an all-out hostile bid for the company. But his investment gave notice that he expected change and soon.

## 1996 annual meeting

Lens attended the annual meeting to speak directly to the board about its concerns over the company's long-term under-performance.

But the company had a surprise of its own. After nearly 30 years as chairman and CEO, Dean Buntrock announced that he would be stepping down as CEO, although he would remain as chairman. Long-serving lieutenant Phillip Rooney, who had also been at Waste since its birth, would replace him.

Though Buntrock's semi-retirement perhaps indicated a change in attitude by senior management, it was clear to Lens and others that there was much still to be done. Although Buntrock was taking a hand off the levers of power, he remained a significant presence as chairman, with long-time insider Rooney moving up a place. In terms of substance, management hadn't changed a bit.

In 1996, there were two shareholder resolutions, both opposed by the company. The first, filed by the Central Pension Fund of the International Union of Operating Engineers and Participating Employers, called for a policy banning directors "from accepting consulting or other fees from the company."

The statement noted that "directors owe their fundamental allegiance to the shareholders of the corporation . . . and not to management." The proposal claimed that consulting fees paid out to directors may have run to hundreds of thousands of dollars a year: "there is an appalling lack of precise information provided to shareholders on the extent of these financial arrangements." The board said: "this rigid restriction is unnecessary and ill-advised."

The second proposal was filed by the Teamsters Pension Plan, calling for annual election of all directors. The resolution argued that the move was necessary because "a number of concerns raise the possibility that WMX management may not be fully attuned" to shareholders' interests.

The Teamsters cited WMX's poor record on executive compensation noting that "[pay] expert Graef Crystal found WMX's CEO scored fifth in rankings of his peers when measuring low performance and high pay."

The board said that the staggered system had received nearly an 80 percent shareholder vote in favor when it was proposed in 1985.

Both proposals were defeated, although the company made the surprise announcement that it would itself propose the same resolutions at the next year's meeting.

## After the annual meeting

In a further meeting, in October 1996, Lens offered the view that the company had never successfully diversified beyond domestic trash. The division still represented half the company's sales, and easily reported the most profit. Rooney countered that he intended to sell $1 billion of under-performing assets by 1998.

Filtering through to analysts, the news of this restructuring sent the stock from the mid-twenties to $34.

Lens continued to press for a revitalized board. In a meeting with Alexander Trowbridge, former secretary of commerce and head of the nominations committee, Lens noted that four directors were up for election in 1997. Lens argued that it was the perfect opportunity to bring in some tough new outsiders. In contrast to the incumbent board, Lens sought independent outsiders who could bring considerable business experience to the table in order to effect a turnaround.

Lens offered four names to Trowbridge, of which the company eventually accepted one – Paul Montrone, who joined the board in January 1997. Mr. Montrone, 55, was the CEO of Fisher Scientific International. He had also been a director of Wheelabrator since 1989.

Despite the promise of streamlining and the improved share price, Lens felt the company was still moving too slowly. It was convinced that the only route to fundamental change lay with new talent at the top of the company. It was inconceivable, in Lens' view, that the company could be restored when top management and the board were made up of long-term insiders.

Lens had a multi-pronged strategy to keep the pressure up. In December 1996, the fund retained Spencer Stuart, the blue-chip recruitment firm, to gather names for a proxy fight for four seats on the board. The involvement of Spencer Stuart was evidence that shareholder activists had achieved mainstream legitimacy. It demonstrated that the shareholders' involvement was credible, and concerned with long-term wealth creation to the benefit of the company and all its shareholders.

But if Spencer Stuart was happy to be associated with Lens, individual director candidates were less happy about getting involved in what could be a high-profile proxy contest. Spencer Stuart identified several people who expressed an interest in serving on the board, but who were unwilling to do so without being asked by the company. Lens forwarded their names to Waste's board.

At the same time, Lens filed a shareholder resolution calling for an independent invest-ment bank to be hired to study the divestment of assets. The resolution was a means of maintaining pressure on the company.

Lens also prepared a full-page advertisement for the *Wall Street Journal* that identified the Waste board as "long term liabilities." The ad, similar to the one directed at Sears in 1992 (see figure 6.1), was another means of needling the Waste board into action. Waste was informed of the ad, and told that dates had been booked for its publication.

*Directors obey the Heisenberg uncertainty principle. Like subatomic particles, they behave dif-ferently when observed. Discuss.*

## THE SOROS EFFECT

George Soros's group, with that $750 million stake behind it, continued to be active.

In December 1996, Stanley F. Druckenmiller, Dusquene's chief investment officer, told *Crain's Chicago Business* that he wished to see an overhaul at the top of the company: "We have become convinced that the only way the inherent shareholder value in the company can be realized is with a change in the current top management."

In the same month, the Soros group filed a statement with the SEC saying that the investors were "frustrated with lack of progress" at the company, and questioned "the resolve of management about enhancing shareholder value."

The company pressed ahead with its streamlining plans. It announced that it would sell its stake in the UK water supply utility, Wessex Water, and pledged to repurchase 25 mil-lion shares. But the moves failed to ignite the stock, which continued to bob around in the high twenties/low thirties.

### Credibility problem

The company was now under considerable pressure to reform and perform. Two events further undermined the incumbent management's credibility.

First, the company was found guilty of cheating a partner in the development of a hazardous waste site.

WMX had purchased the dump from the developers; part of the purchase agreement was that WMX would pay a percentage of the dump's revenue over a period of years. But WMX's creative accounting led to greatly understated revenue and hence a lesser payment to the developers. The court found that the accounting fiddle amounted to $91.5 million.

Though the episode did not concern the top executives, it was embarrassing because it seemed indicative of WMX's approach to financial reporting. Analysts and investors instinct-ively seemed to distrust WMX's numbers. Here, on a small scale, was evidence that they were right to do so.

Second, the company disclosed in filings to the SEC that senior management was cush-ioning itself for a possible change in control. The disclosures revealed that the executives had received large salary increases, hefty stock options, and golden parachute arrangements. Sixteen members of senior management were awarded $13 million in restricted stock that would vest if the employee was terminated.

Rooney himself was blessed with a new five-year contract, a 25 percent increase in base salary, plus options on 350,000 shares – twice the grant he had received the year before. The company said the raise and the options were in recognition of the fact that Rooney had been elevated from COO to CEO.

In August 1996, the company initiated a new three-year rolling contract with James Koenig, the CFO, and Herbert A. Getz, the general counsel, that essentially insulated them from being terminated (except for cause). The contract agreed to pay three years' salary plus annual bonus plus long-term bonus. The proxy estimated that, had the company been taken over on the last day of 1996, the new contract would be worth $1,889,300 to Koenig.

To Soros and Lens, these pay disclosures were evidence that management was further insulating itself from external discipline.

*Analyze these compensation arrangements. Do they align the executive's interests with those of shareholders? How might you design a compensation package for a turnaround situation such as this?*

*If an executive is richly rewarded for failure, what incentive does he have to succeed?*

## RESTRUCTURING

In the early, cold months of 1997, WMX pledged a full restructuring. The market eagerly anticipated what had been demanded for so long – a full-scale retrenchment and consolidation, and a re-focus on the core business.

The *Wall Street Journal* dubbed the day of the announcement as "WMX Tuesday" and described "euphoria" among analysts. The stock was bid up 11 percent in the month leading up to the day.

But WMX Tuesday went less with a bang than a whimper.

The restructuring consisted of a partial retreat back to its core business. Domestic waste would once again be the company's main area of activity, with international operations curtailed (though not eliminated as Lens had requested). Non-core assets to the tune of $1.5 billion would be disposed of, 3,000 jobs cut, and the share repurchase program expanded by 10 percent.

Later in the year, the company simplified operations by taking Wheelabrator off the market. WMX spent about $900 million buying back the shares it did not own.

In a belated recognition that the company had it right first time, WMX announced that it would change its name back to Waste Management. The sexy-sounding "WMX Technologies" had lasted barely four years.

The company also answered one of Lens' early demands – the departure of Koenig. WMX had repeatedly promised he would be removed, but he didn't leave the CFO's office until February 1997, when he was merely reassigned. He remained an executive vice-president.

Although the changes were considerable, it wasn't sufficiently aggressive for the market. The price plunged 9 percent in a single day, down $3 to about $33. The fall indicated that nothing less than an absolute overhaul would satisfy investors, who had waited too long for results.

A further question remained – who was to implement this plan? Lens and Soros continued to press for fresh blood on the board. In February 1997, Lens informed Waste that it would drop the proxy fight if the company immediately appointed two of Soros's director nominees for the board. The Soros group asserted that both Buntrock and Rooney had to go.

In a February 11, 1997, filing with the SEC, Soros nominated four directors to run against the board's nominees for the forthcoming annual meeting, and repeated its call for Rooney's departure. The filing said the group was "even more frustrated with management's lack of progress in enhancing value for shareholders and the apparent inability of management, and its recently announced restructuring plan, to address the issue."

The looming battle was knocked off track by the announcement, on February 18, just one week after Soros's demand for new leadership, that Phil Rooney was resigning from the company. He said he didn't want the company "being distracted by the current public debate over the leadership of the company."

This announcement, coupled with the news that the company would replace two incumbent directors at the forthcoming annual meeting, persuaded investors that the company was serious about initiating change. The share price was bid up nearly $2 to $34.75.

Where did this leave the Soros proxy fight for board seats? The purpose of the contest was to find credible outside directors who, in turn, could select a tough CEO, but this purpose had now been overtaken by events. Although Rooney's departure meant that Buntrock was back in the hot seat as acting CEO, it also provided an opportunity to find a credible outsider. One analyst told Reuters that Rooney was a "sacrificial child to get Soros off their back."[4]

A Soros spokesman told the *Chicago Tribune*: "We would like to see the best possible CEO running the company on a day-to-day basis. We would also like to see that CEO reporting to the strongest possible board of directors."[5] On February 21, the Soros group announced that it was dropping its proxy fight. Soros said that running a proxy fight would only distract the company. The key, said a Soros spokesman, was bringing two new independent directors and the best available CEO.

Gerald Kerner, managing director of Soros affiliate Duquesne Capital Management, explained the decision to pull out of the proxy fight: "We never wanted to drive the bus, and now we believe we are going to get the best driver possible."

> *It is not in shareholders' interests to replace management. It is in shareholders' interests to get the board to do it. Discuss.*

The news surprised the investor community, but most understood that the Soros retreat was a tactical maneuver rather than withdrawal. The Dow Jones Wire asked whether the move constituted "Détente or lasting peace?"

One analyst, NatWest Securities' Paul Knight, said: "They avoided a confrontation now, but if WMX doesn't deploy its strategy with successful result to the stock price, there will be a battle later."

The *New York Times* quoted Leone Young of Smith Barney: "Soros dropped the proxy fight because it is convinced that the board will listen to its suggestions. And that is not the same as backing off."[6]

In other words, Waste had bought itself a breathing space. It now had the opportunity to find an outstanding CEO candidate from outside the industry alongside some new directors. If it failed to do so, the dissident shareholders would undoubtedly be back.

The key, as far as Lens was concerned, didn't stop with the CEO. There was a need for personnel changes that went beyond the chief executive's suite. One of this book's authors, Nell Minow, speaking to Reuters, said that Buntrock should only remain at the company long enough to find a CEO: "Any successor worth his salt is not going to want the job if Buntrock is going to be too involved."

The CEO hunt got under way, with the help of leading search firm Heidrick & Struggles.

Howard H. Baker and Peter H. Huizenga had announced their decisions to retire at the annual meeting. In mid–March 1997, Waste announced two new nominees for the board, to be submitted for election at the May annual meeting.

The first was Robert S. Miller who had unwittingly become something of a crisis management professional. As an executive at Chrysler, he had been part of two major turnarounds under Lee Iacocca. Having retired, he agreed to serve as non–executive director at two troubled companies, Morrison Knudsen and Federal Mogul. At both companies, the incumbent leadership had abruptly resigned and he had taken over as acting CEO.

The second candidate was Steven G. Rothmeier, chairman and CEO of Great Northern Capital. He had also been chairman and CEO of Northwest Airlines, where he had overseen the airline's rapid growth.

Both candidates met the criteria Lens was looking for – they were outsiders, of genuine ability, and had chief executive experience at big companies. There was little chance they would be yes-men.

## Rooney's departure: the aftermath

But if the company seemed to be moving in the right direction, it still managed to upset investors. Waste's proxy revealed that Phil Rooney would continue to be paid $2.5 million a year until 2002. This, after eight months' work as CEO.

The *Wall Street Journal* questioned whether any payment should be made at all. Rooney's contract called for the $2.5 million annual payment but only following "termination by the company." Like anyone else, Rooney wasn't due a dime under his contract if he departed voluntarily. And Rooney had resigned; he had not been forced out.

Furthermore, Rooney went straight to a senior job with ServiceMaster, a subsidiary of Waste's sold only months before – at too low a price according to many. Again, there was a disturbing perception that directors' interests were being placed ahead of the interests of shareholders.

*Crain's Chicago Business* was in no doubt about the message that Rooney's departure sent. It declared "outrage" at the payoff which he was in line to receive for "doing basically nothing." The editorial pointed out that Rooney had been well compensated during his time at WMX. "No parting gifts were necessary. He is out of a job because he wasn't considered responsive to shareholders; now, WMX's board has added insult to investor injury by rewarding him for his ineffectiveness."

*Refer back to chapter 4 and the section headed "Executive Compensation": what does the Rooney episode tell you about the state of executive compensation in corporate America?*

## Towards the annual meeting

Dean Buntrock told the *Wall Street Journal* in April that he was willing to give up a management role in order to bring the right CEO to the company. But he continued to express a desire to remain on the board.

This did not please investors, who not only felt that it would be difficult to select a CEO with Buntrock still a presence in the background, but also continued to press for a more thorough board shake-up.

In advance of the 1997 annual meeting, the Teamsters sponsored a bylaw amendment to provide that the board consist of a majority of independent directors, according to the Council of Institutional Investors' definition.

The Teamsters' proposal complained that Buntrock and Rooney were employees, Flynn, Dempsey, and Huizenga former employees, Baker and Pedersen associates of law firms that receive legal services for the company, and San Juan Cafferty and Edwards employees of universities that might receive grants from the company.

Lens brought its own pressure to bear at the 1997 annual meeting. The fund invited some of WMX's most sizeable investors to attend. Representatives of Alliance Capital Management, Harvard Management, Bear Steams, Capital Research, Lazard Frères, and Goldman Sachs were all present.

This was highly unusual. Institutions of this kind are invariably absent from annual meetings, since they have regular access to management at analysts' briefings and one-to-one meetings. The message Lens intended to send was that the company's shareholders were standing together, a point we will return to below.

Lens principal Robert Monks took the opportunity of the annual meeting directly to address questions to the chairs of the board committees. He said:

> To the chairman of the audit committee, James Peterson. This company has had a history of eight consecutive years of special charges, with almost annual restructurings. What is the audit committee doing to make sure that the company's numbers will be more reliable in future?

Other shareholders asked further searching questions:

One asked the chairman of the search committee, Peer Pedersen, about the status of the CEO search. Another asked Trowbridge whether the nomination committee would again consider shareholder suggestions for board candidates.

Other questions included: What are the independent directors doing to respond to the issues raised by the $91 million fraud judgment against the company? How often do the outside directors meet in executive session, and have they considered retaining their own counsel?"

*Imagine you are a non-executive director of Waste. How might you respond to these questions?*

## A new chief executive

Waste was marking time until the arrival of a new CEO. In July 1997, the company announced the appointment of Ronald LeMay, previously number two at phone provider Sprint.

The stock dropped slightly on the news, demonstrating that investors were anxious for quick results, impatient after a five-month search for the right candidate. The *Wall Street Journal* speculated that Buntrock's continued presence helped depress the stock.[7]

While LeMay was a man of undoubted ability, there were aspects of his appointment that were troubling:

- he didn't purchase any stock;
- he continued to serve on numerous other boards;
- he didn't bring any outside personnel with him, so senior management at Waste remained the same;

- he continued to live at his former home in Kansas, commuting to Waste's head-quarters near Chicago each week.

Investors were also worried by the wealthy nature of LeMay's incentive package. He was granted a salary of $2.5 million, plus options on 4 million shares of stock. This represented plenty of upside potential but little downside risk. LeMay was not required to bet on himself to succeed.

Further, Waste agreed to buy out LeMay's existing stock-appreciation rights at Sprint, at a potential cost of $68 million. In the parlance of executive pay, Waste agreed that LeMay should be "made whole" before leaving Sprint. But again, this strips out any risk. LeMay was not forced to make a commitment to Waste. Indeed, he was not forced to make a choice between Sprint and Waste, since he stood to benefit enormously if either company did well.

The overall impression seemed to be, not that LeMay was eagerly accepting the challenge Waste offered, but that he had to be dragged reluctantly from his former company.

*Shortly after Lee Iacocca joined Chrysler in 1978, he received an annual salary of one dollar a year, no bonus, but a large number of stock options that would only pay out if the share price improved. Ultimately, such was Chrysler's performance, he cashed in option gains of about $43 million. Compare Iacocca's compensation arrangement to LeMay's.*

Early in October 1997, Waste announced that earnings would again be lower than expected. It added that the previous year's third-quarter income statement was overstated and that another charge might be added to the company's long string of write-offs. The market downgraded the stock 10 percent on the news.

Days later, LeMay quit and returned to Sprint. He'd served as the CEO of Waste Management for little over three months. The market was stunned.

LeMay said that he had joined Waste because it offered an interesting set of challenges but that "I have determined, however, that the needs of the company now present different kinds of challenges."

The stock sank like a stone, off 20 percent on the day to $23.25.

On the same day that LeMay rode back to Kansas, the incumbent and former CFOs (James Koenig and his successor, John D. Sandford) also quit the company.

Rumors were rife. The Associated Press commented: "The company's shares tumbled as much as 24 percent as Wall Street was abuzz with speculation that the departed executives had discovered major accounting irregularities that would impede implementation of an aggressive turnaround plan."[8]

The *New York Times* said that "the abrupt turn of events . . . smacked of a story untold – and LeMay was not telling it."[9] LeMay later referred to Waste's accounting as "spooky."[10]

Robert S. Miller was appointed acting chairman and CEO. He was the fourth CEO in less than a year.

It was now Wall Street's worst-kept secret that Waste's books contained some very bad news. Investors would continue to mark down the stock until they knew the truth.

Miller's first job, then, was to convince investors that they had a clear, warts and all, picture of the company's health. He said he knew of no irregularities but that a review of the company's accounting policies was under way. He said: "we'll probably adopt going forward a substantially more conservative philosophy in the way that we record the earnings of the company."

Miller confirmed yet another charge, involving "some pretty big numbers hitting the books," but denied that there was "something terrifying under the covers." "This is not a train wreck," he said.

## Miller's tale

Miller moved aggressively to reconstitute the board. In November 1997, he announced the appointment of two new directors. One of them, Roderick M. Hills, was the former chairman of the SEC. This news intimated that the company was expecting to have to deal with some kind of SEC investigation – again, it seemed like trouble was waiting just around the corner.

The board committees were given a thorough shakeup to put the new outsiders in a dominant position. A new search committee was established to seek a fifth CEO in less than a year. It was made up solely of directors appointed since Lens and Soros had first invested.

The audit committee was entirely replaced, now under the chairmanship of Hills.

The charter of the nominating committee expanded to include board practice and corporate governance issues. And the board's executive committee was reconstituted under the chairmanship of Miller, replacing Buntrock. Dean Buntrock no longer served on a single board committee of the company he had helped to found.

Days later, Miller flew to New York to meet a dozen or so of his largest investors. He traveled alone, accompanied by just an investor relations officer. Miller emphasized that "there's a new board in charge" and told his investors, "you're the owners. I work for you. I want your views."

*Contrast Miller's style to that of Buntrock or Rooney.*

## Fifth CEO

Speculation was rife as to who might take over the poisoned chalice of the CEO suite. A name frequently mentioned was that of Al Dunlap, christened "Chainsaw Al" for his aggressive cost-cutting methods. He had a career of being appointed to failing companies and ruthlessly turning them round. He pruned non-core divisions, eliminated thousands of workers, and often negotiated a merger for what remained. Though many criticized his style, there was no arguing with the results. Dunlap had already effected a successful turnaround at Scott Paper, one of Lens' former investments.

Al Dunlap, speaking to a Bloomberg panel was asked for his views on Waste. He said: "The shareholders would have been better off if they had gotten captured by terrorists . . . There you've had a classic case of a sitting management and a board that's allowed a situation year in and year out to go on without taking the proper corrective action – that's to dramatically change the management."

## More management

Part of Waste's problem, according to *Crain's*, was "too much wasted energy, not enough management."[11] Miller set about applying some management, first by simplifying the complex structure.

Waste's growth had taken place by acquisition, which led to a remarkably convoluted structure. In November 1997, Miller announced that the number of regional headquarters would be cut from 250 to 32. Staff would be trimmed by 1,200, for annual savings of $100 million.

One of those staff members to be trimmed was Dean Buntrock. The company announced he would be gone by the end of the year. The *Tribune* commented: "Perhaps the best thing Dean L. Buntrock did for the company he helped found was simply to leave."[12]

The plan nudged the stock northwards on a day the rest of the market fell. But the 25-cent rise "suggests investors still view the Oak Brook-based waste hauler with caution."[13]

## Restated accounts

At the end of January 1998, Waste finally fessed up. It opened the door on a closet simply stuffed with skeletons.

The company admitted that its misleading accounts went back to 1992, two years earlier than most had anticipated. The company announced a special charge to account for misstated earnings of $3.5 billion pre-tax. This was a whole billion dollars higher than the predicted worst case.

Under the restated earnings, Waste suddenly looked a less healthy company. For example, the company had reported net earnings in 1996 of $192.1 million. In the reviewed accounts, this became a loss of $39.3 million.

In retrospect, the company reported a 1996 loss of $39.3 million, down $231.4 million from the original accounts. The 1995 earnings had to be downgraded to the tune of $263.8 million.

In a press release, Robert Miller said: "The steps we are taking are the strong prescription we believe is needed to acknowledge past mistakes, clarify our financial reporting picture, and begin the process of restoring investor confidence in Waste Management and its ability to prosper in the future."

The *Wall Street Journal* described the adjustments as "mammoth."[14] The *Chicago Tribune* said the results were "startling" and described shareholders as "shocked."[15]

The SEC immediately launched an investigation.

Amazingly, the stock budged just 20 cents on the news of this $3.5 billion problem. This indicated the extent to which investor confidence in Waste had evaporated. The market had such a dim view of the company that *nothing* the company could have announced would have been perceived as bad news.

*Fortune* magazine devoted an in-depth report to how Waste had managed this feat of accounting trickery: "Standard industry practice is to depreciate – or write down – the cost of trucks (about $150,000 apiece) over eight to ten years, with each year's depreciation expense reducing the bottom line. But in the early 1990s, at Rooney's direction and with Buntrock's assent, Waste began stretching the depreciation schedules by two to four years. This lowered the company's annual depreciation charge, boosting earnings."[16]

But that, as *Fortune* revealed, was just the beginning: "Waste also reduced, by as much as $25,000, the starting depreciation amount on each truck, claiming that sum as 'salvage value' – an amount it would recover by selling the vehicles. Standard industry practice is to claim no salvage value. On a North American fleet of nearly 20,000 vehicles, this manipulation added up."

It wasn't just trucks that were dealt with in this way. Waste listed the work life of a dumpster as 15–20 years, while the industry norm was 12. The same kind of shenanigans went on for recycling plants, hazardous waste treatment facilities, everything. Every Waste asset, from the dumpster to the engineering plant, had its working life stretched.

The same technique of making wildly optimistic assumptions was applied to Waste's 137 landfills. Obviously, if a landfill can expand, its useful life is longer and so depreciation and startup capital costs can be spread over a longer time. "So what did Waste Management do?" asked *Fortune*. "Naturally, it claimed that landfill expansions were likely – even when they weren't."

At a site in Atlanta, the company's books counted on a huge expansion even after the state had passed a law barring any expansion. The site's value was inflated by over $30 million.

The sum effect of playing with all these figures was to boost earnings by $110 million a year.

Dean Buntrock told *Fortune*: "To my knowledge, there was proper accounting used on all our financial transactions."

Rod Hills, chairman of the audit committee, pointed the finger at Arthur Andersen, Waste's long-standing auditors. "The SEC is going to find they didn't do their job," he said. An Andersen spokesman sniffed back: "We take exception to preinvestigative inappropriate finger pointing."

## USA Waste

Lens and the Soros group bit the bullet. The company, surely, had hit rock bottom. But there were new people in charge and things could only get better.

In March 1998, the Dow Jones wire reported that the feeling that Waste "is ripe for takeover is gaining momentum . . . There is some talk that USA Waste will make an offer in the low 30s." A critical energy in the merger talks was Ralph Whitworth, one-time boss of the United Shareholders' Association and now principal of Relational Investors, a shareholder activism/turnaround fund.

USA Waste was the minnow in the trash collection pond. It ranked third in terms of size, and was just one-third the size of Waste Management. It had stayed resolutely clear of expansion into non-core businesses, remaining a trash collector, pure and simple, with a sizeable presence in southern and western states but no presence in the north and east where Waste was strong.

Though Waste was the far larger of the two marriage partners, it was USA Waste that walked off with the keys to the new home. John E. Drury would take over as CEO of the combined enterprise, and the headquarters of the merged company would be in Houston, USA's hometown.

The merger was a humiliating end for Waste, once the most exciting of companies. In essence, Waste was being taken over by one of its junior competitors. The *Wall Street Journal* noted: "Though Waste Management's name would live on, the deal would effectively mark the end of one of the great growth stories of the 1970s and 1980s." *Crain's Chicago Business* argued that "the merger represents the best, perhaps only, prospect for Waste's management."

Drury pledged that the new-look Waste Management would go back to basics. He told *Fortune*: "It's a simple business. We don't know that we're real good at a lot of things. But we're damn good at picking up garbage."

## WHAT WENT WRONG?

Waste's story is a sad one. It was a great company, of enormous energy, whose growth dazzled investors. And it ended being merged into a company one-third its size.

We have explained above the accounting trickery that laid Waste low, but it is important to understand that the dodgy accounting was the symptom, not the cause, of Waste's decline. Because Waste's failure was not one of accounting; it was one of management. And management failed because it concentrated too much on the *appearance* of the business and not on the business itself.

This problem started when management continued to insist that Waste was still a growth company despite a maturing market. The *Wall Street Journal* noted that "it became a company as much in the growth business as the garbage business." The paper cited one analyst who compared the company to the movie *Speed* – if it goes below 55 m.p.h. it blows up.

*Fortune* reported "Waste Management did the things it did because it refused to concede that it was no longer a hot growth company. Its desire to retain its status as a Wall Street highflier drove Waste Management not just to inflate its numbers but also to make a whole host of wrong-headed decisions."

The magazine asked: "By the early 1990s, Waste needed to deal with a new reality: it couldn't be a growth company anymore. Or could it?"

*Fortune* lamented the short-term demands imposed by quarterly earnings, and the fact that the stock is punished if predictions are not met. Given these pressures, "the temptation to boost earnings by using accounting gimmicks can be powerful." Buntrock told the magazine: "For 20 years, we had double digit growth. The marketplace and shareholders and even your own employees expect you to continue that."

*Fortune* argued that: "Since going public in 1971, Waste Management has been obsessed with its stock price . . . but then came the 1990s and that obsession became its curse." Satisfying your shareholders is the result of building a successful business, not the route to it. As Robert Miller told the magazine: "The stock should be the product of how you do business, not the god you pay homage to every day."

In an interview with *Business Week*, Miller outlined other roots of corporate failure. His conclusions were:

- accounting and information systems are often to blame for corporate woes;
- no CEO should stay more than 10 years;
- no full-time manager should sit on more than two outside boards;
- few companies can manage diversification.[17]

In a later piece, he also condemned the fad for restructuring charges, arguing that "somebody woke up to the fact that if you take something as a restructuring charge, investors will forgive you immediately."[18]

*How might Waste's history have been different if it had applied Miller's rules from the beginning?*

## HOW WAS IT SOLVED?

The key to the Waste turnaround was shareholder communication. Because, without communication, shareholders cannot act collectively. In the language of Berle and Means (see the section on separation of ownership and control in chapter 2), "ownership" (the shareholders) without communication remains diffuse and powerless in the face of focused and tightly organized "control" (management).

At the beginning of this book we described governance as a set of relationships between three groups – the management, the directors, and the shareholders. In this relationship, management has vastly more power than any other group. It controls the company and, most importantly, it controls the flow of information to the other groups. To a large degree, despite the best efforts of GAAP and other reporting requirements, it is up to management to decide whether the information it discloses is full and accurate – witness Waste's reporting of the most basic issue: its performance.

So too, it is up to management (largely) whether to have a tough, independent board that rigorously checks and balances management, or not.

In the face of such a stoutly defended corporate bastion, shareholders are powerless. Unless they can organize. As owners of the company, they have the legal right to replace the board and the managers. But this right is more myth than reality unless they can act in concert.

Lens set up an "intranet," a private website protected by password and accessed only by those with a genuine interest. The site was made available to nearly 20 of Waste's largest institutional holders, including giants like Alliance Capital Management, Bear Steams, Fidelity, Goldman Sachs, J.P. Morgan, and Lazard Frères, as well as the more "usual suspects" such as CalPERS, New York State Teachers, and CREF.

The website was a device for sharing information and disseminating it rapidly. Notes from meetings with management, thoughts about director candidates, and ideas about how to move the campaign forward could be fed out to investors representing 40 percent of Waste's stock at the touch of a button.

Lens deployed this core group of investors in other ways. When Lens attended its first annual meeting in 1996, it had the air of a pep rally. Dominated by employees, the affair was nothing less than a celebration of the company's success. (The fact that that success was tarnishing rapidly did not seem to be a matter for discussion.)

The following year, as described above, Lens coordinated a group of large investors to attend the annual meeting. This, again, was a remarkable departure from the norm. By attending the annual meeting *en bloc*, Waste's largest shareholders were demonstrating that they were acting together. It was a gesture of solidarity. It showed that the barriers impeding collective action by shareholders had been crossed.

The playing field had been leveled.

*What does the Waste story tell you about the organization of a public company? Who has the power, and how are they held accountable?*

*"Management controls the information." Is this true? And if so, what can shareholders do about it?*

*Who was responsible for Waste's astounding success? And who was responsible for its decline?*

## Waste Management: A Postscript[19]

A happy ending? In corporate governance?

Waste Management's future, folded into USA Waste, looked secure. After all, Waste's problem was that it spent too much time expanding its empire and not enough time consolidating it. As one critic said, there was too little management. Now it was merged with the acknowledged management maestros of the trash sector, surely it could put its grim history of special charges behind it.

Apparently not.

By August 1999, the three members of the rescue team who remained on the board – Relational Investors' Ralph Whitworth, Steve Miller and Rod Hills – were back running the company full-time. USA Waste's reputation for probity and management excellence turned out to be, well, a load of trash.

There was a note of tragedy in this comedy of errors. In November 1998, John Drury was diagnosed with a brain tumor. He promised to be back at his desk within a week of surgery, and doctors' reports were encouraging. Besides, the company appeared to have a ready-groomed successor in COO Rodney Proto.

Drury's remarkable recovery proved to be short-lived. At a March 1999 board meeting, Ralph Whitworth noticed that Drury was "noticeably weaker," and not in full control of his faculties.

But Whitworth noticed something worse – arrogance. Drury and Proto belittled Miller, the chairman, behind his back. When Whitworth proposed that management prepare monthly updates on how the merger was proceeding, his suggestion was brusquely dismissed.

Steve Miller decided to step down early as chairman, and planned to hand over to Drury at the May 1999 annual meeting. Many of the directors were not happy about that, given Drury's health, although at the time of Miller's decision many board members had not seen Drury in two months.

Drury attended the annual meeting in a wheelchair. He had trouble standing to receive the chairman's gavel from Miller. "That's when we should've taken a more aggressive stance," says Hills in retrospect.

Meanwhile, Hills was making himself unpopular with management. The merged company still had the painful hangover of Waste's history to deal with – notably, several shareholder lawsuits and an SEC investigation of Waste's accountancy practice. Hills started to delve deeply into the financials of the combined operation, with the result that, as one director told the *Wall Street Journal*, "he pissed everyone off."

Hills' efforts led him to the conclusion that US Waste had badly overpaid for past acquisitions, both before and after the Waste Management merger. The company was not the spotless star it had appeared.

Out of the blue, in July 1999, the company announced that second-quarter results would fall short of expectations. The stock declined by more than a third. Worse, the company could offer no convincing explanation for the shortfall.

Traditionally, the first quarter is a weaker period, yet the company had come within a penny a share of those estimates. Why had performance dipped in the usually strong second quarter? "For the board, what had been a string of unrelated concerns and annoyances was fast coming together to shatter its trust in management," said the *Wall Street Journal*.

The rescue team's principal concern was that the first quarter's earnings had been dressed up with some undisclosed one-time earnings. Their suspicions hardened when it was revealed that Proto and a dozen other managers had sold significant chunks of stock in the weeks before the profits warning. Proto himself had sold 300,000 shares for more than $16 million. Had they kept the share price pumped up in the first quarter, giving them time to offload stock, before the company's true financial picture emerged? There is no proof that any of the directors acted so coldly, but for an already impatient board, it was a management failing.

The board named Whitworth interim chairman. He made it his task to extract the truth from the financial department, keeping at them until they conceded that the first-quarter earnings had included undisclosed one-time items and would have to be restated.

Drury and Proto were dismissed; Miller was appointed acting CEO for the second time.

USA Waste, it transpired, had suffered the same disease as Waste Management – it was too fixated on the stock price to devote sufficient attention to the day-to-day operations of the company.

The *Journal* concludes: "Since the early 1970s, the formula at publicly traded garbage companies has been to use stock to buy up smaller, privately held haulers. Add profits. Boost the stock. Fund more deals. Actually integrating the operations and running the company efficiently became a secondary consideration. Industry consolidation pushed up acquisition prices, making it harder to boost profits without using some aggressive accounting. At some point, nearly all the big players stretched too far to do deals."

Whitworth was determined to extract a warts-and-all picture of Waste Management's financial position – a problem that all thought had been fixed. He was told that every operation had its own financial controller – 600 of them. How long would it take them to bring their books up to date? Some said 400 hours.

The company brought in 1,160 outside auditors from Arthur Andersen and PricewaterhouseCoopers, the firm's auditor, at a cost of $3 million a day. The real numbers finally arrived – $211 million in uncollectable bills, $305 million in unrecorded expenses; $226 million miscellaneous.

In late 1999, Waste Management took a third-quarter charge of $1.76 billion. Would its history of special charges never end?

The board recruited a new CEO – Maurice Myers, CEO of trucking company Yellow Corp.

Rod Hills now has an extra pile of litigation, and a renewed SEC investigation. One of the shareholder lawsuits? From Dean Buntrock, who alleged that Hills and Miller had mismanaged the company, and owed him $12 million in pension benefits.

## NOTES

1.  *Washington Post*, Apr. 22, 1997.
2.  *Wall Street Journal*, Jan. 30, 1997.
3.  WMX 1995 proxy statement.
4.  Reuters wire, Feb. 18, 1997.
5.  *Chicago Tribune*, Feb. 19, 1997.
6.  *New York Times*, Feb. 22, 1997.
7.  *Wall Street Journal*, July 18, 1997.
8.  Associated Press wire, Oct. 30, 1997.
9.  *New York Times*, Oct. 31, 1997.
10. *Business Week*, Nov. 18, 1997.
11. *Crain's Chicago Business*, Nov. 10, 1997.
12. *Chicago Tribune*, Nov. 13, 1997.
13. Ibid.
14. *Wall Street Journal*, Feb. 24, 1998.
15. *Chicago Tribune*, Apr. 25, 1998.
16. This cite, and all *Fortune* cites below, are taken from the May 25, 1998 issue.
17. *Business Week*, Mar. 19, 1998.
18. *Business Week*, Oct. 5, 1998.
19. All references are to the "Star Rescuers Take On Waste Management – and End Up Tarnished," *Wall Street Journal*, Feb. 29, 2000, p. A1.

# Stone & Webster

## STONE & WEBSTER:
## THE COMPANY THAT BUILT AMERICA

The work of Stone & Webster can be found in the very fabric of the United States of America. As an engineering and construction business, the company helped build the super-structure for the Manhattan project which developed the atom bomb in World War II, the New Jersey turnpike, the Statue of Liberty restoration, and the Washington, DC sub-way system.

In the 1970s the company continued its success, constructing nuclear power plants to US utilities. The company has built more such plants in the US than any other company, except for one.

In its 1994 annual report, the company made much of its place in American corporate history: "Stone & Webster is a century old group of integrated and interdependent engineering, construction and consulting businesses. We have, for more than 105 years, been providing technological vision and innovative solutions to the changing world of energy, petroleum, petrochemicals, environmental responsibility, and infrastructure."

But, as we saw in the Sears and General Motors case studies, a glorious past is no indicator of future success. Indeed, a company accustomed to success may find its entrepreneurial spirit replaced by a sclerotic institutional culture. Past glory may even be an inhibitor of future performance.

Stone & Webster was known for being old and prestigious. It was also renowned for being secretive and defensive.

The *Boston Globe*, writing in November 1994, tried to talk to some Wall Street engineering and construction analysts to give it insight into Stone & Webster. The *Globe* found that no analyst tracked the company. The company's policy, it seemed, was not to brief the market on the company's prospects. Stone & Webster was also the only company in its industry which did not release backlog data, an indicator of future performance.

The *Globe* continued: "Its [the company's] critics say Stone & Webster clung to the past, refusing to acknowledge that its once highly profitable nuclear business was dead," and added: "It's a culture, say those who have worked there, where the boss is always right."

The newspaper identified the cause of this corporate culture. One former executive told the *Globe*: "They had been very successful in the past, so there was no reason to change. The more money they made, the more conservative they got."

Certainly in the case of Stone & Webster, the proud words of the 1994 annual report bore little relation to the facts. The company's core engineering business had been losing money for several years, a fact reflected in several key areas. By the mid-1990s, for example, the company's permanent staff had fallen to 6,000 from the 15,000 of less than a decade previously. Profits flattened and the stock price fell from the mid-forties to the high twenties at a time of consistently rising markets.

From 1989 to 1993, the stock of Stone & Webster fell 11.4 percent per annum, compared to a 7.1 percent per annum increase in the S&P 500 index, and an annual advance of 7.5 percent in the S&P Engineering and Construction index.

These poor figures were caused by continued poor performance of the company's central business. Stone & Webster had, in the early to mid-1980s, done considerable business building nuclear power plants. The business was conducted on a lucrative "cost plus" basis, and the company's profits boomed.

The "cost plus" system, under which the company is paid the cost of the project plus a percentage, may indeed have damaged the company's ability to compete. This system does not require a company to keep costs down. It does not create an incentive to find quicker, cheaper, or innovative ways of completing a project. Indeed, since the company's fee is based on a percentage of the cost, there is an incentive to drive up costs as high as possible. The system positively promoted ill discipline.

The nuclear power market collapsed, however. Following the incident at Three Mile Island in 1979, followed by the Chernobyl disaster seven years later, US utilities lost interest in nuclear power. The last two nuclear power plants in the US were ordered in 1978 but later canceled.

The fact that Stone & Webster was slow to react to the decline of its central business is perhaps part explained by the diverse nature of the company's operations. In addition to central heavy engineering, the company also had significant, but unrelated, interests in cold storage warehousing, oil and gas exploration and production, oil and natural gas gathering and transportation, office building management and real estate development.

The assets were as diverse as the operations. The company owned four office buildings in Boston, New Jersey, and Houston (the last was under construction); three cold storage facilities in Georgia; 13 facilities for natural gas gathering and transporting in Texas, Louisiana, and Oklahoma; a portion of the land and buildings in a 1,000-acre used office park in Tampa; mineral interests in the US and Canada; several inactive drilling rigs; and a portfolio of government securities and common stock.

The center of this sprawl? A holding company in New York City. Despite the fact that the engineering headquarters were in Boston, the company still maintained expensive office space in midtown Manhattan.

Stone & Webster, then, was a diverse misconglomeration, in which the central business had under-performed for several years.

*Whose job is it to identify and rectify this problem?*

In a public company, there are three obvious layers of accountability:

1. the disclosure of accounts: this forces a company to disclose answers on the most basic question – how is the company doing?;
2. the board of directors: it is their job to replace management if it fails;
3. the shareholders: they can replace the directors if they don't do their job.

We will see that Stone & Webster was able to subvert each of these three mechanisms for promoting accountability. As a result, the company continued to live in denial.

## The balance sheet

In business, numbers aren't meant to lie. Performance is reflected in the fabled "bottom line." But because accountancy can sometimes be more art than science, this is not always the case.

A casual glance at Stone's balance sheet would have shown a company reporting healthy, albeit diminishing, profits. Stone & Webster diligently met all the rules of accounting disclosure. But the numbers hid the true story.

The failure of the core business was disguised by the contribution of income from other sources. The most significant non-core addition to the company's income came from its overvalued pension fund.

In the 1970s and early 1980s, thanks to the "cost plus" contracts they secured, Stone & Webster contributed generously to the company's employee benefit plans, especially the pension fund. After all, pension contributions were part of the "cost" which increased the ultimate fee to the company.

Participants in the plan did not become fully vested until they had been employees for ten years – and few jobs lasted that long.

Thus, in the good years, the pension fund outgrew the company. But as the workforce dwindled in the 1980s, there was no commensurate shrinkage of the plan. Large sums deposited earlier for pensions of terminated employees remained in the plan and became available for the company's relatively few ongoing employees.

In the late 1980s, the excess assets in the plan passed the $100 million mark – far more than was needed for existing employees. The company amortized a portion of this surplus, and each year this portion represented an addition to the company's income.

The adjustment, it should be noted, was an accounting device and did not represent the transfer of any cash from the pension plan. Rather, it represented a reduction in the company's operating expenses. None the less, it increased the company's reported earnings by an average $14.4 million per year from 1988 to 1994.

For example, in 1993 the company recorded a $2 million profit. But what the accounts did not state was that it benefited from a $14 million credit from the pension fund surplus, or 5 percent of the company's gross earnings. Aside from core engineering, this was the biggest single contributor to the company's income. The credit was not itemized in the income statement, as permitted by accounting standards.

From 1987, when Stone & Webster first began the practice, the pension fund credits were responsible for reducing operating expenses by a total of $101 million. Without the adjustment, the company would have lost money every year except 1991.

The pension fund credit was not the only item propping up the balance sheet. As discussed above, there were other considerable passive assets completely unrelated to the company's core business. For example, the company's real estate portfolio was worth $169 million. The company also owned $38.2 million in Tenneco shares (a shipbuilding and automotive parts manufacturer) and $55 million in US government bonds.

Stone & Webster asserted that the risky nature of the engineering and construction business made it essential to maintain substantial reserve assets in order to win new business. The company had no plans to liquidate these investments and reinvest them in the core operations, or simply pass them back to shareholders. Rather, the profits from these non-core investments were deployed to support the drifting central business.

These profitable sidelines allowed management and the board to ignore the reality of the company's disastrous performance in its core business, and masked its failure to master a changing business environment.

*In your opinion, did Stone & Webster have an acceptable business structure?*

*Had Stone & Webster been a company made up solely of that core division, would the market have tolerated its failure for long?*

*Why would investors buy into a failing engineering business to enjoy the fruits of investing in government bonds and Tenneco?*

*Who is responsible for ensuring that a "warts and all" analysis of the company's health is reported to shareholders? The directors? The auditors? The audit committee of the board?*

## The board

Clearly, in the first instance, it is the job of management to confront sustained under-performance. That Stone & Webster's management allowed the company to drift in this way is perhaps partly explained by the fact that managers were largely career Stone & Webster employees: Bill Allen had been with the company since the end of World War II and Bruce Coles had started at Stone & Webster 26 years previously.

As we have seen in other case studies, it is often difficult for career insiders radically to alter a company's direction and strategy. It is often easier for an outsider, who lacks the historical and emotional connection to the company, to effect a fresh start.

In such circumstances it is particularly vital to have a strong board, one that can demand a tough response to poor performance from long-term insiders. As we have explained in chapter 3 in this book, it is the responsibility of the board to select management, ensure they have the right strategy for success and, if necessary, replace them if they don't.

But the Stone & Webster board was not capable of fulfilling this function.

In addition to the three inside directors, there were nine outside directors. With the exception of J. Angus McKee (chairman and CEO of Gulfstream Resources, Canada), none of the outside directors was a full-time executive in either business or finance.

Moreover, the ability of some of the outsiders to bring an independent perspective was compromised by the length of their tenure. William Brown had served for 25 years, John A. Hooper for 20, and Peter Grace (who was 80 years old) for a whole half-century. One director who stood down at the 1994 annual meeting, Howard L. Clark, had served for 25 years.

Of the nine outsiders, four were affiliated to the company via consulting arrangements. Kent F. Hansen received $60,000 in consulting fees from the company in 1993. Fred Dalton Thompson, who resigned from the board in 1994 to make a successful run for the US Senate, was a partner at a law firm that had billed Stone $134,000 in legal fees in 1992. Also in 1992, the company received fees of $481,000 from Canadian Occidental Petroleum, of which Mr. McKee was president and CEO; and the company received $88,000 from W.R. Grace & Co., of which Peter Grace was chairman.

These arrangements meant that there wasn't a majority of independent outside directors on the board.

Of the four non-affiliated outsiders, three were over 70 years of age (in addition to the octogenarian Peter Grace) and retired. One was a foundation executive and one was an academic.

**Table 6.1**  Earnings – before and after adjustment

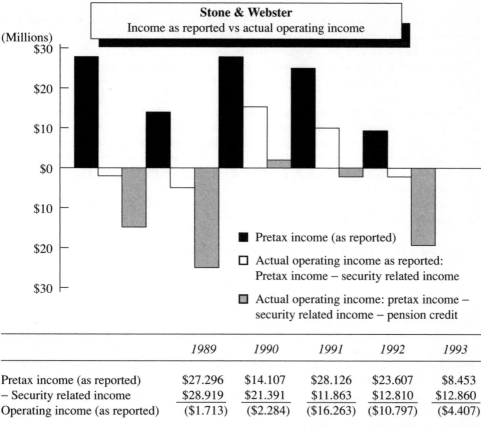

|  | 1989 | 1990 | 1991 | 1992 | 1993 |
|---|---|---|---|---|---|
| Pretax income (as reported) | $27.296 | $14.107 | $28.126 | $23.607 | $8.453 |
| – Security related income | $28.919 | $21.391 | $11.863 | $12.810 | $12.860 |
| Operating income (as reported) | ($1.713) | ($2.284) | ($16.263) | ($10.797) | ($4.407) |
| – Pension credit | $13.939 | $15.247 | $15.318 | $13.751 | $13.953 |
| Actual operating income | ($15.652) | ($22.531) | $0.945 | ($2.954) | ($18.360) |

But, most worrying, was the stock (or lack of it) owned by many of the directors (see table 6.1). Aside from Peter Grace, none of the outside directors owned more than a token amount of stock. For example, William L. Brown had served on the board for nearly 25 years but had amassed a holding of just 400 shares. Meredith L. Spangler, although she had served on the board for just three years, had nevertheless purchased only 100 shares.

The annual director's retainer was $20,000. In 1994, four directors owned less than $10,000-worth of stock.

It is also noteworthy that, until late 1993, there was no nominating committee so there was no focus or energy to bring on fresh, independent non-executive directors.

Finally, the 1994 proxy revealed that Peter Grace did not attend 75 percent of meetings. Outside directors have a responsibility to provide a fresh, independent perspective, one that challenges the status quo if necessary.

*Were Stone's outsiders capable of performing such a role?*

## The shareholder role

Directors, of course, are elected by shareholders. A board that fails to serve shareholders' interests may find itself voted from office. But here again, another layer of protective insulation stood between the company and its owners.

Thirty-seven percent of the company's stock was held by the employee stock option plan (ESOP), an incentive arrangement designed to reward long-term employees at all levels in the company.

The trustee of the ESOP was Chase Manhattan Bank, which had a longstanding commercial relationship with Stone management. Chase received significant compensation for its services as a commercial and investment banker, a relationship that was strengthened by interlocks at board level. John Hooper, an outside director of Stone & Webster, was also a member of Chase's board. A previous Stone & Webster CEO had been a member of Chase's board.

As trustee of the plan, Chase was responsible for voting the shares in the ESOP in the best interests of the beneficiaries.

*How can an ESOP trustee selected by management protect itself from conflicts of interest?*

## A shareholder invests

The two authors of this book are principals of the Lens Fund, an activist investment group that targets under-performing companies and seeks to use the rights available to shareholders to bring about change. In mid-1993, Lens began purchasing the company's stock. By year end, it owned about 172,000 shares of Stone & Webster, or about 1 percent of the outstanding common stock, a stake worth about $6.4 million.

Having researched and analyzed the company, Lens concluded that the company was insulated from the discipline of the marketplace by the unreality of GAAP, a somnolent board, and a friendly block shareholder.

*Do you agree with this conclusion?*

## A shareholder's strategy

Lens's first act was to seek a meeting with the company's management, asserting that constructive dialog is a key element of the governance process.

The first meeting took place in September 1993 with the company's CEO, COO, and CFO. Management insisted that they were unwilling to consider asset sales, insisting that they needed to keep the reserves on hand in order to compete effectively for sizeable construction jobs.

The Lens principals asked how the company could justify holding on to the Tenneco stock. The company replied that it didn't cost it anything. Lens argued that there was an opportunity cost if the Tenneco stake was tying up capital that could be more productively used elsewhere. Furthermore, it noted that the benefit of the capital markets was that companies could seek finance as and when they needed it.

One of the authors of this book, Robert A.G. Monks, noted after the meeting: "It was a striking case of corporate stasis." Later, the Lens principals wrote to the company suggesting that perhaps the company should privatize, with the ESOP buying out all the other investors. Lens wrote: "If a company cannot offer shareholders a competitive rate of return, it seems to me the company can determine whether it can justify having public shareholders at all."

The company didn't respond to this letter for two months, by which time it was too late for Lens to file a shareholder resolution.

Instead, Robert A.G. Monks proposed himself and Joseph Blasi, an expert on ESOPs, as members of the board. The company replied that the nominations committee (formed some months previously according to the company, although no announcement had been made) felt there would not be time to review their candidacies.

Lens also wrote to the trustee of the ESOP, Chase Manhattan Bank, suggesting that it was the trustee's fiduciary duty to consider their candidacy for the board. They received the following reply: "The resources available to Chase enable us to fulfill our fiduciary responsibilities through internal means. Accordingly, we thank you for your interest in this matter but do not feel that it is necessary at this time to meet with your company."

*Do you consider that the above consists of constructive dialog?*

## The law

Lens filed a lawsuit against the company, its directors, and Chase, claiming that the company had committed fraud by failing to disclose that its engineering division had been operating at a loss and to identify its source of reported surplus from the pension fund. In essence, the suit demanded that the company disclose its financial position according to accounting principles that weren't merely generally accepted, but offered a true view of the company's performance.

In a statement Lens said: "We've spent the last eight months asking Stone & Webster to conduct its affairs like a publicly owned company. It prefers to enjoy the benefits of the public market, but without the responsibility of full or accurate disclosure. With management and its agent Chase controlling 37 percent, we've turned to the court to help before its too late."

The suit asked for two things – accurate financial disclosure, and that the company postpone its annual meeting to permit a proxy contest or solicitation of "no" votes for election to the board. Finally, the suit asked the court to remove Chase as trustee of the ESOP because it had failed to vote the shares for the exclusive benefit of the employee members.

The court declined to postpone the annual meeting and Lens eventually lost the suit. However, in 1995, Stone & Webster restated its figures in precisely the way Lens had requested (see table 6.1), and in a second court case, Lens was successful in an effort to secure access to internal company documents.

## 1994 annual meeting

At the annual meeting in 1994, the company announced that William Allen was retiring as chief executive (to be replaced by Bruce Coles) but that he would continue to serve as chairman for another year.

Lens withheld its votes from the director candidates, and explained why. Nell Minow said that Bruce Coles, as president of the company and CEO-elect, was part of the management team that had let the company drift.

A second executive, William Egan, was also a candidate. As the company's executive vice-president and CFO, he had been responsible for the decision to combine the pension surplus with the operating earnings.

Of the non-executives, Lens withheld its votes from Kent Hansen, who owned only 200 shares, despite having served since 1988. His consulting fees from the company had been disclosed in past proxies but not in that of 1994. Further, Mr. Hansen was chairman of the nomination committee, which the company claimed was made up of outside directors, although Mr. Hansen received twice as much in consulting fees as he did in director's fees.

Finally, Nell Minow pointed out that Donna Fitzpatrick, joining the board to replace Howard Clark, had purchased only 100 shares.

In a press release, Lens defended its decision to withhold its votes: "This board needs a message that shareholders will not support a board that hides negative earnings in the pension surplus, a board that fails to respond to five years of unacceptable performance."

## Uniting the shareholders

Lens was not alone in finding the performance of Stone & Webster unacceptable. Frank Cilluffo, a private investor, owned or represented nearly 6 percent of Stone & Webster's stock, a holding worth over $23 million.

At the 1994 annual meeting, Mr. Cilluffo said: "As a shareholder for the past three years I have continually had to wrestle with the question of defining our identity. Are we an engineering firm, an investment company, an oil and gas company, an REIT, or a cold storage enterprise? It appears from our past performance that it has been very difficult to optimally manage the performance of all these industry segments. Any concerned shareholder must wonder whether it would behoove the company to focus on a single industry segment."

He offered a seven-point recovery plan:

1.   the sale of the non-engineering businesses;
2.   the sale of under-utilized real estate assets;
3.   possible consolidation of various engineering and management offices;
4.   the sale/lease back of owned real estate offices where appropriate;
5.   maintenance of tighter employment levels, reflective of current levels of business;
6.   appointment of additional knowledgeable outside directors;
7.   a mandatory retirement age of 67 for management and directors.

Following a similar agenda, and owning between them nearly 8 percent of the stock, Lens and Mr. Cilluffo represented a strong voice for change. How did the company respond?

## A year of little progress

Between 1994 and 1995 the company's performance went from bad to worse – in 1994, it lost money in net terms for the first time in 60 years. It laid off one-sixth of its employees.

Over the course of the year, there was incremental change. But not the thorough, immediate action that Lens pressed for.

The company agreed to sell the Tenneco stock, and proposed to buy back up to 1 million shares. Some of the company's excess real estate was put on the market, and the company's structure streamlined. The company asserted that the changes would account for

$55 million in annual cost savings. William Allen, the chairman, also announced that he would step down following the annual meeting. The company announced that Kent Hansen would replace him. Lens expressed concern that Mr. Hansen only owned 200 shares.

William Egan, the CFO, also announced his departure as both executive and director. Peter Grace also chose not to stand after a half-century of service.

The company proposed two new directors. First, Frank Cilluffo, a candidate warmly welcomed by Lens. As the owner of a stake now worth over 10 percent of the company, he had a vital interest in the performance of the company – an interest that had been lacking in the boardroom for too long.

Another new director was Elvin R. Heiberg, the president of his own consulting firm. In contrast to Mr. Cilluffo, he owned just 100 shares.

At the 1995 meeting, the CEO Bruce Coles said: "We have new incentive compensation, a new CFO, and our Cherry Hill facility is on the market. We have brought our cost structure into line with revenues. The first quarter we have recorded a profit of 32 cents a share. In the first quarter of 1994 we had a loss of 86 cents a share. Some would say we've been averse to change. I say we've embraced change."

The moves weren't enough for Lens, who pressed for revolutionary rather than evolutionary change. While it welcomed the sale of the Tenneco stock, it felt the asset divestment was proceeding at too slow a pace. When it pressed the company to take more urgent action, Lens was advised that Goldman Sachs was keeping the company's capital structure under review and advising on divestments.

Lens replied that, unless it knew the scope of Goldman's inquiry, it could not know how effective the bank's advice would be. Lens continually pressed for details of Goldman's remit. No answers were forthcoming.

The issue was later raised by Lens in a letter to the board: "We have no idea what it is you asked Goldman Sachs and Co. If you had asked them for a plan of maximization of shareholder value, with full license to consider disposition of corporate assets, that would be one thing. If on the other hand, they were asked to approve a management plan (the elements of which we are in ignorance) that would be another."

*Do you feel that shareholders of a company in a turnaround situation should be privy to the company's strategic plan?*

*To whom was Goldman Sachs accountable? Who were they were working for? What kinds of conflicts might the bank have faced?*

In advance of the 1995 season, Lens again sought to use the proxy process as a device for airing their concerns. Lens and Lens' contacts filed no fewer than ten shareholder proposals calling for such items as annual election of the board of directors, a requirement that there be a minimum share ownership by the directors, and asking that the company retain an independent investment bank to study asset divestment.

In a filing the size of a Manhattan phonebook, the company appealed to the SEC to have the resolutions excluded. Some of its arguments were petty at best. For example, it argued that Lens' statement that Peter Grace had served on the board for half a century was factually inaccurate. In fact, Mr. Grace had served 49 years and several months at the time Lens filed its resolution, and by the time of the annual meeting he would indeed have served for 50 years.

To Lens, the company's response to the resolutions was excessive, an unproductive use of company resources, and yet further evidence that the board wished to remain insulated from external discipline.

But Stone & Webster won the day. The SEC proxy rules allow for only one resolution per shareholder. The company argued that in essence all ten resolutions were effectively from the same source – Robert A.G. Monks, principal of Lens.

*What do you think is the purpose of the shareholder resolution process? Is it to allow concerned shareholders a cheap and effective way of communicating with their fellow investors? Is it a level playing field?*

The company made it difficult in other ways for Lens to advance its concerns. Monks asked to address the annual meeting from the podium; the request was declined. He tried to respond directly to the CEO's summing up for the year, but was told he had to route all his remarks through the chairman. He sought to ask questions directly of the nominees for the board; the chairman said he would first ask the nominees if they wished to respond. Monks' aim, of course, was to expose the director candidates to some tough questions – the kind of questions that the non-executive directors should have been asking for some time.

And when Monks asked one director for an example of the way the board carried out self-evaluation, the chairman intervened, saying that Monks had asked a question he had not submitted in advance. Another shareholder interrupted to demand an answer, saying "Are you allowed to answer a question that hasn't been pre-screened?"

To Lens, this all represented further evidence that the management was unwilling to engage in meaningful debate about the company's future. But what does a company have to fear from its shareholders? Presumably a company's managers and its shareholders want the same thing – the long-term prosperity of the firm. So what does a company gain by attempting to silence its critics?

The 1995 Stone & Webster annual meeting speaks volumes about corporate democracy, or rather the lack of it. In this instance, management controlled the timing and procedure of the annual meeting, and could afford the vast resources of the company's legal department and outside counsel to ensure that an outsider couldn't compete on level terms.

*Does the Stone & Webster story tell you that the current system favors one group over another? How might the system be improved?*

Luckily, Lens had prepared a back-up in case (as happened) all its resolutions were dismissed. An investor called Alan Kahn had filed, with Lens' assistance, a resolution calling for the company to hire an independent investment bank to study divestment. This was the critical question in Lens' view, since it required management rigorously to justify the sprawling conglomeration of unrelated assets to a credible external agency with no conflict of interest.

Mr. Kahn asked Robert Monks to propose the resolution on his behalf.

Mr. Monks said the company cried out for a thorough examination from an independent, outside source – a description not met by the company's use of Goldman Sachs. Monks agreed that Goldman was the ideal institution to carry out the inquiry but only if the company asked them the right questions.

But the resolution went beyond the immediate issue. Rather, it was a device for framing shareholders' wider concerns about the company's performance. It was a peg on which to hang concerns over the company's asset dispositions, the quality of the board, the defensiveness of management, and ultimately the long-term under-performance. Given the repeated failed overtures between Lens and the company, both in their meetings and in the courts,

Monks said: "voting for this resolution is the only way we can articulate our concern for the company." The resolution, in a wider sense, became a vote of no confidence in the board.

The company's CFO replied that the company was doing a lot of things Lens wanted. He said the charge that the company was hiding the pension credit was "an out and out lie." He said that hiring another investment bank, given Goldman's assignment, was unnecessary.

The resolution won 35.6 percent of the vote. If the votes of the employee plan, voted by Chase, are stripped out, the resolution won over 55 percent of the vote – a demonstrable vote of no confidence.

The resolution's success was based, in part, on the fact that it was supported by Frank Cilluffo, from inside the boardroom. His position as a director, backed by his sizeable stake, meant his support had substantial credibility.

## First progress

Within three months, Bruce Coles quit the company. Given that Allen, after a 50-year career at Stone & Webster, had also departed at the annual meeting, the company had an opportunity to bring in new, outside blood. Lens pressed for further independent outside directors to join Mr. Cilluffo and asked the company to search for a CEO from outside the company with Lens' help. The company agreed to these requests.

But Lens continued its aggressive pursuit of the company, even seeking purchasers for the company. Fluor Corp. and Raytheon both investigated the possibility of a merger.

In September 1995, Lens issued a press release entitled: "Lens Tells Stone & Webster to Sell the Company." In a letter to the board, Lens wrote: "We must conclude that the only way to realize full value of assets and the jobs of skilled professionals is to sell or merge the company. We are now past the point of studying the divestiture of assets. This company needs to put itself on the market as the best chance to realize full value for shareholders."

Stone & Webster understood that it might soon find itself in play. According to one account, Goldman informed the company that its assets were indeed more than its market value – hence it was ripe for takeover.

> *Does there come a point where a company is unable to change organically and internally, and requires an external agent to effect change? Is a takeover an effective means of accomplishing this, or is it a symptom of a governance system that has failed?*

Under greater pressure than ever to perform, the board continued to make changes – it agreed to pay directors in stock, and consulted Lens on the criteria for new board candidates and a new CEO.

## New management

In February 1996, the board appointed a new CEO, H. Kerner Smith. His first job was to call all the major investors and engineering analysts, reversing the company's traditional policy not to talk to anyone. Analysts began to follow the company once again.

The Bloomberg business news wire reported in June 1997 that the new CEO was bullish on the company's prospects and viewed analysts' estimates as conservative. Bloomberg noted: "The Boston based company is starting to court securities analysts and investors as never before. In May 1996, about three months after Smith joined the company, Stone & Webster provided analysts with its first earnings guidance in its 108 year history."

Smith's other extraordinary discovery was the lack of an overarching strategic plan. Instead, he found separate business plans for the four core engineering businesses. He initiated what Lens had been requesting for so long – a review of the company's capitalization and outline for the most effective deployment of assets. He put in place an *ad hoc* board committee to study the issue. Within a year, the company estimated that Smith's strategy was worth about $55 a share. The company continued to sell off non-core assets and replaced a third of top management as a means of trying to deinstitutionalize the company's culture.

The 1996 proxy statement demonstrates that this new broom reached the boardroom. Three directors retired at the annual meeting – William L. Brown (after 26 years), John A. Hooper (22 years) and Kenneth G. Ryder (9 years).

Joining the board in their place were John P. Merrill (chairman of Merrill International, international project development), Peter M. Wood (former managing director of JP Morgan), and Bernard W. Reznicek (former chairman and CEO of Boston Edison) – all experienced businessmen. Later in the year, an additional non-executive director was added, David N. McCammon, a retired finance executive from Ford.

By the time of the 1996 annual shareholders' meeting, the only directors remaining from 1994 were Angus McKee and Kent Hansen.

It was not all good news, however. Merrill and Wood only bought 200 shares, showing questionable confidence in the company's future.

The 1996 proxy reveals further reforms. The board adopted confidential voting, allowing the ESOP votes to be cast in secret. And the company announced that, effective from January 1997, directors would be remunerated in stock. Each non-executive would receive an annual retainer of 400 shares and $8,000 in cash. The directors could also elect to receive all meeting fees in stock.

## The final pieces fall into place

In October 1996, Stone & Webster announced a "major operational and financial restructuring." The key components were:

- *Headquarters consolidation.* Stone & Webster's corporate headquarters in New York City were consolidated with the Boston offices of the company's principal operating subsidiary, Stone & Webster Engineering. The Manhattan office space was offered for sublease. The company finally admitted that its commitment to clients "does not require us to continue to own substantial real estate holdings or to maintain extensive space in a high-cost midtown New York location."
- *Streamlined organization.* The company reshaped its line management, saying that the company's "structure has been flattened and broadened to improve accountability and encourage a more entrepreneurial environment."
- *Real estate sale.* Stone & Webster announced the sale of its Boston headquarters building, and the planned sale and restructuring of other real estate in Boston.

The good news continued. In February 1997, the company announced:

- a revised compensation plan, based on the company's objective of achieving shareholder returns in the top quartile of the engineering and construction industry;

- a reformed nominating committee, with an expanded remit, renamed the governance committee;
- formal procedures for an annual review of CEO performance.

In May 1997, the board appointed Kerner Smith chairman as well as CEO. Kent Hansen, the caretaker chairman, was appointed lead director. At this point, the board consisted of 11 members, including nine outsiders. Of that 11, all but two had been appointed since 1992.

Kerner Smith celebrated his appointment by projecting a 15 percent increase in earnings per share over the previous year. The stock hit a high in the mid-fifties in response.

Lens took considerable credit for the changes that had taken place in over four years' involvement with the company. In its 1997 annual report, the fund stated: "Lens has played a role in changing virtually every aspect of the governance of Stone & Webster, ranging from the replacement of eight directors and two CEOs to the divestment of non-core businesses, the fundamental recasting of the financial reporting, the creation of a nominating committee, and the adoption of confidential voting, especially important in a company with its ESOP as the largest owner. The company's focus on its engineering business has been strengthened. The Tampa land development, oil and gas holdings, the cold storage business and the Boston office buildings have been sold or are scheduled to be sold. The company has moved out of its expensive and redundant New York headquarters office, and Stone & Webster is on its way to becoming a world competitor in its field. The stock price has appreciated 52 percent over the past 12 months."

And Kerner Smith's view of the fund's involvement? "Lens keeps us on our toes."

*Could these changes have taken place without the involvement of an energetic outside shareholders motivated to improve performance?*

## POSTSCRIPT

In 2000, the company filed for bankruptcy. While it prospered for a while following Smith's reforms, upheavals in the Asian markets and other reversals were insurmountable obstacles.

# Mirror Group/ Trinity Mirror

*The following case study was prepared by Paul Lee. Permission for use granted by Hermes. All rights reserved.*

In 1998, Mirror Group had under-performed the market for several years. Although its core business was fundamentally sound it appeared to be wasting shareholders' money on non-core and non-performing businesses. Policy and personalities had led to major splits on the board. These splits were severe enough to contribute to the failure of talks about a merger with another newspaper group. By strengthening the position of the non-executive directors at Mirror HFAM (Hermes Focus Asses Management) believes that it enabled the group to resolve the stalemate on the board, to focus and proceed with its strategies for the good of long-term shareholder value.

When the merger with Trinity was completed, HFAM realized a significant profit, cashing out of 40 percent of our investment, but remained invested to enjoy the benefits of renewed focus on the core newspaper business. We have continued to test management's thinking and helped encourage what we believe have been positive steps forward in realigning the internet strategy and operational improvements in the regional newspapers. The new chief executive has announced a strategic review and aims to further enhance the value of the business. Her arrival has been received well by investors.

HFAM became interested in the Mirror Group in 1998, having identified it as a fundamentally strong company in spite of years of under-performance relative to the market. The *Mirror* was the second national mass-market newspaper title and the group's Sunday titles were ranked second and third in the UK. Though these nationals were facing the long-term decline shown by the UK newspaper market, they were highly cash-generative. The *Daily Record* was Scotland's leading daily tabloid and the group's regional newspaper concern had a leading market position in the Midlands while developing a significant position in Northern Ireland. The company also had some young growth businesses, in specialist magazines and exhibitions, which we believed had some potential.

In HFAM's opinion, however, there had been a recent failure to implement a coherent strategy for developing the group. The management seemed to be paying less attention to these core businesses than to peripheral unconnected divisions, mostly added by acquisition in recent years. These included Live! TV, Scottish Media Group, Blink TV, and Reg Hayter. Those acquisitions which might have had some strategic value had been poorly timed and priced, and value had been lost. In considering the Mirror Group's recent

**MIRROR GP. DEAD – DEAD 22/11/99**  16/3/01

PRICE
PRICE REL. TO FTSE ALL SHARE – PRICE INDEX
HIGH 243.50 27/5/98, LOW 55.50 16/9/92, LAST 144.00 30/9/98

Source: DATASTREAM

**Figure 6.2**  Performance to October 1, 1998 (first investment)

history, HFAM calculated an erosion of shareholder value of over £200 million in the previous five years attributable to what we regarded as a number of poor financial and/or strategic decisions.

Mirror had purchased Midland Independent Newspapers (MIN) for £355 million in July 1997. Though this was a strong business and very much in Mirror Group's core area – and the management had done a very good job of making the promised cost savings and boosting profits – it seemed to be an expansion into another mature area at the top of the advertising cycle. We estimated the current value of MIN at around £400 million. Though this was higher than the price paid, the value had increased by less than the 22 percent rise in the media sector over the same period. Furthermore, Mirror Group's ill-fated investment in Independent Newspaper Publishing had resulted in net losses to shareholders of over £50 million.

In addition, the unimpressive Live! TV seemed to be a sink for shareholders' funds, in a business which had at best limited synergies with the rest of the group. We estimated the value destroyed by this investment and the ongoing losses at around £50 million. And finally, the company's 19 percent stake in Scottish Media Group also seemed to have under-performed. It was then worth £85 million compared to its £62 million cost, even though the media sector had leapt 85 percent over the same period. We estimated the loss to shareholders at £30 million, though we recognized that the stake might have some strategic value in a further round of television consolidation. Further to these specific losses, we were concerned about the small unconnected acquisitions – of Blink TV and Reg Hayter – which did not seem to make any strategic sense.

In the light of these concerns, and our understanding that there were splits within the board, the focus of our shareholder program was the role of chief executive David Montgomery. Although he had done a tremendous job in his early years as CEO, cutting costs and making sense of the company in the wake of the Maxwell scandal, it seemed that shareholders had lost faith in Montgomery's ability to make strategic decisions that would generate shareholder value. HFAM believed that if the company was to have an independent future there was need of a new chief executive in whom shareholders had confidence.

For us, the company's strategic discussions needed to include consideration of: disposing of the Scottish Media Group stake, disposal of Live! TV, and disposal of peripheral assets to avoid further management distraction. The objective was to restore value to the existing core business before reconsidering longer-term strategic issues such as the possibility of a merger with another regional newspaper group. HFAM made its first investment in October 1998.

## JANUARY 1999

Our shareholder program was launched on January 11, 1999. Trinity, the UK's largest regional press group, revealed that it had broken off merger talks with Mirror Group for the second time in a year. Despite reports that the merger, if it were to go ahead, would yield annual cost savings of up to £20 million, there were two sticking points, according to the City rumor mill. The first centered on the rumored bid price of 155p, approximately 0.375 of a Trinity share. The second focused on reports that Trinity's insistence that David Montgomery would take a limited role in any new venture had split the Mirror board. Trinity indicated that merger talks would not resume until they were convinced that Mirror's board was united.

It was this internal split and the fear of an unacceptably low opportunistic bid for the Mirror Group that triggered HFAM's shareholder program. In an attempt to strengthen Mirror's position, HFAM felt that shareholders would unite behind a campaign for a new chief executive who could keep open all future strategic options – a continuing independent Mirror, a merger or a cash sale.

The following two weeks were some of the most hectic in the life of HFAM as we had multiple meetings with shareholders and various members of the Mirror board. We needed to act particularly quickly because the company was facing a low opportunistic bid – announced on January 18 – from Regional Independent Media (RIM). This offered 200p a share, well below what we believed was the true value of Mirror Group.

Having taken soundings from shareholders representing over 50 percent of Mirror Group equity, and following discussions with some of the non-executives, on January 20 we wrote to the chairman, Victor Blank, formally requesting the non-executive directors "as a matter of urgency, to consider the appointment of a new Chief Executive committed to realising value for shareholders over time." In our discussions with the executive board members it became apparent that the divisions on the board extended beyond the disagreement over the Trinity merger; in fact it seemed that there had been a breakdown in relations between the chairman and chief executive.

On January 21, we agreed to bring forward a planned meeting with Montgomery to the following day. Later that afternoon, Blank asked HFAM to sign a requisition for an EGM[1] to remove Montgomery in case this was needed. We agreed. Montgomery resigned on January 26.

The Mirror Group had already rejected the bid from RIM, and on March 1 it also rejected a 215p-a-share offer from Trinity. Subsequently, both RIM and Trinity made formal applications to the Secretary of State for consent to the transfer of ownership of newspaper titles and newspaper assets owned by Mirror – a necessary process before any merger or takeover could be completed.

HFAM's activities in the intervening period made clear to the board of Mirror Group that we would lend our support to whichever one of three strategies the board agreed on. We believed that each of these strategies – a merger with a rival media group, a cash bid, or an independent Mirror Group – could achieve our target valuation. HFAM confirmed to the Mirror executive directors that we would support a well-reasoned decision for the Mirror Group to be maintained as an independent company if that was the board's view. We also held a number of meetings with Trinity directors to consider the desirability of a merger from a Mirror shareholder perspective in advance of the competition committee's announcement.

## JULY 1999

That announcement came on July 23: the committee gave its consent for the proposed transfer to Regional Independent Media Holdings and to Trinity, on the condition that Trinity divest its titles in Northern Ireland. A week later, the boards of Trinity and Mirror Group announced that they had reached agreement on a proposed merger to form Trinity Mirror plc. Under the terms of the merger, Mirror Group shareholders would receive 0.325 New Trinity shares and 82p in cash for each Mirror Group share. Trinity and Mirror Group shareholders would hold approximately 48.4 percent and 51.6 percent respectively of the merged group's issued share capital. On this date, the terms of the merger valued each Mirror Group share at approximately 271.5p and the whole of Mirror Group at £1.2 billion.

Trinity declared the offer for Mirror Group wholly unconditional on September 6, 1999. The new Trinity Mirror shares were admitted to the Official List. HFAM sold a portion of its stake in the weeks either side of this transaction, but we retained the majority of our holding because we believed that the combined Trinity Mirror had potential to add real shareholder value. In particular, the new company had an attractive strategic position from its increased scale in the rapidly consolidating regional newspapers market. What was more, we believed that the company's unique material gave it an opportunity fully to exploit the burgeoning internet marketplace.

In meetings with Trinity Mirror management around the time of the merger, we made it clear that we believed one key strategic issue for the company was how to exploit its content and market position in the internet age. In particular, we argued that the company should consider splitting off its internet operations from the old-economy activities, perhaps through a partial flotation. We continued to emphasize the need for a focused internet strategy throughout the remainder of 1999 and into early 2000. Unfortunately, the management were understandably distracted from these challenges by the need to carry through the complex integration of Trinity and Mirror. Furthermore, the company's share price was depressed by rising newsprint prices, which pushed the whole sector downwards, and by a company-specific problem over circulation irregularities in Birmingham which came to light in November 1999.

The full announcement of a detailed internet strategy was only made in March 2000, alongside the company's preliminary results. We continued to raise concerns about the

PRICE
PRICE REL.TO FTSE ALL SHARE – PRICE INDEX
HIGH 269.00 6/9/99, LOW 137.00 9/10/98, LAST 269.00 6/9/98

Source: DATASTREAM

**Figure 6.3**    Mirror Group performance from October 1, 1998 to merger

internet strategy over 2000 in meetings with both the senior management and the divi-sional executives. Our assessment was that, while Trinity Mirror had some very sensible internet businesses which fitted with its existing divisions and content – in sports and betting it had IC Sport, and it also had various sites for specific local and regional inform-ation – we doubted that the other businesses had any real strategic fit. We also believed that they would continue to be substantially loss-making. In particular, the company's operation of an internet service provider, IC 24, was effectively paying customers to use it, and the company was unable to articulate any competitive advantage in this field. The other sites – IC Showbiz and IC Choice – similarly seemed expensive and non-core.

## SEPTEMBER 2000

By September 2000 it appeared that the management had begun to agree with our assess-ment. It seemed likely that the company would sell IC 24 and refocus the company's internet efforts on sports and betting, and the regional sites. Over the following months, HFAM suggested that the portal could simply be shut down rather than kept alive with further injections of shareholders' funds until a possible but very uncertain sale.

However, the next news from the company was the surprise purchase of Southnews, a rival local and regional newspaper publisher based in the south-east. Announced at the end of October, the deal cost £285 million. While it made great strategic sense, filling a gap in Trinity Mirror's coverage countrywide, we had concerns about the price Trinity was paying – a premium of nearly 60 percent over the former share price, or around

£100 million. The executives worked hard to provide HFAM and the rest of the market with evidence that the price, though full, was not out of line with previous similar deals. They also argued that they could make enough cost savings, particularly in printing, to justify the price paid.

In March 2001, Trinity Mirror finally announced changes to its internet strategy. Overall, it was to scale back its investment in the area. In particular, it announced it would sell IC 24 and its 50 percent stake in the sporting site Sportinglife.com which it co-owned with the Press Association – freeing itself to concentrate on its wholly-owned sports and betting websites. The stock market reaction was highly favorable.

# JUNE 2001

The year as a whole, however, turned out to be a difficult one for the company. It was hit hard by the market-wide fall in advertising revenues: in June it announced a 10 percent year-on-year decline, in line with that faced by the whole media sector. In December it revealed that the figure for the national papers was nearly 21 percent. Throughout the year, Trinity had therefore focused on cost-cutting and operational management. In particular, the company had great scope to enhance the returns at its regional papers, which had always been run as separate businesses, frequently with up to 15 percent differences between cost levels in specific areas at the different businesses. By sharing best practice, the company had huge scope to close the margin gap with its competitors. This "From Biggest to Best" program was headed by Joe Sinyor, who at the end of 2000 had been appointed chief executive, newspapers, reporting to overall CEO Philip Graf.

HFAM agreed this focus on operational matters was the best way forward for the company. There were rumors in the market that the company was considering selling its national newspaper titles, and also unhelpful rumors about possible changes to the executive management of the group. In our meetings and communications with the company, we argued that any such deal should not be rushed into until the operational improvements had been achieved. A November letter to Graf made these views particularly plain: while we backed the operational focus he was leading, we emphasized the need to work harder at turning around City opinion about the company. Our discussions with analysts made it clear that City perceptions were driven by the company's historic tendency to dealmaking. Analysts were waiting on the next deal, so the company's new focus on operational matters needed to be explained more clearly. Only then would perceptions change and the stock be revalued.

# FEBRUARY 2002

The company's hard work on operations began to pay off in early 2002. The market responded well to Trinity's preliminary announcement in February, despite a £150 million write-down of assets which pushed the company into loss. A particularly positive piece of news was the £16 million cash released from cost-cutting – and the further £22 million promised for 2002. It seemed the "Biggest to Best" program in the regionals was bearing fruit. Importantly, Trinity also announced a relaunch of the *Mirror* and *Sunday Mirror* titles, distancing them from the fiercely competitive so-called "red-top" market and giving up the rather fruitless aim of winning readers from rival titles. Instead, the focus was to be on retaining existing readers and encouraging them to read the titles more often. This, the company predicted, would drive more value for shareholders. Costs would also be cut as the Mirror papers' advertising departments were to be placed into a joint venture with those of the Telegraph Group newspapers.

This news triggered the awaited re-rating of Trinity Mirror, and HFAM began selling down our stake slowly from the start of March. This process was, however, hampered by volatile and illiquid markets which made any substantial selling impossible. HFAM remained bound by our usual sales discipline of selling once a stock has reached our calculation of fair value, but not selling if the only price practically available on the market is 5 percent below this.

The difficulty in selling was exacerbated as the market began to lose confidence in the strategic relaunch of the *Mirror*. This loss of confidence was sparked by price cuts. Though these were said by the company to be an integral part of the relaunch and associated marketing spend, aiming to build loyalty and ensuring readers became more regular purchasers, it seemed to the market to run counter to the stated intention of abandoning competition with long-time rival the *Sun*. The *Sun* more than matched the cuts, and launched a marketing campaign to bolster its position. It appeared to the market that Trinity Mirror was overspending on a mistaken pricing strategy.

Over mid-2002 we tested the reasoning behind the board's decision to offer price cuts in various meetings. The debate also brought into sharp focus the division between the regional and national newspapers. The regional business was (even given the tough advertising market the company faced) a strong one, with scope for substantial increases in profits as the "From Biggest to Best" program fed through to cost savings and revenue growth. In contrast, managing the nationals business remained an issue largely of limiting decline and controlling its consequences. We explored the possibility of splitting these businesses with board members and other investors. We were assured that the board had considered this option, but had not received any offers for the national papers that would have enhanced the value of the group.

Further uncertainty was added to the market's perception of Trinity Mirror by the announcement that finance director Margaret Ewing was leaving the company to join BAA plc. Concern mounted over the summer, as it became apparent that the price-cutting strategy was not sustaining the *Mirror*'s circulation, but that the *Sun* continued to gain readers at its expense. The market was losing confidence in the existing management team to take the business forward.

## SEPTEMBER 2002

The tail end of September 2002 saw the announcement that long-standing chief executive Philip Graf would be leaving in the summer of 2003 to pursue other interests. This was followed a week later with the embarrassment and further disruption of Ewing's appointed successor Ric Piper in effect being sacked even before having joined the company. The Trinity board evidently felt that his joining the company would not be taken well in the market because of his former role as finance director at WS Atkins, which had just issued a profits warning which had undermined its share price. Piper has now reached a settlement with Trinity Mirror over loss of income.

Sly Bailey was announced as Graf's replacement in December. Bailey is well respected in the magazine publishing business, having risen rapidly through publisher IPC to the role of chief executive shortly after the company had come under the ownership of private equity house Cinven. At IPC, Bailey had been charged with readying the business for sale

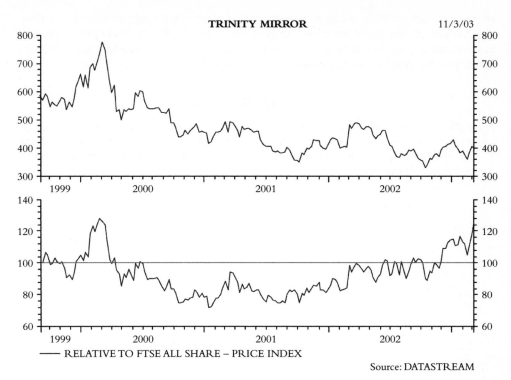

**Figure 6.4**  Trinity Mirror absolute (upper) and relative (lower)
share price performance since merger (September 1999)

| | |
|---|---:|
| IRR of Mirror/Trinity Mirror investment (across all funds): | 8.1%★ |
| IRR of same cashflows if invested in the FTSE All-Share index: | −8.5%★ |
| Current profit on investment at given date (across all funds): | £ 9,589,821★ |
| Current profit on investment relative to FTSE All-Share index: | £22,023,494★ |

★ these are all unaudited figures produced by HFAM's own internal model all figures to
February 28, 2003

within three years, something she achieved in only two when she sold the company to
AOL Time Warner.

Bailey joined Trinity in early February 2003. Her arrival was preceded by the expected
departure in January of Joe Sinyor, who had been a rival for the role of CEO. Bailey
released unspectacular annual results at the end of February, which again showed evidence
of continued slow progress on efficiency and merger benefits within the business.
However, the numbers were again marred by a substantial impairment charge and the continuing decline in circulations at the nationals. Bailey faces a substantial challenge in ending those declines, continuing to make efficiency savings, and making clear what the synergies
are between the two halves of the business. She announced a strategic review and took
the sensible step of abandoning the failed price-cutting strategy. She also halted the move
to link the *Mirror* and *Telegraph* advertising departments.

Bailey's arrival and initial meetings were well received in the market. This, combined
with the continuing operational improvements, led to strong share price outperformance
in early 2003. The fact that the price had outperformed in 2002 in the face of a difficult

advertising market was a credit to the impressive operational progress over time. There was also a small speculative bid premium in the price based solely on a story that the board had rejected approaches from private equity firms in late 2002. HFAM's sales discipline means that we continue to sell down our stake as and when the market allows.

## NOTE

1. Under UK law, shareholders holding 10 percent of a company's issued share capital can require a company to call an Extraordinary General Meeting to discuss resolutions that the shareholders propose. These resolutions can include the removal of any current member(s) of the incumbent board.

# Adelphia

From "The Adelphia Story" on Adelphia's website:

> In 1952, John Rigas borrowed money from family and friends to buy a small movie theater in Coudersport, Pa., not far from his hometown of Wellsville, N.Y. To cover expenses and repay his debts, he kept his day job and spent evenings at the box office selling tickets and popcorn and running the projector.
>
> Many nights, he curled up on a cot in the theater to catch a few hours of sleep before driving back to work early the next morning.
>
> An RKO film salesman urged him to take advantage of a local cable franchise that was for sale. After months of prodding, John reluctantly bought his first cable franchise for $300, a sum that seemed like a steep price for admission into an industry that did not yet exist. The next year he took his first steps toward constructing and operating a cable television system, one of the first in rural Pennsylvania.
>
> In 1972, the company was incorporated under the name "Adelphia," derived from the Greek word for "brothers." A glorious growth spree would follow. Adelphia built its success on a strong commitment to customer care. "We strive to earn our customers' trust by making sure that every customer is satisfied with the outcome of every contact he or she has with our people and the service we provide," says Adelphia's founder John Rigas. "With this philosophy, we've grown up from a company with one customer, then 100, to the company we are today." By 1998, Adelphia passed the 2 million-customer milestone and now serves approximately 5.6 million cable television customers nationwide.

Rigas was known to be ambitious and to be willing to take on enormous risks. He overdrew his bank account to get the $300 to make his first cable franchise acquisition and borrowed heavily to finance his expansions. He continued to leverage heavily. "In 1996, Adelphia's debt was 11 times its market capitalization, an off-the-chart number. (By contrast, Comcast's ratio was 1.28; Cox Communication's was 0.45.)"[1] Rigas made a lot of acquisitions, some for Adelphia, some for the family's private holdings.

On March 26, 2002, Adelphia had 5.7 million subscribers in 32 states and Puerto Rico. Five members of the nine-member board of directors were members of the Rigas family: founder John Rigas, his sons, Michael, Timothy, and James, and his son-in-law, Peter Venetis. The stock was trading at $20.39 a share, half of its high.

The next day, Adelphia disclosed that the Rigas family had borrowed $2.3 billion through various family-owned partnerships off its balance sheet. Adelphia's stock dropped 18 percent. A day after that, on March 28, Adelphia acknowledged that it might be liable for as much as $500 million in debt it had guaranteed for Adelphia Business Solutions Inc. a telephone service company spun off from the parent and run by James Rigas. It had filed for bankruptcy protection. On April 1, 2002, Adelphia said in an SEC filing that it needed more time to review its accounting and would not meet the deadline for filing its annual financial statement. The stock closed at $13.12.

On May 23, 2002, Rigas and sons Timothy, Michael, and James resigned as directors. The family agreed to turn over $1 billion in assets to help cover loans, to turn over $567 million in cashflow from other cable companies the family owned, and to pledge all stock held by the family as collateral. Adelphia estimated it was liable for $3.1 billion in family debts. The stock was delisted by NASDAQ a week later. It was trading at 70 cents a share. On June 25, 2002, Adelphia filed for bankruptcy, saying that it could not meet the $7 billion in outstanding loans.

According to an article in *Fortune*,

> Adelphia inflated subscriber numbers. Routine expenses like service calls had been booked as capital items, inflating Adelphia's reported cash flow. But what was perhaps most unsettling was the unabashed manner in which the Rigases had helped themselves to shareholder dollars. Adelphia financed the family's $150 million purchase of the [Buffalo] Sabres [hockey team]. It paid $12.8 million in 2001 for office furniture and design services provided by Doris [Mrs. John] Rigas . . . [T]he primary source of income at Rigas' farm wasn't honey sales; it was providing landscaping, snow removal, and other maintenance duties for Adelphia.[2]

Adelphia shareholders also paid for the New York apartment occupied by Ellen Rigas (daughter of John and wife of Aldephia director Peter Venetis) and funded the $3 million production costs of her movie, *Songcatcher*. They put $65 million in the Praxis Capital fund run by Venetis. They paid her brother Tim's $700,000 membership fee at the golf club at Briar's Creek. And they guaranteed $1 billion in loans to a Rigas family partnership, which used the funds to buy stock.

A month after the bankruptcy, five executives, including three members of the Rigas family, were arrested and led away in handcuffs, charged with looting the nation's sixth largest cable television company "on a massive scale." The SEC filed a related fraud complaint. James B. Comey, US Attorney for the Southern District of New York, made a statement concerning the Adelphia indictments on September 23, 2002:

> The Indictment charges that, from 1999 through May 2002, the defendants participated in a scheme to defraud Adelphia's creditors and investors by, among other things, making false and misleading statements concerning (1) Adelphia's "off-balance-sheet" debt; (2) the company's purported deleveraging through a variety of securities transactions; (3) Adelphia's operating performance, as reflected in such metrics as its EBITDA (earnings before interest, taxes, depreciation and amortization), basic cable subscriber growth and plant rebuild progress; (4) Adelphia's compliance with various covenants and financial ratios required under its loan agreements and the indentures related to its bonds and other debt securities; and (5) the unauthorized and unreimbursed use of Adelphia's funds and assets by the Rigas Family.
>
> According to the Indictment, Adelphia was one of the most heavily indebted companies in the cable television industry, in part as a result of its rapid expansion through

a series of highly leveraged acquisitions of other cable companies. According to the Indictment, Adelphia faced intense pressure from investors, lenders, securities analysts and credit rating agencies to generate high levels of earnings to service its staggering debt load, and to reduce its leverage.

However, according to the Indictment, Adelphia consistently failed to meet Wall Street's expectations and in order to conceal that failure, and avoid such consequences as a decline in Adelphia's stock price, inability to access the capital markets and default on its debts, the defendants perpetrated a scheme to create the false appearance that Adelphia's operating performance was consistently in line with Wall Street's expectations, and that Adelphia was systematically deleveraging through, among other means, sales of equity securities to the Rigas Family.

The Indictment charges that the Rigas Family used billions of dollars in Adelphia's funds and assets for their own benefit. Among other things, the defendants allegedly caused Adelphia to pay more than $250 million in connection with personal loans to the Rigas Family. From 1999 through April 2002, John J. Rigas, Timothy J. Rigas, Michael J. Rigas and other members of the Rigas Family allegedly took unauthorized and undisclosed cash advances from Adelphia, totaling more than $50 million. In addition, the Rigas Family spent approximately $13 million in corporate funds to construct a golf course located on land primarily owned by them, it was charged. Such uses of Adelphia's funds and assets by the Rigas Family were not presented to or authorized by Adelphia's Board of Directors, and were not disclosed to the non-family members of the board or to the public, according to the Indictment.

The Indictment seeks forfeiture of at least $2.533 billion of the proceeds of the scheme to defraud.

[Coney said that the] scheme charged in the Indictment is one of the most elaborate and extensive corporate frauds in United States history. The Rigas defendants and their co-conspirators exploited Adelphia's byzantine corporate and financial structure to create a towering façade of false success, even as Adelphia was collapsing under the weight of its staggering debt burden and the defendants' failing management of the company, and the Rigas Family lined their pockets with shareholder dollars. The defendants used many of the most sophisticated tricks in the corporate fraud playbook, including concealing Adelphia's billions of dollars of off-balance-sheet liabilities, using dishonest pro forma reporting, and manipulating unaudited metrics such as EBITDA and subscriber growth statistics. Although the defendants for years deceived some of the most sophisticated financial professionals on Wall Street, the Indictment in this case demonstrates that this Office, along with its law enforcement and securities enforcement partners, will quickly get to the bottom of even the most complicated corporate frauds and bring swift justice to CEOs and other executives who use their positions to deceive investors and victimize public companies.

The company's director of accounting and vice-president of finance pled guilty to fraud charges and promised to cooperate with prosecutors working on the charges against the members of the Rigas family.

Adelphia itself sued the Rigas family and the auditors, alleging that the majority presence of the Rigas family on the board should have made it a "high risk" audit and therefore subject to additional scrutiny – and skepticism. The company (represented by its remaining directors), alleged that Deloitte knew, but didn't tell the board, that the Rigases regularly took funds from Adelphia's cash management system. If the "unorthodox cash system" had been revealed, the Rigases' "massive self-dealing could have been and would have been prevented, saving Adelphia hundreds of millions, if not billions, of dollars in damages."

They also alleged that, despite reasons to be wary, Deloitte consistently gave Adelphia a clean bill of health. On March 26, Deloitte told the board that the 2001 audit "was one of the best audits they had ever had," with only "four minor issues." The report was scrapped the next day after Adelphia disclosed the co-borrowing deals, as lenders and investors challenged company debt figures.

In its statement to the press, Deloitte said, "the board, including its independent directors, knew and approved of many of the acts complained of." It noted that it was considering its own lawsuit against Adelphia and current or former executives and directors "who supplied Deloitte with erroneous and incomplete information."

The IRS noted that it, too, was investigating the Rigas family for failure to report the alleged payments as income.

Even though the new CEO was "a consummate Rigas family insider,"[3] he and the other "independent" directors, believing they had been lied to, hired David Boies, the lawyer who represented the US government in the Microsoft case, to look into the books. They told the Rigases that if they did not sign over voting control to the independent directors, they would resign and go public with everything they had uncovered. After the Rigases relinquished control, the company was able to get a $1.5 billion bank loan. The acting CEO hopes to be able to restructure to regain solvency.

## What Happened?

This was a modern-day version of the story of the emperor's new clothes, the story about the two con men who tell a vain emperor that they have cloth so rare that it cannot be seen by those who are stupid or unfit for their jobs. Everyone, even the emperor, is unwilling to admit that the emperor isn't wearing anything because they think that everyone else can see it.

John Rigas was a very big man in a very small town. Coudersport, Pennsylvania had a population of just 2,600, and every single one of them knew John Rigas and almost everyone had a reason to be grateful to him. Rigas, a benign "Lord Bountiful" for the town, brought in a symphony orchestra to play at the Christmas party he gave for Coudersport, sent busloads of children to Sabres games, and used the corporate jet to fly sick people to get treatment.

The *Fortune* article speculates that "There were things that John Rigas and his sons got away with in Coudersport that would never have been tolerated anywhere else." Adelphia was such an overwhelming presence in the town that no one had the incentive, the ability, or the energy to take it on.

The family was very close. Two of the Rigas sons moved back in with their parents after they graduated. A third lived away for a year and then returned to Coudersport. After they all went into the business, it began to grow dramatically. *Fortune* quoted an executive: "Decisions were made at the dinner table rather than in a boardroom or somebody's office."

And no one was there to provide any oversight. "Adelphia was a relatively rare hybrid: a publicly held company whose economic interest was owned by thousands of holders of its common stock, but whose management interest was controlled almost entirely by the founding family."[4] Because it was set up with a dual-class voting structure, the Rigas family had 11 percent of the economic stake in the company but controlled 56 percent of the votes.

That meant that the family controlled the board. Rigas, his sons, and his son-in-law held five of the nine seats on the board. The other four were held by friends and business associates who knew that, if they rocked the boat, they would be replaced. Perhaps that's why no one mentioned that it might be a problem to have Tim Rigas as both CFO and chairman of the board's audit committee.

When the Coudersport tax collector noticed that the real estate taxes of both Adelphia and the Rigas family were paid with a single check, she, like everyone else in Coudersport, thought that the Rigases must know what they were doing. No one wanted to speak up for fear of being thought a fool or not suited for his job.

The Rigases routinely ignored calls from analysts. When a high-yield bond analyst said he could not figure out where the money was coming from for the stock purchases committed to by the family, they refused to answer. Then on March 27, 2002, in a footnote on the last page of Adelphia's quarterly earnings press release, the company disclosed that it was liable for $2.3 billion in off-balance-sheet loans to the Rigas family. Even after that disclosure, there was another $175 million withdrawal from the company's cash management system to cover margin loans. And even after he had resigned as chairman and CEO, he showed up at a board meeting, only to be told that he had to leave. The emperor was finally told that he was not wearing any clothes.

## NOTES

1. At this writing "The Adelphia Story" can still be accessed through the Internet Archive at <http://web.archive.org/web/20020601222356/www.adelphia.com/story/index.cfm>.
2. Devin Leonard, "The Adelphia Story," *Fortune Magazine*, Aug. 12, 2002.
3. Ibid.
4. Daniel Gross, "Adelphia's Family Fools," *Slate Magazine*, July 2, 2002.

# Arthur Andersen

Before there was Arthur Andersen, the $9.3 billion international accounting and con-
sulting firm, with offices in 84 countries and 85,000 employees, there was Arthur
Andersen, the 28-year-old son of Norwegian immigrants, who left Pricewaterhouse to
open up his own accounting firm in Chicago with just one other partner. It was 1913
and the combination of industrial expansion and the introduction of the new income tax
made the prospects promising for specialists who were more than bookkeepers. Andersen's
announcement of the new firm offered clients help with "the designing and installing of
new systems of financial and cost accounting and organization."

In his first year in business, Andersen told a railroad executive that there was not enough
money in the city of Chicago to make him approve a set of books that had not adequately
recorded operating expenses. The railroad went bankrupt a few months later, helping to
establish the young firm's reputation for integrity. And that story was told to all of the
accountants who attended the firm's intensive training program over the decades to teach
them the standard they were expected to uphold and carry forward.

Before long, many other stories of the uncompromising integrity of AA's auditors were
added to the list. They were on the right side of many of the twentieth century's most
memorable financial scandals. After the stock market crash of 1929, they helped to unwind
the pyramiding financing structure of Samuel Insull's power companies, keeping them
out of bankruptcy. The post-crash reforms requiring independent audits boosted their
business. As AA grew, Andersen kept tight control of its work through the "one firm,
one voice" concept, telling employees and clients that services and results must be utterly
consistent. In order to make that work, AA established extensive in-house training facilities, ultimately taking over an entire college campus.

Another of Andersen's innovations was the "Blueback" memo, commentary from the
audit partner to the client about any issues that might be of interest to the client regarding its operations.

Andersen died in 1947. His successor, Leonard Spacek, presided over AA's growth into
the foremost accounting firm in the world. Instead of affiliating with other firms abroad,
he opened up AA offices, so that the "one firm" concept would apply worldwide. By
1963, they had 55 offices in 27 countries, staffed with locals who had been through AA's
rigorous training. All partners shared in the global revenues, so all were committed to the
success of the entire firm.

It was Spacek's idea to make the symbol of the firm its heavy mahogany doors. He said that they represented "confidentiality, privacy, security and orderliness." Identical doors were installed in every AA office throughout the world and the doors were incorporated into the firm's logo. The original doors were selected by Arthur Andersen's son-in-law (who told Andersen that they cost $200 instead of the real price of $1,000). They were such a powerful symbol of the firm that they were moved to AA's corporate training center to inspire all who came to learn what AA stood for. In 2000, AA abandoned Spacek's mahogany doors for a new and non-representational symbol – a glossy orange sphere – that was intended to impart some dotcom-era sizzle. This change was itself symbolic of AA's loss of its core identity.

Spacek "honed the firm's sense of itself as the financial world's answer to the Marine Corps."[1] In his efforts to impose consistency in appearance and performance throughout the organization, no detail was too small. In one legendary memo, he wrote, "Everyone should make it a habit to be busy all the time and avoid any appearance of being inactive or unoccupied. When walking in the halls, walk briskly."

A former partner who started work at AA in 1951 remembered that on their first day, the young men were given five dollars to buy a hat. They were told to wear felt hats from Labor Day to Memorial Day and straw hats in the summer. (No woman would make partner until 1976. By 1998 only 7.5 percent of the partners were women.[2])

Arthur Andersen continued to maintain its reputation for integrity. It resigned all of its clients in the savings and loan industry before the very accounting tricks AA refused to bless led to a series of massive failures and several criminal convictions.

But, just 15 years later, AA abruptly failed, after several of its clients were involved in massive accounting scandals and after AA itself was found guilty of obstructing justice in connection with its destruction of documents relating to its work for Enron. On August 31, 2002, AA issued a statement that was simple but which had a devastating effect: "As of this day, Arthur Andersen LLP has voluntarily relinquished, or consented to revocation of, its firm permits in all states where it was licensed to practice accountancy with state regulators."

## ANDERSEN CONSULTING

AA was a pioneer in non-audit consulting. It began as a way to help its clients. In 1954, it set up one of the original Univac computers at GE to help with its payroll, and AA was soon selling its services as systems analysts in bringing computer technology to its customers. At first, the consultants were all accountants and were required to spend two years in audit practice before being permitted to do consulting work. When that rule was rescinded in the late 1960s, it stopped time being wasted on training people who were not going to stay in accounting, but it eliminated the common ground and culture that had kept both sides feeling as though they were on the same team.

Some time in the 1970s, the consultants became more profitable per partner than the auditors. "The opposing forces of a stagnating audit business and a rapidly growing consulting business created a 'stress' fracture along these practice lines."[3] As one insider described it,

> The solid, trustworthy, proudly boring way of the accountants began to lose its appeal as auditing revenues plateaued. And the stability and respectability of Arthur Andersen was losing its pull as the booming economy gave young business majors many different career options. Slowly, a mighty culture was disintegrating into a soulless cult behind those doors, and I stumbled right into the middle of it.[4]

The firm had always had a clear idea of its values – and its value. The defining story about Andersen's refusal to sign off on the railroad executive's books set the stage for AA's view of itself and its uncompromising integrity. That was more than just a corporate value. It was the key corporate asset. Clients would come to a firm whose name on the audit provided an extra sense of confidence and comfort to investors, regulators, and employees. But that began to change when the two sides of AA fell into bitter sibling rivalry. The audit side still controlled the firm's management, and the consultants chafed at being told what to do by people who were not part of their group. They chafed even more at subsidizing the less profitable side. They felt they were paying for much more than they were getting.

Spacek's successor in 1970 was Harvey Kapnick. He was concerned about the possible ethical conflicts that might arise between the consulting and audit sides. His concerns were practical and political – after being called to testify before a Senate committee on the issue of potential conflicts between accounting and consulting, he concluded that the government would require a split and that AA should do it first. He proposed a spin-off of the consultants into a separate firm at the partners' meeting of 1979. But he handled the issue poorly, and failed to get the approval of the partnership. The partners thought they would be at a competitive disadvantage if they split. And they didn't want to lose the lucrative fees. "The audit partners loudly refused to let go of the consulting golden goose."[5] Kapnick was forced out.

Kapnick's successor, Duane Kullberg, did his best, and it worked for a while. But hostilities between the two sides of the firm continued to simmer. When Kullberg was given a copy of a memo the consultants drew up that showed an estimate of their value as a separate entity, the relationships deteriorated further. To make things more confusing, the audit side of AA set up its own consulting divisions.

The two groups became separate in operations and marketing in 1989 – so much for the concept of "one firm, one voice." The Andersen Consulting offices did not even have the trademark mahogany doors. It was like a bad marriage. They tried counseling, bringing in mediators, but it did not work. At an April 1997 meeting in Paris, for the first time the nearly 2,800 partners had a contested election for head of the firm, with one candidate from consulting and one from the audit side. Both lost, neither gaining the required two-thirds majority. In December, the consulting partners voted unanimously (with one abstention) to split themselves off from AA. The final split was accomplished through arbitration of a thicket of legal and financial disputes.

Andersen Consulting changed its name to Accenture and omitted any mention of AA in the corporate history on its website. The audit side was deeply bitter. It also left them with less money; $100,000 per partner had to go to the consulting side according to the terms of the arbitration.[6]

Both pride and pocketbook pushed what was left of AA to become much more aggressive in seeking and expanding business, and that meant rebuilding the consulting practice. Auditors became salesmen. They were already under a lot of pressure to meet specific revenue goals. In an absurd 1989 partnership pep talk, audit chief John Edwards brought a live tiger on stage while the *Rocky II* theme song "Eye of the Tiger" boomed out, as he urged the accountants to go for the gold.

AA was determined to show Accenture that it could do better and make more money without them. And you can't do that if you are going to tell a client that there isn't enough money in Chicago to make you sign his cooked books.

## A CONFORMIST CULTURE

AA specifically sought new hires who were malleable and inclined to conform. Job applic-ants were evaluated across a complex set of metrics, but positive indicators of a prospect's ability to "fit in" included being the first one in the family to attend college. Young people without first-hand observation of the professional working world were considered easier to mold into the "one firm's" idea of how to do the job. The firm had a strong bias for hiring people just out of school and rarely brought in outsiders with established careers and who might have their own ideas about how to do things, until the 1990s.

At the firm's St. Charles training facility, all new hires learned the AA system for doing an audit in a sort of accounting "boot camp," with the idea that, no matter which office was in charge, any other accountant in the firm would be able to open up the schedule and find every document and number in the same order as every other audit in every other office.

The idea of "one firm, one voice" promoted not just consistency but conformity. Instead of unanimity in upholding the highest standards, it led to a lowest common denominator approach. One-time partner and organizational behavior and corporate ethics specialist Barbara Ley Toffler said that her experience at AA led her to understand the connection between the words "culture" and "cult." She said that the highly conformist employees were jok-ingly referred to as "Androids," and that "it would never occur to them to question any practice, despite the cosmic changes taking place both inside and outside the Firm."[7] Toffler attended a class called "Transitions" to teach lateral hires how to adapt to life at AA. The class outlined six "CLMs" (career-limiting moves), the first of which was "overcustomiz-ing your office."[8] Two more were "trying to do it all alone" and "sugarcoating the truth," but in practice there was no incentive to raise questions or problems with anyone senior. On the contrary, "If a person had a problem, that was prima facie evidence that that person didn't fit here at AA," according to one executive.[9]

The consequences of this "do what the partner wants without asking questions" culture were tragic when David Duncan, the lead partner for Enron, told the staff to comply with the firm's document destruction policy following the revelations of account-ing problems at Enron. Whether it was what he intended to imply or not, this direction led to the destruction of more than a ton of documents and roughly 300 emails and com-puter files, more shredded in three days than the firm normally destroyed in a year. Duncan was there and made no effort to stop it. "Andersen staffers were seen huddled around file cabinets, rifling through desks and picking through piles of paperwork in the Houston office's common workspaces, their hands stinging from papercuts."[10]

## WHO WATCHES THE WATCHERS?

Harvey Kapnick created a prestigious Public Review Board made up of outside experts like the former chairman of the Securities and Exchange Commission to visit AA facilities throughout the world and review their practices to make sure that they were meeting the highest standards of integrity. After the consulting/audit split, the board was discontinued, and no equivalent mechanism was ever established.

For most of AA's history, its internal "Professional Standards Group" (PSG) had the final word on any ethical dispute or question on the application of accounting principles. The group's head until 1980, George Catlett, had an office no more than 50 feet from the office of the CEO.[11] But that ended in 1992. The PSG called for the increasingly popular form of executive compensation, stock options, to be expensed at the time of the award. It was overruled, and from that time on, its power was severely diminished. One of the group's partners, Carl Bass, was removed from the Enron account at the client's request, after he challenged the way Enron wanted to characterize the sale of options owned by one of the partnerships managed by CFO Andrew Fastow. "Andersen was the only one of the Big Five where a local partner could overrule the Professional Standards Group. In retrospect, the system for airing such conflicts at Andersen seemed designed to ensure that top executives never learned of them. Instead, they were handled several layers down in the organization by people with clear and strong incentives to maximize revenues."[12]

AA and KPMG were the first of the then Big Six accounting firms to offer consulting on ethics, compliance, and risk management to their clients, but AA never set up an in-house ethics officer or created any of the other structures it was being paid to develop for others. There was an "Independence and Ethics" office to distribute the required disclosure forms (auditors had to disclose their mortgage companies, banks, investment firms, and stock holdings) and to raise questions if there appeared to be a potential conflict of interest with a client. AA underwrote the development of an ethics training module for business students. But the extensive training for the staff did not cover those issues. An auditor who thought something was wrong was discouraged from raising his concerns. "[N]o matter what you thought privately, a partner still always outranks a manager, and to challenge that hierarchy with uncomfortable questions just wasn't done. Anyone who dared got the equivalent of a public spanking."[13]

AA became so enmeshed with Enron that AA insiders and former insiders were responsible for the internal and external audits of the company. "By the fall of 2000, the two business giants were so enmeshed that dozens of the Chicago accounting firm's most ambitious auditors reported to work each day at Enron." Auditors from both firms took vacations together and played fantasy football against each other over the Enron computer system. "'It was like these very bright geeks at Andersen suddenly got invited too this really cool, macho, frat party,' said Leigh Anne Dear, a former senior audit manager at Andersen who worked in Enron Tower . . . One executive still at Enron describes the allure: 'It's like Patty Hearst, you start identifying with your kidnappers.'"[14] The Independence and Ethics office did not interfere. Indeed, an in-house video shown to the partners commended the close relationship with Enron – and the $58 million in fees in 2000 alone – as a model for other audit clients.

AA was involved in a series of accounting scandals even before Enron and WorldCom: DeLorean, Sunbeam, Waste Management, and the Baptist Foundation of Arizona, the largest religious foundation bankruptcy in US history. But instead of auditing its own practices, it seemed to consider each an isolated incident for which it bore no responsibility, and none was considered serious enough to require a systemic evaluation or any structural changes. The US Attorney who prosecuted AA for destroying Enron documents met the firm's pleas that the entire partnership should not be punished for the actions of a few rogue employees with one word, based on this history: "Recidivists."[15]

By the time AA failed, seven layers of management separated the Professional Standards Group from the office of the CEO.[16]

## CORPORATE GOVERNANCE

AA, as a limited partnership, had little independent oversight. As noted above, it had a Public Review Board which was shut down when the firm split, and it overruled and then marginalized its internal standard-setters when they disagreed with the clients about accounting for stock options.

The firm's own governance and compensation structures created incentives that benefited individual outposts and partners over the good of the firm as a whole.

The 20-year battle over the relationship between the auditors and the consultants demonstrated the limitations of trying to run a large, complex organization as a partnership. Toffler's book documents the almost unthinkably enormous partners' meetings at which the "election" of a new leader was in reality determined ahead of time. Worse was the one dreadful meeting that foreshadowed the fall of the firm, when neither of the candidates received the requisite number of votes, creating great uncertainty and disruption. The firm's CEO at the time of the Enron revelations was Joseph Bernardino. His "emphasis on growth over audit quality, his reluctance to walk away from big clients with questionable accounting, and a stunning ignorance of potentially crippling issues all contributed to the firm's undoing," according to *Business Week*'s John Byrne in an August 12, 2002 cover story. But they were as much a reflection as a cause of what was wrong at AA at the end.

## HUBRIS

AA's failure has been described in epic terms. According to *Chicago Tribune* columnist David Greising, it was the force which has led to documented implosion and destruction since the days of the ancient Greeks – hubris. He wrote:

> Hubris dictated Andersen's decision in the 1980s to assume it could turn auditors into salespeople and not undermine auditor independence. Hubris caused the firm to deny or minimize errors in failed audit after failed audit, and particularly in the Enron disaster. Hubris ultimately caused Andersen to gravely underestimate the threat it faced in [Department of Justice prosecutor Michael] Chertoff, or the outrage of an investing public who felt scammed by Andersen's poor work . . . The firm seemed utterly incapable of recognizing that it had seriously failed in its core mission of protecting investors against fraudulent financial reporting – and the consequences of that failure.[17]

Arthur Andersen, the founder of the firm that lasted for almost 90 years, said that he wanted to "measure our contribution more by the quality of service rendered than by whether we are making a good living out of it." Quoting this high aspiration in a 1995 letter to partners, then chief executive of the worldwide audit and tax practice Dick Measelle said that Andersen Consulting partners were more like "merchants" while the auditors were more like "Samurais" (concerned more with honor and loyalty than with profits). He encouraged the partners to be both, setting a path with tragic consequences.

"A firm that made its name auditing the performance of others in the end faced the ultimate accounting for its own failings."[18]

## NOTES

1. Flynn McRoberts, "The Fall of Andersen," *Chicago Tribune*, series beginning Sept. 1, 2002. Additional reporting by Delroy Alexander, Greg Burns, Robert Manor, and E.A. Torriero.

2. Barbara Ley Toffler with Jennifer Reingold, *Final Accounting*, Broadway Books 2003, p. 28.

3. Bela Barner, "Don't Blame Joe Bernardino for Arthur Andersen," *The Story of Business*, 4, (Fall 2002), p. 4.

4. Toffler, *Final Accounting*, p. 39.

5. Barner, "Don't Blame Joe Bernardino."

6. Part of this section is freely adapted from Toffler's chapter in *Final Accounting*, "Cain and Abel Andersen", an excellent history of this struggle.

7. Ibid., p. 39.

8. Ibid., p. 43.

9. Ibid., p. 59.

10. McRoberts, "The Fall of Andersen."

11. Ibid.

12. John Byrne, "Joe Bernardino's Fall From Grace," *Business Week*, Aug. 12, 2002.

13. Toffler, *Final Accounting*, p. 197.

14. McRoberts, "The Fall of Andersen."

15. Ibid.

16. Ibid.

17. David Greising, "On Andersen, the 'Bad Apple' Argument Rots," *Chicago Tribune*, Sept. 4, 2002.

18. Ibid.

# Tyco

## by Robert A.G. Monks

"Power tends to corrupt and absolute power corrupts absolutely." *Lord Acton*

As a director between 1985 and 1994 I have had a front-row seat to watch one good example of corporate success, Tyco Laboratories. Between 1995 and 2001 Tyco became one of the largest companies on the planet. In 2002, it became almost a code word for everything wrong with a corporate culture.

Let's start at the beginning. In the creative atmosphere of greater Boston in the 1950s, it was said that two men, a wheelbarrow, and an abandoned textile mill were all that was needed for a successful new venture. Throw in a few PhDs, at a million dollars a pop, and you could have a successful public offering of the nascent company's stock. Arthur Tyler's idea was to provide organization and financing for inventors, and thus Tyco was born. The company has been far afield, from joint ventures with Mobil and virtual war with the Russians over deep-water lobstering to a variety of attempted hostile takeovers before the concept was popular.

The company grew rapidly in the middle 1980s, under the leadership of John Franklin Fort, into an integrated worldwide leader in automatic sprinkler equipment. With worldwide sales of $3.5 billion, it was one of the Fortune 200. Fort, a Princeton engineering graduate with an industrial management degree from the Massachusetts Institute of Technology, had risen through the operating ranks of the company. There were no corporate jets, there were no corporate clubs, and there were only 35 employees at the corporate headquarters in Exeter, New Hampshire. A simple incentive system was key to the decentralized management style. Compensation was based on the profits of individual business units. The company did not believe in options. Restricted stock was issued to executives and the company loaned them money to pay their taxes. Compensation was direct and to the point; there were no footnotes on the corporate balance sheet for yachts, farms, consultancies, and the like, just direct grants of stock on top of a modest cash base. Thus, the executives' net worth and their attention were focused on creating shareholder value at Tyco.

Tyco's acquisition record in the late 1980s was impressive. All four of its acquisitions over those years fit its current business mix and offered genuine merger benefits without causing dilution of earnings. Acquisitions were made to increase size; they were made to further industrial integration and to improve profits.

The company demonstrated many of the elements that gave American business its deservedly high reputation in the years following World War II. These included strong leadership from a chief executive officer who focused on technology, operations, and profits. The company had an industrial purpose. Corporate resources were not diverted to unrelated technologies.

As Fort approached his tenth year as CEO and his thirtieth as a Tyco employee, he told members of the board of his desire to retire early in 1991 and his recommendation that Dennis Kozlowski succeed him as CEO. Shortly thereafter the possibility of expanding Tyco's business worldwide through the acquisition of Wormwold surfaced. In order to help consummate what was the most important transaction in Tyco's history to date, Fort stayed on beyond his desired retirement date. In July 1992, Kozlowski became CEO. Fort stayed on as a director.

Under Kozlowski, the rate of growth accelerated to hyper-speed. Tyco acquired so many companies in such rapid succession that keeping score was difficult. The emphasis evolved from an industrial strategy to a financial one, buying bloated businesses, stripping them of excess personnel and facilities, and treating the associated costs as non-recurring in the company's income statement. Investors embraced the 'slash and burn' *modus operandi*, believing that as long as new acquisitions were made, growth could continue indefinitely. It seemed that Tyco, like the universe, was infinite and expanding. Kozlowski appeared on the cover of *Business Week* as America's "most aggressive" CEO.

Tyco branched out into the medical care business with the Kendall acquisition in 1992, and it moved its corporate domicile to Bermuda with the "reverse acquisition" of ADT in 1997 (see the discussion of Bermuda reincorporation in chapter 5). During this period, it made over 70 "bolt-on" acquisitions to further integrate its existing lines. The pace of acquisitions became frenzied, and by year-end 2001 Tyco had acquired a finance company and was credibly seeking to rival GE, widely viewed as the finest company in the world.

Although not as diversified as GE, Tyco's manufacturing and services operations comprised electrical and electronic components (year end 1991 – $13,572 billion), disposable medical supplies ($8,812 billion); fire detection and suppression systems ($7,471 billion); and flow control products ($4,179 billion). Tyco became one of the most valuable corporations in the world in the relatively short term of Dennis Kozlowski's leadership.

This vast expansion placed severe strains on Tyco's governance structure. Extracts from letters that I wrote to the CEO at various times prior to my resignation from the board will give some indication of the struggle for governance structure within a culture of virtually limitless expansion.

## April 26, 1990 – to JFF

The boards of directors of a Massachusetts corporation are given the ultimate responsibility for conducting the business of the enterprise. In discharging this responsibility, the Tyco Board of Directors over the years has made certain implicit and explicit decisions as to its *modus operandi*. The Board's authority stems from the shareholders and the Board directs the venture with the objective of maximizing the long-term value of its owners. The Board has consciously adopted an informal mode of operation. The Board has considered a number of different modes for conducting its business and has decided that, under the circumstances now prevailing and the personalities involved at Tyco, the best results can be obtained by having the Chief Executive Officer both preside at meetings and be initially responsible for the preparation of an agenda. The Board has decided not to adopt a formal strategic plan for Tyco, preferring instead to communicate continuing concerns directly at meetings. Directorial concern focuses on long-term value optimization for shareholders. This involves an aggressive policy with respect to acquisitions; the Board has been particularly concerned that close attention be focused on stand alone operating divisions; that periodic assessments of value be made; and that management be alert to the preservation of values. Management reports (other than detailed financial statements) are oral rather than written; there are no formal agendas for meetings, although any subject that an individual director wishes to discuss is routinely entertained; formal votes, with motions and seconding, are customarily not taken; the mode is one of board consensus with individual directors having the opportunity to express disagreement at all parts of the process; communication among directors both during and outside of meetings is encouraged.

*Is this a bit informal for a $5 billion company?*

## June 7, 1990 – to JFF

The Board has adopted a formal meeting schedule so as (i) to enable the continuance of the present pattern of 100% attendance by members; (ii) certainty as to times when subjects necessary for Board review can be dealt with; and (iii) a concern not to have meetings that are not necessary for the efficient conduct of Tyco's business. The Chief Executive Officer presides at Board meetings. The Board has adopted this mode of operation after consideration of (i) the character and operating style of the Chief Executive Officer; (ii) the needs of Tyco at this stage in its growth; and (iii) a preference for efficient, non bureaucratic procedures to as great an extent as possible. *The Board, of course, has the continuing responsibility to review its mode of operation in light of changing personnel and circumstances.* (emphasis added)

*Casual, yes, but attentive.*

We are embarking upon a period involving the need for mastering several significant new challenges simultaneously [Wormwold acquisition, in particular]; I feel that the Board should take the time carefully and thoroughly to review its functioning and to conclude how best to discharge its responsibilities in the new environment.

*How should a director compel attention to governance matters?*

## September 19, 1990 – to JFF

(i)   There is disagreement as to whether the CEO should also be the presiding officer of the Board . . . Review it periodically.

(ii)   The Board is, in my opinion, paid too much for what it presently does, and too little for what it should be doing henceforth.

(iii)   [Board] [T]erms should typically be for a fixed period of time, and be renewable.

*At what point does a director become obtrusive in pressing a point of view on to management?*

## September 26, 1991 – memorandum to the board

#5 – The board will need to become more effectively involved:

(i)    There is immediate need for two additional directors – ideally one with top level
       U.S. manufacturing experience, another with European (continent) contacts and
       experience.
(ii)   Need to focus on executive succession – a new #2 person.
(iii)  There is need for capability in the area of compensation . . .
(iv)   There is need for financial information in aid of an understanding of the cash flow
       situation of Tyco.
(v)    The board chairman and the CEO should be different persons. We need to probe
       further to assure that all the directors are timely getting the information they may
       reasonably require. *There should be discussion and formal legal action making clear the
       scope of authority delegated to the Board by top management.* (emphasis added)

*The informality of board functioning is no longer tolerable. How can this be made a part of
the agenda for action?*

## March 2, 1992 – to LDK

#3 – As we add new directors, we have the chance to add procedures. I feel that the
board should evaluate its own performance and that of the individual directors once a
year . . . We can't expect the guys down the line to react constructively to evaluation if
we do not have a comparable discipline all the way to the top. Also, the board should
annually assess the CEO. . . . Directors should not expect to serve indefinitely. They should
have explicit understanding – say three years – that their service will be reexamined
periodically.

*Will the new CEO be interestable in governance questions? If not, what are a director's options?*

## April 21, 1992 – to LDK

#3 – At the beginning of the meeting in Wisconsin, I asked the "insiders" to leave so
       that the Board could better consider the questions of compensation. The insider direc-
       tors neither addressed my request, nor did they leave. This put me into a most difficult
       position. Either I had to press my point, which would tend to introduce a confrontation
       element into our board culture for the first time in my experience, or acquiesce. In
       doing the latter, I am conscious of having tolerated, even encouraged, a coerced and
       impoverished discussion of the compensation issues. I, personally, tried to make clear
       as tactfully as possible that I have been very uncomfortable with the level of com-
       pensation to "X". Candor tends to get lost in politeness . . .
#5 – . . . At the very least, there is confusion arising out of a lack of direction and clar-
       ity as to what we expect from various committees (and their relationship to the board)
       and as to the relative roles of insiders and outsider directors in this determination . . .
#8 – It is apparent to me that we need standards and an evaluation process for directors.
       Clearly, outside directors should not be considered as having a lifetime job.

*Confrontation is inevitable. Will it be productive? What are a director's options at this stage?*

## August 21, 1992 – to LDK

(1)    The board has not defined for itself a role. The board has not jelled as a group . . .
       The board does not have sense of itself . . .

(5)     The board has not set a mission for itself. There is no scheduled review. The board does not evaluate its own performance . . .

(13)    The boardroom atmosphere has been strained. The meetings have not been led. The mode has been a monologal meandering with occasional directorial interjections. Increasingly, the board's desire to question has encountered resistance, even hostility. At best − no leadership in the boardroom; at worst − an atmosphere of anger . . .

(18)    I am still a bit uncomfortable as an outside director with extra-board communication with Tyco principals. I have limited myself to letters to the CEO, leaving with him the complete discretion as to what use may want to make of the contents. We need a definite policy as to (i) periodic and occasional meetings between outside directors; (ii) a definition of who is and who is not an "outside" director of Tyco; and (iii) the designation of a particular individual as the "convener" of such meetings.

*The need to avoid acting like a "cabal" prompts the desire to have "legitimate" meetings of outside directors.*

## November 2, 1992 − to LDK

#2 − Tyco directors are unwilling to adapt to any kind of self evaluating process . . .

#6 − The committee structure of the board is in shambles. The Audit committee is poorly led. . . . The Compensation committee worked hard in August . . . and came up with recommendations that were largely ignored or overruled. X decline to take a cut in pay; and it is unclear what survives of the Committee's actions. There are no minutes . . .

#10 − The board lacks leadership and the will seriously to address the company's problems . . . X has no use for the Board. It is becoming clear that the Board has no use for itself. . . . The Board apparently will not insist on a role for itself.

*The board is dysfunctional. See also the "anonymous" memo from a director to the CEO in chapter 3. It is from co-author of this book Robert Monks to the then CEO.*

## August 30, 1993 − to LDK

What can the board do that will be most helpful to Tyco? Is there benefit in having an energy in the board apart from management that sets the agenda, conducts meetings and is responsible for informing directors between meetings? Do we want to make changes in the structure and personnel of the board at this time? My own sense is that the board will be relatively useless in the absence of a commitment to self examination and criticism.

*An appeal to the CEO: the board will be useless unless you personally pay attention.*

## January 3, 1994 − to LDK

What is wrong [about a board] is to have no defined role, no mission, no explicit benchmarks against which performance of the board can be evaluated. This is what I worry about here . . . We should also have regular meetings of the outside directors in executive session at least twice a year . . .

*I resigned as a director shortly after this note.*

The transition of Tyco from an impressive but modest-sized conglomerate to one of the 25 largest companies in the world and a "name that will be known in infamy" has been well documented. It is not our purpose here to more than note the plethora of allegations of criminal and civil conduct by certain top officers of Tyco. We are focused on certain elements of board culture that I experienced some eight years before Tyco became a household word and before any of the conduct that is the content of the allegations occurred.

At the behest of certain Tyco directors in early 2002, the firm of David Boies Esq. conducted an exhaustive forensic audit of the company's finances and governance. Its conclusions of December 30, 2002 included:

> Board of Directors. As previously reported, the entire Board of Directors appointed at the last Annual General Meeting ("AGM") has agreed not to stand for re-election at the next AGM. A number of Directors have already resigned and been replaced and Board Committees have been reconstituted. The Board of Directors has reviewed all of its responsibilities to ensure that it has procedures to assure that it is receiving sufficient information to fulfill its obligations. This includes a formal review of all equity compensation plans, compensation programs, and other similar programs with written approval or disapproval. For any delegated responsibilities to committees or officers, the Board will ensure that the delegation fits within certain parameters and that the Board regularly reviews the performance of the committee or officer to whom the responsibility has been delegated. At least annually, the Board and an appropriate committee will review charitable contributions, compensation to officers, loans to employees, and the use of corporate assets. The Board is preparing and will approve detailed written charters for each of the committees of the Board that clearly articulate the committee's duties and responsibilities.

*Is there a resonance of concerns noted earlier?*

*What conclusions can be drawn about the desirability, for example, of an "independent" chairman of the board whose entire responsibility is to assure the integrity of board proceedings?*

*Who had the opportunity to recognize the pending problems and who had the opportunity to act?*

# WorldCom

## by Beth Young

Spurred by the failures of Enron, Tyco, Adelphia, and other companies amid allegations of self-dealing and fraudulent accounting and disclosure, in early 2002 the US House of Representatives passed legislation authored by Michael Oxley (R – Ohio) which was regarded by many as easy on both the accounting profession and companies. In the Senate, Banking Committee chairman Paul Sarbanes (D – Maryland) sponsored a much tougher bill that provided for an independent accounting oversight body and effected significant reforms related to the gatekeepers – including boards of directors, auditors, and securities analysts – that had failed to protect investors.

By June, however, the smart money had Senator Sarbanes' bill dead in the water. But all of that changed, almost overnight, when the biggest scandal yet broke. On June 25, WorldCom made an announcement that shocked even investors jaded by the prior melt-downs: WorldCom had improperly and intentionally capitalized as assets $3.8 billion in expenses over five quarters, and had paid down expenses with money from reserve accounts earmarked for other purposes, artificially boosting WorldCom's income. (After further investigation, the estimate was raised to $9 billion. Ultimately, WorldCom took a write-off of $79.9 billion, the biggest one-time write-off any US company has ever taken. WorldCom wrote off its entire $45 billion in goodwill and reduced the $44.7 billion value of its property, plant and equipment, and other intangible assets.)

The announcement came on the heels of the April 2002 resignation of WorldCom's CEO, Bernard Ebbers, amid questions over personal loans from WorldCom, and the March 2002 initiation of an SEC investigation into WorldCom's accounting. Since the announcement, several WorldCom executives – although not CFO Scott Sullivan – have pleaded guilty to criminal charges related to the fraud.[1]

Outrage about WorldCom breathed new life into the Sarbanes legislation (dubbed Sarbanes–Oxley after it emerged from conference). It was quickly passed in Senate by a unanimous vote, despite an intense lobbying campaign by the accounting industry, and was signed by President Bush.

WorldCom's place in history was not limited to a well-timed legislative intervention, however. In July 2002, WorldCom became the largest US company ever to file for bankruptcy protection. As of this writing, WorldCom intends to emerge relatively intact from bankruptcy protection and carry on its business under the name MCI, taken from its 2000 merger partner. Whether it can do so in a flagging telecommunications market is unclear.

How did a company of WorldCom's stature end up engaging in such blatant accounting chicanery? A combination of an overly enmeshed relationship with Wall Street, poor corporate governance, and lax oversight by auditors created a culture that prioritized WorldCom's stock price over all else and undermined the monitoring mechanisms necessary to prevent fraud.

## GROWTH BY ACQUISITION

Founded in 1983 as Long Distance Discount Services, WorldCom relied heavily on acquisitions to fuel its growth. From its founding through 2001, WorldCom made over 60 acquisitions on its way to becoming the second-largest long-distance company in the US. Almost all of WorldCom's acquisitions were paid for with WorldCom stock.

Initially, WorldCom was in the voice telephony business, but increasing competition and new technology reduced revenues and profits in that business.[2] WorldCom thus sought to diversify itself in the mid-1990s, acquiring companies that enabled it to enter the markets for data and satellite communications, internet services and web hosting, among others. Those businesses, however, then experienced their own slowdown, making it difficult for WorldCom to meet its own revenue and earnings forecasts.[3]

WorldCom's growth-by-acquisition strategy had four important implications for the company and its investors. One was simply that the company grew very rapidly. Such rapid growth involving far-flung operations posed a significant management challenge, straining WorldCom's resources and internal controls. Unfortunately, WorldCom's internal audit department, which should have been responsible for ensuring that appropriate controls were in place, was focused primarily on operational matters and was significantly understaffed.[4]

Second, WorldCom's constant stream of acquisitions made it very difficult for investors to compare results from one period to another. A report by bankruptcy court examiner Dick Thornburgh (the Thornburgh Report) stated that WorldCom's "unprecedented and unceasing growth may have obscured the ability of investors to focus upon and evaluate objectively the actual strength and financial performance of the Company at various junctures."[5] The opacity of WorldCom's accounting thus may have increased the temptation to manipulate the numbers. It has even been claimed that WorldCom's feverish dealmaking was in fact designed to create reserves that enabled WorldCom to manage its earnings.[6]

The third consequence of WorldCom's acquisitiveness was that the price of the WorldCom stock used as acquisition currency was of paramount importance. Analyst earnings expectations were a frequent subject of discussion at meetings of WorldCom's top management. Indeed, the Thornburgh Report concluded that "a major criterion in WorldCom's strategy formulation and in its choice of transactions was to meet analysts' expectations as to earnings and stock price."[7] Before WorldCom began misclassifying expenses outright, it engaged in various "earnings management" techniques to boost earnings, although as of this writing details about those practices have not been released due to the ongoing government investigations.[8]

Finally, WorldCom's frequent acquisition and financing transactions made WorldCom a sought-after corporate finance client for investment banking firms. The Wall Street firm that received the most engagements from WorldCom over the five-year period ending in early 2003 was Salomon Smith Barney (SSB). A complaint filed by New York's Attorney General alleged that SSB received over $107 million in fees from WorldCom between October 1997 and February 2002. That complaint also alleged that SSB's telecommunications analyst, Jack Grubman, made overly optimistic predictions regarding WorldCom's stock price – he gave WorldCom stock SSB's highest rating until April 2002 – in order to secure investment banking business for SSB. Minutes show that Grubman attended WorldCom board meetings as a "financial advisor" to the company, a role that was clearly inconsistent with providing unbiased advice to investors.

New York's Attorney General has also alleged that SSB allocated shares being issued in initial public offerings to SSB accounts maintained by WorldCom CEO Bernard Ebbers and other WorldCom directors in order to win investment banking business from WorldCom, a practice known as "spinning." The Thornburgh Report asserts that those IPO shares were sold for an aggregate profit of more than $18 million.[9] Regulators are currently evaluating whether WorldCom executives and directors may be liable for theft of corporate opportunity – whether they personally benefited from attempts to win company business – and other legal theories of possible liability.

## WORLDCOM'S BOARD OF DIRECTORS

With the challenge of integrating multiple global businesses and the pressure on WorldCom to perform to Wall Street's expectations, it was imperative that the board of directors fulfill its duty to monitor WorldCom's management and, in particular, its financial reporting. It appears, however, that the board did not vigorously safeguard shareholder interests, but, rather, asked few questions and tended to "rubber stamp" management's decisions.

The Thornburgh Report opined that CEO Ebbers, prior to his resignation, "appears to have dominated the course of the Company's growth, as well as the agenda, discussions and decisions of the Board of Directors."[10] A former board member put it this way: "Rule No. 1: Don't bet against Bernie [Ebbers]. Rule No. 2: See rule No. 1."[11] The Thornburgh Report attributed this attitude to Ebbers' past successes and the stock price appreciation that directors, many of whom owned large stakes, experienced during Ebbers' tenure. The board's passivity was especially evident in the behavior of the crucial audit and compensation committees.

Although not directly related to the financial reporting misconduct that propelled WorldCom into bankruptcy, the apparent failure of the compensation committee to tie top executive pay to company performance, as well as its approval of hundreds of millions of dollars in loans to Ebbers, provide a window onto the board culture at WorldCom. The Thornburgh Report concluded that appointment to the compensation committee "largely was influenced by Mr. Ebbers, in consultation with the Nominating Committee."

Committee chairman Stiles Kellett enjoyed an undisclosed arrangement with WorldCom beginning in 2001, when he leased a jet from WorldCom on terms that the company's Corporate Monitor has characterized as non-arm's-length.[12] Kellett was also a co-investor with Ebbers in VirtualBank, a privately held company.[13] Kellett has since resigned from the board.[14]

WorldCom's senior executive compensation was extremely generous, even in the two years before the company declared bankruptcy, when the company's performance was deteriorating. During the three years from January 1, 1999 through December 31, 2001, Ebbers was paid more than $77 million; that same period saw the company's market capitalization shrink by more than $140 billion. His severance package provided for a $1.5 million per year cash payment for life, lifetime use of the corporate jet, insurance benefits, and an interest rate subsidy on a $408 million note payable to WorldCom. An unusual "retention bonus" program was implemented in 2000, including $10 million payments to Ebbers and CFO Scott Sullivan; the payments were not staggered over time, as is customary in order to ensure that executives stay with the company.

Most notably, WorldCom's compensation committee approved a series of loans to Ebbers which eventually totaled over $400 million. The circumstances surrounding these loans are in dispute, with Ebbers insisting that the compensation committee originally suggested the loans so that Ebbers could avoid selling WorldCom stock he had pledged as collateral for personal loans in order to meet margin calls. Compensation committee chairman Kellett has asserted that Ebbers approached him first.

Preliminary evidence indicated that the full board was not apprised of the loans before they were made. It is unclear whether the compensation committee considered whether Ebbers would be able to repay WorldCom or whether the loans would violate any of WorldCom's debt covenants. The interest rate on the loans was significantly below-market, and there is evidence that Ebbers used some of the loan proceeds for personal purposes rather than just to meet margin calls on existing loans. Tensions resulting from Ebbers' financial condition and the loans from the company ultimately led to Ebbers' termination in April 2002.[15]

The audit committee, which was directly responsible for monitoring WorldCom's financial reporting, seems to have fallen short as well. The audit committee did not take part in any planning by the internal audit department, which increased the ability of management to steer the internal audit department away from sensitive areas. The audit committee also took no action to require correction of identified deficiencies in WorldCom's internal controls, including problems discovered five years earlier.

Max Bobbitt, the audit committee's chairman, reportedly initially delayed relating concerns brought to him by WorldCom internal audit head Cynthia Cooper, whose group uncovered the fraud. According to an article in the *Wall Street Journal*, Bobbitt asked Cooper to contact KPMG, WorldCom's new outside auditor, and did not inform the rest of the board of her concerns at a meeting the next day.[16]

## WORLDCOM'S AUDITOR

A company's outside auditor is charged with ensuring that the financial statements "fairly present" the company's financial position, results of operations, and cashflows. The auditor may rely on a company's internal controls only if it has reason to believe that those controls are adequate. There is evidence that Arthur Andersen, WorldCom's auditor, did not probe the sufficiency of WorldCom's internal controls.

The Thornburgh Report "found little evidence of substantive interaction between Arthur Andersen and [WorldCom's] Internal Audit Department." If this is true, Arthur Andersen would have violated Generally Accepted Audit Standards if it relied to any extent on WorldCom's internal audit function for monitoring and assessing WorldCom's internal controls. As of this writing, the extent of such reliance was under investigation.

Arthur Andersen had access to reports by WorldCom's internal audit department detailing weaknesses in WorldCom's internal controls. Despite the fact that weaknesses were identified, with some remaining uncorrected for years, Arthur Andersen told the audit committee and the full board that there were no material weaknesses in WorldCom's internal controls system.[17] Reportedly, Arthur Andersen initially refused to respond to some of the questions raised by Cynthia Cooper, telling her that the firm had approved some of the accounting methods.[18]

The work papers supporting the 1999, 2000, and 2001 audits show that Arthur Andersen considered WorldCom to be a "maximum risk" client, based on the predominance of historical purchase accounting adjustments to income, the company's prior misapplication of GAAP, and its use of multiple billing systems. A memo in the 1999 work papers stated that WorldCom management had "taken aggressive accounting positions, particularly in the area of purchase accounting." In risk assessments, Arthur Andersen singled out "Accounting and financial reporting risk" and "Overly aggressive revenue or earnings targets" as areas of "significant" risk.

WorldCom's failure illustrates the importance of strong, well-functioning gatekeepers – boards of directors, auditors and securities analysts – in protecting investors. During market and sector expansions such as the one WorldCom benefited from in the 1990s, such checks may seem superfluous, or even burdensome. But they are essential to ensure that managements like WorldCom's, confronted with competitive pressures and a shaky business model, do not succumb to the temptation to fudge the numbers.

## NOTES

1. See e.g. Jerry Markon, "WorldCom's Yates Pleads Guilty," *Wall Street Journal*, Oct. 8, 2002; Susan Pulliam and Jared Sandberg, "Two WorldCom Ex-Staffers Plead Guilty to Fraud," *Wall Street Journal*, Oct. 11, 2002.
2. "When Big Is No Longer Beautiful: Big Telecoms in Big Trouble," *The Economist*, Dec. 16, 2000.
3. Robin Goldwyn Blumenthal, "WorldCom's Woes: It Cuts its Forecasts, Unveils a Restructuring," *Barron's*, Nov. 6, 2000.
4. See First Interim Report of Dick Thornburgh, Bankruptcy Court Examiner, at 57, *In re WorldCom, Inc.*, Case No. 02-15533 (SDNY Nov. 4, 2002), comparing WorldCom's internal audit department to those of peer companies. The final report had not been released as of this writing. This case study draws heavily from the first interim report.
5. Ibid. at 12.
6. Thomas Catan and Stephanie Kirchgaessner, "How WorldCom's 'Big Fraud' Began," *Financial Times*, Dec. 24, 2002. (After the collapse of the Sprint merger, "'They had to do another deal to refill reserves because the cookie jar was running low,' says a person with detailed knowledge of the company.").
7. Thornburgh Report at 63.
8. Ibid. at 106.
9. Ibid. at 82.
10. Ibid. at 6.
11. Jared Sandberg, "Six Directors Quit as WorldCom Breaks with Past," *Wall Street Journal*, Dec. 18, 2002.
12. Thornburgh Report at 64, 70.
13. Walid El-Gabry, "WorldCom to Begin Search for Chief Executive," *Financial Times*, Sept. 11, 2002.
14. Joann Lublin and Jared Sandberg, "WorldCom Director Kellett Quits under Pressure from the Board," *Wall Street Journal*, Oct. 29, 2002.
15. Susan Pulliam et al., "Easy Money: Former WorldCom CEO Built an Empire on Mountain of Debt," *Wall Street Journal*, Dec. 31, 2002.
16. Susan Pulliam and Deborah Solomon, "Uncooking the Books: How Three Unlikely Sleuths Discovered Fraud at WorldCom," *Wall Street Journal*, Oct. 30, 2002.
17. Thornburgh Report at 58.
18. Pulliam and Solomon, "Uncooking the Books."

# Gerstner's Pay Package at IBM

## by Paul Hodgson

### THE ANATOMY OF A CONTRACT

Louis V. Gerstner Jr. was appointed as IBM's chairman and CEO in March 1993, after leaving RJR Nabisco, where he was also chairman and CEO. He was recruited using an employment agreement with what must then have been very generous compensation and an array of "special payments" – to compensate for lost income that might have been earned from his previous employer. He was hired at a salary not only more than double that of his predecessor CEO at IBM but also well above market levels even for a company the size of IBM.

All aspects of Mr Gerstner's 1993 compensation were governed by this employment contract. The board "approved Mr Gerstner's employment agreement after an extensive search . . . with the assistance of two executive search firms." The compensation committee report in the 1994 proxy goes on to say "in settling the final compensation amounts" the board focused on hiring a CEO "with an outstanding business record who could provide the leadership necessary to improve IBM's competitiveness and profitability."

Despite the enormous cost of employing Gerstner over the nine years from his appointment, stockholders appear to have received value for this, as they have experienced an increase of 938 percent in total shareholder return (TSR) during his tenure.

The purpose of this section is to investigate the effects of contractual provisions on his compensation history.

### The compensation elements of the 1993 contract

- Base salary: $2,000,000.
- Target annual incentive: $1,500,000, with a guaranteed three-quarter target bonus in 1993 of $1,125,000.
- Target long-term incentive award: $500,000.
- Eligibility for stock option awards and other equity-based awards.
- Benefit programs including, without limitation, pension, profit-sharing, savings, and other retirement plans, medical, dental, hospitalization, short- and long-term disability and life insurance plans, accidental death and dismemberment protection, travel accident insurance and any other retirement or welfare plans that the company may adopt.

- Supplemental pension: a retirement benefit that supplements pension to the level he would have been eligible for from Nabisco had he remained there until age 60 (i.e. increases it to the level of $2,447,867 per annum).
- Reimbursement of business expenses.

In addition, Gerstner was granted 500,000 stock options in 1993, to vest over four years, and a target award of 10,301 performance stock units, dependent on the company's performance against EPS and cashflow measures over three years.

As can be seen, the only elements not strictly "guaranteed" by the contract are the level of award of equity-based incentives such as restricted stock or stock units, or stock option grants. Indeed, in his nine-year tenure, Gerstner has received only two awards of restricted stock units, and, as table 6.3 shows, there were three years, including the latest, when he did not receive a stock option award. No comment is ever made about the lack of such awards in any of the relevant compensation committee reports.

Other elements of additional compensation not specified in the original contract were covered by the catch-all phrase "any other benefit program." These included the ability to defer up to 100 percent of salary, and certainly that part of it above $1,000,000, following the introduction of Section 162(m) of the Internal Revenue Code. A summary of the deferral programs in operation at the company is given later in this section.

All other payments, and this is made quite clear in the first few compensation reports during his term of office, are based on contractual provisions and not, as is the case with most of the other executives at the company, on market influences or compensation surveys.

### Each contractual amendment required further compensation

But there have been three amendments to the contract, each resulting in additional compensation – sometimes as a direct enticement for Gerstner's agreeing to them. The first amendment, in 1996, reduced his salary, but increased his target annual and long-term incentives. The next, in 1997, was to retain his services as chairman until his planned retirement in 2002 and instituted a ten-year consultancy agreement following on from this. A special award of 2 million stock options was made. Finally, in 2002, this arrangement was again amended to encourage him to agree to delay his retirement one more year and Gerstner received a restricted stock unit award of over 125,000 shares. Each of these amendments will be discussed in more detail in the course of the report, and their potential costs, which went far beyond the immediate expense, will be analyzed.

### "Special payments": compensation for "forfeited" income from previous employer

Before going on to detail the whole of Gerstner's compensation history, the special payments will be looked at in detail. The contract also set out a range of special payments to be made to Gerstner, in order to gain his services from his former employer. Again, the 1994 proxy offers an explanation of these elements of the contract: "The board also recognized the need to consider Mr Gerstner's compensation at his former employer as well as the value of benefits under various plans of this former employer that would be forfeited upon his resignation." And elsewhere, while total compensation for other executive officers is targeted at the upper quartile of the competitive market, "for officers recently recruited, compensation rates reflect the need to recruit them." This is standard practice: most executives move to another job only if the challenges or the rewards are greater than those of their present position. Mr. Gerstner's compensation at his former employer, however, was a salary of around $1,200,000, bonus opportunity, stock option and restricted stock unit grants, and pension. The package offered to him by IBM was well in excess of this.

### Special payments to Gerstner

- Gerstner held options over 3,171,320 Nabisco shares with an exercise price of $5, and 40,000 Nabisco shares with an exercise price of $7.50. The contract guarantees him a sale price of $8.125 per share, and will make up any shortfall. This cost IBM $7,752,854, and was paid out in 1994.
- $725,000, equal to the amount of spread on unexercisable Nabisco options, forfeited on his termination with Nabisco.
- $1,478,750 for an award of performance shares forfeited on his termination with Nabisco.
- $500,000, representing his first-quarter bonus from Nabisco.
- $1,381,764 for forfeited benefits under his Personal Retirement Account.
- $25,000 for financial and tax-planning services that would have been paid by Nabisco.
- $637,500, representing the difference between $8.125 and the price realized upon selling 300,000 shares of Nabisco stock.
- An aggregate of $176,582 for other expenses, including legal fees, relating to his change of employment, payments to purchase the automobile provided by Nabisco and tax gross-ups.

### Improper principle

While the above sums, totaling $12,677,450, seem small compared with some of the "compensation for lost income" that has been paid out lately, for example by Home Depot and Verizon, it should be remembered that this was nine years ago. And however small or large the sums involved, the improper principle that lies behind the practice is constant. Incentives are not forfeited if an executive leaves a company: they are not earned. Compensation for this so-called forfeiting is an unjustifiable part of any employment offer. Either incentives are a reward for performance or they are an expected part of compensation. If they are the former, then there should be no "compensation" for them. If the latter, then companies should not be claiming relief for them under IRC Section 162(m), as they are not truly performance-related.

While none of these special payments is justified, the least defensible is the guarantee of a stock price of $8.125 for any Nabisco shares that Gerstner sells. This affected two elements of his "lost" income. First, his 3,211,320 vested stock options are guaranteed to be worth $8.125 when he sells them. Nabisco stock was not at this level when he exercised the options, and IBM had to pay out just over $7.75 million in compensation. The second element affected was Gerstner's holding of 300,000 Nabisco shares. These were sold at only $6 each, costing IBM $637,500 in compensation. But these shares were sold because they were collateral for a loan taken out by Gerstner from Nabisco, and the purpose of the loan was to buy these shares. One cannot imagine an equivalent situation for any other class of stockholder.

In total, comprising payments from Nabisco that included annuities to fund his pension, the special payments and his regular IBM compensation, Gerstner received $22,854,329 from employment in 1993.

## The contract in practice

Table 6.2 gives us the details of Gerstner's compensation at IBM for the nine years from 1993 until the latest available information for fiscal year 2001. The elements include: base salary; annual bonus – typically based on one or more financial targets such as profit, earnings, or cashflow as well as other qualitative measures; long-term incentive awards in the form of performance stock units based on EPS and cashflow targets; and any value realized from the exercise of stock options. The columns giving other annual compensation and all other compensation consist of several different kinds of payment. As footnotes 1 and 3 explain, in the first years of his employment, they largely represent contractual obligations which the company entered into at the time of his recruitment. Later, however, other annual compensation came to represent the cost of benefits such as the use of corporate aircraft or company vehicles. The first explanation of the amounts given was in 1999, when $27,354 covered use of corporate aircraft and $15,191 the use of a company car when commuting. In 2000, the amount included $36,778 for aircraft usage and in 2001, $43,101.

Following 1994, and the final "special payment," all other compensation was entirely made up of company matching contributions to an all-employee deferred savings plan and an executive plan. The all-employee plan is a deferred income plan set up according to IRS guidelines, under which employees may defer up to 15 percent of their income (up to a maximum level). The company then matches these at the rate of 50 percent for the first 6 percent of compensation deferred. The second plan, as amended in 1994, allows executives whose salary exceeds $1 million to defer a large proportion of their income, matched on the same basis as the all-employee plan, but invested only in IBM stock units. The effects of Gerstner's increasing salary excess over $1 million can be seen in the increasing cost of company matching contributions. Full descriptions of these schemes are reproduced later in the section.

## Gerstner's stock option grants

Table 6.3 details the history of stock option awards for Gerstner. Figures have not been recalculated to take account of the two stock splits, in 1997 and 1999. If they had, the effect would have been to render the 1997 awards, for example, combined at 4,400,000. Some of the option grants are exceptional. The 500,000 stock options awarded in 1993, for example, were part of the employment agreement. The special grant of 2 million options, in 1997 was partially in recognition of a further amendment to his employment agreement – part of an initiative to retain his services and "to recognize his outstanding performance and leadership." It also appears to have taken the place of grants in 1998 and 1999, but no information is given on why grants were not made in those years. In addition, the grant in 2000 of 650,000 options was made with an accelerated vesting condition. The options become exercisable in two equal installments over two years, so that they would all vest before his planned retirement in March 2003.

While the pattern of one-off, multi-year awards for Gerstner is a defensible compensation practice, these awards, even annualized, were far in excess of awards made to board colleagues. But, assuming one of the primary purposes of the stock option scheme is to align Gerstner's interests with those of stockholders by increasing his stockholding following the exercise of options, table 6.4 demonstrates that this has not really occurred.

**Table 6.2** Compensation 1993–2001

| Year | Base salary $ | Annual bonus $ | Other annual compensation $ | Restricted stock $ | LTIP payout $ | Stock option profit $ | All other compensation $ | Total compensation $ |
|---|---|---|---|---|---|---|---|---|
| 2001 | 2,000,000 | 8,000,000 | 82,888 | 0 | 2,190,819 | 115,130,197 | 300,000 | 127,703,904 |
| 2000 | 2,000,000 | 8,000,000 | 96,400 | 0 | 3,585,407 | 59,887,423 | 276,000 | 73,845,230 |
| 1999 | 2,000,000 | 7,200,000 | 66,376 | 0 | 5,250,717 | 87,732,699 | 285,000 | 102,534,792 |
| 1998 | 1,875,000 | 7,500,000 | 12,384[1] | 0 | 4,145,419 | 32,801,922 | 191,250 | 46,525,975 |
| 1997 | 1,500,000 | 4,500,000 | 5,081 | 0 | 2,094,018 | 6,705,008 | 102,600 | 14,906,707 |
| 1996 | 1,500,000 | 3,270,000 | 5,938 | 0 | 2,072,567 | 3,489,228 | 128,250 | 10,465,983 |
| 1995 | 2,000,000 | 2,775,000 | 0 | 7,044,375[2] | 1,274,663 | 132,859 | 138,000 | 13,364,897 |
| 1994 | 2,000,000 | 2,600,000 | 0 | 0 | 0 | 0 | 7,755,055[3] | 12,355,055 |
| 1993[4] | 1,500,000 | 1,125,000 | 160,130[5] | 0 | 0 | 0 | 4,924,596[3] | 7,709,726 |

[1] There is no indication what this amount represents, nor why amounts have now been included for 1996 and 1997 which, in previous proxies, had been given as zero.

[2] Represents the provisional award of 65,000 restricted stock units, which vested after five years (i.e. when the stock price was between $100 and $120, and there had been two stock splits. Value at vesting likely to have been in the order of $28 million.)

[3] Special payments in connection with forfeited income from previous employer

[4] Appointed part-way through the year, salary and bonus for part year only.

[5] Income tax reimbursement on special payments.

**Table 6.3** Stock option grants 1993–2001 – non–adjusted

| Year | Stock option award | Exercise price | As a % of all options granted | Value with 5% annual stock price appreciation | Value with 10% annual stock price appreciation |
|------|-----|-----|-----|-----|-----|
| | No. | $ | % | $ | $ |
| 2001 | 0 | 0 | 0 | 0 | 0 |
| 2000 | 650,000[1] | 109.62 | 1.53 | 44,811,000 | 113,559,000 |
| 1999[2] | 0 | 0 | 0 | 0 | 0 |
| 1998 | 0 | 0 | 0 | 0 | 0 |
| 1997 | 2,000,000 | 103.56 | 10.02 | 130,260,000 | 330,100,000 |
| 1997[3] | 200,000 | 72.13 | 1.0 | 9,071,000 | 22,989,000 |
| 1996 | 300,000 | 126.69 | 3.91 | 23,901,000 | 60,573,000 |
| 1995 | 100,000 | 74.63 | 1.55 | 4,693,000 | 11,894,000 |
| 1994 | 225,000 | 60.94 | 3.24 | 8,622,000 | 21,852,000 |
| 1993 | 500,000 | 47.88 | 2.8 | 15,055,000 | 38,155,000 |

[1] Grant becomes exercisable in two equal installments, not the normal four.
[2] Stock split in 1999, original figures given.
[3] Stock split in 1997, original figures given.

**Table 6.4** Stockholding history, 1993–2001

| Year | Stockholding | Increase/decrease over previous year | Increase/decrease over previous year | Options exercised |
|------|-----|-----|-----|-----|
| | No. of shares | No. of shares | % | No. of shares |
| 2001 | 799,624 | −103,193 | −11.43 | 1,253,156 |
| 2000 | 902,817 | −63,169 | −6.54 | 703,156 |
| 1999 | 965,986 | 21,252 | 2.25 | 803,156 |
| 1998 | 944,734 (472,367 prior to stock split) | 75,898 | 8.74 | 602,772 (301,386 prior to stock split) |
| 1997 | 868,836 (434,418 prior to stock split) | 144,316 | 19.92 | 202,680 (101,340 prior to stock split) |
| 1996 | 724,520 (181,130 prior to stock splits) | 150,108 | 26.13 | 205,956 (51,489 prior to stock splits) |
| 1995 | 574,412 (143,603 prior to stock splits) | 342,588 | 47.78 | 11,632 (2,908 prior to stock split) |
| 1994 | 231,824 (57,956 prior to stock splits) | 110,000 | 90.29 | 0 |
| 1993 | 121,824 (30,456 prior to stock splits) | | | 0 |

## Managing from the perspective of an owner

As the table demonstrates, the largest gains in stockholding were during the first four years of Gerstner's tenure. In fact, new stock ownership guidelines were introduced in 1994. For the CEO, the requirement was to own four times base salary within five years. Gerstner had exceeded his guideline by 1995, even with the higher salary then in operation. Indeed, his early commitment to stockholding is demonstrated by the following passage taken from the compensation committee report detailing his nine months of employment:

> Of the 30,456 shares listed as owned by Mr. Gerstner in the Beneficial Ownership of Shares table, none was part of the terms of Mr. Gerstner's employment agreement. Thirty thousand of these shares were purchased by Mr. Gerstner in the open market from April 1993 through January 1994 with his personal funds. The rest had been acquired prior to his employment by IBM.

In 1997, the stockholding guideline was increased to four times the sum of annual salary and target annual incentive. Gerstner's holding was still in excess of this, and it shows that he was following one of the company's key compensation guidelines: "managing from the perspective of an owner with an equity stake in the business."

## Stock acquired through exercise of options not retained

Following 1997, however, and despite a series of very substantial option exercises, the growth in Gerstner's stockholding slowed significantly and then went into reverse. While this does not inspire confidence in either stockholders or the market, it should be remembered that, even with the lower stockholding, at the 2001 fiscal year end – before the stock price went into decline – his holding was worth $97,626,094.

What seems surprising is that Gerstner's stockholding was not built from the exercise of stock options, but rather from other forms of stock acquisition or award. Certainly some of it will have resulted from the restricted stock awards that made up half of any eventual long-term incentive payment. But this cannot have accounted for all the acquisitions. Indeed, far from using stock option awards to build stockholding, as soon as he began to exercise large numbers of stock options these appear to have been immediately sold.

## 1995

Compensation during 1993 and 1994 has already been covered in detail in the preceding sections describing the immediate effects of the contract. Below, we will examine the progress of compensation year by year. 1995, was the year that saw the first restricted stock unit award, some 65,000 were granted, which vested over the next five years. It was also the first year that Gerstner received a payout from the long-term incentive scheme awarding performance stock units. The award vested at the maximum, 13,391 units, rather than the 10,301 target award. This was paid out half in cash and half in shares restricted for a further two years. It also saw the first exercise of any options by Gerstner, though the number of shares and the value realized was relatively small (see table 6.2 for details). Finally, as in the previous year, the annual incentive award was above target. Only one change to the way compensation was delivered was made during the year. A deferred income plan was amended to allow salary in excess of the new $1 million cap to be deferred.

## 1996

In contrast, 1996 was a year of very significant change. Effective from 1 January, Gerstner's employment agreement was amended, ostensibly to further align his compensation with

**Table 6.5**  Increase in target total compensation

|  | Target total compensation ($) 1995 | Target total compensation ($) 1996 |
|---|---|---|
| Base salary | 2,000,000 | 1,500,000 |
| Target annual bonus | 1,500,000 | 2,000,000 |
| Target long-term incentive | 500,000 | 1,500,000 |
| **Target total compensation** | **4,000,000** | **5,000,000** |

the performance of the company. His salary was reduced from $2,000,000 to $1,500,000 and his target incentive awards were increased. The target annual bonus was increased from $1,500,000 to $2,000,000 and the target long-term incentive from $500,000 to $1,500,000. This led to an exchange of $500,000 fixed pay for a target potential variable pay of $1,500,000. While it has to be admitted that the incentive element of this exchange is at risk, and therefore in theory needs to be higher to compensate, the calculations do not present an equivalency. The change ties in more of his pay to the company's performance, but the board's decisions regarding levels have the result of protecting his compensation level. And the end result is a 25 percent increase in target total compensation (see table 6.5). What is made apparent by setting the figures out in this way is that company and individual performance could be below target, worse than the previous year, and Gerstner could still earn as much as he would have done for on-target performance under the previous arrangements.

## Altruistic presentation

Of course, performance never fell below target, so this never occurred. Nevertheless, the changes are presented altruistically, as if Gerstner is sacrificing salary in order to tie his interests closer to those of the other stockholders. The end result, however, is merely increased potential to earn. It should also be remembered that, by 1999, his salary had risen to $2 million again. Furthermore, from 1997 onwards, any severance benefits continued to be based on his original salary.

In addition, the target level of the long-term incentive is misleading. The amendment indicates that it will be increased to "at least $1,500,000." But as can be seen from table 6.2, in 1999, the year when the LTIP award dating from January 1996 eventually paid out, the target was worth considerably more than $1,500,000. With a payout of $5,250,717 representing 108 percent of the original 13,929 stock units, adjusted for stock splits, the award was valued using the stock price in the January of that year. But even looking at original grants, it is quite obvious that the target award is used as a minimum. Prior to the stock split, the January 1997 share price averaged at around $160. Using this stock price to value a target award of 20,798 stock units, at grant the units were worth just over $3 million – which is technically "at least $1,500,000."

It has been said that each amendment to the contract resulted in further compensation for Gerstner. Although there is rarely any direct association made between special awards and contract changes, the connections are still fairly evident. For example, the compensation committee does not specifically relate any "extra" compensation to this first in the series of amendments. Undoubtedly, however, several special one-off awards facilitated the changes.

First, the 65,000 restricted stock units already referred to were awarded in the year in which the contract was renegotiated. And secondly, a special award of 300,000 stock options was made in the year the amendments became effective. This award, larger than normal, contained a delayed vesting feature. The options were not exercisable until three years from the grant date, to encourage Gerstner to continue in employment with the company.

## Policy and disclosure changes

The compensation report for the 1996 fiscal year also contained a change either in compensation policy or disclosure policy or both. First, the report ceased to indicate whether targets for the annual bonus had been met or exceeded. Instead, a detailed synopsis of IBM's performance is given to justify the ever-increasing compensation levels. In addition, the scope of targets appears to have been widened, or perhaps disclosure has just improved. In previous reports, only the financial measures were described in any detail. Qualitative targets were referred to, but not listed. In the report for 1996, however, the qualitative targets are given in full. They include: product and technology leadership; growth in market share; revenue growth; implementation of key business programs; and customer satisfaction. Table 6.6 shows the difference in disclosure, and also provides a record of the level of achievement and incentive payout at the company during Gerstner's term of office.

## 1997

Gerstner's employment agreement was further amended in November 1997 to ensure he remained with the company as chairman until he reached the age of 60 in March 2002.

**Table 6.6**   IBM's performance record

| Year | Performance record |
|------|--------------------|
| 1993 | Operational targets met, Gerstner's bonus was guaranteed |
| 1994 | Above-target performance led to above-target annual incentives, no payout from the long-term incentive due |
| 1995 | Above-target performance again led to above-target annual incentives. Maximum number of stock units paid out for three-year performance |
| 1996 | Targets appear to have been met, but an extra cash award was made based on the highest-ever reported EPS from operations, record high revenues, and a significant increase in market capitalization. Maximum number of stock units paid out for three-year performance |
| 1997 | Attainment of targets "certified," revenue growth, EPS increase, and further rise in market capitalization. Maximum number of stock units paid out for three-year performance |
| 1998 | Very large growth in stock price and market capitalization, very large annual bonus payouts, but only 80% of the performance stock units due were awarded |
| 1999 | Record revenues, record after-tax profit, record EPS and another very large bonus payout. 108% of target stock units earned |
| 2000 | Record revenues, record after-tax profit, record EPS and another even larger bonus payout. 120% of stock units earned |
| 2001 | Another very large annual bonus payment, based on continued good performance in the face of an industry downturn, performance in excess of the DJIA average. 112% of the performance stock units paid out |

Also part of this second amendment was a consultancy agreement to retain his services for a further ten years beyond his retirement. In recognition of this latest amendment, Gerstner received a special award of 2 million stock options, and his termination arrangements were amended so that he would receive his "without cause" benefits following any termination with the consent of the board. The contract also indicated that these termination benefits would be based on his original $2 million salary, rather than the $1,500,000 he was currently receiving as base pay.

## Severance benefits for termination without cause

The following is a summary of the severance payments, taken from the 1993 contract, which Gerstner would have received had he been terminated.

- Base salary through termination date.
- Further three years' base salary, or until age 60, whichever is the shorter.
- Long-term incentive awards will vest at target pro rata with the salary continuation period.
- The balance of any unpaid incentive awards.
- Stock options vest in full on termination date and remain exercisable for their respective terms.
- Supplemental pension benefit vests in full.
- Payment in full of all remaining "special payments."
- All accrued benefits from all benefit programs, including all deferred compensation.
- Unpaid business expenses.
- Continued accrual of supplemental pension benefit for the salary continuation period.
- Continued medical, dental, hospitalization, life insurance, and any other benefit plans until the end of the salary continuation period or until equivalent benefits are provided by a subsequent employer.
- Any other benefits.
- He is under no obligation to seek other employment and there shall be no offset against due amounts on account of remuneration received from subsequent employment.

## Consultancy contract details

Full details of the terms of the consultancy contract were also given at the time of the employment agreement amendment. Gerstner will receive fees with a daily rate based on his pre-retirement salary (which by then will have risen back up to $2 million). He will also be reimbursed for reasonable expenses. A seemingly exhaustive list of benefits that he will receive during the consultancy was also given:

> access to Company aircraft, cars, office, and apartment, and to financial planning and home security services and he will be reimbursed for club expenses for Company business. He will also be treated as a retired employee of IBM, including for purposes of pension, retiree medical benefit coverage for him and his spouse, stock options (which will vest and remain exercisable for the remaining term) and long-term incentive performance awards (which will be paid based on Company performance over the entire performance period for such awards).

The contract amendment also introduced a range of confidentiality and non-compete clauses. For the ten years of the consultancy contract and an additional ten years following this, Gerstner must abide by these new competition agreements.

## 1998–2001

In the years following the second contract amendment, Gerstner's bonuses increased exponentially over past awards. While amounts received rose steadily throughout his tenure, 1998 saw a large increase up to $7,500,000 (see table 6.2 for details); and bonuses of $8 million were received in 2000 and 2001. In 1999, the company sought reapproval of the terms of the annual incentive program. The description of the annual scheme reveals that the maximum bonus for executives, Gerstner included, is not based on any percentage of salary, or absolute cash figure, but a calculation based on the company's net income for that year. The extract is given below:

> Each year, each covered executive may be entitled to a maximum award equal to three-tenths of one percent of the Company's earnings before income taxes as reported in the Company's consolidated financial statements, but before taking into account any losses from discontinued operations, extraordinary gains or losses, the cumulative effect of accounting changes and any unusual, nonrecurring gain or loss.

1998 was also the first year of four successive extremely substantial option exercises, culminating in 2001, when he realized a value of $115,130,197 on the exercise of 703,156 options. In 1999, the company also introduced a new long-term incentive plan. But this was only one of three times during Gerstner's tenure that the long-term incentive plan had to be put up for shareholder approval. On each occasion, the number of shares available for award was increased and the maximum number of options or stock subject to other awards for individual participants was raised. In 1993, a further 5 percent of outstanding stock was reserved for award, in 1997 another 5 percent was reserved and the maximum number of options that could be awarded was increased to 2,500,000. In 1999, the increase in the reserved shares was set higher, at 6.5 percent of stock, and the ceiling on option awards was doubled to 5 million.

### Deferred compensation plans

Gerstner's contract set his retirement benefits, and the structure and funding of these appears to have changed little since 1993. But besides the retirement plans, there were two other deferred compensation plans at IBM for which Gerstner is eligible, which have been amended several times, most recently in 2002. The first of these schemes is an all-employee plan – the Tax Deferred Savings Plan, which is now called the TDSP 401(k) plan. The second is the Executive Deferred Savings Plan, formerly the Extended Deferred Tax Savings Plan. Most of the amendments that have occurred during Gerstner's time at IBM were made to improve his and other executives' tax situation, as well as to equalize plan benefits between the all-employee and the executive schemes. The first amendment has already been referred to, which allowed the deferral of salary in excess of the $1 million salary cap. A further amendment to the executive plan allowed participants to defer and have matched up to 15 percent of all income, in order to match the structure of the all-employee plan. In the latest change, from 2002, participants in the all-employee plan can defer up to 80 percent of their total pay up to IRS limits. The text describing the schemes is given below:

### Other deferred compensation plans

Effective January 1, 2002, the IBM TDSP 401(k) Plan (the "TDSP") (previously known as the IBM Tax Deferred Savings Plan) allows all eligible employees to defer up to 80% of their income on a tax-favored basis into a tax exempt trust pursuant to Internal Revenue Service guidelines. IBM matches these deferrals at the rate of 50% for the first 6% of compensation deferred. The employee accounts are invested by the plan trustee in a selection of investment funds, including an IBM Stock Fund, as directed by the employees. Corporate officers participate in the TDSP on the same basis as all other employees. For 2002, Internal Revenue Service limits on the TDSP preclude an annual investment of more than $11,000 ($12,000 for participants who are at least age 50 during 2000) or an eligible compensation base of more than $200,000 for any one employee.

IBM established the IBM Executive Deferred Compensation Plan (the "EDCP") in 1995. The EDCP allows any U.S. executive, including officers, to defer additional monies and receive a Company match on the same basis as the TDSP except that the Company match for the EDCP is credited only in units of IBM common stock which are not transferable to other investment alternatives during employment. In addition, participants can defer all or a portion of their annual incentive until termination of employment under the EDCP. In the event that the salary of a Company officer who is subject to the limits of section 162(m) of the Code exceeds $1,000,000, such officer may defer up to 100 percent of his or her salary. The EDCP is not funded and participants are general creditors of the Company. All investments in the EDCP earn income based on the results of the actual TDSP funds' performance, but the income is paid out of Company funds rather than the actual returns on a dedicated investment portfolio.

The Company also provides executives with the opportunity to defer payout of certain restricted stock unit awards on terms similar to the EDCP. These deferrals are recorded as deferred units of Company stock. These amounts are not transferable to any other investment alternatives until paid out, and are not funded (participants are general creditors of the Company). There is no Company match on these amounts.

## 2002

In 2002, the employment agreement was again amended, to extend Gerstner's period of chairmanship until March 2003, at a salary of $2 million – the same as his salary as chairman and CEO – and an annual incentive to be determined. Nothing is said about any further long-term incentive awards, though at the end of fiscal 2001 he still held: 64,954 performance stock units and 40,057 restricted stock units having a combined value of $12,702,131; and 5,767,492 exercisable and non-exercisable options worth a total $382,125,236. In connection with the latest amendment, and on his move to the chairman position alone, he received a special restricted stock unit award covering 125,000 shares valued at around $13 million, to vest on retirement.

It should also be noted that, since his relinquishing of the CEO position, IBM's stock price has been in almost permanent decline. Ignoring other business and financial matters, there are two opposing, but obvious potential causes for this: (1) the market has no faith in IBM without Gerstner at the helm, or (2) the market has no faith in the new CEO's ability to manage the company while Gerstner stays.

# Premier Oil: Shareholder Value, Governance, and Social Issues

## Background

By late 2000, Premier Oil had become a *cause célèbre* amongst those concerned with governance and more particularly with the social, ethical, and environmental responsibilities of business.

Its share price was languishing, and it appeared unable to deliver on its stated strategy. Working with the company, with other shareholders, and with NGOs, Hermes helped the company to resolve these issues.

Hermes accelerated its engagement with Premier Oil in mid-2000. For several years previously Hermes had communicated its concerns over the company's board structure and had voted against the re-election of several of the non-executive directors whom we did not regard as being independent. On the governance side, the fundamental problem was that the company was dominated by two major shareholders, Amerada Hess, a US company, and Petronas, the Malaysian National Oil Company, each of which held 25 percent of the shares. Not content with the control and influence they wielded as such major shareholders, each of them also had two non-executive directors (NEDs) on the board. Two further NEDs were also deemed non-independent.

These board problems were reflected in a failure by the company to address some of the severe problems that Premier was facing. The strategy was not clear to us as shareholders: it appeared that the strategy proposed in November 1999 when Petronas invested in the company (and on the basis of which independent shareholders had approved that investment) was not being followed, and it was not apparent to investors that an alternative had been developed. The company was in a strategic hole: it was not large enough to compete in production and downstream work with the emerging super-major oil companies, but it was also not as lightweight and fleet of foot as it needed to be in order fully to exploit the exploration opportunities opened up by the super-major's focus on larger-scale fields. Its freedom of action was also limited by the company's high level of gearing.

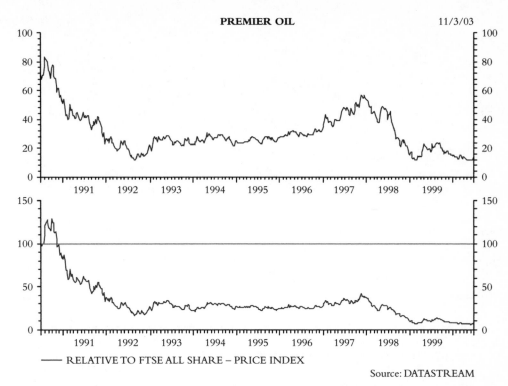

**Figure 6.5** Premier Oil absolute (upper) and relative (lower)
share price performance for 10 years to start of engagement (July 2000)

In addition, the company had allowed itself to become exposed to major ethical and reputational risks as a result of being the lead investor in the Yetagun gas field in Myanmar. Myanmar, formerly known as Burma, was a country ruled by a military dictatorship which had refused to accept the results of democratic elections in 1990, where summary arrest, forced labor, and torture where widely reported, and which had therefore become a pariah state. Premier's involvement in the country had brought public criticism of the company from a range of sources, including Burmese campaigners, Amnesty International, trade union groups, and, not least, the UK government. It was not clear to us as shareholders that the company was effectively managing the reputational and ethical risks it faced as a result of its involvement in Myanmar.

To begin exploring these concerns, we held a meeting in mid-2000 with Dr. Richard Jones, Premier's corporate responsibility director, and the company's finance director John van der Welle. This was an opportunity for us to understand Premier's considerable positive work on the ground in Myanmar – which included building schools, funding teachers, AIDS education, and environmental remediation. While we recognized that positive work, we had continuing concerns. The board had not publicly stated that it believed it was effectively managing all the risks that were associated with its presence in Myanmar, and nor did we have the confidence that the board as currently constituted could give shareholders the reassurance that they needed in that regard.

When we had analysed all these issues, it came as no surprise to us that, in the absence of a clear strategy and with a restrictive capital structure, with the lightning rod of its

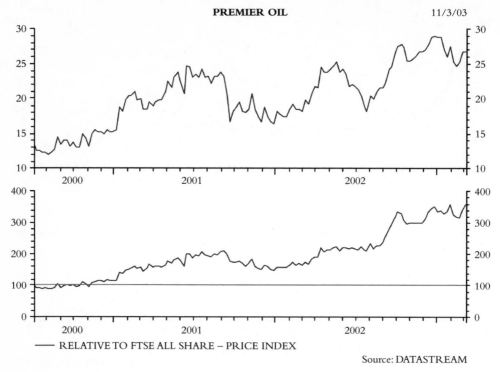

**Figure 6.6**   Premier Oil absolute (upper) and relative (lower)
share price performance since start of engagement

involvement in Myanmar not being clearly managed and a board which did not seem
designed to address these issues in the interests of all shareholders, that Premier's share
price had dramatically under-performed the market for several years.

## Why we chose Premier Oil

With the combination of these issues – governance, strategic, capital structure, ethical,
and share price under-performance – Premier Oil was a natural choice for our first year's
selection of companies for a Core Shareholder Program (CSP). As a fund manager with
predominantly index-tracking mandates, Hermes believes it is in our clients' interest to
become closely involved with companies where we perceive there to be problems. In a
sense, these actions are simply putting into effect the stewardship which our clients, as
partial owners, should exercise over investee companies. Hermes has a tradition of intervention at under-performing companies, but the 2000 CSP was our first attempt to establish a more formal and structured basis for determining where we should intervene. Those
companies where we had consistently voted against re-elections of directors but had not
seen any sign of reform, and where share price performance remained poor, formed the
basis of the ten stocks chosen for the first year of the CSP. Premier Oil was among these.

As we did with the other CSP companies, we wrote to the chairman of Premier, Sir
David John, requesting a meeting to discuss the full range of our concerns.

While we were awaiting that meeting, Hermes was approached by two separate groups asking it to engage on the social, ethical, and environmental (SEE) issues raised by Premier. The first group was our clients, principally led by trade union pension fund trustees. The second was from other NGOs who were focusing on disinvestment from Myanmar. It is worth considering Hermes' position relative to these two groups.

As regards the trade unions, Hermes believes it is appropriate that they, as client trustee representatives, should take a keen interest in the stewardship of their investment, including investee companies' response to SEE issues. We were invited by Brendan Barber of the Trades Union Congress (TUC) to address the international body which co-ordinates trade union/shareholder campaigns. At that meeting we explained that Hermes could not support trade-union campaigns based on a "special interest." We would, however, be happy to engage where failure to address SEE issues was as the result of poor governance, and threatened long-term shareholder value. Premier was one such case.

The second group that encouraged us to take action was the NGOs. We were invited to a meeting organized by other fund managers with representatives from the Burma Campaign UK and Amnesty International. Alongside the UK fund managers with strong ethical investment mandates, a US-based investor with a reputation for activism on social, environmental, and ethical matters was represented at this meeting.

We were somewhat surprised to find that the purpose of the meeting was to discuss proposing a shareholder resolution criticizing Premier for its involvement in Myanmar, something which most at the meeting seemed willing to countenance, despite the fact that they had yet to meet the directors of the company to discuss this proposed plan of action. In any case, Hermes (by reason of our passive, index-tracking mandates) was the only fund manager around the table that held a substantial stake in Premier Oil; indeed most held no shares at all.

At the meeting we took what we felt was the responsible attitude of a part-owner of the Premier Oil business. We argued against the proposal of any immediate shareholder resolution, pointing out that there were much better ways to raise issues with the board which would not of themselves inspire confrontation. We volunteered to lead the engagement.

The meeting did provide us with the opportunity to make contact with some of the NGOs active in Myanmar and among the Burmese people. Notably, we began regular discussions with the Burma Campaign UK, explaining to them the different courses of action which the company might take. We also continued to hold regular discussions with other interested institutional investors. As part of our due diligence, we also accessed publicly and privately other sources of insight, such as the UK government, academics, consultants, brokers, and journalists. This gave us as rounded a view as possible.

## *Our engagement*

The meeting with Sir David John took place in January 2001, and was a frank and honest one. It was rapidly apparent to us that Sir David understood our concerns. In December, the firm had already added a new, fully independent NED, in the person of Scott Dobbie, chair of Crestco and a director of the Securities and Futures Authority. Sir David assured us that further developments on the governance side were in train. We approved of these developments, but said that we doubted that they would ultimately be adequate to address concerns. Sir David was also willing to discuss our strategic and ethical concerns. Importantly, he agreed to our request personally to meet representatives of the Burma Campaign UK (until that point their contact with the company had only been through Richard Jones).

We followed up this meeting with a detailed and direct letter outlining our concerns and asking Sir David to begin addressing them in the interests of all shareholders. Sir David's prompt response assured us that the board would continue to work for a solution to "enable the true value of the company to be reflected in the share price." In March 2001, Premier Oil added another fully independent non-executive. This was Ronald Emerson, a banking executive with extensive experience in Asia, and Malaysia in particular.

At the May AGM, Sir David made a very important public statement with regard to the shareholding structure of the company. It was an acknowledgement that the presence of two 25 percent shareholders was a burden on the company's share price – a point we had clearly made in our meeting with him – and a statement of intent about seeking a resolution to this problem. He said: "We believe that the current share price remains low relative to the underlying value of the business partly as a result of the concentration of share ownership. The board is continuing to seek ways to reduce the discount on assets for the benefit of all shareholders."

Further positive steps occurred in October 2001. The company began to clarify its strategic position by selling assets in Indonesia and restructuring its position in Pakistan, having gained shareholder authority at an EGM.

Throughout this time we were in close contact with pension funds in the United States who were engaged with Amerada Hess over their shareholding in Premier, and hence their involvement in Myanmar. We pointed out to them that Amerada's statements appeared to be at odds with our understanding of UK law, and with statements made at the time of Premier Oil's shareholders circular at the time of its refinancing. Separate discussions were thus begun privately with Amerada to progress these issues.

Over 2001, we worked with other institutional investors on their proposal for a statement on how our investee companies should deal with any involvement in Myanmar. We argued that this document should follow the language of the guidelines we had developed with other institutional investors, which were later published by the Association of British Insurers in October 2001. We felt that Myanmar should not be singled out as an issue above all others – while the risks of involvement there are significant, there are other countries and other issues where risks are at a similarly high level – and we were not keen to see companies overburdened with a variety of different disclosure requests on a range of issues. Furthermore, we believed that had we signed up to the sort of document that was being proposed it would have been harder for us to achieve the level of access and open conversations we had achieved at Premier Oil. We therefore dropped out of the discussions on this document. The other institutions persevered and eventually published their statement in December.

## *Moving matters on*

The first year of our engagement had brought some progress but had failed fully to address Premier's fundamental problems. We met Sir David and Charles Jamieson, the CEO, in early 2002. This was an impressively frank meeting, where they were willing to be more open with us about the work they had been undertaking to resolve Premier's problems. Over the years since 1999, they had proposed a number of solutions to the company's strategic impasse, but each had been in some way barred by one or other of the major shareholders. They were, however, confident that both shareholders now had a different attitude and that a resolution in the interests of all investors could now be achieved – though it might take a number of months.

Following this meeting we sent Sir David a forthright letter expressing our concerns at the actions of the major shareholders and putting in writing our offer to lend him our support in the negotiations, should that prove valuable. We formally offered to call on our contacts at global institutions and share with them our concerns that certain of the directors of Premier had not proved themselves to be the friends of minority investors. We hoped that the implication of potential difficulties this might cause for fundraising by companies those directors were involved in could bolster Sir David's hand in negotiations. We also raised again our concerns that public statements by Amerada – that its investment in Premier was somehow ring-fenced from Myanmar and that its directors did not participate in any discussions on the company's involvement in that country – seemed to us out of line with UK company law and the fiduciary duties of directors to all their shareholders.

The company's preliminary results announcement on March 13 highlighted the positive progress the business was making operationally, but more importantly it detailed the progress being made in relation to the company's fundamental problems. It made clear the roadmap the company was using to solve its problems, talking about shedding mature assets in return for the exit of the major shareholders and turning itself into a focused, fleet-of-foot exploration company once again. The statement read: "We are in specific discussions with our alliance partners on creating a new Premier, better balanced to achieve our objectives. While the restructuring process is complex and involves careful balancing of the interests of all shareholders, we are committed to finding a solution before the end of this year and I am hopeful this will be achieved."

As part of our usual series of financial analysis meetings following preliminary or final announcements, we next met representatives of the company – this time Jamieson and John van der Welle – on March 27. This meeting gave us further encouragement that genuine progress was being made, as they suggested to us that the major shareholders both now clearly understood that any deal that they agreed would have to be approved by independent shareholders without them having the right to vote. Therefore, any deal would have to offer minorities full value to be allowed to proceed. The implication that we took away from this meeting was that negotiations were now on track to reach a resolution.

That resolution was announced in September 2002. Premier Oil said that it was to "swap assets for shares," with Petronas taking the Myanmar operation and a share of Premier's Indonesian activities, and Amerada a further segment of the Indonesian interest (in which Premier retained a stake). This was in return for cancelling their 25 percent shareholdings, and losing their right to appoint NEDs – as well as a substantial cash payment from Petronas. Thus the shareholding and governance issues were resolved in one step, and the cash was to be used to dramatically cut Premier's debt burden. By the same action, Premier reduced its oil and gas production activities and focused on "fleet-of-foot" exploration. Finally, it had withdrawn from Myanmar in a way which was fully acceptable to the Burma Campaign Group, other NGOs, and the UK government.

But, most critically, the share price of Premier Oil rose 10 percent on the announcement. Indeed, news of Premier's change in direction had been anticipated by the market for many months. As a result, Premier Oil's share price doubled (relative to the oil and gas sector) during the period of our engagement, netting an excess return to Hermes clients of over £1 million, and more than 50 times that sum to other minority shareholders.

# Appendix

## OVERVIEW OF CORPORATE GOVERNANCE GUIDELINES AND CODES OF BEST PRACTICE IN DEVELOPING AND EMERGING MARKETS

by Holly J. Gregory[*]

When a firm's management is separate and distinct from the providers of the firm's capital, managers have a responsibility to use assets efficiently in pursuit of the firm's objective. Ensuring that they do so is important to a firm's successful economic performance as well as to its ability to attract long-term, stable, low-cost investment capital. This is true whether the firm is publicly traded, privately held, family-controlled or state-owned. (It is only when the managers of a firm themselves own the entire firm – and are committed to relying solely on their own capital – that managers generally are free to apply corporate assets, as their own private property, inefficiently or for non-productive uses.) The fundamental concern of corporate governance is to ensure the means by which a firm's managers are held accountable to capital providers for the use of assets.

The responsibilities and functions of the corporate board in both developed and developing nations are receiving greater attention as a result of the increasing recognition that a firm's corporate governance affects both its economic performance and its ability to access patient, low-cost capital. After all, the board of directors – or, in two-tier systems, the supervisory board – is the corporate organ designed to hold managers accountable to capital providers for the use of firm assets. The past five years have witnessed a proliferation of corporate governance guidelines and codes of "best practice" designed to improve the ability of corporate directors to hold managements accountable. This global movement to emphasize that boards have responsibilities separate and apart from management, and to describe the practices that best enable directors to carry out these responsibilities, is a

---

[*] Holly J. Gregory is a partner in the international law firm of Wail, Gotshal & Manges LLP.

manifestation of the importance now attributed to corporate governance generally and, more particularly, to the role of the board.

Corporate governance guidelines and codes of best practice arise in the context of, and are affected by, differing national frameworks of law, regulation and stock exchange listing rules, and differing societal values. Although boards of directors provide an important internal mechanism for holding management accountable, effective corporate governance is supported by and dependent on the market for corporate control, securities regulation, company law, accounting and auditing standards, bankruptcy laws, and judicial enforcement. Therefore, to understand one nation's corporate governance practices in relation to another's, one must understand not only the "best practice" documents but also the underlying legal and enforcement framework.

Some governance codes are linked to listing or legally mandated disclosure requirements. Others are purely voluntary in nature, but may be designed to help forestall further government or listing body regulation. In the developing nations, governance codes are more likely to address basic principles of corporate governance that tend to be more established in developed countries through company law and securities regulation, such as the equitable treatment of shareholders, the need for reliable and timely disclosure of information concerning corporate performance and ownership, and the holding of annual general meetings of shareholders. However, in both developed and developing nations, codes focus on boards of directors and attempt to describe ways in which boards can be positioned to provide some form of guidance and oversight to management, and accountability to shareholders and society at large.

## OVERVIEW

The modern trend of developing corporate governance guidelines and codes of best practice began in the early 1990s in the United Kingdom, the United States, and Canada in response to problems in the corporate performance of leading companies, the perceived lack of effective board oversight that contributed to those performance problems, and pressure for change from institutional investors. The Cadbury Report in the UK, the General Motors Board of Directors Guidelines in the US, and the Dey Report in Canada have each proved influential sources for other guideline and code efforts.

Over the past decade, governance guidelines and codes have issued from stock exchanges, corporations, institutional investors, and associations of directors and corporate managers. Compliance with these governance recommendations is generally not mandated by law, although the codes linked to stock exchanges may have a coercive effect. For example, listed companies on the London and Toronto stock exchanges need not follow the recommendations of the Cadbury Report (as amended in the Combined Code) and the Dey Report, but they must disclose whether they follow the recommendations in those documents and must provide an explanation concerning divergent practices. Such disclosure requirements exert a significant pressure for compliance. In contrast, the guidelines issued by associations of directors, corporate managers and individual companies tend to be wholly voluntary. For example, the GM Board Guidelines simply reflect an individual board's efforts to improve its own governance capacity. Such guidelines can have wide influence, however. In the case of the GM Guidelines, institutional investors encouraged other companies to adopt similar guidelines.

In developing nations, both voluntary guidelines and more coercive codes of best practice have issued as well. For example, both the Code of Best Practices issued by the Brazilian

Institute of Corporate Directors and the Code of Corporate Governance issued by the Corporate Governance Committee of the Mexican Business Coordinating Counsel are wholly aspirational and not linked to any listing requirements. Similarly, the Confederation of Indian Industry Code and the Stock Exchange of Thailand Code are designed to build awareness within the corporate sector of governance best practice, but are not, at this time, linked to stock exchange listing requirements. In contrast, Malaysia's Code on Corporate Governance, the Code of Best Practice issued by the Hong Kong Stock Exchange, and South Africa's King Commission Report on Corporate Governance all contemplate mandatory disclosure concerning compliance with their recommendations.

Some of the key elements of governance guidelines and codes of best practice, particularly as issued in developing nations, are summarized below.

## THE CORPORATE OBJECTIVE

Variations in societal values lead different nations to view the corporate objective or "mission" distinctly. Expectations of how the corporation should prioritize the interests of shareholders and stakeholders such as employees, creditors, and other constituents take two primary forms. In the Anglo-Saxon nations – Australia, Canada, the UK, and the US – maximizing the value of the owners' investment is considered the primary corporate objective. This objective is reflected in governance guidelines and codes that emphasize the duty of the board to represent shareholders' interests and maximize shareholder value. Among developing nations, the Brazilian Institute of Corporate Governance Code, the Confederation of Indian Industry Code, the Kyrgyz Republic Charter of a Shareholding Society, the Malaysian Report on Corporate Governance, and the Korean Stock Exchange Code of Best Practice all expressly recognize that the board's mission is to protect and enhance the shareholders' investment in the corporation.

> The mission of the board of directors is to maximize shareholder value. *Brazilian Institute of Corporate Governance Code of Best Practice at 1*

> The Board of Directors represents the shareholders of the Society, and it has a duty to act in the interests of the shareholders. *Charter of a Shareholding Society (Kyrgyz Republic) 17.1*

> The single overriding objective [of] all listed companies . . . is the preservation and enhancement over time of their shareholders' investment. *Report on Corporate Governance (Malaysia), Introduction § 1, 3.3*

In other countries, more emphasis is placed on a broader range of stakeholders. However, this view is not strongly advocated in the governance guidelines and codes emanating from developing nations, although some documents recognize that stakeholder interests should be considered. (For example, the King Report from South Africa states: "Directors must act with enterprise and always strive to increase shareholders' value while having regard for the interests of all stakeholders," ch. 5:27.7.) This may be due to a convergence in perceptions about the corporate objective. There is a growing recognition that shareholder expectations need to be met in order to attract patient, low-cost capital. Likewise, there is growing sensitivity to the need to address stakeholder interests in order to maximize shareholder value over the long term. As the General Motors board of directors mission statement recognizes, "the board's responsibilities to shareholders as well as customers, employees, suppliers and the communities in which the corporation operates are all founded upon the successful perpetuation of the business." Simply put, shareholder and stakeholder interests in the success of the corporation are compatible in the long run.

## BOARD RESPONSIBILITIES AND JOB DESCRIPTION

Most governance guidelines and codes of best practice assert that the board assumes responsibility for the stewardship of the corporation and emphasize that board responsibilities are distinct from management responsibilities. However, the guidelines and codes differ in the level of specificity with which they explain the board's role. For example, Canada's Dey Report, France's Viénot Report, Malaysia's Report on Corporate Governance, Mexico's Code of Corporate Governance, South Africa's King Report, and the Korean Stock Exchange Code all specify board functions such as: strategic planning; risk identification and management; selection, oversight and compensation of senior management; succession planning; communication with shareholders; integrity of financial controls; and general legal compliance, as distinct board functions. The Kyrgyz Republic Charter sets out a detailed list of matters requiring board approval. Other governance guidelines and codes of best practice are far less specific. For example, the Hong Kong Stock Exchange Code simply refers to directors' obligations to ensure compliance with listing rules as well as with the "declaration and undertaking" that directors are required to execute and lodge with the Exchange. The different approaches among codes on this point likely reflect variations in the degree to which company law or listing standards specify board responsibilities, rather than any significant substantive differences.

The main functions of a board are:

* to direct the company both as to strategy and structure;
* to establish from time to time a strategy for the company, including a determination of the businesses that the company should be in and those that it should not be in;
* to ensure that the executive management implements the company's strategy as established from time to time;
* to ensure that the company has adequate systems of internal controls both operational and financial;
* to monitor the activities of the executive management;
* to select the chief executive, ensure succession and give guidance on the appointment of senior executives;
* to provide information on the activities of the company to those entitled to it;
* to ensure that the company operates ethically;
* to provide for succession of senior management;
* to address the adequacy of retirement and health care benefits and funding.

*The King Report (South Africa), ch. 4:1*

## BOARD COMPOSITION

Most governance guidelines and codes of best practice address topics related to board composition, including director qualifications and membership criteria, the director nomination process, and board independence and leadership.

## *Criteria*

The quality, experience and independence of a board's membership directly affect board performance. Board membership criteria are described by various guidelines and codes with different levels of specificity, but tend to highlight issues such as experience, personal characteristics (including independence), core competencies, and availability.

> Every non-executive director must ensure that he can give sufficient time and attention to the affairs of the issuer . . . and satisfy the Exchange that he has the character, integrity, experience and competency to serve as a director of a listed company. *The Hong Kong Stock Exchange Code, Code of Best Practice 90 and Guideline A.5*

> The board should have a diversity of background, knowledge and experience. *The Brazilian Institute of Corporate Governance Code of Best Practice at 3*

> [Non-executive directors should] know how to read a balance sheet, profit and loss account, cash flow statements and financial ratios, and have some knowledge of various company laws. *The Confederation of Indian Industry Code, Recommendation 4*

> [A] candidate should have integrity and independence of thought; the courage to express their independent thought; a grasp of the realities of business operations; an understanding of the changes taking place regionally, nationally and internationally; [and] an understanding of business and financial "language." *The King Report (South Africa), ch. 9:8.2*

## *Director nomination*

The process by which directors are nominated has gained attention in many guidelines and codes, which tend to emphasize a formal and transparent process for appointing new directors. The use of nominating committees is favored in the US and UK as a means of reducing the CEO's influence in choosing the board that is charged with monitoring his or her performance. (See, in the US, the Report of the National Association of Corporate Directors Commission on Director Professionalism (1996), and the General Motors Board of Directors Guidelines (1994); in the UK, the Hampel Committee Report (1998)). The Malaysian Corporate Governance Report expresses a similar view: "[T]he adoption of a formal procedure for appointments to the board, with a nomination committee making recommendations to the full board, should be recognized as good practice" (explanatory note 4; see also Korean Stock Exchange Code of Best Practice 11.3). At the same time, however – and as advocated by the King Report (South Africa) – it is generally agreed that the board as a whole has the ultimate responsibility for nominating directors.

## *Mix of inside and outside or "independent" directors*

Most governance guidelines and codes of best practice agree that some degree of director independence – or the ability to exercise objective judgment of management's performance – is important to a board's ability to exercise objective judgment concerning management performance. In the US, UK, Canada, and Australia, although not required by law or listing requirements, best practice recommendations generally agree that boards of publicly traded corporations should include at least some independent directors. This viewpoint is the furthest developed in the US and Canada, where best practice documents call for a "substantial" majority of the board to be comprised of independent directors. Elsewhere best practice recommendations are somewhat less stringent and seek to have a balance of executives and non-executives, with the non-executives including some truly independent directors. (Although "non-management" or "non-executive" directors may be more likely to be objective than members of management, many code documents recognize that a non-management director may still not be truly "independent" if he or she has significant financial or personal ties to management.) Nonetheless, a general consensus is developing throughout a number of countries that public company boards should include at least some non-executive members who lack significant family and business relationships with management.

> The board shall include outside directors capable of performing their duties independently from management, controlling shareholders and the corporation. *Korean Stock Exchange Code of Best Practice at 11.2.2*

> The majority of the board members should be independent. *Brazilian Institute of Corporate Governance Code of Best Practice at 3*

> No board should have less than two non-executive directors of sufficient calibre that their views will carry significant weight in board decisions. *The King Report (South Africa), 2.2*

> [I]t is recommended that Independent Directors represent at least 20% of the total number of Board members. *Mexico Code of Corporate Governance, Principle at 6*

Definitions of "independence" vary. For example, according to the Brazilian Institute of Corporate Governance, a director is independent if he or she: has no link to the company besides board membership and share ownership and receives no compensation from the company other than director remuneration or shareholder dividends; has never been an employee of the company (or of an affiliate or subsidiary); provides no services or products to the company (and is not employed by a firm providing major services or products); and is not a close relative of any officer, manager, or controlling shareholder.

> Every listed company should have independent directors, i.e. directors that are not officers of the company; who are neither related to its officers nor represent concentrated or family holdings of its shares; who, in the view of the company's board of directors, represent the interests of public shareholders, and are free of any relationship that would interfere with the exercise of independent judgment. *Malaysian Report on Corporate Governance, Explanatory Note 4.23*

> In February 1998, the Korean Stock Exchange adopted a listing requirement that will mandate that outside directors soon comprise at least a quarter of the board of every listed company. Included among the list of persons who do not qualify as "outside directors" are: controlling shareholders; a spouse or family member of a director who is not an outsider; current or recent officers and employees of the corporation, its

affiliates, or of corporations that have "important business relations" with the corporation; and persons who serve as outside directors on three or more listed companies. *Article 48–5 KSE Listing Regulation*

In comparison, the Cadbury Code simply refers to directors who – apart from their fees and shareholdings – are independent from management and free from any business or other relationship which could materially interfere with the exercise of independent judgment. And many of the best practice documents – such as the Cadbury Report and the National Association of Corporate Directors Report on Director Professionalism (US) – view the ultimate determination of just what constitutes "independence" to be an issue for the board itself to determine.

## Independent board leadership

Independent board leadership is thought by some to encourage the non-executive directors' ability to work together to provide true oversight of management. As explained by the National Association of Corporate Directors (US): "the purpose of creating [an independent] leader is not to add another layer of power but . . . to ensure organization of, and accountability for, the thoughtful execution of certain critical independent functions" – such as evaluating the CEO, chairing sessions of the non-executive directors, setting the board agenda, and leading the board in responding to crisis.

Many guidelines and codes seek to institute independent leadership by recommending a clear division of responsibilities between chairman and CEO. In this way, while the CEO can have a significant presence on the board, the non-executive directors will also have a formal independent leader to look to for authority on the board. Documents that place less emphasis on the need for a majority of independent directors seem to place more emphasis on the need for separating the role of chairman and CEO. For example, the Indian Confederation Report expressly relates the two concepts – recommending that if the chairman and CEO (or managing director) are the same person, a greater percentage of non-executive directors is necessary (Recommendation 2). The Malaysian Report on Corporate Governance similarly emphasizes that "[w]here the roles are combined there should be a strong independent element on the board" (Best Practice AA-II). This is in accord with the Cadbury Report, which states that, where the chairman is also the CEO, "it is essential that there should be a strong and independent element on the board" (section 1.2).

## BOARD COMMITTEES

In developed nations, it is fairly well accepted that many board functions are carried out by board committees. For example, a nominating committee, an audit committee, and a remuneration committee are recommended in Australia, Belgium, France, Japan, the Netherlands, Sweden, the United Kingdom, and the United States. While composition of these committees varies, it is generally recognized that non-executive directors have a special role.

The functioning and composition of the audit committee receives significant attention in most guideline and code documents because of the key role it plays in protecting shareholder interests and promoting investor confidence.

Special emphasis has been placed on the need for all listed company boards to establish audit committees to ensure the effective and efficient control and review of a company's administration, internal audit procedures, the preparation of financial statements and the general disclosure of material information to investors and shareholders. *President's Message, Stock Exchange of Thailand Code and Guidelines, pp. iv–v*

[There should be] a mechanism that lends support to the Board in verifying compliance of the audit function, assuring that internal and external audits are performed with the highest objectivity possible and that the financial information is useful, trustworthy and accurate. *Mexico Code of Corporate Governance, Recommendation at 12–13*

Certain countries specifically recommend the size of an audit committee. In India, the minimum size recommended is three members, as it is in Malaysia and the United Kingdom. Also, South Africa and India both emphasize the extra time requirements demanded of audit committee members, and the importance of written terms of reference for this committee. Malaysia also refers to the need for written terms of reference for audit and other board committees.

## DISCLOSURE ISSUES

Disclosure is an issue that is highly regulated under securities laws of many nations. However, there is room for voluntary disclosure by companies beyond what is mandated by law. Most countries generally agree on the need for directors to disclose their own relevant interests and to disclose financial performance in an annual report to shareholders. Generally this is required by law, but some guidelines and best practice documents address it as well. Similarly, even though directors are usually subject to legal requirements concerning the accuracy of disclosed information, a number of codes from both developed and developing nations describe the board's responsibility to disclose accurate information about the financial performance of the company, as well as information about agenda items, prior to the annual general meeting of shareholders. Many codes also itemize the issues reserved for shareholder decision at the AGM. Generally, guidelines and codes of best practice place heavy emphasis on the financial reporting obligations of the board, as well as board oversight of the audit function. Again, this is because these are key to investor confidence and the integrity of markets. South Africa lays out the key points that the directors must comment on, whereas other countries do not go to this level of detail, but the distinction is not necessarily substantive since disclosure tends to be heavily regulated in many nations through securities laws.

## SUMMARY

This brief review of the primary principles addressed by various guidelines and codes indicates that there is no single agreed-upon system of "good" governance. Each country has its own corporate culture, national personality, and priorities. Likewise, each company has its own history, culture, goals, and business cycle maturity. All of these factors need to be taken into consideration in crafting the optimal governance structure and practices for any country or any company. However, the influence of international capital markets will likely lead to some convergence of governance practices.

As regulatory barriers between national economies fall and global competition for capital increases, investment capital will follow the path to those corporations that have adopted efficient governance standards, which include acceptable accounting and disclosure standards, satisfactory investor protections and board practices designed to provide independent, accountable oversight of managers. *Report to the OECD by the Business Sector Advisory Group on Corporate Governance, April 1998 (the Millstein Report)*

This convergence is evident in the growing consensus in both developed and developing nations that board structure and practice are key to providing corporate accountability – of the management to the board and the board to the shareholders – in the governance paradigm.

# INDEX

Index entries are to page numbers. Alphabetical arrangement is word-by-word, where a group of letters followed by a space is filed before the same group of letters followed by a letter, e.g. "market value" will appear before "marketplace". Initial articles, conjunctions and prepositions are ignored in determining filing order.